INDIGENOUS STRUGGLE AND THE BOLIVIAN NATIONAL REVOLUTION

Indigenous Struggle and the Bolivian National Revolution: Land and Liberty! reinterprets the genesis and contours of the Bolivian National Revolution from an indigenous perspective.

In a critical revision of conventional works, the author reappraises and reconfigures the tortuous history of insurrection and revolution, counterrevolution and resurrection, and overthrow and aftermath in Bolivia. Underlying the history of creole conflict between dictatorship and democracy lies another conflict—the unrelenting 500-year struggle of the conquered indigenous peoples to reclaim usurped lands, resist white supremacist dominion, and seize autonomous political agency. The book utilizes a wide array of sources, including interviews and documents to illuminate the thoughts, beliefs, and objectives of an extraordinary cast of indigenous revolutionaries, giving readers a firsthand look at the struggles of the subaltern majority against creole elites and Anglo-American hegemons in South America's most impoverished nation.

This book will be of interest to students and scholars of modern Latin American history, peasant movements, the history of U.S. foreign relations, revolutions, counterrevolutions, and revolutionary warfare.

James Kohl is an independent scholar based in Connecticut, USA. He has contributed articles to many journals: *Hispanic American Historical Review*, *The Journal of Peasant Studies*, *Inter-American Economic Affairs*, *Latin American Research Review*, *American Historical Review*, *The Nation*, and *The Progressive*. He is the co-editor of *Urban Guerrilla Warfare in Latin America*.

INDIGENOUS STRUGGLE AND THE BOLIVIAN NATIONAL REVOLUTION

Land and Liberty!

James Kohl

NEW YORK AND LONDON

First published 2021
by Routledge
52 Vanderbilt Avenue, New York, NY 10017

and by Routledge
2 Park Square, Milton Park, Abingdon, Oxon, OX14 4RN

Routledge is an imprint of the Taylor & Francis Group, an informa business

© 2021 Taylor & Francis

The right of James Kohl to be identified as author of this work has been asserted by him in accordance with sections 77 and 78 of the Copyright, Designs and Patents Act 1988.

All rights reserved. No part of this book may be reprinted or reproduced or utilised in any form or by any electronic, mechanical, or other means, now known or hereafter invented, including photocopying and recording, or in any information storage or retrieval system, without permission in writing from the publishers.

Trademark notice: Product or corporate names may be trademarks or registered trademarks, and are used only for identification and explanation without intent to infringe.

Library of Congress Cataloging-in-Publication Data
Names: Kohl, James V., author.
Title: Indigenous struggle and the Bolivian National Revolution : land and liberty! / James Kohl.
Other titles: Land and liberty!
Description: New York, NY : Routledge, 2021. | Includes bibliographical references and index.
Identifiers: LCCN 2020022569 (print) | LCCN 2020022570 (ebook) | ISBN 9780367471521 (hbk) | ISBN 9780367471392 (pbk) | ISBN 9781003033813 (ebk)
Subjects: LCSH: Bolivia—History—Revolution, 1952—Causes. | Bolivia—Politics and government—1938– | Indians of South America—Bolivia—Government relations. | Indians of South America—Land tenure—Bolivia. | Indians of South America—Civil rights—Bolivia. | Peasant uprisings—Bolivia—History—20th century. | Nationalism—Bolivia—History—20th century. | Chaco War, 1932–1935—Influence.
Classification: LCC F3326 .K64 2021 (print) | LCC F3326 (ebook) | DDC 984.05/1—dc23
LC record available at https://lccn.loc.gov/2020022569
LC ebook record available at https://lccn.loc.gov/2020022570

ISBN: 978-0-367-47152-1 (hbk)
ISBN: 978-0-367-47139-2 (pbk)
ISBN: 978-1-003-03381-3 (ebk)

Typeset in Bembo
by Apex CoVantage, LLC
Visit the eResources: www.routledge.com/Indigenous-Struggle-and-the-Bolivian-National-Revolution-Land-and-Liberty/Kohl/p/book/9780367471392

*To the Memory of
Antonio Mamani Álvarez
aka
Antonio Álvarez Mamani
For my parents
Virgil and Maryon Kohl*

CONTENTS

List of Illustrations   *viii*
List of Maps   *ix*
List of Tables   *x*
Preface   *xi*

	Introduction	1
1	War: The Generation of the Chaco	10
2	Revolution	47
3	Counterrevolution	88
4	The Sexenio	112
5	Revolution: Redux, 1952–1965	159
6	Agrarian Reform	203
7	Sindicato and Revolution	250
8	The "Revolution of Restoration"	289
	Epilogue	343

Bibliography   *380*
Index   *399*

ILLUSTRATIONS

1.1	Bolivia Rushes Its Troops to the Chaco Front	13
2.1	Antonio Mamani Álvarez (wearing striped poncho) with Chipana Ramos to His Left	74
3.1	Honor Guard at Lamp Post Where Martyred President Gualberto Villarroel Was Hanged in 1946	103
4.1	Antonio Mamani Álvarez (second from left) Holding Photo of Martyred President Villarroel	118
4.2	Loyalty March in La Paz Against MNR Rebels in 1949	144
4.3	Cochabamba Police Station Bombed by Rebels in the 1949 Civil War	147
5.1	Antonio Mamani Álvarez Speaking at Solidarity Rally with Gabino Apaza on His Left	173
5.2	Cross-marking Site of Slain Hacendado at Pojo, Cochabamba Department	189
7.1	Peasant Comportment in the Face of an Armed Invasion	255
7.2	Ucureña Campesino Central	265
8.1	Repurposed USAID Tear Gas Containers, La Paz	291
9.1	Coca Terrace, Yungas	364

MAPS

1.1	Bolivia	11
1.2	Bolivia Map with Territory Lost in Wars with Chile, Brazil, and Paraguay	18
4.1	La Paz Department; light-gray shaded area is the altiplano	120
4.2	Cochabamba Valleys	127
6.1	Ecological Zones	213
6.2	Number and Distribution of Community Indians in Bolivia, 1854	222
6.3	Number and Distribution of Community Indians in Bolivia, 1900	224
7.1	Northern Potosí	270
9.1	Major Ethnolinguistic Groups	372

TABLES

6.1	Services Rendered by the Colonos of Compi	206
6.2	Distribution of Land in Bolivia in 1950	207
6.3	Land Ownership by Type of Unit, Bolivia 1950	208
6.4	Classes and Strata in the Bolivian Countryside, 1950	212
6.5	Articles, Quantities, and Value of Most Commonly Acquired Goods Among Bolivian Peasants in North Highlands Before 1952	216
6.6	Articles, Quantities, and Value of the Most Commonly Acquired Goods Among Bolivian Peasants in North Highlands in 1966	217
6.7	Agrarian Structure in Bolivia After 10 Years of Agrarian Reform	237

PREFACE

Che Guevara and I arrived in Bolivia at the same time. My objective was to study the National Revolution overthrown three years earlier in 1964. Che's objective was to begin a revolution—to ignite "Two, Three, Many Vietnams" radiating from the heart of South America. Neither of us knew much about the Bolivian National Revolution. But Che's fateful choice of the remote and sparsely populated scrubland of southeastern Bolivia as the site of operations was fatal.

A reading in 1969 of Noam Chomsky's "The Responsibility of Intellectuals" caused me to question myself as an accessory to American imperialism, interrupt my study of the role of the peasant in the Bolivian National Revolution, and become a supporter of the ELN (*Ejercito de Liberación Nacional*: Army of National Liberation), the urban reincarnation of Che's guerrilla war. *Urban Guerrilla Warfare in Latin America*, co-edited with the unforgettable John Litt in 1974 and dedicated "To the Second War of Independence," embraced this strategy for resistance to tyrannical dictators and U.S. imperialism. Together with a close friend, the enigmatic Joe David Sanderson, I did what I could to support resistance to the U.S.-supported dictatorship of General Hugo Banzer Suárez. Deported from Bolivia along with the Maryknoll Nun Mary Harding, Joe was later killed in combat as a member of the revolutionary FMLN resisting the U.S.-backed military junta in El Salvador.

Decades passed as a boat captain in Alaskan waters, fishing guide, Oregon tree farmer, and peripatetic professor before I resumed my interest in the National Revolution. Much had changed in the intervening years. The landing strip at El Alto, on the Altiplano above the city of La Paz, was rudimentary in 1967. Once the site of a massive indigenous rebellion against the Spanish residents below in the city of La Paz, today's El Alto is now home to two million Aymara urbanites and the steep decline from the Altiplano to the city below, previously only negotiated by motor vehicles or afoot, is now served by modern gondola lifts. A testament to Bolivia's social revolution is the appearance of a marvelous corpus of scholarship by university-educated Aymara and Quechua scholars dedicated to writing history from an indigenous perspective. Their contributions together with those of talented foreign scholars who have deeply enriched our knowledge of Bolivia, its peoples, and their revolution will be evident in the chapters and footnotes of this book.

Porfirio Díaz Machicao was helpful in locating newspapers at the Universidad Mayor de San Ándres as were the librarians at the Biblioteca Municipal Mariscal Ándres de Santa Cruz in La Paz, and Don Gunnar Mendoza, the Director of the Archivo y Biblioteca Nacionales in Sucre. The staff at the U.S. National Archives in College Park, Maryland, and librarians at the Library of Congress in Washington, DC, and the New York Public Library were most helpful. A Ford Foundation Grant supervised by Professor Edwin Lieuwen at the University of New Mexico supported my initial research in Bolivia. The Massachusetts Institute of Technology, American Philosophical Society, National Endowment for the Humanities, and a summer fellowship at the Stanford-Berkeley Latin American Institute. Professor Carl Solberg's National Endowment for the Humanities Summer Seminar on Latin America was instrumental in reenergizing my attention to this book. Many thanks to Kimberley Smith and Emily Irving, my editors at Routledge, the book's project manager Autumn Spalding, and Archivist Mike Murphy at the New Canaan Historical Society for his assistance in preparing the *Tesis de Caranguillas* for the book's online appendix. I am most grateful to the book proposal's three anonymous readers for their incisive questions and comments that sharpened my focus and enhanced my perspective.

William Appleman Williams, with whom I shared an interest in American imperialism, the Oregon coast, and Kentucky bourbon, was a source of inspiration. My thanks to Professors Jerry Simich and Thomas Wright for their conversations, questions, and fellowship over the years. I am most appreciative of the computer assistance from my digital-era children Maia and Max who came to my rescue countless times during the writing of this book. Maia tirelessly rescued me from myself and buoyed my spirit as she and her husband James endured my prolonged presence in their home while I fashioned the manuscript—and experienced the joy of daily life with them and my grandchildren Oliver, Charlie, and Evie. My thanks to Mike and Dawn Kohl for the use of their beautiful house overlooking Lake Pend Oreille, Idaho, and to my dear friends Gage and Nance Kiesling of Corvallis, Oregon for their wonderful hospitality, invaluable support, ready assistance, and many kindnesses during my time in Corvallis.

I have had the good fortune to meet many extraordinary people: Bolivian presidents and indigenous revolutionaries, Nobel Prize winners, brilliant intellectuals, screenwriters, playwrights, professional athletes, U.S. Special Operations officers, and assorted criminals and outlaws. This book is dedicated to the most remarkable man encountered in my many years: the Kallawaya and indefatigable revolutionary Antonio Mamani Álvarez (aka Antonio Álvarez Mamani) whose struggle for "Land and Liberty" in Kollasuyu captured my imagination on every occasion we met.

INTRODUCTION

This book is the history of a social revolution, a rarity in world history and a singular event in twentieth-century South America. The Bolivian National Revolution began in 1943 with a coup d'état executed by military officers dedicated to modernization of the oligarchic state. Overthrown three years later by a counter-revolutionary cabal of oligarchs, mine owners, senior military officers, Trotskyists, and Anglo-American hegemons, a six-year reactionary interregnum ensued (1946–1952) before the revolution resumed in 1952, following an urban insurrection organized and led by middle-class civilians.

Although terminated by a military coup in 1964, the process of change set in motion by the revolution—universal suffrage, the Indian's right to education, to land ownership, to organize unions—continues into the present. Indeed, after five centuries of creole rule, an Indian coca farmer was elected president of the renamed Plurinational State of Bolivia in 2006.

The election of the Aymara president Evo Morales Ayma resulted from the relentless struggle of the nation's indigenous majority against the domination of the creole minority. Indigenous resistance before, during, and after the epic National Revolution is a major theme of this book and essential to understanding the backdrop to the historic rise and fall of President Evo Morales.

Chapter 1 traces the proximate cause of Bolivia's social revolution to the Chaco War (1932–1935), fought by Indian conscripts and lost by incompetent creole generals. The nation's ignominious defeat in the war exposed the ancien régime as rotten to the core: racist, incompetent, corrupt, dishonorable. The war proved to be a catalyst for revolution by those who returned from the trenches determined to overthrow the Old Order. Yet there was also another war: an undeclared war of indigenous resistance against mistreatment by creole-mestizo *hacendado*s and government functionaries (Indians dragooned, their livestock and foodstuffs seized, lands stolen, human rights violated). Opposition to the Old Regime included revolts against hacendados, attacks on towns, draft evasion, desertion, anti-war demonstrations, opposition to forced labor and contrived wartime taxes, an attempt to create a multiethnic counter-state; as well as the efforts of educators to combat the enforced illiteracy imposed on the Indian peoples.[1]

Indigenous education—harshly repressed by criollo overlords for centuries—was understood by both the oppressor and the oppressed as a key to freedom. But, would education lead to liberation and the decolonization of an oppressed people? Or would it result in assimilation and the loss of indigenous culture? While Indian leaders were not of one mind on this topic, the novel and exemplary appearance of indigenous "nuclear schools" in the highland departments met with strident hacendado opposition and their eventual destruction. This chapter looks at a number of indigenous educators, and the rise and fall of Warisata—the innovative Aymara *ayllu* (indigenous community) school and its relationship with *vecinos* (townspeople) in the nearby Altiplano town of Achacachi.

The postwar years were remarkable for the interplay between the various sectors of Bolivian society radicalized by the trauma: creole-mestizo army officers, lawyers, office workers, journalists, artisans, shopkeepers—and the Indian conscripts who returned from the trenches, still denied the rights of citizenship, education, and a vote.

The political and social ferment of the postwar era and the revolutionaries who attacked the legitimacy of the state in a war of words in the legislature, the opposition press, and in popular literature are essayed. The first assault against the Bolivian state came from army officers who seized power (1936–1939), with the intention of diverting criticism of the military for the Chaco defeat, co-opting radical civilian dissent, and restoring the honor of the military institution. These "military socialists" nationalized the Standard Oil Company and granted amnesty to Indians imprisoned for desertion, draft evasion, and sedition; they also initiated a host of reforms—granting hacienda *colonos* (peons) the right to organize *sindicatos* (agrarian unions) and to rent municipal and religious estates; mandating schools for haciendas, mines and factories; social security, pensions, and accident insurance for workers; prohibiting child labor and the arbitrary firing of workers; and legalizing the right to collective bargaining.

A seminal development in indigenous history occurred when colono veterans returned to a hacienda in Cochabamba Department and with the support of a school teacher, a lawyer, and a Trotskyist militant formed a sindicato. Their collaboration eventuated in the unprecedented idea of the colonos themselves leasing the hacienda and thereby, ipso facto, escaping the chains of servitude. This iconoclastic venture would soon come to naught because of oligarchic obstruction: yet the praxis of the agrarian sindicato would be enormously consequential to the struggle against the hacienda system (*colonato*).

Chapter 2 analyzes another iteration of military nationalists who initiated a social revolution in 1943. This phase of the revolution (1943–1946), begun by a military lodge (*Razón de Patria*: RADEPA) of nationalist Chaco War veterans, is given short shrift in accounts of postwar developments. Sullied by propaganda portraying them as fascist anti-Semites, their program for economic diversification, national integration, legal rights, and social justice has been belittled, maligned, or ignored by journalists and scholars.[2] The objectives of the RADEPA revolutionaries and their civilian allies in the Nationalist Revolutionary Movement (MNR) were difficult to implement, given the opposition of Bolivian oligarchs, mining magnates, Stalinists, and Anglo-American hegemons. Despite propaganda to the contrary, RADEPA President Gualberto Villarroel refused to institute a dictatorial regime, or impose repressive measures to assure the survival of the revolution.

The Villarroel regime (yet another creole-mestizo government) was also pressured by subaltern nationalists intent on decolonization of the state. As indigenous resistance to the postwar regimes spread throughout the Andean highlands, a shadowy "Indigenous Committee" of Aymara and Quechua leaders appeared. The Committee sought to organize sindicatos throughout the country, recover lost lands, and allow Indians to live as citizens with legal and social rights. The Committee initiated hacienda sit-down strikes to resist the excesses of the colonato and in 1945 organized a National Indigenous Congress, where President Villarroel issued decrees to mitigate the conditions provoking the strikes. Predictably the decrees (whose enforcement remained the prerogative of rural officials beholden to landlords) heightened tensions on the haciendas.

Chapter 3 evaluates the overthrow of the RADEPA revolution by a cabal of oligarchs, mining magnates, and Stalinists (self-referenced as the *Frente Democrático Antifascista*), abetted by Anglo-American hegemons in 1946. British spycraft forged documents to give the false impression that the Radepistas were fascists and U.S. diplomacy crippled the regime by withholding diplomatic recognition, manipulating the dependent Bolivian economy, imposing economic sanctions, and disseminating propaganda to abet President Villarroel's bloody overthrow. In a critical revision of conventional works, which date the National Revolution from 1952–1964, this chapter argues that the revolution began in 1943, was overthrown in 1946, and resumed in 1952. The revolution is thus divided into a moderate phase (1943–1946), a counter-revolutionary interregnum (1946–1952), and a radical redux (1952–1964).

The 1946 overthrow of the RADEPA revolution is ignored in *all* accounts of U.S. orchestrated counterrevolutions. This chapter seeks to redress this oversight through a reconstruction of the fateful events surrounding the Bolivian overthrow. The "Good Neighbor" policy is unmasked as a clever ruse: nationalists branded as bad neighbors, unilateralism disguised as multilateralism, Bolivia portrayed as "an immense concentration camp." Comparisons are made with the counterrevolutionary schemes of the Anglo-American hegemons in the 1910 Mexican Revolution and against the Iranian nationalist Mohammad Mossadegh in 1953. The case is made that the Bolivian counterrevolution had much in common with the modus operandi deployed by the C.I.A. in Iran: publicized statements to isolate the regime, portraying it as anti-democratic; inciting mass demonstrations against the regime; imposing economic sanctions to weaken the regime;

branding the regime as dictatorial and on the brink of economic collapse; and granting immediate economic aid and assistance following the regime's overthrow.

Chapter 4 surveys the resistance of Indian and creole-mestizo revolutionaries during the *Sexenio*, the six-year oligarchic counterrevolution (1946–1952). Faced with draconian repression, the MNR disseminated propaganda, staged protests, recruited mine and factory workers to broaden its base, and introduced a clandestine cell structure to ensure the party's survival. When numerous coup attempts failed (together with an insurrection that devolved into a disastrous civil war), the *Movimientistas* opted to pursue an electoral strategy. After Víctor Paz Estenssoro was elected president in 1951 (but denied the presidency by a military takeover of the government), the MNR once again plotted an insurrectionary path to power.

The varieties of indigenous resistance to the colonato are discussed. As colonos insisted on implementation of the martyred Villarroel's decrees, instances of dual power arose when colonos refused to accept the authority of hacienda administrators and replaced them with their own leaders. Anarcho-syndicalists appeared at Altiplano haciendas to educate colonos and promote sit-down strikes. A revitalization movement in Cochabamba and Chuquisaca Departments educated Indians, while proselytizing resistance to the dominant creole-mestizo culture and a return to the indigenous culture of the Andean "First People." Indigenous resistance to the Sexenio reached its apogee in the "Great Rebellion" of 1947. Beginning with assaults on hacienda houses in the highland *serranía* of Cochabamba Department, the rebellion spread to Chuquisaca Department before the rebels were attacked by warplanes and infantry troops—women raped, houses razed, livestock and food stolen, crops burned—in a vicious campaign to terrorize the Indians. Other rebellions erupted in the Altiplano only to be repressed by military and para-military forces as the Old Regime confronted widespread agrarian resistance with the greatest military mobilization since the Chaco War.

Introduced in this chapter is an extraordinary indigenous manifesto, the *Tesis de Caranguillas*. Written during the Sexenio, the document is a revolutionary call for a return to the greatness of the pre-Columbian past. The *Tesis* includes an extensive critique of the creole state, foreign ideologies (Fascism, Trotskyism, Stalinism), capitalism, and imperialism together with a detailed prospectus for a multiethnic society and polity without private ownership of the means of production, and organized in a system of cooperative labor based on the traditional Andean practice of labor reciprocity (*ayni*).

The second half of the book (Chapters 5–8) focuses on the MNR redux of the National Revolution (1952–1964). Chapter 5 examines the organization, strategy, and tactics of the MNR insurrectionary seizure of power and demonstrates that the overthrow (April 9–13, 1952) of the ancien régime was the result of a carefully planned insurrection rather than the mythical "popular insurrection" found in many accounts. Once in power, the MNR instituted landmark decrees emasculating the military institution, nationalizing the tin mines, abolishing servitude, enfranchising the Indian, expropriating haciendas, and redistributing lands to colonos. The chapter surveys the ensuing struggle for control of the revolution that arose as right and left-wing MNR factions clashed over the substantive issues within the decrees. Should the military institution—the sword of repression—be reduced or eradicated? The tin magnates indemnified? The hacienda lords compensated for their expropriated fiefs? The schism between MNR reformists and revolutionaries which precipitated a revolt by right-wing Movimietistas in the early days of the revolution would continue to bedevil the National Revolution and contribute to its demise in 1964.

The fate of the revolution was determined by President Paz Estenssoro's insistence on retaining the military institution against the opposition of the MNR leftists Ñuflo Chávez, Juan Lechín, and fellow labor leaders, who advocated a co-government of armed worker and peasant sindicatos (unions). The creation of the *Central Obrera Boliviana* (COB) trade union confederation controlled by Marxist revolutionaries was the apogee of leftist influence in the National Revolution. Dedicated to co-government of miners and peasant sindicatos, the COB was the bête noir of the MNR right-wing. The origins and development of opposition by creole-mestizo elites and U.S. diplomats to Lechín, the COB, and indigenous workers and peasants is a topic in this and the following chapters.

An underlying thread in the National Revolution (and this book) is the continued domination of three million Indians by the MNR—yet another creole-mestizo regime. The revolution offered a momentous opportunity for the indigenous majority to overthrow their masters. The number of sindicato militias was multiplying, and many were organized by military veterans and Marxists indoctrinated with the doctrine of class struggle. The fact that these militias were armed, more numerous, and more experienced than the military's conscripts gave the agrarian revolutionaries the historic opportunity to seize haciendas and redistribute the land strictly among themselves. Instead, as is demonstrated in this chapter, the agrarian revolution failed to realize its potential and an Agrarian reform was decreed by the creole-mestizo élites, for their own ends. The continuation of creole-mestizo domination under the MNR regime depended on the ability to control the awakening agrarian revolution and subvert indigenous political agency. The history of the National Revolution is the history of indigenous resistance and those who organized and led it.

The MNR waged an undeclared war against Indian revolutionaries: utilizing a rural police force to enforce order; issuing supreme decrees to enforce colono labor on haciendas; publicizing "sanctions" against "agitators," and denunciations of sit-down strikes by government spokesmen, including Ñuflo Chávez (the onetime minister of peasant affairs). As rural violence spread in the highlands, the creole-mestizo vecinos faced assaults by ex-colonos against their urban enclaves. Intra-ethnic violence, exacerbated by the power vacuum in the backlands, intensified conflicts over boundaries, clashes between colonos, ex-colonos, and ayllu *comunarios*, and factional struggles over sindicato leadership erupted as a new generation of leaders emerged. The ex-colono José Rojas appeared as jefe of the agrarian revolution in Cochabamba Department; Sinforoso Rivas, an acculturated *cholo*, likewise rose to prominence as a Cochabamba sindicato leader. One month before enactment of the 1953 Agrarian Reform Decree, President Paz Esetenssoro mandated the reinstitution of the armed forces to counterbalance the sindicato militias and quell the forcible seizure and redistribution of hacienda lands by agrarian revolutionaries.

Chapter 6 explores the ramifications of the momentous Agrarian Reform Decree: the MNR's attempt to transform Indians into small farmers subsumed into a capitalist economy and integrated into urban Hispanic culture and society. Regional aspects of land tenure under the colonato are discussed, as well as the obstacles to implementation of colono and comunario land claims. The chapter considers the particularities of the agrarian reform process in the highlands, the attempts by the MNR to quell an indigenous revolutionary awakening, the Indian leaders' resistance to creole-mestizo hegemony, and the role of factionalism among the creole-mestizo elites and the indigenous peoples. Contrary to early accounts of the Bolivian agrarian reform which conflate de facto with de jure (e.g., "The Indian Gets the Land"), the legal decree and its implementation were two different creatures: one a mandate; the other a process undertaken, against all odds, by the emancipated Indians.

This chapter analyzes the problematics and consequences of the decree. The decree offered comunarios a limited opportunity for restitution of usurped ayllu lands; allowed colonos to acquire small plots; made a faint, failed gesture toward creation of agrarian co-operatives; and mandated a serious attempt (under the aegis of USAID) to colonize the lowlands of the Oriente. The MNR commitment to colonization presaged a historic shift in demographic and political power to the Department of Santa Cruz and away from the highland departments. The irony of the Agrarian Reform Decree—granting small plots to colonos, but due to fate, circumstance, and primogeniture—resulting in minifundismo remains a legacy of the revolution. The exodus of peasants from the Andean highlands to urban shantytowns or to the Oriente is yet another result of this transformative decree.

Chapter 7 examines the consequences of the Agrarian Reform Decree: the exacerbation of tensions among ayllu comunarios, hacienda colonos, and ex-colonos; conflicts between Indians and creole-mestizo vecinos; and the rise of Indian caudillos contesting for power at the departmental level, leading to internecine violence between conflicting factions. The interplay of factious agrarian sindicatos, MNR left and right-wing sectors, and Trotskyist, Stalinist, and Fascist militants is also considered. While the regime struggled to control the countryside and co-opt the agrarian revolutionaries, it also lost its urban middle-class supporters to staggering inflation, a government spoils system and nepotism, together with a catastrophic decline in tin ore content and government revenue. How, facing bankruptcy, the MNR regime lost its moral compass, betrayed its revolutionary principles, made a pact with the devil, and capitulated to become a neo-colonial satrapy of the North American empire is made evident in this chapter.

The attempts of President Hernán Siles (1952–1956) to tame both the COB and the agrarian revolution (per the dictates of U.S. policy) are traced as is the "divide and conquer" strategy employed against the COB sectors; the co-optation and neutralization of peasant caudillos; the appointments of right-wing Movimientistas to departmental prefectures; support of vecino militias; military deployments to zones of revolutionary contention; and propaganda campaign against militant Indian "troublemakers." Agrarian sindicato history during this period of confrontation between indigenous revolutionaries and the creole-mestizo regime is discussed. The role of political patronage (clientelism), the rise of regional strongmen (*caudillos*), and factional conflict is analyzed: racketeering and turf wars between caudillos, their conflicts with vecino adversaries, and relationships with mineworkers' sindicatos. Two agrarian revolutionaries: José Rojas, the Cochabamba caudillo, and his Mexican counterpart Emiliano Zapata are compared. Note is made of the influence of communist indoctrination in the case of Rojas and the deployment of Ucureña militiamen to extend hacienda seizures and land redistribution beyond local and regional horizons into the departments of Chuquisaca and Potosí. Twice appointed Minister of Peasant Affairs, Rojas exemplifies the perquisites of MNR patronage and co-optation while Zapata, who held steadfast to his principles, was assassinated.

Chapter 8 chronicles the fateful conjuncture resulting from the regime's descent into authoritarianism: the role of the U.S. government in supporting the tyranny under the guise of the Alliance for Progress, the struggle among MNR leaders for control of the revolution, the machinations of disaffected military officers in the Bolivian High Command, and the conduct of U.S. diplomats and military attachés backing these factions. The internecine conflicts between peasant caudillos are scrutinized with an eye to the ways in which creole-mestizo élites thwarted indigenous political agency in the Cochabamba valleys, the Altiplano, and Northern Potosí.

The densely populated Cochabamba valleys gave rise to brutal and protracted syndical conflicts between rival Indian caudillos. The social and historical roots of the bitter feud between the Ucureña sindicato and the nearby sindicato at Cliza, a town of conservative vecinos, hacendados, merchants, and small farmers with little to gain from an agrarian revolution is essayed, as is the manner in which these indigenous caudillos were co-opted by competing factions within the MNR élite. The resultant war between the Ucureña and Cliza sindicatos confounded the government and led to reliance on a revived military institution to control the conflict. The MNR regime's use of the armed forces to quell warring agrarian sindictos, recalcitrant miners, and fascist rebellions is examined as the harbinger of the restoration of the military institution to praetorian rule.

The chapter also focuses on the factional conflicts in the region surrounding the Altiplano town of Achacachi in La Paz Department. Reminiscent of the Cochabamba conflict between Ucureña and Cliza, a history of hostility existed between the Warisata ayllu and Achacachi vecinos and absentee landlords, eventuating in the destruction of the extraordinary Warisata nuclear school by Achacachi hacendados.

The conflicts between the Warisata sindicato and its vecino adversaries at Achacachi and elsewhere are detailed, as is the rise of the Achacachi caudillo Toribio Salas. Salas is noteworthy for his resistance to creole interference in his domain (including the assassination of a prominent Movimientista), his support of Juan Lechín's opposition to Paz Estenssoro's rule, and his eventual eclipse by the resurgent military in the twilight of the National Revolution.

Potosí Department is the third locus of indigenous factionalism exacerbated by the National Revolution. Although intra-ethnic factionalism, clashes over land, and local quarrels over sindicato leadership persisted as elsewhere in the highlands, the province of Chayanta in northern Potosí Department emerged as the epicenter of clashes among ayllu comunarios, hacendados, ex-colonos, and vecinos. Much of the convoluted history of the regional conflict involved the town of San Pedro de Buena Vista and the attempts of its resident hacendados and vecinos to maintain their dominion over comunarios and ex-colonos in the surrounding countryside. The deeply rooted feuds between vecinos and rebellious Indians resulted in murder, massacres, and mutilation of victims. How the agrarian reform process and the rise of indigenous syndicalism intensified the violence among comunarios, colonos, and vecinos is examined, together with the *Sangre de Venganza* (the intra-ethnic feud among Jukumani, Laymi, and Kakachaka ayllus), and the use of Jukumani comunarios as proxies in a scheme concocted by Paz Estenssoro and USAID agents to end the resistance of Indian miners to the neo-colonial regime.

The chapter concludes with an assessment of the factors contributing to the demise and overthrow of the National Revolution: the factionalism within the MNR inner circle; the use of the Alliance for Progress as a cover for U.S. imperial machinations; the introduction of U.S. counter-insurgency doctrine, including Civic Action projects to win the support of the peasantry; the implementation of the Mann Doctrine as a U.S. counterpoise to resource nationalists; the use of U.S. military attachés to influence Bolivian officers and USAID agents to implement schemes to crush the resistance of indigenous miners and peasants to Paz Estenssoro's authoritarian regime; the cooptation of peasant sindicatos by General René Barrientos Ortuño; the ascendency of the Bolivian armed forces to power, and the overthrow of the National Revolution.

The Epilogue summarizes the legacies of the National Revolution for the indigenous majority (agrarian reform, enfranchisement of adult men and women, universal education, syndicalism, colonization of the Oriente). The economic, demographic, and political implications of the agrarian reform process are discussed in the context of the 500-year resistance of the indigenous populace against creole domination. The post-revolutionary period of praetorian rule is surveyed: the militarized modernization policy of the Alliance for Progress (1964–1971); the resultant shift of national power to the Oriente; creation of a terrorist-state by the Santa Cruz President, General Hugo Banzer Suárez, and the awakening of indigenous resistance to the tyranny (1971–1978); the creation of Latin America's first narco-state (1980–1981) by the Santa Cruz "Cocaine King" and military narcotraffickers, abetted by Nazi war criminals, the CIA, DEA, and the NSA's Colonel

Oliver North. The following period of indigenous mass resistance to neo-liberal rule leading to the election of the Aymara President Evo Morales and the Plurinational State of Bolivia is analyzed, as is the overthrow of the historic 14-year regime by racist creoles from the Oriente supported by the North American hegemon.

Notes

1. The once hidden history of indigenous resistance during the Chaco War has been illuminated by the Bolivian scholars Carlos B. Mamani Condori, *Taraqu, 1866–1935: Masacre, Guerra y 'Renovación' en la biografia de Eduardo L. Nina Qhispi* (La Paz, 1991) and René Danilo Arze Aguirre, *Guerra y conflictos sociales: el caso rural boliviano durante la campana del Chaco* (La Paz, 1987).
2. The image of a brutal, totalitarian regime in the Andes covered the entire political spectrum of U.S. print media (*New York Times, Washington Post, Newsweek,* the *Nation, New Republic, New Masses, Daily Worker*). As the labor activist Ernesto Galarza noted: "There is probably no example on record of such thorough going indoctrination by Nazi and Fascist news and propaganda agencies under Hitler and Mussolini as this almost perfect example of controlled public opinion achieved through the free press" Ernesto Galarza, "The Case of Bolivia," *Inter-American Reports*, 6 (May 1949), 21.

1

WAR

The Generation of the Chaco

Bolivia at mid-twentieth century was a country frozen in time. A nation of extremes: lofty Andean peaks, tropical jungles, a vast Altiplano 4,000 meters above sea level; the most inequitable land tenure system on the planet; three million Indians ruled by a creole oligarchy; an army whose only victories were against its own people. "What is certain is that there is no other country of its size which contributes so little to the general stock of information of the reasonably well-informed," opined a foreign observer in 1953: "Even in the neighboring countries there are few among the general public who know or wish to know more of it than fanciful and slightly malicious gossip."[1] But change was afoot.

In the crucial decades 1932–1952, Bolivia's ancien régime began to self-destruct. The catalyst was an ill-advised and ill-fated war with Paraguay over the expansive Chaco Boreal.

The Chaco War (1932–1935) was a turning point in Bolivian history, a conflict that exposed the decadence, corruption, and incompetence of the oligarchy, not only in the eyes of a generation of creole-mestizo elites but also to those peasants and workers who survived the ordeal. The war was a travesty: creole generals notorious for cowardice and gross ineptitude and an army of peasants and workers sacrificed in a contest whose real lesson would come to involve questions of race and class. The bloody fiasco was a catalyst to the destruction of the traditional order—and the coming of South America's singular social revolution.

The backdrop to the Chaco War lies in President Daniel Salamanca's response to the collapse of the tin-based export economy occasioned by the Great Depression. Revenue from tin exports fell, government deficits rose, unemployment in the mines and cities grew, and a credit crunch bankrupted overextended landlords.[2] The answer to these difficulties was economic diversification: weaning the economy from tin and developing the country's petroleum reserves as a strategic resource. The locus of Bolivian oil production was in the *Oriente*, the eastern lowlands where the Standard Oil Company drilled and refined oil on hundreds of thousands of acres of leased land. In 1929, Argentina refused landlocked Bolivia's request to construct a pipeline to the Atlantic Ocean. The remaining option was to build a pipeline from the Bolivian oil fields, through the scrublands of the Chaco Boreal to a port on the Rio Paraguay, and export the oil downstream to the Atlantic. However, claims to the Chaco were disputed with Paraguay. Skirmishes became more frequent between the countries as Bolivia's President Salamanca assumed a bellicose position. The belligerents reinforced their border outposts.

MAP 1.1 Bolivia

Source: Courtesy of the U.S. Central Intelligence Agency.

Bolivia's claim to sovereignty of the Gran Chaco dated from the Spanish Empire and therefore presumably included in the nation after independence.[3] Paraguayan sovereignty rested on right of occupancy by settlers, with the influential Argentine *estancieros*, estate owners, raising cattle and harvesting *quebracho* (wood used in wine and leather processing) on nearly a million acres of the Gran Chaco.[4] Wars waged in the nineteenth century were failures for both nations. Bolivia fought a war against Chile from 1869 to 1873, resulting in the ignominious loss of 200,000 square kilometers, including its seacoast along the Atacama Desert.[5] A second nineteenth-century war with Brazil over the rubber forests in the Department of Acre led to the loss of some 187,800 square kilometers. The shame of defeat has remained a thorn in the side of Bolivian nationalists.[6] Paraguay was halved in size following the genocidal War of the Triple Alliance (1864–1870) that pitted the megalomaniac Francisco Solano López's army against the combined forces of Argentina, Brazil, and Uruguay. The result was catastrophic: two-thirds of the population killed—more deaths per national population than any war in modern history.[7] For Paraguay, defeat in the Chaco was not an option: failure could spell the demise of the nation itself.

Bolivian interest in the Chaco focused on access to the Atlantic through the Rio Paraguay and the chimerical dream of potential oil reserves in the region. Paraguay initially fought to defend its remaining patrimony: but as its armed forces pushed beyond the disputed border, deep into Bolivian territory, strategy shifted to a war of conquest. Paraguay benefited from troops acclimated to the arid region, familiarity with the terrain, superior leadership, and logistics. The military historian Matthew Hughes argues convincingly that Paraguay's superior logistical infrastructure was instrumental to its success on the battlefield. Paraguay purchased war materiel from manufacturers in 13 countries, evidencing prescient strategic planning (as well as a competitive advantage in quality and price of armaments).[8]

Bolivian efforts were severely hampered by chronic political infighting between President Salamanca and his General Staff, the refusal of Argentina and Chile to allow shipment of supplies through their territories, and the logistical difficulties of delivering war material to the distant Chaco. In a grievous affront, the Standard Oil Company violated its petroleum contract with Bolivia and refused to increase oil production or refine aviation fuel. The Standard Oil Company, claiming neutrality, capped wells and moved equipment from the Bolivian oil fields to Argentina.[9] These difficulties were compounded by the monumental failures of the officer corps: ignorance of the terrain (e.g., cavalry troops reduced to infantry after their mounts died of thirst), chronic breakdown of logistical support, and poor communication within the largely illiterate, ill-equipped, and untrained conscripts. Reliance on the British manufacturer Vickers proved fatal to the war effort: much of the equipment (generally of poor quality) never arrived; what did arrive (estimated at one-fourth to one-third of the contract) was delayed reaching the front because of Bolivia's abysmal transportation infrastructure.[10] The American aircraft manufacturer Curtiss-Wright Corporation sold Bolivia 34 warplanes in 1933. But President Franklin Roosevelt, honoring a League of Nations mandate, imposed an

FIGURE 1.1 Bolivia Rushes Its Troops to the Chaco Front

Source: Courtesy of the U.S. National Archives (Photo: 306NT- 933F2). *New York Times*, 26 January 1933.

arms embargo on sales to the Chaco belligerents and only a few of the warplanes arrived in Bolivia.[11]

The two poorest nations in South America fought with armies largely comprised of Indian conscripts. In the early months of the war (June–December 1932), patriotic creole-mestizos fought alongside Indian peasants, miners, and urban workers. But as casualties mounted, patriotic fervor dwindled as did the number of volunteers. Initially the generals drew upon urban reservists because they were more accessible, more likely to be literate, and easier to train and transport than rural Indians.[12] The war was devastating; of the 77,000 Bolivian soldiers mobilized in the first year of combat; 14,000 were killed in action; 10,000 were captured; 6,000 deserted; and 32,000 were lost to wounds, sickness, and disease. Death, desertions, and casualties accounted for the loss of over 80 percent of the conscripts. In one year of combat, the army was reduced to 7,000 soldiers in the front lines, and another 8,000 (primarily creole-mestizos) who served behind the lines were removed from harm's way.[13]

Besides the high numbers of prisoners and deserters, which roughly doubled by war's end, the number of casualties due to illness is shocking.[14] Dehydration, starvation, disease (yellow fever, smallpox, dengue fever, malaria, cholera, typhus, typhoid fever, bacterial diarrhea, hepatitis), and illness resulting from extreme vitamin deficiency decimated the troops who arrived at the front after an arduous trek on foot for hundreds of miles.[15] Illness and disease contributed to 85 percent of the deaths reported at the Villa Monte hospital in 1932; malaria infected 899 patients. Avitaminosis, the most common disease (1,999 cases reported at the hospital in 1933), caused by extreme or chronic vitamin deficiency, contributed more casualties than malaria and tuberculosis combined. One in four patients deemed unfit for service suffered from tuberculosis, and gastrointestinal infections from foul food and polluted water were the cause of two-thirds of the deaths at the San Antonio Military Hospital.[16] Psychological disorders (depression, self-mutilation, and suicide) took their toll among those who could no longer endure the nightmare.

The Chaco's extreme temperatures debilitated the Andean conscripts. The arid Chaco Boreal is without rain for eight to nine months of the year. "They say we were fighting a war for oil in the Chaco," recalled an Indian miner, "We weren't fighting for oil; we were fighting for water. Over each puddle we waged a war with the Paraguayans because we were dying of heat in that blazing sun."[17] An ethnic divide plagued the Bolivian military and hampered its effectiveness, as the Kallawaya veteran Antonio [Mamani] Álvarez, recounts: "The war was a failure because nobody was able to communicate. The campesinos didn't know how to operate any kind of armaments, the climate didn't favor them and nobody was anybody's friend. There was still much regionalism, the Aymaras together on one side and the Quechuas on the other and they insulted each other in their dialects. . . . [T]hose who didn't know how to speak another language other than their own, weren't able to understand."[18]

The casualties of war also include the surviving victims of the call to arms. The impact of disease—on the primarily Indian soldiers—was compounded as the pathogens were carried home. Bolivian health care, such as it was, served the urban populace and ignored the nation's rural majority. On the eve of the war, an outbreak of yellow fever devastated the Colorado regiment while stationed in Santa Cruz. Miserable living conditions for the troops—overcrowded barracks, poor sanitation, the lack of potable water, and mosquito netting—created the ideal environment for the spread of infectious disease. Smallpox ravaged both civilians and conscripts because of government failure to inoculate the population. At the war's end in 1935, a smallpox epidemic spread from troops to residents in Santa Cruz Department, underscoring the continued inability to inoculate either soldiers or civilians. Typhus, borne by lice, ravaged the country.[19]

A truce signed in 1935 ended the conflict. Bolivia lost 52,397 combatants, failed to secure access to the Atlantic, and ceded three-quarters of the Chaco Boreal to Paraguay. Twenty percent of the 25,000 prisoners held captive in Paraguay died from wounds and sickness.[20] The lessons of the war, as with the sickness and disease contracted in the Chaco, infected those who survived the terrible ordeal of struggle and loss. One-fourth of the adult male population had been pressed into the armed forces. As casualties mounted untamed *colonos*, militant mine workers, urban labor leaders, and political gadflies were sent to the trenches.[21] Recruits were drawn disproportionately from *ayllu* communities rather than haciendas where colono labor was indispensable to creole-mestizo landlords. Consequently, ayllus weakened by the loss of adult males were besieged by opportunistic *hacendados* encroaching on communal lands. Press-gangs roamed the highlands in search of Indians, wreaking death and destruction on those who resisted the brutal demands of recruitment.[22] Families split asunder by a rapacious war machine and forced to eke out subsistence without male labor were preyed upon by corrupt *corregidores* (local officials), ostensibly collecting taxes and food for the war effort.

The War Within

An internal war of resistance to the depredations of creole-mestizo rule ensued behind the lines of the Chaco. Rape, murder, massacre, and pillage of homes and villages were visited upon those who resisted the requisition of livestock, foodstuffs, and contrived taxes.[23] Creole-mestizos were able to evade the killing fields of the Chaco through government exemptions, by serving behind the lines via political connections, bribery, enlisting in the ranks of the carabineros, police, or the paramilitary *Legión Cívica*, a creole-mestizo supremacist organization created in 1932.[24] Dedicated to rooting out Indian deserters, draft dodgers, and fugitives, the *Legión* became a useful tool for landlords to rid themselves of troublesome Indians accused of subversive or, worse yet, "communist" behavior.[25] The irony of Legionnaire draft-dodgers professing patriotism—while dragooning Indians to fight for them— epitomizes the cynicism and racism of the Old Order.

The Tin Barons managed the exemption of mine workers with the exception of labor militants, but the conscription of leftists resulted in the diffusion of anti-war and anti-oligarchic ideas among the troops.[26] Hacendados lobbied for the exclusion of colonos, arguing their necessity for food production vital to the war effort (thereby shifting recruitment and taxation toward the *ayllu comunarios*). The *Sociedad Rural*, a hacendado interest group, lobbied for military recruitment based on Indian population density—a clever maneuver to focus on *ayllu* comunarios and away from hacienda colonos whose labor was essential to agricultural production and war profiteering.[27] Consequently, ayllu comunarios were targeted for conscription. Aside from political lobbying and bureaucratic machinations, hacendados employed a gamut of ploys to avoid loss of *colonos* to the army, including bribery of recruiters and *corregidores*, sale of forged documents, and falsification of a colono's age. The Ministry of Government reported in 1934 that the majority of provincial government authorities created obstacles and failed to cooperate with army patrols.[28]

Local authorities, generally *corregidores* whose sinecure was dependent on the will of the hacendados, pursued Indian draft dodgers.[29] The more enterprising local officials were quick to monetize conscription, conjuring a variety of schemes to extort profit from Indians caught evading their "patriotic" duty.[30] As early as March 1933, incidents involving the capture and extortion of Indian deserters occurred in La Paz Department; Indians in Chuquisaca Department fled to the mountainous *serranía* to avoid entrapment by corregidores. Urban Indians also sought the safety of the serranía, increasingly populated by fugitive colonos and comunarios.[31]

Retaliatory attacks on corregidores began in early 1933 and by April the High Command confessed its inability to pursue draft evaders and deserters because of a manpower shortage. The exodus of Indians escaping recruitment raised the fear of a potential food shortage in the cities—a dire threat to creole-mestizo urbanites.[32] Revolts and land conflicts continued in the Andean highlands, including disputes over boundaries between ayllu and hacienda properties; expansionist land grabs by hacendados; attacks by colonos and comunarios on hacendados, their property, and their representatives (*mayordomos*, corregidores); and uprisings—imagined, threatened, and real—against creole-mestizo townspeople. A climate of fear engulfed the countryside fed by paranoid rumors of vengeful Indian hordes meting out punishment against innocent city folk. Suspected uprisings, reported by local officials and sensationalized in newspapers, fed the great fear of Indian rebellion.

Conflicts between opportunistic landlords, emboldened by the absence of colonos and comunarios serving at the front, erupted in the early years of the war. The lacustrine region of La Paz Department had been swept by an earlier uprising in 1932 and suspected leaders were quickly rounded up by creole-mestizo militias from Guaqui, Viacha, Tiwanaku, and Puerto Acosta. Colono and comunario revolts, real and rumored, were reported during June–July and October–November 1932 in the Altiplano provinces of Omasuyos, Sikasika, Ingavi, and Murillo.[33] Similar rumors circulated in the Departments of Potosí, Oruro, and La Paz. President Salamanca, fearful of a widespread rebellion, authorized the emergency recruitment of 800 carabineros to enforce the conscription levies, and the prefect of Cinti Province (Chuquisaca Department) confronted with strident resistance by Indians to military conscription and to forced labor for road construction utilized police for enforcement.[34]

The murder of five comunarios by an Altiplano hacendado during a dispute over usurped ayllu lands precipitated a widespread uprising in Ingavi Province (La Paz Department) in January 1934, after Carlos Pereira, a hacendado notorious for his depredations against *ayllu* communities, murdered the comunarios: three from the Ikiyaka ayllu and two from ayllu *Q'atawi*. Incensed comunarios besieged the nearby town of Pucarani in June 1934. Soon after Pereira was killed in a fracas with *Q'atawi* comunarios and his body thrown into an arroyo; his mayordomo was killed in a separate attack. The murders precipitated a government massacre of comunario men, women, and children, slaughtered by infantry and strafed from above by warplanes. Leaders of the two ayllus were executed.[35]

Sporadic revolts erupted in the smoldering war of resistance on the Altiplano. The town of Guaqui was invaded and telegraph lines were cut, docks destroyed, and the railroad station and a locomotive damaged. The Indian rebels were then attacked by military air and ground strikes.[36] This was something new: the use of warplanes to terrorize a conquered people. Tiwanaku was surrounded by hacienda colonos, and townspeople were taken hostage; a shootout in the canton of Vilaque left five townspeople and four Indians dead. The following day the town of

Pucarani was attacked and a rectory burned. Authorities in Achacachi, anticipating an attack, pleaded for rifles and ammunition from La Paz.[37]

The government was now conducting a war on two fronts. As the war progressed, the creole-mestizo rulers of the Amerindian nation increasingly drew upon Indian conscripts, while in the Andean highlands Indian soldiers were deployed to defend hacendados and *vecinos* (townspeople) from colonos and comunarios guilty of resisting domination. Rumors of dreaded rebellions fueled by lurid stories of murdered landlords, sacked haciendas, and besieged towns continued throughout the Chaco War. Indians who questioned authority, resisted onerous demands, or insisted on social and legal rights (whether colonos, comunarios, or dwellers in urban shanties) were accused of agitation, inciting rebellion, collusion with the enemy, or "communism"—a recurrent if nebulous opprobrium. Government officials and urban newspapers ceaselessly referenced the communist threat. Indigenous agitation was equated with class warfare rather than a continuation of the age-old struggle for restitution of usurped lands or as a response to intolerable wartime depredations. Senator Jaime Mendoza, demanding amnesty for Indians imprisoned for alleged communist agitation, pointed to the conflation of communism with indigenous resistance: "Communism . . . is an accommodating vocabulary in Bolivia employed for whatever motive. Thus, for example, we call the hungry communists because they ask for bread."[38]

While the communist threat was exaggerated, vanguard militants of the fledgling PIR (*Partido de la Izquierda Revolucionaria*; Party of the Revolutionary Left) and POR (*Partido Obrero Revolucionario*; Revolutionary Workers Party) did indeed focus on organization of indigenous peasants and proletarians in preparation for class struggle. Comunarios, however, because of the prevailing Marxist dogma, were left to their own devices. Both hacienda and ayllu would have to disappear, according to historical materialist theory, for the nation to achieve the requisite stage of capitalist development preparatory to the ultimate stage of communism.[39]

Peasants on the march brandishing Red Flags were reported on the Altiplano and anarchist militants, active among the Aymara in the Department of Oruro, urging passive resistance to military conscription, were charged with treason and imprisoned. The anarchist *Federación del Trabajo de Oruro* (FOT) declared: "Antipatriots are not those who oppose the massacre of the people and the complete ruin of the country. The antipatriots, the traitors to the Fatherland, are those that have sold pieces of the national territory; those who have sold the seacoast to Chile, those who have sold Acre to Brazil; those who have mortgaged the rest to the bankers of North America."[40]

The Generation of the Chaco

The Chaco War forged a passion for change among a generation who would no longer countenance the misrule of a tainted oligarchy. The war drew conscripts from the various departments: enlisted, drafted, dragooned, the nation of Indians, *cholos*, mestizos, and creoles—riven with class, racial, ethnic, linguistic, and regional

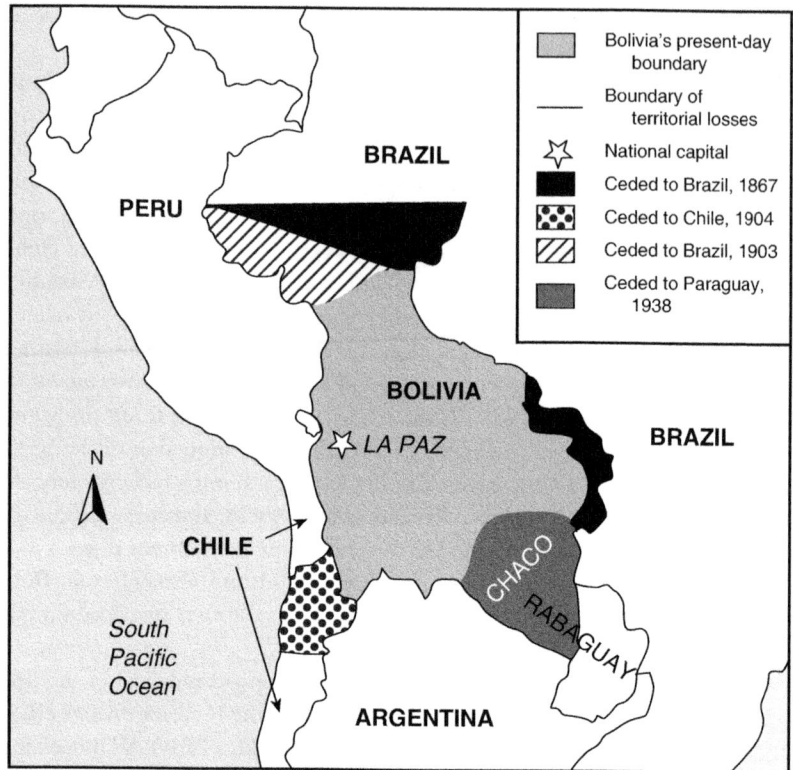

MAP 1.2 Bolivia Map with Territory Lost in Wars with Chile, Brazil, and Paraguay
Source: Courtesy of the U.S. Library of Congress.

divisions—would never again be the same. Nationalism, spawned in the trenches and in Paraguayan concentration camps, became the focus of intense debate, provoking coups, revolts, and rebellions in the postwar years and culminating in a social revolution. The "Generation of the Chaco" generally refers to the creole-mestizo elites who responded to the misrule of a tainted oligarchy with an outpouring of creativity: *Indigenista* literature, investigative journalism, political tracts, and polemics.

Yet another "Chaco Generation" arose in the hinterland as radicalized Indians joined the ranks of organizers engaged in resistance to the Old Order. Santos Marka T'ula, Eduardo Leandro Nina Qhispi, Antonio Mamani Álvarez, and José Rojas Guevara were but a few of the better known leaders (*dirigentes*) in the struggle for indigenous rights. Marka T'ula and Nina Qhispi advocated social rights, education, and land revendication in the prewar decades, organized passive resistance to hacienda excesses, and the conscription and impressment of Indians. Mamani Álvarez and Rojas Guevara, politicized by war and imprisonment, typify the indigenous Generation of the Chaco. Rojas would come to epitomize the *sindicato* (union) movement that emerged in the post-Chaco years; Mamani Álvarez would exemplify pan-indigenous nationalism, a millenarian sensibility of autochthonous identity and political agency, to be awakened through literacy and education.

The postwar period is remarkable for the interplay among the various sectors of Bolivian society radicalized by the trauma: military officers, middle-class intellectuals, journalists and novelists, artisans and shopkeepers, miners, peasants, and urban laborers. Upstart newspapers excoriated mine owners and hacienda oligarchs referred to as the *Rosca* (a kernel; nucleus). *El Universal* and its predecessor *La Republica* introduced investigative journalism to the urban middle class.[41] In a war of words, readers were privy to the inner world of entrenched and corrupt special interests with a daily skewering of the rich and powerful: the jingoism, the Chaco misadventure; the phony patriotism of the nation's rulers, and their failures in diplomacy and war. Dispatches from correspondents at the front chronicled the realities and incongruities of a rich man's war and a poor man's fight: the plight of impoverished Indians suffering in the trenches as their families struggled to eke out an existence with husbands and fathers absent while hacendados and speculators profited. Both newspapers were closed on multiple occasions and ultimately shut down.

Among the war correspondents exposed to the dismal realities of the Chaco were Augusto Céspedes and Carlos Montenegro, who (along with Armando Arce, their editor at *El Universal*) continued their odyssey from the closure of the paper to its reinvention in 1936 as *La Calle*. The two were to become icons of the Generation of the Chaco. Céspedes's acclaimed *Sangre de Mestizos: relatos de la guerra del Chaco* (1936), based on dispatches as a war correspondent for *El Universal*, drew the reader into the plight of the common man, mestizo and Indian, amid the agony of the Chaco: a fight as much against scorching heat and unquenchable thirst as against the enemy. This and later works would establish Augusto Céspedes as the most celebrated writer of his generation. Carlos Montenegro, also a war correspondent, returned from the war to pen *Nacionalismo y coloniaje*, a systematic critique of Bolivian underdevelopment that would infuse a spirit of nationalism among the generation of the Chaco. The contributions of Céspedes and Montenegro at *La Calle* together with Armando Arce's editorials established the newspaper's reputation as the relentless voice of opposition to the Rosca.

A literature emerged that exposed the dark underside of the conflict. *Repete*, a memoir written by the Quechua author and *Ex-Combatiente* Jesus Lara, is noteworthy for its portrayal of life and death in the Green Hell but also for the denial and resentment the book elicited from military and civil authorities.[42] Sale of the book was forbidden in the Department of Cochabamba ("prohibited for concepts injurious to our army and that damage our national honor"). Indeed, an irate army colonel, his honor besmirched by *Repete*, challenged Lara to a duel.[43] Lara's trilogy of revolutionary novels *Surumi* (1943), *Yanakuna* (1952), and *Yawarninchij* (1959) focuses on creole and vecino exploitation of the Indians of the Cochabamba valleys and their redemption in a communist state.[44]

The author Fernando Diez de Medina (who joined the MNR after the 1952 Revolution), published a scathing criticism of the mining *superestado* in *Pachakuti y Otras Páginas Polémicas: Con la Denuncia por defraudación de impuestos contra los multimillonarios Patiño y Aramayo* (1948), notable for the inclusion of a conversation between the author and the tin magnate Carlos Víctor Aramayo. The later *Siripaka: La Batalla de Bolivia* (1950) and *Ainoka: Ideario del Pachakutismo* (1950) augmented Diez de Medina's nationalist and Indianist perspective, attracting a following to the idea of *Pachakutismo*, that included the journalist Carlos Serrate Reich, later appointed Minister of Education during the National Revolution.[45]

Military Socialism

Resistance to the Old Order was not confined to civilians. Combat officers returned from the war infused with a desire to oust the Rosca and modernize the nation. Their experience is of a piece with that of France, Russia, Germany, and China, where the political scientist Chalmers Johnson notes, "Defeat in war, as an accelerator [of dysfunction], shatters the myth of sovereignty, exacts sacrifices—even the supreme sacrifice—from a society's members of an unpopular system, and completes the crippling of an already creaking system; *most important, it opens the doors to revolution because of its effects on the army.*"[46] (emphasis added) For those who fought—army officers, middle-class intellectuals, peasants, miners, workers, artisans—a return to the status quo ante bellum was unacceptable.

After President Salamanca was ousted by a military coup in late 1934, Vice President José Luis Tejada Sorzano assumed the presidency and the impossible task of negotiating a surrender, ceding a vast expanse of the Chaco to Paraguay, and demobilizing potentially mutinous troops. The president was also confronted by the *Legión de Ex-Combatientes* comprised exclusively of Chaco veterans (primarily Indian peasants and workers) with a radical agenda of demands: nationalization of the means of production, pensions for ex-prisoners of war, investigation of war profiteering, a purge of the judiciary, rent control, creation of a socialist university.[47] Likewise, the demands of the militant postwar trade unions vexed the president: 100 percent salary increase for employees; 50 percent reduction in the price of consumer goods; regulation of working hours; aid for veterans and benefits for war widows; unionization of labor; freedom of assembly; freedom of the press; and suspension of a state of siege.[48] Tejada Sorzano's decision to resort to martial law, amidst a general strike, led to his downfall. Army officers frustrated by his inability to control civil society deposed him as they had his predecessor. But this time there would be no handoff of power from the army to another feckless civilian.

The Military Socialists

A duo of young officers, Colonels David Toro (1936–1937) and Germán Busch (1937–1939), seized power and instituted military rule. The colonels ruled for a combined three years; their agenda of nationalist-populist policies, subsequently labeled "military socialism," sought also to divert criticism of the military institution and co-opt the growing influence of radical leftists.[49] President Toro increased workers' wages, created a Department of Labor, and recognized the Bolivian Workers' Union Confederation (*Confederación Sindical de Trabajadores Bolivianos*) as a legal entity. Toro also nationalized the Standard Oil company in 1937 (a year before the better known oil nationalization in Mexico). A symbol of U.S. imperialism, Standard Oil had refused to support the Bolivian war effort in the Chaco by refining aviation fuel. The company also failed to honor a provision in its contract specifying increased output in the event of war, capped oil wells, and shipped its trucks and equipment to Argentina. Furthermore, Standard Oil was accused of criminal behavior related to the allegations of the theft of Bolivian oil from 1925 to 1928, lying about the purloined petroleum (shipped via a secret pipeline to Argentina), violation of contract, fraud, and tax evasion.[50] The issue of indemnification continued to fester in the public eye even after a formal settlement in 1942.

The military socialists recognized that linguistic differences within the army created serious failures in communication and command. Thus, education of the Indian to forge a more effective soldier and worker was considered a national priority. "The incorporation of the autochthonous races into all activities of national life is the first responsibility of the state because of its importance in the present and future of Bolivia."[51] Following up on President Tejada Sorzano's earlier fiat establishing 16 "nuclear schools" to be constructed by Indian communities, President Toro called for the creation of schools on "haciendas, agricultural enterprises, mines and industry" and authorized a "free school" for the Checa ayllu in Loyaza Province (La Paz Department).[52] Toro authorized the organization of peasant sindicatos on municipal and church properties, prohibited the expulsion of colonos (who failed to comply with personal obligations) if they had worked on the haciendas for two consecutive or three discontinuous years, and legalized marriages performed by clerics.[53] The military socialists traced Bolivia's backwardness to the "Indian problem" (not the landlord problem), hence the objective was literacy and education rather than indigenous freedom.[54] The question of "personal obligations" was left to the interpretation of colonos and hacendados (did the decree condone refusal to perform *pongueaje*, the despised work, as a servant in the landlord's house?), yet enforcement remained in the hands of a judicial and law enforcement system controlled by hacendados. The decree consequently exacerbated tensions within the *colonato* (hacienda: manorial system).

President Busch decreed August 2nd as the "Day of the Indian." A holiday dedicated to "appreciation of the Indian masses" seemed an appropriate gesture after the Chaco sacrifice. The rhetoric of the decree ("elevating the social, moral and cultural level of the autochthonous masses") suggests the military socialist approach to the "Indian question." Regarding specific structural changes to the quasi-feudal relations of the colonato, the military socialists were mute: the question of land tenure was avoided as were the issues of incorporation of the peasantry into the money economy or payment for field work.[55]

President Busch's brief tenure was highlighted by significant reforms. A labor code (*Código del Trabajo*), later to be known as the *Código Busch*, legalized collective bargaining and the right to strike, limited workday hours and the arbitrary dismissal of workers, mandated social security, pensions, paid vacations, accident insurance, safeguards for women workers, and prohibited child labor. A second decree targeted the Rosca's control of the economy, mandating that foreign exchange earnings (*divisas*) from the tin mines be deposited in the Central Bank, taxed, and then remitted in *bolivianos*. Non-compliance was considered treason, punishable by death. Busch's decree prompted an attempted revolt financed by the tin magnate Carlos Víctor Aramayo and led by the capricious ex-president Colonel David Toro.[56]

The 1938 Constitution

A constitutional convention convened in 1938 addressed questions of race (the Indian), land tenure, the role of the state, and the rights of property ownership. Radical legislators argued that the right to property depended on its social function. The notion of property rights based on "social function" was inimical to the existing legal definition of property as the right of the individual as defined in the 1880 Constitution. It was argued that property was a social right to be determined by its use.[57] Applied to the quasi-feudal domain of lords and peasants, the criterion of legitimacy determined by social function inevitably raises the question of agrarian reform. What form this change might assume—penny capitalist or Andean collectivist—elicited impassioned debate at the constitutional convention. The Deputy Wálter Guevara Arze argued forcefully in favor of cooperative farming as opposed to individual ownership—a question later resolved by the 1953 Agrarian Reform Law in favor of individual ownership, but with some sections of common lands to be worked cooperatively.

The radicals also attacked the Rosca and their foreign counterparts for looting the nation's oil and mineral resources. The case for state ownership of subsoil rights as essential to economic development was forcefully argued by the economist Víctor Paz Estenssoro. In any such scheme the state would necessarily assume primacy over the individual, resulting in a redefinition of land tenure relationships, subsoil rights, and mine ownership. Both Paz Estenssoro and Guevara Arze considered nationalization of the mines and agrarian reform as essential to the modernization of the nation. The Tin Barons responded to the threat of expropriation through their control of the media, subjecting newspaper readers to an onslaught of propaganda conflating nationalism with communism.[58]

The 1938 Constitution was the apogee of military socialism. Implementation and enforcement of the proposed laws would have been tantamount to a revolution of the nation's socioeconomic structure. But most of the proposals to modernize the nation came to naught. Personal service was declared illegal (Article 5), and yet the myriad forms of indigenous degradation remained undefined and without provision for enforcement.[59] Article 165 recognized the legality of the ayllu community, but it failed to address the question of restitution of lost lands; it also did not define the means by which the ayllus would be protected against hacienda encroachment.[60] Article 167 reflected creole-mestizo interest in the creation of nuclear schools among the peasantry. The question of agrarian reform was brought to a vote, but it was rejected by a majority of the legislators. Nevertheless, the debate represented a significant foray into the forbidden realm of land tenure in a country noteworthy for the most inequitable relationship between man and land on the planet.

Indian Education in War and Peace

Discussion and debate at the constitutional convention tied citizenship to literacy. After four centuries, Indians remained disfranchised. In Cochabamba Department, Indians who owned small parcels of land met the property requirement necessary for suffrage, and yet were excluded from joining the enfranchised 2 percent of the male population because of illiteracy; women, another majority, also remained disenfranchised. Bolivian hacendados resisted Indian education because literacy propagated potential litigants conversant in the language of the judicial system.[61] However, literacy was promoted by the military to reduce the linguistic divide between creole-mestizo officers and Indian recruits that hampered combat in the Chaco. Francisco Chipana Ramos and Antonio Mamani Álvarez, who would become revolutionaries, served as aides and translators for Majors Germán Busch and Gualberto Villarroel.

The quest for literacy and education was inextricably linked to the indigenous struggle for social rights and land restitution. The ability to read and write was crucial to the *apoderado* movement, the network of Aymara and Quechua legal experts dedicated to resistance against hacienda encroachments on ayllu lands since the Disentailment Law (*Ley de Exvinculación*) of 1874.[62] The result was the catastrophic loss of two-thirds of ayllu territory between 1880 and 1930; the dispossessed comunarios were obliged to work as hacienda colonos, mine workers, or migrate to the cities.

The touchstone for revendication of usurped lands was an ancient codification ("Titles of Composition of the Crown of Spain") granting legal title to Indian communities. Literacy was necessary for interpretation of the Spanish documents essential to litigation of threatened lands and restitution of lost territory.[63] The fixation on legal redress—on belief in ancient documents so egregiously ignored by creole governments throughout the Americas—led the Mexican novelist Carlos Fuentes to suggest, "It would be tempting to interpret Mexican history as a battle between sacred texts and profane reality."[64] Fuentes recalled a prophetic meeting with a peasant later murdered in defense of communal lands: "With great care he unfolded the almost golden sheets of paper. 'These are our titles to the common lands of Tlaquiltenango. The land was ours in Indian times. The King of Spain recognized it as ours.... They prove our right to exist. And I will never lose them, even if it costs me my life.'"[65] The nexus between Spanish colonial documents, literacy, and revendication of communal land is underscored in the novelist's epitaph for the martyred peasant: "but they had not been able to destroy the papers, the one concrete piece of evidence of the reality of communal existence, work, memory and hope. Stronger than murder, the titles to the land were even stronger than justice, since justice itself could be founded only upon that holy bit of parchment signed by an ancient Father, the King . . . the final proof of legitimacy: the written word."[66]

Indigenous resistance to disentailment in Bolivia took various forms: episodic violence, occasional revolts, rebellions, and legal opposition by apoderados contesting the legitimacy of the *revista* decisions. Apoderados fashioned written legal defenses and presented arguments before government representatives: "In other words, they constructed a system of ideas and strategies that used history and memory to influence the present," notes Aymara historian Waskar Ari.[67] By the turn of the twentieth century, a wide network of apoderados stretched throughout the Andean highlands and into villages in the tropical lowlands. Instrumental in the growth of the movement was Martín Vásquez, a comunario from La Paz Department who, together with a sympathetic mestizo lawyer, began an archival search to discover the lawful title to threatened ayllu lands.[68] The search was successful, the ayllu lands protected, and Vásquez recognized as a leader (*apoderado general*) by comunarios in the Altiplano provinces of Pacajes and Ingavi (La Paz Department). Accused of inciting a rebellion over usurped land, opposition to taxes, forced labor obligations, and demands for Indian participation in government, Martín Vásquez was imprisoned: his influence and authority diminished, Vásquez selected a fellow comunario to lead the movement.[69]

The choice was Santos Barco, the descendant of a *cacique de sangre*, a blood relative of a colonial ayllu chieftain (*mallku*) who held legal title to land. Santos Barco assumed the name Santos Marka T'ula in the belief that adopting the name of an ancestor would be useful in the search for land titles that would be in ancestor's name.[70] In addition to archival research, Santos Marka T'ula and other apoderados produced and circulated *garantías*, evidentiary documents based on colonial law guaranteeing indigenous rights and protection. In the garantías, Marka T'ula and other apoderados referenced themselves as "first Bolivians" to legitimate their claims and justify their contention that Indians should separate themselves from creole-mestizos.[71]

In order to propagate future leaders, Santos Marka T'ula founded an Indian school in urban La Paz, the *Centro Cátolico de Aborígenes Bartolomé de las Casas*, as well as numerous schools in the countryside. His educational network included Indian urban migrants, but also attracted sympathizers, including Catholic priests, Protestant evangelicals, the anarchist *Federación Obrero Local* (which in 1926 appointed Marka T'ula as Secretary of Peasant Affairs), and Tristán Marof (Gustavo A. Navarro) and the *Grupo Tupac Amaru* who advocated destruction of the colonato.[72] Santos Marka T'ula was repeatedly harassed by the government: arrested in 1916 following demands for a resurvey of ayllu and hacienda boundaries; imprisoned for sedition (1923–1926); and again for complicity in the 1927 Chayanta Rebellion. Opposition to hacendado abuses during the Chaco War brought charges of disloyalty, communism, and treason.[73] In 1933, Marka T'ula and other indigenous leaders were arrested, tried, and sentenced by a military tribunal for agitation related to a colono uprising on haciendas near the Altiplano town of Guaqui (La Paz Department). Resistance to a war that utilized Indian soldiers as cannon fodder—and in their absence allowed opportunistic hacendados to usurp their land—led to civil disobedience. Santos Marka T'ula was arrested again in 1935 for leadership of an anti-war demonstration in La Paz by Aymara women protesting the war and demanding the return of their men and land usurped during their service in the Chaco.[74]

There were also activists who had come to believe, after years of work in Marka T'ula's network, that little had been gained by litigation and that the focus on ayllu comunarios ignored the concerns of hacienda colonos; furthermore, they believed that cooperation with priests, missionaries, and labor leaders threatened indigenous people with the danger of acculturation into the creole-mestizo world. Schooling and literacy in Spanish carry the seed of deculturation: the metamorphosis of the indigenous peasantry into a lumpen proletariat eking out subsistence in urban barrios. Led by Toribio Miranda and Gregorio Titiriku, these apoderados referred to themselves as *Alcades Mayores Particulares* (AMP) and focused on indigenous religion and culture in contradistinction to Marka T'ula's fixation on literacy in Spanish as a prerequisite for legal restitution of ayllu lands. Titiriku "argued . . . that colonial land titles are evil pathways written with the blood of our grandparents" and opposed the fixation on property titles "because he did not want the Indian struggle to be restricted to a fight for lands and property within the framework of the dominant sectors' laws."[75]

The Republic of Kollasuyu

Perhaps the most fascinating development of the tumultuous Chaco era involves Eduardo Leandro Nina Qhispi's evolution from a focus on indigenous schooling to the conception of a counter-state—the Republican Society of Kollasuyu (*Sociedad República del Kollasuyu*)—a democratic, multiethnic republic to be founded on the recognition of the rights of all citizens, political representation of the indigenous peoples, and restitution of usurped ayllu territories. Nina Qhispi's odyssey from a remote ayllu to national prominence began after the violent seizure of his community's land (Ch'iwu ayllu) near the Altiplano canton of Santa Rosa del Taraqu (Ingavi Province, La Paz Department) by a murderous hacendado. Nina Qhispi understood that the abuses committed daily against his people in places distant from the purview of higher authorities were perpetrated with impunity. Accused of participation in a subsequent uprising, Nina Qhispi joined the throngs of similarly dispossessed comunarios living in the barrios of urban La Paz.[76] It was there that the Aymara autodidact conceived of education as a weapon for revendication of a lost patrimony.

The genesis of what would become a seminal accomplishment in the history of indigenous resistance began with Nina Qhispi's agreement to tutor neighborhood children: "I who have felt in my heart the sobbing cry of a vexed race . . . understand the benefit that leaving the rough road of slavery would give us." Nina

Qhispi worked as a baker by day and taught a class in the evening to the children of the butcher's guild.[77] What began with a group of some 20 students in 1928 piqued interest: as enrollment swelled, alumni were utilized to teach the eager students. Within two years, Nina Qhispi formally instituted the *Sociedad Centro Educativo Kollasuyu* (Kollasuyu Central Education Society). Imbued with a broader vision and a wider calculus, the Society sought to incorporate the whole of Kollasuyu in a network of schools. The focus on children was strategic. Youths were the future of the subaltern people and their education was crucial to the defense and survival of indigenous society and culture, human rights and personal dignity, restitution of usurped land and lost national territory.

Nina Qhispi perceived education as a pedagogy for the oppressed: vital to the preservation of the indigenous ethos and a prerequisite to restitution of the land that sustained Kollasuyu society.[78] The underlying principle was respect for others and for one's culture: "*Jach'a jaqirus, jisk'a jaqirus, jaqirjamaw uñjañaxa*" ("Whether big persons or small persons, they are to be seen as people").[79] The 1930 "Congress of Indigenous Teachers" sponsored by the Kollasuyu Educational Society in La Paz is suggestive of Nina Qhispi's vision: indigenous caciques, including Guarani tribal leaders from distant Santa Cruz and apoderados from the Marka T'ula network, convened in a demonstration of solidarity to discuss mutual interests in education and land revendication.[80] The success of the Society and its message did not go unnoticed by its enemies. The Kollasuyu Educational Society was charged with subversion and Nina Qhispi accused of communism by hacendados and the creole-mestizo Civic Action League. In November 1932, government agents confiscated Nina Qhispi's correspondence together with documents from the Kollasuyu Educational Center. Arrest and torture of members of the organization followed.[81]

The Kollasuyu Society's focus on education and the restitution of indigenous territory underwent further refinement during the Chaco War. Nina Qhispi's quest for the return of usurped lands, reenvisioned as the multiethnic Republic of Kollasuyu, was antithetical to the creole-mestizo state as was Nina Qhispi's passive resistance to the war. His comparison of land usurped by hacendados in their internal war against comunarios—with the land surrendered by inept creole oligarchs in their international wars—was an additional irritation. In *Flood of Fire* (*Aluvión de Fuego*), a popular novel published in 1935, a government minister is handed a broadside calling for the creation of an Indigenous Republic of Kollasuyu:

> Manifesto of the Indigenous Nationalities of Kollasuyu. For the Return of Their Land to the Indigenous Communities, For the Boycott of a War that the Indian Neither Perceives Nor Understands, We do Not Want to be Mere Cannon Fodder Defending the Interests of Our Oppressors, For the Indigenous Right to Elect His Own Authorities, Against the Landlords and the Landlords' Governments, For the Socialist Republics of Workers, Soldiers and Peasants. Bread, Land, and Liberty.

"What stupidity!" opines the minister, to which his aide replies:

> What do you think, my lord! . . . [T]his [i]s the work of foreign agitators, aided by enemies from within, which are the opposition! The communists, friend, the communists! That miserable band of wretches . . .! "It is necessary to take measures, señor minister!"[82]

The creole government found Nina Qhispi's ideas intolerable. His envisioned Republic was multiethnic and pluralistic, based on the democratic self-determination of a literate and educated citizenry.[83] The armed forces would no longer serve as a colonial force of occupation, but would instead deal with external threats to national security. Nina Qhispi understood that the abuses committed daily against his people in places distant from the purview of higher authorities were perpetrated with impunity regardless of legal appeals for justice. He perceived the issue of land titles and boundaries as a national question, rather than as a parochial dispute between hacendados and Indians. His demand for re-adjudication of boundaries and land titles was referenced in comparative terms; just as the Bolivian government had searched the Spanish colonial archives for proof of territorial claims to the Chaco, Nina Qhispi argued that a national archival survey of properties was essential to restitution of comunario territory granted by the Spanish Crown.[84]

The government would not countenance a challenge to its legitimacy by the incipient Republic of Kollasuyu, nor would it allow the apoderado network to continue agitation for boundary surveys. Accused of a "vast subversive network" in late 1933, Nina Qhispi, Manuel Colque, Julian Cruz, and a number of other influential leaders of the Republic of Kollasuyu were sentenced to six years in prison for sedition. News of the arrests sparked a widespread uprising in La Paz Department.[85] Eduardo Leandro Nina Qhispi was released from prison together with other political prisoners by an amnesty decree issued by the President Toro in 1936. We are reminded by his biographer, Carlos Mamani Condori, that for Nina Qhispi the "renovation" of Bolivia was not the "civilization" of the Indian envisioned by creole-mestizo reformers, but the "radical territorial restitution and political self-determination of indigenous society."[86] The evolution of Nina Qhispi's genius, from his initial conception of education as essential to the struggle for land and rights, through the articulation of a strategy for subaltern political agency culminating in the multiethnic Republic of Kollasuyu, represents the zenith of indigenous critical thought and action during a defining era in Bolivian history.

Warisata: The Ayllu School

In April 1931, the educator Elizardo Pérez was offered the position of Director of the Indian Normal School in Miraflores, a creole-mestizo La Paz suburb. After some consideration, Don Elizardo declined the opportunity: "the trap of teaching the sons of the *gamonales* [pejorative: hacendados] in Miraflores and converting them into new exploiters of the Indians."[87] Instead, Elizardo Pérez formulated an alternative approach. Instead of "civilizing" Indian children, utilizing education as a means of divesting a non-western people of their indigenous culture, Pérez decided to empower them by developing a heightened sense of their native culture and identity:

> The Indian school ought to be located in the Indian ambience. . . . [I]ts function ought to be highly active and provided with a clear social content. . . . [T]he parents should co-operate in the construction with their own labor and cede land as a tribute to the work of their own culture; the school should radiate its action to the life of the community and serve the harmonious and simultaneous development of all the child's skills in their education.[88]

Herein one discerns Don Elizardo's praxis: the wedding of education and indigenous culture. The school was not to be a separate entity but to be integrated into the life of the community. An encounter with Avelino Siñani Cosme, a respected elder of the *Warisata* ayllu near the Altiplano town of Achacachi (Omasuyos Province), was fortuitous. The two men shared a dream that eventuated in the genesis of Warisata, the ayllu school that was to reform Indian education.[89] As a member of the Warisata *Consejo de Amautas* (Council of Elders), Avelino Siñani enlisted his colleagues' support and guidance in the school project. The incorporation of the elders was, in itself, an initial step in the revitalization of the ayllu.[90]

Avelino Siñani's lifelong commitment to education began in childhood with a four-hour commute on muleback to the village of Huarina, where he was tutored by altruistic mestizos. Once conversant in Spanish, Siñani began teaching Indian children. Schoolwork involved the gathering of variously colored stones for writing and the collection of seeds for use in counting. Indian schooling was necessarily a clandestine activity: educational materials were prohibited and their possession was considered proof of subversive activity. Siñani's efforts did not go unnoticed. Repeatedly beaten and jailed, a friendly mestizo teacher observed, "The thieves, the assassins, walk freely in the streets, instead Avelino Siñani, undergoes a sentence just for wanting education."[91]

A day after the Warisata school was founded in August 1931, 150 Aymara children enlisted in a regimen that combined literacy and academics together with the work of constructing the school together with their families. Pérez contributed shovels and a wheelbarrow from his house in La Paz, his labor, and funds from the Education Ministry. Leading by example, living an existence similar to theirs, he gained the confidence of the Warisateños.

> In fifty days we had won two great battles in the relentless war against ignorance and we began the feud. The first was accomplished more by perseverance than by persuasion, by personal example, by hard work, by the daily effort, for the love of the cause. So, we won the spirit of the Indian and incorporated him into the homework of his own redemption.[92]

The other "battle" involved "the feud" with hostile creole-mestizo vecinos. Soon after the inception of Warisata, the Achacachi corregidor arrested and berated two comunarios known for their support of the school and administered a flogging to one as a lesson to the ayllu community. Arrests, beatings, and harassment of colonos and comunarios would continue as interest in the ayllu school spread across the highlands. It could not have been otherwise; as Elizardo Pérez adduced, "Warisata, from its beginning, was placed against the order of existing things . . . because all the representative organisms of feudalism saw it as an attempted threat against the laws that determined the subsistence of their privileges."[93] Within weeks of the school's inception, Achacachi hacendados initiated a legal campaign against Warisata, punctuated by intimidation and violence against the ayllu comunarios that continued for a decade.[94] The decision to hold a market to sell foodstuffs and crafts produced at the school (a competitor to the Achacachi market) and the replication of the indigenous school model beyond La Paz Department exacerbated vecino and hacendado opposition.

As interest in Warisata spread, the initial concept of the ayllu school underwent refinement, resulting in a nuclear school matrix with a core school surrounded by smaller satellite schools in outlying communities.[95] This iteration of the nuclear school was publicized by the Bolivian delegation to the First Inter-American Indigenous Congress convened in Pátzcuaro, Mexico, in April 1940, and the tenets of the Warisata nuclear school were adopted in a formal resolution issued by the Congress. The nuclear school model was later replicated in Mexico, Guatemala, Educador, and Peru.[96]

Leafing through photos in *Warisata: La Escuela-Ayllu*, one is struck by the enormity of the accomplishment: the community's construction of the building complex, students and families working the land together, fields planted in potatoes, wheat and quinoa, the preparation of chuño, a completed irrigation canal with children playing in the water, ovens for cooking and firing bricks, girls weaving on looms, dormitory rooms, and photos of sports and fiestas. Only by enlisting the support of Avelino Siñani together with fellow amautas and by winning the confidence and support of the community through mutual effort (*minka*) did the school project come to light. My good fortune was to room next door to Don Elizardo in a La Paz *pensión* in 1967 where I was struck by the stream of Indians paying respects to the aging visionary who believed so fervently in them.

A visit to Warisata in May 1933 by Vice President Tejada Sorzano brought an influential ally to the school cause. Tejada Sorzano saw in the nuclear school the possibility of "assimilating our autochthonous races into civilization" and in August 1935 called for the creation of 16 nuclear schools in the highlands as well as in the lowlands of Beni and Santa Cruz: one year later Warisata's "most determined supporter" contributed $250,000 to the school.[97] As word of Warisata spread, Indians from various communities made the trek to observe the ayllu nuclear school experiment where hygiene and sanitation (e.g., use of soap and disinfectants) were taught along with horticulture, animal husbandry, handicrafts, reading, writing, and arithmetic. Reading and writing were taught by a dedicated staff, including the writers Juan Anawaya, Eusebio Karlo, and the poet Maximo Wanuico. The novelist Raul Botelho Gosalvez taught at Warisata and the experience shaped his acclaimed novel *Altiplano*, an exploration of the vicissitudes of life in an ayllu on the shore of Lake Titicaca.[98] Botelho Gosalvez witnessed the provincial legal system at work in Achacachi, where vecino pettifoggers victimized illiterate Aymara litigants. *Altiplano* recounts the telling episode of a shyster who presented an Indian seeking legal advice with two books of unequal size from which to choose. The price for use of the larger tome was 600 pesos, but less for the smaller book: the assumption being that the success of litigation was proportional to the size of the law book. After declining the shyster's legal services, the Indian stranger in a strange land is nevertheless obliged to pay 50 pesos for the attempted chicanery and warned of the legal repercussions should payment be refused.[99]

The lesson inferred from the aforementioned situation is that a literate peasantry, possessed of rudimentary education, threatened the ancien régime. Presidents might decree mandates from above, but legal enforcement at the local level was suborned by hacendado obstruction. The history of Warisata is at once the history of a unique experiment—and of the unremitting assault upon the ayllu school—and those associated with it. The school was accused of inciting anarchy, fostering insolence, incubating communism, and levying personal service on Warisata men, women, and children (because of their participation in the construction and activities of the school). Corregidores sought to dissuade Indians from involvement in the ayllu schools through beatings, arrests, and confiscation of personal property (soon to become corregidor pawn items).[100]

Sindicato and School

The Chaco produced a generation like no other in the nation's history. The war affected everyone and exposed the gross dysfunction of the Old Order, the ordeal demonstrated the patriotism of indigenous soldiers, brought a disparate population together through shared military service, radicalized veterans, and engendered creative responses to national problems. Colonos returning from the war were aware that their servitude was but part of a wider system and that change was possible through organized resistance. The postwar genesis of peasant sindicatos and introduction of the nuclear school model to Cochabamba Department attest to the historic role of the Chaco generation.

Colonos returning to the Hacienda Santa Clara (Cliza Province) were shocked to find that in their absence the *patrón* (landlord), a Catholic priest, had tightened control over the hacienda operation, instituted harsh enforcement, and expelled elderly colonos from their plots. While this bitter homecoming was not uncommon, what would eventuate at Hacienda Santa Clara was momentous. The colonos of Hacienda Santa Clara lived and labored on land held for centuries by the Convent of Santa Clara that leased the hacienda and the colonos, in five-year terms. The leaseholder during the Chaco era, the Catholic priest Juan de Dios Gamboa, was resented by the colonos because of his harsh administration. Father Gamboa utilized the war as a convenient means to rid himself of unruly colonos who were shipped off to the front as cannon fodder.[101]

For those veterans who returned, the hacienda regimen was intolerable. Gamboa ran a tight ship controlled by an administrator, three mayordomos, and eight *kurakas* to supervise work gangs. The colonos responses to the harsh conditions included insubordination, disobedience, evasion, sabotage, and a sit-down strike (*huelga de brazos caidos*).[102] When word reached the hacienda that Gamboa was to renew his lease for another five years, the enraged colonos planned to burn the hacienda house to the ground. Only the timely intercession of troops from Cochabamba on 12 October 1935 prevented their attack on the house, a symbol of hacienda authority. But the colonos had exhibited a capacity for concerted action. Among their leaders were the brothers Desiderio Delgadillo Vasquez, an Ex-Combatiente and veteran of a Paraguayan POW camp, and Pedro Delgadillo Vasquez, also an Ex-Combatiente and POW, who remembered the lesson of the Chaco—"we learned that time [imprisoned in Paraguay] that united we were able to be respected."[103]

After the October upheaval, the colonos reassessed their situation. For centuries, Indian rebellions were followed by repression and a return to the status quo. What developed at the Hacienda Santa Clara was anomalous. The colonos at Santa Clara sidestepped the cycle of rebellion and repression; the Delgadillos, together with Ex-Combatientes from the sector of the hacienda known as Ana Rancho, began meeting with mestizo political contacts: the schoolteacher Andrés Dávalos Valencia (a Trotskyist militant); a local attorney; and Antonio Revuelta, a mestizo small farmer and Ex-Combatiente. The upshot was the creation of a clandestine union, the agrarian *Sindicato de Huasacalle*, formed in April 1936, and a precursor to the revolutionary *Sindicato de Colonos del Valle de Cliza* (Union of the Colonos of the Valley of Cliza).[104] An epiphany followed: the idea of leasing the property themselves, cutting out Father Gamboa as the middleman, and thereby eliminating the traditional obligations of the colonato.[105] The meetings also generated the idea of presenting their case to Eduardo Arze Loureiro, the Secretary of Campesino Affairs in President Toro's newly formed Ministry of Work, Health and Social Security. The son of an illustrious Cochabamba family and a founding member of the Trotskyist POR, Arze Loureiro proved to be a vital contact.[106]

Also fortuitous were two decrees issued by President Toro in late August 1936 mandating creation of rural schools on haciendas, commercial farms, mines and factories, and unionization of peasants as a corporate sector within the military socialist polity. The peasant sindicato at Hacienda Santa Clara was thus legitimated and the cause of the colonos strengthened. When landlord thugs attacked colonos at a fiesta near the hamlet of Ucureña, sindicato emissaries together with the PORista teacher were dispatched to La Paz to discuss the situation with Eduardo Arze Loureiro. Sympathetic to the peasants' plight, Arze Loureiro arranged a meeting with Minister of Labor Waldo Álvarez where the novel idea of the lease of monastery lands by the sindicato was discussed. Favorably impressed by the sindicato representatives, Minister Álvarez set up an audience with President Toro where the sindicato representatives related their troubled history with Father Gamboa and the recent attack by his henchmen at the Ucureña fiesta. The President appeared sympathetic to their proposal to lease the monastery land themselves at double the amount paid by Father Gamboa.

The social networking bore fruit. On 5 November 1936, President Toro issued a Supreme Decree authorizing a lease between the Monastery of Santa Clara and the Sindicato de Colonos del Valle de Cliza. The support by the military socialist government for a lease between the colonos and the monastery, unprecedented in Bolivian history, was reinforced by another decree issued two months later that required "municipalities and religious orders to cancel the action of intermediaries [e.g., Gamboa] in the development of land and property . . . to promote the rehabilitation of the colonos and teach them cooperative systems of exploitation of the land [and] . . . an opportunity to show their aptitude for management of agrarian labor."[107]

The struggle would transcend the Hacienda Santa Clara and spread throughout the countryside. Sindicatos were formed to facilitate the lease of municipal property in the Department of Tarija by colonos on the haciendas Higuera-Huayco in March 1937 and Iscayachi in July 1937. At the haciendas Coca-Marca in Arque Province and Kochi in Punata Province (Cochabamba Department), sindicatos were formed and petitioned the prefect for permission to lease municipal and church properties in mid-1937.[108]

Vacas: An Indigenous School

The municipality of the City of Cochabamba held title to a vast estate: a legacy of Spanish colonial rule, comprised of 13 haciendas nestled in the serranía to the east of Hacienda Santa Clara.[109] The isolation of the haciendas distanced their colonos from the political ferment engendered by the war. In 1935, the Vacas hacienda was chosen as the site for the *Escuela Indigenal de Vacas* (Vacas Indigenous School) by the indigenista educator Toribio Claure Montaño who soon ran afoul of local officials for alleged "crimes against collective security" and "rousing Indians against the renter-patrón señores."[110] The confrontation between the municipal representative of the oligarchs and the socialist school director is indicative of the contradictions of President Toro's government. Claure presented himself to the *alcalde* (mayor) as a defender of Indian rights sanctioned by the military socialist government ("to which you are obligated to unconditionally serve") and whose authority superseded that of the alcalde.[111]

The Prefect of the Department, Colonel José A. Capriles, then presented a hacendado *denuncia* (legal demand) accusing Claure of nefarious activities, to which he questioned the legitimacy of the allegations. "It is a monument of falsehoods, Señor Prefect, a fruit of the spite of the patrones, who have believed that the property of the State is a fief destined for the exclusive exploitation of the capitalist rosca . . . enjoying and erecting riches based on Indian misery."[112] Colonel Capriles warned Claure that he could be imprisoned for espousing "extremist propaganda" and scheduled a hearing for 25 January 1937 to consider accusations of "preaching communism," embezzlement of colono school funds, and fomenting disrespect among the colonos.[113] He was ordered to bring all documents requisite to his defense, together with representatives of the Indian communities, to the scheduled hearing at the Prefecture. At this hearing, Claure informed the Colonel of his address to the *Primera Asemblea de Directores Indigenistas* (First Assembly of Indigenist Directors), recently convened in La Paz and attended by President Toro. There, persuaded by Claure's argument that municipal land (much as church property) should be leased to the colonos who worked it, the president promised to transfer the municipal land to the colonos.

Serendipitously, days before the scheduled hearing with the Prefect, President Toro issued his 22 January 1937 Decree granting colonos, when organized in agrarian sindicatos, the right to lease the municipal or church property on which they worked.[114] A month earlier the colonos had founded the *Sindicato de Trabajadores Agrarios de Vacas* (Union of Agrarian Workers of Vacas) "under the aegis of the will of the Socialist Government to defend our class rights in pursuit of the common welfare and national progress."[115] Fortuitously aligned with the dictates of the military socialist government, Claure and the Vacas colonos presented themselves to the Prefect.[116] The colonos vouched for the integrity of their school funds that were to be deposited in the *Banco Central* following the hearing. Claure deftly countered the accusations lodged against him and presented himself as an advocate of the military socialist cause of social justice.

The Prefect dismissed all charges. The indigenista school, born under military socialism and tied to the sindicato, had survived the formal assault of the Old Order. But the hacendados wielded extra-legal power via rumor and intimidation. Rumors circulated in the Vacas *chicherías* (chicha bars) of a scheme to murder Toribio Claure and Eduardo Arze Loureiro, who narrowly escaped harm at the hands of "The Cenáculo," a clandestine cell comprised of powerful Cochabamba hacendados determined to maintain the traditional order.[117]

In 1937, the Sociedad Rural intensified its propaganda campaign. Newspaper diatribes demonized indigenista teachers as extremists, "communists," and "agitators"; Indians as "lazy" and "avaricious"; and the schools as a threat to the national welfare. The teaching of crafts, it was argued, was an impetus to urban migration—and the specter evoked of *mestizaje* (racial mixing) in cities overrun by Indians.[118] Rumors circulated in Cochabamba of a city without food in the event colonos abandoned haciendas. The Cochabamba Sociedad Rural intensified its opposition to the military socialist support of sindicatos. Hacendados opposed the opening of the Santa Clara school and successfully pressured the Director of Indigenous Education to require an administrative council for school governance consisting of hacendado representatives, the Sub-prefect of Cliza, and the school director. Two consecutive school directors were undermined by hacendado obstructionism; Carlos Dorado was accused of embezzlement of school funds and inciting revolution.

The hacendado denunciation of the school teachers as agitators and extremists was well-founded. Dorado expounded a version of "the land for those who work it" at a public hearing before an inspector from the Ministry of Education. The hearing, attended by a large colono audience, gave rise to debate regarding the renewal of the monastery lease versus the option of purchasing the property. Title to the land, it was argued, was the exclusive right of the colonos who worked it: and not the hacendado lessees.[119] The idea of leasing the monastery land was revolutionary as was the notion of a land purchase as a collective endeavor: lease or purchase of the land, ipso facto, would eliminate pongueaje, the humiliating degradation ritual. Carlos Dorado was subsequently replaced as school director by the dedicated PIR militant, Juan Guerra, who would play an important role influencing an agrarian revolution in Cochabamba.

The Sociedad Rural reacted quickly to the developments at Santa Clara and Vacas. Carabineros dispatched from Cochabamba City arrived at Ucureña (a rancho within Santa Clara) and arrested sindicato leaders for instigation of the strike. The school director, threatened with imprisonment by the Cochabamba Chief of Police for inciting "disobediencie" among the colonos, was admonished to stick to school affairs.[120] On 31 May 1938, the quixotic President Busch issued a decree dissolving the Sindicato Agricola de Colonos de Cliza in favor of a land sale to an influential clique (the "Cináculo") that previously had leased the property. The sale involved a corrupt scheme that included Bishop Tomas Aspe and the Minister of Agriculture and Colonization, Jorge Mercado Rosales, who was handsomely bribed for his role in expediting the deal.[121]

In response to the presidential reversal of fortune, the Santa Clara colonos enlisted their mestizo supporters, including Antonio Revuelta and the influential Eduardo Arze Loureiro, who again demonstrated his powers of persuasion with President Busch—who reversed himself, yet again, with a presidential decree to be issued on 9 September 1939. The decree countermanded the president's previous approval of the monastery land sale to the Cochabamba hacendados, authorized the land purchase by the Santa Clara sindicato, and included a loan from the Central Bank to facilitate their purchase of the property. Unfortunately, President Busch's suicide on 23 August 1939 left the document unsigned. And while Busch's successor, General Carlos Quintanilla, would later sign the decree found amidst papers on the presidential desk, it was summarily revoked.

Schooled in the military world of order and obedience, yet impetuous by nature, Busch's success on the battlefield could not be transposed to politics. Frustrated with factional politics and the obstruction of the Tin Barons, the young president abandoned constitutional niceties, dismissed parliament, and in April 1939 proclaimed a dictatorship.[122] A confrontation with the Tin Barons over his decree granting the central bank control of tin exports and taxes, dramatized by the kidnapping of the intransigent Mauricio Hochschild, flummoxed the mercurial young president. Bedeviled by the complexities of political combat, the frustrated Colonel Busch committed suicide.[123]

German Busch's death terminated the brief era of military socialism. Because of the inability of the military socialists to enforce their fiat, the decrees issued by presidents Busch and Toro remained but symbols of intention. The "rehabilitation" of peasants and proletarians was left to indigenista educators and a growing movement of radical supporters. The ancien régime retained control over the rural hinterland. Yet the cause undertaken by the colonos of Santa Clara would not be easily suppressed. The evolution of their empowerment was unprecedented. The lease of land by an Indian sindicato, the near enactment of Busch's decree authorizing purchase by the sindicato, and the de facto elimination of pongueaje resulting from the lease or sale of land were harbingers of change to come.

Resurgence of the Old Order: The Concordancia, 1939–1943

In the wake of Germán Busch's suicide, the oligarchy quickly reasserted itself through the *Concordancia*, a coalition of conservative political parties represented by two generals elected president: Carlos Quintanilla (1939–1940) and Enrique Peñaranda (1940–1943). Both generals had served as senior officers in the Chaco War where they were distanced from the carnage of the front lines. At the service of the resurgent oligarchy, they erased all military socialist legislation, save for Busch's iconic labor code (albeit the Código Busch would remain unenforced).

The Sociedad Rural capitalized on Busch's suicide and intensified their opposition to the nuclear schools. In late 1939, two rural schoolteachers working at a Warisata satellite school in the hamlet of Patapatani were assailed by Achacachi hacendados. Shots were fired at the teachers as they fled along a mountain path: pursued by their assailants in the dead of night, they fell into a precipice where one was killed and the other was gravely injured.[124] The hacendado assault on nuclear schools escalated in the press and by the government. In January 1940, the office of General Director of Indigenous Education (*Director General de Educación Indigenal*) was eliminated and replaced by a National Council of Education dedicated to destruction of the nuclear schools.

Vacas was one of three nuclear schools to escape the Council's purge. Much to the consternation of Elizardo Pérez and his former nuclear school compatriots, Toribio Claure was a member of the Council. The Council revived creole-mestizo fears that education would promote urbanization of unwashed Indian hordes, to the detriment of food supplies from a depopulated countryside. The latent potential of Indians scattered in disparate hamlets, but organized in a network linked to the primary Matrix schools, was a threat to the Sociedad Rural and its Council.[125] Questions of student hygiene served as the pretext to close the schools.[126] In a country with appalling rates of infant mortality (estimated at 50 percent for 1967!), the nuclear school attention to hygiene, evidenced by the victory over scabies at Warisata (overlooked by the school's inquisitors), was as tangible a success as that achieved in literacy, education, or vocational skills in agronomy, animal husbandry, and crafts.[127] Despite protests, Warisata was closed in 1940 and its physical infrastructure carted off to La Paz. On his deathbed, dying of cholera, Avelino Siñani's words to his daughter afford a fitting epitaph to Warisata: "My daughter, the Indians who have permitted the enemy to come to the school, soon will regret it when they see our work sacked and destroyed. All the fruit of our labor will perhaps then be in vain, when the thieves and intruders take the last blade of straw. And the same ones who have come to accuse us will speak and put flowers on my grave."[128]

In Cochabamba, hacendados moved quickly to reassert their power. On 1 April 1940, the colonos were given three days to vacate their plots. Those who opted to return to the yoke of the colonato were relocated to the margins of the estate; those who objected were evicted, others arrested, or fined. Within a month, a dozen militant colonos were imprisoned at Chimoré in the eastern lowlands. The arrival in June 1940 of a new school director, Juan Guerra, revitalized the colono cause. A vanguard member of the communist *Partido de la Izquierda Revolucionaria* (Party of the Revolutionary Left: PIR), Guevara's appearance presaged a radicalization of the struggle against the Old Regime within the context of Marxist–Leninist class struggle.

Guerra's organizational flair and deft maneuvering reinforced the position of the sindicato. Following the return of imprisoned colono leaders in 1941, the sindicato held a meeting at the school house in Ucureña where the union was reorganized with Guerra as a director.[129] No longer required to function with hacendado representatives in attendance, the sindicato addressed the question of additional land purchases. Meanwhile, hacendado opposition to the sindicato continued: Angel Jordan, their ringleader, evicted 40 colono families from his leased property and replaced them with compliant *pegujaleros* (temporary renters). Colonos were also arrested for tapping water in a dispute over irrigation rights. Juan Guerra assisted the sindicato's defense of rights violated by the hacendados (illegal expulsion of pegujaleros, personal abuses, and confrontations over pongueaje).[130]

Guevara initiated a campaign to expose a corrupt deal behind the hacendados' purchase of the monastery land. The "affaire," as it came to be known, was roundly criticized in the press, and the colonos were supported by influential PIRistas on the law faculty at the Universidad de San Simón in Cochabamba. In April 1942, the Supreme Court ruled the land sale fraudulent and sentenced Minister Mercado Rosales to a brief prison term. Bishop Aspe was posted to Argentina and the monastery lawyer briefly detained for his role in the deal. Although the court did not rule that the colonos had the right to purchase the property, 51 of the original sindicato colonos managed to purchase the coveted land following the court's decision. The price paid was exorbitant, but the collective endeavor by which the colonos purchased land and gained freedom from personal servitude was unprecedented. With the stroke of a pen, colonos were transformed from *pegujaleros* into *piqueros*, small farmers.[131] The "implications" were revolutionary and included freedom to travel, to work wherever one chose, and avoidance of the host of obligations required by the colonato regimen.

The sindicato underwent reorganization, yet again in 1942, to become the *Sindicato de Agricultores y Educatores de Cliza* (Union of Cliza Farmers and Educators), with Guerra and the school teachers formally included in the organization. Fears for the future of the sindicato prompted the inclusion of teachers, which allowed association with the departmental federation of teachers and workers. Support also came from the University of San Simón student federation, influential PIRista members of the university law faculty, and the MNR journalists at *Última Hora* and *La Calle*.[132] As the conflict gained a wider audience, urban laborers (including Indian migrants from the countryside) found common cause with the embattled colonos. The influence of Juan Guerra was decisive to the success of the sindicato.[133]

Summary and Conclusions

The Chaco War exposed the vulnerability of the oligarchic state and exacerbated the dysfunction within the ancien régime. The holocaust devastated the indigenous population: eight of every ten conscripts died in the first year of hostilities; 62,000 of the 77,000 troops mobilized never returned from the "Green Hell." The 32,000 deaths from illness, disease, and dismal medical care exceeded the 30,000 killed in action. The oligarchs profited from the war, utilizing deferred Indian labor in mines, factories, and haciendas, while war profiteers and a rapacious bureaucracy extorted bribes in money, animals, and crops from colonos and comunarios.

The causes of the defeat were evident to the junior officers who commanded troops at the front and recognized the imperative of "rehabilitation" of the indigenous majority. Education and acculturation of the Indian, divided by language, culture, and region, was a strategic goal of the postwar military socialists whose influence would transcend their brief rule. As presidents, Colonels David Toro and Germán Busch issued decrees to ameliorate the blatant abuses of the traditional order: landlords were prohibited from evicting colonos (who had worked the land for two consecutive or three discontinuous years), or for failure to comply with "personal obligations" (e.g., pongueaje and mitanaje). Ayllus and sindicatos were recognized as legal and corporate entities in the military socialist state, schools were mandated for haciendas and factories, the legality of church marriage for Indians decreed, and August 2nd was declared the "Day of the Indian," a national holiday in recognition of the indigenous race.

Radicalized by a disastrous war and a callous government, the postwar "Generation of the Chaco" sought to transform the nation by reform or revolution. Indian and indigenista reformers, as well as Stalinists, Trotskyists, Fascists, and nationalist revolutionaries came to the fore. The Constitutional Convention convened in 1938, a crucible for postwar social, political, and economic debate, set the stage for over a decade of political disputation, culminating in a social revolution. In a departure from the liberal Constitution of 1880, with its emphasis on personal property rights, the 1938 Constitution vested property rights in their social utility and employed the metric of "social function" to determine these rights.

The vagaries of social function as applied to the colonato system threatened the legitimacy of the hacienda based on the rights of personal property and added to instability in the countryside, whetting indigenous dreams of a return of the land to those who work it. Article 5 of the Constitution declared personal service illegal; and although undefined and unenforced, the article fueled Indian desires for freedom, quickening resistance to the colonato. Article 167 mandated nuclear schools to promote the military socialist interest in "rehabilitation" of the Indian: literate in Spanish, acculturated, and integrated into the creole-mestizo state.

But the military socialist reforms lacked procedural mechanisms for implementation: moreover, hacendado control of local and regional governments hindered enforcement. Although the military socialists failed to alter the land tenure system, incorporate the peasantry into the money economy, or introduce wages as payment for hacienda labor, their decrees played a significant role in catalyzing indigenous expectations for change and accelerating resistance to the colonato.[134]

Far from the entrenchments of the Chaco, Indian colonos and comunarios waged an internal war of resistance against creole-mestizo depredation. Radicalized by mistreatment, privation, and death within their families, Indian women opposed the war with civil disobedience. Indigenista educators confronted the illiteracy and enforced ignorance imposed by the ancien régime on the Indian. The apoderados Marka T'ula and Nina Qhispi recognized the necessity of literacy and education to the quest for legal restitution of usurped ayllu lands. Their struggle reveals an exemplary commitment to the Amerindian "battle between sacred texts" (the ancient Spanish documents granting land titles to their communities) "and the profane reality" of subjugation, usurped lands, and enforced ignorance.

Eduardo Leandro Nina Qhispi believed in education as a prerequisite for a future generation of revendicationists. The Republic of Kollasuyu, the incipient multiethnic and democratic counter-state promoted by Nina Qhispi (which prefigured the twenty-first century Plurinational State of Bolivia) was interpreted by the Rosca as a seditious attempt at indigenous dual power.[135] His comparison of territory lost by war and ayllu territory stolen in peace threatened creole-mestizo suzerainty as did his demand for a national survey of rural land titles to determine the legitimacy of boundaries and restore usurped ayllu territory. Tried as subversives, Nina Qhispi and influential leaders of the Republic of Kollasuyu joined Santos Marka T'ula and countless others imprisoned for sedition.

The Chaco experience catalyzed awareness. Experience in combat and as prisoners of war demonstrated the power of unity and survival through collective effort. The formation of the Legión of Ex-Combatientes, limited to combat veterans and thus largely comprised of Indians, functioned as a veterans' advocacy group; it also facilitated communication and organization for resistance to the oligarchy. The role of colono Ex-Combatientes at the hacienda Santa Clara was crucial to the formation of a land group sindicato mandated by the military socialists as a legal entity in the corporatist state. Discussions among the Indian Ex-Combatientes, a PIRista teacher, and mestizo sympathizers led to the novel idea of the colonos *themselves* renting the church property: Ipso facto, exempt from personal service, free to travel and work outside the confines of the hacienda. Unfortunately, a corrupt deal concocted by the oligarchs terminated what would have been a dangerous threat to their suzerainty.

The postwar ferment extended beyond the political agitation of Indian and mestizo reformists and revolutionaries. Indigenista novelists such as the Quechua communist Jesus Lara, a Chaco veteran, came to the fore with topics of Indians exploited by creole-mestizo rule in war and peace. Mestizo writers publicized the travesty of lives lost in the Green Hell where patriotism was an Indian and mestizo monopoly. Indigenista educators devoted themselves to teaching a generation of students to read and write in Spanish while respecting their native culture at Warisata, Vacas, and a host of other nuclear schools. Opposed as a danger to the traditional order, the creole-mestizo oligarchs succeeded in closing and dismantling the ayllu schools.

After President Busch's suicide and the return of the Old Order (viz., Concordancia), the military socialist reforms were reversed, illegal expulsion of colonos from their hacienda plots multiplied, and hacendados reaffirmed the personal service obligations required of colonos. Yet, despite heightened repression, indigenous resistance continued among a generation forged in war who recognized the strength of group solidarity. The ancien régime could not for long contain the postwar revolutionary forces: the Generation of the Chaco would not be denied their rendezvous with destiny.

Notes

1. Harold Osborne, *Bolivia: A Land Divided* (London, 1964), 1. The first edition written in 1953 was published in 1954. A pair of articles by Laurence Whitehead provide astute critiques of Bolivian statistics as exemplary of problems inherent in conclusions derived from the data of an underdeveloped country. See Laurence Whitehead, "Basic Data in Poor Countries: The Bolivian Case," *Bulletin of the Oxford University Institute of Economics & Statistics*, 31. 3 (1969), 205–227, and "Altitude, Fertility and Mortality in Andean Countries," *Population Studies*, 22.3 (November 1968), 335–346.
2. See Laurence Whitehead, "The Impact of the Great Depression on Bolivia," *Atti del XL Congreso Internazonale degli Americanisti*, 4 (September 1972), 375–393.
3. The legal argument is based on the Spanish *uti possidetis* of 1810, "The doctrine that old administrative boundaries [e.g., the colonial Audiencia of Charcas] will become international boundaries when a political subdivision achieves independence." Bryan Garner, ed., *Black's Law Dictionary*, 7th ed. (St. Paul, MN, 1999), 1544.
4. Stephen Cote, "A War for Oil in the Chaco, 1932–1935," *Environmental History*, 18.2 (October 2013), 741–742, 747–749.
5. Defeat in the War of the Pacific with Chile (1879–1883) resulted in the loss of a seaport at Antofagasta and Bolivia's claims to the Atacama Desert: a source of nitrate deposits required for the manufacture of gunpowder, of strategic value to the imperial powers in the nineteenth century before German chemists developed a synthetic substitute.
6. See Carlos Montenegro, *Nacionalismo y coloniaje* (Buenos Aires, 1967), 207.
7. A papal dispensation was granted to Paraguayan Catholics to allow for polygamy, as the 28,000 remaining males set about the task of repopulating the decimated nation. For the demographic disaster, see Thomas Whigham and Barbara Potthast, "The Paraguayan Rosetta Stone: New Evidence on the Demographics of the Paraguayan War, 1864–1870," *Latin American Research Review*, 34.1 (1999), 174–186.
8. Matthew Hughes, "Logistics and the Chaco War: Bolivia versus Paraguay, 1932–1935," *The Journal of Military History*, 69 (April 2005), 415–416. On Bolivia's logistics predicament, see the prescient warning by Lieutenant Colonel Angel Rodríguez, "Commissioned to Study the Routes of Entry to the Gran Chaco, to the Señor Minister of War," in Sinclair Thomson et al., eds., *The Bolivia Reader* (Durham, NC, 2018), translated by Alison Spedding, 195–199.

9. Cote, "A War for Oil in the Chaco, 1932–1935," 748. Herbert S. Klein, *Parties and Political Change in Bolivia, 1880–1952* (Cambridge, 1969), 260–263.
10. Hughes, "Logistics and the Chaco War," 418–421.
11. Only a few of the warplanes arrived, but their case made its way to the U.S. Supreme Court. Robert A. Divine, "The Case of the Smuggled Bombers," in John A. Garraty, ed., *Quarrels That Have Shaped the Supreme Court* (New York, 1966), 210–221.
12. Elizabeth Shesko, "Mobilizing Manpower for War: Toward a New History of Bolivia's Chaco Conflict, 1932–1935," *Hispanic American Historical Review*, 95.2 (2015), 306–311, 313.
13. Klein, *Parties and Political Change*, 180–181; Shesko, "Mobilizing Manpower for War," 305.
14. *La Calle* reported the news in July 1936 that 16,000 Bolivian deserters, represented by a National Union of Exiles, had taken up residence in Argentina. Cited in Jerry Knudson, *Bolivia: Press and Revolution, 1932–1936* (Lanham, MD, 1986), 23.
15. Bruce W. Farcau, *The Chaco War: Bolivia and Paraguay, 1932–1935* (Westport, CT, 1996), 20. Recruits making their way to the front also contended with attacks by bandits, deserters, and indigenous tribes. See René Arze Aguirre, *Guerra y conflictos: El caso rural boliviano durante la campana del chaco* (La Paz, 1987), 119–133.
16. Ann Zulawaski, *Unequal Cures: Public Health and Political Change in Bolivia* (Durham, NC, 2007), 62–63.
17. June Nash, *We Eat the Mines and the Mines Eat Us: Dependency and Exploitation in Bolivian Tin Mines* (New York, 1979), 37.
18. Claudia Ronabaldo, *El camino perdido: biografía del dirigente campesino kallawaya Antonio Álvarez Mamani* (La Paz, 1988), 65–66. See also Roberto Querejazu Calvo, *Masamaclay* (La Paz, 1965), 123–124.
19. Zulawaski, *Unequal Cures*, 70–74.
20. David H. Zook, *The Conduct of the Chaco War* (New Haven, CT, 1960), 240; J. Valerie Fifer, *Bolivia: Land, Location, and Politics Since 1825* (Cambridge, 1972), 220; Klein, *Parties and Political Change*, 187.
21. Radical mineworkers accused of protests against the war were summarily conscripted and sent off to the trenches, an implicit death sentence. Nash, *We Eat the Mines*, 41.
22. Eric D. Langer, *Economic Change and Rural Resistance in Southern Bolivia, 1880–1930* (Palo Alto, CA, 1989), 87. The popular novel, *Aluvión de Fuego* (Santiago, 1935), recounts the exploits of government troops waging a war of repression against comunarios, see in particular, 102–111. Impressment of Indians facilitated by priests and local authorities often took place at rural fairs and fiestas. See Alfredo Guillén Pinto's, novel *Utama* (La Paz, 1945), 151–153.
23. The internal war between oligarchs and Indians during the Chaco War is illuminated by the Bolivian scholars René Danilo Arze Aguirre, *Guerra y conflictos*, and Carlos B. Mamani Condori, *Taraqu, 1866–1935: Masacre, Guerra y 'Renovación' en la biografía de Eduardo L. Nina Qhispi* (La Paz, 1991). This chapter owes much to the insights of these scholars.
24. For the various loopholes utilized by creole-mestizo elites to avoid military service, see Shesko, "Mobilizing Manpower for War," 316, 319–322.
25. Vitalino Soria Choque, "Los caciques-apoderados," in Vitalino Soria Choque et al., eds, *Educación Indigena: ¿ciudadania o colonización?* (La Paz, 1992), 72, 74.
26. Shesko, "Mobilizing Manpower for War," 319.
27. Ibid., 55.
28. Arze Aguirre, *Guerra y conflictos*, 68; see also 69, 72, 73.
29. Shesko, "Mobilizing Manpower for War," 316–317.
30. In October 1932, the government prohibited corregidores from collecting money from Indians; a month later corregidores in Chuquisaca and Tarija were accused of providing documents for exemption of military service in exchange for cash, livestock,

and foodstuffs. Arze Aguirre, *Guerra y conflictos*, 48–49, 65–67, 70; also, Mamani Condori, *Taraqu*, 106.
31. Arze Aguirre, *Guerra y conflictos*, 46, 56, 68, 87–89.
32. Mamani Condori, *Taraqu*, 108; Arze Aguirre, *Guerra y conflictos*, 92.
33. Arze Aguirre, *Guerra y conflictos*, 83–88.
34. Ibid., 109–111. The indignities of race and class pervaded the military institution that consisted of Indian peasants, proletarians, and the indigent who were forced to perform manual labor, working on haciendas, performing menial tasks for army officers, and constructing public works projects in addition to breaking strikes and repressing hacienda uprisings. See Elizabeth Shesko, "Constructing Roads, Washing Feet, and Cutting Cane for the '*Patria*': Building Bolivia with Military Labor," *International Labor and Working-Class History*, 80 (Fall 2011), 7–13.
35. Roberto Choque Canqui, *Historia de una lucha desigual* (La Paz, 2005), 93–94.
36. See Mamani Condori, *Tiraqu*, 121–122. See also James Dunkerley, *Origines del poder militar en Bolivia* (La Paz, 1987), 168.
37. Arze Aguirre, *Guerra y conflictos*, 96, 101–102.
38. Ibid., 113. Jaime Mendoza, an early Indianista and a voice of sanity in the legislature, also counseled comunarios seeking assistance in disputes with hacendados. Arze Aguirre, *Guerra y conflictos*, 32, fn. 7. For examples of Mendoza's point, vis-à-vis the communist label, see Arze Aguirre, 87, 89, 94–95, 114; Mamani Condori, Tiraqu, 143, 147, 149; see also Soria Choque, "Los caciques-apoderados," 56, 60.
39. Carmen Soliz, "'Land to the Original Owners': Rethinking the Indigenous Politics of the Bolivian Agrarian Reform," *Hispanic American Historical Review*, 97.2 (2017), 280–282.
40. Dunkerley, *Origines del poder*, 169. The incipient efforts of libertarian anarchists would be reprised in resistance to creole-mestizo repression during the years of the Sexenio (1946–1952). See Zulema Lehm and Silvia Rivera Cusicanqui, *Los artesanos libertarios y la ética del trabajo* (La Paz, 1988), 42–61, 84–97.
41. *El Universal* reached a circulation of 34,000 paid readers in a nation of 50,000 voters. Knudson notes the important distinction between newspaper readers and newspaper sales, citing evidence of a 4:1 ratio of readers to buyers. Knudson, *Bolivia: Press and Revolution*, 20.
42. Jesus Lara, *Repete* (Cochabamba, 1938). *Repete* ("repeat") was the nom de guerre of the Indian soldier whose limited knowledge of Spanish included repetition of the word *repete* while in the chow line. See Dunkerley, *Origines del poder*, 169.
43. The second edition (1938) includes the official prohibition of sale of the book, printed opposite the title page, together with Lara's sardonic response to a duel as a "bourgeois aftertaste." Most interesting is the defense of the book ("a true exposition of the events of the campaign") by the Superior Executive Committee of the Association of Ex-Combatientes of the Colorado Regiment.
44. Jesus Lara was a member of the Stalinist PIR. Murdo J. Macleod. "The Bolivian Novel, the Chaco War, and the Revolution" in James M. Malloy and Richard S. Thorn, eds., *Beyond the Revolution: Bolivia Since 1952* (Pittsburgh, PA, 1971), 341–365.
45. "The Quechua-Aymara term *pachakuti*," note Forrest Hylton and Sinclair Thomson, "can be interpreted as a profound turning or transformation of the world (space and time)." Forrest Hylton and Sinclair Thomson, *Revolutionary Horizons: Past and Present in Bolivian Politics* (London, 2007), 28. For its modern usage, see Felipe Quispe Huanca, "In the Time of Pachakuti," in Sinclair Thomson et al., eds., *The Bolivia Reader*, translated by Alison Spedding (Durham, NC), 563–574.
46. Chalmers Johnson, *Revolution and the Social System* (Palo Alto, CA, 1964), 14. Johnson cites the fall of Napoleon Bonaparte after his 1871 defeat by the Prussians and observes: "Defeat in war also accelerated dysfunctional conditions to the flash point in Russia (1905 by the Japanese, and 1917 by the Germans); in Hungary, Germany and Turkey in 1918; in China and Yugoslavia during World War II . . .," 13.

47. Dunkerley, *Origines del poder*, 179; see also Klein, *Parties and Political Change*, 208–209; Gotkowitz, *A Revolution for Our Rights* (Durham, NC, 2007), 111; Kevin A. Young, *Blood of the Earth: Resource Nationalism, Revolution, and Empire in Bolivia* (Austin, TX, 2017), 22–23.
48. Klein, *Parties and Political Change*, 225.
49. James Dunkerley, *Political Suicide in Latin America* (London, 1992), 32.
50. See Steven Cote's revisionist article, "A War for Oil in the Chaco, 1932–1935," 738–758; Klein, *Parties and Political Change*, 260–263; Knudson, *Bolivia: Press and Revolution*, 58.
51. Article 44 prescribed "sanctions with all the rigor of the law" for hacendados who impeded enrollment of children in the schools. José Flores Moncayo, *Legislación Boliviana del Indio* (La Paz, 1953), 354: for Tejada Sorzano, 349–353 and David Toro, 354–370.
52. Ibid., 370.
53. Germán Busch next legitimized Indian marriages previously performed by the church (a revision of liberal anti-clerical legislation codified in the 1880 Constitution). Flores Moncayo, *Legislación Boliviana del Indio*, 381. See also Roberto Choqui Canqui and Cristina Quisbert Quispe, *Educación indigenal en Bolivia: Un siglo de ensayos educativos y resistencias patronales* (La Paz: UNIH-PAKAXA, 2006), 116–118.
54. Military support for Indian schools was solicited by the caciques apoderados in an appeal to Chief of Staff General Hans Kundt, ostensibly to facilitate improved communication between officers and their troops. In fact, their motive was to gain military support for protection of their schools and defense of their lands. See Humberto Mamani Capchiri, "La educación India en a vision de la sociedad criolla: 1920–1943," in Vitalino Soria Choque et al., eds., *Educación Indigena: ¿ciudadania o colonización?* (La Paz, 1992), 85.
55. Luis Antezana E. and Hugo Romero B., *Historia de los sindicatos campesinos: un proceso de integración nacional en Bolivia* (La Paz, 1973), 65.
56. Knudson, *Bolivia: Press and Revolution*, 64.
57. Klein, *Parties and Political Change*, 284.
58. Ownership of the major dailies by the three Tin Barons was as follows: Carlos Aramayo, *La Razón*; Mauricio Hochschild, *Ultima Hora*; and Simon Patiño, the majority share of *El Diario*.
59. Gotkowitz, *A Revolution*, 127.
60. This reversed the 1874 disentailment law that revoked ayllu communal landholding rights in favor of individual property rights.
61. Toussaint L'Ouverture, Benito Juárez, and Frederick Douglass attest to the transformative power of literacy in the language of the oppressor.
62. Soria Choque, "Los caciques-apoderados," 60–75; Gotkowitz, *A Revolution*, 46–51.
63. On the Composición Titles of the Spanish Crown as the touchstone for indigenous land revindication in Bolivia, see Santos Marka Tola and the Caciques Apoderados, "The Laws of the Land," in Sinclair Thomson et al., eds., *The Bolivia Reader*, translated by Alison Spedding (Durham, NC, 2018), 327–330.
64. Carlos Fuentes, "Viva Zapata: Zapata and the Mexican Revolution," *The New York Review of Books*, 13 March 1969, 5.
65. Ibid.
66. Ibid. That an indigenous people should place such abiding faith in a judicial system established by colonial interlopers and enforced by their descendants appears ironic. Indeed, this would be a point of factional contention between the *Alcades Mayores Particulares* leaders and Santos Marka T'ula.
67. Waskar Ari, *Earth Politics: Religion, Decolonization, and Bolivia's Indigenous Intellectuals* (Durham, NC, 2014), 35–36.
68. Soria Choque, "Los caciques-apoderados," 44–45.
69. Gotkowitz, *A Revolution*, 48.
70. Ari, *Earth Politics*, 41–42.

71. Ibid., 45, see also 46–47. For an example of the caciques-apoderados' legal appeal for revendication of usurped lands, see Santos Mark Tola and the Caciques-Apoderados, "The Laws of the Lands," in Sinclair Thomson et al., eds., *The Bolivia Reader* (Durham, NC, 2018), translated by Alison Spalding, 327–330.
72. Soria Choque, "Los caciques-apoderados," 63–68; Ari, *Earth Politics*, 42–43; Gotkowitz, *A Revolution*, 57.
73. Arze Aguirre, Guerra y conflictos, 31.
74. Gotkowitz, *A Revolution*, 108. For the role of Aymara women in the resistance, see Ari, *Earth Politics*, 44.
75. Ari, *Earth Politics*, 48, see also 50–53, 81–85, 96–99.
76. The decade of the 1920s was marred by violent seizures of ayllu land that sparked revolt and rebellion in the fertile lakeside communities coveted by aggressive creole-mestizos. Thousands of displaced Indians, including Nina Qhispi, found their way to the urban barrios of La Paz. See Esteban Ticona Alejo, "Conceptualización de la educación y alfabetización en Eduardo Leandro Nina Qhispi," in Soria Choque et al., eds., *Educación indígena*, 100–101; Soria Choque, "Los caciques- apoderados y la lucha por la escuela (1900–1952)," in Soria Choque et al., eds., *Educación indígenal*, 69–70; Choque Canqui and Quisbert Quispe, *Educación indígenal*, 70–78; and also Mamani Condori, *Tiraqu*, 128. The history of the Aymara struggle to recover their land and preserve their culture owes much to these historians. I am indebted to their painstaking research and incisive perceptions.
77. Mamani Condori, *Tiraqu*, 128.
78. Nina Qhispi's use of education as a means to decolonization of the creole-mestizo state would have later reverberations in the Brazilian priest Paulo Freire's *Pedagogy of the Oppressed*, and in the liberation theology movement within the Latin American Catholic Church.
79. Ticona Alejo, "Conceptualización de la educación," 105.
80. Mamani Condori, *Tiraqu*, 132.
81. Roberto Choque Canqui, "La escuela indigenal: La Paz (1905–1938)," in Soria Choque et al., eds., *Educación indígenal*, 24–29; Soria Choque, "Los caciques-apoderados," 72–74; Ticona Alejo, "Conceptualización de la educación," 104.
82. Oscar Cerruto, *Aluvión de Fuego* (Santiago, Chile, 1935), 97–100. *La Razón* accused Nina Qhispi's Republic of Kollasuyu of the "propagation of exotic ideas among the Indian race," cited in Mamani Condori, *Taraqu*, 147.
83. The Republic of Kollasuyu was not the first iteration of indigenous nationalism. Aymara comunarios formed the ephemeral counter-hegemonic Republic of Peñas in Oruro during the nineteenth-century civil war between creole liberals and conservatives. See Ramiro Condarco Morales, *Zarate, El "Temible" Willka: Historia de la Rebelión Indígena de 1899* (La Paz, 1965), 359–393. See also Soliz, "Land to the Original Owners," 266–267.
84. As Nina Qhispi contended in a letter to President Salamanca, "almost all these lands have been expropriated violently from their owners." Mamani Condori, *Taraqu*, 144.
85. Choque Canqui, "La escuela indigenal," 25–29; Arze Aguirre, *Guerra y conflictos*, 94–96; Mamani Condori, *Tiraqu*, 29, 30–31,142.
86. Mamani Condori, *Tiraqu*, 131.
87. Elizardo Pérez, *Warisata: La Escuela Ayllu* (La Paz, 1963), 82. Don Elizardo granted himself some poetic license here: Indian education as practiced in the rural normal schools was not in the interest of the gamonales because it fostered resistance to the colonato and emigration to La Paz or the mines. For the history of the rural normal school, see Choque Canqui and Cristina Quisbert Quispe, *Educación indígena*, 91–119, and Karen Claure, *Las Escuelas Indigenales: otra forma de resistencia comunaria* (La Paz: Hisbol, 1989), 39–53.
88. Pérez, *Warisata*, 80. See also Soria Choque, "Los caciques-apoderados," 57–58, and Choque Canqui and Quisbert Quispe, *Educación indígenal*, 119–123, 134–135.

89. Research by Aymara scholars has retrieved the indigenous pursuit of literacy and education from the shadow of the past. As Víctor Hugo Cardenas observes in a Prologue to the seminal *Educación Indigena,* "Little by little, in the period before the Warisata experience, appear the names of important drivers of school education, the majority illiterate and very few knew how to write." He cites a lengthy list compiled by Vitaliano Soria that reveals the names of Julian and Avelino Siñani, Santos Marka T'ula, and Eduardo L. Nina Qhispi among educators from Oruro, Cochabamba, Chuquisaca, Potosí, and Santa Cruz. Soria Choque et al., eds., *Educación Indigena,* 13.
90. Pérez, *Warisata,* 100–103.
91. Ibid., 130. Avelino Siñani's son Miguel and brother Julian, also teachers, were persecuted for their efforts. Miguel died at the age of 18 following incarceration in the Achacachi jail. Julian, who served a ten-year sentence for teaching was once forced to walk from Achacachi to Sorata dragging heavy chains on his feet while horsewhipped on the 30 mile ordeal. Ibid. The cause of Indian education would continue to be a fatal attraction, as evidenced by the murder of a dirigente caught by vecinos at a school inauguration and hung in the town plaza at Pocoata in 1947. Olivia Harris and Javier Albó, *Monteras y Guardatojos, Campesinos y mineros en el norte de Potosí* (La Paz, 1976), 36.
92. Pérez, *Warisata,* 91; see also XIV.
93. Ibid.
94. Ibid., 91–93. Pondering his experience, Don Elizardo recalled the problematics of the ayllu school experiment: "Thirty years have already passed and we are able to say that our constructive action commenced at the margin of legality, that it was eminently revolutionary in its content. It could not be otherwise. If we had waited for the land needed for the school to be turned over to us, or the materials delivered to us by the usual bureaucratic routes, I am certain that Warisata would not have existed . . ." Pérez, *Warisata,* 91. See also Soria Choque, "Los caciques-apoderados," 58; Choque Canqui, "La escuela indigenal," 30–35.
95. Pérez, *Warisata,* 116–119.
96. Ibid., 101.
97. Ibid., 137–138,192–194; Flores Moncayo, *Legislación Boliviana,* 349–353.
98. The name of a hacendado protagonist in the novel, Dr. Bautista Las Casas, leaves the reader to conjecture whether the author is satirically melding Bautista (after Bautista Saavedra, a prominent Altiplano landlord, author, President, and massacrer of Indians) with Bartolome de las Casas, the "Apostle of the Indians," famous for his defense of the indigenous peoples before the Spanish Court of Ferdinand and Isabella.
99. Raúl Boetlho Gosálvez, *Atliplano* (Lima, 1967), 100.
100. Choque Canqui and Quisbert Quispe, *Educación indigenal,* 168–171.
101. Antezana and Romero, *Historia de los sindicatos,* 4.
102. Luis Antezana E., *El movimiento obrero Boliviano* (La Paz, 1968), 6–7; Dandler, *El Sindicalismo,* 64. The huelga de brazos caidos was a precursor to the sit-down strikes of the 1940s and early 1950s.
103. Dandler, *El Sindicalisimo,* 67. The Delgadillos are referred to as first cousins by Dandler and as brothers by Antezana and Romero, *Historia de los sindicatos,* 12.
104. Antezana and Romero, *Historia de los sindicatos,* 8, 12.
105. As Joel Migdal argues, peasants follow "a mimimax strategy, maintaining control over their environment with a minimum of risk. . . . Innovations were looked upon skeptically, for the peasant was aware that so-called advances could leave him worse off than before, and this could bring an intolerable risk to those hovering on the brink of survival." Joel S. Migdal, *Peasants, Politics, and Revolution: Pressures Toward Political and Social Change in the Third World* (Princeton, NJ, 1974), 53.
106. Eduardo Arze Loureiro received a master's degree in anthropology from Michigan State University, and sharpened his perspective on Bolivian society during a four-year hiatus in Santiago, Chile, while living in a pension with another Cochabambino, the

brilliant Trotskyist, José Aguirre Gainsborg. Converted to Trotskyism, Arze Loureiro wrote the agrarian thesis (under the pseudonym J. Delgado) for the POR's founding congress in 1935 and was a member of the party Central Committee. See Steven Sandor John, "Peasant Revolution in the Altiplano: Bolivian Trotskyism, 1928–2005," Ph.D. dissertation, City University of New York, 2006, 87. Gustavo Navarro (aka Tristan Marof), the noted POR ideologue, referred to Arze Loureiro as "the most capable and respected in the party." Antezana and Romero, *Historia de los sindicatos*, 8. After the 1952 Revolution, Eduardo Arze Loureiro served on the Agrarian Reform Commission, preparing the historic Agrarian Reform Decree of 1953.

107. See Antezana and Romero, *Historia de los sindicatos*, 64–65. A paternalistic cant is evident in the decree: "rehabilitation" translates as acculturation to a western capitalist ethos (equated with "civilization" by ethnocentric urban creoles); the notion of "teaching cooperative systems of land exploitation" to peasants dispossessed of their traditional ayllu territory likewise reveals a dismissive ignorance of Andean indigenous culture.
108. Ibid., 74–77. As the authors note, the appearance of sindicatos in Tarija and in the Cochabamba provinces of Arque and Punata contradicts the idea of the Santa Clara sindicato as the singular outlier prior to the 1952 Revolution.
109. In the early days of the republic, lease fees collected by the municipality from the sweat of colono labor were designated to fund schools in villages throughout Cochabamba Department. Antezana and Romero, *Historia de los sindicatos*, 39–43.
110. Toribio Claure Montaño, *Una escuela rural en Vacas* (La Paz, 1949), 142.
111. Ibid., 143.
112. Ibid., 144.
113. The "interests" threatened by the school were the maintenance of the colonato as conveyed with the lease of the municipal land. For the denunciation of the educator, including the accusation of "preaching communism," see Claure, *Una escuela*, 146–148.
114. Flores Moncayo, *Legislación*, 378–380.
115. Antezana and Romero, *Historia de los sindicatos*, 56.
116. Claure's recollection of the hearing in an ornate salon at the Prefecture affords a vivid sense of a society at odds with itself: the hacendados sitting "silent and pompous, cynically communicative" with each other, and Claure accompanied by the Vacas colonos. "The room filled with the unmistakable odor of the Indian: smell of sweaty armpits, of chewed coca, of rawhide sandals, of wet wool." Claure, *Una escuela*, 151.
117. Ibid., 140. The Cenaculo cabal is referenced in "The Chronicle of Cochabamba" (the Cochabamba Municipal Council blog: cronistacochabamba.blogspot.com).
118. Presumably the close proximity of the races in cities would lead to miscegenation. See Carlos Salazar Mostajo's discussion of the topic in his prologue to Pérez, *Warisata*, XX, and also, 251–254.
119. Dandler, *El Sindicalismo*, 85–89.
120. Ibid., 88–89.
121. The conspiracy, referred to as the "Affaire," revealed the interrelationship of three pillars of the ancien régime: hacendados, Church (Bishop Aspe), and government (Minister Mercado Rosales). See Dandler H., *El Sindicalismo*, 92–93; the details of the scheme are traced in Dandler's footnotes: 140 (fn.137), and 142 (fn. 142).
122. An examination of the German Foreign Ministry's diplomatic correspondence reveals that Busch sought Nazi consultation and assistance before deciding on a Bolivian dictatorship. The Germans, preoccupied elsewhere, opted for non-involvement. Cole Blasier, "The United States, Germany, and the Bolivian Revolutionaries," *Hispanic American Historical Review*, 52.1 (February 1972), 28.
123. Elizardo Pérez recalled that when he heard President Busch had "lodged a bullet in his skull. . . . The news of his death touched every fiber of my being, because, as I said, his fall was also the fall of the cause of the Indian." Pérez, *Warisata*, 328.

124. Ibid.
125. On the destruction of the indigenous schools, see Karen Claure, *Las Escuelas Indigenas*, 56–60, and Larson, "Capturing Indian Bodies," 186. For an extensive post-mortem on the nuclear schools, see Pérez, *Warisata*, 3810421. Ironically, the destruction of the schools by traditional educators in the service of the hacendados began while Elizardo Pérez was in Mexico touting Bolivia's nuclear school program at the First Inter-American Indigenista Congress.
126. As Ann Zulawski reminds us, "under certain circumstances, hygiene becomes a means of maintaining the existing social hierarchy." Ann Zulawski, "Hygiene and the 'Indian Problem', Ethnicity and Medicine in Bolivia, 1910–1920," *Latin American Research Review*, 35.2 (2000), 116–117; see also Stephenson, *Gender and Modernity*, 118–128, and Larson, "Capturing Indian Bodies," 194–195.
127. Laurence Whitehead, "Altitude, Fertility and Mortality in Andean Countries," *Population Studies*, 22.3 (1968), 343.
128. Choque et al., eds., *Educación Indigena*, 133; a slightly different version appears in Pérez, *Warisata*, 400.
129. The nuclear school matrix was begun in May 1937 under the indigenista Director Leonidas Calvimontes who had worked on Altiplano nuclear schools with Elizardo Pérez; the central school was situated at Ucureña with secondary schools in outlying hamlets. Dandler, *El Sindicalismo*, 82 and 140, fn 140.
130. Ibid., 104.
131. Dandler, *El Sindicalismo*, 101.
132. Antezana and Romero, *Historia de los sindicatos*, 71, 74; Dandler, *El Sindicalismo*, 96–98, 105–106.
133. Guevara's acumen is evident in a letter regarding the colonos: "They considered themselves free and secure in their property rights . . . but after recent abuses, arrests and growing opposition, they have realized that as individuals perhaps they are in a less secure position than when they were colonos. . . . They understand that their strength lies in their unity of group and sindicato." Dandler, *El Sindicalismo*, 106–107.
134. Antezana and Romero, *Historia de los sindicatos*, 65.
135. Laura Gotkowitz underscores the threat posited by Eduardo Leandro Nina Qhispi, Santos Marka T'ula, and the network of Aymara and Quechua apoderados who challenged the legitimacy of the Old Order while developing dual power in the countryside: "The caciques apoderados, in short, assumed a parallel structure of government: the effort to recuperate land went hand in hand with the struggle for local power." Gotkowitz, *A Revolution*, 71.

2
REVOLUTION

In the early hours of 20 December 1943, officers of a clandestine military society captured President Peñaranda and his senior officers. The rebels, who identified themselves as members of "Cause of the Fatherland" (*Razón de Patria*: RADEPA), then occupied the Palacio Quemado. The Arsenal of War and the central arms depot at Plaza Antofagasta were taken by a RADEPA force, the army regiments in La Paz neutralized together with the guards assigned to the General Staff, and the carabineros responsible for government security. Radepistas seized control of the artillery regiment at Viacha and after the air base at El Alto was secured, a squadron of aviators flew from Santa Cruz to La Paz to support the coup.[1] The RADEPA operation was also flawlessly executed in Cochabamba and other departmental capitals. The Rosca diplomat Alberto Ostría Gutiérrez marveled at the perfection of the "lightning revolution," likening it to a Nazi blitzkrieg.[2] Yet the RADEPA leadership remained a mystery as was their nexus with the Nationalist Revolutionary Movement whose militants had seized control of the radio and telecommunication centers in La Paz.[3]

The RADEPA officers issued a lengthy Manifesto to the nation proclaiming a new era: "The people and the young men of the Bolivian Army incited to rebellion by the disorder of the fallen regime, by the constant illegality of its acts, by the criminal deceit with which it has misused the public faith, by the wanton misuse of public funds and the complete neglect in which it has left Bolivian interests . . ., have taken up arms of vengeance with which Bolivia, condemned hitherto to oligarchic domination, may once more save its constitution, its liberties and its destinies."[4]

RADEPA and the Bolivian National Revolution

The inception of the RADEPA Revolution can be traced to a prisoner of war camp in Asunción, Paraguay, where a clique led by Second Lieutenant Elías Belmonte Pabón enlisted select junior officers in the secretive lodge. Membership was later extended to other officers who met the qualifications of "known patriotic morality, were under age forty-five and who belonged to no other lodge, masonic or international, willing to completely renounce the military hierarchy."[5] The brotherhood devoted itself to the Cause of the Fatherland, expressed in the maxim "Honor, Patriotism, Valor."

The Radepistas questioned the patriotism of their military and civilian leaders who had served the fatherland so poorly and espoused a fervent nationalism and a virulent anti-imperialism. This attitude was also common among many of the 15,000 Chaco War POWs. The shared rage of these veterans is evidenced in a manifesto published in March 1936 by the *Asociación de Ex-Prisoneros*, remarkable for its searing resentment toward the "choir of angels in certain rear posts . . . the failed jefes, the strategists and tacticians of simulation." Their voice would be heard: "We prisoners who have suffered absence from our native soil are not satisfied with the patria that we encounter; it does not seem to us the same; its pain, its silence, its passivity, its indifference, discourage our patriotism. If we ex-prisoners remain silent in this historic moment, we would indict ourselves as guilty."[6]

RADEPA officers became influential in the advanced School of War established in postwar Cochabamba where their curricula included geopolitics, international law, political economy, and social science.[7] Among these officers (known within the military as the "Cochabamba Group") was Major Gualberto Villarroel. Although never a prisoner of war, Major Villarroel was nonetheless accepted by RADEPA whose numbers are estimated at 68 on the eve of their 1943 coup d'état.[8] Assignment to the advanced war college afforded the Radepistas a bully pulpit for proselytization of their revolutionary agenda.[9] This agenda was the goal of President Gualberto Villarroel's Nationalist Revolution (1943–1946). Much of the RADEPA agenda was shared by the MNR and would reappear during the later (1952–1964) redux of the Nationalist Revolution (see Chapters 5 and 6).

Gualberto Villarroel and the National Revolution

The 1943 coup introduced Major Gualberto Villarroel, the RADEPA eminence grise, into the public eye. A Cochabambino graduate of the *Colegio Militar*, Villarroel served as Commander of the Ayacucho Battalion in the Chaco front lines where the incompetence and decadence of the General Staff disgusted him. The defeats at Picuaba and Villamontes in 1935—suffered while General Toro and fellow whore-mongering senior officers debauched themselves in drunken orgies safely behind the lines—so incensed the idealistic Villarroel that he considered assassinating the general.[10] Víctor Andrade, who would later play a significant role in the National Revolution, recalls his initial encounter with Major Villarroel while assigned as a liaison to the Eighth Division. Conveying orders from the General

Staff, Lieutenant Andrade presented himself to Colonel Ayoroa, Commander of the Ayacucho Regiment:

Colonel Ayoroa: "*Since when does headquarters send us only 'college boys' for such an important position? Do you realize, Lieutenant, that the mission which you propose to carry out belongs to a higher-ranking career officer?*"

Lieutenant Andrade: "*Colonel, I am merely following an order from headquarters.*"

In a corner of the field tent, an officer . . . sat up. He [Major Gualberto Villarroel] intervened firmly, "*Colonel, there is no cause to reproach Lieutenant Andrade. He is only trying to fulfill the mission with which they have entrusted him. Here we are all Bolivians who do what we can, and it is not up to us as professional officers to reject the efforts of the civilians who wear a uniform and who have earned their rank by sacrificing so much.*"[11]

Major Villarroel's acumen is evident here: a sensitivity to the arrogance of rank and power of professional officers, together with a cognizance of the necessity of an alliance between military and civilian patriots. The encounter initiated a friendship critical to the genesis of the National Revolution. Gualberto Villarroel would emerge as RADEPA's leader, while Víctor Andrade was to lead the veterans' organization, *Estrella de Hierro* (Iron Star). Collaboration between the two led to the formation of the *Mariscal Santa Cruz Lodge*, a stalking horse for RADEPA in the civilian sphere led by Andrade and comprised of veterans in La Paz, Cochabamba, Potosí, and Sucre. Because neither the RADEPA officers nor the MNR civilians were independently capable of ousting the *Concordancia* and governing the nation, a marriage of convenience had been arranged. As the American Embassy in La Paz noted, "The marriage between the [RADEPA] Villarroel group and the MNR was one of the shot-gun variety because it was felt within the Villarroel group that civilian support was necessary. . . . [I]t was realized within the Villarroel group that it in itself was not strong enough so it was decided to take in the MNR."[12] Major Gualberto Villarroel was an unknown, whereas his MNR counterpart Víctor Paz Estenssoro was renowned as a brilliant orator (and a consummate politician with a preternatural gift to wheel and deal, divide and conquer). The fateful collusion, based on an "affinity of ideals," was allegedly agreed upon between Gualberto Villarroel and the MNR's Víctor Paz Estenssoro at Andrade's La Paz residence in August 1943.[13]

The Provisional Government legitimized the "December Revolution" with elections in 1944. The RADEPA Major Gualberto Villarroel was elected President and three MNR founders, including Minister of Finance Víctor Paz Estenssoro, were accorded cabinet positions. With a majority elected to the 1944 parliament, the MNR was able to select the nation's vice president: the choice was Major Clemente Inofuentes, a RADEPA officer respected for his character, intelligence, and revolutionary commitment. But this was not to be. Minister of Defense Colonel Celestino Pinto overturned the choice and Major Inofuentes was summarily posted abroad. Colonel Pinto, a favorite of the U.S. State Department, next used his influence to deny the vice presidency to the MNR leader Víctor Paz Estenssoro.[14]

Rifts among the Radepistas festered. Symptomatic of this predicament was President Villarroel's inability to control the plotting of a right-wing clique within RADEPA, determined to isolate militant Radepistas and minimize MNR influence in the regime. Colonel Pinto's rejection of Major Inofuentes as Vice President was seen by Movimientistas as an early example of the Colonel's perfidy. Colonel Francisco Barrero, a RADEPA cabinet member, found Pinto's "incalculable influence on the unhinging and disorientation of Radepa and the Villarroel government" treasonous, a charge validated by Pinto's defection to the conservative Illimani Lodge in February 1944.[15]

Villarroel's reply to the question of a fifth column within his government is revealing. In response to a query on the topic by *La Calle's* Armando Arce, the President hinted at an ulterior presence in his government: "What you say is evident, Víctor [Paz] also informed me and asked me the same thing more than once; but I can't do it [remove the conspirators] because the comrades don't want to do that." Arce mused: "Who were . . . those comrades that in a form so decisive and fatal influenced the spirit of President Villarroel and forced him to be an impotent spectator of events that had to lead him to the sacrifice of his life."[16] By 1944, RADEPA was no longer a unified cohort. The U.S. government was well aware of the factionalism. Secretary of State Cordell Hull reported, in a March 1944 telegram to the American Embassy in La Paz, that in a meeting with the Bolivian Military Attaché Colonel Oscar Moscoso, the Colonel had lobbied for the removal of his Commander in Chief. "He was not certain what changes should be made among the military members of the Junta although he threw out, obviously to get a reaction, which was not forthcoming, the removal of Ponce and Villarroel."[17]

Non-recognition of the Junta Revolucionaria

Diplomatic recognition by the United States was a prerequisite to the sale of tin; hence, the first order of business for the Junta was to assure the continued supply of tin and other raw materials vital to the Anglo-American cause in World War II. A telegram to the Secretary of State from the U.S. Embassy in La Paz opined that the Provisional Junta was "national in character rather than in response to any foreign impulse or ideologies," yet the State Department ordered Ambassador Boal to avoid contact with the Junta, and the War Department ordered its military attaches to be circumspect in conversations with Bolivian officers.[18] The objective of Anglo-American diplomacy was to oust the *Junta Revolucionaria* and return the Rosca to power; the modus operandi included: (1) non-recognition of the Junta; (2) isolation of the Junta, alleging that it was a nest of Nazi subversion, a threat to the security of its neighbors and the Allied cause; (3) delay of tin contracts, and curtailment of imports and foreign aid to impair the Bolivian economy.

The non-recognition campaign led by Secretary of State Cordell Hull culminated in the assembly of an "Emergency Committee for Political Defense" on 28 January 1944 in Montevideo, Uruguay. The Committee for Political Defense, originally formed in 1942 to coordinate a united stand against Axis influence in the Americas, was a front for United States policy, "secretly manipulated by the North American delegate . . . and limited to retroactive approval of unilateral measures already adopted in Washington."[19] Under the guise of multilateralism, the United States cajoled 19 Latin American nations to withhold diplomatic recognition from the fledgling regime: a transparent maneuver well understood by Víctor Andrade, the Bolivian Ambassador to the United States. "The U.S. plan was to make non-recognition of the new Bolivian government a phase of the action against the Axis powers."[20] The State Department upped the ante against the Junta, issuing an order "to withhold action on all export license applications for Bolivia . . . to hold all requests for freight space for goods destined to Bolivia; to prevent the shipment of rubber and quinine to Argentina from Bolivia; to continue suspension of tin negotiations; and to refrain from undertaking any activities relating to procurement of war materials from Bolivia."[21] Meanwhile, the tin magnates utilized their newspapers to influence public opinion and opened their coffers (via the Association of Mining Industrialists) to retain the lobbyists essential to garnering support in the U.S. Congress.[22]

Evident at this early date was the unequal relationship between a great power and a weak and dependent nation, which is illustrated in the "Strictly Confidential" memo of 24 March 1944 from the U.S. State Department's Office of American Republic Affairs regarding recognition of the RADEPA government. "Thus, according to the Embassy, all of the MNR members will resign from the Junta and the first of three conditions for recognition . . . will have been fulfilled. It is also reported that Major Ponce [a key RADEPA leader] will probably resign, thus fulfilling the second condition. The third and final condition has already been fulfilled by a call for general elections."[23] North American hegemony, wielded indirectly through the Brazilian Minister of External Relations, is evident in a query from Brazilian Foreign Minister Oswaldo Aranha to U.S. Ambassador Caffery: "Please ask Mr. Hull just what he wants done in Bolivia and we will do it."[24] Diplomatically isolated, economically squeezed, besieged at home and abroad by a hostile press, the Provisional Junta was forced to jettison three MNR cabinet ministers objectionable to the United States. Two of the three, Secretary of Agriculture Carlos Montenegro and Augusto Céspedes, the Secretary General of the Junta, were MNR founders with fascist sympathies. To assure diplomatic recognition, the Junta acquiesced again in April and jettisoned the three remaining MNR ministers: Víctor Paz Estenssoro, Wálter Guevara Arze, and Rafael Otazo.

U.S. Special Ambassador Avra Warren arrived in La Paz the following month to personally assess the reconstituted Junta purged of its MNR ministers. Pursuant to Warren's subsequent demands, the Junta traded 81 German and Japanese citizens in exchange for diplomatic recognition; the unfortunate pawns were deported aboard a squadron of U.S. military DC-3s destined for North American internment camps. "It was hard to argue that a few Germans left alone in Bolivia posed a threat to the Western Hemisphere or to the Allied war effort in 1944," notes diplomatic historian Max Paul Friedman, "Instead, deporting Germans became a means for the Bolivian government to meet the standards for legitimacy established unilaterally by the United States."[25] Dr. Humberto Palza, representing the Bolivian government in Brazil, expressed his frustration with the policy. "Bolivia may have committed mistakes in its revolution, but certainly she has been spanked for it. The spanking has lasted for more than three months now and the country has not only promised to behave, but has demonstrated and is demonstrating by deeds that her original intentions were good. . . . Now we are in the position of begging to be Allies, and refused by our friends'."[26]

Bolivia surrendered the rights of a sovereign nation by acceding to the dictates of the United States, including the right to determine the fate of its citizens in its own courts. After six months of genuflection, the provisional Junta was at last granted diplomatic recognition by the United States, Britain, and the nations of the Anglo-American bloc.

The non-recognition policy was but the continuation of opposition to the RADEPA–MNR nationalists earlier dramatized by the infamous "Putsch Nazi" episode—a clever piece of British spycraft—purporting that Major Elías Belmonte Pabón, a RADEPA founder, was involved in a German scheme to overthrow the Peñaranda government.[27] The "Belmonte Letter" was unmasked as a fake intended to besmirch the reputation of the nationalists, casting them as Nazis—a fact that was not lost on Bolivian cognoscenti.[28] After an exegesis of diplomatic records relevant to the non-recognition policy, a former U.S. Foreign Service officer concluded: "It would be hard to find a more dramatic case of foreign political influences being used to determine the composition of another country's government than the U.S. non-recognition policy towards Villarroel in 1944."[29]

The fledgling regime was also undermined by Rosca obfuscation, attempted coups, and rogue elements within RADEPA. The kidnapping of tin baron Mauricio Hochschild after a thwarted coup in April 1944 provided grist for the media. Time magazine reported, "The Bolivian regime of Provisional President Gualberto Villarroel last week discovered and scotched a plot to overthrow it. Warned in the nick of time, the Government caught one conspirator actually handing out cash to soldiers. Bigger fish captured were ex-Minister of War Ernesto Hertzog, two generals, and Lawyer Nestor Galindo, charged with distributing a 20,000,000 $boliviano ($450,000) corruption fund. Biggest fish . . . Tin Magnate Mauricio

Hochschild, jailed as principal."[30] Hochschild had been previously arrested by the Provisional Government following a secret meeting with U.S. officials where he offered his cooperation to "destroy the regime."[31] A string of shocking events followed, including the attempted assassination of the PIR leader José Antonio Arze, beatings administered to a number of prominent opposition politicians, and the execution of 12 Rosca conspirators in November 1944 following a failed coup centered in Oruro.

Newspaper readers were feted to lurid repetition of the brutal torture and execution of the 12 "November Heroes" by Indian soldiers, stoking fears among the creole-mestizo middle class of retribution by the subaltern masses. The November executions were endlessly repeated in the Rosca press, together with warnings of fascist totalitarianism, inciting misgivings among middle-class supporters of the revolution who identified with the "martyrs" allegedly murdered by savage Indians. Villarroel's defenders argue that the president was unaware of the executions and thus exonerated of guilt.[32] Of far more relevance is the RADEPA creed, pledged by its members, to defend the revolution from its enemies. Were the perpetrators thus patriots for eliminating the Rosca reactionaries caught attempting to overthrow the National Revolution? As the RADEPA Generals Eliodoro Murillo Cardenas and Gustavo Llarrea Bedregal have it, the Radepistas swore an oath to defend the "Cause of the Fatherland" and "punishing with the death penalty those Bolivians who betray our sublime desires . . . the sacred essence of our beloved Patria," and thus:

> There were certain things that were without doubt. . . . [T]hose in charge of the State knew of the macabre plans of the counterrevolutionaries. They knew, for sure, that these plans contemplated the physical elimination of the President, of the members of his Cabinet and of their closest collaborators. . . . It is logical that whoever ordered the [November] shootings of Chuspipata and Caracollo knew such plans. . . . They knew that it was a mode of legitimate defense.[33]

The kidnapping of the tin baron Mauricio Hochschild, the attempted assassination of the PIRista Jefe José Antonio Arze, and the execution of a dozen Rosca conspirators after a failed coup attempt, all presumably the work of extremists within RADEPA, added to the estrangement of the RADEPA–MNR collaborators. Senator Manuel Frontaura Argandoña would later remark on the estranged relationship of the RADEPA–MNR partners, citing "Differences of caste, mutual contempt . . . personal antipathy, intellectual imbalance, practice and theory, realism and utopia, each way of seeing things was different within the gubernatorial family, and there they were Villarroel and Paz Estenssoro to calmly confront the storms that beset them every day both in substance and in detail." It was said, noted the senator, that only the two could sustain the unity of the National Revolution, and that the flawed RADEPA–MNR marriage could ill afford a divorce: should ether falter, the revolution would collapse.[34]

Meanwhile, President Villarroel increasingly appeared a hapless figure removed from the political realities of governance. His aloofness, a source of consternation to his MNR allies, was epitomized by the president's response to political queries, as noted by the Movimientista José Fellman Velarde upon overhearing Villarroel's response to a political question: "Politics? No, I don't understand politics. Why don't you speak with the Minister of Government?" Fellman later recalled, "That sentence alone, in the mouth of a President like him, summarizes his tragedy."[35]

The Nationalist Revolutionary Movement

The Nationalist Revolutionary Movement was remarkably homogeneous. Virtually all of the MNR founders were young creole or mestizo lawyers and journalists from La Paz or Cochabamba. Primarily graduates of the *Universidad Mayor de San Andrés*, many also had attended the American Institute in La Paz (a Methodist preparatory school), most were veterans of the Chaco War, and some had served in the military socialist governments of Colonels Toro and Busch.[36] The party appealed to disaffected members of the middle class whose aspirations were limited by the constraints of life in a quasi-feudal society wracked by postwar inflation, rife with nepotism, and under the sclerotic thumb of the oligarchy.[37]

Two factions were at work within the MNR: a fascist group that included the *La Calle* journalists Augusto Céspedes, Carlos Montenegro, José Cuadros Quiroga, Armando Arce, and a Marxist clique led by Víctor Paz Estenssoro, Hernán Siles Zuazo, and Juan Lechín Oquendo. Bolivian nationalists, rankled by the domination of hacendados, tin barons, and their Anglo-American hegemons, were receptive to fascist and Marxist critiques of capitalism and imperialism.[38] Fascism was a dynamic force in the post-Chaco years. Nationalist, anti-imperialist, and anti-communist notions of national will, national purpose, and national integration influenced RADEPA officers and MNR militants. The Bolivian iteration of fascism, the Bolivian Socialist Falange (*Falange Socialista Boliviana*: FSB) dedicated to "God, Fatherland, Honor," founded in 1937 by Catholic creoles and led by the irrepressible Oscar de Unzaga de la Vega, sought to defend the traditional order against communism (perceived as a threat to family, religion, and property). As the historian Timothy Snyder puts it, "The fascists don't really have concepts. They have attitudes . . . they don't start out with a set of ideas that they then apply to the world."[39] An attitude shared by both the Falange and MNR fascists was a disdain for the foreigners in their midst, expressed in the anti-semitism of the German-subsidized MNR newspapers *Inti* and *La Calle*.

Bolivia attracted German geopolitical attention in the 1930s (as it did Che Guevara in the 1960s) because of its strategic position at the center of the continent, contiguous with five countries. German attachés advised the Bolivian armed forces; Condor Airlines flew throughout the Andes; German businesses, schools, and cultural centers were prominent fixtures in major cities; Bolivian newspapers were given free access to the German wire service; and *La Calle* received financial support from the German legation.[40] British diplomatic records reveal official concerns regarding German influence, particularly in Cochabamba: "The Germans found themselves thoroughly at home there. . . . [T]he military connection (most provincial authorities being army officers) and the air network were used to their full value and a close knit and well-organized politico-commercial domination of almost the whole Eastern part of Bolivia was built up with Cochabamba as the centre of the web."[41]

Bolivia's subservience to the Colossus of the North—a raw nerve inflamed by the Standard Oil scandal and the martyred President Busch—wounded Bolivian national pride. Hence, many Bolivians saw German opposition to Anglo-American imperialism as a kindred struggle. "Really there was a sympathy in Bolivia for the cause of Germany, not for the Nazi-Fascists, but as an enemy of our oppressor, the United States. Germany was not our oppressor," noted Augusto Céspedes in a retrospective interview.[42] Víctor Paz Estenssoro viewed the Allies-Axis confrontation as a war between competing imperialisms and not as a conflict between democracy and totalitarianism: "Behind the phrases such as the new order of the Germans, and of democracy, human rights, and the liberty of the Allies, there is nothing but the struggle of two imperialisms that try to divide the world in order to acquire zones of production of raw materials and of markets to absorb the production of manufactured goods."[43]

Movimientista legislators assailed the failings and machinations of the Rosca as did the MNR journalists writing in *Inti* and *La Calle*. Both newspapers were blacklisted by the Department of State and subsequently denied U.S.-controlled newsprint.[44] They were also shut down when the Rosca decided to deflate criticism. The synergy of an opposition party energized by its own newspapers was unprecedented in Bolivia. Augusto Céspedes, Carlos Montenegro, José Cuadros Quiroga, and Armando Arce treated readers to a daily dose of exposes and satire in a relentless pillorying of ruling class peccadilloes. President Peñaranda's expensive taste in wine and spirits subsidized with public funds, the spoils of office and political patronage, war profiteering, the lies and deceptions of the tin barons and their newspapers, *The Monos of Wall Street and Yanquilandia*, as well as the Stalinist PIR were all subjected to relentless criticism. *La Calle* also trumpeted the radical MNR agenda: separation of church and state, socialized medicine, reform of the educational system (including Indian education and vocational schools), enforcement of the Busch Labor Code, agrarian reform, pay raises for teachers and workers, and construction of low-income housing.[45]

The MNR shared the RADEPA belief in the necessity of modernization, so evident after the humiliation of the Chaco War. Nationalization of the mining *superestado* was a sine qua non for economic development, as was reform of the seigneurial system. Yet the middle-class MNR leaders were loath to initiate a revolution from below—unleashing the latent power of three million peasants and proletarians—in a violent and uncontrollable confrontation with their masters. Instead, they sought a moderate formula of modernization within a capitalist framework. Publication of Carlos Montenegro's *Nacionalismo y coloniaje* (*Nationalism and colonialism*) in 1943 presented a vivid synopsis of the country's underdevelopment and history of subservience to its foreign masters ("International capitalism . . . nailed its harpoon in our mountains").[46]

Montenegro painstakingly essayed the tragedy of a nation betrayed by its ruling class—the subjugation of its people by ruthless oligarchs, the loss of territory through ill-fated wars, the surrender of precious natural resources to predatory monopolists and of sovereignty to imperialism. But there is an ironic twist here: Montenegro (an urban creole) railed against neocolonialism, yet ignored the proverbial elephant in the room—the topic of the indigenous majority's historic struggle against internal colonialism. Nonetheless, the work provided the creole-mestizos with a systematic critique of the ancien régime together with a rationale for change: not a revolution to destroy capitalism, but instead reform of hacienda exploitation and nationalization of the mining superestado.

Alberrto Mendoza López's *La Soberanía de Bolivia* (*The Sovereignty of Bolivia*), published in 1942 (with a prologue by Carlos Montenegro), presented MNR critiques of the Rosca, Anglo-American imperialism, and Russian communism. Mendoza López's signature essay "Bolivian Socialism" states the MNR case for socialism, and argues that Soviet communism "proclaims the suppression of the right to private property . . . the abolition of religion . . . the destruction of the family . . . the institutions and sentiments most dear to nationality."[47]

The MNR's founding manifesto, *Movimiento Nacionalista Revolucionario: sus bases y principios de acción inmediata*, written in 1942 by the fascist-inspired journalist José Cuadros Quiroga, is a paean to nationalism delivered via a spate of demands: "We demand the union and effort of the middle class, worker and peasant in the struggle against the antinational superestado and its servants . . . to extirpate the great private monopolies . . . that operate outside the Bolivian state."[48] The *Bases* demands an end to the favoritism accorded to foreign businesses and calls for regulation of working conditions in international (e.g., mining) companies and registration of their personnel under the "vigilance" of the Army General Staff. The legacy of the Chaco appears in demands for the retirement of officers over age 55, exclusion of foreign officers commanding Bolivian troops, purchase of modern armaments, and instruction of a "sense of nationalist political culture" in civil–military education. The *Bases* defined Bolivia as an "indo-mestizo" nation and advocated Indian education, agrarian reform, social justice, social security, colonization of undeveloped lands, and modernization of the national transportation and communication infrastructure.[49]

The nationalism of *Bases y principios* is not without a xenophobic cant: fears of spies and espionage recur together with a call for the end of foreign influence in the press, which begs the question of German influence in the MNR propaganda organs *La Calle* and *Inti*.[50] The Janus face of nationalism appears in the demand for prohibition of Jewish immigration as well as the conflation of Judaism with international communism in a thinly veiled attack on the rival Stalinist and Trotskyist parties. "We denounce as anti-national every possible relation between international political parties and the maneuvers of Judaism."[51] *Bases y principios* is critical of the influx of cosmopolitan European immigrants advantaging themselves among creole-mestizo rubes in the poorest of South American countries:

> The destroyed ones of Judaism, thrown out of Europe by Hitler, who have arrived in Bolivia do not constitute for this country anything but a parasitic group that begins by contending for the necessities of life with the middle and working classes [and ends up] consolidating itself in a new exploitative class. That will weigh . . . upon the Bolivian people.[52]

The anti-Semitism of *Bases y principios* is restrained when compared to the vitriolic *La Calle*. The newspaper lambasted the millions of dollars pocketed by corrupt diplomats through the sale of Bolivian passports to European Jews fleeing Nazi persecution. The "Passport Affaire" proved to be a propaganda bonanza exposing the venality of the Old Regime while fueling middle-class paranoia of inundation by tens of thousands of Jewish business competitors as illustrated in an anti-Semitic rant by Augusto Céspedes: "The immense national majority, the foundation of democracy, opposes and repudiates the ominous big-nosed immigrants . . . to fall like a ravenous invading horde upon the cities of Bolivia."[53]

A Social Revolution in the Andes

The RADEPA coup d'état escalated the confrontation between the Old Order and the forces of modernity. A harbinger of momentous upheaval, the 1943 coup initiated South America's singular twentieth-century social revolution. Its course was tortuous: initiated by the RADEPA government of Gualberto Villarroel (1943–1946), truncated by a counterrevolution (1946–1952), and reignited in the momentous years of radical political, social, and economic transformation (1952–1964).

This periodization is at odds with the traditional narrative in which the nationalist revolution is portrayed as originating with the April 1952 MNR defeat of the ancien régime and ending with the 1964 overthrow by a military coup de état: an erroneous schema that endures as the standard rendition of conventional wisdom.[54] The Bolivian National Revolution began, in fact, with the RADEPA coup of 1943 and not with the MNR insurrectionary triumph of 1952. It bears note that utilization of this revised periodization reveals parallels with the 1910 Mexican Revolution:

- Both social revolutions originated in Amerindian nations with politically moderate precursors: the Bolivian military nationalist Gualberto Villarroel and the Mexican reformist Francisco Madero.
- After a brief period, the moderates Villarroel (1943–1946) and Madero (1910–1913) were martyred in violent episodes orchestrated by the ancien régime in league with foreign imperialists (the United States and Great Britain) during eras of the World War (Mexico, World War I; Bolivia, World War II).

- Counterrevolutionary coups then returned both countries to oligarchic rule: Bolivia (President Enrique Hertzog's "*Sexenio*," 1946–1952); Mexico ("The Usurper" General Victoriano Huerta, 1913–1914).
- The revolutions next began a radical transformative phase of violent assaults by the subaltern masses against the remnants of the oligarchic state (Bolivia: 1952–1964 and Mexico: 1914–1930s).

Application of the conventional Bolivian typology to Mexico would necessitate omission of the initial moderate phase of the revolution under Madero as well as General Huerta's counterrevolutionary interregnum—and therefore require the recalibration of the Mexican Revolution as 1914–1940, instead of the conventional 1910–1940 periodization. (Comparisons of the two revolutions are to be found in Chapters 3–5 and 7.)[55]

Objectives of the RADEPA Revolution

President Villarroel's primary interest was modernization of the nation through technical expertise and administrative efficiency. That he is remembered for his martyrdom—rather than for his attempt to modernize an underdeveloped and dependent nation—is the tragedy of the man. The objectives of RADEPA's National Revolution were (1) "redemption" of a nation dishonored by a perfidious oligarchy; (2) reform of the military institution to include a mobile corps of professional troops imbued with esprit de corps, reinforced by an army of trained reservists equipped with modern weaponry; (3) economic independence; (4) nationalization of oil and mineral resources; (5) modernization of the national infrastructure; development of telegraph, telephone, and postal communications; and construction of highways, railways, and airfields; (6) foreign policy determined to reclaim the Pacific seacoast and an outlet to the Atlantic, unrealized by the Chaco War fiasco; (7) "redemption" of the Indian through education; (8) implementation of a "rational system of land parceling" to those who work it; (9) economic and technical assistance for agriculture; (10) development of the Oriente lowlands through colonization and migration; and (11) reduction of the government bureaucracy. Many of these RADEPA objectives would reappear during the 1952–1964 redux of the Nationalist Revolution.[56]

The Villarroel regime enforced the labor code enacted by Germán Busch and the *fuero syndical*, granting formal recognition of labor's right to organize without fear of dismissal, coercion, or transfer; and supported the country's first national labor union (*Federación Sindical de Trabajadores Mineros de Bolivia*: FSTMB), numbering upward of 40,000 miners led by the Movimientista Juan Lechín, a charismatic leader destined to influence the future of the mine workers and the National Revolution.[57] The regime also pushed for parliamentary support of social security for Bolivian workers and issued decrees mandating payment of back wages, extra pay for night work, paid vacations, a rent reduction law, and a Christmas bonus (*aguinaldo*) for blue- and white-collar workers to be funded, in part, by corporate contributions.[58] The creation of a "Department of Efficiency and Administrative Reorganization" was a step toward modernization of the country's archaic *empleocracía*, the bureaucratic web of sinecures, where "Each one of the administrative branches was independent and determined its own actions, ignoring the existence, needs and problems of the others."[59] Three months after the inception of the revolution, Villarroel asked the U.S. Embassy for a copy of the report prepared by Rowland Egger (the manager of the Bolivian Development Corporation), with recommendations for the administrative reorganization of the Bolivian government, including the "systematizing of classes of public employees" and the institution of a merit system for advancement within the bloated bureaucracy.[60]

Social Rights and Social Welfare

The president's technocratic approach is also apparent in a census undertaken to determine mine workers' salaries and day wages, the nature of their work, and the length of their service—data essential to determination of minimum wages, overtime, and disability payments.[61] The employment of social workers for the investigation of socioeconomic problems was unprecedented in Bolivian government. The regime's adjudication of strikes rewarded workers with increased wages. A January 1944 Decree raised salaries for the lowest-paid workers (earning 6.5 bolivianos a day) by 20 percent and the highest-paid workers by 10 percent. Strikes by railroad workers on the La Paz–Antofagasta line, La Paz factory workers, and miners in the Patiño and Aramayo mines were adjudicated by the president who increased wages 30 percent and 10 percent, respectively, for the lowest- and highest-paid workers.[62]

The regime's commitment to the welfare of the Bolivian worker is also evident in the budgetary increase for social welfare programs initiated by the MNR Finance Minister Víctor Paz Estenssoro. The government began a study to determine the dietary needs of working-class families in 1945 and introduced a General Directory of Maternity and Social Assistance to assist in protection of mothers and children. Maternity and infant clinics were under construction in Puerto Acosta and plans drawn up for clinics in Sacaba, Charana, Guaqui, Villazón, Puerto Suarez, Guayaramerín, and Yacuiba. Hospitals were built in Capinota and Trinidad and a surgical wing added to the Miraflores hospital in La Paz. The government launched campaigns against bronchopneumonia, tuberculosis, smallpox, malaria, yellow fever and venereal disease and opened laboratories and dispensaries in Potosí, Tarija, Beni, and Santa Cruz. Social assistance for the widows and orphans of the Chaco War was also a concern of the regime that provided free housing for war widows visiting La Paz in search of pensions. Public housing projects were constructed for workers in Potosí and Tarija and other projects planned for Cochabamba and Sucre.[63]

The quest for social justice elicited a debate over social conventions: concubinage (*concubanato*), paternity, child equality, and children's welfare. Questions regarding sexual consequences and paternal responsibility addressed social mores deeply rooted in Latin American patriarchal society. Agitation for equal rights posed a direct challenge to traditional sexual and social power—an exclusively male domain. Many of the offspring of illicit sexual unions, such as the MNR leaders Hernán Siles and Juan Lechín, were mestizos born of criollo fathers and Indian mothers. A law granting concubines legal rights was a victory for social justice, and *La Calle* admonished its opponents: "you are not defending the common women; you are acting with prejudice to maintain a privilege of caste, or better said, the privileges of the rich."[64] The wide-ranging commitment of the Villarroel regime to workers' rights, social welfare, and public health are often overlooked in narratives that focus on the MNR, RADEPA's junior partner in the initial phase of the National Revolution.[65]

Resource Nationalism, Sovereignty, and National Integration

A paramount concern of the National Revolution was control of the economy dominated by the mining superestado. Instead of reaping the advantage of wartime demand for tin, the ore was sold at one-tenth fair market value. This contributed between $600 and $900 million to the U.S. war effort: considerably more than the total U.S. aid to Bolivia since the war.[66] A rare opportunity to fund the dream of modernization and national integration was missed. Compounding the inability to capitalize on unprecedented wartime demand, Bolivia found itself pauperized by the postwar drop in demand for tin, wolfram, antimony, lead, and zinc.

Tin revenue accounted for 65–70 percent of the value of Bolivian exports between 1929 and 1949, but had fallen from a high in 1939 to its lowest level in 1944–1945.[67] Thus, in 1945, President Villarroel ordered enforcement of Busch's 1937 decree granting the nation total control of the *divisas* (foreign exchange earnings) of tin.[68] The law allowed the state to directly tax corporate earnings, threatening the Rosca's profits and power. Additionally, Víctor Paz Estenssoro, appointed Minister of National Economy, sought payment of millions of dollars in unpaid taxes owed by the tin magnates. Revenue from control of the tin divisas and Paz's strict control of the budget delivered a surplus that allowed construction of the Camiri–TinTin petroleum pipeline and bolstered the reserves of the Banco Minero and the Agricultural Bank. However, while Paz raised taxes on the tin magnates and increased funds for social welfare, he also reduced expenditures for economic development[69]

President Villarroel directed the Banco Minero to acquire machinery abandoned at inoperative mines and redistribute the equipment to operative producers. In an attempt to gain administrative authority over the mining sector, the Banco Minero catalogued and registered some 8,000 mineral concessions and created a development office to foster production of the country's 700 gold mines. Control of subsoil rights was also tightened over the national oil corporation *Yacimientos Petrolíferos Bolivianos* (YPFB).[70]

The RADEPA officers considered the agglomeration of regional bureaucracies (controlled by caudillos and opportunistic local officials) a hindrance to national integration and regionalism a threat to national security given the history of territorial losses suffered at the hands of acquisitive neighbors. President Villarroel called for unity among "men from all latitudes of the country in the same faith, creating a national consciousness."[71] The primitive state of Bolivian infrastructure, so woefully apparent in the Chaco War (poor to non-existent roads, railroads, bridges, airfields, radio, telegraph, meteorological, and mail services), was yet another focus of the regime's commitment to modernization and national integration.

The Ministry of Public Works and Communications undertook construction projects to develop and integrate a national system of transportation and communication. Construction of a highway linking Cochabamba and Santa Cruz was accelerated and plans were projected for roads linking Santa Cruz to Camiri and La Paz to Beni.[72] Construction of the Santa Cruz–Corumbá railroad added 180 kilometers of track with another 220 kilometers under construction in 1945.[73] International accords for railroad connections with Brazil and Argentina were ongoing to link regional, national, and international systems. Installation of radio-telephone service modernized communication between Cochabamba, Camiri, Cobija, Oruro, Potosí, Puerto Suarez, Reyes, Riberalta, San Borja, Santa Cruz, Sucre, Tarija, Todos Santos, Trinidad, Tupiza, Vallegrande, Villamonte, Villazón, and Yacuiba.[74] Aviation was put to the service of national integration: airmail and meteorological services were instituted and flights initiated to transport agricultural products from far-flung regions to urban markets; the Air Force utilized photo reconnaissance to facilitate studies of sources of potable water, terrain suitable for cattle ranching, and the delineation of national boundaries.[75]

Indigenous Social Rights

The regime's concern for a formal definition of the rights and responsibilities of colonos and landlords was reflected in an agrarian law for the Department of Tarija. Enacted in December 1944, the law defined contractual agreements and regulations between landlords and colonos, renters, and agricultural workers. Contracts, per Article 6, were to be entered into in "good faith" without compromising production and with respect for the "dignity of the campesino" (an early substitution of the word *campesino* for *indio*, with its pejorative connotation). The law guaranteed peasants water rights (Article 8), indemnification for property improvements (Article 9), preferential grazing rights for livestock (Article 11), and equal division of harvests between peasant renters and landlords (Article 13). It defined the colono as the "absolute owner of his harvest, to be sold in free commerce, without restrictions" (Article 15).[76] The law also stipulated that disputes between landlords and peasants were to be presented to the police within eight days with unresolved cases to be determined by a Departmental Labor Judge.

The Tarija Agrarian Law underscored the moderation of the Villarroel regime, granting peasants a number of legal rights while assuring landlords control over their fiefdoms. The law was an attempt to guarantee colonos' rights, regulate rural labor relations, mitigate instability on haciendas, and ensure harvests without interruption of sabotage or strikes. But the law failed to prescribe penalties for violations by landlords (left in control of local courts, police, and *carabineros*). However, it stipulated substantial penalties for non-compliance by colonos and renters who faced fines of Bs$3000 for leaving a hacienda. Personal services rendered to the hacendado were defined as "obligations established by custom" and affirmed as a legal obligation of the colono.

Indigenous Nationalism

Five months after enactment of the Tarija Agrarian Law, in mid-May 1945, thousands of colonos and comunarios attended a National Indigenous Congress in La Paz. The Congress was a milestone in indigenous history. President Villarroel issued four Supreme Decrees that redefined agricultural labor relations between lord and peasant. If implemented, the Decrees would ameliorate the centuries of creole domination dating from the Spanish Conquest. When he signed the historic decrees, the president knew he had signed his death warrant. "This decree-law will not die. I may disappear, surely they will kill me like a dog. My days are numbered. But this law will last no matter who becomes president."[77]

The National Indigenous Congress was the work of two nationalisms: the creole-mestizo version of modernization, resource nationalism, national integration, indigenous assimilation, and land privatization; and another version of nationalism expounded by indigenous revolutionaries who sought freedom from servitude, restitution of lost land, education, social rights, and legal legitimation as citizens. A proliferation of sit-down strikes in the Andean highlands provided the backdrop to the Congress; overt resistance to the Old Order was no longer confined to isolated local uprisings, but instead had become a widespread movement in the decade of the 1940s.

Passive Resistance: The Sit-down Strike Movement

The sit-down strike (*huelga de brazos caídos*), a tactic borrowed from factory and mine workers, posed a serious threat to hacendado domination and jeopardized hacienda production. Contemporaneously in India, nationalists employing passive resistance bedeviled the British Empire, and eventually brought an end to colonial rule. If implemented during harvests, evolving from a local tactic to a widespread strategy, the work stoppages would create dire food shortages in the cities and give colonos control over the fruits of their labor.[78] The sit-down strikes had the potential to bring the urban creole-mestizos to their knees and force an end to the colonato.

President Quintanilla's Ministry of Government had reported four huelgas de brazos caídos on haciendas in 1939 and the Oruro Rural Society attributed the plight of four haciendas "affected by communist propaganda" to the handiwork of PIR agitators.[79] In 1943, the Peñaranda government claimed that the PIR was responsible for sit-down strikes on 43 haciendas. Resistance to labor and personal service obligations grew in scope as strikes spread to the Departments of Oruro, Cochabamba, Potosí, Chuquisaca, and La Paz. Hacendados were alarmed by the widening arc of insurrection; in four years the strikes had multiplied tenfold.[80]

The Rural Society condemned the strikes as the handiwork of "agitators," "ringleaders," "communists," and "demagogues," but President Peñaranda's labor minister stated that the underlying cause of the strikes was the latifundia system where "The Peasant is almost a slave."[81] A legal complaint filed by the colonos of Hacienda Yayani in the Cochabamba Upper Valley on 24 April 940 affords a glimpse into the backdrop of the sit-down strikes:

> Since our youth we have been colonos and servants of the proprietor of the Yayani estate, for whom we have always reserved the utmost respect and consideration. But, not content with our servile attitude and taking advantage of our condition as natives . . . he commits all sorts of crimes against our persons and the little property we have. So it is that with frivolous pretexts and without our having provided any justifiable motive, he violently takes from us the animals that are exclusively ours, and furthermore, commits abuses and exactions which now make intolerable our situation as colonos on that property.[82]

Coercion rather than reform of the colonato excesses was the answer to the wave of passive resistance by the hacendados who viewed the strikes as a problem to be solved through government intervention and imprisonment of the movement's leaders. President Peñaranda issued a State Security Decree with sanctions for "agitators that infiltrate haciendas and communities, disturbing agricultural work [where] they incite and contribute to desertion from work or to passive resistance."[83] Peñaranda's decree failed to end the hacienda strikes that continued after his overthrow in 1944. Press coverage of resistance to hacienda depredations focused on "agitators," the "degenerates of the peasant masses," and "the demagogues and reformists of the universe," while avoiding discussion of the social origins of the sit-down strikes.[84] The Oruro Rural Society, amidst five years of sit-down strikes in the department, averred that "personal service or obligations of the colono" was an inherent right of the landlord as his private property. Worrisome to the *Sociedad Rural*, a disparate network of agrarian revolutionaries pressed for education, restitution of stolen land, and an end to pongueaje/mitinaje and other colonato obligations. There were those who believed that their cause would be realized.

The National Indigenous Committee

Presidents Busch and Villarroel had utilized literate Indian conscripts serving under their command in the Chaco as translators and liasons. Two of these men, Francisco Chipana Ramos and Antonio Mamani Álvarez, were personally acquainted, and each had a similar history: born in Aymara villages in the Altiplano highlands of La Paz Department, they were multilingual, had served time in Paraguayan prisoner of war camps, and were destined to play significant roles in the organization of a nationwide indigenous movement. Mamani Álvarez recalls a conversation with the then major Villarroel who told him: "Now you are charged with a mission: as you talk to everyone, tell them to learn to read and write and take note of everyone you know, that are your friends. Some day you will be able to go forward with us and when we rise to power, we are going to support those who aid the peasantry."[85] Meeting surreptitiously at secretive hideouts high in the mountains, slipping into remote haciendas and communities in the dark of night, Indian militants argued the cause of resistance to the ancien régime. They wove a network of supporters and sympathizers to safely navigate the vast countryside of varied ethnicity, language, and terrain. Imprisoned over a half-dozen times, Mamani Álvarez networked with *Ex-Combatiente* prisoners, making converts, discussing strategy and tactics with other peasant and labor revolutionaries, and plotting his escape.

Francisco Chipana served as aide-de-camp to the then major Germán Busch. Before the war he had left the Challapata ayllu in the Altiplano Province of Camacho for the city of La Paz where he worked as a household servant for a family who taught him to read and write Spanish and supported his education at a city school. After the war, President Busch enlisted his former aide to traverse the countryside, reporting information gathered from Indian militants engaged in resistance to the colonato. He continued the work for President Villarroel, serving as a liason with indigenous leaders, reporting on rural developments, and extending his contacts to militants in the proletarian labor movement. President Villarroel recognized Chipana Ramos's loyalty to the revolution when he appointed him to the leadership of a National Indigenous Congress to be held in La Paz and organized by a National Indigenous Committee.[86]

The National Indigenous Committee consisted of a core group, including Chipana Ramos and some 20 other peasant leaders who had worked together in the struggle for indigenous rights since the late 1930s. The Committee represented a leap forward in the development of the indigenous movement, organizing hundreds of Indian leaders in the highland departments. While the Committee enjoyed the tacit support of President Villarroel, its members were nevertheless subject to harassment and incarceration by the provincial authorities controlled by the rural oligarchy. The majority of the members were Aymara caciques and apoderados from Oruro and La Paz Departments and Quechua alcaldes and colonos from Cochabamba Department. They maintained contact with each other and with colonos, comunarios, and Indian vecinos living in towns and cities. The Committee widened the range of resistance (evidenced in the growth of the sit-down strikes), and developed links with urban migrants beset with discrimination, and immiserated workers in mines and factories. The widening network also included contacts with the creole-mestizo world of lawyers and PIR, POR, and MNR revolutionaries.[87]

Dionisio Miranda, a colono from Hacienda Chacapaya, another Committee member with connections throughout the highland provinces of Ayopaya and Tapacari, was involved with the alcalde Hilarión Grájeda (also a Committee member), the brothers Julio and Nicolas Carrasco, and other colonos in a confrontation turned violent in 1940 at the Hacienda Yayani in Ayopaya Province.[88] Grájeda's severely beaten brother was a plaintiff in the criminal charges brought by Grájeda and the Yayani colonos against the patrón and mayordomo of the hacienda (quoted earlier) is noteworthy for its appeal to a legal system known by the colonos to be rigged against them. The Yayani colonos would not always be as patient in seeking redress for hacienda abuse. Neither Grájeda nor Miranda would be dissuaded in their struggle against the colonato. Both were destined to play significant roles in the movement.

The éminence gris of the National Indigenous Committee, Luis Ramos Quevado, was the son of a *piquero* (small landholder) near the village of Sipe Sipe in Cochabamba's Ayopaya Province. The most dynamic of the indigenous revolutionaries of the 1940s, known as *Rumi Sonk'o* ("Heart of Stone") for his machismo and courage, Ramos Quevado devised brilliant stratagems to catalyze the peasant movement, bringing relentless pressure to bear upon President Villarroel (as he had done earlier with the Concordancia presidents).[89] Cagey and impervious to co-optation, Ramos Quevado exposed the vulnerability of creole-mestizo governments, including the RADEPA–MNR regime.

He emerged as the architect of the sit-down strikes erupting in Yayani and Morochata in Ayopaya Province. "The campesinos in the valleys obeyed his orders when they didn't want to work their *chacras* (land plots) or to tend the patron's livestock because he said the Indians should work for themselves," Antonio Mamani Álvarez recalled.[90] The La Paz departmental prefecture attributed work stoppages at the haciendas Calacala and Vilaque to Ramos Quevado's influence.[91] Ramos Quevado also networked with Luis Bustamonte, an Indian *valluno* (town dweller) and ex-miner from Sipe Sipe. Bustamante's work and travel introduced him to the radicalism infusing the Rosca's mining towns and to the Stalinist, Trotskyist, and MNR revolutionaries organizing a proletarian vanguard. An early member of the Indigenous Committee, Bustamante provided a link with Committee members involved in sit-down strikes at Chacapaya, Ayopaya, Tapacarí (Cochabamba Department), and beyond.[92]

Luis Ramos Quevado extended his influence to the colonos and comunarios of Oruro Department where supporters in the region of Lipiani and Caracollo initiated the sit-down strikes that would become the epicenter of his mercurial rise as strategist and spokesman for the Indigenous Committee. Ramos Quevado was a founder and secretary of the anarchist Oruro Federation of Union Workers (*Federación de Obreros Sindicales*: FOS) and together with the Aymara cacique Victoriano Condori Mamani (a fellow Committee member), organized the 1941–1942 work stoppages in Oruro that continued into the Villarroel years 1944–1945.[93] "He defended the caciques who fell prisoner," notes Antonio Mamani Álvarez, "and collected ramas in order to cover the expenses of his followers who traveled from one zone to another, carrying the pamphlets and periodicals of their struggle."[94] The Sociedad Rural held him responsible for sit-down strikes in

Oruro, La Paz, Cochabamba, and Chuquisaca. His arrest in early May 1944 was appealed by 20 alcaldes who traveled to La Paz to request that President Villarroel release the man they recognized as the "Secretary General of Indigenous Affairs" of the Oruro FOS.[95]

Ramos Quevado, Condori Mamani, and other Committee members, including Hilarion Grájeda and Dionisio Miranda, arranged a meeting with President Villarroel in September 1944 to gain his support for an indigenous congress.[96] Scarcely a month later, Ramos Quevado addressed the 1944 National Convention, speaking as the Secretary General of Indigenous Affairs of the Oruro FOS, he urged an end to pongueaje (per Article 5 of the Constitution), requested guarantees for alcaldes and Committee leaders harassed by provincial authorities, and demanded an end to a law dating from the 1920s prohibiting Indians from use of urban streets and plazas.[97] The president of the National Convention, Alberto Mendoza López, supported Ramos Quevado's demand. In November 1944, Minister of Government Major Alfonso Quinteros ordered government officials to guarantee Indians the right of free transit in all the nation's streets and plazas. A month later Quinteros issued an order granting the right of "committees, sindicatos, representatives, delegates, Apoderados and Alcaldes escolares" to organize the Congress.[98] Ramos Quevado and the Indigenous Committee achieved a remarkable victory: their cause was gaining momentum.

Ramos Quevado met with President Villarroel and Minister of Government Major Edmundo Nogales in December 1944 after which safe conduct papers bearing the president's signature were issued to members of the Indigenous Committee. The president's imprimatur was a tacit endorsement of the Committee and a boon to the movement's organizational efforts.[99] The countryside was soon leafleted with 25,000 copies of an eight-page bulletin—written, printed, and distributed by the National Indigenous Committee—announcing a forthcoming National Indigenous Congress scheduled for 25 December 1944. The Bulletin's 27 points demanded rights and guarantees, laws and lawyers for the Indian, an end to pongueaje and mitinaje, the return of land to "those who work it," as well as requests for education and assistance for Indians to adapt to western dress.[100]

President Villarroel recognized the initiative behind the publication, as well as the Committee's role in the indigenous awakening. When the government rescheduled the event for February 1945, in an attempt to interject a measure of control over the Congress, a thousand colonos and comunarios from the highlands of La Paz, Oruro, Cochabamba, and Potosí arrived in La Paz to meet with President Villarroel. Uninvited, the assemblage met with the president and pressed their demands for resolution of disputed land claims, a survey of property titles and boundaries, the end of pongueaje, mitinaje, and other forms of personal service, and technical assistance for agriculture.[101]

In early Februry1945, the Sociedad Rural requested government intervention to halt the sit-down strikes, referred to as an "anachronism of the epoch," and reaffirmed the claim that personal service by colonos was an inherent right of a landlord's property ownership. The National Indigenous Convention, it was argued, would provoke conflict. Hacendados reported *cabecillas* (agitators) making the rounds, telling colonos that the government was going to give them land. The landlord of Hacienda Queraya in Quillacollo (Cochabamba Department) decried the "paralysis of peasant labor on which lives the landlord, the Indian, the consumer and the merchant." Minister Nogales recognized the impending problems with the year's harvest and in late February instructed the Oruro prefect to order subprefects to tell the colonos to return to work because their issues would be addressed at the forthcoming National Indigenous Congress.[102]

The Sociedad Rural accused Luis Ramos Quevado and agitators from the Oruro FOS of distributing propaganda, soliciting money, holding "illegal" gatherings, and urging resistance to "services recognized by ancestral custom that favor the *terratenientes* (large landholders) on whose properties they live and farm."[103] Charges initiated in September 1944 against seven agitators were broadened to include Victoriano Condori and Ramos Quevado, who was accused of soliciting funds (*ramas* and *cuotas*) from caciques and alcaldes; implicit here is the presumption that the money was used for personal gain and not to cover the Committee's organizational expenses.[104] The Rural Society's accusations were absurd: the urban populace was led to believe that the *patrones* were concerned about colonos being bilked for cash when the reason for the charges was to defund the indigenous resistance movement.

The press releases of the Sociedad Rural belied their true intent: a refocus from defense of the status quo and the scare tactics of privation and food shortages, insurrection, and race war to an offensive strategy attacking the financial underpinning of the movement and its leaders. The Sociedad sought to gain the moral high ground by besmirching the reputation of prominent Committee leaders, portraying them as opportunists who cheated Indians out of what little money they had via a propaganda campaign to discredit the indigenous movement. Lawyers, translators, scribes, tinterellos, and government bureaucrats charged Indians for their services and dirigentes relied on funds (viz., ramas) to support their cause; thus, the creole judicial system made it illegal for indigenous leaders to collect money to finance their efforts.

The National Indigenous Congress was postponed to May 1945 at the request of the National Indigenous Committee, whose leaders reported hundreds of organizers jailed after a sit-down strike at Hacienda Siquilini near the Yungas town of Chulamani, continuing strikes in Cochabamba and Oruro, agitation in the environs of Lake Titicaca and at the hacienda Chacoma Grande near the Altiplano railroad juncture of Viacha where the administrator "fled for his life."[105] In a speech to hacendados and colonos in the troubled lake region, a government spokesman announced that there would be no land redistribution, affirmed the government's respect for private property, advised the colonos to ignore the "propaganda of unscrupulous agitators," and to inform authorities of such activities. They were also reminded of the fate of agitators imprisoned in La Paz for subversion and collection of ramas.[106]

Luis Ramos Quevado drew the ire of the regime. The *official mayor* of government claimed that Ramos had "printed and sold fake property titles to Indians, and used the money to purchase property for himself."[107] Minister of Government Nogales stated that the government did not authorize the "propaganda" circulated by Ramos Quevado who, he claimed, had "agitated" and "swindled" the peasants for years.[108] The minister's statement signaled the regime's decision to rein in the movement's most prominent leader. Nogales next ratcheted up the pressure on Ramos Quevado, stating he was an agitator who had not been authorized to recruit indigenous representatives to the congress, and had illegally collected quotas: "On account of these shenanigans, Ramos Quevado was detained and later transported to Beni, from whence he managed to escape to Brazilian territory."[109]

Questions arise regarding the disappearance of Luis Ramos Quevado. Did he drown while allegedly crossing the river into Brazil? Did he perish in the jungle? Or was he "disappeared" by his government captors while imprisoned at remote Riberalta on the banks of the Rio Beni? Certainly, the disappearance of the brilliant strategist and organizer of the indigenous resistance movement was convenient to the government and to the Sociedad Rural. Because most Indian leaders at one time or another were incarcerated, only to return to the struggle, Luis Ramos Quevado's eclipse remains an enigma.

The leadership void for the forthcoming National Indigenous Congress was summarily filled by Antonio Mamani Álvarez. The choice initially appeared to have much to recommend it: the most worldly of the indigenous leaders, the peripatetic Kallawaya had traveled throughout the west coast of the Americas. He was familiar with the creole-mestizo world, with Major Gualberto Villarroel with whom he served as a liaison in the Chaco, with influential members of the RADEPA–MNR government, and with leaders of the Indigenous Committee. Meetings with President Villarroel and Minister Nogales confirmed his commitment to indigenous education and abolition of personal servitude; he down-played the more radical views of land revendication or agrarian reform of the latifundia that directly threatened the hegemony of the oligarchy and the stability of the regime.[110]

Antonio Mamani Álvarez and the Second Indigenous Committee

Antonio Mamani Álvarez was instrumental in the formation of a Second Indigenous Committee in early March 1945 at Machacamarca in La Paz Department's Aroma Province. The Committee, per Mamani Álvarez's conversations with Villarroel and Nogales, espoused the goals of abolishing pongueaje and mitanaje and promoting education "so that they [campesinos] are able to make contact among themselves and later to unite in a singular organization." He pointed out that the Second Committee included members of the First Indigenous Committee, incorporated their plans, and organized the Congress.[111] It was then, as the General Delegate of the Department of La Paz to the Bolivian National Indigenous Congress, that Mamani Álvarez assumed the task of organizing the forthcoming event to be held in La Paz during 10–15 May 1945. A manifesto announcing the convocation of the National Indigenous Congress was written in March 1945 with the assistance of Leonardo Chirino from Aroma Province and 50,000 copies were distributed by Ex-Combatientes directed by Julio Apaza Mamani from Oruro together with Mamani Álvarez's prison acquaintances, MNR contacts in the La Paz Departmental Command, and *chaskis* (messengers) from the Indigenous Committee.[112] The resourceful Kallawaya also mobilized supporters among the diverse indigenous movement, including leaders associated with Ramos Quevado and the First Indigenous Committee, as well as influential members of RADEPA and the MNR, including Víctor Paz Estenssoro, Hernán Silez, and Rafael Otazo.[113]

Mamani Álvarez achieved notoriety with the publication of his "Manifesto of the General Delegate from the Department of La Paz to the First Indigenous Congress of Bolivia." The Manifesto did not demand agrarian reform nor mention the issue of revendication of usurped lands. It did, however, reveal that Antonio *Álvarez* Mamani (who used the occasion to switch, from the matronymic Antonio Mamani *Álvarez*, to his patronymic surname) would be no easier for the regime to control than was the deposed Luis Ramos Quevado. The Manifesto surpassed the regime's narrow focus on highland colonos and addressed all of the "indigenous class"— colonos and comunarios of the Andean highlands, the Guarani and peoples of the tropical forests, dwellers of river banks, rubber tappers, the Urus of the shores of Lake Titicaca, and miners toiling underground—who were to be excluded from the government's National Indigenous Congress. It also called for "Revendication of the inherent rights of the class humiliated and exploited for centuries"; "suppression of pongueaje . . . and other gratuitous services and degradations to the dignity of MAN"; enforcement of Article Five of the Constitution prohibiting slavery and the Supreme Decree of August 1936 obligating hacendados, mine, and factory owners to establish schools on their properties; enforcement of the February 1937 Supreme Decree that prohibited eviction of colonos from haciendas after two continuous years of residence on the property; and enforcement of the government order of November1944 that Indians be permitted free access to streets and plazas. The Manifesto also demanded that in cases of "involuntary leave" (viz., expulsion) colonos be paid, as were factory and industrial workers, and called for establishment of Free Legal Assistance offices in departmental and provincial capitals, Rural Inspectors and Tribunals in the countryside, and the creation of linguistic institutes.[114]

Mamani Álvarez also used the Manifesto to advance a sectarian agenda. Cloaked within an appeal to the future of the "Indian Race" and the "future of the Patria" is a denunciation of the "Idols of Clay," a reference to the *Caciques Inkaicos* (also referred to as the *Consejo de Amautas*), the venerable revendicationist organization headed by Santos Marka T'ula. Mamani Álvarez respected the Caciques Inkaicos for their long-standing struggle and influence (primarily among comunarios), but considered them hidebound illiterates at the mercy of *tinterellos* (sidewalk attorneys), creole-mestizo bureaucrats and lawyers—exploited by those from whom they sought assistance and trapped within a redundant cycle of legal appeals for restitution of land usurped by the very system from which they sought redress—"faithful to all the bad habits of tradition, ready to return to the odious servility of yesteryear, pongos and lackeys of the feudal señores," as he put it in a gratuitous screed on the first page of his Manifesto.[115]

Mamani Álvarez held other members of the Indigenous Committee such as Luis Ramos Quevado and Hilarion Grájeda in high regard because of their aggressive leadership that led to the rapid growth of the hacienda sit-down strikes. He shared Ramos Quevado's belief in the necessity of education as fundamental to the development of a revolutionary consciousness among the peasantry and respected Ramos Quevado's address to the national legislature calling for an end to pongueaje, his demand for indigenous access to the nation's streets and plazas, his manipulation of President Villarroel through publication of the Bulletin that set both the date and the agenda for the National Indigenous Congress, and his aggressive strategy of indigenous organization while Secretary General of the Oruro FOS.

Publication of the Manifesto brought Mamani Álvarez to the fore: indefatigable, and resourceful, independent, zealous, single-minded, possessed with a powerful sense of mission and self-confidence (as evidenced by the author in visits with him in La Paz, 1970–1971). These traits, necessary for success in politics and war, can equally spell failure. The regime needed an indigenous leader who would follow its lead but Mamani Álvarez could never play another's tune. His Manifesto with a call to *all* Indians beckoned to a wider audience. The regime attempted to constrain the movement, eliminating Luis Ramos Quevado because of his independence. Yet, Antonio Mamani Álvarez proved to be no different as evidenced in his public defense of Ramos Quevado after his arrest for collecting ramas. Mamani Álvarez's enemies labeled him a *ramero* (slang: one who collects ramas) and a "Quedavista" after his defense of Ramos Quevado.[116]

Antonio Mamani Álvarez was animated by a belief in the potential of education to empower the indigenous peoples of Kollasuyu, the Inka designation for what centuries later creoles would call Bolivia. With his network of Ex-Combatientes (referred to in his Manifesto as the future of the movement), he epitomized the indigenous iteration of the Chaco Generation. Just weeks after issuing the Manifesto, he resigned his position as General Delegate to the National Indigenous Congress because of a disagreement over the Congress's perspective. This was inevitable for the zealot whose beliefs, including his insistence that all indigenous people be represented at the National Indigenous Congress, were non-negotiable. His defense of Ramos Quevado published in *La Calle* on 10 March 1945 elicited this public indictment by the regime:

> A dangerous mestizo is acting as representative of the natives to the Congress. The District Attorney requests that Antonio Álvarez Mamani be restricted from congressional activities on account of his abominable precedents . . . [he] recently published a manifesto. . . . The District Attorney says the aforementioned delegate does not belong to the indigenous class, since

even his last name reveals his mestizo status; [he] has problems pending with the Courts for various crimes . . . in different parts of the department. He therefore cannot and should not become the voice of the entire indigenous element of La Paz. . . . The exclusion of Álvarez Mamani from all indigenous activities is suggested, preventing if at all possible his contact with the native masses, whom he deceives and tries to represent for inequitable purposes.[117]

The government's wording was straightforward. The Kallawaya was tainted as a dangerous mestizo who had published an indigenous manifesto, avoided criminal charges, and should be prevented from leadership of the indigenous movement. The use of the racialized accusation that the Kallawaya was a mestizo (i.e., Antonio *Álvarez* Mamani) and not an Indian (Antonio *Mamani* Álvarez) delegitimized his position as an Indian activist and legitimated his persecution by the government. In November 1945, Mamani Álvarez was imprisoned on Coati Island, surrounded by the frigid waters of Lake Titicaca, 13,000 feet above sea level. This was not his first imprisonment, nor would it be his last.

The National Indigenous Congress

It was essential that the government find a suitable Indian leader for the upcoming National Indigenous Congress. The available man was Francisco Chipana Ramos, who had been enlisted by President Busch to develop contacts with colonos and comunarios and gather intelligence on the situation in the countryside. This dangerous work continued during the Villarroel years. The rural oligarchy (*gamonales*) controlled the countryside through a web of interconnections (*gamonalismo*) among local and regional bureaucracies. The hazards of indigenous activism are evident in this vignette from the highlands of Cochabamba Department:

> During our activities, we had to be very careful with the people whom we permitted to participate in our meetings. Beforehand, one had to go through a special ceremony, in which we swore before Grájeda and other leaders never to reveal what was heard or spoken; but there was always some squealer [soplón] among us who would tell the administrator or some relative what we had talked about. Almost always, the day after the meeting, the administrator would know that we had gathered or that someone had visited us from the outside.[118]

Despite official credentials from President Villarroel, regional authorities harassed the organizers of the National Indigenous Congress. Tasked with the mission of selecting two delegates from each hacienda and ayllu to represent their community at the Congress, they were assisted by chaskis who slipped in and out of hacienda communities bearing news of the movement and of the forthcoming National Congress. Skilled in operating in an enemy-controlled environment, the chaskis survived through intuition and experience. To fail meant a beating, arrest, incarceration, or worse. They employed *quipus*, the knotted mnemonic device invented by the Incas to record information, but with an added twist: a black quipu signaled danger, the more knots, the more dangerous (e.g., cancellation of a rendezvous); red signaled a potential problem; an unknotted white quipu indicated no danger. Antonio Mamani Álvarez often traveled in disguise. "My compañeros gave me clothes: a campesino from Cochabamba gave me an old poncho, another from Oruro a hat from his zone, another from Potosí gave me a pair of sandals and in this way I was able to contact peasants as if I was looking for work."[119] In an age in which Indians wore traditional clothes, handwoven, with *dibujos* (Andean designs) particular to their ayllu, the authorities were able to spot outsiders and ascertain their provenance, thereby controlling the movement of the subaltern population. A master of guile, the Kallawaya was an elusive revolutionary.

Regional congresses catalyzed the National Indigenous Congress. The "First Indigenous Congress of Quechua Speakers" convened in Sucre (Chuquisaca Department) on 6 August 1942. The date commemorated Bolivian independence (6 August 1825) and afforded a reminder of who had gained independence—and who had not. Indians from Chuquisaca, Cochabamba, Oruro, and Potosí attended the congregation of Quechua-speaking peasants and workers. The delegates excoriated the colonato system ("harassed by the Corregidor, exploited by the tinterillo"), demanded the end of restrictions on the movement of Indians throughout the country, abolition of pongueaje-mitinaje, and restitution of community lands. Sponsored by the Stalinist PIR, the Anarchist FOS, and supported by Santos Marka T'ula, the Congress melded Quechuas from ayllus, haciendas, and mines with cadre from the urban parties in an attempt to forge a peasant-worker alliance. The FOS promoted the use of sit-down strikes to force hacendados to desist in the practice of pongueaje-mitinaje, and representatives of Santos Marka T'ula traversed the highlands urging work stoppages where landlords had refused to comply with the laws.[120]

A "Second Congress of Indigenous Quechua, Aymara, Guarani and Others" held in 1943, attended by Melitón Gallardo, Antonio Garcia, and Mariano Qhispe representing the *Alcaldes Mayores Particulares*, was followed by a host of regional congresses in the departments of La Paz, Cochabamba, Sucre, Oruro, and Tarija in 1944 and 1945. The congresses called for an agrarian labor code, labor inspectors and judicial offices to provide free legal assistance for Indians, a national review of land boundaries and expropriations, and reexamination of court decisions in which ayllu lands were usurped by hacendados.[121] President Villarroel attended two of the congresses in Cochabamba where he presented his notion of colonato reform and payment for agricultural labor.[122]

As residents of La Paz braced for an invasion of thousands of visitors (invited and uninvited) to the National Indigenous Congress, the government instituted measures to control the event. Weeks before the Congress government agents and local authorities apprehended hundreds of Indians en route to the event. Those caught without proper documentation, after perfunctory appearances before local kangaroo courts, were sent to a labor camp.[123] Nevertheless, over

1,500 colonos and comunarios arrived for the Congress, including 800 Ex-Combatientes: some stayed in military barracks, others set up camp at El Alto on the heights overlooking the city. Most were unable to enter the congress that was limited to official delegates, referred to in the press as "authentic Indians."[124] The massive turnout rekindled creole memories of La Paz besieged by an Indian army encamped above the city during the eighteenth-century Tupac Katari rebellion.

The Villarroel regime determined the leadership, agenda, and participants in the National Indigenous Congress, convened during 10–15 May 1945. When Francisco Chipana Ramos, chosen as President of the Congress, addressed the assemblage at the city's Luna Park, he validated the government's faith in his anointed role: "the indigenous people are assembled thanks to President Villarroel. . . . [T]he government has trusted in them, and therefore they ought to trust in it. . . . [T]he nation needs labor and peace, and . . . everything makes one think that the hour of redemption has arrived for the indigenous people."[125] These words could not have been better scripted by the regime as it sought to control the restless countryside. When Chipana Ramos spoke of the delegates as "sons of the Inca," he also averred: "We are Bolivians and he [President Villarroel] is our governor. . . . [H]e wants us to know how to work better in order to live better so that the harvests are better and everyone is content; so that everyone can read and be clean and their souls can be good."[126]

The delegates included the Aymara President Chipana Ramos, Vice President Dionisio Miranda (a Quechua Colono from Cochabamba), and Secretary General Desiderio Cholina, representing the peoples of the tropical lowlands. They were joined by over 1,600 delegates who weathered the elements and impediments to participate in the historic event. *Los Tiempos* lambasted the event as the work of the "fuhrers of the MNR" convened by "the hierarchs of criollo nazi fascism . . . who spent much money from the National Treasury to obtain some applause from . . . some Quisling indigenas against the terratenientes."[127]

The internal contradictions of the regime were evident at the Congress. President Villarroel could proclaim his readiness to "die like a dog" for the Indians, while Minister of Government Edmundo Nogales, a fellow Radepista and also a landlord, controlled the Congress, permitting five members of the Sociedad Rural to sit in on official meetings.[128] Certainly, this would have been unacceptable to Luis Ramos Quevado, Antonio Mamani Álvarez, and Hilarion Grájeda. The official government agenda omitted the all-important questions of land tenure and restitution of indigenous lands while addressing the topics of rural labor and personal services, indigenous legal defense, a rural police force, education and agricultural cooperatives. Clearly, the regime intended to prevent an agrarian revolution that would overturn the colonato and return *all* hacienda lands to colonos and comunarios.

The government's priorities were evidenced in the major speeches delivered at the Congress. The keynote speech by the head of the government planning committee attributed rural unrest to the colonato, the exploitation of Indians

FIGURE 2.1 Antonio Mamani Álvarez (wearing striped poncho) with Chipana Ramos to His Left

Source: Courtesy of Antonio Mamani Álvarez.

by corregidores, police, and tax collectors, and the lack of laws and courts to adjudicate conflicts. The Minister of Labor decried the pernicious excesses that gave root to indigenous agitation and argued the role of law as the protector of Indians and a safeguard against insurrection. The Secretary General of the organizing committee attributed rural unrest to the dearth of legislation defining the legal relationship between patrón and colono.[129] Questions of this nature were of concern to the regime as it struggled to control the indigenous awakening while amidst the counterrevolutionary pressures of hacendados, tin barons, and hostile political parties. On the last day of the conclave, President Villarroel presented the response of the National Revolution to the crisis in the countryside: the historic Supreme Decrees of 15 May 1945.

The Supreme Decrees of 1945

As the grand finale of the First Indigenous Congress, President Villarroel issued four decrees intended to bring order and stability to the rural hinterland. The first decree abolished gratuitous personal service, citing as precedent Simón Bolívar's Supreme Resolution of 1825 suppressing the practice.[130] All non-agricultural labor by colonos was prohibited: labor, aside from hacienda work, was illegal without the consent of the colono. If agreed to by the colono, the landlord was required to pay for the work (Article 2). Article 3 decreed remuneration for personal or domestic services (*cacha, apiri, islero, aljiri, hilado, tejido, mukeo, lavado*, etc.) "that are not part of agricultural chores." This article invited disputation over the definition of what were and were not considered agricultural chores.

Transport of hacienda products by a colono would require consent and agreement regarding payment. Disagreements were to be resolved by the intervention of the nearest political authority (Article 4). The authorities, of course, were influenced by the hacendados. The colono remained exempt from hacienda labor for the duration of time spent in performance of service as muleteer, vaquero, or field hand (Article 5). In a concession to the Sociedad Rural, this article explicitly confirmed the continuation of these services by colonos. Article 6 declared the colono to be the "absolute owner" of his harvest, able to sell it at the current price in a free market. Payment by colonos for the *catastro* (hacienda land tax) was prohibited (Article 7). Violence or ill-treatment of Indians by hacendados, administrators, or other persons could result in arrest and indefinite suspension from duty (Article 12). This begs the question as to just what authority was to sanction the offending "authority" because the rural oligarchs dominated local and regional government. Non-comunario Indians were prohibited to sell their land without written government authorization (Article 13). All complaints by Indians regarding land claims were to be presented to the Office of Free Legal Assistance to aid in their preparation (Article 14).[131]

This momentous decree, while restricting the dominion of the colonato, aimed to mitigate the underlying sources of rural agitation and instability. It granted hacendados legal recourse against "instigators and agitators" who (per Article 10) were to be held financially responsible for damages incurred as a result of their failure to fulfill labor obligations. Article 11 struck at financial support of the indigenous movement. Collection of "ramas" in the form of money or goods solicited to defray the expenses of Indian organizers was prohibited and violation punishable by fines. This article additionally mandated fines for purveyors of false copies of laws or land titles—a measure intended to curtail the indigenous movement through the oligarchy's control of the provincial legal system. The draconian Article 9 granted landlords the right to banish colonos who failed to comply with their labor obligations to forced labor colonies (together with their families) in the distant and inhospitable jungle.

A second decree declared that, per the constitution, slavery did not exist in Bolivia and that "each person has the right to just remuneration for the work that he voluntarily undertakes."[132] The decree abolished the practices of pongueaje and mitinaje that required colonos to perform household chores for the patrón. The male *pongo* (a derivation of the Quechua *punkurina:* doorman) was required to serve a set number of days working about the hacienda big house and sleep in a doorway with the household dogs. The practice was rotated on a regular basis among the hacienda colonos as was mitinaje, the personal service rendered by Indian women and girls serving the hacendado household. Mitanaje placed Indian females at the disposal of the hacendado and allowed for sexual abuse—yet another odious form of enforced racial domination. Violation of the decree was punishable by fines of Bs$500 (US$11), a pittance for landlords.

The decree also prohibited authorities (administrative, judicial, ecclesiastic, provincial, cantonal) from obligating colonos, comunarios, and urban Indians to perform personal service (Article 2). Officials guilty of violation of the decree would be removed from office: but again, by whom? A third decree mandated fines (Bs$1,000–5,000) for owners of haciendas, mines, and factories found to be in non-compliance with the 1936 military socialist decree establishing schools. A period of 60 days was set for compliance; again, enforcement was a moot question. Taxes were to be assessed on rural properties, per a Villarroel law signed in October 1944, to subsidize public works and school construction.[133] A fourth and final decree mandated formulation of an agrarian labor code by 31 December 1945 specifying "rights and obligations" between colonos and landlords. In the intervening period, hacienda labor was limited to four days per week, excess work was to be paid by landlords at the prevailing day-labor rate, and colonos were not obligated to work outside the hacienda property on which they resided (labor outside the estate was set at a daily rate of Bs$20 per day). Colonos could provide a substitute to fulfill labor obligations when agreed to by landlords. Annual contracts between landlords and renters were required to be in writing and minors under 14 years of age were prohibited from service as shepherds. Again, the question of enforcement arises. The requirement of written contracts would appear to be a legalistic safeguard against hearsay, but this stipulation advantaged the hacendado with the resources to draw up a legal contract written in Spanish. And whoever writes a contract gains the initiative and advantage of its wording and content.

Repercussions of the Supreme Decrees

Villarroel's Supreme Decrees were the pinnacle of the revolution's attempt to reform relations between lord and peasant. The statutes granted colonos and comunarios many of the demands that precipitated the revolts and rebellions since the Spanish invasion.[134] But the intent of the regime was to ameliorate the more egregious conditions underlying indigenous resistance to the colonato rather than to abolish the system itself and ipso facto the dominion of the hacienda oligarchs. The interest of the National Revolution was not the return of ayllu lands, but the modernization of labor relations from quasi-feudal to capitalist wage labor.

The decrees sought to promote national integration through assimilation of the indigenous majority into a modern version of a creole state. Toward this end, the Indian was to become a "civilized" (i.e., acculturated), educated, Spanish-speaking, petty capitalist farmer producing a surplus to supply the urban markets. The creole-mestizo leaders viewed the Indian from a paternalistic perspective. Speaking in his inaugural address to the Congress, President Villarroel stated that the peasant "must be treated like a son by the government: he will be protected, he will have schools, he will have guarantees, but he will be obligated to work, loyally fulfilling his debts and obligations."[135] Citizenship would be the reward for assimilation and integration into the modernizing creole-mestizo state.

Delegates returning from the Congress with news of the decrees were disappointed to find that little had changed. Provincial police and judicial authorities dismissed Indian land titles as fakes; refused to enforce the decrees; levied fines on insistent Indians; and harassed, intimidated, and arrested leaders bearing news of the laws (printed in Spanish, not in Quechua, Aymara, or Guarani).[136] Despite edicts from the distant capital, the hacendado domination of the countryside continued. The failure to enforce the decrees, thwarted by chicanery and repression, exposed the limitations of legal reforms as a means of emancipation.

Resistance and rebellion continued in the backlands during the fateful months preceding the overthrow of the Villarroel regime. In January 1946, *Los Tiempos* reported that peasant agitation "stretched to all the Altiplano and adjacent valleys of Cochabamba and Chuquisaca" and in "every district where there exist native populations of Aymara and Quechua families." Readers were warned of a possible race war and of impending food shortages because of work stoppages on haciendas in Potosí and Cochabamba Departments.[137] Sit-down strikes proliferated between February and May with foci in Potosí Department and the Provinces of Ayopaya, Capinota, Mizque, and Tapacari in Cochabamba Department. Government troops repressed a rebellion at Hacienda Lachiraya, after killing three colonos and wounding a score of others. The arrest of 40 "ringleaders" in March 1946 and their imprisonment at Chimoré, the dreaded jungle prison in Chapare Province, underscored the contradiction between law and justice.[138]

After the National Indigenous Congress, Francisco Chipana Ramos resumed the agrarian struggle with a series of estate seizures in La Paz Department. The Rural Society accused him of the expropriation of Hacienda Taracoca in the environs of Timusi, a canton in Muñecas Province (La Paz Department).[139] In May 1946, provincial authorities apprehended, tried, and sentenced him to prison. The regime ignored the plight of the "President of the Indians" whose personal ties to President Villarroel dated from the Chaco War. As with Luis Ramos Quevado who had met the same fate, Chipana Ramos was an expendable nuisance. He remained imprisoned in the Panóptico Nacional after the overthrow of the regime.

Six months after the Indigenous Congress, a major disturbance over interpretation of the decrees erupted between a terrateniente and colonos at the hacienda Las Canchas in Potosí Department. Per usual, an army detachment was dispatched to "solve" the problem and "come to an understanding of the scope of the decrees of 15 May." After failing to reach an accord, a second detachment armed with machine guns arrived "to pacify the uprising" that had grown to 2,000 Indians armed with "some firearms, clubs, and sharp weapons." The upshot was a massacre: 28 colonos were killed, another 26 wounded, and 30 "ringleaders" apprehended and jailed in Potosí. The massacre was the work of provincial authorities, allegedly without President Villarroel's knowledge.[140]

Despite the decrees, little had changed in the countryside. Without adequate provision for implementation, their promise would go unfulfilled. The National Congress failed to ratify the decrees or draft a labor code. The Villarroel government vetoed a law passed by the National Convention in October 1945 to halt ongoing lawsuits to evict colonos and prohibit further evictions on the grounds that the law disadvantaged landlords and threatened agricultural production.[141] The decrees were limited to questions of labor relations while avoiding the divisive question of agrarian reform. The MNR leaders Hernán Siles Zuazo, Ñuflo Chavez, Wálter Guevara Arze, and Víctor Paz Estenssoro pushed for land reform and understood its potential as the ultimate weapon against the oligarchy.[142] But the MNR was inconsistent on the question of land. José Cuadros Quiroga ignored the topic in the *Movimiento Nacionalista Revolucionario: sus bases y principios de acción inmediata* published in 1942, and Alberto Mendoza López's *La Soberanía de Bolivia*, published in the same year, evidenced little interest in land restitution or in a radical change of the manorial system. Indeed, his later *Doctrina del movimiento nacionalista revolucionario* completely ignored the question.

Factional constraints within RADEPA and the appointment of hacendados to cabinet positions suggest the influence of conservative elements within the regime opposed to an agrarian revolution. President Villarroel saw the land question as a problem to be solved, not by the restitution of indigenous property usurped by hacendados but as a matter of organization: "the indigenous problem is not land itself but of regimen, because there are sufficient lands and what it takes is to organize the social and economic system of the Indian. . . . [T]he Indian has no exact concept of property because throughout history he never was a property owner."[143] This statement, issued months after the National Indigenous Congress, gives no indication as to the president's notion of how the land tenure regimen might be altered or implemented. It suggests RADEPA's interest in moderate reform in contradistinction to the radical positions of Movimientista and Marxist revolutionaries to destroy the colonato. Rather than delivering order and stability to the countryside, the Supreme Decrees of May 1945 whetted indigenous expectations, exacerbated tensions between lord and peasant, and intensified factionalism among RADEPA officers and their MNR compatriots within the regime.

Summary and Conclusions

The RADEPA revolution was a harbinger of the decolonization struggles and wars of national liberation in Latin America, Africa, and Asia during the last half of the twentieth century. Third World nationalists understood the pious and hypocritical preachments of the American and European imperial powers ("self-determination," "Four Freedoms") enshrined in the rhetoric of the United Nations as mere platitudes.[144] The Bolivian National Revolution was antithetical to the interests of U.S. hegemonic interests and thus a threat to be eliminated. Besieged by the Rosca, Wall Street, and Washington, the Villarroel government was also pressured by indigenous nationalists seeking an end to internal colonialism, eradication of the colonato system, restitution of land, social rights, and the recognition of three million Indians as citizens of the republic.

The RADEPA–MNR revolution aroused the desires of those struggling to accomplish the eternal quest for "Land and Liberty" but failed to deliver its promises. The supreme decrees issued by President Villarroel at the National Indigenous Congress were subject to the interpretation and implementation of a bureaucracy controlled by hacendados and selectively enforced to benefit their interests. Ironically, the unintended result of Villarroel's decrees was the reinforcement of creole hegemony over colonos and comunarios. As with a similar experience with land tenure legislation in Peru, "The effect of the measure is a good illustration of what might be called Ford's law of Peruvian land tenure . . . [T]hat the law's effects were exactly the opposite of its nominal intent. . . . [T]he surest way to perpetuate a practice by landowners in Peru was to pass a law forbidding it."[145] The 1945 decrees subsumed the 1930s mandates of the military socialists, the 1938 Constitution, and Simon Bolivar's Supreme Decree delivered at the birth of the Republic—all summarily unenforced in the countryside. The decrees sowed uncertainty and discontent, exacerbating the problems they were intended to solve. Moreover, more often than not the laws were ignored.[146]

The Villarroel regime was the initial iteration of the National Revolution—in 37 months and against all odds—instituting a campaign for social justice, economic diversification, and national integration.[147] The laws of the military socialists were invoked and new laws enacted to abolish personal service by hacienda colonos and grant workers the right to organize trade unions. Reforms were undertaken to streamline the government bureaucracy, secure increased revenue from mineral and petroleum resources, diversify agriculture, and modernize the nation's transportation and communication infrastructure.[148] Intent on the creation of a modern, nationally integrated state, the RADEPA–MNR regime was beset with the opposition of domestic elites in league with the Anglo-American hegemons to suborn the nationalist revolution as a matter of "national security" via a host of foreign policy options: diplomatic machinations (unilateralism under the guise of multilateralism), subterfuge (the Belmonte letter, Putsch Nazi), and economic sanctions (together with stalled tin negotiations) under the pretext of instilling or restoring democracy.

The success of Villarroel's regime (as will be seen in Chapter 3) was fatally compromised by its moderation, its decision to allow the Rosca media free reign to sow discord, and President Villarroel's fatal refusal to use armed force to defend the National Revolution. In this the idealistic Villarroel was akin to Mexico's President Francisco Madero, another moderate revolutionary betrayed by his naiveté. The nationalist revolutionaries may have seized power effortlessly, but fulfillment of their promise of modernization and national integration ultimately brought them face to face with the forces of their destruction. Gualberto Villarroel's rendezvous with destiny is an exemplary chapter in the history of the struggle of weak nations to escape the shackles of imperial suzerainty. The RADEPA and MNR agenda and the commitment of the Villarroel regime to modernization, national integration, and social rights were a watershed in Bolivian history.

Notes

1. Eliodoro Murillo Cárdenas and Gustavo Larrea Bedregal, *Razón de Patria, Villarroel y Nacionalismo Revolucionario* (La Paz, 1988), 103–111. Generals Eliodoro Murillo Cárdenas and Gustavo Larrea Bedregal (junior officers at the time) played key roles in the "December Revolution."
2. Far from congratulatory, the clever diplomat's intention was propagandistic, equating the RADEPA "lightning" coup with a Nazi blitzkrieg (lightning war). See Alberto Ostría Gutiérrez, *The Tragedy of Bolivia: A People Crucified* (New York, 1958), 6.
3. Regional commandos of 20 or so members founded by the MNR in the major cities, as was the commando organized by José Cuadros Quiroga, comprised "all from the youth of the middle class, distinguished in Cochabamba society." Christopher Mitchell, *The Legacy of Populism: From the MNR to Military Rule* (New York, 1977), 19.
4. RADEPA Manifesto, Woodward to Secretary of State, 21 December 1943, NA824.00/1430.
5. Augusto Céspedes, *El Presidente Colgado* (Buenos Aires, 1966), 113–114; Colonel Francisco Barrero, *RADEPA y la Revolución Nacional* (La Paz, 1976), 396–397; Murillo and Larrea, *Razón de Patria*, 229–230; Luis Antezana Ergueta, *Historia secreta del Movimiento Nacioalista Revolucionario*, Vol. 1 (La Paz, 1984), 82–90; Jerry Knudson, *Bolivia: Press and Revolution, 1932–1964* (Lanham, MD, 1986), 120–121. For the cell structure of the lodge, see Elías Belmonte Pabón, *RADEPA: Sombras y refulgencias del pasado* (La Paz, 1994), 42–46. The restrictions on age and membership in other lodges would exclude senior officers associated with the Rosca, many of whom belonged to the elite Ayacucho Lodge. Villarroel was rumored to be a Mason, as was Víctor Paz Estenssoro, yet the Radepistas explicitly excluded Masons from inclusion in the Lodge.
6. Herbert S. Klein, *Parties and Political Change in Bolivia, 1880–1952* (Cambridge, UK, 1969), 247–248.
7. Céspedes, *El Presidente*, 110, Barrero, *RADEPA*, 64.
8. Céspedes, *El Presidente*, 113–114; Knudson, *Bolivia: Press and Revolution*, 120–121; Barrero, *RADEPA*, 107.
9. Barrero, *RADEPA*, 386–395; Murillo and Larrea, *Razón de Patria*, 209–229; Major Alberto Candia Almaraz, *Razón de Patria ante la historia* (Cochabamba, 1957), 3–21.
10. James Dunkerley, *Origines del poder militar en Bolivia* (La Paz, 1987), 176–177.
11. Víctor Andrade, *My Missions*, 14–15.
12. Interview with the Bolivian Minister of Economy by U.S. Embassy staff member, in Adam to Secretary of State, NARA, 19 February 1944, 824.00/2-1946.
13. This account is based on Víctor Andrade's recollection: Ibid., 15–16. The fateful meeting followed initial contacts between Víctor Paz, Augusto Céspedes, and Carlos

Montenegro with RADEPA officers in January 1943. See Charles Weston, Jr., "An Ideology of Modernization: The Case of the Bolivian MNR," *Journal of Inter-American Studies*, 10 (January 1968), 94. The "revolutionary command" was comprised of Major Gualberto Villarroel, Lieutenant Colonel José Celestino Pinto, Lieutenant Colonel Manuel Vaca Roca, Major Antonio Ponce Montán and the MNR's Víctor Paz Estenssoro, Carlos Montenegro, and Augusto Céspedes, and the independent Gustavo Chacón (later to be a foreign minister in the Villarroel government). See Murillo and Larrea, *Razón de Patria*, 103.
14. See NARA, 824.01/764; 824.01/769A; 824.00/1967. See also Armando Arce, *Los fusilamientos del 20 de noviembre de 1944 y el Movimiento Nacionalista Revolucionario* (La Paz, 1952), 9; Barrero, *RADEPA*, 98–99; José Fellman Velarde, *Víctor Paz Estenssoro: El Hombre y la Revolución* (La Paz, 1955), 128–129; Céspedes, *El Presidente*, 114; Manuel Frontaura Argandoña, La Revolución Nacional, 116, 119; Mitchell, *The Legacy of Populism*, 22.
15. Barrero, *RADEPA*, 114.
16. Armando Arce, *Los Fusilamientos*, 16.
17. Department of State telegram (29 March 1944), NARA, 824.01/769A. Colonel Moscoso also recommended the removal of MNR cabinet members.
18. Telegram, La Paz Embassy to Secretary of State, Department of State files U.S. National Archives and Records Administration, College Park, MD (hereafter cited as NARA), 3 January 1944, 24.00/1432. See also Max Paul Friedman, *Nazis and Good Neighbors: The United States Campaign Against the Germans of Latin America in World War Two* (Cambridge, UK, 2002), 127.
19. Friedman, *Nazis and Good Neighbors*, 122, 128–129. The *New York Times* reported that the Bolivian Junta resulted from "one act committed by a general subversive movement having for its purpose steadily expanding activities on the continent." *New York Times*, 25 January 1944, 1, 11.
20. Andrade, *My Missions*, 21. Andrade's vignette of the U.S. Embassy in La Paz is revealing: "The U.S. embassy in La Paz isolated itself completely, creating a *sui generis* situation in which its officers adopted the mentality of the besieged. The paranoia of Ambassador Boal led him to order all high and low-ranking functionaries of the embassy to leave their offices frequently during the day, go to a brick storage site, and secretly bring many of these bricks, wrapped in newspapers, into the embassy. He then began to build parapets where, in his fantasies, he would see his followers defending democracy to the bitter end against this creole brand of Nazis." Ibid., 18.
21. Blasier, "The United States, Germany, and the Bolivian Revolutionaries," 42. See also Ernesto Galarza, "The Case of Bolivia," *Inter-American Reports*, 6 (May 1949), 26.
22. Andrade, My Missions, 137.
23. Caffery to Secretary of State, 12 April 1944, NARA, 824.0/1780.
24. Caffery to Secretary of State, 31 March 1944, NARA, 824.01/766.
25. Friedman, Nazis and Good Neighbors, 133. The expulsion of prominent Germans, resisted by President Peñaranda, had a deleterious effect on the Bolivian economy: 70 percent of wholesale and retail businesses were German-owned. Ibid., 125, 129.
26. Attaché W.A. Wieland, in John F. Simmons to Secretary of State, 29 March 1944, NARA, 824.01/769.
27. The choice of Major Belmonte as the target of the British artifice is significant. An ardent nationalist who had served as Minister of Government in Busch's military socialist regime, Belmonte was also a founder of RADEPA: indicating British knowledge of the ultra-secret military lodge.
28. Bryce Wood, *The Making of the Good Neighbor Policy* (New York, 1962), 195–196. Cole Blasier's detailed examination of the forgery based on archival research in Germany and the United States confirmed the earlier suspicions of Bolivian nationalists. See Blasier, "The United States, Germany, and the Bolivian Revolutionaries, 1941–1946," *Hispanic American Historical Review*, 52.1 (February 1972), 32–33. For details of the shadowy world of espionage written by the British agent behind the plot, see H. Montgomery

Hyde, *Room 3603: The Story of the British Intelligence Center in New York During World War II* (New York, 1963), 153–160; see also, Friedman, *Nazis and Good Neighbors*, 58–59, 126 and Stephen Kinzer, *The Brothers: John Foster Dulles, Allen Dulles, and Their Secret World War* (New York, 2013), 65.
29. Blasier, "The United States, Germany, and the Bolivian Revolutionaries," 53; Friedman, *Nazis and Good Neighbors*, 131.
30. *TIME*, 8 May 1944. The magazine also informed its readers that Don Mauricio "eats hugely, spills cigar ashes on his stomach, claims a stock of 2,000 jokes in various languages . . . is charitable to nuns, priests, Jews, and likes to hand out expensive cigars as if they were calling cards" while also reporting his commitment to "hold miners' wages and standards of living to the lowest possible level."
31. Friedman, *Nazis and Good Neighbors*, 132.
32. In his summary of the Rosca's strategy for the overthrow of the National Revolution, Armando Arce (editor of *La Calle*) notes the propaganda value afforded the enemies of the revolution because of the executions. Armando Arce, *Los Fusilamientos*, 145–146.
33. Murillo and Larrea, *Razón de Patria*, 180–181, 231; also see René González Torres and Luis Iriarte Ontiveros, *Villarroel, Mártir de sus ideales y el atisbo de la revolución nacional* (La Paz, 1983), 86–92.
34. Frontaura Argandoña, *La Revolución Nacional*, 113, 118.
35. Fellman Velarde, *Víctor Paz Estenssoro*, 124.
36. Mitchell, *The Legacy of Populism*, 17–19. The Methodist church was not only associated with education of the MNR creole-mestizo elites but also had a significant influence on education in the northern Altiplano where missionaries "specifically sought to create an 'economic transformation' in Aymara lives. . . . They determined to increase skills, economic opportunities, and the Aymara's ability to legally defend themselves from social abuse." Libbet Crandon-Malamud, *From the Fat of Our Souls* (Berkeley, CA, 1993), 102.
37. Studies of social revolutions point to the disaffection of intellectuals as a causal factor when a "lack of social mobility . . . leaves a large portion of the intrinsic elite barred from the use of their talents, or denied appropriate rewards." Crane Brinton, *The Anatomy of Revolution* (New York, 1965), 33. Brinton also notes, "One might well argue *a priori* that in Western societies any approach to a rigid caste system which would bar the possibility of rise to the able but-low born, any serious stoppage of what [Vilfredo] Pareto calls the *circulation of the elites* . . . would be a very important preliminary symptom of revolution." Ibid., 60, 64; see also George Sawyer Pettee, *The Process of Revolution* (New York, 1938), 11.
38. Weston, Jr., "An Ideology of Modernization," 100–101. Hernán Siles Zuazo personified the eclecticism of the MNR, combining a Marxist critique of capitalist imperialism with admiration for German National Socialism; pro-German articles were a recurrent theme in *Inti*, the opposition newspaper edited by Siles Zuazo. Knudson, *Bolivia: Press and Revolution*, 121–122, 130. Knudson also notes, "*La Calle* was openly sympathetic to the Republican [Spanish Civil War] cause, which partially refutes those who charged later that the early MNR was oriented toward the Axis powers in World War II." Ibid., 60–61.
39. Timothy Snyder with Tony Judt, *Thinking the Twentieth Century* (London, 2012), 159; for an engaging dialogue on European fascism, see 161–163, 165–167, 169–170.
40. Weston, Jr., "An Ideology of Modernization," 92–93.
41. The note is from an embassy secretary in La Paz, cited by Laurence Whitehead, "Bolivia Since 1930," in Leslie Bethell, ed., *The Cambridge History of Latin America* (Cambridge, UK, 1991), 526. Nazi influence was not limited to Bolivia. John Foster Dulles, an early admirer of National Socialism, signed paperwork with "Heil Hitler" while employed as an attorney for the influential Wall Street firm Sullivan and Cromwell, where he brokered deals with German corporations vital to the development of Adolph Hitler's military ascendency. Stephen Kinzer, *The Brothers* (New York, 2013), 49–54.

42. Knudson, *Bolivia: Press and Revolution*, 117. "Fascism claimed to provide the ideological basis for a new integration of society, which resolved the conflicts inherent in both the capitalist and Communist systems. For a political party such as the MNR, which was to some extent both anti-capitalist and anti-Communist, fascism seemed to be a possible 'third way.'" Weston, Jr., "An Ideology of Modernization," 92.
43. Ibid., 94. This perception was soon to be echoed by Juan Perón's "Third Position" toward the contending imperialisms.
44. Ibid., 122.
45. Ibid., 44–45, 52–53.
46. Carlos Montenegro, *Nacionalismo y coloniaje* (Buenos Aires, 1967), 209. The book was first published in 1943.
47. Alberto Mendoza López, *La Soberanía de Bolivia* (La Paz, 1942), 51, 41.
48. José Cuadros Quiroga, *Movimiento Nacionalista Revolucionario: sus bases y principios de acción inmediata* (La Paz, 1942), reprinted in Mario Rolón Anaya, *Política y Partidos en Bolivia* (La Paz, 1966), 274. Cuadros Quiroga is inconsistent: while demanding the "extirpation of the great monopolies," he also calls for the "absolute subordination of the great enterprises [mining superestado] operating outside the Bolivian state."
49. Cuadros Quiroga, *Bases y principios*, 274–275.
50. Rolón Anaya, *Política y Partidos en Bolivia*, 273.
51. Ibid.
52. Knudson, *Bolivia: Press and Revolution*, 120.
53. Ibid., 112–113.
54. See, for example, Herbert S. Klein, *Bolivia: The Evolution of a Multi-Ethnic Society* (Oxford, 1982); James M. Malloy, *Bolivia: The Uncompleted Revolution* (Pittsburgh, PA, 1970); Mitchell, *The Legacy of Populism*, Laura Gotkowitz, *A Revolution for Our Rights: Indigenous Struggles for Land and Justice in Bolivia, 1880–1952* (Durham, NC, 2007); Thomas C. Field, Jr., *From Development to Dictatorship: Bolivia and the Alliance for Progress in the Kennedy Era* (Ithaca, NY, 2014).
55. Alan Knight's thoughtful comparative analysis of the Bolivian and Mexican social revolutions references "the revolution of 1943 and the Villarroel regime; and the final, discordant swansong of the Rosca after 1946." Yet, "without entering into this complex narrative," sidesteps consideration of the Sexenio, the 1946–1952 Bolivian counterrevolution that is comparable to the Huerta counterrevolutionary interlude in Mexico. Alan Knight, "The Domestic Dynamics of the Mexican and Bolivian Revolutions Compared," in Merilee S. Grindle and Pilar Domingo, eds., *Proclaiming Revolution: Bolivia in Comparative Perspective* (London, 2003), 66.
56. Tcnl. Gualberto Villarroel, *Mensaje a la H. Convención Nacional de 1945* (La Paz, 1945), 4; Murillo and Larrea, *Razón de Patria*, 213–229.
57. Klein, *Parties and Political Change*, 375–376; Mitchell, *The Legacy of Populism*, 23; Steve Volk, "Class, Union, Party, 188–189; González and Iriarte, *Villarroel, Mártir de sus ideales*, 197–200.
58. Klein, *Parties and Political Change*, 378; Gotkowitz, *A Revolution*, 175. These benefits were later introduced in Argentina by Juan Perón.
59. Villarroel, *Mensaje*, 4, 9; Golzálaz and Iriarte, *Villarroel, Mártir de sus ideales*, 221–222.
60. Robert F. Woodward, Charge d'Affaires, United States Embassy, La Paz, Bolivia to Secretary of State Cordell Hull, 11 April 1944, "Interest of Bolivian Provisional Government in Administrative Reorganization," NARA, 824.01/785. See also, Murillo and Larrea, *Razón de Patria*, 158.
61. Villarroel, *Mensaje*, 60, 62. The 75 percent completion of a questionnaire distributed by these workers is suggestive of the success of the Department's pioneering mission. Gonzalaz and Iriarte, *Villarroel, Mártir de sus ideales*, 221.
62. Knudson, *Bolivia: Press and Revolution*, 91; Villarroel, *Mensaje*, 60–61.
63. Villarroel, *Mensaje*, 64–66.
64. Gotkowitz, *A Revolution*, 178.

65. See, for example, the introduction to chapter eight ("Revolutionary Currents") in Sinclair Thomson et al., eds., *The Bolivia Reader* (Durham, NC, 2018), 324.
66. Steve Volk, "Tin and Imperialism," *NACLA, Latin American and Empire Report*, 8.2 (February 1974), 17. Volk estimates United States aid to Bolivia from World War II to 1961 as $220 million. This was one-fourth to one-third of the fair market value of tin exported during the war years. Ibid., 16.
67. Wilkie, *The Bolivian Revolution*, 30–31.
68. Knudson, *Bolivia: Press and Revolution*, 91.
69. Young, *Blood of the Earth*, 201, fn. 86; Klein, *Parties and Political Change*, 377–378.
70. Villarroel, *Mensaje*, 24–25, 44–46; Frontaura Argandoña, *La Revolución Nacional*, 119–121.
71. Villarroel, *Mensaje*, 4.
72. Frontaura Argandoña, *La Revolución Nacional*, 49–50.
73. Ibid., 56.
74. Ibid., 57–58.
75. Ibid., 41, 69.
76. José Flores Moncayo, *Legislación Boliviana del Indio* (La Paz, 1953), 414–418.
77. Fermin Vallejos, *Tata Fermin: Llama viva de un Yachaq* (Cochabamba, 1995), 10. Seemingly hyperbolic at the time, Villarroel's words would prove to be an understatement.
78. Luis Antezana and Hugo Romero note the early use of the sit-down strike on the Altiplano fomented by Republican politicians against hacendado rivals in the intra-elite squabbles with Liberals in the early years of the 1920s. Antezana and Romero, *Historia de los Sindicatos*, 80–81.
79. Ibid., 90.
80. Ibid., 89, 91, 94.
81. Ibid., 93.
82. Jorge Dandler and Juan Torrico A., "From the National Indigenous Congress to the Ayopaya Rebellion, 1945–1947," in Steve J. Stern, ed., *Resistance, Rebellion, and Consciousness in the Andean Peasant World, 18th to 20th Centuries* (Madison, WI, 1987), 340.
83. Ibid.
84. Ibid., 96.
85. Claudia Ranaboldo, *El camino perdido: biografía del dirigente campesino kallawaya Antonio Álvarez Mamani* (La Paz, 1988), 64; César Peon E., *Historia y mito en la conciencia de un líder campesino boliviano* (Buenos Aires, 1995), 32–33.
86. Dandler and Torrico, "From the National Indigenous Congress," 343.
87. For an excellent discussion of the Indigenous Committee, see Gotkowitz, *A Revolution*, 198–210.
88. Dandler and Torrico, "From the National Indigenous Congress," 342.
89. Ibid., 341–342, 348–350; Gotkowitz, *A Revolution*, 198–205.
90. Ranaboldo, *El camino perdido*, 84.
91. Roberto Choque Canqui, *Historia de una lucha desigual: los contenidos idelógicos y politicos de las rebeliones indigenas* (La Paz, 2005), 109.
92. Dandler and Torrico, "From the National Indigenous Congress," 342.
93. Gotkowitz, *A Revolution*, 199; Waskar Ari Chachaki, *Earth Politics: Religion, Decolonization, and Bolivia's Indigenous Intellectuals* (Durham, NC, 2014), 56.
94. Quoted in Ranaboldo, *El camino perdido*, 83.
95. Antezana and Romero, *Historia de los Sindicatos*, 97; Ranaboldo, *El camino perdido*, 83–84.
96. The nuances of the meeting are elucidated by Laura Gotkowitz, *A Revolution*, 198–206; see also Antezana and Romero, *Historia de los Sindicatos*, 102.
97. Antezana and Romero, *Historia de los Sindicatos*, 103.
98. Gotkowitz, *A Revolution*, 199, 201–203.
99. Ibid., 199.
100. Ibid., 199–201, 203–207.

101. Ibid., 208–209.
102. Antezana and Romero, *Historia de los Sindicatos*, 103–105.
103. Ibid., 106.
104. Ibid.
105. Ibid., 101–110.
106. Ibid., 108; also see Gotkowitz, *A Revolution*, 210.
107. Ibid., 211.
108. Antezana and Romero, *Historia de los Sindicatos*, 107, Gotkowitz, *A Revolution*, 210–211. Ramos Quevado may not have been the culprit. Antonio Mamani Álvarez claimed that Victoriano Condori Mamani had lost or stolen $60,000 bolivianos contributed by indigenous supporters of the Committee in Cochabamba Department. See Ranaboldo, *El camino perdido*, 96.
109. Antezana and Romero, *Historia de los Sindicatos*, 107–108; Dandler and Torrico, "From the National Indigenous Congress," 350; Gotkowitz, *A Revolution*, 210–211.
110. Ranaboldo, *El camino perdido*, 92.
111. Ibid. The Second Committee also attracted peasant militants formerly associated with Ramos Quevado and the First Indigenous Committee. This allowed for utilization of their organization and logistics (e.g., chaskis and a network of local supporters and sympathizers).
112. The undertaking was underwritten with an inheritance from his father, a prominent Kallawaya who had treated, among others, a Peruvian president and workers afflicted with malaria during construction of the Panama Canal. The funds were utilized to pay for food and lodging for the chaskis and the printing of handbills. Ibid., 102.
113. Ibid., 66, 81.
114. Ibid., 99–101.
115. Ibid., 97–99, 84–86. Mamani Álvarez also found it ironic that the Caciques Inkaicos published the weekly *Claridad* even though their constituency was illiterate. Ibid., 85.
116. Ibid., 83, 96, 104–105.
117. Dandler and Torrico, "From the National Indigenous Congress," 350. In fact the debt was stacked against Mamani Álvarez the moment Colonel Edmundo Nogales, a RADEPA officer, was appointed Minister of Government. Nogales owned three haciendas in Bautista Saavedra Province (La Paz Department), with designs to expand his holdings. Mamani Álvarez's nearby family property was coveted by the Minister who was ill-disposed toward the indigenous revolutionary. See Ranaboldo, *El camino perdido*, 103 and Peon E., *Historia y mito*, 27, 28.
118. Dandler and Torrico, "From the Indigenous National Congress," 348.
119. Ranaboldo, *El camino perdido*, 102. Ibid., 86. The Kallawaya also spoke of his subterfuge in recollections with the author in La Paz (1971).
120. Antezana and Romero, *Historia de los Sindicatos*, 86–87. See also, Ari Chachaki, *Earth Politics*, 129–130; Ranaboldo, *El camino perdido*, 131–132.
121. Ibid., 91–92; Dandler and Torrico, "From the Indigenous Congress," 345; Gotkowitz, *A Revolution*, 210; Ari Chachaki, *Earth Politics*, 130.
122. Gotkowitz, *A Revolution*, 210, 195.
123. Gotkowitz notes, "By the end of April, the government had placed between 150 and 399 people in 'preventative detention' . . . . Since few men possessed the certificates [of military service], the government found this an effective means to limit the numbers of colonos and comunarios who would reach the capital for the congress." Ibid., 212.
124. Ranaboldo, *El camino perdido*. 103.
125. Dandler and Torrico, "From the Indigenous Congress," 352.
126. Aside from the obeisance to presidential paternalism, the historian Elizabeth Shesko finds these "words also contained a revolutionary backdrop: they also represented the Congress as a contract between the government and the delegates. Chipana promised the delegates that 'now further abuse is not allowed from anyone against anyone'."

Elizabeth Shesko, "Hijos del inca. El congreso indigenal de 1945," *Fuentes, Revista de la Biblioteca y Archivo Histórico de la Asamblea Legislativa Plurinacional*, 4.6 (2010), 5.
127. *Los Tiempos*, 10 January 1946, 7. The editorial perceptively claimed that the MNR was ignorant of history ("The Indian was never a property owner under the Inka collectivist regime") and that the MNR sought "to parcel and increment the land under individual ownership, making an ostentatious . . . labor of subversive agitation in the countryside, arousing the hatred of the colono against the patrón . . . [while] pretending to be redeemers of the aboriginal masses . . . to exact their entrance to the Nationalist Movement."
128. Gotkowitz, *A Revolution*, 213, 216.
129. Ibid., 216–218.
130. Miguel Bonifaz, *Legislación Agrario-Indigenal* (Cochabamba, 1953), 520–521.
131. Ibid., 521–523.
132. Ibid., 524–525.
133. Ibid., 411–414. The 1945 Supreme Decree mandated that 50 percent of the land tax was to be designated for the school projects. Penalties were prescribed for violation of the law. However, "modification" by departmental prefects was permitted and therefore enforcement was still determined by the creole oligarchs.
134. Over 60 uprisings were reported in the highland provinces from 1901 to 1917. Their underlying causes were resistance to the seigniorial system, conflicts over land, or the revendication of lost lands. See Gonzalo Flores, "Levantamientos campesinos durante el perodo Liberal," in Fernando Calderón and Jorge Dandler Hanhart, eds., *Bolivia: La Fuerza Historica del Campesinado*, Geneva: Instituto de Investigaciones de las Naciones Unidas, 1984, 122–132. But Elizabeth Shesko's recent research suggests that Flores' number is far too low: "Conscripts thus marched into indigenous communities and rural properties at least forty times between 1912 and 1925 in just the Department of La Paz." Elizabeth Shesko, "Constructing Roads, Washing Feet, and Cutting Cane for the *Patria*: Building Bolivia with Military Labor, 1900–1975," *International Labor and Working-Class History*, 80 (Fall 2011), 10. Luis Antezana estimates: "Between 1866 and 1953 there were 6,000 indigenous uprisings." Antezana, "La reforma agrarian campesina en Bolivia (1956–1960)," *Revista Mexicana de Sociología*, 2 (April–June 1969), 309.
135. Dandler and Torrico, "From the National Indigenous Congress," 352.
136. Ibid., 356–360.
137. *Los Tiempos*, 9 January 1946, 3; 14 February 1946, 3.
138. Dandler and Torrico, "From the Indigenous Congress to the Ayopaya Rebellion," 358.
139. Roberto Choqui Canqui and Cristina Quisbert, *Líderes indigenas Aymaras: lucha por defensa de tierras* (La Paz, 2010), 32. See also, *Los Tiempos*, 2 March 1946, 3.
140. *Los Tiempos*, 10 January 1946, 7; 15 January 1946, 7. Luis Antezana argues that the incident at Las Canchas was part of a PIR plan to provoke a "violent wave of agitation" in the mines and Potosí countryside to elicit government repression: this distraction was to be followed by a PIR coup d'état in La Paz. Luis Antezana E., *Historia secreta*, Vol. 3, 765. For a different interpretation, see Céspedes, *El presidente colgado*, 193.
141. Gotkowitz, *A Revolution*, 230.
142. Hernán Siles avered "our greatest problem is of the land, our land that should belong to he who works it." *La Calle*, 11 May 1945, as cited in Antezana and Romero, *Historia de los Sindicatos*, 113.
143. *La Calle*, 27 July 1945, cited in Antezana and Romero, *Historia de los Sindicatos*, 115.
144. *The Shark and the Sardines* (New York, 1961), written by Guatemalan President Juan José Arevalo after his 1954 overthrow by the CIA, comes to mind.
145. Jeffrey Paige, *Agrarian Revolution: Social Movements and Export Agriculture in the Underdeveloped World* (New York, 1975), 151–152.
146. The anthropologist Dwight Heath found, "It is noteworthy that the Aymara of the yungas seem to be unaware of this event or these laws. There is no evidence that hacendados anywhere obeyed the letter of the laws, but a nod in the direction of their

spirit may have been the reduction of unremunerated labor requirements (from four days a week to three)." Dwight B. Heath, "New Patrons for Old: Changing Patron-Client Relationships in the Bolivian Yungas," *Ethnology*, 12.1 (January 1973), 96. Laura Gotkowitz points out that the decrees rather than being transmitted by national government officials to local authorities were left to diffusion by the indigenous delegates following the congress. Gotkowitz, *A Revolution*, 223.

147. As a pair of RADEPA generals adduce: "he methodically developed his plan with extraordinary statistical vision, with admirable honesty and unshakeable firmness, consecrated to the service of the highest interests of the nation. These virtues were recognized even by his most bitter detractors after his cruel sacrifice." Murillo and Larrea, *Razón de Patria*, 146; for the generals' 30-page compilation of the RADEPA agenda, see 147–177.

148. The Potosí Senator Manuel Frontaura Argandoña recounts the MNR rendition of the regime's accomplishments in *La Revolución Nacional*, 122.

3
COUNTERREVOLUTION

The Anglo-American hegemons considered the Villarroel regime a threat to the Allied war effort. Counterrevolutionary schemes were afoot. The forged "Belmonte letter" was a strand in a propaganda web spun by British agents to deceive the U.S. State Department and induce President Franklin Roosevelt to enter the war and prevent a German invasion of the British Isles. British intelligence officers also fabricated a map illustrating German plans for reorganization of South America into a Nazi fiefdom of five vassal states that threatened the U.S. Panama Canal Zone.[1] The map was foisted on the F.B.I. and then turned over to President Roosevelt who revealed the details in a speech on Navy Day 1941.[2]

Tin, wolfram, rubber, and quinine were essential to victory in the war against fascism. The British propaganda campaign sought the overthrow of the Villarroel regime and the return of the Rosca to assure control of the strategic raw materials.[3] The necessity of Bolivian raw materials, strategic to the Allied War effort, reveals the Roosevelt Administration's "Good Neighbor Policy" as the continuation of hegemony, sans the obvious "big stick" of Marine invasion and occupation associated with the earlier era of "Dollar Diplomacy." U.S. foreign policy was directed toward mitigation of resource nationalism to prevent expropriation of American-owned mines, oil wells, factories, plantations, and forests.[4]

Anatomy of a Counterrevolution

The National Revolution was dedicated to the reclamation of Bolivian sovereignty as stipulated in both the RADEPA and MNR statements of principles. The professed commitments of the Villarroel regime to a nationalist agenda, including Bolivia's sovereign rights to subsoil resources, were inimical to the tin magnates who controlled nearly 90 percent of Bolivian foreign exchange, together with a monopoly of the nation's media, and influence in the North American world of business and diplomacy. Threats to foreign ownership of natural resources also drew the concerted opposition of U.S. corporate interests during the Mexican Revolution and the later nationalist regimes of Mohammed Mossadegh (Iran), Juan José Arévalo (Guatemala), Fidel Castro (Cuba), João Goulart (Brazil), Salvador Allende (Chile), Hugo Chávez (Venezuela), Evo Morales (Bolivia).[5] Prime Minister Mossadegh's words echoed the views of Latin American nationalists: "The oil reserves of Iran, like its soil, its rivers and mountains, are the property of the people of Iran. They alone have the authority to decide what shall be done with it, by whom and how."[6]

The opposition of Bolivian oligarchs, Tin Barons, and Anglo-American hegemons, as well as the objectives and accomplishments of the Villarroel regime are minimized or ignored in most accounts of the RADEPA–MNR revolution (1943–1946). The intent of this chapter is to redress this error. It will be demonstrated that the overthrow of the RADEPA–MNR regime, symbolized by the sensational murder of President Gualberto Villarroel, was not the spontaneous uprising of workers and students as publicized in the contemporary media.[7] The overthrow of the Villarroel regime was not a revolution, a victory of democracy over dictatorship, or the downfall of a Nazi-fascist government as portrayed in contemporary accounts originating in the Rosca press and reiterated by North American media. It was a *counterrevolution* meticulously planned and orchestrated by the Rosca and abetted by the U.S. government to overthrow the Nationalist Revolution.

Overthrow: The Modus Operandi

The Anglo-American plan for the overthrow of Iranian Prime Minister Mohammad Mossadegh, executed seven years after the overthrow of the Villarroel regime, reveals marked similarities with the Bolivian experience: both nationalist governments were committed to the perilous mission of redressing the problems of underdevelopment through the exercise of sovereign rights to recover control of subsoil resources. Mossadegh's overthrow by the Anglo-American hegemons is well-known. Yet the Villarroel overthrow remains in obscurity and overlooked in the history of U.S.-sponsored coups in Latin America. Both overthrows were followed by authoritarian regimes characterized by systematic repression of nationalist opposition, only to beget a more radical reprise: the Bolivian National Revolution (1952–1964) and the Iranian Islamic Republic (1979–present).

The modus operandi for the overthrow of both regimes is instructive. Examination of the CIA's declassified history of the coup against Mossadegh ("Plan TPAJAX") reveals the congruence of tactical objectives in the overthrow of the two nationalist regimes, illustrates the continuity of Anglo-American imperialism, and documents the overlooked history of the United States in the overthrow of President Villarroel.[8]

Plan TPAJAX provides a template for comparison of the counterrevolutions in Bolivia and Iran. The primary components of the plan are (1) isolation of the regime through public statements by U.S. spokespersons linking suspension or denial of foreign aid and economic assistance to antidemocratic influence; (2)

application of economic sanctions to weaken the regime and create the belief that the regime's policies are leading the country into economic collapse; (3) a propaganda barrage portraying the regime as dictatorial and foreign-influenced, thereby transforming nationalists into *anti-nationalists*; (4) support for mass demonstrations against the government; (5) collusion between U.S. military attachés and dissident military officers to overthrow the government; (6) and immediate financial aid following the counterrevolution. (The Iranian component of Plan TPAJAX is abridged here: for the complete text, see endnote number 8.)

Isolation of the Regime Through Public Statements Linking Suspension or Denial of Foreign Aid and Economic Assistance to Antidemocratic Influence

Bolivia: On 10 January 1944, Secretary of State Cordell Hull issued a memorandum telegraphed to U.S. embassies in Latin America, repeating allegations that the Bolivian nationalists were fascist anti-Semites funded and influenced by Germany. Hull then convened an "Emergency Committee for Political Defense" in Montevideo on 28 January 1944 to increase pressure against the RADEPA–MNR government. Stigmatized as proto-Nazi by Hull's pronouncements, the government was denied diplomatic recognition by the United States, Britain, and their Latin American allies for six months. Recognition was only granted after the demands of the United States were met: removal of prominent MNR cabinet ministers, removal of the labor inspector for the tin mines, and the deportation of German citizens.[9]

The United States applied further pressure to isolate and weaken the fledgling regime by delaying the purchase of tin, denying visas to government functionaries, impeding importation of American products, halting lend/lease shipments, and suspending technical assistance programs. It is noteworthy that U.S., economic aid and assistance, together with an immediate contract for tin purchases—at an increased price—were promptly extended to the counterrevolutionary government following the overthrow of President Villarroel.

Iran: *"In the United States high-ranking US officials were to make official statements which would shatter any hopes held by Premier Mossadeq that American aid would be forthcoming."*[10]

Economic Sanctions

Bolivia: Economic sanctions were levied against the National Revolution to weaken the Bolivian economy, introduce economic hardship to the citizenry, and create discord among the populace and factionalism within RADEPA and the MNR, threatening the survival of the regime. Carl B. Spaeth, the head of the Western Hemisphere Division of the *Board of Economic Warfare* (emphasis added), in a secret memorandum to Spruille Braden, the Assistant Secretary of State for Western Hemisphere Affairs, suggested alternatives to bring the Villarroel government to heel: "An extreme course would include economic pressures to be exercised through the tin contract and possibly in connection with the delivery of products required by the Bolivian economy."[11]

Bolivia was particularly vulnerable to economic pressure because of the dominant role of tin exports essential for funding the government and funding plans for national development. The use of economic sanctions "to take measures to bring about a *readjustment* (emphasis added) in Bolivia" is outlined, in a March 1944 note to Secretary of State Edward Stettinius Jr., from Philip W. Bonsal, the head of the State Department's Division of the American Republics, who recommended:

> A freezing of Bolivian assets within this country. . . . Once this has been done, and to follow, if necessary, as soon as reactions have been observed, a reduction in the tin price paid Bolivia. . . . A complete stoppage of all supplies and equipment going directly or indirectly for the use of the Bolivian Army. Lend-Lease has already been stopped. . . . It may be that as an alternative to this step by step procedure above outlined consideration should be given to putting all points of the program into effect simultaneously.[12]

Negotiations over renewal of the contract for U.S. tin purchases began after the RADEPA coup in 1943 and continued until the counterrevolution in 1946. These negotiations reveal an identity of purpose on the part of the tin magnates and their allies in the State Department.[13] The proposal by Mauricio Hochschild representing the tin barons, and repeated by Assistant Secretary of State for American Republic Affairs Spruille Braden, called for Bolivia to reduce taxes on the mine owners (who owed the Bolivian government an estimated $200,000,000 in back taxes) and devalue the Bolivian peso by 10 percent. This was to be accompanied by an initial payment of US$0.67 per pound with periodic decreases until a June 1946 price of US$0.58.[14] Devaluation of the peso would reduce salaries, create economic hardship, and cause discontent and resentment among the populace, providing grist for propaganda portraying the Villarroel regime as ineffectual and thus contributing to labor and middle-class alienation.[15] The proposal posed a threat to the revolution because the regime would be forced to curtail projects for social welfare, modernization, and national integration.

Aware of the historic parallel between the earlier military socialist confrontation with the tin magnates and their danger to the National Revolution, Bolivian Ambassador Andrade noted:

> During the administration of President Busch, the mining companies had reduced tin production to less than nineteen thousand tons annually on the pretext that resources were being exhausted. In doing so, they had strangled the government, the forerunner of the revolution. This time they devised a new plan: they would take advantage of the United States' unwillingness to increase prices, in order to force a reduction in the fiscal resources of Bolivia at a time when price inflation would make the crisis even more serious. While punishing the Bolivian people for daring to want freedom,

they would establish as an indisputable principle the mine owners' right to international protection.[16]

Iran: *"While Mossadeq [is] in power no aid for Iran from United States." "Mossadeq is leading the country into complete economic collapse through his unsympathetic dictatorship."*[17]

Propaganda Campaign

Bolivia: Key leaders within RADEPA and their MNR allies were branded as Nazi-fascists, an accusation reinforced by the Belmonte and Nazi map forgeries.[18] Duplicitous labels were treated as facts and repeated ad infinitum, accomplishing what Adolph Hitler termed the "big lie." Branded with the stigma of Nazi-fascism, the Villarroel government was then refused diplomatic recognition by the Anglo-American hegemons and their Latin American satraps. U.S. foreign policy toward Latin America during the 1940s ironically labeled the "Good Neighbor Policy," labeled nationalists "bad neighbors."[19] What, then, of the accusations that the National Revolution behaved as a bad neighbor? As Ambassador Andrade put it:

> Having brought free trade unionism into the mining camps, having confiscated the property of Axis nationals and sent many prominent German and Japanese residents to the United States for internment, having endured continuous attacks from the establishment press, having diligently supplied the Allies with all the strategic raw materials the country could produce at what most Bolivians considered to be subsidized prices, and having played an active part in the creation of the United Nations, how could the Bolivian government continue to be classified as 'Nazi'?[20]

President Franklin Roosevelt's Good Neighbor Policy sought to disassociate itself from the unilateralism of the Monroe Doctrine and Dollar Diplomacy and create the image of a multilateral policy based on a Latin American consensus. Secretary of State Cordell Hull's comments at the Inter-American Committee for Political Defense conference in Montevideo (1944) are illustrative of the contrived Nazi-fascist contagion. "It is my information that by the consultation now in progress [among 18 American Republics] there is already taking place considerable exchange of information regarding the origin of the revolution in Bolivia. . . . The information available here increasingly strengthens the belief that forces outside Bolivia and unfriendly to the defense of the American Republics inspired and aided the Bolivian revolution."[21] Following Hull's announcement *TIME* magazine informed its readers: "To diplomats, this turgid language was as clear as Hull's curse. It meant that: (1) the U.S. would not recognize the revolutionary regime of Bolivia's new President, Major Gualberto Villarroel; (2) the U.S. blamed Argentina and Nazi Germany for putting the Villarroel junta in power; (3) a hemispheric united front was being formed to smash it."[22] Underlying the ostensible multilateral workings of the American republics was the continued unilateralism of the United

States: "the strategy of using cooperative delegates from other countries as fronts to present . . . proposals, so that these would not seem to have originated with the United States—a tactic the United States had already used successfully at the summit meetings."[23]

The Villarroel regime came to power six months after a clique of colonels with corporatist leanings had seized control of Argentina. Under the charismatic leadership of Colonel Juan Domingo Perón Argentina remained neutral in the Allied-Axis conflict, playing the opposing powers against each other to gain economic advantage in the export of agricultural products (beef, leather, wheat), resulting in a favorable balance of trade. Perón's "Third Position" of non-alignment was considered a breach of hemispheric solidarity against the Axis threat. North American propaganda equated Argentine neutrality with fascist totalitarianism and created the image of the Bolivian nationalists as Peronist marionettes. "So effective was the campaign that this opinion of Villarroel was accepted by liberals, churchmen, publishers, teachers and labor leaders." After an exhaustive examination of the propaganda campaign "to stigmatize Villarroel as a stooge of Hitler, Mussolini and Perón," concludes Ernesto Galarza, the Pan American Union's former Director of Labor and Social Information: "There is probably no example on record of such through going indoctrination by Nazi and Fascist news and propaganda agencies under Hitler and Mussolini as *this almost perfect example of controlled public opinion achieved through the free press of the America's* [sic]."[24] (added emphasis).

U.S. propaganda against Perón was epitomized in the notorious "Blue Book" released by Ambassador Spruille Braden in 1945.[25] The pamphlet alleged Nazi influence in the Perón regime and associated the Bolivian nationalists Víctor Paz Estenssoro and Major Elías Belmonte with Nazi-fascism through repetition of claims made in the earlier British forgeries. The propaganda attack against Belmonte and Paz Estenssoro was repeatedly used in the press and by the U.S. State Department as illustrated in the following Confidential Office Memorandum:

> By the information released in the section concerning Argentine-Nazi efforts to subvert the Bolivian Government . . . we give notice to Bolivia and the world at large, of not only the activities of Major Belmonte in the Argentine-Nazi plot to subvert this Hemisphere, but also implicate Victor Paz Estenssoro, the present Bolivian Minister of Finance, and the MNR, in having been in collusion with the Argentines and the Nazis. . . . Tomorrow the memorandum with its particulars regarding the MNR and the Belmonte clique will fall like a bombshell in the [sic] Bolivian politics. It will give to the opposition powerful ammunition against the Government and as well, to the military group antagonistic to the MNR, if that group so choses to use it.[26]

The days of both Gualberto Villarroel and the National Revolution were numbered. The MNR understood that publication of the State Department's contrived Blue Book "gave the green light to proceed with the insurrection."[27] Bolivia had become a pawn in a broader diplomatic—diplomatic strategy to defeat Juan Perón's nationalist government. The Blue Book, bereft of evidence to support a compendium of unsupported claims, notes Ernesto Galarza, "has already passed into diplomatic history as one of the most unusual incidents of inter-American relations in the past half-century."[28] Another fanciful propaganda gem, *Una revolución tras los Andes*, written by the Rosca diplomat Alberto Ostria Gutierrez warned of impending Nazi danger: "The Bolivian altiplano is the world's largest and best natural airfield. Hitler and his agents know it. And any day the swastika could appear flying over the wilderness, before the astonished eyes of the condor and the llama."[29]

In addition to a deluge of propaganda attacks, the Villarroel government also withstood a series of revolts in November–December 1944, April–May 1945, and June 1946. The execution of a dozen conspirators following a failed revolt in Oruro in November 1944 resulted in a propaganda bonanza for the Rosca. The conspirators were prominent members of the oligarchy, including a general, two former government ministers, and two senators. Constant repetition of sensationalized accounts of their execution by the opposition press transformed the victims from reactionary oligarchs into heroes. Labeled the "November Massacre," the counterrevolutionaries who exemplify what Edward Herman and Noam Chomsky categorize as "worthy victims" received constant repetition in the Rosca newspapers, often accompanied by photos, whereas massacred peasants and miners remained "unworthy victims," faceless, and ignored.[30]

Labeled the "Assassins of 1944," President Villarroel's government was subjected to a relentless propaganda onslaught in opposition leaflets, pamphlets, newspaper columns, and graffiti on city walls. An article in the popular New York tabloid *PM*, "Americas to Protest Bolivian 'Terror'," echoed the branding of the Villarroel regime as tyrannical.[31] A propaganda masterpiece contrived by Gustavo Navarro (aka, Tristan Maroff) described in graphic detail the grisly torture, mutilation, and execution of the creole prisoners by Indian soldiers, arousing the paranoid fantasies of creole-mestizo readers.[32] Condemnation of Villarroel's "reign of terror," originating in the Rosca dailies (*El Diario, La Razón, Última Hora*) was parroted in Latin American and U.S. newspapers and magazines. Former Under Secretary of State Sumner Welles claimed that President Villarroel "had turned Bolivia into an immense, concentration camp" gave the aura of legitimacy to the propaganda onslaught.[33]

Bloody corpses of students and workers appeared in the La Paz barrios of the urban poor "to incite popular anger and create an atmosphere of indignation" among illiterate inhabitants, and faked rumors of 17 students hung in the municipality were circulated to stoke popular opposition against the "Nazi-fascist" government.[34] On the eve of the counterrevolution, a spurious radio broadcast with duplicitous assertions capped the Rosca's disinformation campaign to drive a wedge between the MNR and RADEPA.[35]

Iran: "*In Iran, CIA and SIS* [British] *propaganda assets were to conduct an increasingly intensified propaganda effort through the press, handbills, and the Tehran clergy in a campaign designed to weaken the Mossadeq government in any way possible.*"[36]

Mass Demonstrations

Bolivia: Utilization of a mass demonstration against the targeted government is the pièce de résistance of tactical objectives when each of the opposition stakeholders assumes a critical role in the final phase of the overthrow. Domestic opponents to the National Revolution formed the Democratic Anti-Fascist Front (*Frente Democratica Antifascista*: FDA). The FDA encompassed an unlikely alliance of bedfellows: the tin magnates,[37] hacendados, and the oligarchic political parties (*Partido Liberal, Partido de la Unión Republicano Socialista, Partido Socialista, Partido Republicano Genuino*) together with the Stalinist PIR led by José Antonio Arze and Ricardo Anaya with strength among the teachers and labor unions (*Confederación Sindical de Trabajadores de Bolivia*: CSTB) and university students (*Federación Universitaria Boliviana*: FUB) centered at the Universidad Mayor de San Andrés (UMSA) in La Paz.[38]

After an unsuccessful attempt to participate in the National Revolution, the PIR opted for a pact with the devil: "The enemy of my enemy is my friend."[39] The evidence suggests that Arze, Anaya, and the PIR were more opportunistic than communistic as they worked in league with the Rosca and the United States to overthrow the RADEPA–MNR revolution. The PIR assumed leadership of the organization and execution of the overthrow. The party's "Political Bureau" orchestrated the coordination of "brigades" assigned with specific objectives: contacts with the FDA leadership, direction of university student and teacher agitation, contacts with labor unions to influence the timing of an anti-government strike in La Paz, distribution of propaganda to foment disinformation and destabilize the regime, culminating in the seizure of targeted media (Radio Illimani; the newspaper *La Cumbre*).[40]

RADEPA and MNR leaders were targeted for death by PIR militants during and after the insurrection. Víctor Paz Estenssoro narrowly escaped an assassination attempt when assailants broke into a neighbor's dwelling, severely wounding the wrong man, and Roberto Hinojosa, the director of *La Cumbre*, was among those beaten to death during the insurrection and hanged on a lamppost in Plaza Murillo.[41] PIR militants spearheaded the street demonstrations in La Paz to foment instability and provoke confrontations with police, carabinero, and military forces. Student provocateurs led by PIR militants were supported by the UMSA Rector Héctor Ormachea Zalles, the alleged "intellectual author" of the FDA conspiracy, Masonic Grand Master, and prominent member of the Liberal Party.

A strike for increased wages by the teachers was concocted as a provocation for the overthrow.[42] On 10 July 1946, armed PIRista students and FDA provocateurs attacked Radio Illimani, the Prefecture, and the Palacio Quemado, injuring carabineros and townspeople before they were repulsed by police tear gas and bullets. A student was allegedly killed: the conspirators now had their bloody shirt. The populace was incited to rebellion with a torrent of leaflets and fake newspaper stories of murders and hangings of students in Plaza Murillo. The FDA propaganda incited popular indignation against the "Nazi-fascist" regime and called for another demonstration. On 13 July, a funeral procession ceremoniously paraded a casket to internment at the La Paz cemetery. In the resultant melee, a transit policeman and a carabinero were killed by the demonstrators; the injured included four carabineros and two traffic policemen, two students, and four workers.[43]

By 16 July, student militants were organized in 37 "primary revolutionary combat groups" supported by the university Rector Ormachea Zalles and commanded by PIRistas A general strike announced by *La Razón* on 17 July was boycotted by 20,000 miners, railway, and factory workers. This contradicts the narrative of Villarroel's overthrow by a spontaneous rising of students, teachers, and workers.[44]

On 19 July, Defense Minister Pinto (in the role of mediator) led a demonstration at the Plaza Murillo demanding the removal of the MNR from the government with the intent of fracturing the RADEPA–MNR regime. Pinto then joined President Villarroel and other officers in addressing the demonstrators when armed provocateurs opened fire. A shootout with carabineros and police left some 20 dead and wounded. In this, as in the "student" funeral demonstration, creole women led by Señora Maria Teresa Solari Ormachea, the niece of university Rector Ormachea Zalles, were conspicuous participants.[45]

The crescendo of demonstrations continued until the final mass demonstration leading to an attack on the Palacio Quemado and overthrow of the regime on 21 July 1946. The conspirators' propaganda legacy—that the counterrevolution was a spontaneous revolution of students, teachers, and workers—lives on in the historiography of the topic. Ernesto Galarza's judicious study of the event documents a contradictory scenario:

> This Report examines the background of the July 1946 revolution to determine . . . whether it was in fact a "workers" revolution. *The conclusion, which is substantially supported by the facts now known, is that the July revolt was not a revolution of workers, students and teachers*[46] (added emphasis).

Iran: *"Station political action assets also contributed to the beginnings of the pro-Shah demonstrations." "Supported by CIA local assets and financial backing, [the coup] would have a good chance of overthrowing Mossadeq, particularly if this combination should be able to get the largest mobs in the streets and if a sizeable portion of the Tehran garrison refused to carry out Mossadeq's orders."*[47]

Collusion Between U.S. Military Attaches and Indigenous Military Officers to Overthrow the Government

Bolivia: A "fifth column" of senior military officers hostile to the MNR revolutionaries and their radical vision of modernizing the nation played a decisive role in the overthrow of President Villarroel. The clique led by Colonel José Celestino Pinto forced the removal of Major Clemente Inofuentes who had been selected by the MNR parliament as Vice President of the revolutionary government. Pinto next opposed Víctor Paz Estenssoro's candidacy for the office and then supported the demand of the United States for the removal of the MNR ministers as a precondition for diplomatic recognition.

The objectives of the Pinto military clique, the Rosca, and the United States were one and the same: the elimination of MNR influence in the Villarroel regime. A "Secret Memorandum for the Assistant Chief of Staff, G-2" (U.S. military intelligence) on 3 February 1944 noted the régime's precarious situation due to economic dependency: "Ninety-five percent of Bolivia's exports are minerals which can be absorbed at the present time only by the United States." The memorandum also revealed the U.S. interest in an overthrow of the nationalist revolutionary regime: "That complete overthrow of the existing junta is not presently feasible. That it is desirable that a compromise solution to the present impasse be effected by working to accomplish replacement of the more undesirable members of the Junta. That the personnel of our military and air missions are suitable media for the transmission to acceptable junta members of the conditions under which United States recognition would be extended, and are available to act in such capacity."[48]

Meetings by Pinto and Ponce with U.S. military attaches were duly noted by the American Embassy and information and commentary immediately routinely forwarded to Washington.[49] Ambassador Flack's telegram (sent the day after the counterrevolution) illustrates the embassy's interest in the FDA's military faction: "Humberto Torres Ortiz designated Chief of Staff had been in arrest. Is friendly to US and had been anti-government. Lieut. Col. Víctor B. Alarcón, Acting Commander Region Number 1 (La Paz). Pro-student commander [i.e., FDA] designated for Sucre regiment which may be put on police duty later today."[50]

The military, with its monopoly on armed force, is the historic arbiter of Bolivian politics. General David Toro, a persistent protagonist in plots against the Villarroel regime, epitomized the penchant for caudillismo, the synergistic relationship between arms and politics that defines the military institution.[51] President Villarroel found himself treading water in a veritable sea of sharks—staving off a half-dozen coup attempts led by military officers in league with the Rosca. As Augusto Céspedes observed, "The offices of the Ministry of Defense and the General Staff were converted into a barracks of the counter-revolutionary chiefs and officials" and concluded, "demoralized by military sabotage, divided by caudillista ambitions, crippled by the confusion they [FDA] sowed, some leaders were incompetent to understand the value of the Bolivian revolution and others were corrupted by contact with the Rosca."[52]

On Saturday, 20 July 1946, President Villarroel summoned military officers to a meeting in the Palacio Quemado that continued into the early morning of the following day: traitors were unmasked, passions inflamed, pistols drawn, epithets hurled. The event was a turning point in the revolution. The confrontation between loyalists and counterrevolutionaries revealed that the idealistic goals of the RADEPA national revolution had given way to the traditional praetorian avarice and intrigue. A crucial moment for both President Villarroel and the National

Revolution came to the fore when commanders of key garrisons in the city stated that their regiments (Loa, Sucre, Lanza, Bolívar) would not fire on demonstrators (viz., not defend Villarroel and the National Revolution).[53] But Gualberto Villarroel refused to call his RADEPA loyalists to arms. Instead, he ordered them to stand down.

Iran: "*The branch task force was able to draw up a plan designed to neutralize the Tehran garrison and to isolate all other brigades in Iran. . . . [O]ur first staff plan was based on the use of the Third Mountain Brigade for the capture and arrest of the offices assigned to the Chief of Staff, as well as the arrest and neutralization of all other forces in the city of Tehran.*"[54]

Financial Aid to Counterrevolutionary Government

Bolivia: The United States withheld diplomatic recognition and economic assistance to strangle the Bolivian economy. A new contract for tin exports had come to naught before the counterrevolution. But three days after the overthrow, Ambassador Flack was notified by the State Department of an "agreement in principle reached a few days ago between the RFC [Reconstruction Finance Corporation] and Bolivian producers covering deliveries . . . through balance of the calendar year."[55] On the day of the counterrevolution, Flack telegraphed news of the coup and urged "that we be prepared [to] ship any food necessary on any terms to prevent this democratic movement falling victim to Fascist reaction because of people's hunger. Also that tin negotiations be brought to prompt satisfactory conclusion as soon as recognition is accorded."[56] Secretary of State James F. Byrnes immediately replied: "Dept exploring possibility food shipments should occasion arise. RFC already informed that Dept has no political objections to conclusion [of] tin contracts as soon as situation permits. RFC considering possibility [of] some interim arrangement."[57]

President Truman agreed with Ambassador Flack's request for immediate recognition of the counterrevolutionary junta "to bolster the return of liberal constitutional oligarchy," as the diplomatic Historian Glenn Dorn has it, "recognition did pave the way for emergency food shipments, military sales, and the final ratification of Ambassador Andrade's tin contract—all of which would strengthen the authority of the new government."[58]

Iran: "*US-UK financial aid will be forthcoming to successor government. Also the Department of State wanted to satisfy itself that an adequate amount of interim economic aid would be forthcoming to the successor government before it would finally approve decisive action.*"[59]

Postmortem

President Villarroel had presided dispassionately throughout the drama in the Palacio Quemado with an occasional comment to quench the rancor among his officers. And thus, the question arises: what had become of his commitment to the ideals of RADEPA and the National Revolution? In the meeting at the Palacio, the counterrevolutionary officers and their conspiracy were revealed. His supporters had taken the key military conspirators captive, and with decisive leadership from Villarroel, they could have parlayed this into defense of the revolution. But Colonel Villarroel, president and commander in chief of the armed forces, squandered a perfect opportunity to neutralize the mutinous officers, declare them a treasonous threat to the revolution, and squelch the counterrevolution.

Instead, the president dithered. The officers, loyal and disloyal, were excused from the Salon Rojo, leaving the Palacio to Villarroel, his aide de camp Captain Ballivian and Secretary Uria de la Oliva. Reports from the street were ominous: armed mobs gathering, talk of lynchings, and of garrisons suborned. On the morning of 21 July, a radio broadcast by Defense Minister General Rodríguez announced "the army has been confined to quarters and will not agree to the defense of their Captain General [Villarroel]." The police were withdrawn from the streets and students began sacking an arms cache from the unguarded municipal building.[60] By midday, the Loa Regiment, in accord with a pact agreed to earlier with the FDA, committed itself to the counterrevolution.

The Palacio Quemado was defenseless. Within hours the Palacio would be stormed by an armed mob, Villarroel, Ballivian, and Uria hurled from the windows of the palace, and in a macabre demonstration of mob violence their bodies brutalized and hung on lamp posts in the Plaza Murillo. They were soon joined by others.[61] Gualberto Villarroel, as with his military socialist predecessor Germán Busch, was defeated by the Rosca—and ultimately by himself—when he failed to fight for the National Revolution. Instead, as foretold in his prophesy to indigenous supporters, he died "like a dog." The "Hanged President" and his handful of subordinates in the Palacio Quemado were but the first victims of the counterrevolution. The resurgent Rosca would purge countless adherents of the National Revolution, including hundreds of indigenous activists during the "Sexenio," the six-year interregnum (1946–1952) of oligarchic rule, before the redux of the National Revolution under the stewardship of the MNR (1952–1964).

A Historiographical Note

The overthrow was accomplished by the FDA coalition: the Tin Baron's Mauricio Hochschild and José Carlos Aramayo, the oligarchs Héctor Ormachea Zalles and Señora Maria Teresa Ormachea Solari, the PIRistas José Antonio Arce and Ricardo Anaya, the Pinto clique and senior officers within RADEPA. The conversations and concerns of the Rosca–PIRista plotters are amply revealed in the U.S. State Department memoranda in contradistinction to the dearth of communication between the U.S. Embassy and the RADEPA–MNR leaders. The foregoing account of the overthrow of the National Revolution documents the strategy and tactics of the counterrevolutionaries. It also calls into question the conventional narrative of North American historians. Consider the assertions in the standard work, *Parties and Political Change in Bolivia, 1880–1952*, by the eminent historian Herbert S. Klein:

- *"After the Oruro massacre of the previous November, anti-government plotting continued at an ever-increasing pace."*

   A massacre is defined as the killing of a large number of people, Reference to the "12 November Martyrs" was a constant refrain in the Rosca newspapers (the victims included Hochschild's bagman with US$500,000 in cash, two senators, two generals, and assorted Rosca conspirators), and contributed significantly to the FDA strategy of eroding urban support for the regime.

- *"With RADEPA breaking down under the strains of governing, and the lack of any other cohesive military elements, the army itself was becoming disorganized and was increasingly ineffective in the suppression of mounting popular agitation."*

   The "strains of government," as we have seen, resulted from the concerted Rosca and U.S. opposition to the government, including the military fifth column within the regime. Meanwhile, Villarroel refused to censor the press or utilize violence to suppress the FDA-inspired demonstrations.

- *"At the same time the MNR showed little sympathy for the radical left, the CSTB, or the student movement, which were utterly hostile to the régime."*

   The radical left included PIR conspirators, leaders of the CSTB [union], and PIRista-led student provocateurs hostile to the MNR revolutionaries in the régime.

- *"Strikes by teachers were bitterly contested and the MNR instigated a full-scale assault on the university and many of its instructors."*

   The Universidad Mayor de San Andrés was a focal point of anti-government agitation. The Rector, Héctor Ormachea Zalles, was a leader of the FDA counterrevolutionaries, and PIRista-led students used the university as a base for attacks on the regime. PIRistas and Movimientista militants engaged in shootouts at the university and elsewhere.

- *"The net result of this action was to force the traditional parties . . . to form a common defence with the PIR and a formal anti-government Frente Democrática Antifascista was established by the two extremes of the political spectrum. . . . [T]here is no question that the deliberate attacks on the party by the MNR and RADEPA forced the PIR to adopt a united anti-government front in self-defence.*

   In fact, the FDA was formed in 1945 by the Rosca–PIRista conspirators as a counterrevolutionary offensive against the nationalist revolution and a "self-defense" of the ancien régime (aka FDA).

- *"Constant acts of brutality and the inability of the military to carry through a coherent programme made revolution inevitable."*[62]

   The "inevitable" revolution arrives bereft of the schemes of the Rosca, oligarchs, Tin Barons, Stalinist opportunists, and Anglo-American statecraft to subvert the cause of the nationalist revolutionaries. It was, in fact, a counterrevolution. The Rosca's concerted resistance to the revolution is ignored and the victim is blamed. If one were to argue inevitability vis-à-vis the counterrevolution, a better argument might be made regarding Villarroel's tolerance of the Rosca-Stalinist opposition and his unwillingness as commander in chief of the armed forces to employ armed force against the regime's enemies, ergo his inevitable martyrdom.

- *"No military leaders defected and no troops were suborned. Rather, building on the momentum of the teachers' strike . . . and on the university movement, the anti-fascist front succeeded in turning a mass protest movement into a revolt."*[63]

The anti-government demonstrations were fomented by the FDA as part of an overthrow strategy contrived to cripple RADEPA, unravel the RADEPA–MNR alliance, and suborn army regiments in La Paz. The defection of army garrisons in La Paz following a broadcast on Radio Illimani by General Ángel Rodríguez, a key military conspirator, was a crucial tactical instrument in the FDA strategy for counterrevolution.[64]

Klein's primary source is *Bolivia bajo el terrorismo nazifascista*. Penned in 1945 by the Stalinist José Antonio Arze, *Bolivia under Nazi-fascist terrorism* constituted the PIR contribution to the FDA propaganda campaign to defame and delegitimize the Villarroel government.[65] Arze presents the counterrevolutionaries as defenders of the nation against a despotic RADEPA–MNR regime, labeled as Nazi-fascist. But, as we have seen, the Rosca-Stalinist "Anti-Fascist Democratic Front" was a counterrevolutionary contrivance and the students, teachers, and workers were led by PIRista militants. It was only after the rejection of José Antonio Arze's bid to join the RADEPA–MNR government that the PIR entered into the FDA conspiracy to overthrow the National Revolution.

Klein's narrative is echoed in Laura Gotkowitz's masterful *A Revolution for Our Rights*. "Against a backdrop of urban strikes, rural unrest, and acts of state repression, an unlikely alliance was formed. . . . This multi-class movement . . . toppled the government without any collaboration from the police or the army"[66] Gotkowitz follows Klein's lead and ascribes the army an apolitical role in the overthrow, an interpretation at odds with the foregoing account of the counterrevolution, as is the notion that the Rosca–PIRista alliance was contrived as a result of strikes, unrest, and state repression. The "alliance" was neither "multi-class" nor a "movement" or a "popular revolt" as portrayed in counterrevolutionary propaganda. Contrived by the Tin Barons and *Concordancia* oligarchs in league with Stalinists embedded in the university and unions, the unholy alliance was not the "popular revolt" against repression portrayed in counterrevolutionary propaganda. As we have seen, the FDA was a conspiratorial front whose strategy was to foment strikes and incite violence to provoke government repression, thereby demonstrating the brutality of the regime. The Rosca newspapers were then able to popularize the RADEPA–MNR nationalists as Nazi-fascists: a clever propaganda transposition of the nationalists into creole Nazis that continues to bewitch the history of the National Revolution.

Gotkowitz claims the United States "erroneously labeled Villarroel's government Fascist."[67] The fascist label was indeed erroneous, but purposely so (viz., the fake Belmonte letter, Putsch-Nazi propaganda, Nazi map forgeries), conjured by Anglo-American diplomats to stigmatize the nationalist revolutionaries. The FDA overthrow of the National Revolution is also erroneously labeled a revolution rather than a counterrevolution, a "popular multi-class movement," rather than a Rosca-Stalinist conspiracy assisted by a cabal of senior army officers, and abetted by the U.S. government.[68] Unfortunately, the misrepresentation of the Villarroel regime persists among U.S. historians.[69]

Overthrow

Gualberto Villarroel ignored the counsel of MNR radicals. When Víctor Paz Estenssoro met with the beleaguered president in the final hours of the revolution, Villarroel disregarded his pleas for decisive action. The discussion between the RADEPA and MNR leaders is recounted by the Movimientista Alfonso Finot who accompanied Paz Estenssoro in the final hours of the regime. The RADEPA and MNR leaders were at odds. Villarroel wanted Paz Estenssoro and the other MNR leaders to resign their positions in the government as demanded by the FDA. Paz Estenssosro understood that this would be tantamount to a surrender of the revolution, a validation of the opposition strategy of divide and conquer. Paz then urged the use of armed force to defend the revolution: "For me the only formula to solve things is dissolving the demonstrations and not throwing us out. That is all Gualberto, and now I'm going." Frustrated, the MNR leader abruptly left the meeting. In a much-debated episode, he allegedly ordered the telephone line to the presidential palace cut.[70]

Paradoxically, Villarroel the decorated war veteran, refused to fire on the civilian mob mobilized by his enemies. During the contentious gathering of the military leadership at the Palacio where conspirators were unmasked and plans laid bare, Villarroel eschewed the opportunity to seize the initiative, arrest the conspirators, and defend the National Revolution. Lt. Colonel Francisco Barrero, a RADEPA founder and Villarroel's Minister of Government, portrayed the president as "passive . . . naïve at times when the government needed an implacable politician or a decisive, hard military man," "incapable of initiative regarding his bitter and powerful opponents," "innocuous" whose "kind-heartedness accelerated the ruin of the Revolution."[71] Villarroel rejected the pleas of loyal RADEPA aviators to spirit him to the safety of the El Alto airbase above the city. His indecision was a disservice to the revolution and ultimately cost him his life: defenestrated, murdered, and mutilated by the mob that stormed the Palacio Quemado. Ironically, in his pocket a note was discovered in which he renounced the presidency.[72]

Villarroel's dithering and indecision, as evidenced in the tragi-comic confrontation between traitors and loyalists during the fateful final night at the Palacio

Quemado, revealed a man whose worst enemy was himself—a leader who would rather die like a dog than fight like a lion defending the RADEPA "Cause of the Fatherland." Perhaps Víctor Paz sensed that Villarroel might better serve as a martyr than as a politician when he allegedly ordered a subordinate to cut the telephone lines to the Palacio, leaving him to his fate.

FIGURE 3.1 Honor Guard at Lamp Post Where Martyred President Gualberto Villarroel Was Hanged in 1946

Source: Photo by author.

Summary and Conclusions

This chapter details how the Colossus of the North exercised power over a weak and impoverished country dependent on the sale of tin. It argues that beneath the sophistry of the Good Neighbor Policy, U.S. diplomats continued to oppose regimes whose plans for resource nationalism and anti-imperialist policies threatened U.S. economic interests. The overthrow of President Gualberto Villarroel and the Bolivian National Revolution is a neglected chapter in the history of U.S. interventionism. It was a victory in the war against Latin American nationalism and a harbinger of things to come in Guatemala (1954), Brazil (1964), Chile (1973), and Nicaragua (1985–1987).[73] The modus operandi of the counterrevolution in Bolivia shared much in common with the later Iranian overthrow orchestrated by the Central Intelligence Agency; a revived nationalism would later spark more radical iterations in both Bolivia (1952) and Iran (1979).

The enemies of President Villarroel conspired to subvert plans for modernization of the oligarchic state.[74] The suppression of modernity, education, and social justice for the indigenous majority was fundamental to continuation of the Old Regime: a "liberal constitutional oligarchy,"[75] anti-modern, stultified, based on servile labor, unconcerned with the health or welfare of workers in field, mine, and factory, lacking in scientific knowledge, dependent on the export of raw materials to the industrial powers, its sovereignty compromised, its leaders preoccupied with peddling political favors and repression of internal opposition.

President Villarroel's May 1945 decrees remain synonymous with the RADEPA phase (1943–1946) of the National Revolution. Conveyed by delegates from the National Indigenous Congress to the rural hinterland, the decrees aroused colono expectations and hacendado hostility. The Villarroel regime had allowed the *Sociedad Rural* a measure of influence in shaping the content of the decrees and their enforcement remained subject to the decisions of government officials influenced by powerful hacendados. The colonato continued unabated. Creole-mestizo authorities continued to persecute and imprison indigenous revolutionaries. The Las Canchas Massacre was a reminder of how little had changed despite the president's brotherly words. *Los Tiempos*, the Cochabamba daily owned and edited by a prominent hacendado, attributed Las Canchas to the "fuhrers of the MNR" whose "crass ignorance regarding economic questions" led to "subversive agitation in the countryside, arousing the hatred of the colono against the patron."[76]

The regime's toleration of a "free press" granted journalistic license to enemies of the revolution. Villarroel's Supreme Decrees, continued *Los Tiempos*, were the root of rural agitation, the work of MNR "hierarchs of creole nazi fascism . . . who convoked the great Indigenous Congress . . . [and] spent much money from the National Treasury to obtain some applause from the delegates [referred to as "native Quislings"].[77] Likewise, an editorial in *El País* (another Cochabamba opposition newspaper) claimed that peasant unrest was the result of the Indigenous Congress, ignoring the government's failure to enforce provisions of the decrees favorable to amelioration of hacienda labor relations.[78]

The RADEPA–MNR government refused to harness the latent power of the peasantry to end the *colonato*. Instead, the National Revolution denied the political agency of the indigenous majority and continued the oppression of their leaders. Luis Ramos Quevado, Antonio Mamani Alvarez, and Hilarión Grajéda—men of great imagination and unswerving conviction—were imprisoned for leadership of the indigenous nationalist movement. Neutralized by the traditional power of the hacendados, the National Revolution failed to enforce its mandate in the countryside.

The overthrow of President Villarroel was not the spontaneous revolution of teachers, students, and workers touted by the international media; it was a carefully planned and well-executed counterrevolution devised by the Tin Barons, oligarchs, and Stalinists abetted by the Anglo-American hegemons. Propaganda from the tin magnates' newspapers reverberated abroad, resulting in a virtually universal repetition of the Rosca narrative parroted, for example, in *The Nation, New York Times, Washington Post*, the *Daily Worker* and in academic accounts of the overthrow. The counterrevolution shared strategy and tactics with U.S. interventions in Mexico and Iran. Yet the U.S. role in the Bolivian overthrow remains an outlier in the chronicles of North American counterrevolutions.

Amid accusations of Nazi-fascism, the Villarroel overthrow was conducted in the incipient period of postwar Soviet imperialism. Curiously, the "Democratic Anti-Fascist Front" was directed by the Stalinist PIR and abetted by the U.S. government. The U.S. State Department's collusion with the PIRista Jefe José Antonio Arze (who incidentally taught at Williams College) appears to have been of little concern. The sordid history of the PIR during the "*Sexenio*," the six-year rule of the "Democratic Anti-Fascist Front" is treated in Chapter 4.

Notes

1. The Assistant Secretary of State for Latin American Affairs noted, "I believe that the British Intelligence probably has been giving attention to creating as many 'incidents' as possible to affect public opinion here," Ibid., 170 173; see also Max Paul Friedman, *Nazis and Good Neighbors: The United States Campaign Against the Germans of Latin America in World War II* (Cambridge, UK, 2003), 58.
2. Roosevelt may have been complicit in the map affair and not a dupe of British espionage. See R.A. Humphreys, *Latin America and the Second World War*, Vol. 1 (London, 1981), 132; see also "Roosevelt: Conniver or Country Bumpkin?" in William E. Breuer, *Deceptions of World War II* (New York, 2001), 59–60; John Nicholas Cull, *Selling War: The British Propaganda Campaign Against American Neutrality* (Oxford, 1996), 170–173; James Siekmeier, *The Bolivian Revolution and the United States, 1952 to the Present* (University Park, PA, 2011), 25.
3. "The full effort . . . stands as one of the most diverse, extensive, and yet subtle propaganda campaigns ever directed by one sovereign state at another." Cull, *Selling War*, 4.

106 Counterrevolution

4. Kevin Young differentiates "resource nationalism" with its demand of sovereignty over the extraction of natural resources, from nationalism (associated with patriotism, chauvinism, natavism, anti-imperialism) in his recent book *Blood of the Earth: Resource Nationalism, Revolution, and Empire in Bolivia* (Austin, TX, 2017), 3; for U.S. opposition to resource nationalism, see Ibid., 53–57, 61.
5. The disastrous results of the CIA coups in Iran and Guatemala and their bloody aftermaths continue as a legacy of the Eisenhower administration's interest in covert warfare. See Stephen Kinzer, *The Brothers: John Foster Dulles, Allen Dulles, and Their Secret War* (New York, 2013), 119–174.
6. Stephen Kinzer, *All the Shah's Men* (New York, 2003), 124. As a former CIA officer put it, Mossadegh was a "nice fellow who made a mistake: he thought the oil under the soil was Iranian." Ray McGovern, former CIA officer in the video, "Speaking Frankly," *Cinema Libre Studio*, Vol. 3 (9 October 2007).
7. "The university students, who operate in spontaneous, well-disciplined cadres of ten, haven't had much sleep either." *TIME* magazine 5 August 1946. Students had played a similar role in the 1930 oligarchic coup against President Hernando Siles. Jerry Knudson, *Bolivia: Press and Revolution, 1932–1964* (Lanham, MD, 1986), 98.
8. United States Central Intelligence Agency, Donald N. Wilber, "Overthrow of Premier Mossadeq of Iran, November 1952–August 1953," *Clandestine Service Historical Paper 208*, March 1954 (nsarchive2.gwu.edu/NSAEBB/NSAEBB28).
9. As Max Paul Friedman notes, "The entire exercise predictably offended Latin American opinion, since it showed the Colossus of the North resolutely reverting to the old ways." Friedman, *Nazis and Good Neighbors*, 134.
10. *CIA Clandestine Service History, Plan TPAJAX*, Appendix A, 2.
11. Spaeth noted that to levy these sanctions would doubtless create blowback within Latin America because of the obvious unilateralism, inconsistent with the Good Neighbor image. Spaeth to Braden, 13 July 1946, NARA 824.00/7–1346.
12. Bonsal to Stettinius, 6 March 1944, NARA 824.01/750. See also the memorandum, Chargé d'Affairs McLaughlin to Secretary of State, 14 July 1944, NARA 824.00/1544.
13. Cole Blasier, "The United States, Germany, and the Bolivian Revolutionaries, 1941–1946," *Hispanic American Historical Review*, 52.1 (February 1972), 51; Glenn J. Dorn, *The Truman Administration and Bolivia* (University Park, PA, 2011), 45–46; Ernesto Galarza, "The Case of Bolivia," *Inter-American Reports*, 6 (May 1949), 27–29; and also the revealing "Attitude of Mining Interests Toward Present Bolivian Junta," Division of the American Republics, Department of State, 21 March 1944, NARA 824.01.
14. Andrade, *My Missions*, 114.
15. Ambassador Andrade observed, "Hochschild had another purpose . . . by forcing the government to lower taxes and devalue the currency. On this third front every weapon was employed, including psychological pressures and intimidations. For the tin barons, the contract negotiations were only one aspect of a comprehensive plan. They tried to use the negotiations to strike a blow at the Villarroel government." Andrade, *My Missions*, 115.
16. Ibid., 115–116.
17. *CIA Clandestine Service History, Plan TPAJAX*, A-2, 7.
18. "BOLIVIA: Professor Paz Takes Over," *TIME*, 27 December 1944, replays the Belmonte deception: "The professor's record was not reassuring. Once Minister of National Economy, he was arrested 20 July 1941, for implication in a German plot to Nazify Bolivia" (*TIME*, 28 July 1941). He has recently been in Argentina, where he could hardly help hearing about her anti-U.S. "Co-prosperity Sphere" (*TIME*, 20 November 1941); and again, "The MNR had a Nazi smell. Two years ago Dr. Paz Estenssoro was arrested when Peñaranda's government charged him and German Minister Ernst Wendler with plotting its overthrow." *TIME*, "Good Neighbor Trouble," 3 January 1944.
19. Hostility to the National Revolution also violated the precepts of the Atlantic Charter, signed by Churchill and Roosevelt in 1941, proclaiming Allied principles of self-determination, sovereignty, economic development, and social welfare. *TIME*,

"BOLIVIA: Good Neighbor Trouble," 3 January 1944, "BOLIVIA: Threatened Epidemic," 10 January 1944 and "PARAGUAY: Friend Lost," 3 April 1944, afford insight into adaptation of the Good Neighbor yardstick.
20. Laurence Whitehead, "Bolivia since 1930," in Leslie Bethell, ed., *The Cambridge History of Latin America*, Vol. 8 (Cambridge, 1991), 533. See also, Galarza, "The Case of Bolivia," 26–27.
21. *TIME*, "BOLIVIA: Counterattack," 17 January 1944.
22. Ibid.
23. Friedman, *Nazis and Good Neighbors*, 122.
24. Galarza, "The Case of Bolivia," 21. Ernesto Galarza's exhaustively documented indictment against the U.S. government, the Rosca, and the PIR in the overthrow of the Villarroel government finds: "The conclusion, which is substantially supported by the facts now known, is that the July revolt [overthrow] was not a revolution of workers, students and teachers. Rather it was the result of a complicated and obscure process in which Bolivia's tin barons—Carlos Víctor Aramayo, Simón Patiño, and Mauricio Hochschild; the extreme left-wing political party, the [Stalinist] PIR, and certain officials of the Department of State of the United States played important roles. Their object appears to have been the return of the government of Bolivia to the same forces that have exploited its people and resources for decades." Ibid., 5.
25. Spruille Braden was heir to his father's Chilean copper mines and five million acres in the Chaco sold to the Standard Oil Company in 1921. Braden later worked as an agent of Standard Oil in the Bolivian venture. See Margaret Marsh, *The Bankers in Bolivia* (New York, 1928), 57. As a shareholder and a paid lobbyist for the United Fruit Company, Braden was involved in the 1954 overthrow of the Guatemalan government following the attempted nationalization of the vast United Fruit plantations.
26. Espy to Flack, U.S. State Department Office Memorandum, 11 February 1946, NARA 824.00/2–1246. President Villarroel's reaction to the allegations was telegraphed from the U.S. Embassy in La Paz to the Secretary of State. "It has been learned unconfirmedly [sic] that Paz Estenssoro offered his resignation to the President as a result of the charges against him in the Blue Paper. The President is reported to have rejected resignation on grounds that the proof was inadequate and his presence in the Government was necessary to the welfare of the country." Adam to Secretary of State, 14 February 1946, NARA 824.00/2–1446.
27. Augusto Céspedes, *El Presidente Colgado* (Buenos Aires, 1966), 207.
28. Important is the conclusion of Galarza's exegesis of the Blue Book's disinformation: "Thus, the proof repeatedly offered by the American Government was never divulged. Nor could it be published without great risk to the prestige of the [State] Department. Any competent analysis of the text of the memorandum would have quickly revealed its flaws and inconsistencies. It turned out to be the better part of discretion, if not of diplomatic courage, to file and forget the devastating 'indictment'." Galarza, "The Case of Bolivia," 23.
29. Alberto Ostria Gutierrez, *Una revolución tras los Andes* (Santiago, Chile, 1944), 55.
30. "The devotion of our leaders and the media to this narrow set of victims," Herman and Chomsky find, "raises public self-esteem and patriotism, as it demonstrates the essential humanity of country and people." Edward Herman and Noam Chomsky, *Manufacturing Consent: The Political Economy of the Mass Media* (New York, 2002), liii.
31. "Americas to Protest Bolivian 'Terror'," *PM*, 31 December 1944, 6.
32. Armando Arce, *Los fusilamientos del 20 de Noviembre y el Movimiento Nacionalista Revolucionario* (La Paz, 1952). This detailed account by a founding member of the MNR and editor of *La Calle* affords an excellent critique of the propaganda assault preparatory to the overthrow of the National Revolution, an exhaustive defense of himself and his party against accusations of complicity in the "Shootings of the 20th of November," and an outline of the Rosca strategy for the overthrow (pp. 145–146). For examples of

Rosca propaganda, see F. Priegue Romero, *La Cruz de Bolivia: crónica de la revolución de julio* (La Paz, 1946); Alfredo Sanjines G, *El hombre de piedra y la revolución* (La Paz, 1946); and the photographic paean to the counterrevolution by Carlos Núñez de Arco B, *Relato gráfico de la Revolución de julio de 1946: el pueblo en armas* (La Paz, 1946).
33. Galarza, "The Case of Bolivia," 6–8, 24.
34. Ibid., 37–38, Andrade, *My Missions*, 17.
35. For copies and a translation of the alleged MNR bulletin, together with a note regarding Víctor Paz's denial of the veracity of the document, see Ambassador Flack to Secretary of State, 20 July 1946, NARA 824.00/7–2046.
36. *CIA Clandestine Service History, Plan TPAJAX*, Appendix A, 4–7; Appendix B, 12–16, 18, 22, 24.
37. The financial support of the FDA by the tin magnates is noted in a memorandum by John Edgar Hoover, Director, Federal Bureau of Investigation to Frederick B. Lyon, Chief, Division of Foreign Activity Correlation, Department of State, 14 February 1946, NARA 824.00/2–1346 and Ambassador Henderson to Secretary of State, 2 January 1944, NARA 824.00/1426; for the antipathy of the tin barons toward the RADEPA-MNR regime, see Ambassador Woodward's memorandum from regarding a conversation with Mauricio Hochschild: Woodward to Secretary of State, 20 April 1944, NA824.01/786.
38. Instructive is the 19 July 1946 memo: "Unrest in Bolivia," from John Edgar Hoover, Director, Federal Bureau of Information to Jack Neal, Chief, Division of Foreign Activity Correlation, Department of State, NARA 824.00/7–1946, regarding PIR control of the trade unions and university students as well as the possibility of a factional split within the MNR between members supportive of the strike and others loyal to the regime.
39. Ambassador Víctor Andrade referred to Arze as "the captain of the Chaco War deserters." Andrade, *My Missions*, 18. Arze was later targeted by zealous RADEPA officers in an assassination attempt. Wounded, he was airlifted to a New York hospital for treatment. *TIME* magazine, in an article on 21 February 1944, lauded Arze as "a favorite of the U.S. State Department" referring to him as a "leftist" rather than as a Stalinist. Rebuffed by the RADEPA-MNR provisional government Arze and Anaya joined the Rosca in unsparing opposition to the national revolution: Arze even "asked the United States to send troops to overthrow Villarroel," notes S. Sandor John in *Bolivia's Radical Tradition: Permanent Revolution in the Andes* (Tucson, AZ, 2012), 85 n.39 who neglects mention of the Stalinists' role in the FDA overthrow. Their cozy relationship with the U.S. Embassy is evidenced in State Department memoranda. See, for example, Ambassador Boal to Secretary of State, 2 January 1944, NARA 824.00/1427 (Sections One, Two, Three; telegram of 11 January 1944).
40. See the *La Cumbre* attachment in Hector C. Adam, Jr. to Secretary of State, 18 July 1946, NARA 824.00/7–1846. Extensive personal and organizational details of the PIR membership were provided by FBI Director John Edgar Hoover in a 34-page report forwarded to the State Department's Chief of the Division of Foreign Activity Correlation, the Chief of Naval Intelligence, and the Assistant Chief of Staff of the War Department: John Edgar Hoover to Frederick B. Lyon, 8 February 1946, NARA 824.00/2–846. (Note: the Federal Bureau of Intelligence and the Office of Strategic Services antedated the Central Intelligence Agency, founded in September 1947.)
41. Ambassador Flack to Secretary of State, 15 July 1946, NARA 824.00/7–1546.
42. In fact, the teachers were the beneficiaries of the regime's interest in education: their wages were double their pay during the Peñaranda government and ostensibly the highest in South America. Jeffrey Knudson, *Bolivia: Press and Revolution*, 98. The FDA conspirator Ormachea Zalles was, significantly, an "arbiter" of the teachers' strike. See Carlos Montenegro, *Culpables* (La Paz, 1955), 1–4, 17, 21–22.
43. Movimientista authors Carlos Montenegro and Augusto Céspedes claim the "dead student" in the casket was in actuality a cadaver from the La Paz mortuary, ceremoniously born in the cortege by FDA-led demonstrators—a deja vu of an earlier coup in 1930.

See Montenegro, *Culpables*, 8, 14–15; Céspedes, *El Presidente Colgado*, 222–223; Francisco Barrero, *Radepa y la Revolución Nacional* (La Paz, 1976). *La Razón* reported a government communiqué stating that police and carabineros had fired only tear gas when assaulted by the student mob on 10 July and would be confined to barracks during the cortege demonstration of 14 July. *La Razón*, 14 July 1946, 4.
44. Montenegro, *Culpables*, 4, 7–8, 17–18.
45. The Movimientista Luis Peñaloza claims the melee resulted from "a well hatched plan" to assassinate President Villarroel. Luis Peñaloza, *Historia del Movimiento Nacionalista Revolucionario, 1941–1952* (La Paz, 1963), 91; Montenegro, *Culpables*, 15–16, 19. The U.S. Embassy account of the demonstration differs: "Yesterday afternoon's demonstration was fired on by soldiers stationed in Plaza Murillo when they entered the Plaza. Government announced later that thirty-two men (presumably MNR) were under arrest in Hotel Paris (also in Plaza) for having fired into crowd and also wounding Pinto and Chief of Staff Barreiro [sic, Barrero] with the object of blaming government demonstrators composed chiefly of students apparently unarmed." Ambassador Flack to Secretary of State, 20 July 1946, NARA 824.00/7–2046.
46. Galarza, "The Case of Bolivia," 5.
47. *CIA Clandestine Service History, Plan TPAJAX*, Appendix A, 4–7; Appendix B, 21–22.
48. Memorandum for the Assistant Chief of Staff, G-2, 3 February 1944, NARA 824.01/709.
49. Adam to Secretary of State, 9 February 1946, NARA 824.00/2–946; Adam to Secretary of State, 19 February 1946, NA824.00/2–1946.
50. Flack to SECSTATE, 23 July 1946, NARA 824.00/2–1946.
51. The U.S. Embassy thwarted an assassination attempt on General Toro by RADEPA officers who planned to kill the general in his planned escape by train to Chile after a failed coup. Woodward to Secretary of State, 21 April 1944, NARA 824.01/702, Woodward to Secretary of State, 19 April 1944, NA 824.01/783–1/2.
52. The collaborators included PIR conspirators, FDA leaders Ormachea Zalles and Alfredo Mendizabal, Roberto Arce representing the Patiño interests, and Gastón Arduz representing the Aramayos. Céspedes, *El Presidente Colgado*, 223.
53. Ibid., 237. This summary of President Villarroel's final hours draws heavily from Céspedes' reconstruction of events, much of which appeared in "La Ultima Noche del Gobierno Villarroel," written by General Arenas and Lt. Colonels, Mercado, Ramallo, Rioja, and Major Montero, published in *El País*, 14 August 1946; see also Moises Alcazar, *Sangre en la Historia* (La Paz, 1956), 171–192, and René López Murillo, *Los restaurados* (La Paz, 1966), 36–39.
54. *CIA Clandestine Service History, Plan TPAJAX*, Appendix A, 11; Appendix D, 4.
55. The agreement was formally concluded following the counterrevolution, on 14 August 1946. Cole Blasier, *The Hovering Giant: U.S. Responses to Revolutionary Change in Latin America, 1910–1985* (Pittsburgh, PA, 1985), 51.
56. Flack to Braden, 22 July 1946, NARA 824.00/7–2246.
57. Byrnes to AMEMBASSY, 23 July 1946, NARA 824.00/7–2246.
58. Dorn, *The Truman Administration and Bolivia*, 52–53. See also Galarza, "The Case of Bolivia," 29–30.
59. *CIA Clandestine Service History, Plan TPAJAX*, Appendix A, 2.
60. Ambassador Flack telegrams to Department of State, 21 July 1946, NARA 824.00/7–2146 and 22 July 1946, NARA 824.00/7–2246. Flack referred to General Rodríguez as a "thoroughly devious character"' telegram, 21 July 1946, Department of State, NARA 824.00/7–2146. See also Peñaloza, *Historia*, 92; Montenegro, *Culpables*, 20, 22–24; Barrero, *Radepa*, 239–240.
61. The PIR obsession with hanging had the propaganda effect of identifying the victims with Italian fascism symbolized by the hanging of Benito Mussolini. In Bolivia, hanging was associated with Spanish colonial rule and infrequent after independence. Montenegro, *Culpables*, 25–27.
62. Klein, *Parties and Political Change in Bolivia*, 381–382.

63. Colonel Francisco Barrero notes the role of the suborned military and the use of a tank from the disloyal "Loa" regiment to breach the Palacio doors, allowing the opposition mob to storm the Palacio and murder Villarroel and his aides. Barrero, *Radepa*, 272.
64. In fact, General Rodríguez's radio address (an unusual venue for command) ordering the La Paz regiments to remain in their barracks signaled the desertion of the president's armed forces, leaving President Villarroel and his aides defenseless against the FDA mob.
65. José Antonio Arze, *Bolivia bajo el terrorismo nazifascista; un llamada a la ciudadanía boliviana y la consciencia democrática internaciónal, para reforzar la acción de la Unión Democrática Boliviana* (Lima, 1945). It is worth noting that Arze drew heavily on Spruille Braden's discredited "Blue Book" for much of his argument.
66. Laura Gotkowitz, *A Revolution for Our Rights: Indigenous Struggles for Land and Justice in Bolivia, 1880–1952* (Durham, 2007), 233. The present criticism notwithstanding, Gotkowitz's, prizewinning work is a significant contribution to Bolivian indigenous history.
67. Gotkowitz, *A Revolution for Our Rights*, 234.
68. While highlighting the resistance of street vendors and market women to the Villarroel administration in La Paz and Cochabamba, Gotkowitz downplays the tactical contribution to the counterrevolution by Señora Ormachea Solari and upper-class Paceña women.
69. See, for example, Robert M. Gildner, "Indomestizo Modernism: National Development and Indigenous Integration in Postrevolutionary Bolivia, 1952–1964," Ph.D. dissertation, University of Texas, Austin, 2012, 100; and Maria Carmen Soliz Urrutia, "Fields of Revolution: The Politics of Agrarian Reform in Bolivia, 1935–1971," Ph.D. dissertation, New York University, 2014, 116.
70. Alfonso Finot, *Así Cayó Villarroel y Defensa de mi Relato Así Cayó Villarroel* (La Paz, 1966), 69. Finot, a dedicated MNR militant, fell afoul of Víctor Paz Estenssoro because of his account of the telephone line incident that was later used by reactionaries to besmirch Paz's reputation in the 1951 presidential election. Paz Estenssoro replied to Finot's allegation in an extensive letter published in *En Marcha*, 10 April 1951, much of which is reprinted in Moises Alcazar, *Sangre en la Historia*, 182–185. The alleged incident and its repercussions are noted in Knudson, *Bolivia: Press and Revolution*, 135–137; Antezana, *Historia secreta del Movimiento Nacionalista Revolucionario*, Vol. 4 (La Paz 1986), 1052–1069; Barrero, *Radepa*, 263–265; Peñaloza, *Historia*, 92.
71. Barrero, *Radepa*, 269–270, 292–293. Villarroel's failure of leadership nearly cost Colonel Barrero his life when he escaped death through a hole breached in a bathroom wall of the besieged presidential palace—left defenseless per Villarroel's orders.
72. Colonel Barrero relates a defining moment for Villarroel and the revolution when, with hat and overcoat in hand, the president appeared ready to retreat from the palace under the escort of loyal air force pilots. But when Colonel Nogales questioned his departuere, Villarroel answered, "Nothing's happening, I will remain in the Palace until the end like every captain in his ship!" Barrero, *Radepa*, 270.
73. The 1946 Villarroel overthrow is overlooked, for example, in Chalmers Johnson, *Sorrows of Empire: Militarism, Secrecy, and the End of the Republic* (New York, 2004); Niall Ferguson, *Colossus* (New York, 2004); Stephen G. Rabe, *The Killing Zone: The United States Wages Cold War in Latin America* (New York, 2012); William Blum, *Killing Hope: US. Military and CIA Interventions Since World War II* (Monroe, Maine, 1995); although Blum focuses on post–World War II examples, he does include China 1945, Korea 1945–1953, the Philippines, 1940s–1950s, and the Soviet Union from 1940s to 1960s.
74. To be modern, notes Edward Shils, "means dynamic, concerned with the people, democratic, equalitarian, scientific, economically advanced, sovereign, and influential." Edward Shils, *Political Development in the New States* (Paris: Mouton, 1968), 7; see also Tony Judt, *Postwar* (New York, 2006), 793.
75. This felicitous phrase is taken from Glenn Dorn, *The Truman Administration and Bolivia: Making the World Safe for Liberal Constitutional Oligarchy*.

76. *Los Tiempos*, 10 January 1946, 7. Was President Villarroel unaware of the massacre until after its occurrence? For differing views on the Las Canchas Massacre, see Fausto Reinaga, *Tierra y Libertad: La Revolución Nacional y el Indio* (La Paz, 1953), 33–34; Augusto Céspedes, *El president colgado,* 193; Klein, *Parties and Political Change in Bolivia,* 380.
77. *Los Tiempos*, 10 January 1946, 3; 30 April 1946, 3.
78. "The Congress and the Indian Uprising," *El País*, 19 January 1945, 3.

4
THE SEXENIO

The return of the Rosca was brutal—President Villarroel lynched on a lamp post in the Plaza Murillo, his face stomped to a bloody pulp; Villarroel's secretary hanging from another lamp post, brains oozing from a smashed skull; the president's aide d'camp dangling nearby, intestines spilling from a bayonet gash in his belly. Other lynchings followed in the Rosca's campaign to extirpate RADEPA and MNR survivors. A few members of the regime fled in military aircraft piloted by RADEPA officers to a safe landing in exile. Others sought asylum in foreign embassies. Sixty officers were immediately arrested and 52 RADEPA officers, charged with violations of the military code, were purged by the FDA junta.[1] The Bolivian armed forces were again at the command of the Rosca. The U.S. Ambassador notified the Secretary of State: "A popular revolution in every sense of the word has just occurred in Bolivia. Every indication is that this may prove the first democratic revolution in Bolivian history. Immediate prospects are greatly improved relations with the United States."[2]

Deprived of its founders, the MNR now depended on lower echelon militants for its survival. Vital membership files (names, plans, memoranda) seized in a raid on the party headquarters in La Paz exposed Movimientistas and threatened the existence of the organization.[3] Those ensnared in the ensuing nationwide dragnet were imprisoned. Some succumbed to offers of amnesty, financial incentives, and official perquisites in exchange for the betrayal of party secrets. The loss of the party's documents underscored the need for greater security, resulting in a shift from the vertical structure of *Comandos Departmentales*, operating as an overt organization, into a covert web of compartmentalized cells composed of 10–15 militants and supporters.[4] Survival necessitated evolution of the organization, but problems in conveying information and planning actions within the broader cellular network frustrated MNR strategy and tactics during the Concordancia's six-year reign ("Sexenio").

Luis Peñaloza, a key figure in the MNR resistance, recalls life under the FDA: the "massive blacklists" denying employment to "MNR militants or anti-communist union leaders . . . houses raided without court order . . . deportation and imprisonment without explaining to anybody why . . . the personal enemy of an individual in the streets shouting 'That movimientista to the gallows'!"[5] Peñaloza assumed leadership of the "Emergency Committee" in La Paz to buttress the morale of beleaguered comrades. A memorial staged for the martyred Villarroel at the La Paz cemetery in mid-December 1946 attracted a large crowd and demonstrated that the party, while down, was not out. The Committee decided to participate in the national elections scheduled by the junta for 3 January 1947. Borrowing a propaganda technique from the FDA, they plastered the city with leaflets proclaiming "Glory to Villarroel" and listing MNR electoral candidates.[6] The public display of MNR symbols and slogans drew public attention necessary to revive the party's image.

The MNR participated in the 1947 national elections to demonstrate the party's resilience, although the victory of the FDA candidates was a foregone conclusion: Dr. Enrique Hertzog Garaizabal, a founding member of the Concordancia, won the 1947 FDA-sponsored election and Mamerto Urriolagotia, a powerful Chuquisaca hacendado, was elected vice president; the *Partido Unión Socialista Republicana* (PURS) candidate received 44,700 votes and Luis Fernando Guachalla, the Liberal Party candidate received 44,300 votes. The MNR's Víctor Paz Estenssoro garnered some 13,000 votes.

The composition of Hertzog's administration reveals the return of the Rosca via the Concordancia: Néstor Guillen and Monje Gutiérrez, oligarchs from the Liberal and Republican parties, served as acting presidents of the provisional junta; Luis Gosalvez Indaburu, a partner in the law firm employed by Mauricio Hochschild, appointed Minister of Economy and Treasury; Roberto Bilbao La Vieja, employed by the *Asociacion de Industriales Mineros* (a legal entity of the three tin magnates), appointed Minister of Government; Carlos Muñoz Roldan, manager of the Bolivian Power Company, chosen the Minister of Public Works; and Aurelio Alcoba, the PIR representative, selected as Minister of Labor. The head of the Supreme Court (an attorney employed by the tin barons) annulled the Constitution, suspended habeas corpus, reinterpreted labor legislation to the detriment of workers, and postponed retirement benefits until 1953. Movimientistas employed by the Villarroel government were threatened with seizure of their financial assets along with demands for reimbursement of their salaries.[7]

The Resurgence of the Old Order

President Hertzog adopted a carrot and stick strategy toward the indigenous peoples. Hertzog ordered prefects to make certain that hacendados obeyed laws favoring Indians and said rural inspectors would be sent to the countryside.[8] The apparent paradox of the president's order to enforce reformist decrees may well have been a ploy to mollify rebellious Indians in the backlands as the regime focused on repression of workers in urban factories and mining camps. Hertzog soon began imprisonment of rebellious colonos at work camps in the tropical lowlands. Under the velvet glove of his initial blandishments, there remained an iron fist.[9]

Repression in the mines, where Trotskyists were organizing a revolutionary vanguard among the workers, was draconian. A confrontation between mine workers and tin magnates followed the postwar resumption of foreign competition and reduction in demand for tin. Profits were to be wrung out of the mine workers by revoking the trade union reforms of the RADEPA-MNR regime.[10] President Hertzog artfully maneuvered the Stalinist PIR to do the government's bidding in the mining camps. The Stalinist strategy was both doctrainare and opportunistic. After the end of the Hitler–Stalin pact in 1941, the PIR followed the Moscow line and ceased opposition to the Allied Powers. With the onset of the Cold War, the party followed the Soviet policy of opposition to the United States. Rejected in an overture to join the nascent Villarroel government in 1943, the spurned PIRistas denounced the National Revolution and joined the FDA counterrevolution of 1946. A year later the party reversed its revolutionary role in the mines. In a gruesome reprise of the infamous 1942 Catavi Massacre, the PIR labor minister dispatched infantry troops to crush a strike at Catavi in 1947. Three hundred miners were slaughtered, ending the srike.[11] Hoisted on its own petard, the obvious contradiction between revolutionary rhetoric and authoritarian practice spelled the end of the discredited PIR.

Strange Bedfellows

The MNR continued to pursue electoral politics and developed an appreciation for the organizational strength and solidarity of the tin miners led by the charismatic Juan Lechín Oquendo (elected senator for the Department of Oruro, together with the PORista leader Guillermo Lora). The MNR and POR began an association during the Hertzog presidency (1947–1949) as the MNR sought to establish a political presence among the tin miners—a revolutionary force alien to the urban, middle-class creoles drawn to the MNR in its formative years.

The POR

The clash between Marxism and capitalism was formalized in the revolutionary *Tesis de Pulacayo*. Written by Guillermo Lora and presented at the Fourth Congress of the *Federación Sindical de Trabajadores Mineros de Bolivia* (FSTMB) meeting at Pulacayo (Potosí) in 1946, the Thesis embodied the Trotskyist theory of permanent revolution.[12] Lora's theoretical arguments regarding the role of the POR in the revolutionary vanguard of Bolivian workers might well have been disregarded as rhetorical hyperbole ("You cannot speak of democracy when 60 families dominate the

United States and when these 60 families suck the blood of semi-colonials, such as ourself.")[13] Nevertheless, the document's systematic prescriptions and detailed strategy for the dictatorship of the proletariat could not be ignored. The influence of the Thesis was monumental: a clarion call to revolution that would radicalize opposition to the Old Regime and ultimately contribute to its downfall by the most revolutionary workers in twentieth-century Latin America. "We are soldiers of the class struggle. We have said that the war against the exploiters is a war to the death."[14]

The POR blueprint for revolutionary change in the mines is spelled out in ten specific demands: (1) *Vital Basic Salary* ("that is to say, a salary that permits a family to live an existence that can be called human") with a *Sliding Scale* that would adjust for inflation; (2) *40 Hour Week*; (3) *Occupation of the Mines* ("posing the question who is the true owner of the mine: the capitalist or the workers"); (4) *Collective Contract* ("revocable at any time by the sole determination of the unions"); (5) *Union Independence* ("The FSTMB has absolute independence with relation to the bourgeois sectors, to the reformism of the left, and to the government . . . trade unionism is the syphilis of the worker's movement"); (6) *Workers Control of the Mines* ("effective control by workers of all aspects of the functioning of the mines"); (7) *Armaments for the Workers* ("If we wish to avoid repetition of the Catavi Massacre we must arm the workers . . . up to the teeth against the armed bourgeoisie." "Have we forgotten that we work daily with powerful explosives?" "Every strike is the potential beginning of a civil war and we ought to go to her properly armed"); (8) *Strike Fund* ("the strike has its worst enemy in the hunger that strikers suffer"); (9) *Regulation of the Pulpería* ("the system of the company store permits the improper enrichment of the patrón at the cost of the worker's salary"); (10) *Abolition of Contract Labor* ("We need to break this new capitalist maneuver that is used for purposes of plunder" and " set the single salary system for day labor").[15] The Thesis called for direct action of the masses through a tactical alliance with peasants, artisans, and the petty bourgeoisie sector (that would eventuate in collaboration with the MNR), as well as participation in electoral politics via a parliamentary "Miners Bloc."

The fiery rhetoric of the POR was put to the test at the Catavi-Siglo XX mines in August 1947 when the FSTMB initiated a strike after the dismissal of union leaders by Antenor Patiño. The mine workers, who had earlier demanded wages of 32 cents a day, lived in squalid huts without plumbing or sanitary facilities.[16] Patiño answered the strike with massive layoffs of workers and reduced the wages for miners rehired as *pirquineros* (contract laborers). The miners' only victory was in the realm of public opinion where Patiño's assault on the mine workers was labeled the "White Massacre," because the result was a loss of jobs and not of lives.

The MNR

The survival of the National Revolutionary Movement depended on strategic and tactical innovation, the resilience of its militants and supporters, and management of factionalism among the party elite. The Movimientistas were pursued mercilessly:

murdered, imprisoned, exiled, extorted, their houses seized, offices ransacked, and equipment stolen. Peñaloza notes, "The finances of the M.N.R. could not be worse. All the militants were without work. Nobody had economic resources."[17]

Command and control remained in the hands of the Comité Politico in La Paz. Regional commandos operated with the Comité Central in La Paz and with local partisans throughout the country. The relentless assault on party members led to the formation of an autonomous cell structure to withstand the capture of a member without compromising other cell members. It was crucial that captured cell members withstand torture without disclosing information about the cell to prevent its destruction.[18] Later additions to the party organization included the "special sectors, such as the *sector feminino* ("women's sector"), the *sector militar* ("military sector"), and the *sector obrero-artesano* ("worker-artisans sector").[19] The appearance of these specialized sectors indicates a broadened constituency in the evolution of the National Revolutionary Movement.

MNR strategy during the Sexenio was replete with failed conspiratorial alliances and attempted coups involving opportunistic politicians, military and carabinero officers, and fascists of the *Falange Socialista Boliviana* (Bolivian Socialist Falange: FSB). Luis Peñaloza, the executive secretary of the MNR Comité Politico, attributed these failures to insufficient resources of men and arms, overenthusiasm, and lack of discipline among militants who "never before and hardly ever after obeyed the orders of the Comité Politico."[20] The party's foray into alliances with urban laborers and factory workers (*fabriles*) concentrated in La Paz and railroad workers (*ferroviarios*) encamped around the major railway lines was a significant strategic development.[21]

Yet the 8,300 factory workers organized in La Paz's National Union of Factory Workers (USTFN) were wary of the middle-class Movimientistas. The USTFN's opposition to the Urriolagotia government's currency devaluation, together with repression of union activities, culminated in a general strike—repressed by a military assault on the working-class barrio of Villa Victoria—and the massacre and arrests of hundreds.[22] Numerous USTFN strikes backed by the MNR fared no better than their ill-conceived coup attempts because of difficulties coordinating actions between the bourgeois urban cells and the proletarian labor unions; moreover, the Movimientistas occasionally failed to support union protests against the regime.[23]

The MNR also faced internal conflict. A factional confrontation between Rafael Otazo and Víctor Paz Estenssoro over the direction and control of the party surfaced in 1947. In an open letter published in Patiño's *El Diario*, Otazo publicly argued that the party should take refuge and seek accommodation with the Rosca, exposing a rift in party strategy. To publicize internal conflict is to reveal weakness. Rafael Otazo, together with Alfonso Finot and Fausto Reinaga, were among the 23 members expelled from the party in the January 1948 National Convention.[24]

Meanwhile, the MNR leaders were at work building the mass base necessary for victory by armed struggle as they devised an imaginative variety of propaganda techniques to give the appearance of a much larger entity and enhance its opposition to the Rosca.[25] A hunger strike by MNR prisoners at Coati forced the government to lift a state of siege and reinstitute the right of habeas corpus. Taking a cue from the FDA, Movimientistas utilized black propaganda in response to an embryonic "Agrarian Party" organized to reinforce hacendado domination of the backlands. The ploy involved the fabrication of fake leaflets signed by the "Agrarian Party" replete with the slogans, "Kill an Indian, Kill a Cholo."[26] The agrarian party was stillborn.

The Crisis of the Hacienda

Organized resistance to the dominion of the hacienda by *cabecillas* ("ringleaders") such as Chipana Ramos, Hilarión Grájeda, and the Carrascos was fraught with difficulty. The dehumanization and demoralization of colonos, reinforced with violence exercised by the master and his minions, perpetuated the seigneurial system. The mission of indigenous revolutionaries was to cajole peasants from accommodation to resistance: to insist, for example, on enforcement of Villarroel's decrees ending the practice of pongueaje and mitanaje. The social landscape within the hacienda was a maze of differential relationships among the colonos: *originarios* who originally held land within the ayllu and continued to work the parcel after the ayllu was subsumed by a hacienda; landless *utawawas* who worked for *originario* families; day laborers (*jornaleros*); renters (*arrenderos*); *arrimantes* who worked for *arrenderos*; and squatters subsisting on the margins of the estate. Each relationship was influenced by status within the hacienda ayllus supervised by *jilakatas*, *mayordomos*, the *patrón*, and his administrator.

The indigenous struggle for land and liberty invited confrontations with hacienda administrators, including the mayordomo and *jilakata* representing the subsumed ayllu community. Sit-down strikes (often referred to as "uprisings" in newspapers) at haciendas in the province of Capinota (Cochabamba Department) in January 1946 were attributed to the "abuses by some patrones with the collaboration of their favorites that hold the posts of Hilicatas." This editorial also noted, "the ringleaders occupied the post of mayordomos in substitution of those that the patrones had appointed."[27] The replacement of hacienda mayordomos and subservient jilakatas by colono "ringleaders" indicates the appearance of dual power: the rejection of the illegitimate authority of the Old Order and its replacement by indigenous representatives.[28] Resistance to the colonato, fueled by the National Indigenous Congress, together with President Villarroel's decrees and martyrdom—exacerbated by the revolutionary exhortations of anarchists, communists, nationalists, and indigenous revindicationists, millenarians, and messianic prophets—contributed to a crisis of the hacienda. Few, if any, knew this was the twilight of the Old Order. Many would sacrifice their lives to assure that it was.

118 The Sexenio

FIGURE 4.1 Antonio Mamani Álvarez (second from left) Holding Photo of Martyred President Villarroel

Source: Courtesy of Antonio Mamani Álvarez.

The Great Rebellion

The Rosca counterrevolution was won in the cities; La Paz, Oruro, Cochabamba, Potosí, Santa Cruz, and Sucre easily fell to the FDA insurgents. Movimientistas suffered severe repression in the major cities as they struggled to regroup and resist the Rosca onslaught. The isolated mining encampments, seething with revolutionary ferment, were kept under heel by government troops. Yet the cities and mines accounted for only a fraction of the population, a few hundred thousand souls in a nation of 3.5 million. The agrarian countryside of hacienda colonos, ayllu comunarios, small farmers, and cholo and mestizo townspeople comprised the remaining majority of the population. Here the penultimate chapter in the 400-year rule of the colonato would be scripted during the tumultuous Sexenio.

The Rosca-Concordancia faced widespread agrarian unrest in 1947, as a storm of revolts swept an area of 160,000–200,000 square kilometers in the highlands of Cochabamba, La Paz, Oruro, Chuquisaca, and Potosí. This "Great Rebellion" would continue for nearly a year; sporadic peripheral revolts continued for four years. President Hertzog mobilized the full panoply of resources at his disposal in confronting the indigenous threat. The Rosca regime relied on the support of the Concordancia and Señora Teresa Ormachea's ladies of the Unión Civica Femenina to stage anti-Indian demonstrations in La Paz, the Rural Society's "Rural Guards" to enforce the colonato, and the PIR to assist in repression of rebellious miners. To this Hertzog utilized carabineros, infantry detachments, a motorized 300-man rural police force, a cavalry detachment, civilian militias, rural vigilantes, and aerial bombing to terrorize the countryside. Hertzog ordered the massive imprisonment of "agitators" and the forced "rehabilitation" of hundreds of rebellious leaders and their families in distant concentration camps.[29]

The president displayed imaginative statecraft in a variety of schemes—trumpeting the creation of "agricultural cooperatives" (viz., concentration camps), manipulation of Villarroel's decrees regarding rural labor relations, the proposed introduction of agrarian statutes to redefine landlord–colono relations, and promotion of paid agricultural labor—abetted by the power of the Rosca propaganda apparatus. The hacendados also redoubled efforts to retain cultural domination of the colonos through the safety net of reciprocal patrón–client relations and continuation of pongueaje and mitinaje, together with a host of other personal obligations to perpetuate the submission of colono to patrón.

La Paz Department

President Hertzog referenced the "Great Rebellion" as "one of the most grave rebellions in our history" in his 1947 address to congress: "As is general knowledge, in the course of the past months and through the work of agitation of some extreme elements, that obeying foreign instructions intended to take advantage of the chaos, produced some uprisings among the peasantry of the Altiplano and the valleys of Cochabamba. There were seen . . . cases in which the subterranean work culminated with acts of violence that caused not only just alarm, but the outrage of the citizenry."[30] True to form Hertzog ignored the socioeconomic roots of rebellion, instead he portrayed Indians as ignorant pawns manipulated by shadowy extremists, intent on creating chaos in the countryside. He omitted mention of his ruthless war against Indians in which he deployed the army, air force, carabineros, local police, a rural guard, and regional vigilantes: nor did he address the mass imprisonment of indigenous leaders in jungle prisons, or the forced detentions of community members and their families in tropical concentration camps, euphemistically referred to as "colonies."

Underlying the challenge to the Altiplano hacendados of La Paz Department were two factors: demographics, and a Trojan Horse. Urban migration threatened the racial dominion of creole-mestizos in the segregated city. Indians and cholos were banned from street cars, restaurants, and theaters in La Paz. A national law enacted in 1925 excluded Indians from entering city plazas, and the La Paz municipal government prohibited passengers carrying bags from riding in streetcars (i.e., Indians). Informal dress codes discriminated against Indians wearing traditional homespun pants, poncho, and *lluch'u* (wool hat with earflaps), and segregated barrios divided Indians and cholos from creole-mestizo neighborhoods.[31]

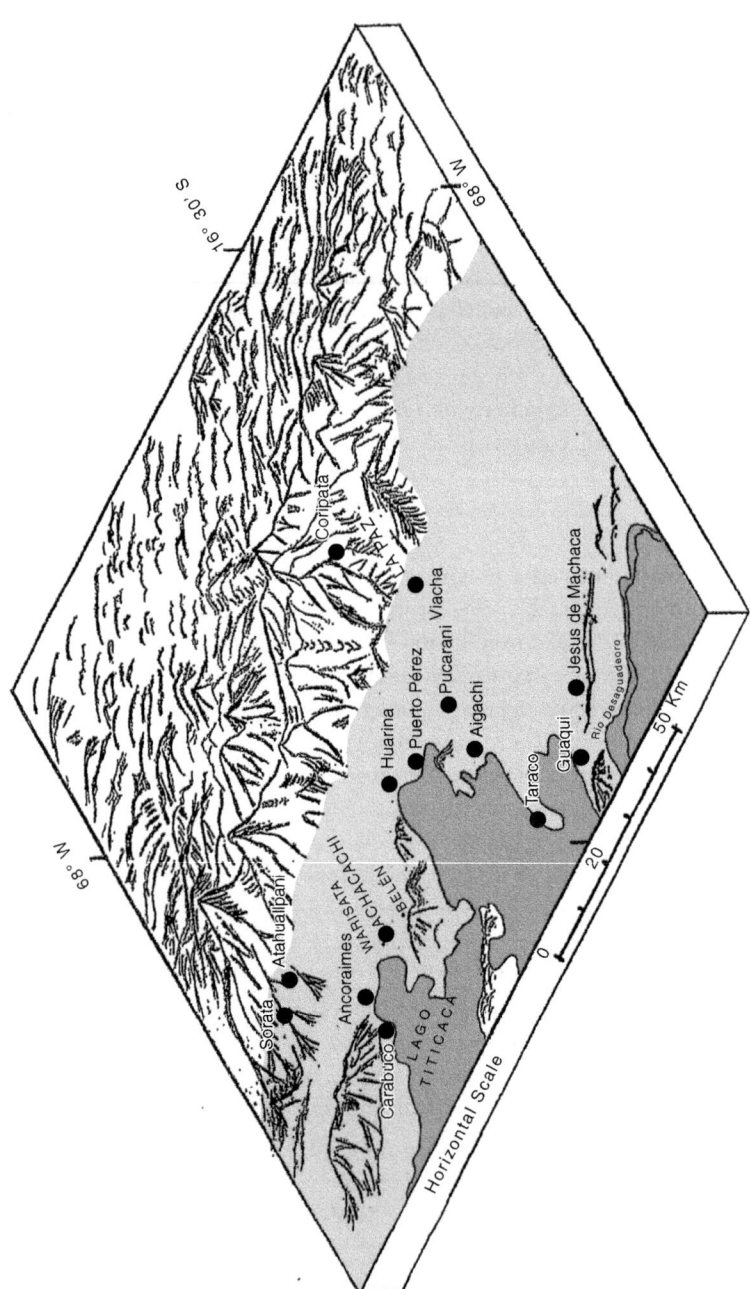

MAP 4.1 La Paz Department; light-gray shaded area is the altiplano

Source: Instituto Geografio Militar, 1973, edited by Ken Franklin and James Kohl.

Organized resistance to discrimination and segregation had come to the fore in the 1920s when Santos Marka T'ula, appointed Secretary of Peasant Affairs in the Oruro Workers Federation (*Federación Obrera de Oruro*), collaborated with the anarchists of the Local Workers Federation (*Federación Obrera Local*: FOL) founded in La Paz in 1926 by the Indian activist Luis Cusicanqui. The subaltern city dwellers, despised by the creole-mestizo elite, now found a political voice of unprecedented potential; inclusion of Indian migrants in the FOL bolstered the strength of the union and fostered unity among the working class.[32] The population of La Paz had doubled following the Chaco War. Rural migrants seeking a better life in the city swelled the shanty-towns in the surrounding heights with butchers and tanners, construction, railroad, factory and print shop workers, artisans, tailors, shoemakers, market women, maids, gardeners, day laborers, street vendors, and produce peddlers.[33] The indigenous invasion of the city increased after the White Massacre layoffs at the Patiño mines in 1947, reviving the eternal creole-mestizo dread of the *indiada*: the Indian masses overwhelming the city.

In May 1946, the FOL embarked on extension of the union's reach into the countryside. Marcelino Llanque, a leader in the 1921 Jesus de Machaca rebellion, was selected "to bring the delegation of the FOL to all of the country" and in August FOL militants left La Paz to reconnoiter the Altiplano for likely sindicato sites.[34] Within two months, union organization was under way in Guaqui, Topohoco, and Q'achuma. By year's end, a newly created Departmental Agrarian Federation (*Federación Agraria Departamental*: FAD) had taken root in the cantons of Laja and Cucuta (Los Andes Province), Guaqui (Ingavi Province), Caquiaviri (Pacajes Province), and Araca (Loayza Province). A solidarity pact between the FOL and FAD signed on 22 December 1946 by 20 indigenous representatives, including Marcelino Quispe Yucra (Secretary General of the FAD) and Esteban Quispe Yucra (Maximum Leader of the Sindicato of Aygachi), announced the anarcho-syndicalist mission. "The components of the FAD are in accordance with the norms of Libertarian syndicalism, taken as a means of struggle for the immediate conquest of their revindications and social transformation. Thus, the FAD declares itself anti-political and anti-capitalist and consequently outside all intervention in politics and parties."[35]

The union demanded compliance with "laws decreed in our favor" (e.g., prohibition of pongueaje), an end to hacienfa evictions of colonos and destruction of their homes, creation of schools on haciendas funded by the patrón and the state, and called for a national peasant congress. To foster unity with the urban workers of the FOL—and erase the division between rural and urban Indians—the FAD referred to colonos as workers and addressed the humiliation of racial discrimination encountered in cities where "everyone has the right to offend us: the chola, the *misti* [creole-mestizo], the gendarme, the rich and even the Indians who have been poisoned by capitalist morals."[36] FOL-FAD labor unions in the Department of La Paz challenged the domination of a people divided between city and countryside, Indian and cholo, Aymara and Quechua, hacienda and ayllu and may well have posed "the gravest threat in the nation's history," in the words of President Enrique Hertzog.

Anarchism found a receptive audience in the densely populated Altiplano surrounding the shores of Lake Titicaca. Hacienda expansion (the seizure of ayllu land and resultant transformation of comunarios into colonos) was comparatively recent, spurred by the railway construction of 1905–1917, connecting the Altiplano with the port of Arica, improving access from Guaqui on the shore of Lake Titicaca to the railhead at Viacha, and the urban and mining markets of La Paz and Oruro. The memory of the dispossessed comunarios remained painful, affording fertile ground for anarcho-syndicalist organizers. In December 1946, colonos at Hacienda Quilluma had declared a sit-down strike in response to the patrón's refusal to repay a loan owed them. The patrón requested government intervention. Equating unionization with rebellion, the authorities violently repressed the strike and arrested 20 leaders, including the FAD Secretary General Marcelino Quispe.[37]

Incidents involving thousands of sindicato members erupted in the first weeks of 1947 at Puerto Pérez, Aygachi, Pucarani, and Carapata (Los Andes Province). Four thousand Indians met at Hacienda Carapata to elect representatives of the *Sindicato de Labradores* (Farmworkers' Union) and present demands to the government that included schools, prohibition of personal service, and official recognition of the union. A thousand Indians wielding guns, clubs, slings, and stones invaded Puerto Pérez, intimidating townspeople. Indians shouting "Down with Pongueaje" and "Viva Syndicalization" surrounded the town of Pucarani in mid-January 1947.[38] A government commission accompanied by a troop of carabineros arrested 20 dirigentes and seized evidence of sindicato activity, including a document dated 11 February 1946 founding the *Unión Sindical de Labriegos del Cantón Aygachi* (Syndical Union [sic] of Farmworkers of Cantón Aygachi) written "in defective Spanish" by "Members of the Syndical Council of the Province [sic] of Pucarani." Printed in Oruro, the leaflet allegedly incited the peasants to organize themselves into sindicatos in order to get schools and guarantee social conquests.[39] FAD sindicatos were founded in Pujsani, Huarina, Pucarani, Viacha, Coripata, and Desaguadero, and the FOL was also busy recruiting rural schoolteachers to instruct the children of union members.[40] Union organizers ("ringleaders") who were arrested and interrogated by the government voiced their objectives: creation of a school for their children, protection against abusive landlords, official recognition of the unions as a legal entity (*personera juridical*). Other FAD demands included abolition of pongueaje (i.e., enforcement of President Villarroel's Supreme Decrees of 1945), prevention of eviction from haciendas of colonos accused of union activities, the inalienability of the domicile, and abolition of compulsory military service and forced labor (*prestación vial*).[41]

The astonishing growth of the FAD among the Altiplano peasantry attested to the popularity of the anarchist message: direct action by workers (e.g., work stoppages) to demonstrate solidarity; abolition of the wage system and private ownership of the means of production (hacienda, mine, factory), replaced by agricultural and industrial cooperatives under workers control (no landlords, no bosses) and organized in decentralized horizontal federations; the end of class divisions and titles (Don, Señor, Jefe, Patrón, Tata, replaced by comrade); solidarity and mutual aid instead of individualist competition ("From each according to his ability, to each according to his needs").[42] Listening to the FAD activists, one could appreciate the congruence of anarchism with native society and conjure the return of a lost world of ayllus and markas, cooperative labor (*mink'a*) and mutual aid (*ayni*), the exchange of goods and services dictated by reciprocity and not money, communities governed by jilaqatas, alcaldes, and kurakas selected from within the ayllu kindred—all without creole-mestizo overlords.

The FAD thrust to unionize the La Paz peasantry quickly spread beyond the lacustrine provinces of Los Andes, Ingavi, Pacajes, Omasuyos, and Camacho; east to Larecaja, south and southeast to Aroma and Loayza; and to the tropical Yungas on the eastern slope of the Cordillera Real. In April 1947, union "agitation" was reported in the vicinity of Coripata (Yungas Province) where landowners complained to the prefect of sit-down strikes and work slowdowns on their estates. The colonos believed that unionization would result in "no more owners or administrators" and the rule "of the Indian for the Indian."[43] Anarcho-syndicalist agitation exacerbated the existing tensions in the countryside: boundary conflicts between ayllu communities, conflicts between ayllu comunarios and hacienda colonos (previously living as comunarios); encroachment of haciendas on ayllu lands; competition for land and water between colonos on contiguous haciendas and between haciendas and ayllus. Demands that the anarchist unions be officially recognized and accorded the legal rights and protection of the nation's courts were a threat to the ancien régime.

On 12 January 1947, the Sociedad Rural alerted readers of *La Razón* to the dangers of the "gestation of an indigenous rebellion" on the Altiplano, foreshadowing a "revolutionary movement in La Paz . . . incinerating the casas de hacienda and their owners" and endangering food supplies to the city.[44] A week later, the corregidor of Cantón Porvenir (Ingavi Province) notified the prefect of La Paz Department that colonos were refusing to work or assume the "obligation of mulero" transporting hacienda goods and warned "for strength they have resorted to the miners' unions." By month's end, the "existence of danger in the altiplano region" and "threats of indigenous uprisings" had become a topic of discussion between the prefect and the General Director of the police.[45] Meanwhile, the vecinos of Guaqui and Jesus de Machaca (Ingavi Province) requested "guarantees . . . because of the threat of revolt" and the police intendant at Guaqui was ordered "to take determined means to guard the public order and the right of property."[46] Private property was, of course, construed to include colonos.

The Altiplano was rife with unrest. Colonos from the haciendas Qhuniri, Mullujawa, Punkini, and Qullawa sacked the hacienda Qina Amaya.[47] Comunarios from the ayllu Jilawi in Pacajes Province invaded the Hacienda Chocorosi, destroying planted fields and stored seeds. Comunarios from Batallas and Seguenca in Los Andes Province sought "guarantees" against the ingression of FOL "emissaries and leaflets."[48] Rebellious colonos murdered the administrator and school teacher at the hacienda Anta near Cantón Caquiaviri (Pacajes Province). The teacher's unpopularity with the colonos proved to be deadly as were the administrator's designs on the land of the neighboring comunarios who participated in the uprising.[49] Complicating events surrounding the violence at Anta was the offer of comunarios from the adjacent Comanche and Caquiaviri communities (wary of the influence of militant colonos on contiguous property boundaries) to assist police efforts to suppress the FAD unionization of the Anta colonos. Caquiaviri vecinos attributed the sensational murders at Anta to FOL and FAD anarcho-syndicalist activists.[50] Army regiments occupied restive areas in La Paz Department. All but the most determined landlords fled Ingavi Province to the safety of La Paz.

In a matter of weeks, 23 colonos accused of FOL affiliation were arrested together with the cabecillas from Hacienda Anta and comunarios from Caquiaviri and Comanche.[51] Police raided the FOL office in La Paz and confiscated "subversive" materials, including anarchist leaflets and pamphlets. The Chief of Police accused the anarchists of collecting ramas (money) from peasants for use in "inciting rebellion" at Caquiaviri, Topohoco, and Caquiaviri Chico. An official commission found evidence allegedly linking a dirigente from the Corocoro mine to the uprising, together with anarchist documents revealing the role of rural teachers as "agitators of the rebellion," and stating the rebels' objectives: abolition of obligatory military service; abolition of prestación vial; termination of the parceling of rural lands; and creation of rural schools. The FOL-FAD answered the regime's repression with the announcement of a forthcoming general strike to free their 70 jailed unionists. President Hertzog subsequently released 40 of the 70 leaders to avert the strike, thus sidestepping a total capitulation to the FOL.[52]

The day after the assault on Hacienda Anta, comunarios attacked the Arica-La Paz train.[53] Far from a random act of violence, the train incident stemmed from the frustration of ayllu communities negatively affected by railway construction. The railways connected the Altiplano with cities and mines and stimulated trade and the growth of haciendas and towns, facilitating commerce and enriching creole-mestizo hacendados and vecinos. These developments were disastrous for the indigenous ayllu communities whose once lucrative trade in charcoal, wool, meat, and vegetables to mines and cities, as well as commerce borne by llama caravans from the Pacific, were supplanted by the railroad companies, merchants, and hacendados.[54] Ayllu communities in La Paz Department, in addition to the invasion of predatory hacendados, now suffered the consequences of the evolving regional transportation and market systems.

In June, sit-down strikes were reported in the vicinity of Puerto Pérez (Los Andes Province) and Achacachi (Omasuyos Province) in addition to "threats of an Indian uprising" in Ancoraimes (Omasuyos Province) and a "certain inquietude" in the region of Carabuco (Camacho Province).[55] An outbreak of shocking violence then occurred at the Hacienda Tacanoca in Los Andes Province: the sensational news of the murder of a patrón and his niece by colonos. The La Paz newspapers feasted on the gruesome details of the torture and execution of the hacendado and his niece (a white woman), abused and hanged by Indians.[56] Mortified by this breach of taboo, creole-mestizo readers were oblivious to the underlying feud between the Tacanoca and Carapata (Q'arapata) hacendados over contiguous land. Allegedly the landlord of Carapata orchestrated the attack by hacienda colonos to facilitate a land grab. Disputes between landlords over adjoining lands were common occurrences in the countryside, and colonos, often used as proxies in these conflicts, were involved in the unrest at Puerto Acosta, identified by the Hertzog regime as a focus of Altiplano agitation.[57]

Violent confrontations over land (as in the preceding instance) and land boundaries between ayllus have occurred in the Andes for a millennium. The latter nineteenth century implementation of liberal laws (*leyes de ex-vinculación*) to privatize land and the arrival of Altiplano railways exacerbated conflicts between ayllu and hacienda. By the 1940s, the peasant awakening increasingly pitted Indians against creole-mestizo hacendados. During the first half of 1947, the oligarchs in the Hertzog regime were particularly concerned with the rise of anarcho syndicalism amid millions of subaltern Indians in the countryside. The implication of FOL-FAD anarch-syndicalist organizers in the violence at Hacienda Tacanoca was alarming to the regime: on 26 May the subprefect of Los Andes Province notified the prefect of La Paz Department that "virtually the entire *indiada*" appeared subversive.[58]

The Tacanoca rebels were quickly apprehended and delivered to La Paz for interrogation. Esteban Quispe Yucra, known as "The General," denied that the rebellion was premeditated, but instead resulted from demands for a union and a school on the hacienda.[59] A rebel witness claimed that the General had shoved the barrel of a gun into the dying landlord's mouth and shouted, "Why haven't you allowed your colonos to belong to a union?" Others said that Quispe Yucra had imparted orders from the FOL to attack the haciendas of Carapata, Cachilaya, Cutusuma, Pantuni, Esquivel, Chojasuni, and Cuyawani. He stated that FOL leaders Simon Zurita and Modesto Escobar from La Paz arrived to direct the planning of the hacienda attack, and that Marcelino Quispe Yucra, Secretary General of the FAD, initiated the abuse of the hacendado's niece.[60] *La Razón* claimed that Zurita and Escobar traveled to the region in April visiting the Talatani, Sunimoro, Aynocollo, Ejra, and Aypa haciendas and the ayllu community of Pujsani to promote hacienda attacks and land distribution.[61]

Meanwhile, on the day of the burial of the slain landlord and his niece, the local police station holding leaders of the insurgent peasant union was attacked. None of this escaped the attention of President Hertzog and the nation's elites. Three thousand Indians marched under the anarchist black and red flag in the FOL-FAD May Day parade in 1947, a reminder to the creole-mestizo inhabitants of the latent power of the native population.[62] The La Paz representative of the Rural Society warned that if the government failed to effectively guarantee the life and property of the landowners, given the "low and repulsive bestial instincts of the aborigine . . . leniency toward the rebels would only provoke greater evils." In Cochabamba, a spokesman for the Society called on the government to banish the "agitators" to agricultural work colonies, noting the precedent for the colonies in the 1945 Villarroel Decrees.⁶³ In fact, Hertzog's "colonies" were concentration camps for unruly Indians.

The señoras of the *Unión Cívica Femenina*, whose previous demonstrations were instrumental to the Rosca counterrevolution, mobilized a march of 10,000 to the doors of the *Panóptico Nacional* (National Penitentiary in La Paz) demanding the death of the colonos accused of the Tacanoca rebellion. Under the pretext of mourning the two Tacanoca hacienda victims, the Minister of Government called for an "energetic hand" to end the uprisings and demonstrators called for revenge against the prisoners in the Panóptico.⁶⁴ The oligarchic media focused on the death of a handful of hacendados and ignored the conditions that gave rise to the violence: the 100-fold deaths of Indian men, women, and children victimized by the regime's murderous repression and the fate of another 1,000 imprisoned in the tropical gulags. In the wake of intensified government repression, a manifesto released by the FOL asked: "Why, for example, have the press and the radios of this city not reported the death by clubs near 'Pujsani' of the seven relatives of Marcelino Quispe, Secretary General of the FAD? Why have they not reported the violation of thirty-one Indian girls . . . by thirty soldiers and a priest?"⁶⁵ The FAD answer to these rhetorical questions addressed the creole-mestizo dehumanization of the subaltern Indians:

> Unfortunately nobody understands us, nobody knows our language, because according to them we are children of the devil. . . . That is why the urban populace sees the burning flames of our rebellion and the sound of our *pututus* [bullhorn trumpets] announcing the vengeance of justice, cry out for help to the authorities and the cities tremble in fear. . . . Because the Indian is fierce, savage and a cannibal whose only desire is to assault, kill and destroy everything they encounter in their path, however in order to defend themselves the *mistis* [mestizos] tightly shut their doors, arm themselves to the teeth, the airplanes undertake their reconnaissance flight and the regiments are put in march to drown in blood the righteous rebellion, killing us . . . razing our fields, forcing us to live in dens, persecuted and imprisoned without a single word heard in our defense: they all condemn us, they all whisper, that the *indio* [pejorative: Indian] must be exterminated, that the *indio* is the disgrace of aristocratic Bolivia.⁶⁶

Cochabamba Department

In the serranía of Cochabamba's Ayopaya Province, colonos received word of President Villarroel's decrees as a blessing. But at the remote Hacienda Yayani, the patrón imposed extra duties on the colonos, toiling under the tyranny of intense labor and servitude exactions, enforced by a brutish administrator and compliant jilakatas. The hacienda administrator taunted the colonos mourning the death of their president, "the thief, just like you, has died . . . that man was condemned by his chicanery"; to which the colonos said, "among ourselves . . . if our father has

Cochabamba Valleys

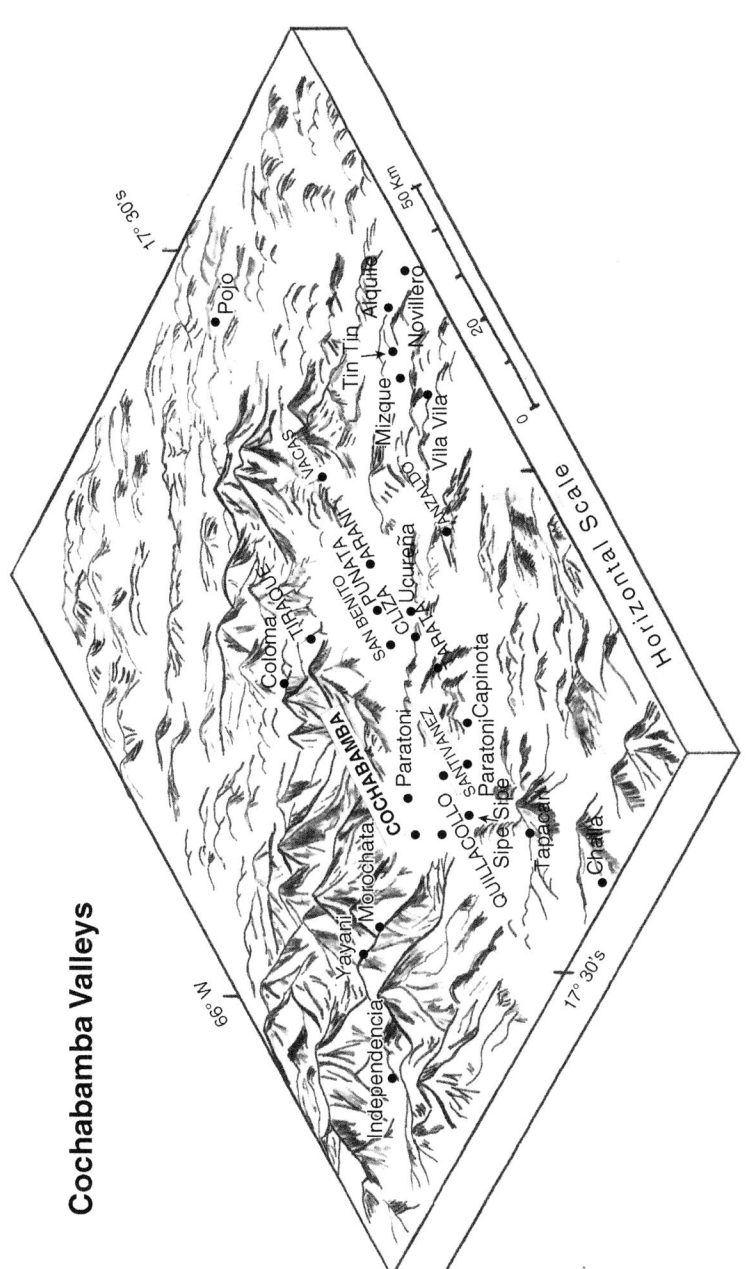

MAP 4.2   Cochabamba Valleys

Source: Instituto Geografio Militar, 1973, edited by Ken Franklin and James Kohl.

died, we too will die; either they will be finished, or we will."⁶⁷ Resistance to the patrón had been ongoing for years, spearheaded by the alcalde Hilarión Grájeda, the brothers Julio and Nicolas Carrasco, together with other delegates to the 1945 National Indigenous Congress. Grájeda had been banished from the hacienda in 1927, but he returned to continue resistance against injustices. A complaint lodged with the Ministry of Labor and Social Welfare in 1942 listed a multitude of grievances including rape, whippings, imposition of "onerous obligations," arbitrary evictions, and changes to usufruct plots. An adroit maneuver by Grájeda resulted in dismissal of the presiding judge (who had assaulted a colono). "All this helps us see that the official responsible for protecting us . . . is instead an instrument of the landlord, who does not just rule against the colonos but actually mistreats them and commits unspeakable abuses."⁶⁸

Driven from the hacienda after the counterrevolution, Grájeda and the Carrascos continued their resistance. Contacts were made with miner and peasant militants outside Ayopaya. A letter sent to Grájeda from Antonio Mamani Álvarez on 13 January 1947 offered his cooperation in organizing resistance, listing the equipment and funds necessary to set up an office and fund a secretary: "I have come here [Vinto, Quillacollo Province] to reach an agreement with all the delegates, and in case you want to continue with this, we need a central office in Cochabamba for everyone."⁶⁹ Weeks later Ayopaya was aflame in rebellion.

Far from a spontaneous flare-up by irate colonos provoked beyond forbearance, the Yayani rebellion was carefully planned. The Yayani conspirators met clandestinely in the dark of night, at a cave high in the serranía, to plot the hacienda assault and to plan a wider rebellion. On the night of 3 February 1947, the key conspirators—Grájeda, a miner Gabriel Muñoz, his wife Lorenza Choque, and a number of trusted colonos gathered at the cave. A participant interviewed by anthropologists Jorge Danhart and Juan Torrico recalled that fateful night:

> Grájeda arrived along with the miner Gabriel Muñoz and a woman [Lorenza Choque—Ed]. . . . [S]he read some pamphlets that night. . . . [W]e leaders had a meeting with them and with other campesinos of the hacienda. . . . [T]here was also a man who was a soothsayer [advino] there and he read the coca. . . . [H]e told us that all would go well. . . . [T]he woman said that if we didn't fight now and get rid of the patrones, we would all die, and our families would lose their lands and die of hunger. . . . [S]he told us the moment had come to defend the president. . . . [A]s we swore before the Congress at La Paz, Villarroel said that he was prepared to die for us, and now we are ready to die for him. . . . [W]e all loved Villarroel like a father.⁷⁰

After the assault on Yayani, in order to avoid identification, the colonos decided to attack haciendas other than their own. They planned to assault haciendas in a widening swath, moving outward and upward in the Ayopaya serranía, and then onward toward Oruro to spark a wider conflagration near the mining centers. Antonio Ramos, a dirigente from hacienda Parte Libre near Yayani, traveled to

Oruro to confer with miners and obtain dynamite, rifles, and pistols for continuation of the rebellion on the Altiplano.[71]

The following night colonos from the four *suyos* (sections) of the hacienda ayllu assembled for the assault on the big house. The miner Muñoz hurled sticks of dynamite as the rebels, primarily wielding farm implements, stormed the residence. In the ensuing melee, a house guest was beaten to death. The patrón's son escaped together with the hacienda administrators. The rebels ransacked the house and seized guns, tools, and foodstuffs before joining rebellious colonos for an attack on a hacienda house at nearby Lachiraya.[72] The rapidity of the insurgency together with the combined action of colonos from different haciendas, united in a common force, evidences concerted planning. On the following day, the haciendas Parte Libre, Punachi, and Quirquiri in the environs of Yayani, were sacked. The haciendas Moyapampa and Llajama were assaulted and in an act of grisly vengeance, the colonos murdered the patrón, Dr. José Maria Coca, and mutilated his body. The doctor's caretaker was also killed and the house looted and burned together with the patrón's property title, documents, legal papers, and law books. "With this symbolic act of violence," as Laura Gotkowitz notes, "they destroyed the legal trappings of the landlord's domain."[73]

The rebellion spilled over into the adjacent mountains of Tapacarí Province where colonos at Hacienda Charapaya, near the cantón of Calchani, sacked the hacienda house. Towns were overrun and the offices of corregidores and chicha tax collectors looted in retribution for personal property appropriated for nonpayment of dubious taxes.[74] This was the high-water mark for the Cochabamba rebellion. As the Yayani rebels began to disband, a contingent led by Grájeda and Muñoz pushed on into Oruro Department where they had hoped to spark a wider rebellion. The rebels armed with farm pitchforks, shovels, clubs, a few sticks of Muñoz's dynamite, and some firearms taken from the haciendas were captured at Ch'alla, near the intersection of the Oruro–Cochabamba highway.[75]

President Hertzog responded to the rebellion with overwhelming force. In addition to local and regional police and carabineros, army detachments from Cochabamba and Oruro were mobilized, supported by warplanes to surveil and hound the rebels as they retreated into the mountain fastness. Within a week, the Ayopaya rebellion had fallen into disarray. Infantry troops pursued the rebels relentlessly and even donned civilian clothes to allay suspicion while combing the serranía in search of the fugitives. Indian women were raped, men tortured, houses razed, crops and foodstuffs stolen, and livestock slaughtered by rampaging soldiers. Police depredations continued after the withdrawal of infantry troops. Months after the rebellion, Julio Carrasco and Luis Bustamente, representing the colonos, met with the Minister of Labor in La Paz to protest "a series of abuses and violences [sic] against the natives . . . there exists a state of violence between the natives and the hacienda."[76] Over 150 colonos from Ayopaya Province were imprisoned in Cochabamba. Grájeda, Muñoz, and other leaders were sent to a Chapare jungle prison.

The Ayopaya rebellion and the courtroom trials that followed (1947–1951) reveal connections between peasant dirigentes and militant miners such as Gabriel

Muñoz. The miners were a source for weapons procurement and news of proletarian resistance to the Rosca. Grájeda had made a desperate appeal for support during the rebellion to the miners' jefe Juan Lechín: "More than fifty soldiers have entered our territory to commit abuses. . . . [W]e are disposed to fight, but let there be help, I beg you to give us the mine workers to help and continue fighting against the roscas."[77] The last-minute request was futile.

The Ayopaya rebellion was the most dramatic indigenous challenge to the oligarchy during the Sexenio. Estimates of the number of rebels vary from 3,000 to 20,000.[78] Whatever the number, the question arises: how could an insurrection by thousands of Indians end with the deaths of only four victims? Apparently the hacendados, frightened by the upsurge in resistance to the colonato, fled their properties to seek refuge with absentee landlords in urban sanctuaries. A climate of hostility (insolence, insubordination, legal challenges, sit-down strikes) had emerged on the haciendas where the authority of the patrón, corregidor, and the state itself was perceived as illegitimate. Colonos had began appointing their own representatives to defend their interests, asserting independent political agency and exposing the disinterest of the state in enforcing laws.[79]

An investigation of judicial records for the Cochabamba provinces of Mizque and Aiquile found that colonos not only delineated the boundaries of their usufruct plots, but also selected their own alcaldes mayores.[80] This appearance of dual power is indicative of an incipient agrarian revolution. Both Lenin and Trotsky noted the appearance of dual power in the Russian Revolution. Lenin commented on similarities with the 1871 Paris Commune where "officialdom" (the bureaucracy, police and army), "institutions divorced from the people and set against the people" are replaced "by the direct arming of the whole people." And Trotsky averred, "The two-power regime arises only out of irreconcilable class conflicts—is possible, therefore, only in a revolutionary epoch, and constitutes one of its fundamental elements."[81] Trotsky's observation is particularly relevant in the context of the Bolivian highlands where a social revolution was brewing. The spread of a revolutionary consciousness, evidenced by the removal of the mental yoke of domination among the colonos, was a far greater threat to the colonato than were the episodic revolts and rebellions routinely repressed by the government for centuries. Indigenous authorities from within the communities began replacing hacienda and state authorities perceived to be illegitimate. This process, most evident in the Ayopaya region, was an underlying cause of the Cochabamba rebellion.

Chuquisaca Department

The Ayopaya rebellion of 1947 was but a part of a growing wave of agrarian unrest. The provinces of Zudañez, Azurduy, Padilla, and Sud Cinti Provinces in Chuquisaca Department also teetered on the brink of rebellion. Agitation, including distribution of leaflets ("Stomp and Crush the Patrones," "The Lands are Ours"), collection of ramas to finance resistance, and sit-down strikes, was prevalent on haciendas in Azurduy and Yamparez Provinces. Resistance in Chuquisaca Department, while unique in its inception, was apiece with the rebellions in La Paz Department, Cochabamba Department, and Charcas Province (Potosí Department).[82]

In June 1947, colonos sacked and burned hacienda houses at Sumala and Yuca-Cancha in Zudañez Province (Chuquisaca Department). As with the Cochabamba rebellions, the influence of militant miners was evident. Antonio Garcia and Felix Vargas "well known agitators" from Oruro were arrested as instigators of the insurrections.[83] The Sociedad Rural and the Rosca press decried the pernicious influence of miners on hacienda colonos. But something was also brewing. Antonio Garcia, a colono from Hacienda Sumala, had worked in the Oruro mines. Yet more important was his role as a member of the *Alcaldes Mayores Particulares* (AMP) organization, an indigenous revitalization movement that called for a return to ancient Andean beliefs and customs, rather than adaptation of foreign theories recited by creole, mestizo, and cholo apparatchiks from the mines and cities.

Toribio Miranda, an Uru-Aymara from the Uru ayllu Phunaqa on the shore of Lake Poopo, initiated the AMP movement, a factional spinoff from Santos Marka T'ula's *alcaldes mayores* organization. Miranda had successfully waged a legal defense (1921–1925) of his Uru community's contested land rights with a neighboring Aymara ayllu. This began the formative period in the personal development of an extraordinary indigenous nationalist.[84] Miranda dedicated his early years to promotion of Santos Marka T'ula's vision of indigenous revindication before forsaking the alcaldes mayors in the 1930s to found the *Alcaldes Mayores Particulares*. Raised among both Uru and Aymara communities, Miranda sensed the unifying cultural and ethnic threads underlying the various highland communities. He developed an interest in what he would call "Indian law" based on utilization of the Spanish Laws of the Indies that he believed were preferable to the laws enacted by creole republicans. He opposed Santos Marka T'ula's reliance on republican law that he considered the law of creole-mestizo oppressors. The Aymara historian Waskar Ari notes that for Miranda, "Indigenous notions of property, culture and religious practices were all centered on the ideas of community and collectivity, which the new [republican] law did not validate."[85] Miranda rejected cholo clothing that aped western fashion. He differed with Marka T'ula's interest in the cholo urban proletariat because he thought they had stopped being Indian. He also disagreed with Santos Marka T'ula's focus on the education of Indians in the Spanish language, arguing that it fostered acculturation, the inexorable disappearance of indigenous society and culture. Toribio Miranda's fundamental differences with Santos Marka T'ula regarding law, culture, and indigenous revindication influenced the evolution of the AMP movement.[86] Miranda's trepidation is affirmed by modern social science theory: "elites control the 'ideological sectors' of Society—culture, religion, education, and media—and can thereby engineer consent for their rule. By creating and disseminating a universe of discourse and the concepts to go with it, by defining the standards of what is true, beautiful, moral, fair, and legitimate, they build a systematic climate that prevents subordinate classes from thinking their way free."[87]

Revitalization and Escuelas Particulares

In the decades of the 1930s and 1940s, Toribio Miranda traversed the haciendas and ayllus of Chuquisaca and Cochabamba as a peddler of goods while delivering his message of indigenous nationalism based on Indian law and native religion. He stopped by Sumala numerous times in a four- to six-month trip from his home near Lake Poopo. Miranda hewed to the Uru belief that they were the "first people," and because the Uru, Aymara, Quechua, and peoples of the Oriente antedated the Spanish interlopers, their descendants' claim to the land was illegitimate. He argued that they should arise and overcome the colonato.[88]

Miranda's charisma attracted a generation of AMP activists who created a widespread network of *escuelas particulares*, clandestine schools for revitalization of an indigenous consciousness grounded in traditional Andean religion and culture. Miranda visited the Sumala hacienda soon after the National Indigenous Congress of 1945 to popularize Villarroel's decrees, distribute Indian law documents, and spread the AMP message of a millenarian, plurinational republic of Indians free of white-mestizo subjugation: "when all Indians eat freely in the main plaza . . . then we will truly be a human race, the montepuchus [Quechuas], quchupuchus [Urus], and chullpapuchus [Aymara]. And it would please Pachamama, the mother earth would be happy. That would be a great day."[89] Among those converted to the AMP movement were local and regional disciples who risked their lives for the cause: Melitón Gallardo, Antonio Garcia, and Manuel Qhispe in Chuquisaca Department; Manuel Andia Colque, Octavio Ferrufino, and Fermin Vallejos in Cochabamba Department; and Gregorio Titiriku in La Paz Department. The escuelas particulares, operating within 500 haciendas and ayllus, constituted a network of cells dedicated to the indigenous revolution, as well as an alliance between the colonos of Mizque-Campero and comunarios in Northern Potosí.[90]

Government officials were particularly concerned with the sit-down strikes organized by Manuel Andia, known as "Atahualpa" or "The Inca," a dynamic leader of regional stature in the Cochabamba provinces of Mizque and Campero, whose sister Berna was the wife of Toribio Miranda. A telegram from the Sub-prefect in Aiquile (Campero Province) to the Cochabamba Prefect in November 1945 requested assistance to capture Andia, referred to as the "constant instigator and agitator" of colonos on haciendas, including Laguna, Quewinal, and Calamarca.[91] The rural police captured Manuel Andia and attempted to silence him by cutting off his tongue. Andia escaped, only to be trapped in Molinero (Mizque Province) where the police set fire to the house in which he had taken refuge and then delivered the coup de gràce with a bullet to the head.[92] Andia's murder in November 1946 incited an insurrection on haciendas (including Quewinal, Novillero, San Vicente, Raqaypampa). Octavio Ferrufino, the "Second Inca," emerged to continue resistance in the region where colonos instituted dual power, suspending work and replacing hacienda administrators with their own leaders.[93]

Prelude to Rebellion

Stretching from the valley floor to the mountainous heights above the cantón of Icla in Zudañez Province lay the haciendas Sumala and Suruma. The expansive and ecologically diverse estates produced a variety of products: citrus, sugar cane, tropical fruits and grapes in the lower elevations; maize, potatoes, and barley in the heights above the temperate valleys; chuño (freeze-dried potatoes), sheep, alpacas, and llamas in the lofty puna. The agricultural potential of the region had attracted indigenous settlers from the Uru and Aymara ayllus of the Altiplano long before the Spanish invasion. The Icla haciendas were among the oldest in the Andes. Coveted by Sucre hacendados and mine owners, they provided foodstuffs for the city and silver mines of Potosí. Following the collapse of the silver boom at the end of the nineteenth century, the haciendas in the region were sought as a hedge against investment in mines. Mine owners caught in the crisis were forced to liquidate their haciendas to solvent buyers. The capital flight from silver to land created a regional boomlet in Yamparaez Province and Northern Potosí at the expense of ayllu landholdings.[94]

The Icla haciendas were sold to foreign buyers dedicated to increasing profits on their investments and transforming the traditional estates (valued primarily for social status rather than economic potential) into capitalist enterprises. Land and labor were committed to cultivation of grapes and production of "Vinos Soroma," a popular and profitable wine. Colonos were forced to work more days a week in the vineyard at the expense of time in their own fields and surrender their best usufructs for grape production.[95] Traditional relations between colono and patrón—the reciprocal exchange of colono labor for patrón-sponsored fiestas and the bonds of fictive kinship between lord and peasant (*compadrazgo*)—were sacrificed to increased demands for profit.[96] The AMP offered an answer to their plight.

Melitón Gallardo was a wanted man. By the mid-1940s, his network of AMP cells embedded in hundreds of haciendas and ayllus posed a threat not only to the dominion of the Chuquisaca hacendados but also to the very existence of the agrarian order. Connected through ties of marriage to Aymara and Quechua kindreds and with contacts among anarchist and leftist organizations in Sucre, Oruro, and La Paz, Gallardo proselytized throughout the highland communities.[97] His message, at once millenarian and Manichean, heralded the rise of a united *original people* to end the domination of white overlords:

> Saxama Achachila [the spirit of Saxama mountain] is coming back to restore the unity among Aymaras and Quechuas. The power of Saxama is so strong that it will shake the world. . . . [T]he broken head of the Mururata Mountain will be restored, as the power of the Qullasuyus will be victorious and the blood of the land will be refreshed . . . and the domination of whites will end. . . . Then, Saxama will rest in peace.[98]

Indigenous clothes, language, and customs were to be celebrated and creole-mestizo language, culture, religion, and laws rejected. AMP congregations, held at night, were ritualistic. Amidst prayers and offerings to Pachamama, incense was burned, white roosters sacrificed, money, birth certificates, and other documents were burned by participants "to mark their passing from white society into the republic of Indians and as a symbol of separation from whites."[99] Gallardo preached unity—colono and comunario, highland and valley, Quechua and Aymara—all were the original people. "Gallardo's discourse promoted a nationalist message by connecting the idea of 'Indian blood' with land rights. By representing a subaltern nation of Indians opposed to the dominant racial system, he racialized the content of his discourse but used race in a counter-hegemonic way." Thus, continues the Bolivian historian Waskar Ari, "Gallardo's argument cast the hacienda owners and their administrators as Spaniards or whites who should return the land to the *jallp'a sangres* [Quechua/Spanish: blood of our lands; viz., native people]. In this way he used an earth politics to rebel against the powerful haciendas."[100]

Desperate to quell the rising millenarian tide flooding haciendas and ayllus, landlords burned down the houses of suspected activists and the escuelas particulares. Melitón Gallardo survived an attempted assassination on the grounds of Hacienda Sumala in November 1946 by a killer contracted by the hacendado. The landlord of the nearby Hacienda Suruma murdered Marcelini Mamani. Mariano Qhispe, another AMP activist at Suruma, died in a tropical prison.[101] Resistance at Sumala and Suruma reached a crescendo in 1947. After the June assaults on the hacienda houses, President Hertzog's rural police were summoned to forcibly reimpose order. An altercation broke out as soldiers rounded up hundreds of colonos and an officer was killed. In the ensuing fray, troops fired into the crowd killing two colonos and wounding dozens. The repression failed to force capitulation. Instead, the bloody incident ignited a regional rebellion that spread to northern Potosí and the Chuquisaca provinces of Zudañez and Azurduy. A number of hacienda houses were razed before three days of bombing quelled resistance. Numerous AMP leaders, including Antonio Garcia and Mariano Qhispe, were captured and remanded to jungle death camps. As a reminder of the price of defiance, their houses were burned down. Meliton Gallarado managed to escape the Rosca repression, only to be imprisoned later.[102]

The Counterrevolutionary as Counterinsurgent

President Enrique Hertzog realized that if a peasant revolution was to be averted, reforms were necessary to mitigate the causes of the agrarian unrest. Campaigning for the presidency, he had promised to create agrarian cooperatives utilizing modern agronomy and technology. He also spoke of "defense of the indigenous communities" and stated that the "agrarian problem" could be solved with an "agrarian statute" in which the rights and obligations between colonos and hacendados were clearly defined and "remunerated work" (paid labor) would be instituted in the countryside.[103] Revisiting the topic in 1949, Hertzog proposed the introduction of a wide range of reforms to ameliorate the conditions underlying rural unrest: agricultural cooperatives with schools teaching literacy and agronomy, a more equitable distribution of harvests between hacendado and colono, abolition of pongueaje and mitanaje, creation of schools financed by hacendados, protection of Indians from abuse by landlords and townspeople, formation of a commission to examine land titles toward the end of returning fraudulent titles to the ayllus, and rural credits made available to Indians for land purchases.[104]

President Hertzog grasped the paradox that because of their resistance to agrarian reform, the hacendados were the perpetrators of violence in the countryside and not the victims.[105] Yet he steadfastly denied that the rebellion stemmed from an oppressive land tenure system. Instead, he claimed that the Indians were "unconscious victims" of subversive agitation by the MNR, POR, and FOL. Faced with the Great Rebellion, Hertzog had continued to talk of reform as he ratcheted up repression and sent Indians to prison camps in the Oriente.[106] Ill-adapted to survive in the hot and humid jungle, many of the prisoners never returned, including Marcelino Quispe, the Secretary General of the FAD.[107]

In the course of the six-month rebellion, the Hertzog regime wielded the combined power of the state. Never in the twentieth century had a Bolivian government unleashed such an unprecedented combination of military power to terrorize the indigenous populace. The rebellion ended with an estimated 700 Indian leaders imprisoned. The Yayani rebels Hilarión Grájeda and Gabriel Muños received death sentences.[108] The indiscriminate use of state terror unleashed by President Enrique Hertzog's war against the peasantry appeared to have quelled indigenous resistance to the Rosca. A communiqué from the Sociedad Rural Boliviano, issued in the first week of July 1947, advised its members that it was safe to return to their haciendas. Following an earlier insurrection, it was decided that the Indians were "pacified," that conditions on the haciendas were "normal," and the colonos "content."[109] President Hertzog freed Indian rebels imprisoned at the Ichilo death camp, released the FOL prisoners in the Panóptico Nacional, proposed colonization and cooperative schemes (e.g., transforming ayllus into cooperatives), urged hacendados to be more generous in the division of harvests with colonos, and, in a finishing touch, affirmed the need to enforce the Villarroel decrees abolishing personal service. These measures were palliatives designed to defuse much of what had provoked the rebellion and ensure the survival of the colonato.[110]

Indigenous resistance to the colonato continued despite Hertzog's reformist ploy as evidenced by the appearance of the Pachakamak movement and the radicalization of Chipana Ramos. Once the symbol of moderation, the "President of the Indians" had come to believe that the oppressor had to be exterminated. As Antonio Mamani Álvarez's put it, "Chipana Ramos in those years was leading an indigenous uprising that wanted to finish off the white[s], whatever their social status, economic or religious, all white[s] had to disappear."[111] Chipana Ramos was not alone in his resistance to the colonato. Six colonos killed a landlord in a dispute over labor obligations at a hacienda near Culpina (Chuquisaca Department). In Cochabamba Department, a landlord was murdered by an enraged pongo after the patrón threw a glass of spoiled milk in his servant's face.[112] Indians led by Virgilio

Vargas, the "Son of God," murdered another Cochabamba hacendado while en route to Tarata.

Agrarian conflict was not confined to confrontations between patrón and colono. Violent clashes were reported in Potosí Department between the Kakachaka and Pari ayllus, the Cakaj Ana and Incumbris ayllus, and the Coroma and Tomave ayllus. Conflicts between ayllu comunarios also continued in La Paz Department where a boundary dispute between the Sillcatiti and Konko ayllus near Jesus de Machaca resulted in one death and six injuries, and five houses were razed during a boundary feud between Ayca and Italaque comunarios. A confrontation between colonos on the haciendas Janco Jaqui and Tutuni led to one death and nine injuries and carabineros were ordered to quell a conflict between colonos of the Arapa and Sairi Chiruni haciendas. Other less violent confrontations were common occurrences. Excessive work demands occasioned a conflict between colonos and the landlord of Hacienda Goitia in La Paz Department and a prolonged sit-down strike at Caramarca (Cochabamba Department). Curiously, an ongoing dispute at Hacienda Quiviquivi (Potosí Department) over the colonos' refusal to perform personal service led to the patrón's decision to hand administration of the estate to the military.[113]

Government authorities continued to combat "agitation" and "subversion" by MNR, FOL, and PIR militants and indigenous revolutionaries. Movimientistas were accused of distributing mimeographed materials "inciting revolution" among the peasantry in Chuquisaca, promoting land seizures in Potosí, and collecting contributions (ramas) in Nor Chichas (Potosí Department). Anarchists supported indigenous opposition in La Paz, Potosí, and Oruro to a proposed 1950 census that would levy increased taxes on Indians. Sixty-three FOL militants accused of agitation on the Altiplano were jailed and another 75 FOL and FAD leaders were arrested in March 1948 accused of sedition, provoking Indian land seizures, distribution of literature inciting rebellion, soliciting funds for arms purchases, and traversing the region "under the pretext of founding rural schools."[114] Local authorities arrested José Rojas, the Secretary of the Sindicato Agrario of Cliza (Cochabamba Department) and Antonio Mamani Álvarez continued distributing leaflets urging resistance to the Rosca. He also signed a pact agreeing to enlist literate Indians to vote for the MNR in the forthcoming presidential election and in return the MNR accepted his principles of agrarian revolution set forth in the *Tesis de Caranguillas*.[115]

The *Tesis* of Caranguillas

Six months after the Great Rebellion, a "Second Bolivian Indigenous Congress" assembled at Caranguillas, a hamlet in Oruro Department, far from the repressive tentacles of the Rosca. There Antonio Mamani Álvarez, the self-designated "Chief Executive of the Bolivian Peasantry," called for agrarian revolution. An indigenous manifesto, the *Tesis de Caranguillas*, accompanied the Congress. Written by Asto Warachi Condorcanqi (designated the "Intellectual Leader of the Bolivian

Peasantry"), the manifesto presents an indigenous blueprint for revolution, replete with a lengthy historical justification.[116] Antonio Mamani Álvarez recalled the date of the Congress as 25–27 December 1947, although the *Tesis* (written beforehand) refers to the date as "x of the initial year of the Agrarian Revolution." Likewise, the manifesto's reference to "4,800 Representatives of the Peasant Class" at the Congress is a questionable number given the fact that the document antedated the event. This number exceeds the 4,500 representatives that attended the 1945 National Indigenous Congress convened under the Villarroel regime, thereby enhancing the image of the Caranguillas event, held in an isolated location and reported ex post facto. The majority were Aymara peasants from Oruro department where the Kallawaya dirigente Antonio Mamani Álvaraz had developed a strong following.

The *Tesis of Caranguillas* is an indigenous counterpoint to the Trotskyist *Tesis de Pulacayo*; to read the *Tesis of Caranguillas*, go to www.routledge.com/Indigenous-Struggle-and-the-Bolivian-National-Revolution-Land-and-Liberty/Kohl/p/book/9780367471392 and click on eResources. *Section One* of the manifesto essays the history of a conquered race in six vituperative chapters ("Our Glorious Past"; "The Conquest"; "The Usurpation of Our Lands"; "The Revolution of Tupac Amaru"; "The Republic: From Slave Economy to Oligarchic Despotism"; "Under the Yoke of Yankee Imperialism"). The intent of this lengthy section (nearly two-thirds of the *Tesis*) is to demolish the legitimacy of the ancien régime, as well as justify and incite an indigenous revolution.

This section targets a perennial pair of evildoers: the corregidor ("petty exploiter") and the priest ("The Black Shadow of the Indian"). The vast landholdings of the Franciscan and Jesuit missions in the Oriente, usurped from indigenous tribes, and the church's enrichment through Indian levies (*diezmos, primicias, capellanías, mandas de misa*) are assailed together with the corregidor and his minions: "The Corregidor has at his service various slaves with supposed subaltern titles; their principal instruments of domination were the caciques and jilacatas, those who have replaced the authority of our ancient curacas." The *Tesis*'s history of invasion and conquest, domination and resistance, national despotism and international imperialism completes the bill of particulars adduced to validate an indigenous war for independence.

Section Two proffers a plan for revolution ("Fundamental Principles of the Revolution"; "Ayni: Cooperation"; "The Revolution: Basic Objectives"; "Individualism: Its Inapplicability"; "Cooperativism: Our Anchor and Redemption"). These chapters are noteworthy for their anarchist parallels and censure of capitalism, Trotskyism and Stalinism.

Section Three provides programmatic details for a revolutionary state ("Syndical Organization"; "The Revolution: Immediate Realizations"; "Function of the Revolutionary State"; "Rationalization of Agriculture"), syncretizing ayllu cooperativism with anarchist precepts. "Our resurgence consists in the valorization and rationalization of autochthonous elements that, when fused with modern matters of contemporary civilization, produces the constituent formulas for a new doctrine; a doctrine essentially ours, whose realization allows us to reconstruct a Nation that . . . resembles the great Tawantinsuyu. (*Tesis*, 20)

Introduced at the onset of the Congress were a number of resolutions. The "Day of the Unknown Slave" (May 18), designated to honor fallen comrades in the struggle for freedom, was proposed to commemorate these martyrs. Another resolution, inspired by the recent rebellions, pledged support to guarantee the security of peasant "jefes and dirigentes" and, in the event of death or imprisonment, provide assistance to their families. Other resolutions demanded enforcement of the laws enacted by the martyred President Villarroel, ratified the *Federación Syndical Agraria de Bolivia* (FSAB) and the precepts of the Pachakamak revolutionary doctrine, proclaimed Antonio Mamani Álvarez as Chief Executive and Asto Warachi Condorcanqi as Secretary General and Intellectual Leader of the FSAB, and stipulated the convocation of a Third Bolivian Indigenous Congress. The manifesto's impassioned critique of creole domination provides the requisite polemics to inflame revolutionary consciousness:

> It is time to demonstrate to our enemies that we are tired of their despotism and of their demagogic chatter; that their depravity and shamelessness causes our repugnance; that we are tired of their lies and their felony. It is time to demonstrate to the vampires of the antinational Rosca that we will give them no more blood to suck; that now the fury of the justice of a Nation will fall over the heads of the tyrants.
>
> (*Tesis*, 22)

Centuries after the Spanish invasion, little had changed for a conquered race: "neither the wars of independence . . . nor the later revolutions . . . nor the laws, nor institutions, nor political and economic forms . . . are made for us." The FSAB summoned the native peoples to take back their patrimony, to throw off the chains of servitude, and to create a new form of government representative of indigenous culture. "Our movement aspires to stimulate an organic revolutionary action among all the oppressed classes of the country: an action sustained by the Indians, the proletarians, the artisans, and all the working forces of the Nation." Mindful of the nation's demographics, with five of every seven inhabitants an Indian, and the remainder primarily mestizos, the *Tesis* proclaims, "Without our emancipation there can be no national emancipation; for, we ourselves constitute the Bolivian Nation . . . our Redemption and that of the fatherland necessarily has to be our exclusive work." Emancipation could only come about through termination of the Rosca's control of creole-mestizo minds.

> The Rosca cunningly primes the fear and hatred of the urban populations against us; their debased press, through systematic campaigns, frightens the inhabitants of the cities and towns with the spectre of Indian attacks against the cities, looting, beheadings of the whites, destruction of cities and other frauds, presenting us as savages, bloodthirsty and hungry for revenge. To these fabricators of lies we answer: our revolution is not racial, nor regional, nor partisan. Our only enemies are those that withhold our rights and liberties,

our goods and patrimonial riches; those that enslave and exploit us; those that exploit the national wealth and impoverish the country. In a word our enemy is the imperialistic Rosca.

(*Tesis*, 21)[117]

The *Tesis* warned that another enemy lurked within the psyche of the dominated race, "the disastrous sentiment of weakness and inferiority in which we collectively fall," and called for an end to this "suicidal temperament" through revitalization of revolutionary spirit. The Pachakamak doctrine offered the millennial dream of a return to the greatness of the Inca Empire. Notice was served to "Those great Rosca imperialists (Trusts), that have adopted all the Rosca capitalists of the world, determined to keep humanity tied tightly to their bastard conceptions"; "It is time to demonstrate to *roscakutismo* that we Indians do not need the 'protection and aid' of the oligarchy, nor will we admit to be considered as if we were 'underage children,' nor accept the favor of 'certain conditions of guarantee'";

It is time to demonstrate to the *prioporismo* [sic, *piroporismo*: Stalinism/Trotskyism] *rosquero* that the Indians are not begging to accept the charity of their 'economic plots' or the colonization of 'collective farms' in unhealthy zones, nor are we little rabbits for experimentation that piroporismo seeks to subject to the materialistic formulas of Asian [i.e., Russian, Soviet] ferment. The piroporistas can go to Russia with their decadent Agrarian Reform. Here in Bolivia they are unnecessary, when the Indians are making the AGRARIAN REVOLUTION.

"It is time to demonstrate to the *falangista* puppies that . . . it does not have to be a fascist dictatorship to which we Indians subordinate ourselves and serve."

The "Pachakamak" doctrine is presented in the second and third sections of the *Tesis* through discussion of the stages of the Agrarian Revolution: (I) "Conquest of Political Power"; (II) "Revindication of Land"; (III) "Possession of Economic Power."

Conquest of Political Power

The *Tesis* critiques the failure of indigenous revolution from Tupac Amaru to the recent past: the isolated rebellions, lacking firm objectives, basic theory and revolutionary tactics, badly organized and poorly equipped with weapons of war. The proposed remedy is the FSAB sindicto federation organized and cooperating in secrecy throughout the countryside, awaiting the moment to strike in unity. "People considered individually are incapable of setting in motion any revolutionary engine . . . Consequently, we postulate the syndicalization of the Bolivian indigenous class, as a first and necessary step to make the Revolution. Given the persecutory rage unleashed against us and [as] no guarantee exists on our behalf, the peasant syndical organization will have a distinctly secret character." (*Tesis*, 36)

Sindicatos of colonos and comunarios, artisans, and small industrialists were to conjoin in a national confederation and function according to the dictates set forth in the *Tesis*. The revolutionary leaders (*cabecillas revolucionarios*) selected from among the sindicatos would both instruct and direct their constituents. Deception and secrecy are stressed as essential to the organizational stage of the revolution—preparatory to the insurrectionary stage launched simultaneously by sindicatos throughout the country.

> The FSAB cautions that during the organizational stage of the sindicato cadres, strikes of any kind do not take place, neither is the work of agitation discovered, nor isolated and discordant uprisings declared. . . . We cannot put in motion any revolutionary mechanism, as long as we have not consolidated our sindicato forces on solid doctrinal and disciplinary bases. For centuries we have awaited the hour of our restoration; now that we have it within our reach, we can well wait for the time we need to prepare it and take it to fruition.
>
> (*Tesis*, 37)

The emphasis on secrecy and concerted action of a unified organization rising up as a whole, at a given moment, reflects Mamani Álvarez's criticism of the FAD rebellions as premature and isolated events destined to failure with the needless sacrifice of insurgents.[118] The Pachakamak state would be limited to control of social functions, regulation of economic development and protection of the common interests, to avoid a return to the control of the few over the many as under the Rosca capitalists and Stalinist communists. "The duties of the Revolutionary state are the ones created by our own collective and common needs" (*Tesis*, 39).

Land Revindication

The Pachakamak doctrine proposed a solution to the sordid paradox of a country rich in land and minerals, but a nation where the indigenous majority are homeless and landless: "two million Bolivians . . . wandering as pariahs without a Fatherland, or home, within their own Native Land, dragging their misery and pain." The *Tesis* disparages the quest for agrarian reform as a ploy to divert the focus of the Indian to a legal paper chase. All palliatives, "revisionism, reformism, protectionism," were to be rejected. "Agrarian Reform is a symbol of slavery; the Agrarian Revolution is a symbol of Redemption." The sectarian feud between the alcaldes mayores and Alcaldes Mayores Particulares is considered a distraction from the Agrarian Revolution. "Within our revolutionary conceptions the titles of property or possession of the land granted by the Spanish Crown have no value, nor [do those] conceded by the republican oligarchy. All those are insulting for us and contrary to our authentic rights. The only property titles that from now on must have a true value will be those arising from our Revolution." (*Tesis*, 27)

Immediately after the victory of the revolution, a cadre of Cabecillas Revolucionarios representing the sindicato network would begin implementation of measures to consolidate power. "At the triumph of our Revolution, there ought not be left a single landowner . . . fiefs, latifundios, religious missions, vacant land, all Bolivian soil will be unfailingly claimed by our Revolution. However, lands cultivated directly by their owners will be respected, organized in cooperative societies." There would be no parcelization of land because it would allow a regression into minifundisimo, an unsustainable vestige of the Old Order.[119] Expropriated lands would be farmed by agrarian sindicatos, "community cooperatives" of self-governing families.

> Cooperativism represents a revolutionary tendency of global potential. It destroys the capitalist principle of competition that engenders wars; eliminates the capitalist fundamental of profit that causes the exploitation of man by man; destroys class hatred, because it replaces individual predominance by the solidarity of equality; it gives an end to social conflicts, because it annuls autocratic privilege; and all those who participate in the Cooperative take their part in initiative, control, responsibility . . . to emancipate ourselves from the yoke of the Rosca capitalists, and to free the Bolivian Fatherland from the imperialistic yoke of the Yankees; [there is] nothing more suitable than Cooperativism for the revindication of our lands, for the manumission of our labor force from capitalistic domination."
>
> (*Tesis*, 24)

Individualism and competition would be eliminated in the cooperativist society. "Scientists, intellectuals, professional and artistic elements; production and distribution, public services, culture, technology; all the elements of civilized life should be collectivized and put to the service of the revolutionary majority. Our doctrinal principles do not admit the survival of capitalistic individualism. . . . Consequently the FSAB will ensure that not a single individual, nor entity, will remain isolated from the body of our cooperativist organization." (*Tesis*, 38)

Possession of Economic Power

Restitution of the land was envisioned as the basis for a society founded on ancient Andean cooperativism, but utilizing modern techniques to realize the potential virtually untapped by the hacienda system. "From here it follows that the modern Cooperation is nothing other than our primeval Ayni; Ayni rationalized, converted into the science of humanity, that establishes the norms and indicates the road to follow to reach higher standards of living, without rich, or poor, without rich or poor, without executioner or oppressed, without wars or fratricidal strife; where everything is justice, abundance and happiness."

Agricultural and technical schools would be opened for the study of agronomy, animal husbandry, resource management, and associated trades. The goal of increased production (in a nation that imported food) through mechanization would be funded through the creation of a "Bolivian Agrarian Cooperative Bank" to finance, distribute, import, and export.[120] "The decisive factor for the imposition and the subsistence of our new Revolutionary order is in production. Only with intense and prodigious work will we be able to face and conquer the tremendous crisis that will come to the Revolution, like a posthumous revenge of the overthrown capitalist Rosca."

The *Tesis* forewarns that consolidation of the revolution would be dependent upon the will of the emancipated peasantry to dedicate their collective labor to the development of the new order. "Once victorious we must redouble our efforts in order to overcome the ordinary levels of our productive capacity. Only thus can we prevent our Revolution from being born dead. . . . We will have thus established the fundamentals of a new society, of a society based on brotherhood and justice; and we will have reconstructed the ideal form of Indian Republic, on the fundamental pillars of cooperative democracy and of social peace." (*Tesis*, 40)

Beginning with "Our Glorious Past" and woven throughout the *Tesis de Caranguillas* is the millenarian dream of a return to the glory of the Inca Empire. The summons to recreate an idyllic lost world of communal ayllus bound together through collective labor is invoked as a remembrance of the past and an inspiration for the future.[121] The path to fruition delineated by Pachakamak lies in man's relationship to the land. The Pre-Colombian socioeconomic model had much to offer: sustainable agriculture adapted to diverse ecological niches, domestication of a plethora of plants micro-adapted to the unique environments of the Andean highlands, irrigation and aqueducts, and terracing and raised fields farmed by ayllu kindreds.

Indigenous agronomy supported the fluorescence of Andean states and the largest empire in the Americas before the invasion of an alien race and the imposition of a foreign, ill-adapted agricultural system focused on political domination rather than economic production. As the *Tesis* observes, the result was the utter failure of the colonato system to feed the populace and a nation forced to import food. In contradistinction, 25–95 percent more land was farmed in the Andes prior to the European invasion.[122]

The *Tesis*'s argument for a fusion of the indigenous ayllu with modern agricultural and industrial cooperatives, abolition of private ownership of the means of production, and the substitution of cooperativism (ayni) and mutual aid (minká) for capitalist individualistic competition is suggestive of anarchist principles.[123] The *Tesis de Caranguillas* is a more radical document than the better known Mexican treatises, the Zapatista *Plan de Ayala* and Agrarian Reform Law of 1915. The *Tesis* and the Zapatista manifesto demanded the expropriation of latifundios, but the Mexican Agrarian Law allowed the continuation of capitalism and individual ownership of private property. The Pachakamak doctrine would abolish capitalism and replace it with collectivization in a federation of communal cooperatives controlled and managed by workers. The Mexican indigenous *ejido* was to replace the hacienda, but with selective implementation (e.g., based on proof of legal title prior to 1856) and expropriated properties were to be indemnified. With its complex provisions (35 Articles), the Mexican Agrarian Law was a lawyer's dream.[124]

The *Tesis of Caranguillas* eliminates capitalism, expropriates private property without indemnification (with the exception of owners of small agricultural plots), and aims not only to return the land to those who till it but also to recreate a pre-Columbian world of group cooperation without individualistic competition, money, middle-men, banks, loan sharks, and the tyranny of a plutocracy over an impoverished majority. Issued in the wake of the 1947 Great Rebellion, Pachakamak called for an agrarian revolution to arise, Phoenix-like, from the ashes of rebellion and deliver the people of Kollasuyu a bountiful future free of creole domination and oppression.

The Twilight of the Ancien Régime

Violence had become endemic in the Sexenio. Unremitting states of siege, arrests, "interrogations," beatings, executions, imprisonment, and exile made for an extremely difficult existence for Movimientista militants and their families. The MNR response was pragmatic. After three days of discussion, the Comité Politico agreed to pursue an electoral victory or, if necessary, "the seizure of political power by violence."[125] As the MNR recouped strength in Cochabamba, Santa Cruz, Potosí, and Oruro central planning became a critical component for the success of the revolution in a country traditionally beset by regional antagonisms. Thus, the question of consultation by regional commandos with command and control in La Paz became a critical matter for discussion.

In late 1947, the MNR National Convention met and voted to expel Rafael Otazo for his attempt to unseat Víctor Paz as party Jefe Máximo. The Otazo affair had no sooner ended after months of internal party turmoil when the Taborga affair began. It would also end badly. Colonel Alberto Taborga, the head of the Transit Police, had proffered 300 rifles, machine guns, and men to the MNR in exchange for a major role in an impending insurrection. Taborga's intrigue coincided with plans for a major offensive involving an assault on the city of Villazón together with an uprising at the Catavi mine designed to set off widespread rebellion, sparking a revolution. When Taborga's insistence on meeting with the Comité was rebuffed, he found himself unable to discover the particulars of the plan that he intended to offer the Rosca. Nevertheless, his intrigue led to the arrest of Luis Peñaloza. Taborga then began personal attacks on party Jefe Víctor Paz to generate factionalism within the MNR.[126]

The MNR schemed with whoever might offer men, arms, or preferably both, as in its ongoing negotiations with the Falange. Comprised primarily of urban middle- and upper-class students, more atavistic than ideological ("Instead of intellectuals, we are fighters"), the Falange never attracted a mass base. As the party Jefe Oscar Unzaga de la Vega averred, "Democracy is an artifice of words for the distraction of the people."[127] In April 1948, the MNR Comité initiated meetings with the Falangista leaders Unzaga de la Vega and Hugo Roberts to gain the support

144 The Sexenio

FIGURE 4.2 Loyalty March in La Paz Against MNR Rebels in 1949
Source: Courtesy of the U.S. National Archives (Photo 306NT- 933F1), *New York Times*, 5 September 1949.

of Falangista junior officers in Cochabamba considered necessary for a planned revolution in 1949.

Elections were allowed by the Rosca to legitimize the regime as "democratic." The result inevitably favored Enrique Hertzog's PURS. Despite this foregone conclusion, the elections were rich in opportunities for the opposition: public speeches, charismatic speakers, and mass demonstrations made for a propaganda bonanza. The trick was in the reversal of fortune, creating success out of foreordained defeat, as illustrated by MNR participation in the parliamentary elections of 1 May 1949. The MNR was victorious in the departmental capital cities, but lost in La Paz; the MNR lost in La Paz by 300 votes due to PURS chicanery.

A post-election demonstration staged by Movimientistas resulted in the massacre of 168 Movimientistas. A demonstration by workers the following day was machine-gunned by the army. President Hertzog was traumatized by the violence. Rumor had it that he fled the Palacio Quemado fearing that the demonstration in Plaza Murillo was the beginning of a revolution. A week later, claiming ill-health, Hertzog stepped aside and Vice President Mamerto Urriolagoitia, a brutal hacendado from Sucre, assumed the presidency.

Simultaneous with the electoral contest and the Taborga affair, the MNR focused on a grand strategy for a revolution. Initiated by a general strike, the plan called for a rebellion in the Patiño mines, the seizure of the town of Villazón on the border with Argentina, followed by insurrections in the major cities. The plan was ill-fated. The general strike of miners, telegraph, bank, railroad, and factory sindicatos was suppressed. The Catavi uprising was crushed. Over 1,000 miners, their families, and a handful of foreign hostages were slaughtered by government artillery, machine guns, and warplanes. The Villazón attack failed because of miscalculation and misfortune. Augusto Céspedes, José Quadros Quiroga, and Luis Peñaloza were captured by Argentine gendarmes as they attempted to cross the border at Villazón. Unable to operate their radio-transmitter, the Movimientista leaders found it impossible to contact their comrades in the mines and cities to warn them of the fiasco.[128]

What the regime gained in containment of the insurgency was lost in public opinion and popular support. The militarization of violence, successful in the suppression of urban insurgency, demonstrated the brutality of government repression and alienated the populace. But, President Urriolagoitia was more concerned with the survival of the Old Order than with public opinion. Two regiments of carabineros equipped with radios and assault rifles were deployed in La Paz along with military detachments strategically situated to isolate and strangle insurgents. The vital Bolívar Regiment in Viacha was also modernized. By the end of May, hundreds of Movimientistas were imprisoned and others, including party luminaries (Juan Lechín, José Fellman Velarde, Mario Diez de Media), had fled the country.

The MNR augmented party membership among the working class by enlisting the support of influential labor union leaders. Juan Lechín commanded the loyalty of the FSTMB, the powerful miners' federation, and in June 1949 the La Paz factory workers elected a Movimientista as their Secretary General. The growth of MNR cellular organization within the working class continued apace, but coordination of these cells with the middle-class urban cells was difficult. There were instances when the middle-class cells failed to support the actions of the workers' cells. Yet, as the MNR militant Lydia Gueiler Tejada recalls, the doors of the "humble huts of the popular [workers'] barrios of Munaypata, Villa Victoria, Los Andes, Puente Negro" were open to the revolutionaries.[129] Lydia Gueiler joined the MNR in January 1948 beginning a lengthy commitment to the party and the incipient cause of women's liberation. As in other revolutionary movements, women played a vital role in the MNR. Less likely to arouse suspicion, women militants and supporters were invaluable in securing and conveying information, facilitating logistics, smuggling arms and ammunition, and ultimately carrying out revolutionary armed struggle.[130]

The Civil War

In a remarkable sign of resilience and confidence, the MNR planned a revolution for August 1949. Movimientista militants, organized in clandestine revolutionary cells of 7–14 members, implemented the tactics of the Comité's strategy: "think, address, organize, create and distribute propaganda, take to the street in demonstrations," and "convince the citizens, one by one, to give money for these activities."[131] Few cell members knew the names of the Comité Politico and vice versa to prevent the disclosure of cell members in the event of betrayal or torture. At a given moment, the cells would be alerted to meet within an hour's notice.[132] Unfortunately, there were glitches in communication and coordination within the cellular organization. The forthcoming revolution was doomed at its inception: a member of the La Paz Comité Revolucionario, Lieutenant Juan Monje, was a government mole. Privy to the inner workings of the Comité, Monje conveyed details of the MNR plot—the existence of the cellular network, weapons depots, safe houses, communication techniques, propaganda workshops—to the government. Unbeknownst to the Comité, their plans compromised by Lieutenant Monje's espionage, the Movimientistas prepared for the coming insurrection that would devolve into a Civil War.[133]

The strategy for the August 1949 revolution was an expanded reprise of the Villazón strategy. La Paz, Oruro, Cochabamba, Potosí, Santa Cruz, Sucre, and Tarija were to be simultaneously assaulted by Movimientistas supported by workers, FSB cadre, and military officers. A rebellion from the mines was to accompany the urban insurgency. But what of the revolutionary potential of the three million Indians, restive under the heel of the oligarchy? Silvia Rivera Cusdicanqui notes that after the 1947 rebellion, hundreds of "Indian agitators" were recruited by the MNR in an attempt "to turn the Indian movement into a 'peasant movement.'"[134] Indeed, among the prisoners at Puerto Grether on the Rio Ichilo was Guillermo Muños de la Barra, a MNR militant snared in a government roundup of Indian rebels, who proselytized his fellow prisoners on the subject of revolution and agrarian reform.[135]

As Augusto Céspedes pointed out many years later, the MNR leaders planned to institute agrarian reform when they seized power, but in the interim it was decided to downplay their intention lest they alienate landowners living in the cities "who were an important factor" in the overthrow of the regime.[136] Víctor Paz Estenssoro (in an interview with the author) stated that Movimientistas, including the militant Zenón Barrientos Mamani, planned to seize control of Villazón in the August Revolution and then march to the Hacienda Mojo, where they would expropriate and redistribute the land to the colonos.[137] The indigenous revolutionary Antonio Mamani Álvarez distributed 5,000 copies of "A Call to Bolivian

Indians" on 30 August 1949 urging peasants on the Altiplano to join the insurrection. He also cut the Oruro-Potosí telephone line, severing government communication between the cities.[138]

A bomb explosion was the signal for the insurrection in La Paz, but the bomb failed to detonate, compromising the scenario: by midnight 200 militants were arrested and a number of arms caches seized. The MNR cell structure stymied the interrogation and torture of prisoners whose information was limited to La Paz.[139] Meanwhile, the Movimientistas outside of La Paz continued preparations for a revolution. The insurrection in Oruro was a failure before it began. Movimientistas approaching the barracks of the Camacho regiment (to cement a conspiracy between MNR and regimental officers) were attacked. Some were captured, others fled the city. Government troops savagely suppressed the miners' revolt at Catavi. Bombed by the air force, shelled by artillery, and assaulted by an infantry regiment, over 1,000 men, women, and children were massacred.[140] The Altiplano secured, Urriolagoitia was free to focus on the Movimientista insurgents in Potosí, Sucre, Cochabamba, and Santa Cruz.

Cochabamba was captured on 27 August by Movimientista commandos. The MNR Revolutionary Committee in charge of the city included retired and active duty pilots; noteworthy among the air force collaborators was Captain René Barrientos Ortuño, who would play a heroic role in the ensuing Civil War. MNR commandos in Santa Cruz led by Ñuflo Chávez, the scion of a prominent family,

FIGURE 4.3 Cochabamba Police Station Bombed by Rebels in the 1949 Civil War

Source: Courtesy of the U.S. National Archives (Photo: 306NT-933F3), *New York Times*, 5 September 1949.

occupied the police barracks, forced the surrender of army officers, seized control of the air base, and expropriated money from the National Bank.

Potosí also fell to the MNR. Movimientista commandos backed by miners forced the surrender of the police and accepted the word of the Manchego Regiment's commanding officer to remain neutral. A contingent of miners then appropriated weapons from the army garrison.

Erroneous in the belief that President Urriolagotia had been overthrown, government officials in Sucre released their MNR prisoners, surrendered to them, and pledged fealty to the revolution. A detachment of miners and a company from the Manchego regiment were dispatched from Potosí to assure control of the city. The August Revolution had reached its apogee. In control of Cochabamba, Santa Cruz, Potosí, and Sucre, the MNR formed a "National Revolutionary Government Junta" with Víctor Paz Estenssoro as President.[141]

Urriolagoitia's generals initiated a counterattack spearheaded by regiments from Oruro and La Paz and supported by bombers from the El Alto airfield. Cochabamba was bombed on 1 September. The MNR abandoned the city the following day and retreated east to Santa Cruz. In a stroke of luck, Movimientistas captured the government bomber pilots when they landed at Camiri to refuel. The oil fields at Camari were occupied as part of MNR strategy. Camiri, Valle Grande, Villa Montes, and Yacuiba formed a north–south axis in the Gran Chaco stretching from Valle Grande to the Argentine frontier at Yacuiba.

Desperate for provisions, members of the Junta Revolucionario flew from Santa Cruz to Yacuiba and crossed the border in search of arms, ammunition, food, and clothes. It was too little and too late.[142] The August Revolution morphed into a war for the cities. Potosí was besieged in September and the airstrip and surrounding barrios pulverized by warplanes. Officers in the Manchego Regiment then disavowed their pledge of neutrality, and PIRista informants joined the government offensive as snipers. After two days of combat, the revolutionaries were overwhelmed by government forces. Twenty-eight Movimientistas were executed.[143]

Sucre next fell to the Rosca offensive. The Sucre Movimientistas then retreated to Camiri where they were joined by hundreds of the oil workers and peasants. Within a week, the revolutionaries fled Camiri and hundreds of oil field workers and peasants escaped to Argentina. Those less fortunate were captured and executed. The news from Camiri prompted the MNR leaders in Santa Cruz to fly to safety in Argentina. After two weeks of combat, Santa Cruz fell on 16 September 1949. The Civil War was lost.

The Civil War was a military disaster for the Movimientistas, but much was gained from the experience. The seizure of the departmental capitals demonstrated the ability of the party to operate on a national level. The MNR cell structure prevented penetration and disruption of the insurrectionary scenario outside of La Paz. The failure of the insurrection in La Paz decided the fate of the August Revolution. Thwarted by government espionage, the insurrection failed to launch and the revolution degenerated into an unwinnable conventional war for the cities. The Rosca won the Civil War, but lost the support of the middle class.

The wanton savagery of the regime—bombings of civilians, massacres, torture, executions—incensed the urban populace. MNR strategy would seek to exploit their alienation and resentment.

Endgame

President Urriolagoitia's Civil War victory was the high point of his career and of the Concordancia's PURS party. Ironically, the greatest challenge to Urriolagoitia and the PURS would come from within the regime as the coalition began to self-destruct. Tin was no longer a strategic priority after World War II. The decline in demand for tin was followed by a drop in price and production. Export tonnage in 1949 was at its lowest in a decade. In 1950, it dropped even lower. The Tin Barons' responded by cutting costs; the Hochschild mines fired 40 percent of their workers and cut production by 20 percent. The decline in tin exports was calamitous for President Urriolagoitia who found that the reduction in tin output translated as reduced tax revenue and government layoffs. Already beset with inflation, the support of the urban bourgeoisie became questionable. In April 1950, with government revenue reduced by 50 percent, Urriolagoitia decreed that all foreign exchange from tin would be appropriated for government needs.[144]

The tin magnates and the PURS no longer shared a common objective. Confronted with an economic crisis, the alienation of the middle class, and the obstruction of the tin barons, Urriolagoitia found himself at a loss. A rift occurred within the regime in May 1950 when Urriolagoitia fired his ministers of government and labor after they raised workers' wages, circumventing the president's mandated wage freeze.[145] The regime next lost its ally in the U.S. State Department. Thrown to the wolves of the market, Urriolagoitia and the tin magnates were forced to contend with a host of U.S. government bureaucracies seeking to drive down the price of tin.

The Rosca began to unravel because of the competing needs of the Tin Barons and the PURS-led oligarchy. When President Urriolagoitia had demanded $500,000 from Patiño to help defray the cost of the Civil War, the mining corporation refused. Nor was assistance forthcoming from the United States. The Munitions Board informed the State Department that "no one tin-producing area is considered absolutely essential to the defense of the United States" and was advised by the National Strategic Resources Board to respond to Urriolagoitia's entreaties in a manner "sufficiently blunt to awaken the Bolivians to the realization that the divine intervention of the U.S. could not be counted on to alleviate their difficulties." In February 1950, the State Department concluded "nothing can be done to give the Bolivian tin industry special assistance" and predicted "a drastic reduction in the production of tin as well as violent political and social disturbances."[146] The economic downturn exacerbated inflation, decreased the purchasing power of the urban population, forced large numbers of workers into unemployment, and drew the urban middle and working class to the opposition. In May 1950, MNR demonstrators demanded a 60 percent wage increase for workers, the release of political prisoners, and threatened a general strike in La Paz unless Urriolagoitia complied. Falangista military officers attempted a coup d'etat. And rebellious students in La Paz demanding amnesty for political prisoners occupied the *Universidad Mayor de San Andres* and the *Centro Boliviano-Americano*, burned the offices of *La Razón*, and engaged the police in a shootout at the Plaza Murillo.[147] A strike by the La Paz *fabriles* on 17 May that began with a march to the Plaza Murillo escalated into an insurrection when workers, armed and led by MNR militants, were driven into the working-class barrio of Villa Victoria. After a two-day assault by infantry and carabinero forces and air force bombing, Villa Victoria was conquered. Casualties were estimated at over a thousand. The U.S. Embassy believed the government was nearing its end and recommended the exodus of U.S. technicians in the mines.[148] Ridiculed as a lackey of the Tin Barons, a stooge of U.S. imperialism, and frustrated by political infighting within the PURS coalition, Urriolagoitia's only hope was the presidential election scheduled for May 1951.

The parties within the PURS coalition assumed that the MNR did not constitute an electoral threat. This was a fatal mistake. Despite imprisonment, torture, executions, and losses in the Civil War, the numbers of Movimientista militants and their supporters were increasing. Daring escapes from the La Paz Panóptico Nacional and Coati prisons demonstrated the resilience of the party and the incompetence of the government. Women MNR militants from across the country led efforts to assist wives and mothers to provide food, clothing, and moral support for imprisoned loved ones. Utilizing limited financial resources and adroit political tactics, the MNR fashioned a formidable propaganda campaign against the Rosca. An "indefinite hunger strike" by Movimientista women begun on 20 April 1951 drew public attention to the plight of the prisoners and their families.[149]

The MNR staged dramatic events designed to undermine government credibility. Coverage of the events in the Rosca newspapers gave the Movimientistas an invaluable forum illustrating the regime's tyranny. When the MNR announced the arrival of Paz Estenssoro to El Alto on 14 April 1951, thousands of supporters flocked to the airport—only to be disappointed by the government's decision that the airliner be turned back to Paraguay—whereupon police tear-gassed the angry crowd. Likewise, the appearance of Hernán Siles Zuazo from exile to a surprise appearance on the floor of the Chamber of Deputies dramatized Movimientista panache.

Riven by opportunism and factionalism and seemingly ignorant of impending disaster, the PURS coalition continued down the road to ruin. President Urriolagoitia's decision to foist Gabriel Gosalvez on the PURS as a presidential candidate fractured the Concordancia. Denied their choice of a presidential candidate, the Republican Socialists deserted. The Liberal Party refused to join a "democratic front," instead of opting to attack the dismal economic performance of the regime. Tin magnate Carlos Víctor Aramayo's decision to promote Guillermo Gutiérrez (his personal secretary and former editor of the Aramayo daily *La Razón*) as a presidential candidate further divided the Rosca. Attacks on Gosalvez in the Aramayo newspaper unwittingly played into the hands of the opposition. Desperately in search of an ally, Urriolagoitia's ambassador beseeched the United States for assistance against the MNR, alleging that the party was a communist pawn of the Soviet Union and warned that unless the United States enforced the Truman Doctrine, Bolivia would become "their first satellite state" in the Americas.[150] The U.S. State Department ignored the artifice.

The Mamertazo

The election of 6 May 1951 was a momentous victory for the MNR. Víctor Paz Estenssoro garnered 54,049 votes; Gabriel Gosalvez, 39,940; Bernardino Bilbao Rioja of the FSB, 13,180; Guillermo Gutiérrez, 6,559; and the candidates of the Liberal Party and the PIR, a total of 11,611. Government electoral suppression in the mining districts denied the MNR an even greater victory. Hernán Siles won the vice-presidential election and Juan Lechín and a handful of MNR candidates were elected to the senate.[151] The Rosca was forced to either concede and hand over the reins of power to their nemesis or reunite and contrive a solution to the disastrous election. Rather than attempt to deny the MNR victory on constitutional grounds (because Paz Estenssoro failed to win a majority, the election was to be determined by the legislature), the oligarchy decided on a more certain solution. Ten days after the election, President Urriolagoitia renounced the presidency and "to preserve the public order and the security of the citizenry" handed the government to General Hugo Ballivian and a coterie of generals. Without a shot fired, the armed forces were once again in power and the MNR forced to consider the only remaining option.

Conclusions

The Sexenio gave rise to a cornucopia of indigenous revolutionary movements evidenced in brilliant stratagems for cultural revitalization, territorial revindication, and political resistance to creole-mestizo domination. The Sexenio was also the ancien régime's last stand against a revolution by the Movimientistas who responded to repression with resolve and ingenuity. Command and control of the organization was strengthened, a revolutionary cell structure formed, propaganda contrived to promote mass participation, insurrections and a civil war attempted, a successful electoral campaign undertaken, and Víctor Paz Estenssoro elected president. President Urriolagoitia's denial of the Movimientista electoral mandate (via the Mamertazo) left armed struggle their only option to overthrow the Rosca.

The internal war between the Old Regime and the nationalist revolutionaries of the Chaco Generation exemplifies the tri-continental struggle in twentieth-century Latin America, Africa, and Asia for decolonization, national self-determination, and legal and social rights for the majority of the populace. But Bolivian nationalism was a double-edged sword. Creole-mestizo nationalists espoused sovereignty, modernization, indigenous acculturation, and social integration of the nation;

indigenous nationalists sought the sovereignty of the ayllu, restitution of usurped communal lands, freedom from the colonato, and recognition of their legal and social rights as citizens. But indigenous nationalism was far from monolithic. Santos Marka T'ula and the alcaldes mayores movement believed education and literacy in Spanish were essential to revindicationist efforts in locating, reading, interpreting, and documenting legal claims to purloined lands, as did the Kallawaya Antonio Mamani Álvarez. Yet Toribio Miranda and the Alcaldes Mayores Particulares differed. They believed literacy in the language of the oppressor to be a siren song: a gateway to acculturation into the creole-mestizo world and the ultimate destruction of indigenous culture and society.

In Bolivia as elsewhere, the revolutionary nationalists were forced to confront traditional elites supported by foreign hegemons. The strategic value of tin during World War II predisposed Allied support for the Rosca and opposition to the anti-imperial struggle for sovereignty and self-determination waged by revolutionary nationalists. The Rosca, who had previously enlisted U.S. aid in the overthrow of the RADEPA–MNR nationalists—under the guise of combating Nazi-fascism—next branded the Movimientistas as communists to fit the ideological climate of the Cold War. But the North Americans were more interested in making a profit on Bolivian tin than in assisting the Rosca's questionable plea to fight communism. It is noteworthy that the U.S. manipulation of the tin contract was previously wielded as a weapon to aid the Rosca overthrow of the RADEPA National Revolution in 1946.

The conflict between tradition and modernity engendered a crisis of the colonato. The decrees of the martyred Villarroel were countermanded by hacendados, but indigenous revolutionaries challenged the legitimacy of the seigneurial system of lord and peasant. Colonos began to select authorities (jilakatas, alcaldes, and even corregidores) from within their own communities, giving rise to dual power in the countryside. The mestizo corregidores representing government authority in towns and villages served as a constant reminder of the corruption and illegitimacy of the state: levying taxes on *chicha* and *muk'o*, collecting fines, and confiscating the personal possessions of hapless Indians unable to make payment.

In the crucial decade of the 1940s, an indigenous awakening confronted the ancien régime. As Marxist militants in mining camps and haciendas spoke of class consciousness, the Indigenous Committee organized hacienda sit-down strikes throughout the highlands as the *Alcades Mayores Particulares* stressed the commonality of the *first people* and founded clandestine schools to revitalize indigenous religion and culture as a means of combating creole-mestizo domination. Anarchists conjoined the aspirations of urban and rural Indians into schools and sindicatos, and the Pachakamak ideologues sought the unity of indigenous peoples organized into a national system of cooperatives within a multicultural state. Indigenous resistance to creole-mestizo hegemony, epitomized in the Great Revolt of 1947, was a harbinger of change and a precursor to the agrarian rising in the Andean highlands following the restoration of the National Revolution in 1952.

Notes

1. Augusto Céspedes, *El president colgado* (Buenos Aires, 1956), 248. *Los Tiempos*, 4 August 1946, 7; Luis Peñaloza, *Historia del Movimiento Nacionalista Revolucionario, 1941–1952* (La Paz, 1963), 100–103.
2. Flack to SECSTATE, 22 July 1946, U.S. National Archives 824.00/7–2246.
3. Peñaloza, *Historia*, 118.
4. Ibid., 118–119.
5. Ibid., 131.
6. Ibid., 118–121.
7. Ibid.
8. Laura Gotkowitz, *A Revolution for Our Rights: Indigenous Struggle for Land and Justice in Bolivia, 1880–1952* (Durham, NC, 2007), 236. On Hertzog's rural inspectors, see Luis Antezana E. and Hugo Romero B., *Historia de los sindicatos campesinos: un proceso de integración nacional en Bolivia* (La Paz, 1973), 145.
9. Glen J. Dorn, *The Truman Administration and Bolivia: Making the World Safe for Liberal Constitutional Oligarchy* (University Park, PA, 2011), 78.
10. Laurence Whitehead, "Bolivia since 1930," in Leslie Bethell, ed., *The Cambridge History of Latin America,* 8 (Cambridge, UK, 1991), 536.
11. James Dunkerley, *Rebellion in the Veins: Political Struggle in Bolivia, 1952–1982* (London, 1984), 35; Herbert S. Klein, *Parties and Political Change in Bolivia, 1880–1952* (Cambridge, UK, 1969), 388–389.
12. James Dunkerley observes that the Thesis, with contributions by Lora's comrade Fernando Bravo, is "in essence an application of Trotsky's 1938 'Transitional Programme' to Bolivian conditions and with special reference to trade-union objectives." James Dunkerley, *Rebellion in the Veins*, 17.
13. Guillermo Lora, *Tesis de Pulacayo* (La Paz, 1959), 16.
14. Ibid., 27. See also Steven Volk, "Class, Union, Party: The Development of a Revolutionary Union Movement in Bolivia (1905–1952)," Part 2, *Science and Society*, 39.2 (Summer 1975), 192–197.
15. Ibid., 19–25.
16. Dunkerley, *Rebellion in the Veins*, 14.
17. Peñaloza, *Historia*, 136.
18. For a dramatic portrayal of the revolutionary cell under attack, see the *The Battle of Algiers*, Gillo Pontecorvo's cinematic tour de force on urban counter-insurgency.
19. James M. Malloy, *Bolivia: The Uncompleted Revolution* (Pittsburgh, PA, 1970), 137.
20. Peñaloza, *Historia*, 144. For details and criticism of the party's failed coup attempts by the Executive Secretary of the MNR Comité, see Ibid.136–139, 144–149, and Malloy, *Bolivia: The Uncompleted Revolution*, 136–137.
21. Malloy, *Bolivia: The Uncompleted Revolution*, 139.
22. Kevin Young, *Blood of the Earth* (Austin, TX, 2017), 118–119.
23. Christopher Mitchell, *The Legacy of Populism in Bolivia: From the MNR to Military Rule* (New York, 1977), 29.
24. Peñaloza, *Historia*, 133–135, 143. Alfonso Finot (Paz's aide) claimed in *Asi cayó Villarroel*, his personal account of Paz's role in Villarroel's final hours, that Paz had ordered the telephone line to the Palace to be cut: this provided sensational grist for the Rosca propaganda war against the MNR.
25. Malloy, *Bolivia: The Uncompleted Revolution*, 136–137; Dorn, *The Truman Administration and Bolivia*, 78; Malloy, *Bolivia: The Uncompleted Revolution*, 133–135.
26. Peñaloza, *Historia*, 132–133.
27. Antezana and Romero, *Historia de los sindicatos campesinos*, 124.
28. Luis Antezana Erguita, *Historia secreta del Movimiento Nacionalista Revolucionario*, Vol. 5 (La Paz, 1986), 1281–1286.
29. Ibid., 1260–1267, 1270–1271.
30. Enrique Hertzog, *Mensaje al H. Congreso Ordinario de 1947* (La Paz, 1947), 21, 25.

31. Ari, *Earth Politics*, 81–96.
32. Ibid., 94.
33. Ibid., 92; Gotkowitz, *A Revolution for Our Rights*, 249–250.
34. Zulema Lehm and Silvia Rivera Cusicanqui, *Los artesanos libertarios y la etica del trabajo* (La Paz, 1988).
35. Ibid., 84–85.
36. Gotkowitz, *A Revolution for Our Rights*, 254.
37. Lehm and Rivera, *Los artesanos libertarios*, 86–87.
38. Antezana and Romero, *Historia de los sindicatos campesinos*, 134; Roberto Choque Canqui and Esteban Ticona, *Historia de una lucha desigual: los contenidos ideológicos y políticos de las rebeliones indígenas* (La Paz, 2005), 104,121.
39. Antezana and Romero, *Historia de los sindicatos campesinos*, 135.
40. Lehm and Rivera, *Los artesanos libertarios*, 88–89.
41. Antezana and Romero, *Historia de los sindicatos campesinos*, 136; Lehm and Rivera, *Los artesanos libertarios*, 88, 91.
42. The FOL Anarchists were doubtless cognizant of developments that transpired a decade earlier in Spain: "Anarchosyndicalist peasant unions were composed, at the outbreak of the war, almost entirely of laborers and indigent farmers who had been fired by the philosophy of anarchism. For these zealots, rural collectivization was the foundation stone of the new regime of anarchist, or libertarian communism, as it was called . . . a regime of 'human brotherhood that would attempt to solve economic problems without the state and without politics in accordance with the well-known principle, 'from each according to his abilities, to each according to his needs.' . . . [A] regime without classes, based on labor unions and self-governing communes, that would be united into a nationwide confederation, and in which the means of production and distribution would be held in common." Burnett Bolloten, *The Spanish Civil War: Revolution and Counterrevolution* (Chapel Hill, NC, 1991), 65.
43. Gotkowitz, *A Revolution for Our Rights*, 251–252.
44. Antezana and Romero, *Historia de los sindicatos campesinos*, 137.
45. Choque and Tiquina, *Historia de una lucha desigual*, 123.
46. Ibid., 123–124.
47. Ibid., 124.
48. Ibid.; Antezana and Romero, *Historia de las luchas campesinas*, 151, 163.
49. Gotkowitz, *A Revolution for Our Rights,* 252; Antezana and Romero, *Historia de los sindicatos campesinos*, 146–147.
50. Antezana and Romero, *Historia de los campesinos revolucionarios*, 147.
51. Lehm and Rivera, *Los artesanos libertarios*, 90–92.
52. Antezana and Romero, *Historia de los sindicatos campesinos*, 147–149.
53. Ibid., 147.
54. Silvia Rivera Cusiquanqui, *Oprimidos pero no vencidos* (Geneva, 1986), 27–29.
55. Antezana and Romero, *Historia de los sindicatos campesinos*, 149.
56. Ibid.,152–154. See also Choque and Ticona, *Historia de una lucha desigual*, 126; Lehm and Rivera Cusiquanqui, *Los artesanos libertarios*, 93; Antezana, *Historia secreta*, Vol. 5, 1260, 1269, 1275.
57. Gotkowitz, *A Revolution for Our Rights*, 253–254, Antezana and Romero, *Historia de los sindicatos campesinos*, *147, 153;* Choque and Ticona, *Historia de una lucha desigual, 126.*
58. Choque and Ticona, *Historia de una lucha desigual*, 126.
59. Antezana, *Historia secreta*, Vol. 5, 1269.
60. Antezana and Romero, *Historia de los sindicatos campesinos*, 153–154.
61. Ibid., 151.
62. Lehm and Rivera, *Los artesanos libertarios*, 89.
63. Antezana and Romero, Historia de los sindicatos campesinos, 152.
64. Ibid., 151. Lehm and Rivera, *Los artesanos libertarios*, 93.
65. Lehm and Rivera, *Los artesanos libertarios*, 95.

66. Ibid., 87–88.
67. Interview with ex-colono Esteban Cruz in Dandler and Torrico, "From the National Indigenous Congress to the Ayopaya Rebellion," in Steve J. Stern, ed., *Resistance, Rebellion, and Consciousness in the Andean Peasant World, 18th to 20th Centuries* (Madison, 1987), 363.
68. Gotkowitz, *A Revolution for Our Rights*, 150.
69. Dandler and Torrico, "From the National Indigenous Congress to the Ayopaya Rebellion," 375–376. Xavier Albo notes parenthetically that the MNR "instigated the well-known rebellion of Ayopya in 1947" but provides no more than the assertion. Xavier Albo, "From MNRistas to Kataristas to Katari," in Stern, ed., *Resistance, Rebellion, and Consciousness*, 383.
70. Ibid., 365–366. See also José Gordillo, *Campesinos revolucionarios en Bolivia: Identidad, Territorio y Sexualidad en el Valle Alto de Cochabamba, 1952–1964* (La Paz, 2000), 206.
71. Antezana and Romero, *Historia de los sindicatos campesinos*, 140–141.
72. Dandler and Torrico, "From the National Indigenous Congress to the Ayopaya Rebellion," 364.
73. Gotkowitz, *A Revolution for Our Rights*, 237–238.
74. Ibid., 237.
75. Dandler and Torrico, "From the National Indigenous Congress to the Ayopaya Rebellion," 365; Choque and Ticona. *Historia de una lucha desigual*, 121–122.
76. Quoted in Dandler and Torrico, "From the National Indigenous Congress to the Ayopaya Rebellion," 368.
77. Gordillo, *Campesinos revolucionarios*, 204.
78. Antezana and Romero's estimate is 20,000 rebels: *Historia de los sindicatos campesinos*, 138; Gotkowitz's estimate is 3,000–10,000, see *A Revolution for Our Rights*, 237.
79. Gotkowitz, *A Revolution for Our Rights*, 247.
80. Ibid., 245; 142–153. The dirigente Manuel Andia together with a number of miners fomented the unrest at Mizque. Antezana and Romero, *Historia de los sindicatos campesinos*, 143.
81. V.I. Lenin, *Collected Works* (Moscow, 1964), 38–41; Leon Trotsky, translated by Max Eastman, *The History of the Russian Revolution* (Chicago, 2008), 149.
82. Antezana and Romero, *Historia de los sindicatos campesinos*, 138, 144, 146, 149, 156–157, 161.
83. Ibid., 161.
84. Waskar Ari Chachaki, *Earth Politics: Religion, Decolonization, and Bolivia's Indigenous Intellectuals* (Durham, NC, 2014), 193–197. I am indebted to this Aymara historian's impressive contribution to Bolivian indigenous history.
85. Ari, *Earth Politics*, 57–58, 77.
86. Ibid., 64–68.
87. James C. Scott continues this argument initiated by Antonio Gramsci, "In fact, for Gramsci, the proletariat is more enslaved at the level of ideas than at the level of behavior. The historic task of 'the party' is therefore less to lead the revolution than to break the symbolic miasma that blocks revolutionary thought," quoted in Scott, *Weapons of the Weak*, 39.
88. Ibid., 63, 73, 77.
89. Juan Félix Arias [Waskar Ari], "La politica y sus modelos en la relacion estado boliviano y el movimiento indígena del sur de Cochabamba (1936–1947)," in Regalsky, ed., *Tata Fermin: Llama viva de un Yachaq* (Cochabamba, 1995), 65, 68. Waskar Ari translates the Inca precept as "*ama sua, ama llulla, ama khella*: Don't steal, don't lie, and don't be lazy." Ari, *Earth Politics*, 108, 227.
90. Ibid., 67.
91. Ibid., 24–25 and Ari, *Earth Politics*, 68. For official correspondence regarding work stoppages fomented by Andia and hacendado requests for government intervention against the AMP leader, see Arias, "La politica y sus modelos," 26–27.
92. Ibid., 71, 73.

93. Ibid., 30, 71.
94. Eric Langer, *Economic Change and Rural Resistance in Southern Bolivia, 1880–1930* (Palo Alto, CA, 1989), 50.
95. Ari, *Earth Politics*, 124.
96. Langer, *Economic Change and Rural Resistance*, 60, 171, 179. An extreme example of this trend in Chuquisaca occurred at Hacienda La Candelaria, where a Harvard-educated agronomist sought to maximize production by increasing labor demands through elimination of all of the above hacienda customs. Ibid., 172–174. See also Arias, "La politica y su modelos," 66.
97. Ari, *Earth Politics*, 67, 69–70, 75, 152; see also Gotkowitz, *A Revolution for Our Rights*, 67–68.
98. Ari, *Earth Politics*, 125.
99. Ibid., 135, 132.
100. Ibid., 126.
101. Ibid., 116, 133.
102. Ibid., 75–76, 133. Melitón Gallardo remained in prison after the 1952 overthrow of the ancien régime. Maria Carmen Soliz Urrutia, "Fields of Revolution: The Politics of Agrarian Reform in Bolivia, 1935–1971," Ph.D. dissertation, New York University, 2014, 136.
103. Antezana and Romero, *Historia de los sindicatos campesinos*, 128–129, 145.
104. Ibid., 143–144, 157, 181–184; Lehm and Rivera, *Los artesanos libertarios*, 89.
105. Whitehead, "Bolivia since 1930," 538.
106. In addition to a prison on the banks of the Rio Ichilo and another at Puerto Grether in Santa Cruz, Asunta in the Sud Yungas (La Paz Department) also held indigenous rebels; Antezana, *Historia secreta*, Vol. 5, 1276, 1292; Antezana and Romero, *Historia de los sindicatos campesinos*, 133.
107. Peñaloza, *Historia*, 177; Lehm and Rivera, *Los artesanos libertarios*, 96.
108. Dandler and Torrico, "From the National Indigenous Congress to the Ayopaya Rebellion," 377.
109. *Los Tiempos*, 14 February 1946, 3. But appearances can be deceiving: "An alternative interpretation of such quiescence might be that it is to be explained by the relationship of forces in the countryside and not by peasant values and beliefs. . . . Agrarian peace, in this view, may well be the peace of repression (remembered and/or anticipated) rather than the peace of consent or complicity." Scott, *Weapons of the Weak*, 40.
110. Antezana and Romero, *Historia de los campesinos revolucionarios*, 181–182. The benign side of Hertzog's plans for agricultural cooperatives is evidenced in his Supreme Decrees of 1948 granting Indians in the Oriente the mission lands on which they toiled. Miguel Bonifaz, *Legislación Agrario-Indigena* (Cochabamba, 1953), 534–539.
111. Ranaboldo, *El camino perdido*, 161. The dehumanization of racism, it was argued during the African struggle against white domination, could only be extirpated through violent retribution. See, for example, Frantz Fanon, *The Wretched of the Earth* (New York, 1963) and Albert Memmi, *The Colonizer and the Colonized* (New York, 1965).
112. Antezana, *Historia secreta*, Vol. 5, 1285–1286.
113. Antezana and Romero, *Historia de los campesinos revolucionarios*, 177–178, 188, 198–199.
114. Ibid., 173–174.
115. Ranaboldo, *El camino perdido*, 144, 154–155, 163, 166–168, 171, 179–180, 184–185, 193.
116. The Kallawaya averred that Luciano Catari Tito (aka Asto Warachi Condorcanqi) and Julian Apaza Mamani (aka Agustín Warachi), "one of the most prepared among my dirigentes," aided in the composition of the *Tesis*. Ronabaldo, *El camino perdido*, 149. In an interview with *El Diario* on 26 September 1950, Mamani Álvarez stated that the Pachacamac Party was proclaimed on 27 December 1947.
117. The *Tesis* welcomes foreign immigrants but excludes Jews as "useless and prejudicial to the nation" and in a chilling note adds, "*of whom we will have to cleanse the country.*" (emphasis added) (*Tesis*, 20)

The Sexenio **157**

118. Ranabaldo, *El camino perdido*, 140, 146.
119. The *Tesis* is congruent here with Spanish anarchist principles: "We Anarchosyndicalists . . . believed from the very beginning that individual farming would lead directly to large properties, to the domination of political bosses, to the exploitation of man by man, and finally to the reestablishment of the capitalist system." Bolloten, *The Spanish Civil War*, 64; whereas, "Collective labor . . . banishes hate, envy, and egoism and opens the way for 'mutual respect and solidarity because all those who live collectively treat one another as members of a large family." Ibid., 63.
120. Antonio Mamani Álvarez, a persistent advocate of indigenous education, intuitively understood the importance of collectivization and mechanization for the peasantry. In the words of the Spanish Anarchist, Abad de Santillan: "The greatest disadvantage of individual farming, which occupies all able-bodied members of the family: the father, the mother, the children . . . is the excessive amount of labor. . . . There are no fixed hours of work, and the expenditure of physical energy is unlimited. . . . It is essential that he [the peasant] should have the time and energy to educate himself and his family, so that the light of civilization can illuminate life in the countryside." Bolloten, *The Spanish Civil War*, 63.
121. In fact, the peoples of Kollasuyu were vassals of the Inca, requisitioned to provide forced labor (*mit'a*) in mines and the construction of extensive public works projects, were forcibly relocated (*mitimaqs*) and compelled to adopt Quechua, the lingua franca of their conquerors. Revolts and rebellions were commonplace and retribution was carried out with a vengeance.
122. Michael E. Moseley, *The Incas and Their Ancestors: The Archaeology of Peru* (London, 2001) 227. In the highlands of Kollasuyu, "It was not long before the sophisticated agricultural techniques worked out by the natives of the high plateau over the millennia were lost to the world. The population that survived the conquest was not large enough to justify investment in terraces and dams, dikes and aqueducts. The Spanish overlords were more interested in precious metals, cattle, and a few crops that fueled their mining industry. . . . The once innumerable banks of fertile agricultural terraces fell gradually into disuse, the once vast herds of llamas and alpaca dwindled to nothing, and the once bustling network of caravans and colonies atrophied, bringing isolation to the native populations. . . . The native Andean peoples have persisted in this state of marginality to this day." Alan L. Kolata, *The Tiwanaku: Portrait of an Andean Civilization* (Cambridge, MA, 1993), 301.
123. Discussion of anarchist-related topics often appear in quotations, but the *Tesis* is a revolutionary manifesto bereft of citations and not an academic treatise. The *Tesis* reprises Mamani Álvarez's criticism of the FOL-FAD Anarcho-syndicalist experience in La Paz Department as precipitous in execution—insurrections deficient in the ideological preparation necessary to inspire revolutionary struggle—and inexorably doomed to failure. The *Tesis* reflects the Kallawaya's input as the most worldly of the Indian revolutionaries, but the composition is the work of his collaborators, referred to as the "more prepared" of his followers, doubtlessly influenced by Bolivian Anarchists and indirectly, by the contemporaneous Anarchosyndicalist experience of the Spanish Civil War (1936–1939).
124. See Articles 1–21, 24–31, 33–34 of The Agrarian Law in John Womack, Jr., *Zapata and the Mexican Revolution* (New York: Vintage, 1968), 405–410.
125. Peñaloza, *Historia*, 154.
126. Ibid., 163, 183–184. The U.S. embassy's observations of March 1949 on the Taborga faction (*Movimiento Nacionalista Revolucionario Villarroelista*) note that Taborga "worked as an informer for the police" and had been expelled from the MNR. See the declassified CIA File, U.S. National Archives (released 9 September 1999): CIA-RDP82-00457ROO2400250008-28.
127. Richard W. Patch, "The Bolivian Falange," *American Universities Field Staff Report*, 14 May 1959, 5–6. For the Falange's "Program of Principles," see Mario Rolon Anaya, *Politica y Partidos en Bolivia* (La Paz, 1966), 243–247. It is noteworthy that the FSB

embraced the "Redemption of the Indian" through education and agrarian reform in a proposed "New State." Ibid., 246.
128. Ibid., 181–183, 186–191; also, Luis Antezana, *Historia secreta*, Vol. 5, 1405–1407.
129. Lydia Gueiler Tejada, *La mujer y la revolucion* (La Paz, 1959), 39.
130. Ibid., 27–35.
131. Ibid., 157.
132. Ibid., 157–158, 171–172.
133. Ibid., 196.
134. Silvia Rivera Cusicanqui points out that the Indian leaders "were to be passive receivers of the [MNR's] new civilizing proposals" as they "slowly abandoned their ethnic attachment and assimilated the illusion of equality among citizens." Silvia Rivera Cusicanqui, *Oppressed but Not Defeated: Peasant Struggles Among the Aymara and Qhechwa in Bolivia, 1900–1980* (Geneva, 1987), 60.
135. Antezana, *Historia secreta*, Vol., 5, 1275–1276.
136. Ibid., 1277–1278.
137. Interview by the author with Víctor Paz Estenssoro, Lima, Peru 27 June 1970.
138. James V. Kohl, "Antonio Mamani Álvarez: 'A Call to Bolivian Indians'," *The Journal of Peasant Studies*, 4 (July 1977), 394–397.
139. Peñaolza, *Historia*, 198.
140. Ibid., 202–203.
141. Ibid., 201–202, 212; Raul Lema Pelaez, *Con las banderas del Movimiento Nacionalista Revolucionario: el sexenio, 1946–1952* (La Paz, 1979), 401–410; Antezana, *Historia secreta*, Vol. 5, 1455–1584.
142. Peñaloza, *Historia*, 208–209.
143. Ibid., 215–219.
144. Dorn, *The Truman Administration and Bolivia*, 104, 108, 111–112.
145. Ibid., 105.
146. Ibid., 111, 113–114.
147. Ibid., 109–110.
148. Peñaloza, *Historia*, 238.
149. Ibid., 235–236, 245–246; Lema Pelaez, *Con las banderas*, 410–416.
150. Dorn, *The Truman Administration and Bolivia*, 132.
151. Peñaloza, *Historia*, 248, Dorn, *The Truman Administration and Bolivia*, 131–132; Malloy, *Bolivia: The Uncompleted Revolution*, 152–153.

5

REVOLUTION

Redux, 1952–1965

Denied their electoral victory, the MNR revolutionaries began preparations for a revolution. Much had been learned from their many attempts to seize power during the Sexenio.[1] The grand strategy would be much the same as that of the 1947 and 1949 insurrections: a propaganda campaign directed at the illegitimate usurpers—public demonstrations to attract popular support; increased recruitment of militants to revolutionary cells; strategic and tactical leadership by a cadre of seasoned party militants; and continued collusion with the FSB, army, and carabinero officers. Significant changes were also instituted. Recruitment was extended to the *fabriles* and "popular classes" of the La Paz barrios, a revolutionary vanguard, *Los Grupos de Honor*, organized, and the party High Command divided into three insulated *Comités*, led by Hernán Siles Zuazo.[2]

The propaganda campaign brought attention to the MNR. When the Junta triumphantly paraded a coffin with the cadaver of Eduardo Abaroa, a hero of the War of the Pacific, through the streets of La Paz (after the Chilean government returned the patriot's remains), Movimientista militants sprang into action and draped the coffin with an MNR banner. The ensuing melee between police and MNR militants undermined the Junta's attempt to associate itself with patriotism while drawing attention to the patriotic resistance of the party. Mass demonstrations staged in departmental capitals were instrumental in associating the nation's food shortage with the Junta's inept governance. A "Hunger March" in February 1952 that led to the arrests of dozens of Movimientistas (followed by the arrests of their lawyers when they sought writs of habeas corpus for the defendants) illustrated the Junta's disregard for the rule of law as well as the tactical ingenuity of the party. A successful hunger strike by women militants freed 31 imprisoned Movimientistas—demonstrating that the effect of a particular action could be compounded through a creative twist.[3]

The MNR also capitalized on the internal disintegration of the Junta Militar. Although General Ballivián posted his most dynamic generals in remote garrisons, the Junta remained a nest of opportunists. Army Chief of Staff General Humberto Torres Ortiz and the Minister of Government General Antonio Seleme Vargas (who commanded the carabinero national police) were ceaseless conspirators— with each other, with the MNR, and with the FSB—at times simultaneously.[4] Movimientista activity was an open secret, as were the conspiratorial doings of Falangistas, Trotskyists, carabinero, and army officers. General Terrazas was soon in contact with Hernán Siles, proposing a new election with Siles as the presidential candidate; General Torres proffered a similar proposal; while Colonel Sánchez proposed a Sánchez-Siles ticket. Negotiations with General Seleme, the Minister of Government, and General Torres soon followed suit. But Siles refused all offers and insisted on recognition of Paz Estenssoro's electoral mandate stolen by the Mamertazo.[5]

General Ballivian's problems were further compounded by negotiations with the United States for the purchase of Bolivian tin. The Reconstruction Finance Corporation (RFC) representing the North American government was directed by Senator Stuart Symington, a bombastic fiscal conservative with presidential ambitions, who launched a personal crusade against the Bolivian Junta and the Tin Barons—equating pennies per pound of tin with extortion and "the ultimate destruction of our free enterprise system." Pennies per pound represented savings for U.S. taxpayers, but spelled economic deprivation and political instability for Bolivia. Symington's initial offer of $1.03 per pound was summarily rejected and negotiations stalled.[6]

The Tin Barons retained the influential Nathanson Brothers ($200,000 per annum) to influence public opinion and lobby against nationalization of the mines. With the advent of the Korean War, they waged a propaganda campaign in newspapers and magazines portraying the Bolivian revolution as a communist threat to the Free World. The technique was reminiscent of the earlier effort contrived to portray the Nationalist Revolutionaries as Nazi-fascists threatening South America.[7]

Symington was forced to resign from the RFC after General Ballivián suggested that the Organization of American States might provide a more favorable arena to plead its case against Yankee imperialism. Negotiation was then resumed by President Truman, Secretary of State Dean Acheson, and their staffs. Ballivián next proposed to end the impasse by selling the tin to the Argentine nationalist Juan Perón. Amid an economic crisis and mounting political opposition, the Junta dispatched a trio of oligarchs to Washington to negotiate a new offer. Agreed to on 7 April 1952, the offer of $1.21 per pound was to be accompanied by a $5,500,000 loan to the Junta together with an Export-Import Bank loan of $8,000,000 for development of aviation facilities, tungsten and oil exploration, and a meat-packing facility.[8]

Two days after the agreement, on 9 April 1952, a revolution erupted in Bolivia. The British Foreign Office attributed the revolution to the United States: "The principal architect of the present coup d'état was Mr. Stuart Symington." The State

Department's Deputy Assistant Secretary Thomas Mann concurred. "We felt very strongly that haggling over a few cents difference in the price of tin might set in motion forces which would lead to the overthrow of a friendly, middle-of-the-road government and precipitate nationalism."[9] The rule of the Rosca was neither "middle-of-the road" nor "friendly" to its subjects, as the nationalism unleashed in April 1952 attests.

Insurrection: 9–11 April 1952

The MNR planned to seize control of the nation's major cities via a series of armed insurrections in yet another reprise of the many failed attempts of the Sexenio (1946–1952). La Paz, the center of governmental power, remained the crucial target. Armed with bolt-action rifles from the Chaco War, the Movimientistas and their supporters faced a daunting task. The army High Command had crafted a Plan of Operations to combat insurrections with an "Iron Ring" of seven regiments deployed around La Paz, supported by artillery batteries above the city at El Alto, where there was also an air base with transport and warplanes. The Plan included a provision for additional regiments to be dispatched from Altiplano garrisons and others to arrive by railway or airlifted from Cochabamba and Camiri to reinforce the troops in La Paz.[10] The regiments wielded considerable firepower: light and heavy machine guns, artillery, mortars, grenades, bazookas. The heights of El Alto afforded a strategic advantage to bombard the city with artillery fire and an air base ideally situated to launch warplanes against insurgents below. The relative disposition of force between the Junta and MNR revolutionaries certainly favored the Junta. How, then, could the Movimientistas hope to prevail against the preponderant armed forces with ground and air superiority?

In three fateful days (9–11 April 1952), a significant chapter in the history of urban insurrectionary warfare would transpire as the MNR armed vanguard, against all odds and leading by example, inspired the urban populace to take up arms. And thus, a social revolution was born.[11]

The groundwork had been laid earlier. To survive the repression of the Sexenio, the MNR necessarily refined their command and control organization, created a clandestine cell structure, instituted urban zonal and barrio commandos, and recruited adherents among army and carabinero officers, miners, factory workers, students, and the middle and working classes. MNR militants had been involved in the 1950 factory workers' strike that was crushed by government artillery and warplane bombs.[12] The memory of the oligarchy's brutality was not forgotten by the residents of the working-class barrios where many of the men were battle-hardened Chaco War veterans. Their morale, tactical experience, and knowledge of the terrain would soon prove decisive in combat against the Junta's battalions led by inept senior officers (who lost the Chaco War), inexperienced junior officers, and Indian conscripts.[13]

On 8 April 1952, General Antonio Seleme Vargas, the head of the national police (*carabineros*), was accused of treason and expelled from the Junta. He then sent a note ("Now or Never") to Hernán Siles who alerted the MNR revolutionary committees, zonal commandos, and Los Grupos de Honor.[14] The MNR had lost the element of surprise. The insurrection planned for 12 April could not wait.

Wednesday, 9 April: Day 1

MNR Objectives: (1) seize and distribute weapons and ammunition from police stations and military arms depots; (2) assume defensive positions to combat the Lanza Regiment and Colegio Militar cadets; (3) neutralize the warplanes stationed at the El Alto airbase; (4) rally the citizenry of La Paz to the MNR cause; (5) occupy Radio Illimani.

By daybreak the Movimientistas began assuming positions to combat the Junta regiments in the city, seizing arms and ammunition from police stations and military arms depots and distributing them to MNR militants and citizen insurgents. The *Unión Sindical de Trabajadores Fabriles* called upon factory militants to mobilize their militias and join the revolution while a detachment of General Seleme's carabineros assembled in the city center. Augusto Cuadros entered the El Alto air base at dawn and with the assistance of Captain René Barrientos (and other members of a secretive MNR military cell) convinced the commanding officer to remain neutral.[15]

Hernán Silez, Juan Lechín, and Etelvina Peña de Córdova occupied Radio Illimani and—in a perfectly executed example of propaganda disinformation—announced the overthrow of the Junta by a coup d'état.[16] Crowds welcomed the news and swarmed the streets. Control of Radio Illimani would be invaluable to the revolution: calling the populace to arms and directing their movement. "The call to the people by means of Radio Illimani," continually transmitted, "to assemble in the barrio of Miraflores and inviting them to form barricades to defend the revolution" against the advance of the Lanza Regiment was noted by *El Diario*.[17]

The Grupos de Honor together with citizen insurgents entrenched atop Laikakota Hill impeded the movement of the Lanza regiment from their barracks at the Estado Mayor toward the city center. MNR cadre, acting in concert with carabineros and bolstered by an influx of citizens, repulsed a detachment of the Lanza Regiment as it approached the city center. Here MNR tactical prowess snatched victory from impending defeat. Adrián Barrenechea seized upon the idea of using dynamite to halt the Lanza advance. Raúl Fortún managed to secure three crates from a friend. After the Movimientistas freed miners from the National Penitentiary to provide expertise with the explosives, the Lanza advance was halted.[18] Suffering serious losses, a desperate call for ammunition by the soldiers went unanswered: because, as the wife of Lanza Captain Rogelio Miranda recalled, "one of the superior officers was committed to the revolution."[19]

By midday, MNR insurgents, including Grupos de Honor militants Lydia Gueiler Tejada and Carmela Ascarrunz de Peláez, occupied the Palacio Quemado.[20] The Federation of University Students called upon the citizenry to meet at Plaza Murillo outside the Palacio to support the revolution, while

Movimientistas took to the streets enlisting adherents to the cause: "Viva the Movement!," "Glory to Villarroel!," "Paz Estenssoro Awaits Power!"[21] Elsewhere, two companies from the Lanza Regiment were engaged in a street battle with carabineros of the Calama Regiment (escaping their overrun barracks) together with aroused citizens after they entered the working-class barrio of Villa Villa. The memory of the 1950 government massacre sparked insurrectionary fervor among the populace—many of whom were combat-hardened Chaco War veterans—in a daylong engagement that shifted to the Triangular Park and then to the environs of the city cemetery.[22]

In mid-morning, the Junta launched a fearsome artillery barrage on the city; this was followed by a second shelling in mid-afternoon targeting Villa Victoria, Villa Nuevo Potosí, Villa Pabón, and other working-class barrios. Surrounded by the military's "Iron Ring" of seven regiments equipped with heavy armaments, the frightening shelling created a crisis of confidence among the MNR leadership. Late that afternoon, General Seleme convened a meeting of Movimientistas and RADEPA officers, including Colonel Edmundo Nogales, the most vociferous defender of the revolution in the final hours of the Villarroel regime. Assessing the Junta onslaught, Seleme asked Nogales to assume command of the insurgents holding the high ground at the cemetery. Nogales refused, claiming the battle was lost. Shaken, General Seleme renounced his leadership in a broadcast on Radio Illimani and fled to the safety of the Chilean Embassy where he joined General Ballivián, his erstwhile adversary, who likewise had chosen expediency over honor: the struggle was not for the faint of heart.[23]

At 11:00 p.m., as another hour of artillery bombardment commenced, Hernán Siles convened a meeting at the Universidad Mayor de San Andrés to assess the situation with student militants and MNR leaders. The mood was initially defeatist. Yet Adrián Barrenechea and Julio Manuel Aramayo voiced their total commitment to the cause as did other Movimientistas and students. Hernán Siles feared a tremendous loss of life if the insurrection continued. A telephone call to General Torres Ortiz was answered with vehemence: surrender or face the full fury of the armed forces and the execution of all survivors. The MNR found itself in a fight to the death. With no way out: morale turned from defeatist to positive.[24]

Meanwhile, MNR militants executed a crucial pair of tactical maneuvers. With weapons and ammunition in short supply, it was imperative to secure armaments. Army Captain Israel Téllez (a member of the MNR Departmental Command) leading a small force assembled five mortars at the Cemetery and unleashed a relentless barrage on the army arsenal at Caiconi (Polvorín de Caiconi). Three hours later, MNR militants and civilian insurgents stormed the armory, seizing 40 million rounds of ammunition that was quickly distributed among their compatriots fighting in La Paz and in the steep canyons beneath El Alto to halt the descent of army regiments.[25] In addition to the Caiconi armory, three other arsenals were taken adding 12,000 rifles to the 4,500 carabinero rifles and ammunition earlier provided by General Seleme. To this was added a trainload of ammunition destined for the Bolivar Regiment: left virtually unguarded at the Viacha railway station, it was easily secured by Movimientistas led by Ángel López España, who with a band of insurgents, began the most audacious campaign of the revolution.[26]

After seizing weapons from a police station and gathering more men, weapons, and ammunition from an arms depot, España's group climbed under the light of the moon toward the left flank of the Junta's entrenched position at "La Ceja" ("The Eyebrow") where artillery batteries were pulverizing the working-class barrios below. They stopped briefly at the *Usina*, the city's electrical plant, to cut the power lines before attacking La Ceja with dynamite, rifle, and machine gun fire.[27] The city fell into darkness and the cannons fell silent.

Thursday, 10 April: Day 2

MNR Objectives: (1) seize and distribute weapons and ammunition; (2) defeat Lanza Regiment; (3) halt descent of Junta regiments from El Alto; (4) defeat Junta regiments entrenched at El Alto.

Workers from the railway, cement factory, and miners from Milluni joined the revolution, together with middle-class sympathizers, university students, and militants from the anarchist FOL.[28] The Lanza Regiment and Colegio cadets were stopped from reaching the city center by the Zeballos Carabinero Regiment, students from the university, the Police Academy, and Paceño insurgents.[29] The Lanza detachments retreated to the fortified stronghold of the Estado Mayor where, despite their superior firepower, they were overpowered in a bloody engagement by dynamite-wielding miners and Paceños firing rifles, machine guns, and mortars.[30] The defeat of the Lanza Regiment resulted in a bonanza of weaponry: rifles, light and heavy machine guns, mortars, and ammunition were quickly put to use in the war for the city. The Pérez and Bolivar Regiments, arriving from the Altiplano, were summarily captured by civilian insurgents as they attempted to negotiate the tortuous descent amidst the steep canyon terrain.[31] Their weapons were quickly distributed among the insurgents.

As the numbers of civilian combatants swelled to mass proportions, the insurrection reached a tipping point—to become a revolution. The conquest of El Alto would deliver the coup de grâce to the ancien régime. As the MNR Chauffeur's Commando, together with MNR militants, ascended the heights to attack the Air Base, insurgents led by López España and Captain Téllez continued their assault on the flanks of the government positions at La Ceja. Outflanked, surrounded, and low on ammunition, the disorganized and dispirited troops were shocked to see some 10,000 armed Paceños swarming the steep inclines—climbing toward them. As the regiments retreated, they found themselves confronted by 200 dynamite-hurling miners.[32] Fearing the worst, General Torres retreated to Viacha, a town 20 kilometers behind his lines, as his demoralized officers and their troops began surrendering en masse.[33] This, together with attacks on the entrenched Junta regiments at El Alto, gave pause to Torres, who fled to the village of Laja near the Peruvian border.

Insurrections also broke out in the departmental capitals. As *El Diario* reported on 9 April, "insurgent forces controlled the situation in the following districts: Cochabamba, Potosí, Oruro, Beni, Tupiza, Sucre. In all these centers, the revolution was consummated by the civilian forces of the MNR in collaboration with units of the National Army and the Corps of Carabineros."[34]

But the newspaper report was misleading: the fate of insurrections in Cochabamba and Potosí had yet to be decided, and Oruro was in the throes of a violent confrontation whose outcome would prove decisive to the outcome of the revolution.

Oruro: A Turning Point

In Oruro, the MNR's 16-member Revolutionary Committee, in concert with General Jorge Blackutt (the Chief of the Oruro Military Region), schemed to take control of the city on 9 April. General Blackutt (who was in league with General Seleme) had taken the precaution of removing the majority of the Altiplano regiments' ammunition and storing it in the Camacho Regiment's barracks in Oruro. General Blackutt's quid pro quo with General Seleme was the position of Prefect of Oruro Department after the overthrow of the Junta. According to plan, early Wednesday morning, the Oruro Revolutionary Committee (including the stalwart Zenón Barrientos Mamani), MNR Zonal Commandos, citizen supporters, university students, workers, and miners seized the prefecture and police headquarters. But as they approached the Camacho Regiment barracks, they were met with a torrent of rifle and machine gun fire. General Blackutt, upon receiving word that the La Paz insurrection was foundering, had shifted his allegiance to the Junta.[35]

This ignited a furious uprising. Loyalist carabineros were overwhelmed and their weapons distributed to the citizenry. Now well-armed, the insurgents besieged the Camacho Regiment throughout the night and into the following day when the soldiers were captured while attempting to escape. Their weapons then fell into the hands of the insurgents who soon put them to use against the Junta's reinforcements. The Ingavi Regiment from Challapata, troops from the Andino Regiment barracked in Uncía, and the Colorado Regiment from Uyuni were on the march to crush the insurrectionists, who were now backed by miners from San José and Huanuni. The decisive battle was joined outside the village of Papel Pampa 74 kilometers west of Oruro.[36] The Junta plan of attack involved a frontal assault by the Andino Regiment, while the Ingavi Regiment circled the insurgents' right flank to come to the aid of the besieged Camacho Regiment in Oruro. Enfiladed with mortar fire, the Ingavi troops quickly surrendered. The Andino Regiment fared no better: uncoordinated, on the run, low on ammunition and out of water, they also surrendered.[37]

A people in arms had defeated three army regiments destined for reinforcement of the Junta's army in La Paz. The fate of Oruro sealed, the insurgents also secured the railhead above La Paz, commandeered a munitions train, occupied the military air base, and threatened the rear of the High Command's position at El Alto. The conflict at this point had taken a toll of 1,600 to 1,800 dead and 5,000 wounded.[38] With the victory of the revolution a foregone conclusion, the Papal Nuncio requested a truce to resolve the conflict and spare the loss of more life. Apprised of the dismal situation by radio, General Torres reversed direction and met with Hernán Siles at the Altiplano village of Laja where on the afternoon of 11 April a treaty was signed.[39] The six-year Rosca interregnum had come to its end.

The Peasantry: A Postscript

But a question remains: why did the MNR fail to enlist the peasant masses in the insurrection? After all, hundreds of thousands were Chaco War veterans: many of whom had returned from the war with their rifles. Conventional wisdom points to the problematic of unleashing the indigenous masses into the revolutionary equation. "Their failure to seek peasant support in 1949 indicates . . . their attempts were vitiated by resistance on the part of the MNR urban commando units and by leaders of the MNR primary party organizations."[40] Reflecting on the revolutionary potential of the peasantry, the MNR militant José Fellman Velarde noted: "some of the leaders of the MNR had scruples about letting loose a peasant movement, the results of which were unforeseeable," but also added an afterthought: "At any rate, the perspective of time shows how necessary it might have been, in those moments when the weights of the scale were still seesawing, to throw all the weight of a peasant insurrection on the side of the rebellion. "[41] The Movimientista strategy was to avoid a peasant revolution: as Porfirio Diaz, the Mexican dictator overthrown by peasant armies, famously remarked, "Madero has unleashed a tiger. Now let's see if he can control it."[42]

MNR militants promoted organization of peasant unions (*sindicatos*) during the Sexenio and the dirigente Antonio Mamani Álvarez issued a "Call to Bolivian Indians" to join the MNR in the 1949 Civil War against the Rosca. In a secret pact with the MNR on 30 April 1951, he pledged the vote of literate peasants for the MNR in the forthcoming national elections and, after an electoral victory, the MNR was to support the demands of Mamani Álvarez's *Tesis de Caranguillas*.[43] However, the MNR strategy for overthrowing the Rosca did not include the mass intervention of a peasantry in arms, unleashing an unknown "tiger" into the fray.[44] In Wálter Guevara Arze's words, "We want to make a Mexican revolution, but without ten years of Pancho Villa.[45] The urban, middle-class Movimientistas were also preoccupied with the potential loss of food supplies to the cities in the event of an agrarian revolution.

The final MNR strategy consisted of two stages: an initial urban insurrection in the departmental capitals; and, if necessary, a contingent stage in which the struggle would be thrown open to indigenous workers and peasants initiating an unpredictable and uncontrollable civil war. As Alfredo Candia later revealed, "The first phase would have the characteristics of the typical revolutionary *golpe* [*golpe de estado*: coup d'état] . . . . The second stage was the most grave. It would be immediately executed when it was known that the revolutionary forces in La Paz had been defeated. . . . [T]he civil war was to begin, on the first day, with the armed uprising of fifty seven provinces, cantons, and mining centers . . . with an uprising of the *indigenas* of La Paz, Oruro, Potosí, Cochabamba, Sucre and Tarija."[46] Although the MNR avoided sparking an indigenous uprising in the April 1952 Revolution, there were nonetheless examples of indigenous insurrectionists in La Paz, including Antonio Mamani Álvarez and comunarios from the Altiplano.[47]

The National Revolution: Redux

After the triumph of the revolution, Hernán Siles delivered a brief speech on the balcony of the Palacio Quemado and reaffirmed the objectives of the National Revolution: "The mandate of the President Martyr Gualberto Villarroel has been completed in the same plaza in which he was sacrificed by the oligarchy. . . . We are going to incorporate the campesino into the Bolivian economy, into the national life, to the end [that] he ceases being an entity despised by his executioners. . . . Viva the Revolution! Glory to Villarroel! Viva Bolivia!"[48] The MNR's objective was the transformation of indigenous colonos and comunarios into campesinos (peasants) incorporated into the national economy as wage laborers or small farmers tilling their former hacienda usufructs. The task was monumental and the resultant transformation would prove unpredictable.

In the next 16 months, the tin mines would be nationalized, Indians enfranchised, universal education proclaimed, agrarian reform mandated, President Villarroel's decrees reinstated, and Indians imprisoned for resistance to the colonato freed.[49] The insurrection was won in three days; the ensuing social revolution that would transfigure the political, economic, and social structure of the nation was years in the making. The revolution exacerbated internal conflicts among the creole-mestizo elites, between the urban elites and the peasantry, and among the peasants themselves. The future of the political economy of the nation was at stake: capitalism or socialism; reform of the hacienda with a regimen of private land ownership; or an agrarian revolution based on cooperative labor and land ownership by the indigenous communities. Would the revolution bequeath indigenous autonomy and independence: or reform and the revival of creole-mestizo dominance? Creation of a modern nation state necessitated stripping control of the economy from the Rosca—divesting the rural oligarchs of their haciendas and the Tin Barons of their mines.

Economic Sovereignty: Resource Nationalism and the Tin Mines

On 31 October 1952, the MNR nationalized the 163 Aramayo, Hochschild, and Patiño mines and created the Bolivian Mining Corporation (*Corporación Minera de Bolivia*: COMIBOL) to control and operate the mines and their 29,000 mine workers.[50] The issue of compensation for the seized properties, chartered in Delaware with U.S. citizens as shareholders, presented a complex subject for negotiation. At issue was the question of Bolivia's sovereign right to nationalize the mines and U.S. insistence, per the Hull Doctrine, on "fair, prompt, and effective" compensation for expropriation of private property. Negotiations were influenced by the urgency of the Bolivian government to secure foreign exchange vital to the economic survival of the nation and to the need of the United States to acquire Bolivian tin and tungsten for the war in Korea. As in the Standard Oil case, the issue of compensation and the determination of "fair" value was complicated by issues involving, for example, valuation based on past tax information provided by the companies. The sum of unpaid legal obligations, per the 1939 Busch decrees, owed by the Tin Barons to the Bolivian government was $218,474,369. According to this metric, the Tin Barons owed the Bolivian government compensation, rather than vice versa.[51]

Tensions within the revolutionary and reformist wings of the party mounted over the issue of financial compensation for the expropriated mines. The MNR left-wing, led by Minister of Mines and Petroleum Juan Lechín and Minister of Labor Germán Butrón, opposed compensation.[52] They argued that paying the tin magnates was an insult to the miners whose blood and sacrifice would be dishonored. The U.S. State Department, aware of the factionalism within the MNR, used the rift to advantage in negotiation of the metals contract in order to diminish the influence of the radicals. The objective of U.S. diplomacy was to prevent the nationalization of strategic mineral and petroleum resources. In a worst-case scenario, nationalization in one nation could spark a contagion: Venezuelan oil; Chilean copper; Brazilian, Central American, and Caribbean banana, tobacco, and sugar plantations.

In the event of nationalization, the State Department sought indemnification of U.S. corporations and their shareholders. Toward this end, the State Department leveraged the power inherent in the unresolved tin and tungsten contracts to pressure Bolivia. As Secretary of State Dean Acheson noted in a memo to the U.S. Embassy in La Paz: "Our tin policy offers the most flexible, effective and appropriate available instrument for influencing decisions."[53] The State Department, alarmed by the power of Juan Lechín and the revolutionary trade unions in the mines, regarded Paz as a centrist hedge against the MNR left-wing. The U.S. Embassy was aware that Paz was quietly purging the government of radical revolutionaries and replacing them with moderates.[54]

Víctor Paz belonged to neither of the party wings. A centrist, the Jefe exercised a pragmatic gift for playing off competing factions and brokering compromises within the party and with the U.S. government. Paz's understanding of Yankee imperialism was grounded in a Marxist analysis of capitalism, by personal experience in the Villarroel cabinet (U.S. diplomatic recognition was contingent on his expulsion), and in the streets of La Paz during the U.S.-supported overthrow of the RADEPA regime. His objectives were to minimize the taint of extremism, toxic to an accommodation with Washington, and to safeguard the National Revolution during the process of nationalization of the mines and expropriation of the haciendas by placating the party radicals and their subaltern constituents. The question of compensation was a foregone conclusion: Paz understood the need to compromise with the United States lest he run afoul of hegemonic policy formulated to protect American investments worldwide.

Mindful of the need for an expedited settlement that would allow for the resumption of a long-term contract for the sale of tin to the United States and utilizing the accounting records of the tin companies, the Bolivian government arrived at the figure of $18,200,000 (without insistence on the unpaid $218,474,369 owed by the companies). No definite agreement was reached on the amount or the terms of compensation; however, by 1960, the three tin companies had received informal payments of $18,000,000 for the mines in which they only had invested $1,000,000 since 1928.[55]

An agreement was never concluded with the Truman administration. Without the input of foreign exchange funds, the National Revolution was kept afloat by selling off the nation's dwindling gold reserves. By the time a long-term contract was signed with the Eisenhower administration in July 1953, the price of tin had fallen from $1.22 to $0.70 per pound, resulting in a significant loss of foreign exchange revenue. Declining tin content in the ore of the nationalized mines, antiquated infrastructure, inefficient operation, and the mass departure of foreign engineers and technicians contributed to decreased profits.[56] The MNR had nationalized a white elephant.

COMIBOL, the government entity in control of the mines, operated as a satrapy of the FSTMB and the *Central Obrero Boliviana* (Bolivian Workers Central: COB) controlled by the labor caudillo Juan Lechín and influenced by Trotskyist and Stalinist politicos imbued with notions of workers' control (*control obrero*) and co-government (*co-gobierno*). Employment was contingent on MNR party affiliation and as is the case with government bureaucracies, power and influence accrued from the size of the organization and its payroll. COMIBOL experienced a dramatic increase in the number of workers. By 1959, nearly half of the labor force was employed aboveground, and in 1967 only 7,600 of COMIBOL's 22,500 employees worked belowground.[57] Production costs also rose astronomically: from $3.64 per worker in 1950 to $10 following nationalization in 1953.[58] Furthermore, COMIBOL revenue was siphoned off to fund projects for economic diversification, particularly exploration and development by the state oil company *Yacimientos Petroliferos Fiscales de Bolivia* (*YPFB*).[59] Nationalization of the mines, while indispensable for Bolivian sovereignty, was not without unexpected consequences—economic, social, and political.

Peasants and Proletarians

Marxist revolutionaries quickly set about the radicalization, organization, and mobilization of workers and peasants. A week after the triumph of the revolution, the inaugural session of the COB trade union confederation was convened in La Paz under the direction of Executive Secretary Juan Lechín, Secretary General Germán Butrón, and Secretary of Relations Mario Torres. Lechín and Torres, also leaders of the FSTMB, had been instrumental in the Oruro and La Paz insurrections, and Butrón had led the factory workers in the battle for La Paz. Ñuflo Chávez soon added the peasantry to the federation. The COB "Program of Principles" stated the demands of the MNR left-wing sector: The immediate nationalization of the mines, without compensation, and under workers' control, and of the railways under the supervision of the railway workers; the occupation of the factories by the workers; the nationalization of the latifundia and their transfer to the organized peasantry for exploitation within a collective system."[60]

These principles borrowed much from the POR *Tesis de Pulacayo*. Capitalism would be extirpated through the "mobilization and the direct action of the masses" organized in sindicto militias. The COB included left-wing Movimientists and Marxist *entristas* who entered the party following the defeat of the Rosca with the intention of radicalizing the National Revolution.[61] The left-wing envisaged a future of nationalized mines operating under workers' control without indemnification, haciendas expropriated without compensation functioning as sindicato cooperatives, the military abolished and replaced by armed peasant, and proletarian militias controlled by the COB.[62]

The dictatorship of the proletariat was hardly in the plans of the urban middle class represented by the MNR right-wing sector who understood that the COB was a force to be reckoned with—the sooner the better. The right-wing reformists favored a restrained revolution of enfranchised Indian farmers, mine and factory workers, artisans and petty capitalists, endowed with legal and social rights. They found the radicalization of the National Revolution outlined in the COB's "Program of Principles" alarming—and its declaration of a People's Republic of Bolivia and call for the takeover of the mines without compensation—evidence of "communist ideas."[63] The initial response of the MNR right-wing was to denounce the COB, drawing a line between nationalism and communism, noting "ninety per cent of the workers are nationalists and belong to the MNR; on the other hand the leaders of the COB are in the majority communist elements from all the Internationals: POR, PIR and Communist Party." The denunciation, published in the 12 September 1952 issue of *Rebelión* and signed by a legion of MNR stalwarts (including Alfredo Candia, Luis Peñaloza, Hugo Roberts, Adrían Barrenechea, Julio Manuel Aramayo, Froilán Calleja, Arturo Fortún, Jorge Rios Gamarra, and Zenón Barrientos Mamani), declared: "the MNR is contrary to the communist postulate of the Dictatorship of the Proletariat," asserted the right of private property, and urged the reorganization rather than abolition of the military.[64] Tensions within the MNR right- and left-wing sectors were exacerbated by the increasing number of leftists employed in the burgeoning party bureaucracy to the detriment of party veterans.

On 6 January 1953, the right-wing responded with an attempted coup led by Alfredo Candia, Luis Peñaloza, Hugo Roberts, and disaffected members of the Grupos de Honor, military, carabinero, and police officers. The conspirators' only success was the kidnapping of Ñuflo Chávez and Lieutenant Colonel Miguel Ayllón, the Army Chief of Staff.[65] The kidnapping of Chávez underscored the trepidation of MNR reformists over the armed mobilization of the peasantry; their concern with subaltern syndicalization was confirmed the following day when peasant and worker militias marching under the aegis of the COB demanded an agrarian revolution, abolition of the army, a people in arms, and worker and peasant co-gobierno. President Paz downplayed the fanfare of the factional fiasco, quietly demoting and exiling the conspirators (the names of many were not publicized until 1956), disarming, disbanding, and purging members of the Grupos de Honor from jobs in the government bureaucracy.[66] Paz's intention was to minimize internal differences within the MNR and mitigate the potential for instability and violence. He also was determined to restrain the rapid growth of the COB.

Universal Suffrage

Three months after the MNR seizure of power, a presidential decree granted universal suffrage: "All Bolivians, men and women over twenty-one years of age, if they are unmarried, or eighteen years if married, regardless of their level of instruction, occupation, or income" were enfranchised. Elections, previously limited to 200,000 literate urbanites, were now open to one million Indian men and women, most of whom (70–80 percent) were illiterate.[67] This act represented a democratic milestone; of course, these enfranchised citizens would doubtless cast their ballots for the MNR, legitimating the rule of the creole-mestizo party.[68] To ensure the electorate's proper selection of candidates, colored ballots were printed bearing the symbols of the various parties, enabling observers to determine the political disposition of those casting a ballot—and also identifying those voting for the opposition.

The Military Institution

The fate of the armed forces awaited determination by the new regime. A strong case would be made to eliminate the institution noted for massacres of Indian peasants and miners, its role in the overthrow of President Villarroel, repression of Radepistas and Movimientistas during the Sexenio, and ignominious defeat in the Chaco War. The dishonorable and duplicitous conduct of army officers in the MNR revolution further besmirched the reputation of the military institution and put its future at risk. As the MNR's Alfredo Candia noted, "the numerous *militares* [military officers] pledged [to the MNR] in more than twelve regiments, did not faithfully fulfill their word of honor. . . . Scarcely five per cent of the pledged *militares* participated in the revolution, the rest switched in favor of the old capitalist army that put themselves opposite the people."[69]

A related question concerned the fate of both the Colegio Militar and its cadets who had fought so ardently against the National Revolution. Were the cadets honorably serving the military institution, loyally following the orders of their superiors, or were they reactionaries, molded by the Colegio as servants of the Old Order? The debate over the fate of the cadets and the Colegio, military officers and the military institution, was contentious. It also exposed another factional rift within the MNR elite. Often forgotten amidst discussion of the MNR's revolutionary decrees, the decision over the future of the military institution would have an indelible impact on the future of the revolution and the Bolivian state.

The very existence of the military was vehemently opposed by MNR leftists, notably Minister of Mines Juan Lechín and Minister of Peasant Affairs Ñuflo Chávez, who represented the two constituencies that had suffered the worst of military depredations. Whether reformed or reconstituted, they feared the institution and insisted it be abolished. Opposition was also voiced by Wálter Guevara Arze, the party's right-wing theoretician, who objected to the institution's authoritarian hierarchy and historic penchant for political power.[70] As Lechín put it, "We must not permit the reorganization of the Army. What more Army do we need than the people? In order to make massacres totally impossible, we must repeat once and a hundred times that we don't want an Army."[71]

President Paz and Defense Minister General Calleja sought retention of a reformed military institution to counterbalance the power of the carabineros and the peasant, miner, and worker sindicato militias. Paz managed a compromise that retained the military institution with a reduced budget, cut troop numbers from 20,000 to 5,000, and instituted a series of purges of reactionary elements within the officer corps.[72] As the president noted in an address to the nation on New Year's Eve: "We have returned dignity and a true function to the Armed Forces, eliminating from its ranks all those who used their arms against the people. At the same time, those officers who had been dismissed due to their loyal cooperation with the popular regime of Villarroel, have been reincorporated into the military institution."[73]

The question of the Colegio Militar also elicited sharp differences among both military and civilian ministers. Mindful of the Colegio's history as an incubator of reactionary graduates and the recent battle between the cadets and civilians in La Paz some MNR leaders pressed for elimination of the institution. "We have reached a dilemma," Paz announced, "either to eliminate the actual Army or to reopen the Colegio Militar in order to give admission to elements of the popular classes, which will be the officers of tomorrow, to defend the people and their interests." The decision, left to Paz, further demonstrated his role as a pragmatic centrist in the party. The Colegio was closed on 7 May 1952 and not reopened until the following year. Renamed after Colonel Gualberto Villarroel, a new curriculum was to be introduced and cadets recruited from the peasantry and proletariat. "It was understood then, in the army, that the rules to which they had been habituated had been changed, that a new power had appeared, resting on the people that saw in the *militares* an instrument of their old oppressors. It would be necessary to adapt themselves to new circumstances, be humble, endure taunts and humiliation. But at the same time it would be necessary to fight to recover the respect and appreciation of the citizenry."[74]

Víctor Paz Estenssoro's decision to retain the military institution constituted the MNR's greatest failure. As ever, the armed forces would continue to be staffed by a creole-mestizo officer corps against the interests of the nation and its indigenous majority.

Agrarian Reform

Popular pressures for agrarian reform surfaced when President Paz Estenssoro, returning from exile in Argentina, was greeted at El Alto Airport by 60,000 enthusiasts, including Indians carrying placards demanding "*Reforma Agraria!*" Addressing the crowd, Hernán Siles traced MNR history from its beginning in 1941, noting a projected program to incorporate the peasant into the economic and political life of

FIGURE 5.1   Antonio Mamani Álvarez Speaking at Solidarity Rally with Gabino Apaza on His Left

Source: Courtesy of Antonio Mamani Álvarez.

the country.⁷⁵ Management of this revolutionary transition would be undertaken by a Ministry of Indian and Peasant Affairs (*Ministro de Asuntos Indios y Campesinos*). The newly created ministry formed a committee comprised of three MNR creole-mestizos (Max Mendoza López, Carlos Ponce Sanjinés, Vicente Álvarez Plata) and three Indian revolutionaries (Chipana Ramos, Antonio Mamani Álvarez, Gabino Apaza) renowned for their role in the Villarroel regime and opposition to the Sexenio.⁷⁶

Ñuflo Chávez Ortíz, a scion of the Santa Cruz oligarchy appointed to head the ministry, presented the objectives of the creole-mestizo Movimientistas: "We are going to orient the agrarian reform around the base of strengthening collective communal property, implementing the capitalist stage in private property, and liquidating feudalism . . . effectively incorporating the two million Indians into civilization."⁷⁷ The ministry was soon renamed the Ministry of Campesino Affairs. The omission of "Indio" with its pejorative connotation ostensibly dignified the indigenous people. However, as will be seen, there was more to the erasure of "indigenous" than might initially meet the eye. A hint of things to come, the MNR plan to transform the Indian majority into a nation of yeoman farmers, campesinos bereft of communal ayllu culture, acculturated and integrated into the creole-mestizo world of capitalist individualism and private property presaged a dangerous threat: as the Aymara historian Sylvia Rivera Cusicanqui puts it,

> One of the fundamental contradictions generated by the revolution of 1952 was the failure of the project of attaining cultural homogeneity. The country of *indios* governed by *señores* was to disappear with the revolution. The *señores* converted into bourgeoisie of democratic and progressive mentality and *indios* into citizens, integrated in the solid foundation of the internal market and Castilinization. The *indio* should disappear with *mestizaje*, education, migration to the urban centers and the parcelization of the communities, and his vestiges disappear into the museums and cultural documents of the new nation. The word *indio* would also disappear from the official language in order to express this transition to citizenship longed for by the conductors of the revolution.⁷⁸

Minister Chávez also affirmed the MNR's commitment to enforcement of the Villarroel decrees abolishing pongueaje, mitinaje, and other forms of personal service. Violations were to be presented to the local authorities (still influenced by hacendados). He also stated his opposition to subdivision of hacienda lands into small parcels (*minifundios*) on the grounds that the division would be detrimental to agricultural production.⁷⁹ The process of *minifundismo*, the diminution in the size of property inherited by successive heirs, would inevitably result in insufficient land to sustain a campesino family and spawn migration to urban shantytowns. However, Wálter Guevara Arze believed minifundismo could be averted through colonization of the Oriente by peasants from the highland departments. Previously an objective of the RADEPA–MNR revolution in the 1940s, colonization offered a panacea for the unproductive minifundios centered in the cold, dry, overpopulated highlands and presented an opportunity for economic development as well.[80] Commercial farming of rice, wheat, sugar, soy, cotton, and cattle ranching in the vast lowlands of Santa Cruz, Beni, and Pando could reduce the country's reliance on food imports as well as foster the possibility of exports.

Indigenous Education

Education was essential to the MNR objective of transforming Indians into campesinos integrated into a modernized nation of capitalist small farmers. Their participation as producers and consumers would at once integrate the peasantry into the monetary economy and free the nation from its dependence on imports resulting from the seigneurial regime. This transformation was contingent on Indian education: literacy in Spanish, reading, writing, arithmetic, and training in handicrafts, horticulture, and animal husbandry. The Ministry of Indigenous and Peasant Affairs was responsible for the execution of this unprecedented task, estimated to require 15,000 schools and 30,000 teachers.[81] Major difficulties in implementation arose from the lack of competent teachers willing to work in the rural hinterland and insufficient funds to support the endeavor.

The transformative power of education and enfranchisement of the indigenous peoples, constituting nine-tenths of the populace, was inestimable (certainly there were few who would believe the nation would be governed by an Indian in 50 years). But the devil was in the details: what would be the net effect of education on indigenous culture and society? Would the students be best served by instruction in Spanish, the language of national government and institutions, or in their indigenous languages? Would literacy and education in Spanish, the language of the dominant white and mestizo minority, inevitably result in acculturation into the creole-mestizo world of individualism, competition, materialism, private property, and the eventual destruction of the communal ayllu? Would acculturation lead to the loss of indigenous identity, transforming the Indian peasant—bereft of indigenous identity, culture, and society—into a poor imitation of city folk? Could education prove instrumental in mitigating regionalism and fostering nationalism as envisioned by Movimientistas and their RADEPA precursors?

The Movimientistas sought an enfranchised, educated, and acculturated electorate that in periodic displays of eternal gratitude would cast their ballots for the MNR. The military nationalists had advocated education as essential to modernization of the armed forces to obviate the problems in command when Indian conscripts were unable to understand their officers, or each other. Indigenous revolutionaries, while not of one mind as to the goals and consequences of education, were nevertheless at odds with the objectives of the creole-mestizo leaders, civilian and military. Antonio Mamani Álvarez and Gregorio Titiriku advocated indigenous education as a means to preserve the collectivism of the ayllu against the privatization of property and the culture of individualism and economic competition. "In opposing ideas inherent to the republican law, like individual property, the AMP made a clear choice to emphasize religion in the Indian law." Indeed, in a petition to the Ministry of Education and Indigenous Affairs, "Titiriku asked indigenous communities to create *escuelas particulares* [autonomous indigenous schools] that taught in Aymara or Quechua to help them live well . . . which included justice, equality, and harmony with Pachamama and nature. Titiriku thus combined the liberal notion of equality with the Aymara notion of collective well-being."[82]

Reform or Revolution

The epic question of reform or revolutionary change in the rural hinterland awaited resolution. The MNR lacked a specific program for agrarian reform. The party's "Bases and Principles of Action" was nebulous: "We demand the identification of all Bolivians with the desires and needs of the campesino, and we proclaim that social justice is inseparable from the rendition of the Indian for the economic liberation and sovereignty of the Bolivian people."[83] The transition from clichés to specifics would be both contentious and factious for the Movimientistas.

One point of agreement was abolition of the colonato: the haciendas were inefficient and unproductive, condemned colonos to farming usufructs for subsistence, and promoted barter rather than cash exchanges, resulting in the exclusion of the majority of the population from the monetary economy while impeding economic growth and national development. Agrarian reform would at once destroy the basis of economic power and free the colonos to labor for cash rather than subsistence. The question of hacienda expropriation engendered contentious debate over the issue of financial compensation. Never a monolithic party, the MNR was divided on the issue. "By all accounts the question of land reform was the most divisive issue to be raised in the loosely knit revolutionary family."[84] Crafted by representatives of right- and left-wing MNR factions, as well as POR and PIR members, the landmark Agrarian Reform Decree proclaimed on 2 August 1953 was a compromise that allowed for both communal cooperatives and individual private plots.

The fate of the ayllu communities also engendered debate. The communal ayllus argued that the creole-mestizos who were to determine their future represented a relic of the Andean past. How would this archaic, pre-capitalist mode of production with its proclivity toward subsistence and barter fit within the modernization agenda of the National Revolution? The MNR leaders, as well as members of the Agrarian Reform Commission, agreed that the ayllus should continue intact, but be induced to forsake subsistence and function as cooperatives integrated into the national monetary economy.[85] The particulars of the ayllu question as framed in the 1953 and 1954 Agrarian Reform Decrees, as well as the comunario responses to the decrees, are discussed in Chapter 6.

Sindicalismo: The Struggle for Agrarian Unions

Agents from the Ministry of Peasant Affairs promoted labor contracts between colonos and landlords during the early months of the revolution.[86] Yet unofficial agents of agrarian revolution—Indian dirigentes and mestizo Marxists—remained at the mercy of local authorities, right-wing Movimientistas, and hacienda informers. A communiqué from an Altiplano sindicato is illustrative: "The Campesino Sindicatos of the district [Guaqui] protest the detention of campesino dirigentes. . . . [O]nce again the intent is to unleash a violent repression against the Indians that fight for social justice."[87] Marxist revolutionaries quickly set about the radicalization, organization, and mobilization of workers and peasants. Trotskyists promoted land seizures without indemnification, and ayllus converted into collective farms managed by the state.[88]

Whether agrarian reform or agrarian revolution, the future of the hacienda would be decided by the emerging Indian sindicatos. Sindicalismo offered the subaltern majority a historic opportunity for freedom. The agrarian sindicatos were organized in groups of at least 30 members at the local level, ascending to regional and departmental COB federations. The COB was the creature of three leftist MNR cabinet members: a mass organization of armed peasants and proletarians prepared to fight for the co-government of peasants, miners, and industrial workers.

Sinforoso Rivas, an enterprising PORista militant, presented the case for peasant unions in Cochabamba to the Labor Minister Juan Lechín. Rivas proposed a peasant federation for Cochabamba Department (*Federación Sindical de Trabajadores Campesinos de Cochabamba*) with a chain of command from the national federation to regional centers (*centrales*) and local land-group sindicatos.[89] Central to Rivas' conception was the inclusion of indigenous political agency: absent in the COB plan where Indians would "receive orders" from the creole-mestizo MNR leaders. As the Bolivian historian José Gordillo notes, both sectors of the MNR intended to control the peasantry: the right-wing attempted to control the sindicatos within the confines of the party, while the left-wing sought control within the confines of the COB.[90]

The FSTCC was founded on 6 August 1952 in joint ceremonies at Sipe Sipe and Mallco Rancho under the direction of Sinforoso Rivas and the veteran Indian dirigente Luis Bustamente. The MNR officials were unaware of the gatherings: "No authority assisted, only two delegates from the COB" were in attendance.[91] The keynote speaker at Mallco Rancho was Ñuflo Chávez, at this time, a passionate advocate of agrarian revolution. Often accompanying Chávez were Antonio Mamani Álvarez, who translated when necessary, and Gabino Apaza, an Indian dirigente also solicited by Chávez as a Ministry representative. Incompatible rivals, the two were necessary as MNR stage props; they were soon to be replaced by an emerging generation of dirigentes.[92]

The Ministry of Peasant Affairs dispatched sindicato organizers throughout the highlands to develop a mass movement. Ñuflo Chávez, Juan Lechín, and Germán Butrón attended the historic cabinet meeting, chaired by President Víctor Paz, to decide whether to pursue agrarian reform or agrarian revolution. Hernán Siles and Wálter Guevara Arze argued for land reform: the diminution of hacienda estates into medium-sized properties surrounding the hacienda house. Chávez and the leftists insisted on the expropriation of the haciendas without the continued presence of the oligarchs on the properties. When Paz put the "Great Debate" between his cabinet members to a vote, the result was a tie; observing the absence of Education Minister Germán Monroy Block, Paz beckoned Monroy to the meeting to cast the deciding vote. Obviously, Monroy's vote was a foregone conclusion to Paz, a proponent of uncompensated expropriation, and a victory for the MNR left-wing. As Chávez aptly put it: "thus with the vote of Germán Monrroy [sic: Monroy] Block the most profound article of the agrarian reform was approved and by this the latifundio in Bolivia was extinguished."[93]

The Peasant Awakening

Indigenous reactions to the revolution varied throughout the countryside. Urged by the government to continue working until codification of the proposed agrarian reform decree, some peasants complied, faithfully fulfilling time-honored labor practices; others refused to work for landlords, citing as legal precedent a Villarroel decree stating that colonos could not be forced to work without previous consent and just reward; some presented legal claims for expropriation of estates; and those less patient, and often organized in sindicatos, forcibly seized the lands. Peasant responses to the revolution were influenced by the particular history of the community and the degree to which the community was either isolated or exposed to external events. The cumulative weight of appeals for redress of hacienda violations of law and human rights, together with the escalation of labor conflicts, eroded the omnipotence of the Old Order as Indians confronted hacendados with a variety of strategies: courting local officials amenable to their entreaties; confounding those in league with the hacendados; manipulating the MNR bureaucracy by playing off one official against another; filing legal demands in one prefecture rather than another where the authorities were known to be oppositional, thereby sowing confusion over jurisdiction; and on occasion, as in the province of Arque (Cochabamba Department), courting a sympathetic sub-prefect.

The case of Arque illustrates the struggle against hacendado hegemony in the countryside. There the Sub-Prefect Emilio Román and his son Franklin, the Jefe of the MNR Provincial Commando, functioned as "Protectors of the Campesinos" in confrontations with hacendados, "evidencing the functioning of a prototype of the model of social control imagined by the party right-wing," as José Gordillo notes.[94] The hacendados countered the Románs by shifting the legal venue from the town of Aiquile in Cochabamba Department to the *Fiscalia General de la Nación* in Sucre, thus "delegitimizing the arguments of social justice presented by Roman and the campesinos, adducing that the revolutionary charges were against the laws of the nation."[95] Román was summarily removed from his position after notifying the prefect of the attorney general's interference in affairs outside his jurisdiction. Despite imaginative legal maneuvers, the entrenched oligarchs continued their domination of the nation's heartland.

There were those who urged extralegal responses to the patrones—forming sindicatos, arming militias, seizing land by force—and their numbers were growing.

The revolution was a latent force awaiting those who seized the opportunity.[96] An incident indicative of the volatility of rural relations and the continued power of the landed elite occurred in December 1952 when colonos of a newly formed sindicato on the Hacienda Seguenca in Los Andes Province (La Paz Department) clashed with carabineros defending the property. Led by the hacendado, the carabineros attacked the colonos as they were "taking possession" of the hacienda, but were rebuffed by the colonos carrying "the guns with which we contributed to the triumph of the revolution."[97] When the colonos brought a carabinero captured in the fracas to La Paz, they were surrounded by a carabinero detachment; 31 peasants were taken prisoner, marched to the barracks of the Calama Regiment, beaten, and then subjected to forced labor.

While the future of the military institution was debated by the MNR creole-mestizos, its domination of the Indians remained inviolate. But the indigenous awakening had arrived on the Altiplano. Not only had the colonos of Seguenca organized a sindicato to defend their interests, but the colonos also demonstrated the capability for concerted action. Furthermore, their action was contagious. Peasant dirigentes from Los Andes Province addressed a letter to President Paz requesting the intervention of the Ministry of Indigenous and Peasant Affairs to adjudicate the matter and demanded the release of the jailed colonos, the arrest of the landlord and carabineros involved, and the patrón fined for damages to the colonos.[98]

In the aftermath of the MNR victory sit-down strikes (*huelgas de brazos caídos*) based on the Villarroel decrees appeared on haciendas in the highland departments. The work stoppages were a continuation of the earlier sit-down strikes of the 1940s that were widespread during the Sexenio. Awakened to their revolutionary potential, colonos began refusing to work, preferring to await the expected decree that was to give them land.[99] Thus, for example, the 180 colonos and 80 *arrimantes* (renters) at the El Convento hacienda in Capinota Province (Cochabamba Department) went on strike in August 1952 over frustration with the administrator's insistence on continuation of personal service obligations prohibited by the 1945 Villarroel decrees. The conflict ended when the administrator fled into the night after the hacienda house was surrounded by militia from the Santiváñez *Sindicato Agrario de Trabajadores Campesinos*.[100]

Legal appeals for redistribution of land continued as always with claims dating back centuries: comunarios of the ayllu Hilata in La Paz Department demanded restitution of usurped lands, presenting documents dating from the Spanish Conquest; the Chrungalla ayllu presented a demand they had pressed for 72 years.[101] Colonos in Chuquisaca Department petitioned for expropriation of the Rosca ex-president Mamerto Urriolagoitia's hacienda; colonos demanded expropriation of lands subsumed by the hacienda Buena Vista in Potosí Department; colonos on the hacienda owned by the Monastery of Santa Clara in Jordan Province (Cochabamba Department) demanded expropriation, claiming that they were forced to work as *muleros* (mule drivers) and *vaqueros* (horsemen) for periods of eight days in violation of the Villarroel decrees. And the MNR seized the Sud Yungas estate of the Junta's chief of police in La Paz.[102] President Villarroel's horrific death was not in vain. His Supreme Decrees bequeathed the hope of freedom.

News of the overthrow of the government sparked resistance in the highlands. A peasant interviewed by the anthropologist Richard Patch recalled the indigenous awakening in the Upper Valley of Cochabamba Department.

> I . . . heard of the revolution of April 9 by way of newspapers given out from the train on its way to Punata. I was happy, and all of us shouted 'Viva Paz Estenssoro!' After the revolution we . . .,went to the hacienda to shell maize for the patrón, Ramon Ladezma. Ledezma took Crisostomo [Crisótomo] Inturias into custody because we had not brought our tools. . . . We told the *patrón* that the law no longer required us to furnish our own tools, but Ledezma forced us off the hacienda. We walked to Cliza and told don Walter Revuelta, the sub-prefect, what Ledezma had done to us. . . . Revuelta could do nothing . . . we threatened to go to the authorities in Cochabamba. . . . In order to threaten Ledezma, we called a meeting of all . . . who were in the Syndicate of Ucurena. More than 20,000 campesinos gathered, armed with axes, machetes, revolvers and shotguns. After this manifestation Ramon Ledezma disappeared to [Cochabamba] and has never returned.[103]

Land seizures, attacks on hacendados, *mayordomos* [overseers], theft, and destruction of estate property intensified in the months before the Agrarian Reform Decree of 2 August 1953. Official reaction to these events, as in the Ledezma affair, was at best inconsistent: ill-equipped to deal with accelerating developments in the countryside, the authorities often ignored the threat of rural violence. After the majority of the landlords had been driven off their estates, power struggles developed among indigenous leaders competing for power, as was most evident in the densely populated Cochabamba valleys. As the revolution progressed in the countryside, violence erupted between indigenous groups: disputes between hacienda colonos and ayllu comunarios; quarrels over land boundaries; religious disputes (Catholic versus Protestant), and conflicts over sindicato leadership at the local and regional level. Typical was a boundary clash reported on the Altiplano between the peasants of Yanacachi and Taipi Peroni in Omasuyos Province (La Paz Department) where two peasants were killed and five wounded; soon after, a shootout erupted between peasants on the hacienda *Nuestra Señora de La Paz*.[104] Ñuflo Chávez personally intervened in a dispute in Cochabamba Department between the colonos of the Vacas and Rancho Santa Clara haciendas over a disputed boundary.[105]

Violent conflicts were most prevalent in the two areas of greatest population density: the Cochabamba valleys and near the shore of Lake Titicaca (La Paz Department). The rich lacustrine soil near the lake and the irrigable land of the Cochabamba valleys created favorable conditions for agriculture. The two regions were the agricultural centers of the country and under the labor-intensive colonato, pressures for production were intense. On the eve of the 1952 revolution, an observer noted, "The static, unhealthy life imposed by the deadhand manorial system has given rise to a huge urban proletariat which has remained largely unproductive, thereby increasing the pressure of population on the Altiplano's meager food supply."[106] Roads and a railway, links to the modern world of La Paz, beckoned the Altiplano peasantry and elicited this prediction penned in 1947: "A third alternative . . . is a revolution that would dispossess the patrones and place the lands in the hands of those that work them. Such a catastrophe is certain to follow if the patrón cannot demonstrate his usefulness to society."[107]

In Cochabamba, the fortuitous combination of climate and irrigable soil in the Valle Alto yielded two to three harvests a year. The bountiful harvests afforded the capital accumulation necessary for the purchase of land.[108] Thus, there were greater numbers of small landholders (*piqueros*), agriculture was more likely to be commercial rather than subsistence-oriented, and the land tenure pattern was more diversified than elsewhere in the highlands. The indigenous population was generally concentrated in small pueblos as a result of the sixteenth-century policy of forced relocation (*reducciones*) into villages and towns where contact was more intensive and social relations more complex among Indians and creole-mestizos.[109] Here sindicatos were more likely to germinate than in the isolated serranía. Indeed, the first agrarian sindicato was organized in the Upper Valley in 1936, a decade and a half before the 1952 revolution. The Cochabamba valleys and the Altiplano lake region were ripe for revolution. After centuries of domination, a power vacuum appeared for those daring enough to see it and seize the moment.

Confrontations, often violent, escalated between colonos and landlords, mayordomos, police, tax collectors, and other local authorities. For those landlords who elected to remain on their estates, this was a time of trial. Certainly, the creole-mestizos were aware of previous Indian uprisings, but seldom in the history of the republic had power relationships been so tenuous. Resistance to the peasant awakening was dangerous: threats and verbal intimidation, beatings, kidnappings, and murder were common occurrences. The patrón of the hacienda Quimsa Maya at Sacaba (Cochabamba Department), kidnapped in November 1952 by a group of colonos, was only rescued by the timely intercession of neighboring hacendados. A month later, the landlady of Hacienda Novillero and her mayordomo were threatened with an invasion by colonos exasperated by the persistence of onerous labor obligations; nearby, at Anzaldo, the patrón and the administrator of Hacienda Chujcuhañusca braced for an imminent invasion.[110] Attacks by peasants were commonplace in the Cochabamba provinces of Aiquile, Anzaldo, Cliza, and Tarata: the haciendas Yerba Buena and La Alcoholería were assaulted in April and the patrón of La Alcoholería was murdered; a landlord at Tarata was beaten and then sequestered at the Sacabamba sindicato; other assaults on hacendados were reported at Cliza, Sacaba, and Ayopampa.[111] In May 1953, a patrón and ten colonos were killed during a battle in Potosí Department, the city of Potosí was invaded by hundreds of colonos searching for a recalcitrant landlord, and attacks on hacienda houses were reported in the provinces of Ingavi and Los Andes (La Paz Department).[112]

Land seizures erupted. At Villa Viscara (Vila-Vila), Sacabamba, Matarani, Machacamarca, Chilicchi, Ayampu, and Skimara in Cochabamba Department colonos ceased working for landlords and began cultivating the land for themselves.[113] Agrarian conflict reached such proportions that the MNR government found it necessary to issue a decree on 30 April 1953 regulating relationships between peasant and patrón, prohibiting agitation, and requiring wages to be paid for colono labor per the obligations earlier set forth by President Villarroel. Concerns arose regarding the agrarian economy and the supply of foodstuffs to the cities. The MNR noted that the "obstruction of some patrones" as well as the "irresponsible work of provocateurs" had led to neglect of the fields and that the decline of the price of tin reduced the funds available for importation of foodstuffs.[114]

Civilization and Barbarism

The small towns that dot the countryside provide a link between the peasantry and the government. In the chain of authority beyond hacienda, ayllu, and village, the town represents creole-urban authority with its host of Spanish-speaking officials of one kind or another, clerics and tax collectors, judges and courts, police and soldiers.[115] A rudimentary road system and Spanish, the language of the bureaucracy, convey government demands: food, labor, and cannon fodder. Towns and cities were hostile territory for Indians, and vecinos were viewed with distrust and derision: "*Walaycho* is today the most commonly used term by which the peasants refer to the non-peasant inhabitants of Villa Serrano [a town in Chuquisaca Department]. It is a Quechua word that has a broad meaning: a scoundrel, a person who is lazy, noisy, and acting the buffoon. More specifically used, it alludes to the fact that *Serranenses* abuse peasant women and maltreat drunken peasants."[116] MNR propaganda referencing the enemies of the revolution ensconced in town and city fostered Indian mistrust of city folk.[117]

As the peasant awakening swept the creole-mestizos from haciendas into towns and cities, the basic antagonism, now openly manifest between lord and peasant, became polarized with the hacendados and vecinos in urban enclaves and the campo increasingly under the control of the indigenous majority. Paranoia gripped the creole-mestizos: "They were convinced that they lived in the midst of unbridled savages, and they responded accordingly. Guns were polished and cocked, ammunition stores were augmented, and a twenty-four-hour street patrol was instituted. Most vecino women and children locked their houses and fled to La Paz." As William Carter, an anthropologist living on the Altiplano, also recalled:

> One afternoon in March, on riding out to a nearby estate, I found the joint owners, a pair of sisters, supervising the barley harvest with whips in their hands and guards at their sides. They were determined to extract profits as long as they could. In the same month a number of trucks, protected by well-armed bodyguards, came through the town carrying estate owners intent on defending their land. When one of these landlord groups did not return for several days, rumor raced through the town that they had all been massacred and eaten in a cannibalistic orgy.[118]

The Sociedad Rural mounted a propaganda offense in the newspapers denouncing the situation in a deluge of polemics reminiscent of their earlier attacks (1943–1946) on the National Revolution.[119] *Los Tiempos* continuously spewed racist editorials noteworthy for their vitriol: "Everyone knows that the Indian . . . ought to possess the same rights of whatever mortal. But, like some medicines that are to be taken in small doses or the opposite result is fatal to the organism, thus also the 'inalienable rights' of the Indian must be proportioned to them gradually and conditioned to a progressive cultivation—an absolute liberty put in the hands of ignorance would produce disastrous and specious effects. . . . A professional agitator is a type without God, Country, or Law."[120]

The Pro-Cochabamba Committee, in hopes of bringing an end to the rural violence that threatened the harvest, proposed a meeting of Indian and landlord representatives to discuss the violence, "especially in the regions of Totora, Mizque, and Independencia, where campesinos assaulted hacienda houses and whipped landlords."[121] But the Committee evidenced no interest in addressing the underlying causes of the conflicts.

The urban paranoia of falling prey to an avenging horde of savage Indians came true in November 1952 at Colomi (a town in Chapare Province to the east of Cochabamba city) when a rumor that the Rosca had overthrown the MNR led to an invasion of the town by 3,000 Indians who believed the Rosqueros intended to exterminate them. A colono from the Hacienda Iluri accused of inciting the uprising claimed that colonos from Iluri and surrounding haciendas had invaded Colomi searching for weapons to defend themselves. The sindicato militants Carlos Montaño and Mario Montenegro, also accused of inciting the rebellion, were arrested by the Colomi police.[122] The Cochabamba Sociedad Rural utilized the occasion to press MNR authorities to dispatch a rural police force to enforce the colonato regimen and "avoid the campesino dictatorship . . . the vanguard of communist materialism."[123] Other assaults followed, most notably the invasion of the city of Cochabamba in January 1953 by Indians searching for weapons. The village of Pojo (Carrasco Province), situated beside the Cochabamba-Santa Cruz highway, was also attacked: colonos under the cover of darkness and amidst the trumpeting of *pututus* (bull's horns) and cries of "Death to the Patrones!" sacked a hacienda house.[124]

Peasants also invaded the Cochabamba towns of Comarapa, Tarata, Cliza, Punata, Arani, and Vila Vila where a gunfight with vecinos ended with 6 dead and 11 wounded. An invasion and a shootout at Tarata resulted in numerous casualties and four deaths; the peasants later forced their way into a Cochabamba hospital menacing vecinos while searching for wounded comrades.[125] Townspeople throughout the backlands were fearful of the unfettering of indigenous frustration and hatred catalyzed by the revolutionary awakening. Vecinos at Acchilla (Chuquisaca Department), fearful of an invasion by hostile Indians, pleaded for "armed forces" to control the situation.[126] An assault on the town of Chayanta (Potosí Department) was averted by the timely joint intercession of MNR officials and Llallagua sindicato dirigentes who sought out and arrested the suspected conspirators.

The plot was noteworthy because it revealed plans for a widespread indigenous rebellion to be coordinated by dirigentes from Charcas, Sacaca, and the surrounding environs.[127]

Syndicalism and Factionalism

The history of the colonos of hacienda Santa Clara is emblematic of the indigenous struggle for land and liberty. Radicalized by a PIRista schoolteacher, the sindicato was led by José Rojas Guevara, a former prisoner of war whose family had been evicted from their home that was then razed as an object lesson for the disobedient. Rojas was a "sharp opportunist," as a sindicato lieutenant put it, also noting that he was a man "who . . . knew how to present demands that were closest to our hearts. He personalized our wishes, while other leaders outside Ucureña were not as campesino as he was."[128] Charismatic and forceful, José Rojas believed that power comes from the barrel of a gun, and organized an aggressive network of armed peasant sindicatos linked to Ucureña. In his words:

> The only lasting thing for a campesino was to be free of the *gamonales* (landlords and other exploiters) and become full owners of our lands. . . . We realized this through our own painful experience of Ucureña. . . . Some of our compañeros achieved their freedom as a unified body in the form of a sindicato before 1952. But even our little school was thought to be a menace to patrones. . . . We tried to unite again with the help of a party (PIR), willing to press total expropriation of the hacienda, but the *gamonales*, oppressors and the Rosca (elite) again conspired against us. . . . We knew they could not go on with such a farce.[129]

The repression of the landlords only reinforced the will of the Ucureños to resist. Encarnación Colque, a Rojas lieutenant, described how a team of dirigentes addressed rallies of hacienda colonos: "I spoke about labor legislations and how they should be clearly understood by everyone and enforced on the hacienda . . . and if the *patrón* did not cooperate, to let Ucureña and other authorities know in order to have it properly implemented. Then [Crisótomo] Inturias spoke how campesinos should organize themselves." Rojas delivered the grand finale, in "a fulminating speech . . . he talked about the coming of the agrarian revolution which would make campesinos owners of the land and free them from the *gamonales*, and in order to accomplish this the campesinos had to become a solid mass (*"como una masa de pan"*—like bread dough), organized into sindicatos. . . . The motto was Agrarian Revolution. . . . [T]hat the campesinos should carry their rifles on their shoulder to defend their rights."[130]

In mid-November 1952, the Ucureña sindicato threatened to invade Cliza with 6,000 militiamen to apprehend a number of recalcitrant hacendados, including Ramón and Bernardino Ledezma, sentenced to death by the sindicato for their unconscionable abuse of colonos.[131] The right-wing MNR prefect Germán Vera

Tapia was forced to meet with the Ucureños who demanded reinstatement of colonos evicted from their hacienda *pegujales* (plots). The prefect's decision to postpone his response to the Ucureña demands was rejected, accompanied by the veiled threat that the Ucureños would not be responsible for the consequences of the delay. Intimidated, Vera Tapia acceded to the Ucureño demands and ordered the patrones to reinstate the colonos on their pegujales.

This victory established José Rojas as a man to be reckoned with; unconstrained by official political parameters, Rojas and the Ucureña revolutionaries operated autonomously in pursuit of revolutionary objectives—hacienda expropriation and redistribution of the land to those who worked it—rather than legal appeals for compliance with the Villarroel labor laws. Within a month of the MNR revolution, the Ucureños had formed the *Sindicato Campesino del Valle*, a regional federation of 24 sindicatos in the provinces of Cliza, Arani, Punata, and Tarata. They next founded an autonomous *Central* and a *Federación Especial* to evade the official sindicato hierarchy (which designated a *Campesino Central* in the capital of each province) because the mandated Central in Cliza Province was the town of Cliza, a bastion of reactionary landlords and vecinos.[132]

MNR departmental officials attempted to reign in the Ucureña revolutionaries. First, Vera Tapia tried co-optation, backing the election of José Rojas as Secretary General of the Ucureña sindicato, but when Rojas continued to act independently, the prefect decided to remove him. Rojas was ousted in a rigged sindicato election and replaced by Simón Aguilar, a dirigente from Santa Clara with pre-revolutionary ties to the MNR. The prefect also supported the formation of another Upper Valley sindicato at San Isidro under the leadership of Agapito Vallejos, a dirigente considered amenable to MNR authority. Undaunted, the Ucureños continued their hostility toward the Cliceños, defied the prefect, and followed Rojas.

Another hotbed of agrarian resistance was the environs of Sipe Sipe, a pueblo in the Cochabamba Valle Bajo (Quillacollo Province), home to a trio of indefatigable dirigentes. Luis Ramos Quevado, Dionisio Miranda, and Luis Bustamente were members of the Indigenous Committee responsible for the wave of hacienda sit-down strikes in the 1940s and representatives to the 1945 National Indigenous Congress where President Villarroel abolished personal service. Dionisio Miranda, a colono from Hacienda Chacapaya, was the Vice President of the Indigenous Congress: a leader in the resistance to the colonato in Ayopaya and Tapacarí provinces, he was involved with the Yayani alcalde Hilarión Grájeda in the 1947 Ayopaya rebellion. Luis Bustamente, an Indian vecino and ex-miner from Sipe Sipe, was a member of the Indigenous Committee as well as a provincial delegate to the National Indigenous Congress. Together with Sinforoso Rivas (also a mine worker from Sipe Sipe), Bustamente was instrumental in the formation of the departmental peasant federation (FSTCC) on 2 August 1953.

Sinforoso Rivas was sponsored by both the COB and the Ministry of Peasant Affairs (MAC) to prepare an agrarian revolution in Cochabamba Department. The son of a colono and a veteran of the Marxist labor movement in the mines, Rivas was also an entrepreneur who parlayed his work and connections in the Patiño mines at Catavi-Siglo XX into a successful business provisioning the company pulperías. Fluent in Spanish and Quechua, Rivas was equally conversant in the company of Indians and creole-mestizo elites. A Trotskyist, a confidant of Juan Lechín, and personally acquainted with President Paz Estenssoro, Rivas soon drew the concern of the MNR right-wing prefect, provincial authorities, the landlords' Rural Society, and the indignation of José Rojas: "These organizations [sindicatos] must be made up of 'real Indians' wearing sandals, not shoes nor using hair fixer," Rojas would emphasize at sindicato gatherings, "Then Rojas would take off his old campesino hat shouting that those campesinos who were for the Agrarian Revolution used such hats to symbolize their poverty, while those who talked of legalities, promises and a peaceful Agrarian Reform showed their bourgeois and high living tendency."[133]

Rivas and Rojas believed the revolution would be attacked by counterrevolutionaries, as had befallen the Villarroel regime, and that a recurrence could only be averted by a national network of peasant and worker sindicato militias. Rivas sought to create a departmental network of sindicatos with organized militias, led by a vanguard cadre of campesino youth selected by their communities, trained by the RADEPA Colonel Eduardo Rivas Ugalde, and formally commissioned as military reservists by the Ministry of Defense. This unprecedented decision was approved in a meeting attended by Rivas, President Paz, and his generals. The FSTCC developed a strategic model for defense of the revolution together with maps of roads connecting the barracks of the army and transit police. President Paz failed to support Rivas with government funds, perhaps to avoid attention to the precedent of an Indian military school operating in Cochabamba. Rivas was thus forced to scavenge revenue from his pulpería business to help fund the FSTCC; rivals from sindicatos in the Valle Alto subsequently accused him of misappropriation of funds.[134]

The FSTCC was conceived as a departmental federation. Rivas labored to extend its domain throughout the Cochabamba valleys and into the serranía, home to the scattered ayllu communities not subsumed by haciendas. The remote haciendas of the serranía were enormous. Hacienda Yayani, famed for its history of colono resistance and rebellion, covered an expanse of 18,000 hectares (44,480 acres); divided into four sections, each worked by colonos, the hacienda spanned three climatic zones from 1,700 to 3,500 meters.[135]

Sinforoso Rivas traversed the highlands to extend the federation into the far reaches of the department, alerting the peasantry to the benefits of syndical organization and the need for preparedness to defend the revolution from the counterrevolutionary patrones. Accompanied by four armed bodyguards, Rivas visited the Valle Bajo provinces aligned with the FSTCC: Ayopaya, Tapacarí, Arque, Capinota, Cerdado, and Quillacollo. He motored by jeep to the canton of Morochata in the serranía of Ayopaya Province to deliver his message, inveighing against hacendados and promoting schools, education, and hard work: "These gamonales are not satisfied with living so many years without working; they have never built schools on their haciendas, instead there are chapels and shrines in all the hacienda houses, to justify himself before God and to justify his exploitation to the dispossessed. The patrones don't want the campesinos to know how to read because for them it is a danger."[136]

Rivas reconnoitered the backlands by foot and muleback visiting, for example, the immense Hacienda Choro (the property of a non-resident German, managed by a Peruvian agronomist), divided into eight *suyos* (sections) worked by 700 Quechua and Aymara colonos. At the Hacienda Yayani (operating under lease to a notorious hacendado), Rivas met with the legendary Hilaríon Grágeda, recently pardoned by presidential fiat for his role in the 1947 rebellion sparked by an uprising at the hacienda. The meeting was symbolic with Rivas the ascendant *valluno* (valley) dirigente, supported by the COB and MAC, paying his respects to the esteemed veteran of the serranía. Embracing an emotional Grágeda, Rivas announced, "I am delighted to have come to these places that are the bastion of the struggle for emancipation by the Bolivian campesinos."[137]

The MNR right-wing officials were vexed by Rivas' genius for operating within the interstices of the MNR bureaucracy: petitioning President Paz for approval of his expansive agenda; legal recognition of the sindicato federation; inclusion of peasant representatives in the preparation of an agrarian reform decree; prohibition of hacienda land sales and eviction of colonos; the return of expelled colonos together and restitution of their plots; dismissal of the administrators of the Convento and Santa Clara haciendas; expropriation of the Ledezma family's haciendas near Ucureña; replacement of provincial authorities subject to FSTCC approval; and the distribution of arms to sindicato militias. To the dismay and consternation of the MNR right-wing and the Rural Federation, Rivas' petition included the signatures of José Rojas, Agapito Vallejos, and Simón Aguilar, thus representing the sindicatos of both the Valle Bajo and Valle Alto. The petition was rightly seen by the creole-mestizos as a dangerous development indicative of a pivotal point in the peasant awakening.[138]

It was not without notice that Rivas' petition had circumvented the authority of the Cochabamba prefect. Public condemnation by the FSTCC of recalcitrant landlords and their supporters within the MNR departmental bureaucracy further demonstrated an agrarian movement, unconstrained and aggressively pursuing a revolutionary agenda independent of official purview. When Rivas enlisted the COB's leftist ministers Lechín and Butrón to attend a FSTCC rally at Sipe Sipe in late 1952 (timed to coincide with a visit to the Valle Alto by Paz Estenssoro under the auspices of the prefect), the prefect was forced to seek the intercession of the influential right-wing Movimientista Wálter Guevara Arze to stymie the affair. The prefect's next maneuver was to publicly question the legitimacy of the FSTCC and orchestrate an official election by 80 sindicato dirigentes to determine leadership of the federation. But Rivas and Luis Bustamente were elected Executive Secretary and Secretary General of the FSTCC, confounding the prefect who unwittingly had legitimated the troublesome federation.[139]

Revolution in the Revolution

An autonomous agrarian revolution was brewing within the National Revolution. While the MNR dithered over the question of agrarian reform or agrarian revolution and departmental officials continued to support the will of the patrones, radicalized campesinos were seizing hacienda lands. The Cochabamba Prefect Germán Vera Tapia, unable to control the radicalization of the countryside, concocted another scheme to unseat Rivas: inserting Emilio Chacón and Carlos Montaño as provocateurs within the FSTCC to vilify Rivas as a puppet of the hacendados. But the mission backfired when the two PORistas went rogue, inciting colonos to rise up, expel the patrones, and seize the land. Finally, the MNR cabinet intervened to remove Sinforoso Rivas from the leadership of the FSTCC. Rivas was accused of misappropriation of funds by PORista militants from Ucureña at a raucous meeting in the FSTCC headquarters in Cochabamba and expelled from the federation; after the syndical coup d'état, the Ucureños looted the FSTCC offices.[140]

Although Sinforoso Rivas was unseated from leadership of the syndical federation, the MNR attempt to combat indigenous agency proved counterproductive. The grassroots approach of Rojas and the dirigentes of the *Central Campesino del Valle* continued: cowing vecinos and local authorities, halting sales of hacienda land, forcing patrones to return lands previously worked by expelled pegujaleros, and seizing and redistributing properties.

The Ucureña modus operandi was evidenced at the village of Pojo where Rojas and Emilio Chácon assembled colonos from the outlying haciendas, denounced the MNR (including Paz Estenssoro) as Rosqueros, and incited the armed invasion of haciendas: "sell all of the cattle to get money to buy guns to defend the Agrarian Revolution" and, if necessary, "make rivers of blood on the streets of the pueblo."[141]

Gabriel Arze Quiroga, Germán Vera Tapia's replacement as prefect, sought the intercession of the leftist ministers Lechín and Chávez to deter the agrarian revolutionaries. At Chávez's bequest, the PORista militants together with José Rojas, Carlos Montaño, and Crisóstomo Inturias were apprehended and remanded to La Paz as political prisoners. The betrayal by the Minister of Peasant Affairs incited a furor within the Ucureña Central, leading to an armed invasion of the city of Cochabamba and an attack on the police station.[142]

An attempt to curtail the radicalization of the Valle Alto had inflamed the situation and once again the prefect requested the intercession of party luminaries from La Paz. Juan Lechín, Ñuflo Chávez, and Minister of Government Federico Fortún Sanjinés traveled to Cochabamba where Lechín denounced the "agitators" as "insolent provocateurs" whose "ignorance was conducive to these attitudes . . . proof of their deceit to the campesinos" and Fortún warned that disrespect of the "principle of authority" would be punished by the "Supreme Government."[143] The indigenous agrarian revolutionaries were betrayed by Movimientistas determined to co-opt the syndical movement.

FIGURE 5.2 Cross-marking Site of Slain Hacendado at Pojo, Cochabamba Department
Source: Photo by author.

Ñuflo Chávez decided that the "centers of rebellion provoked by POR" agitators could be neutralized "by placing the Ucureños under the direct control of Chumacero, Rivas, and Vallejos." Víctor Zannier, the Coordinator of the Ministry of Peasant Affairs, determined that Sinforoso Rivas, Juan Chumacero, Agapito Vallejos, and Simón Aguilar were to be considered the official peasant leaders and as such were responsible for controlling José Rojas and Carlos Montaño. The Prefect Arze Quiroga objected to the scheme as a fool's errand, given the charisma of Rojas and Montaño and the zeal of their followers.[144] The prefect was correct. Within a month Rojas, Colque, and Inturias were once again at work making hacienda appearances, insisting that administrators comply with an order by the Minister of Peasant Affairs limiting colono work obligations from four to three days per week as pursuant a 1945 labor decree. To the distress of the Cochabamba Rural Society, fear of the Ucureña Central compelled many landlords to abandon their haciendas.[145]

The specter of an agrarian revolution again drew the attention of President Paz, who redoubled efforts to reassert MNR control of the countryside. Paz supported a peasant central at Cliza, led by Agapito Vallejos, to counterbalance the hegemony of the Ucureños while Víctor Zannier insinuated himself into an association with the Ucureña Central. In June, the MNR sponsored the First Departmental Congress of Cochabamba Campesinos where Sinforoso Rivas was elected Executive Secretary and José Rojas, Secretary General; dirigentes from the Upper and Lower Valleys were given equal representation in the departmental federation; the 14 provinces were divided equally between Rivas and Rojas factions; and the PORistas Chacón and Montaño were expelled from Cochabamba Department. The unification of the sindicatos was contrived by the MNR creole-mestizos as a tactic to moderate the political agency of the Ucureña revolutionaries through Rivas' now restrained approach to an agrarian reform promoted by the Ministry of Peasant Affairs. At the same time, Paz Estenssoro pursued a divide and conquer strategy in the factional struggle for provincial hegemony between Ucureña and Cliza. The unintended consequences of this stratagem would not bode well for the future tranquility of the region: in half a dozen years, the rivalry between the rival factions would escalate into a bloody war fought by thousands of campesino militiamen.

The *Cliceño* dirigente Agapito Vallejos put aside factional concerns on 2 June 1953 and contacted the Ucureña Central with news of a common threat. Falangistas were rumored to be preparing a coup; as word spread, a mass mobilization of sindicatos began throughout the Cochabamba valleys. Peasant militias searching for caches of arms and ammunition secreted by the counterrevolutionaries invaded towns and terrorized vecinos. In the Valle Alto, gunfire was exchanged at Tarata and at Villa Vila where militiamen entering the plaza were surprised by an enfilade of Falangista machinegun fire. The sindicato mobilization was unprecedented. Weapons and ammunition were discovered. As José Gordillos avers, "this event is a landmark in the campesino political movement because apart from this there was never a repetition of any situation that combined such a high grade of autonomy, with perfect coordination, in a territory of operations so extensive."[146] By 1953, the Ucureña Central had become the undisputed vanguard of the agrarian revolution, aggressively organizing colonos, inciting hacienda occupations, and promoting land seizures.

The Falange and hacendado oligarchs were desperate. In a unique display of dual power by the Ucureña Central, three landlords from the Valle Alto accused of Falangista affiliation were taken into custody in July. An earlier appearance of dual power was reported at the Altiplano Canton of Escoma.[147] The MNR was threatened by an autonomous indigenous revolution within the National Revolution. Víctor Zannier, the MNR's high-level operative in the Ministry of Peasant Affairs observed that the MNR urban politicians "mistakenly pretending to manage the revolution from their desks" were late to comprehend the gravity of the situation.[148] Indians were escaping the grip of the MNR—yet the latest iteration of creole-mestizo rule.

The Lost Road

The saga of Antonio Mamani Álvarez affords a cautionary tale regarding the fate of indigenous dirigentes in the National Revolution. For decades, the outspoken and indefatigable Kallawaya carried the message of indigenous emancipation throughout the Bolivian countryside. A major indigenous voice during the RADEPA–MNR regime as well as the counterrevolutionary years of the Sexenio, Mamani Álvarez (aka Álvarez Mamani) participated in the 1949 and 1952 MNR insurrections and pledged support to the MNR in the 1951 "Pact of Alliance." He was personally acquainted with the MNR elite, Indian dirigentes, ex-combatientes, and every prison, penitentiary, penal colony, and concentration camp in the country. But the revolution that Mamani Álvarez had helped make soon revealed a Janus face.

The Kallawaya was one of the first indigenous leaders to be pushed aside by the creole-mestizos of the National Revolution. Neither the MNR nationalists nor the POR or PIR Marxists could abide Mamani Álvarez's vision of Andean millenarianism with corporate landownership and cooperative labor relations replacing private ownership and individualistic competition. Hence, the inevitable confrontation with the creole-mestizo elites and their imported ideologies. In the initial months of the revolution, often with his rival Gabino Apaza, the Kallawaya appeared at mass demonstrations in support of the Ministry of Indigenous and Peasant Affairs, translating speeches by Ñuflo Chávez into Quechua or Aymara and touting the MNR strategy of restrained agrarian reform: "We also say to them [campesinos] that they should respect the patrones. . . . That they not take their own vengeance, that they not kill, that they not sack. There are laws that protect the indio and the patrón, and because we are all equal, the law is equal for all. We do not permit abuses of the patrones, but neither will we abuse them." He also proposed discussions between Indian dirigentes and the landlord Sociedad Rural to contrive a "plan of cooperation."[149]

Mamani Álvarez differed with the MNR. In a speech delivered on the Day of the Indian (2 August 1952), alongside President Paz Estenssoro, he appealed to indigenous nationalism in addition to the MNR mantra of hard work, increased production, and modernization. "So, our Fatherland constituted by a campesino majority, is unable to progress; because the towns where a minority of families live as parasites of the majority are debilitated, . . . and unable to produce anything good . . . under the empire of the Inca there existed peaceful work and collective wellness."[150] In solo appearances, the Kallawaya often strayed from the MNR reformist program of penny capitalist farmers and into the Pachakamak call to embrace the pre-Columbian world of cooperativism within a multicultural government of Indians, creoles, and mestizos. Outside the pale of the dominant orthodoxies (whether capitalist or communist), this autonomous indigenous vision was unacceptable to the Movimientistas. Two months after the revolution, Juan Lechín and Germán Butrón denounced Mamani Álvarez as an "adventurer, disloyal, and an instrument of the forces that were displaced by the April popular uprising." Thus, "in order to fortify the worker-peasant unity . . . indispensable for the materialization of the agrarian revolution," he was expelled from the MNR left-wing COB.[151]

The marginalization of the Kallawaya Indianist persisted. Ñuflo Chávez ordered the arrest of the "campesino leader of the right of the MNR" on 13 February 1953 for alleged subversive activities, including the charge of illegally collecting money (*ramas*).[152] After insistent requests by Oruro sindicatos and the intercession of President Paz Estenssoro, he was released from jail and "despite death threats" announced that he would continue his "nationalistic position." The Kallawaya then proposed that he and other Indian dirigentes be allowed a place on the Agrarian Reform Commission that was comprised of creole-mestizos, including hacendados and Marxists, but with no peasant representatives. In March 1953, the self-appointed "Maximum Dirigente" of the campesinos restated his position, pointing out that "while many claim that our movement is pro-Indian and directed against the right of property and the patrones . . . this is a profound error." What was wanted, he asserted, was social justice and "the lands that were snatched by . . . the patrones that have extorted my class, which they have molested and depressed into abject misery, have to answer to justice and render account for their acts."[153] He was arrested ten days later.[154]

In the months leading up to the proclamation of the Agrarian Reform Decree of 2 August 1953, frustrated by the MNR leadership, the contentious Kallawaya descended into the factionalism he had once derided. In a spate of public announcements, he excoriated the POR, PIR, COB, Toribio Miranda, Gregorio Titiriku, Victorio Condori Mamani, Luis Bustamente, Sinforoso Rivas, Lucio, and Juan Céspedes Lavayen, and his longtime rival Gabino Apaza (as both an agent of the Rosca and a communist).[155]

After a lifetime of struggle, Antonio Mamani Álvarez was finally silenced by the revolution he had fought to bring about, as a new generation of dirigentes jockeyed for position. This breed of dirigentes, many of them like Sinforoso Rivas of the Cochabamba Valle Bajo and Toribio Salas of Achacachi (La Paz Department), were not peasants, but citified Indians (*cholos*) more adept at maneuvering within the confines of the creole-mestizo revolution. Some had worked in the mines, tutored by communist militants, and versed in the intricacies of class warfare, they nevertheless proved amenable to co-optation by the MNR.[156]

Whereas Mamani Álvarez's forte was the organization of Indian congresses to promote unity, and public proclamations of resistance to the Rosca, the emerging generation of dirigentes commanding sindicato militias represented a force to be reckoned with: hacienda invasions, land seizures, assaults on landlords, and attacks on towns threatened the MNR's tenuous control over the hinterland. The appearance of José Rojas and Sinforoso Rivas presented a quandary for the MNR leaders, themselves riven by the factional conflicts of right- and left-wing sectors, exacerbated by the COB's demands for peasant and proletarian co-government.

The capitalist and individualistic provisions of the landmark 1953 Agrarian Reform Decree were far from Antonio Mamani Álvarez's dream of indigenous cooperativism expressed in the *Tesis de Caranguillas*. Indigenous leadership had passed to the dirigentes and caciques of militarized sindicatos, agile in manipulation of the MNR bureaucracy and inured to the perquisites of power. Marginalized and isolated on the Altiplano, the Kallawaya Antonio Mamani Álvarez was eclipsed by history.

Conclusions

Bolivia's social revolution followed a well-organized, carefully planned, and skillfully executed insurrectionary strategy, accentuated by the tactical brilliance of MNR militants. While the revolution was neither a spontaneous rising of the people or a proletarian overthrow of the oligarchy, it could not have succeeded without popular and proletarian participation. The struggle was a creole-mestizo affair to be settled among conflicting elites, but the majority of the combatants were indigenous conscripts and urban workers. The peasant majority remained on the sidelines: uninvited by the Movimientistas.

The National Revolution democratized the populace: freeing Indians from servitude, allowing purchase of land, enfranchising all adult men and women, mandating universal education, and colonization of the vast lowlands of the Oriente. The MNR would not allow an indigenous agrarian revolution to interfere with their objective of transforming Indians into campesino farmers, tilling individual plots of land, and marketing foodstuffs for cash (not barter) in a capitalist market economy. To accomplish this feat, the MNR creole-mestizos co-opted the agrarian revolutionaries who disrupted their agenda and jeopardized food supplies to the cities.[157] The presumed solution to the turmoil was the 1953 Agrarian Reform Decree, which only exacerbated conflicts in the countryside.

To assert control over the backlands, the MNR adopted measures used by both the Rosca and the earlier RADEPA–MNR iteration of the National Revolution. Local authorities cited provisions in Villarroel's Supreme Decrees regulating patrón–colono labor relations to enforce the colonato. The legal defense of haciendas as private property continued under the National Revolution; sindicato organization was often declared illegal, and the collection of ramas by Indian dirigentes was prohibited.[158] The MNR organized a rural police force "to guarantee private property and agricultural labor," Mobile Brigades reconnoitered the Altiplano investigating peasant agitation, and Regional Labor Inspectors were dispatched to investigate denunciations of indigenous agitation and capture the ringleaders.[159] In April 1953, the MNR issued two Supreme Decrees (03375 and 03376) governing hacienda labor relations and instructing sindicato dirigentes to enforce colono labor required for hacienda harvests and seed planting.

Ñuflo Chávez's denunciation of work stoppages (a mainstay of indigenous resistance to the colonato) by hacienda colonos as "sabotaging the Revolution" and a "betrayal to Bolivia" underscores the taming of the initial postulates of the Ministry of Indigenous and Campesino Affairs and acceptance of the MNR right-wing dogma of agrarian reform promoted by the renamed Ministry of Campesino Affairs. In fact, the "sabotage" and "betrayal" of the National Revolution was the work of the creole-mestizo elite. To counterbalance the burgeoning indigenous campesino, miner, and factory worker militias, President Paz Estenssoro mandated reinstitution of the armed forces in July 1953.[160] It was a terrible decision: as was the creation of *Control Político* the regime's secret police.

Notes

1. Luis Antezana Ergueta, *Historia secreta del movimiento nacionalista revolucinario*, Vol. 5 (La Paz, 1986), 1277.
2. Luis Peñaloza, *Historia del Movimiento Nacionalista Revolucionario, 1941–1952* (La Paz, 1963), 258–259.
3. Ibid., 259–262; Lydia Gueiler Tejada, *La mujer y la revolución* (La Paz, 1959), 43–52.
4. Glenn Dorn, *The Truman Administration and Bolivia* (University Park, PA, 2011), 137. See also General Antonio Seleme Vargas, *Mi Actuación en la Junta Militar de Gobierno con el Pronunciamiento Revolucionario del 9 de Abril de 1952* (La Paz, 1966), chapters 8–9.
5. Peñaloza, *Historia*, 259–264.
6. Dorn, *The Truman Administration and Bolivia*, 138–139.
7. Víctor Andrade, *My Missions for Revolutionary Bolivia, 1944–1962* (Pittsburgh, PA, 1976), 135, 137.
8. Ibid., 158–159.
9. Ibid., 159–161.
10. Antezana, *Historia secreta*, Vol. 7, 1957.
11. An historiographical note: With the rise of indigenous focus in modern (twenty-first century) works by Bolivian scholars has come criticism of "top-down" interpretations privileging creole-mestizo protagonists. The MNR leaders have been aptly targeted for critical assessment. The April 1952 insurrection is a case in point. The Bolivian sociologist Mario Murillo in *La bala no mata sino el destino: una crónica de la insurrección popular de 1952 en Bolivia* (La Paz, 2012) argues that the April victory owed not to the MNR, but rather to the spontaneous rising of civilian Paceños. This oral history of civilian participants is a welcome contribution to the literature: yet Murillo omits information regarding MNR leadership in the planning and execution of the insurrection as evidenced in his selective use of Luis Peñaloza, *Historia del Movimiento Nacionalista Revolucionario, 1941–1952* and Luis Antezana Ergueta, *Historia secreta del movimiento nacionalista revolucionario*, Vol. 7 (La Paz, 1988).

12. Peñaloza, *Historia*, 238 and Herbert Klein (who quotes Peñaloza) in *Parties and Political Change in Bolivia, 1880–1952* (Cambridge, MA, 1969), 391. For a detailed account of the 1950 Villa Victoria massacre, see Murillo, *La bala no mata*, 83–85.
13. On the Bolivian army, see Elizabeth Shesko, "Conscript Nation: Negotiating Authority and Belonging in the Bolivian Barracks, 1900–1950," Ph.D. dissertation, Duke University, 2012. For an insightful summery of the strengths and weaknesses of the army and insurgent forces, see Murillo, *La bala no mata*, 135–148.
14. Peñaloza, *Historia*, 261–265.
15. The following day (10 April), the five Movimientista pilots flew the warplanes away from the conflict to an air base in Cochabamba, preventing the Junta from wreaking a bloodbath on both insurgents and the city's residents. Antezana, *Historia secreta*, Vol. 7, 1914–1917. Murillo notes, to the contrary, that many of his interviewees remember being "bombed incessantly." Did they perhaps conflate 1952 with the 1950 bombings of their barrio? Murillo, *La bala no mata*, 90–91.
16. With this pronouncement the MNR propaganda war against the Junta reached its apogee. *El Diario*, 9 April 1952, 1, *El País*, 10 April 1952, 1; Peñaloza, *Historia*, 269–270; Gueiler, *La mujer y la revolución*, 91–92; Antezana, *Historia secreta*, Vol. 7, 1939.
17. *El Diario*, 9 April 1952, 1. For the "spontaneous," yet scant participation of the Trotskyist POR in the insurrection, see S. Sandor John, *Bolivia's Radical Tradition: Permanent Revolution in the Andes* (Tucson, AZ, 2009), 128–129.
18. Antezana, *Historia secreta*, Vol. 7, 1916–1917.
19. Murillo, *La bala no mata*, 74.
20. Lydia Gueiler would again occupy the Palacio Quemado, as Interim President (1979–1980).
21. *El País*, 10 April 1952, *El Diario*, 9 April 1952, 1, Peñaloza, *Historia*, 270–273.
22. Antezana, *Historia secreta*, Vol. 7, 1928; Murillo, *La bala no mata*, 95–98.
23. On General Seleme's convoluted role in the insurrection, see Antezana, *Historia secreta*, Vol. 7, 1919, 1924, 1930, 1946–1950, and Peñaloza, *Historia*, 274–275; Carter Goodrich, "Bolivia in Time of Revolution," in James Malloy and Richard Thorn, eds., *Beyond the Revolution: Bolivia Since 1952* (Pittsburgh, PA, 1971), 3–5.
24. How stalwart was Hernán Siles in this crucial juncture? For conflicting views of his role, see Antezana, *Historia secreta*, Vol. 7, 1938–1946, 2017–2020; Peñaloza, *Historia*, 277–278; José Fellman Velarde, *Víctor Paz Estenssoro: El hombre y la revolución* (La Paz, 1955), 274–275.
25. Antezana, *Historia secreta*, Vol. 7, 1980–1981, 2024.
26. Ibid., 1934–1935, 1939, 1977, 1979, 1982–1983, 2020, 2024–2025.
27. Ibid., 1940–1941, 1960–1961.
28. Zulema A. Lehm and Silvia Rivera Cusicanqui, *Los artesanos libertarios y la ética del trabajo* (La Paz, 1988), 99. On the Milluni miners, see Murillo, *La bala no mata*, 92–94, 111–112; Antezana, *Historia secreta*, Vol. 7, 1990.
29. The Universidad Mayor de San Andrés was turned into a concrete bunker: manned by students with rifles and a machinegun which was moved from floor to floor to confuse and repulse the advance of the Colegio Militar cadets. Antezana, *Historia secreta*, Vol. 7, 1994–2000.
30. Murillo, *La bala no mata*, 71–77; Antezana, *Historia secreta*, Vol. 7, 1983–1984, 1928–1929, 2002–2015.
31. Luis Antezana notes that a senior officer (a clandestine member of the MNR) sowed confusion in the Junta's Order of Operations by sending only two of the five regiments from El Alto to attack the city, thus allowing the insurgents to defeat the Bolivar and Sucre regiments in detail; likewise, the Avaroa Regiment arriving from Guaqui discovered that mortars were useless because they lacked ignition caps. Antezana, *Historia secreta*, Vol. 7, 1964–1965, 1974, 1987, 1989. Among the army officers taken prisoner

on 10 April 1952 were lieutenants Luís Garcia Meza and Alberto Natusch Busch destined to be future dictators. Ibid., 2028.
32. Antezana, *Historia secreta*, Vol. 7, 1984–1985, 1990–1993, Murillo, *La bala no mata*, 98–103, 111–112.
33. Ibid., Vol. 7, 1963–1965, 1968–1973; Murillo, *La bala no mata*, 106–109.
34. *El Diario*, 9 April 1952, 1–2.
35. *El País*, 15 April 1952, 3. Antezana, *Historia secreta*, Vol. 7, 2032–2047. For personal recollections of the Oruro insurrection, which began with a hail of gunfire from the Camacho Regiment as unarmed demonstrators approached the barracks, see June Nash, *We Eat the Mines and the Mines Eat Us* (New York, 1979), 52–53, and Murillo, *La bala no mata*, 119–120, 122, 125–128.
36. Antezana, *Historia secreta*, Vol. 7, 2047–2054; Murillo, *La bala no mata*, 129–134.
37. An insightful account of the failed effort of the Andino Regiment by an officer in the battle of Papel Pampa may be found in René López Murillo, *Los restaurados* (La Paz, 1966), 136–147.
38. *El País*, 10 April 1952, 1, 8; 15 April 1952, 1, 3; *El Diario*, 15 April 1952, 3 and 11 July 1952, 6. Antezana, *Historia secreta*, Vol. 7, 2023.
39. Peñaloza, Historia, 281–282.
40. Charles Weston Jr., "An Ideology of Modernization: The Case of the Bolivian MNR," *Journal of Inter-American Studies*, 10 (January 1968), 98, and also James Malloy, *Bolivia: The Uncompleted Revolution* (Pittsburgh, PA, 1971), 200 and 370, fn 30.
41. Fellman Velarde, *Víctor Paz Estenssoro*, 228.
42. Michael C. Meyer and William L. Sherman, *The Course of Mexican History* (New York, 1979), 511.
43. According to Mamani Álvarez, the "Pact of Alliance" was signed on either 3 or 6 April 1951 by Federico Álvarez Plata representing the MNR and Mamani Álvarez representing the Indians. Mamani Álvarez pledged electoral support for the MNR; Álvarez Plata agreed to create an agricultural bank for campesinos, give scholarships to Indian university students, publish and distribute news and information in Quechua and Aymara for mass distribution in the campo, and enforce the precepts of the *Tesis de Caranguillas*. *El Diario*, 13 January 1953, 5; Claudia Ranaboldo, *El camino perdido: biografía del dirigente campesino kallawaya Antonio Álvarez Mamani* (La Paz, 1988), 207, 209, 211, 213–214, 260; César Peon E. *Historia y mito en la conciencia de un líder campesino boliviano* (Buenos Aires, 1995), 30; Luis Antezana and Hugo Romero, *Historia de los sindicatos revolucionarios* (La Paz, 1973), 235–236.
44. Peasant participation in the insurrection involved the acquisition and shipment of Argentine rifles from Potosí to Oruro and organizational contacts with factory workers' leaders and carabinero officers in La Paz. Ranaboldo, *El camino perdido*, 191–193. Luis Antezana notes the participation of a number of peasants in the La Paz insurrection: *Historia secreta*, Vol. 7, 1970.
45. Cited in Malloy, *Bolivia: The Uncompleted Revolution*, 234–235.
46. *El Diario*, 21 April 1952, 5.
47. See Ronabaldo, *El camino perdido*, 192; Maria Carmen Soliz Urrutia, "Fields of Revolution: The Politics of Agrarian Reform in Bolivia, 1935–1971," Ph.D. dissertation, New York University, 2014, 306; Antezana, *Historia secreta*, Vol. 7, 1970.
48. *El País*, 15 April 1952, 2.
49. However, despite the MNR's decree, the AMP militant Melitón Gallardo remained imprisoned along with Indians involved in the Great Rebellion of 1947 in Cochabamba and others from Altiplano uprisings in Omasuyos Province (La Paz Department). See Soliz, "Fields of Revolution," 136–137.
50. James Dunkerley, *Rebellion in the Veins* (London, 1984), 58.
51. Andrade, *My Missions for Revolutionary Bolivia,* 151–153.

52. In his memoirs, Ñuflo Chávez reveals that differences within the MNR leadership were sometimes more complex than simple divisions between right and left-wing sectors; see for example, Ñuflo Chávez Ortíz, *Recuerdos de un revolucionario bolivianio* (La Paz, 1988), 77–78.
53. Quoted in Dorn, *The Truman Administration and Bolivia*, 173.
54. A discovery in State Department archives by the diplomatic historian Glenn Dorn reveals the alteration of speeches by labor leaders Juan Lechín and José Lucio Quiros: "someone, presumably from Paz Estenssoro's wing of the party, was working to tone down whatever anti-U.S. sentiments the radicals may have had." Ibid., 171.
55. Ibid., 152, 179; Foreign Area Studies Division, *U.S. Army Area Handbook for Bolivia* (Washington, DC, 1963), 498; NACLA, *Latin American and Empire Report*, 8, 2 (February 1974), 15.
56. Andrade, *My Missions for Revolutionary Bolivia*, 151; Dunkerley, *Rebellion in the Veins*, 58; Jerry W. Knudson, *Bolivia: Press and Revolution, 1932–1964* (Lanham, MD, 1986), 256.
57. See "Table 10: Distribution of the Labor Force in Large-Scale Mining (COMIBOL) 1951–1964," in Richard Thorn, "The Economic Transformation," in Malloy and Thorn, eds., *Beyond the Revolution*, 193; Dunkerley, *Rebellion in the Veins*, 60, 62.
58. Foreign Area Studies Group, *U.S. Army Area Handbook*, 497.
59. Dunkerley, *Rebellion in the Veins*, 62–63.
60. Guillermo Lora, *A History of the Bolivian Labour Movement, 1848–1971*, edited by Laurence Whitehead (Cambridge, UK, 1977), 282. Also see, Gueiler, *La mujer y la revolución*, 119–121.
61. The Bolivian POR pursued the Trotskyist doctrine of *entrismo*: "Their characteristic strategy was 'entryism': working inside larger left-wing organizations (parties, trade unions, academic societies) to colonize then or nudge their policies and political alliances in directions dictated by Trotskyist theory." Tony Judt, *Postwar: A History of Europe Since 1945* (New York, 2005), 402. For entrismo during the Bolivian National Revolution, see Sandor John, *Bolivia's Radical Tradition*, 120, 126, 130–136, 147–153.
62. Lora, *A History of the Bolivian Labour Movement*, 281–285.
63. Ibid., 282–283.
64. Gueiler, *La mujer y la revolución*, 121–122.
65. *El Diario*, 7 January 1953, 7; *El País*, 7 January 1953, 4.
66. Gueiler, *La mujer y la revolución*, 127–129.
67. Herbert Klein, "Social Change in Bolivia Since 1952," in Merilee S. Grindle and Pilar Domingo, eds., *Proclaiming Revolution: Bolivia in Comparative Perspective* (London, 2003), 237. The presidential decree is quoted in Robert J. Alexander, *The Bolivian National Revolution* (New Brunswick, NJ, 1958), 82.
68. See Silvia Rivera Cusicanqui, "Liberal Democracy and *Ayllu* Democracy in Bolivia: The Case of Northern Potosí," *The Journal of Development Studies*, 26.4 (1990), 106.
69. Alfredo Candia G., *El Diario*, 21 April 1953, 5.
70. Walter Guevara's prescient objections to the continuation of the military institution were confirmed in the 1964 overthrow of the National Revolution by the armed forces. See Walter Guevara Arze, *Bases para replantear la Revolución Nacional* (La Paz, 1988), 106–107.
71. Christopher Mitchell, *The Legacy of Populism* (New York, 1977), 52. An outspoken voice for "radical measures" to be taken was Captain René Barrientos Ortuño, a daring pilot and hero of the 1949 Civil War, and a member of the Avaroa Lodge of junior officers aligned with RADEPA. Prado, *Poder y fuerzas armadas*, 45.
72. Prado, *Poder y fuerzas armadas*, 45; Mitchell, *The Legacy of Populism*, 52.
73. William Brill, *Military Intervention* (Washington, DC, 1967), 16. See also Paz Estenssoro's discussion of a reconstituted and reconstructed military institution reported in *El Diario*, 16 September 1952, 7.

74. Víctor Paz Estenssoro, cited in Brill, *Military Intervention*, 48–49; see also *El Diario*, 26 July 1953, 6
75. *El Diario*, 16 April 1952, 1.
76. *Última Hora*, 16–17 April 1952, 5; *El Diario*, 15 April 1952, 4. For discussion of the new ministry, see *El Diario*, 15 April 1952, 4; 18 April 1952, 4; 16 July 1952, 15; 28 July 1952, 8. *Los Tiempos*, 20 April 1952, 4; 26 April 3; 8 June 1952, 3; 16 July 1952, 3; 19 August 1952, 5; *El País*, 19 April 1952, 4.
77. Ñuflo Chávez, *El Diario*, 6 June 1952, 6.
78. Silvia Rivera Cusicanqui, *Oprimidos pero no vencidos* (Geneva, 1986), 4.
79. *El Diario*, 2 August 1952, 6. The MNR leaders were also aware of the loss of communal ejido lands following hacienda privatization in the Mexican Revolution.
80. Matthew Gildner notes Guevara Arze's ingenious theoretical twist: by "transforming Bolivia's human and geographic diversity—long recognized as insurmountable obstacles to national progress—into one of the nation's 'greatest advantages' . . . the revolutionary government could . . . transform Bolivia from a semicolonial republic into a modern, integrated nation-state. Robert Matthew Gildner, "Indomestizo Modernism: National Development and Indigenous Integration in Postrevolutionary Bolivia, 1952–1964," Ph.D. dissertation, University of Texas at Austin, 2012, 132.
81. Ibid., 83.
82. Waskar Ari Chachaki, *Earth Politics: Religion, Decolonization, and Bolivia's Indigenous Intellectuals* (Durham, N.C, 2014), 84.
83. Mario Rolon Anaya, *Política y Partidos en Bolivia* (La Paz, 1966), 275. See also "Bases y Principios del MNR," in Alberto Cornejo S., ed., *Programas políticos de Bolivia* (Cochabamba, 1949), 149, 169–170. Further evidence of early MNR interest in agrarian reform is found to be found in the 1944 speech by Víctor Paz to the Bolivian senate: see Víctor Paz Estenssoro, *Discursos parlamentarios* (La Paz, 1955), 304–311. See also the message from Hernán Siles to the 1945 National Indigenous Congress, in Agustín Barcelli S., *Medio siglo de luchas sindicales revolucionarias en Bolivia* (La Paz, 1957), 167. The question of the MNR's historic interest in agrarian reform and the political realities surrounding the issue, eventuating in the Agrarian Reform Decree, is noted in James Wilkie's interview with Víctor Paz Estenssoro in *Measuring Land Reform* (Los Angeles, 1974), 27–29.
84. James Malloy, "Revolutionary Politics," in Malloy and Thorn, eds., *Beyond the Revolution*, 124.
85. Gildner, "Indomestizo Modernism," 158–160.
86. According to the anthropologist William Carter, "It was agents from the ministry who organized the peasant revolt on the northern Altiplano." Personal correspondence by the author with William Carter, 19 April 1971. Dwight Heath noted the efforts of MNR agents in the Yungas: see Dwight B. Heath, "New Patrons for Old: Changing Patron–Client Relationships in the Bolivian Yungas," *Ethnology*, 12 (January 1973), 83; Soliz, "Fields of Revolution," 142–143, 158. For an analysis of the landlord–colono labor contracts, see Soliz, 185–202.
87. *El Diario*, 4 February 1953, 5.
88. Soliz, "Fields of Revolution," 145, 155.
89. Sinforoso Rivas Antezana, *Los hombres de la revolución: memoria de un líder campesino* (La Paz, 2000), 45–46.
90. José Gordillo, *Campesinos revolucionarios en Bolivia: Identidad, teritorio y sexualidad en el Valle Alto de Cochabamba* (La Paz, 2000), 37.
91. Ibid., 46–47.
92. *El Diario*, 20 April 1952, 11, 25 April 1952, 5; 28 April 1952, 5; *El País*, 30 April 1952, 3.
93. Chávez, *Recuerdos*, 85.
94. Ibid., 40.
95. Ibid., 41.

96. Agrarian sindicatos soon emerged after the April revolution: for Cochabamba Department, see *Los Tiempos*, 23 May 1952, 5; 15 January 1953, 4; 12 April 1953, 5; for Chuquisaca Department, *Los Tiempos*, 3 June 1953, 3; 11 June 1953, 3; 22 August 1952, 3; *La Nación*, 9 May 1953, 3; for La Paz Department, *La Nación*, 17 January 1953, 3; 19 March 1953, 3; 27 June 1953, 3; 19 October 1953, 5; for Potosí Department, *Los Tiempos*, 11 June 1953, 5; 10 August 1952, 4; 24 September 1952, 3; 27 September 1952, 3; 20 June 1953, 3; *La Nación*, 5 December 1952, 5; 27 January 1953, 3. For the incipient sindicato militias, see El Diario, 8 April 1953, 7; 5 May 1953, 5; 22 May 1953, 5; *La Nación*, 25 April 1953, 3; 13 May 1953, 4; 16 May 1953, 3; 11 August 1953, 7; and *Los Tiempos*, 29 April 1953, 3. Sindicatos were also organized by ayllu comunarios: for example, the comunarios of the ayllu Sora (Pantaleón Dalance Province, Oruro Department) formed a sindicato to aid their ongoing boundary conflict with the colonos of a contiguous hacienda, as noted in *El Diario*, 19 July 1952, 15. The continuation of violent conflicts between colonos on haciendas with antagonistic landlords is reported in *La Razón*, 15 January 1952, 8.
97. *El Diario*, 31 December 1952, 7.
98. Ibid.
99. *Última Hora*, 12 November 1952, 4; *El País*, 29 May 1952, 4; 4 July 1952, 4; 20 July 1952, 7; *El Diario*, 27 January 1953, 11, 24 February 1953, 4.
100. *El País*, 14 August 1952, 5; *Los Tiempos*, 12 December 1952, 4; *Última Hora*, 5 December 1952, 4; 6 February 1953, 6.
101. *El Diario*, 13 May 1952, 4; 10 December 1952, 7.
102. *Última Hora*, 9 August 1952; *El País*, 10 August 1952, 5; *Los Tiempos*, 25 June 1952, 2; 13 July 1952, 3; 19 July 1952, 4.
103. Richard Patch, "Social Implications of the Bolivian Agrarian Reform," Ph.D. dissertation, Cornell University, 1956, 107.
104. *El País*, 8 May 1952, 5; See also *El Diario*, 13 May 1952, 4; *Los Tiempos*, 13 May 1952, 3; *El País*, 13 May 1952, 5; *Última Hora*, 12 May 1952, 5.
105. *El Diario*, 17 August 1952, 7.
106. Frank Keller, "Finca Ingavi: A Medieval Survival on the Bolivian Altiplano," *Economic Geography*, 17 (January 1950), 42.
107. David Weeks, "Land Tenure in Bolivia," *Journal of Land and Public Utility Economics*, 23 (August 1947), 336.
108. Specific instances of colono land purchases are noted in Mario Carranza Fernández, *Estudio de caso en el Valle Bajo de Cochabamba: Camarca, Parotani e Itapaya* (La Paz, 1972), 11–12. See also chapters 4 and 5 in Robert H. Jackson, *Regional Markets and Agrarian Transformation in Bolivia: Cochabamba, 1539–1960* (Albuquerque, NM, 1984).
109. Brooke Larson, *Cochabamba, 1550–1900: Colonialism and Agrarian Transformation in Bolivia* (Durham, NC, 1998), 67–74; also see Jackson, *Regional Markets and Agrarian Transformation*, 25–29.
110. *El País*, 21 November 1952, 5; *Última Hora*, 6 November 1952, 4. Also see *Los Tiempos*, 16 November 1952, 5; 9 December 1952, 6; *El País*, 6 December 1952, 5.
111. *Los Tiempos*, 16 April 1953, 5; 19 April 1953, 4; 21 April 1953, 4–5, 25 April 1953, 4; 3 May 1953, 4; *El Diario*, 19 April 1953, 5
112. *El Diario*, 15 August 1953, 7; 16 August 1953, 5; *Los Tiempos*, 12 May 1953, 5; 19 April 1953, 3; *El Diario*, 20 April 1953, 5.
113. *El Diario*, 14 March 1953, 5. The seizure and redistribution of hacienda lands was not confined to the Cochabamba valleys; for example, in Muñecas Province (La Paz Department), see *El Diario*, 20 September 1953, 6.
114. *Los Tiempos*, 3 May 1953, 4. The question of the decline in agricultural production, or the availability of foodstuffs in the urban markets, is addressed in Charles Erasmus, "Upper Limits of Peasantry and Agrarian Reform: Bolivia, Venezuela, and Mexico Compared," *Ethnology*, 6 (October, 1967), 361, and Ronald Clark, "Land Reform and

Market Participation on the North Highlands of Bolivia," *Land Tenure Center Paper*, No. 40 (Madison, WI, December 1967), 15–24.
115. This relationship, intuitively obvious to those familiar with the campo, is graphically presented in the film *Yawar Mallku*, by the Bolivian director Jorge Sanjines.
116. José Havet, "Rational Domination: The Power Structure in a Bolivian Rural Zone," Ph.D. dissertation, University of Pittsburgh, 1979, 131.
117. See the speech by Carlos Serrate Reich, "A los campesinos de Papelpampa," in Serrate Reich, ed., *¿Qué es profoundizar la revolución?* (La Paz, 1964), 54.
118. William Carter, "Revolution and the Agrarian Sector," in Malloy and Thorn, eds., *Beyond the Revolution*, 236.
119. The Cochabamba Rural Federation published a series of newspaper articles presenting the hacendado position toward the forthcoming agrarian reform decree. The thoughts of the creole-mestizo landlords regarding the "aborigines" are best exemplified in the columns of *Los Tiempos*, 3 March 1953, 2; 10 March 1953, 2; 18 March 1953, 2; 25 March 1953, 2; 1 April 1953, 2; 14 April 1953, 2; *Última Hora*, 5 June 1952, 4; 23 September 1952, 5; 26 February 1953, 5; *La Nación*, 29 November 1952, 3. These articles reveal the racist bias of *Los Tiempos* and its use as a propaganda vehicle for the Sociedad Rural by its owner Demetrio Canelas, himself a Cochabamba landlord. For the upshot of this provocative media onslaught, which led to the closure of the newspaper (after an alleged sacking by peasants during the abortive Falangista coup attempt of 9 November 1953), see Jerry Knudson, *The Press and the Bolivian National Revolution, Journalism Monographs*, 31 (November 1973), 31–33.
120. *Los Tiempos*, 24 June 1952, 4.
121. *El Diario*, 28 April 1953, 7.
122. *El País*, 7 November 1952, 5; 10 December 1952, 4; *El Diario*, 11 November 1952, 3–4. The agitation in the environs of Colomi, allegedly incited by the Ucureña Agrarian Federation, continued into 1953: *El Diario*, 6 February 1953, 5; 9 February 1953, 7; 12 February 1953, 5; *Los Tiempos*, 8 February 1953, 7. However, Prefect Germán Vera Tapia claimed that the news regarding Colomi was erroneous and "everything was calm in the region." Solis, "Fields of Revolution," 244.
123. A presidential commission determined that abusive treatment of colonos by the patrón of Hacienda Emusa precipitated the incident. *Última Hora*, 8 November 1952, 5; 12 November 1952, 4; *El Diario*, 10 November 1952, 4. See also Gordillo, *Los campesinos revolucionarios*, 52. Landowners in Loayza Province (La Paz Department) urged the creation of a mobile police force to control widespread indigenous agitation in the region. *El Diario*, 14 June 1952, 6.
124. *El Diario*, 12 January 1953, 5; 18 January 1953, 15; *Última Hora*, 20 January 1953, 4.
125. *Los Tiempos*, 5 July 1953, 3.
126. *El Diario*, 22 October 1953, 5.
127. *El Diario*, 11 July 1953, 5; *Los Tiempos*, 16 July 1953, 1.
128. Jorge Dandler, "'Low Classness,' or 'Wavering Populism?' A Peasant Movement in Bolivia (1952–1953)," in June Nash, Juan Corradi, and Hobart Spalding, eds., *Ideology and Social Change in Latin America* (New York, 1977), 154. See also the biographical sketch, "José Rojas, Líder de los Campesinos," *El Pionero*, 1 (1954), 51–53.
129. Dandler, "Low Classness," 154–155.
130. Ibid., 156–157. For an example of the influence of José Rojas on the spread of syndical formation far afield from Ucureña, see Richard A. Simmons, *Palca and Pucara: A Study of the Effects of Revolution on Two Bolivian Haciendas* (Berkeley, 1971), 132–133, 142–145.
131. *El País*, 3 May 1952, 5. For the conflict with Cliza, see El Diario, 22 November 1852, 5, and Gordillo, *Los campesinos revolucionarios*, 56.
132. *Los Tiempos*, 23 May 1952, 5. See also Gordillo, *Los campesinos revolucionarios*, 56–57.
133. Dandler, "Low Classness," 157.
134. Sinforoso Rivas recounts his life and times in *Los hombres de la revolución: memoria de un líder campesino*: for the Bella Vista project, see 66–70.

135. Jorge Dandler, "Politics of Leadership, Brokerage and Patronage in the Campesino Movement of Cochabamba, Bolivia, 1935–1954," Ph.D. dissertation, University of Wisconsin, 1971, 45–46.
136. Rivas, *Los hombres de la revolución*, 64–65.
137. Ibid., 63. Recently freed from five years in prison, the old revolutionary greeted Rivas with tears of joy.
138. Dandler, "Low Classness," 158; Gordillo, *Los campesinos revolucionarios*, 53–54.
139. Gordillo, *Los campesinos revolucionarios*, 49–50.
140. The insurgents in the FSTCC coup included the Valle Alto caudillo José Rojas, and his lieutenants Emilio Chácon, Carlos Montaño, Crisótomo Inturias, Encarnación Colque, Modesto Sejas (all PORistas), and Andrés Arispe. Sandor John, *Bolivia's Radical Tradition*, 142–145. For an excellent account of these events, and Lechín's betrayal of Rivas, see Gordillo, *Los campesinos revolucionarios*, 59. Rivas' recollections of the tumultuous affair are to be found in his autobiography, *Los hombres de la revolución*, 47–50.
141. The quotes are from official MNR departmental correspondences cited in Gordillo, *Los campesinos revolucionarios*, 60.
142. *El Diario*, 2 February 1953, 3, 6; Antezana and Romero, *Historia de los sindicatos revolucionarios*, 238–239; Sandor John, *Bolivia's Radical Tradition*, 142–143.
143. Gordillo, *Los campesinos revolucionarios*, 63–64.
144. Ibid., 65; see also Sandor John, *Bolivia's Radical Tradition*, 143.
145. This decree antedated by four months the Agrarian Reform Decree of 2 August 1953. Dandler, "Low Classness," 161–162; Gordillo, *Los campesinos revolucionarios*, 67–69.
146. Gordillo, *Los campesinos revolucionarios*, 71.
147. *El Diario*, 1 July 1953, 7; 5 July 1953, 7 and Soliz, "Fields of Revolution," 140.
148. This is a paraphrase of Zannier from an interview by Gordillo, *Los campesinos revolucionarios*, 68.
149. *Los Tiempos*, 18 September 1952, 4 cited in Gordillo, *Los campesinos revolucionarios*, 162.
150. *El Diario*, 2 August 1952, 7 and also, *Los Tiempos*, 3 August 1952, 3.
151. *El Diario*, 26 June 1952, 7; Ranaboldo, *El camino perdido*, 215–217; Peon E., *Historia y mito*, 35.
152. *El Diario*, 13 February 1953, 5; 15 February 1953, 7. For Antonio Mamani Álvarez's recollection of his marginalization, see Ranaboldo, *El camino perdido*, 212, 258–259.
153. *El Diario*, 8 March 1953, 5. Mamani Álvarez also stated: "The Indian is by nature nationalistic, tied to his terrain, and not plagued by extravagant foreign ideologies."
154. *El Diario*, 18 March 1953, 5.
155. Ranaboldo, *El camino perdido*, 196–197, 218–221.
156. Mamani Álvarez recounted the origins of the emergent dirigentes: "Juan Céspedes Lavayen, ex-miner from Catavi . . . Gabino Apaza of Pacajes, ex-miner from Huanuni . . . Toribio Salas of Achacachi, shoemaker, Agapito Vallejos and José Rojas of Cochabamba, artisans, Sinforoso Rivas, merchant." Ranaboldo, *El camino perdido*, 214.
157. *Los Tiempos*, 28 January 1953, 3; *La Nación*, 14 June 1953, 3. The topic of agricultural production is a recurrent feature in newspaper articles during the months leading up to the Agrarian Reform Decree. See, for example, *La Nación*: 27 October 1952, 3; 3 December 1952, 3; 4 April 1953, 3, and Antezana and Romero's compilation (from *El Diario*), in *Historia de los sindicatos revolucionarios*, 217–220, 228, 249, 254, 256–257. A draught during the onset of the revolution made for a shortage of foodstuffs in the first year of the revolution; the slaughter of thousands of cattle after the proclamation of the Agrarian Reform Decree was reported in *La Nación*, 30 August 1953, 3.
158. Peasant dirigentes "accused of intent to organize agrarian sindicatos" in Uchojchi near the canton of Senajo (Chayanta Province, Potosí Department) were arrested by a subprefect enforcing orders "to suppress whatever agitation, that falls under the pretext of organizing agrarian sindicatos." *El Diario*, 12 December 1952, 5. For alleged collection of ramas, see *El Diario*, 12 April 1952, 7; 15 October 1952, 4; 20 December 1952, 5; 21 December 1952, 7; 12 January 1953, 4; 14 January 1953, 4; 23 January 1953, 5; 27

January 1953,6, 1 February 1953, 5,7; *Los Tiempos*, 18 June 1952, 4; 14 January 1953, 5; 7 May 1953, 4; 30 June 1953, 5.
159. *El Diario,* 16 November 1952, 6; 20 May 1952, 7; 18 June 1952, 6; *Los Tiempos*, 15 June 1952, 5; *La Nación*, 26 January 1953, 3. A Regional Labor Inspector was killed by landlords in the Department of Santa Cruz: *El Diario*, 6 February 1953, 3.
160. *La Nación*, 26 January 1953, 3; *El Diario*, 20 May 1952, 7; 18 June 1952, 6. For the MNR Supreme Decrees, see *Los Tiempos*, 3 May 1953, 4. Ñuflo Chávez's remarks—originally published in *Gaceta Campesina*, 2 (1953), 28–30—are excerpted in Antezana and Romero, *Historia de los sindicatos revolucionarios*, 219–220. For the Supreme Decree on reorganization of the armed forces, see *El Diario*, 26 July 1953, 6.

6
AGRARIAN REFORM

Since the Iberian conquest of the Americas, control over land and its tenure has been the root of creole domination.[1] Under the ancien régime Bolivia had the most inequitable concentration of agricultural land on the planet, and it was necessary to import food.[2] The Agrarian Reform Decree of 2 August 1953 addressed the nation's dysfunctional land tenure system. This seminal decree engendered a process of momentous political, economic, social, cultural, and demographic change ongoing into the modern age. It is noteworthy that General Douglas MacArthur, the American proconsul of postwar Japan and architect of the country's economic recovery, insisted on land reform as a prerequisite for modernization of the nation. His biographer lauded "MacArthur's land-reform program [as] probably his greatest achievement in Japan."[3] This is at odds with North American policy in Latin America to thwart agrarian reform in Guatemala (1954), Brazil (1964), and Chile (1973). Although the United States opted for co-optation rather than an overthrow of the MNR regime—its influence over the direction of the National Revolution and the vital issue of agrarian reform—was nonetheless profound and best appreciated within the context of the capitalist world system.

At the time of Bolivian independence in 1825, tribal peoples constituted one-half of the world populace.[4] By the latter half of the nineteenth century, subsistence and reciprocal exchange of commodities began to give way to the developing capitalist system based on individualism, private ownership of property, and a culture of consumption. The transition from subsistence and reciprocity to the commodification of land was considered essential to economic development by creole elites as Eurocentric notions of progress appeared in schemes for agrarian reform throughout the Americas.[5] The Jeffersonian yeoman farmer became synonymous with notions of progress and the emancipation of slaves and peons a cornerstone of nineteenth-century liberal ideals.

In Latin America, liberal laws sought to divest indigenous communities of their lands in Bolivia as well as in Mexico, Guatemala, El Salvador, and Colombia.[6] In Mexico, for example, the 1856 Disentailment Law resulted in the usurpation of Indian communal lands. On the eve of the 1910 Mexican Revolution, less than 1 percent of the populace controlled 85 percent of the land and only 10 percent of Indian villagers on the central highlands still held communal lands.[7] Nineteenth-century disentailment laws produced similar results in Bolivia: by 1950, 92 percent of all agricultural land was held in haciendas of 1,000 hectares or more; 4 percent of Bolivian landowners owned 82 percent of all rural property, while one-half of the rural population owned 0.13 percent of the land in holdings of 3 hectares or less.[8]

The 1953 Bolivian Agrarian Reform Decree harkened back to earlier attempts to radically alter the rural order. "Land privatization was an old creole policy," notes the anthropologist Tristan Platt, "traceable back to Bolivar's 'dictatorial decrees' of 1825, whose implementation had been seriously attempted under Ballivian (1841–1847) and Melgarejo (1864–1870), before reappearing as the main objective of the 'First Agrarian Reform' of 1874 [Ley de Exvinculación]."[9] Land privatization was anathema to the ayllu communities, but considered essential to "progress" by outsiders. For the Indians of Charazani, an ayllu community on the slopes of Mount Kaata, the vagaries of individual ownership represented an existential threat:

> for Kaatans, there is a wholeness in their mountain, which is an ayllu . . . united to each other by social and cultural principles. Kaatans argued in 1598 against the Conquistadores and in 1953 against the Agrarian Reformists that *like a human body, the mountain is composed of parts organically united to each other. The lands of Mount Kaata belong together because they are parts of a social and human mountain* (emphasis added).[10]

The Colonato Regime

Kaata and other "free" highland communities on the Altiplano were interspersed with ayllus that had been subsumed by haciendas—and the ayllu comunarios, ipso facto, transformed to hacienda colonos. Haciendas varied both in size and in number of colonos on the Altiplano as elsewhere: in the Canton of Achacachi (La Paz Department), for example, the largest hacienda encompassed 2,854 hectares with 106 colonos; the 12 largest haciendas (1,000 hectares to 2,854 hectares) averaged 77 colonos; 13 haciendas of 100–999 hectares averaged 43 colonos.[11]

The colonato required fieldwork from a *persona* (Altiplano term for colono) together with personal services rendered by the family. Similar to the ayllu communities, the hacienda lands were worked by a hierarchy determined by wealth and status: the persona in the Altiplano with full usufruct rights; the *media persona* with half the land and labor obligations of the persona; the *yanapaco*, who worked a small parcel; and the *mayoruni*, who farmed a smaller parcel. The poorest peasants, the landless (*utawawa*) families, lived and worked for the wealthier peasants on their plots (*sayañas*). The colonato also imposed a host of personal services; although banned by decree during the presidency of Gualberto Villarroel in the 1940s, pongueaje and mitanaje continued after the president's overthrow. The following list of obligatory services, compiled by the anthropologist Hans Buechler for Aymara colonos in La Paz Department, also applied (with some regional variations) to Aymara and Quechua colonos in Oruro, Potosí, Cochabamba, and Chuquisaca Departments. To the onerous regimen of personal services, additional indignities abounded: for example, services such as *awatiri*, *islero*, and *apiri*, included the liability of replacement cost for any livestock lost while rendering the service. The islero's shepherding involved the care of hundreds of animals and the omnipresent potential for loss. Indeed, loss of livestock was a common cause of emigration to La Paz by unfortunate colonos who also were burdened with payment to the landlord for broken dishes, lost tableware, and underproduction of *chicha*.[12]

The 1953 Agrarian Reform Decree

Sixteen months after the victory of the revolution, President Víctor Paz Estenssoro presented the MNR's Agrarian Reform Decree before thousands of peasants assembled at Ucureña, a hotbed of revolutionary syndicalism. The objectives of the MNR agrarian reform decree were monumental: to "liberate campesino workers from their conditions of serfs, prohibiting gratuitous services"; "transform the feudal system of tenancy and exploitation of the land"; "return to the indigenous communities those lands that were usurped, modernizing their cultivation"; and "incorporate the indigenous population into the national life." Additionally, the agrarian reform sought to "develop agrarian cooperatives, lend technical aid and open credit possibilities," and "promote currents of internal migration of the rural population, now excessively concentrated in the inter-Andean region, with the objective of obtaining a rational human distribution"[13]

The decree cited statistics from the Agrarian Census of 1950 to illustrate the dimensions of the latifundia problem; 5 percent of rural property owners held 70 percent of the land in a "semi-feudal" mode of production. The inequitable land tenure system and the contempt of the landlords for the indigenous peoples resulted in 80 percent illiteracy, dismal agricultural production, and a drain on the economy.[14] The agrarian reform law declared (Article 2) that the state "recognizes and guarantees private rural property when this accomplishes a useful function for the nation."[15]

The *Servicio Nacional de Reforma Agraria* (SNRA) employed rural inspectors, juntas and judges, topographers, surveyors, and other specialists to determine the "social function" of estates after collecting information on their size, system of land tenure, level of capital investment, and degree of market participation. Latifundia were defined as properties of great size, insufficiently exploited with antiquated forms of labor and technology as opposed to agricultural enterprises farmed by the owner and salaried workers with capital invested in agricultural equipment. Latifundia, because of their archaic mode of production, were defined as serving a negative "social function" and hence to be redistributed among their colonos.

TABLE 6.1 Services Rendered by the Colonos of Compi

Name	Description of Service	Number of Persons	Duration of Each Term	Place Where Service Was Rendered
Awatiri	Shepherd of hacienda sheep	1	Six months	Compi
Islero	Cowsherd and swineherd, also cleaned patios and store rooms	1	Six months	Compi
Camani	Elaborated chuno and c'aya (dehydrated potatoes and ocas)	With relatives whom he hired at own cost	One to three months, depending on the harvest	Compi
Ch'iar awatiri	Shepherd of black sheep (reserved for mayorunis)	2	One month	Compi
Mit'ani	Cooked for the patron and administrator	1	One week	Compi
Quesero	Took care of the milk sheep	Together with wife	One week	Compi
Mulero	Herded horses, saddled them; cleaned house, lay the table, etc., brought water from distant spring	1	One week	Compi
Aljiri	Directed other servants from Compi who went to Sorata	1	Six months	Sorata
Wayllpero	Ground chicken feed, fed chickens, tended the bees	1	First 2 weeks, later 1 month	Sorata
Hortelano	Servant in the hacienda house	1	First 2 weeks, later 1 month	Sorata
Apiri	Drove pigs and sheep down to Sorata from Compi	?	Whenever needed	Sorata

Source: Hans Buechler, "Agrarian Reform and Migration on the Bolivian Altiplano" (Ph.D. dissertation, Columbia University, 1966), 34.

TABLE 6.2 Distribution of Land in Bolivia in 1950

Hectares*	Farms	Owned	Cultivated
<1	24,747	10,880	5,715
1	18,130	31,962	18,031
3	8,321	31,036	16,282
5	8,790	59,086	25,953
10	5,881	76,959	26,015
20	3,441	85,764	21,247
35	1,391	56,651	13,164
50	1,881	107,711	19,352
75	895	75,466	15,373
100	2,238	295,114	41,366
200	2,494	756,073	70,462
500	1,539	1,049,332	64,329
1000	2,139	3,290,879	95,364
2500	1,861	5,433,897	71,642
5000	797	5,146,335	55,364
10000	615	16,233,954	85,851
	85,160	32,741,099	645,510
unk	1,217	8,750	8,748
	86,377	32,749,849	654,258

Source: INE, I Censo Agropecuario 1950 (La Paz, 1985), pp. 25–26. Courtesy of Cambridge University Press. Herbert S. Klein, "Social Change in Bolivia Since 1952," in Merilee S. Grindle and Pilar Domingo, eds., *Proclaiming Revolution*, 233.

Note *In this and in the subsequent tables, hectares rounded to the nearest whole number.

Identification of the social function of land with its use resulted in a focus on hacienda productivity rather than the unequal distribution of land between hacendados and colonos. But colono exploitation was at its worst on haciendas exempted as "agricultural enterprises." In addition to operating and maintaining farm equipment, harvesting, transporting, and marketing produce, the colonos also were required to comply with demands of personal service. Colonos found it successful to argue for hacienda expropriation not in terms of size, investment or productivity, but because of the colonato regimen.[16]

The MNR's approach was procedural and legalistic. Because expropriation was decided on a case-by-case basis for each individual hacienda rather than mandating the expropriation of all haciendas per se, many properties were judged exempt. Social function was a subjective judgment determined by SNRA functionaries who were easily influenced by hacendados. The particular circumstances of each case determined the fate of latifundia: per Article 13 of the decree, "The maximum amount of private property is determined by taking into account only the extension economically cultivable."[17] Limits were set for the size of landholdings to be redistributed in all the geographical regions of the country. Soil fertility was used to

TABLE 6.3 Land Ownership by Type of Unit, Bolivia 1950

Number of Hectares

Type	Farms	Owned	Cultivated
Comunidades	3,779	717,844,857	17,010,644
Haciendas	8,137	1,270,107,657	29,016,469
Small Farms*	56,259	952,642,180	12,332,755
Others	18,202	334,390,256	7,065,941
Totals	86,377	3,274,984,950	65,425,809

Source: INE (1985), pp. 25–26.

Note: *Owner operator farms without *coionos* or *jornaleros*.

Source: Courtesy of Cambridge University Press. Herbert S. Klein, "Social Change in Bolivia Since 1950," in Merilee S. Grindle and Pilar Domingo, eds., *Proclaiming Revolution*, 234.

determine the extent of hacienda expropriation: for example, in the well-watered environs bordering Lake Titicaca, the maximum amount of land allowed to a small owner was 10 hectares; in the less productive zone to the south, near Lake Poopo, a small owner was allowed 15 hectares; and in the more arid region further south, a small farmer could have 35 hectares. A small owner with irrigated land in the Cochabamba valleys could receive 6 hectares, while his counterpart with unirrigated land could be granted 12 hectares.[18]

Agrarian Sindicatos

Article 132 of the decree legitimized the growing indigenous syndical movement:

> The campesino sindicto organization is recognized as a means of defense of the rights of its members and of the conservation of the social conquests. The campesino syndicates will intervene in the execution of the Agrarian Reform. They may be independent of or associate themselves with the central organizations.[19]

Where campesino sindicato mobilization was weakest, as in the Departments of Chuquisaca and Tarija, landlords were most successful in staving off expropriation of their estates through chicanery, graft, intimidation, and violence. Land seizures by revolutionary sindicatos proved to be the most expeditious means of redistributing land to those who worked it because the hacendados were unable to recover the properties. Indeed, the potential of an agrarian revolution hastened codification of the MNR's agrarian reform decree some 16 months after the onset of the National Revolution.

Implementation

The transformation of the agrarian sector was stymied by a plethora of complex procedures for confiscation and distribution of land, a reliance on legal procedural formulism in determination of land titles, and a cumbersome and inefficient bureaucratic apparatus that undermined the redistributive process. A Byzantine paper chase awaited those peasants who pursued a formal *expediente* (land claim) to acquire land—a frustrating legal and bureaucratic gauntlet with titles granted only after years of concerted effort and expense. Within the Decree lies a Kafkaesque bureaucracy, a veritable lawyer's cornucopia of 177 articles, seemingly born from Jorge Luis Borges' "Library of Babel." Litigation of land value led to corrupt negotiation of land values, and eroded trust regarding the validity of land titles granted without indemnification.[20] The mitigation of latifundia expropriation because of judicial considerations led the Soviet scholar E.V. Kovalev to conclude, "The utilization by the bourgeois government of Bolivia of such a conservative institution of the bourgeois state as the judiciary as the basic weapon of agrarian reform was one of the principal reasons for the slowness in implementation of the reform."[21]

Implementation was further impeded by a lack of budgetary commitment to the SNRA apparatus (0.4–1.5 percent of the total national budget), by a lack of skilled technicians, surveyors, topographers, and agronomists (of which the SNRA employed a total of three in 1963), by a paucity of basic administrative necessities (equipment, supplies), and inadequate salaries for employees.[22] Ultimately, land would be most readily secured when peasants seized it outright—obviating the complexities of legal procedures—with a fait accompli. Furthermore, giving "the land to those who work it" resulted in distribution according to hacienda usufruct patterns, perpetuating minifundismo.[23]

The ex-colonos and ayllu comunarios were at a disadvantage in the pursuit of land claims. Government agencies were located in towns and cities, necessitating a journey to entreat with lawyers, surveyors, judges, clerks, and the assorted petty bureaucrats who came to encrust the SNRA apparatus. The cost included expenses for travel, payments, payoffs, and time away from the field. Proceedings were in Spanish, the language and culture of government, foreign to illiterate campesinos.[24] As the Peruvian novelist Mario Vargas Llosa notes, "Public enterprises are useful for providing cushy jobs for the protégés of those in power, for feeding the people under their patronage, and for making shady deals. Such enterprises soon turn into bureaucratic swarms paralyzed by the corruption and inefficiency introduced into them by politics."[25] It was within this alien, Spanish-speaking world that the Indian peasantry had to struggle for the opportunity to own land.

The legal contest was unequal and the outcome costly; the labyrinthine and lengthy administrative process was detrimental to the peasants' quest for land while offering hacendados the advantage of bureaucratic shenanigans: for example, the attrition rate due to the disappearance of legal paperwork (through incompetence or fraud) is estimated at 20 percent for the early years of the reform.[26] An expediente was initiated at a meeting with a five-member rural council (either on the estate in question or a nearby town) after which it had to be shepherded through nearly a dozen SNRA offices to determine if the property fit the definition of small, medium, large hacienda or agricultural enterprise, and then to an agrarian judge for a verdict—and ultimately, in the 2–20 years necessitated by the process—to the desk of the president for his signature. It then would wend its way in reverse order back to the recipient.

The strategies utilized to subvert the agrarian reform included outright grants of properties, via the reform apparatus, to the landowners themselves; division of estates into smaller parcels apportioned among family members, thereby escaping the latifundio designation and total expropriation; postponement of the reform process through legal machinations; infiltration of the SNRA bureaucracy as well as peasant sindicatos by landlords and/or their surrogates; intimidation, threats, and violence against peasant leaders who refused to be co-opted by landlords.[27] It was to the patrón's advantage to remain on a property and prolong litigation in a legal war of attrition against the disadvantaged peasant—adding to the insecurity of the ex-colonos as well as their dependency on the MNR regime.[28]

Yet there were instances when the expediente process subverted hacendado machinations. Carmen Soliz's examination of expedients in Omasuyos Province (La Paz Department) found that MNR officials could interpret the intent of the agrarian reform laws as either mandating land expropriation and redistribution to the peasants who worked it, or exempting properties that promoted agricultural production through capital investment in equipment, fertilizer, and the use of animal husbandry.[29] The anomalous act of the Rural Council led by its President Luciano Quispe, a revolutionary who had earlier defied the powerful Achacachi terratenientes and opened an Indian school, is a case in point. Under Quispe's forceful leadership, the Rural Council moved aggressively to expropriate a number of terrateniente (large hacienda) properties together with all their assets. His adroit use of the agrarian reform laws to justify expropriations posed a danger to the creole-mestizo landlords and the MNR's tenuous control of the countryside. Within three months, Quispe was replaced by Toribio Salas, a shoemaker from Achacachi considered to be more moderate and amenable to terrateniente demands and MNR control.[30] As will be seen later, the MNR grossly misjudged Toribio Salas.

In a study of agrarian reform in ten regional sites, the agricultural economist Ronald Clark notes that peasant–patrón conflicts resulted from the "confusion and inefficiency in the expropriation process" and because the law allowed landlords to retain part of their estates, peasants were insecure about the changes related to the reform and fearful that a return to the colonato was in order.[31] Until an expediente was definitively resolved by the SNRA bureaucracy, the landlord prevailed; most peasants continued to work on their hacienda usufructs under colonato and sharecropping arrangements, despite their prohibition under the 1953 decrees.[32] A decade after the agrarian reform decree, sharecropping was found on one in ten estates and wage labor on 41 percent of the estates, where peasants, per decree, were obligated to work for landlords at sublegal wages.[33] Outright purchase would often have benefited both parties and have been the better option for many peasants.[34] As the quantitative historian Paul Turovsky notes, the agrarian reform mollified peasants through granting the rights to obtain their usufruct plots, but it also prevented a radical restructure of the rural order and allowed many hacendados to remain on their land.[35]

The MNR assumed a cautious approach, preferring an orderly restructuring of the latifundia system rather than outright destruction of the colonato, to minimize the potential of revolutionary upheaval and the loss of food supplies to the cities. In the early years of the revolution, disruption of the hacendado-controlled agricultural marketing system resulted in food shortages in the urban markets, necessitating the importation of food staples. Three months before the Agrarian Reform Decree, peasant sindicatos and government inspectors were directed to enforce Supreme Decree 3375, mandating colono labor for harvests.[36] Yet another threat to food supplies was weather: the drought of 1956–1958 was the driest in a decade.[37]

Land Redistribution

Acquisition of land titles was a slow process; the MNR spawned a bureaucratic monster that crept along at its own pace. After factoring in division of lands among family members, property sales, and other hacendado tactics, including intimidation, violence, and co-optation of peasant sindicato leaders, it is evident that landlords emerged from the expediente process with a considerable percentage of their haciendas intact. Indeed, studies of the rate of land distribution undertaken through 1980 reveal that only 20–25 percent of the estates were expropriated.[38] The MNR's desultory commitment to agrarian reform becomes obvious if one follows the money. The National Land Reform Council received less than 2 percent of the MNR budget during the revolution (1952–1964). After six years of MNR rule, 528,369 hectares had been redistributed among 29,216 families. Given the population increase of some 60,000 persons a year during this period, the rate of redistribution failed to keep up with the increase in population.[39]

Agricultural land is most valuable where it is cultivable, and as comparative studies of land tenure demonstrate, domination of the rural sector rests on the control of cultivable land. The land most prized and contested during the revolution contained arable and irrigable soil. As the expropriative process progressed, it became obvious that a significant category of hacienda workers had been overlooked in the agrarian reform decree. Besides the hacienda colonos working usufruct plots, there were landless peasants (forasteros, arrimantes, utawawas) whose numbers (10–12 percent) are estimated to have been equal to those of the colonos. Their presence became obvious with their demands for the hacienda lands they occupied, in particular those portions with prime cultivable land, coveted by the hacendados. Ultimately, these occupations were legalized because of MNR concerns that confrontations would jeopardize their control of the countryside.[40]

Land Restitution

Both hacienda and ayllu were considered archaic forms of land tenure and therefore impediments to the MNR agenda of economic development of the countryside where 70–80 percent of the nation's population, primarily hacienda colonos and ayllu comunarios, worked the land. The intent of the 1953 Agrarian Reform

TABLE 6.4 Classes and Strata in the Bolivian Countryside, 1950

Classification	Units	Number of Hectares Possessed	Number of Hectares Worked	Percentage Worked of Land Possessed
Total	86,377	32,749,849,50	654,258.09	2.00
Owner-operated	56,259	9,527,421.80	123,327.55	1.30
Landowners[a]	8,137	12,701,076.57	290,164.69	2.28
Renters	13,598	1,983,764.63	44,466.68	2.24
Sharecroppers	3.033	382,114.72	5,206.33	1.36
Indian communities	3,779	7,178,448.57	170,106.44	2.37
Peasants[b]	617	105,425.65	1,933.30	1.83
Owners of state lands	818	439,253.74	6,433.83	1.47
Societies and cooperatives	136	433,333.82	12,619.27	2.91

[a]. Operate with colonos and wage workers.
[b]. Those tolerated in Indian communities.

Source: Courtesy of Latin American Perspectives. Uri Mendelberg, "Impact of the Bolivian Agrarian Reform on Class Formation," *Latin American Perspectives*, 12.3 (Summer 1985), 46.

Decree, granting "land to those who work it," was to end the colonato and thereby eliminate the underpinning of the landed oligarchy. While the emancipated colonos were free to lay claim to expropriated hacienda lands, the decree limited comunarios to restitution of lands usurped in the twentieth century.

Exclusion of pre-1900 usurpations excluded the wholesale loss of ayllu properties following the disentailment laws of the late nineteenth century; after four centuries of hacendado usurpation, ayllu communities retained an estimated 22 percent of the nation's rural land. The agrarian reform commission sought to significantly reduce the number of land claims by ayllu comunarios and inhibit the potential growth of communal land tenure considered an obstacle to agricultural development. But it would not be so simple. Comunario demands for land restitution, education, and government loans for agricultural and home improvement—together with seizures of hacienda lands—often sidestepped the parameters mandated by the 1953 agrarian reform decree.

In a surprise move, President Paz Estenssoro issued a second decree in 1954 to mitigate rising comunario unrest. This decree mandated restitution of *all* ayllu land usurped after 1900. The president's decree contravened the intent of the agrarian reform commission to inhibit growth of the non-capitalist ayllus and elicited a host of unintended consequences: an outpouring of appeals resulting in restitution of ayllu land usurped before 1900; exacerbation of land and boundary disputes between comunarios and ex-colonos; invigoration of traditional ayllu sociopolitical organization. Recent archival research by Carmen Soliz documents the success in restitution of usurped lands by comunario use of land titles dating from the colonial period as well as titles based on the late nineteenth-century land title survey (Revista de Tierras) and purchased as a result of the disentailment law.[41]

Regional Land Tenure Variations

Bolivia is a nation of great geographical and ecological diversity: the arid and frigid Altiplano and Andean cordillera, the steep eastern slopes of the Andes whose rivers drain into the Amazonian river system, the highlands and inter-montane valleys of Cochabamba, Potosí, Sucre, and Tarija Departments, and the eastern lowlands and jungles of Santa Cruz, Pando, and Beni abutting the border with Brazil. These regional variations were considered in the agrarian reform calculus, together with the particulars of each expediente initiated with the SNRA (property size, intensity of cultivation, level of production, political influence), in the final determination of the fate of an estate. The following analysis reveals the varied outcomes of agrarian reform in the highland departments.

MAP 6.1 Ecological Zones

Source: Courtesy of the University of Pennsylvania Press. Maria Lagos, *Autonomy and Power*, 13.

Altiplano: La Paz and Oruro Departments

The Altiplano . . . is a place of superlatives: It holds the world's highest navigable lake, Titicaca, and the largest salt flat. It is the second largest mountain plateau in the world, after that of Tibet—a landscape of ice and fire, wind and salt that stretches from northern Argentina to the harsh flatlands of Peru.[42]

Sixty percent of Bolivia's indigenous people, Aymara-speaking descendants of pre-Columbian polities, inhabited the Altiplano Departments of La Paz and Oruro on the eve of the 1952 National Revolution—three quarters of them concentrated in the provinces of Omasuyos and Los Andes in La Paz Department where the alluvial soil near the shores of Lake Titicaca is most advantageous for farming. The pre-revolutionary population density in Los Andes Province, 31 inhabitants per square kilometer, was second only to the Upper Valley of Cochabamba Department with a density of 76 inhabitants per square kilometer.[43] Colonos cultivated potatoes, yucca, oca, quinoa, barley, wheat and raised pigs, sheep, cattle, llamas, and alpacas. Oruro peasants continued the Andean tradition of farming these crops acclimated to the Altiplano, whereas comunarios in the La Paz provinces with access to the tropical Yungas also grew fruits and coca leaves, marketing their surplus in provincial towns or the city of La Paz. Comunarios in Carangas Province (Oruro Department) that borders Peru, traded llamas, *charque* (dried llama meat), and pig lard in Peru and returned with wine, aguardiente, and olives; they also exchanged salt for rice from the Oriente.[44]

Hacienda expansion was spurred by the growth of the mining industry and the construction of railways in La Paz Department between 1900 and 1917. The Altiplano railways constructed during these years facilitated shipment of food and material to the mines in La Paz and Oruro Departments, and the haciendas provided security for loans as well as vertical integration for the mine owners.[45] Prominent politicians, businessmen, attorneys, and mining magnates were among those who usurped over 100,000 hectares of ayllu land between 1878 and 1920.[46] President Ismael Montes, for example, purchased virtually the entire peninsula of Taraco in the surrounds of Lake Titicaca in 1907; his son-in-law, who commanded a regiment at Guaqui violently usurped ayllu lands during the years 1920–1922.[47] The Altiplano ayllu communities continually suffered the usurpation of lands: in 1846, there were reportedly 302 ayllu communities and 79 haciendas in Oruro Department; a century later there were 213 ayllu communities and 224 haciendas in the department.[48]

Violent resistance to encroachments on ayllu communities erupted in Omasuyos, Pacajes, and Sicasica provinces in La Paz Department in 1895 and spread to the provinces of Muñecas, Ingavi, and Inquisivi, and then the Departments of Oruro, Potosí, and Cochabamba before the rebellion was quelled and its leaders executed in 1896.[49] The indigenous leaders who advocated restitution of ayllu lands, an end to further hacienda usurpations, and an autonomous Indian government were summarily executed by the creole-mestizo generals in 1899 following their victory in the Federal War.[50] Yet the despoliation continued after the Federal War in which a large Indian contingent had fought on the side of the Liberal Party elites. Increasing population pressure aggravated conflicts between comunarios and emancipated ex-colonos who laid claim to hacienda usufructs—lands that had once belonged to the ayllu communities.[51] By 1920, over 98,000 hectares of usurped ayllu lands in Pacajes Province (La Paz Department) were in the hands of creole-mestizos!

The stated intent of the 1953 Agrarian Reform Decree was, "To restore to the indigenous communities the lands which were usurped from them, and to cooperate in the modernization of their agriculture; respecting and utilizing, where possible, their collective traditions; liberating the campesino workers from their condition of serfs, proscribing free services and personal obligations."[52] But Article 42 of the subsequent Decree (3732) restricted restitution of communal lands to those usurped after 1900 "when their rights are proven."[53] Significantly, the post-1900 provision excluded ayllu lands lost following the nineteenth-century Disentailment Laws, thereby legitimizing the catastrophic creole-mestizo land grabs following this earlier iteration of "agrarian reform." Thus, the most productive ayllu lands in the fertile valleys and along lake and stream shores usurped in the nineteenth century were to be exempt from ayllu revendication.[54]

However, comunarios, undaunted in their quest for restitution, appealed to local judges as well as President Paz Estenssoro and Minister of Peasant Affairs Ñuflo Chávez for "land to the original owners." Comunario land claims in the departments of La Paz, Potosí, and Oruro were often successful when sympathetic judges altered the time frame for restitution or presented cases as expropriation rather than restitution. Despite the government's objective of transforming Indians into independent farmers, comunario protests and petitions eventuated in the restitution and expansion of comunario landholdings, thereby preserving the communal ayllu.[55]

The agrarian reform emancipated colonos and abolished the onerous custom of unpaid personal services rendered to the landlord. Free of the yoke of servitude, the subsistence oriented colonos were able to participate in the market economy. Once widespread on the Altiplano and elsewhere, barter declined following the development of a market economy driven by cash exchanges.[56] Peasants farming the rich alluvial lands in the environs of Lake Titicaca began cultivation of onions, a labor-intensive but lucrative crop much in demand in the urban marketplace. The irrigable lands in the northern Altiplano yielded two harvests a year, compounding the value of planting onions rather than potatoes.[57] In Pucarani and Batallas, young peasants planted onions, carrots, radishes, lettuce, and turnips.[58] The cultivation of high-value, labor-intensive crops such as onions and carrots also appeared in the Cochabamba Valleys.

On the Altiplano, as elsewhere, the agrarian reform occasioned the collapse of the creole-mestizo agricultural marketing nexus. Indian peasants, *cholos* and *cholas* (urbanized Indian men and women) as well as mestizo vecinos moved into the vacuum and began to restructure a complex web of middlemen, truckers, and peddlers.[59] New towns and markets sprouted along the routes to La Paz as participation in a market economy, once monopolized by hacendados, emerged among a freed peasantry. Houses in these settlements were constructed of adobe bricks, with tile or metal roofs, and the occasional window distinguishing them from traditional rural dwellings of earth with thatched roofs. The new towns were spontaneous settlements by those interested in trade and commerce as well as others seeking urban life and its amenities (electricity, potable water, schools), but more often their impetus came from peasant sindicatos. As David Preston notes, 8 of 12 new towns in the northern Altiplano were initiated by sindicatos, and the sindicato at Umacha owed its inception to the clandestine efforts of the Achacachi caudillo Toribio Salas before the 1952 Revolution.[60]

TABLE 6.5 Articles, Quantities, and Value of Most Commonly Acquired Goods Among Bolivian Peasants in North Highlands Before 1952

Bartered Articles	Quantity	Present Value ($)
Condiments	—	0.65
Cooking grease	3 lbs	0.60
Noodles, etc.	15 lbs	1.50
Pots for cooking	5	1.65
Salt	3 panes	0.75
Wool	4 hides with wool	2.70
TOTAL VALUE OF GOODS ACQUIRED BY BARTER DURING THE YEAR ON A REGULAR BASES		$7.85

Purchased Articles	Quantity	Present Value ($)
Alcohol	5 quarts	3.50
Bread	30 pieces	1.25
Cigarettes	5 packages 10 lbs	0.50
Coca		4.20
Dyes	2 lbs	0.25
Hats	2	415
Kerosene	26 bottles	1.10
Matches	50 boxes (small)	0.85
Pants	1 pair	1.50
Sugar	15 lbs	1.25
Tocuyo (cloth)	10 yards	4.25
TOTAL VALUE OF GOODS ACQUIRED BY CASH DURING THE YEAR		$22.80
TOTAL VALUE OF ALL GOODS		$30.65

Source: Courtesy of University of Wisconsin Press. Ronald Clark, "Land Reform and Peasant Market+ Participation on the Northern Highlands of Bolivia," *Land Economics*, 44 (May 1968), 166.

TABLE 6.6 Articles, Quantities, and Value of the Most Commonly Acquired Goods Among Bolivian Peasants in North Highlands in 1966

Bartered Articles	Quantity	Present Value ($)
Condiments	—	0.65
Pots for cooking	5	1.65
Salt	3 panes	0.75
Other food items in small quantities		2.00
TOTAL VALUE OF GOODS ACQUIRED BY BARTER DURING THE YEAR ON A REGULAR BASIS		$5.05

Purchased Articles	Quantity	Present Value ($)
Alcohol	5 quarts	3.50
Soft drinks	20 bottles	1.75
Beer	10 bottles	2.50
Cooking grease	3 lbs	0.60
Cooking oil	3 bottles	1.25
Fruit and vegetables	various (in season)	2.50
Noodles	15 lbs	1.50
Bread	75 pieces	3.15
Flour (wheat and corn)	50 lbs	3.40
Rice	35 lbs	3.00
Sugar	25 lbs	2.10
Coca	5 lbs	2.10
Cigarettes	20 packages	2.00
Matches	60 boxes (small)	0.95
Kerosene	26 bottles	1.10
Cloth of all kinds	15 yards	7.00
Dyes	—	0.50
Shoes	2 pairs	12.50
Suits	1	12.50
Skirt	1	5.00
Sweaters	1	5.50
Pants	1	5.00
Shirts	2	2.00
Hats	2	8.00
Shawls	1	5.00
Soap	10 pieces	1.50
TOTAL VALUE OF GOODS ACQUIRED BY CASH DURING THE YEAR		$95.90
TOTAL VALUE OF ALL GOODS		$100.95

Source: Courtesy of University of Wisconsin Press. Ronald Clark, "Land Reform and Peasant Market Participation on the Northern Highlands of Bolivia," *Land Economics*, 64 (May 1968), 169.

A study of the effects of the agrarian reform process on peasant market participation in the northern highlands is revealing. Data gathered from interviews with ex-colonos from 51 haciendas indicates that barter declined 35 percent as a result of the agrarian reform process, while items purchased for cash in the money economy increased by 400 percent. The study also indicates a 40 percent increase in number of items purchased, most notably food and drink, cloth and clothes, and bars of soap (perhaps a result of the revolution's promotion of hygiene and public health awareness). The transformative changes resulting from the agrarian reform process are evident in the kind of purchase of foodstuffs (rice, flour, noodles, fruits, and vegetables) suggesting improved nutrition.[61] Purchases of shoes, suits, commercial cloth, shirts, skirts, sweaters and shawls, as well as beer and soft drinks underscore the participation of the former colonos in the market economy.[62]

The agrarian reform improved the material living conditions of rural life. An inventory of some 200 ex-colonos living on an expropriated Altiplano hacienda suggests the material changes wrought by the agrarian reform process: "In 1956 there was one house with a metal roof and one bicycle; now [1968] there are 40 metal roofs and 80 bicycles. In 1952 there were seven sewing machines; now there are 120. In 1959 there was one radio; now there are 100. . . . The above does not include the increased purchases of chairs, tables, beds, plates, knives, forks and spoons, cups, metal pots.[63] The development of markets fostered new settlements along the major roads. In both the new towns, as well as the existing markets in provincial towns, a revolution in marketing drew increasing numbers of peasant women from barter into the cash economy.[64]

Sindicatos, the peasant land groups mandated by the Agrarian Reform Decree, arose as a catalyst for land acquisition. In the initial years of the revolution miners, political militants, and dynamic young Indians, fluent in Spanish and conversant with the workings of the creole-mestizo bureaucracies, appeared as sindicato leaders.[65] The revolution precipitated a transfer in the adjudication of disputes from the local to the departmental level; thus, the ability to effectively function in the Spanish-speaking urban environment became essential for pursuit of land claims and defense of the inevitable boundary disputes. The village leader (Aymara *hilacata*; Quechua *jilakata*), whose status derived from the traditional civil-religious hierarchy, was often superseded by younger urbanized sindicato leaders.

Yungas

The Yungas (Aymara: "warm valleys") is a region of steep valleys plunging from the eastern slopes of the Cordillera Occidental through a temperate zone, and, at lower levels, it becomes a tropical drainage for the vast Amazonian river system. The valleys of Nor and Sud Yungas have provided tropical fruits and coca leaves for the ayllus of the Altiplano for over a millennium. At the onset of the revolution, the *finqueros* (regional term for landlords) often resided in the few local towns, although many favored residence in La Paz. Aymara Indians drawn from the Altiplano served as *peones* (regional term for *colonos*) on the *fincas* (estates). The peon was granted usufruct use of a small plot of land to be worked in exchange for labor by himself and his wife. Labor obligations also included pongueaje and mitanaje, the obligatory personal service required of the peon and his wife in the finquero's house. Additional labor to be rendered included the shepherding of livestock, transportation of coca, coffee, and other produce to market, as well as work on private and public work projects. As was the case throughout the Bolivian countryside, the attempted reforms of President Gualberto Villarroel in 1945–1946 to ameliorate the onerous labor and personal service obligations required of colonos were generally ignored by the landlords.

The temperate and tropical lands of the Yungas attracted migrants from Altiplano ayllus who worked either for the finqueros or for enterprising Indian landholders with spare land to till and a commitment to harvesting a profitable surplus. The Yungas afforded cultivable lands for farming and was sparsely populated at the time of the revolution; labor, not land, was the scarce commodity. Finqueros utilized migrants to work their fields through the exchange of labor for the right to till a small parcel; the system was replicated by peasant small farmers in need of labor. The anthropologist Barbara Leons found the Yungas peasantry "among the best-off peons in Bolivia" because of their high level of participation in the cash market economy.[66]

Most finqueros fled their Yungas estates while awaiting the litigious onslaught of ex-colonos intent on gaining title to lands. The grassroots sindicato movement associated with the Cochabamba Valleys and northern Altiplano was absent in the Yungas. Instead, MNR militants fostered sindicato development and thus "they were under the thumb of the MNR."[67] As elsewhere, the agrarian reform process was strongly influenced by the social and political context surrounding each case. The Yungas sindicatos failed to achieve their potential and thereby allowed landlords to maximize their position. In the Canton of Arapata, despite their lack of capital investment, primitive technology, and use of the colonato, all properties were considered medium-sized and thus escaped expropriation as latifundia. The SNRA not only granted landlords the land worked at the time of the Agrarian Reform Decree, but also awarded them additional land in the Yungas.[68] These plots, while not contiguous and often in the higher reaches of the valleys, could nevertheless be worked if acquired by ambitious peasants. Acquisition of land titles in the Yungas was a tedious process and many peasants still occupied land, de facto, two decades after the 1953 Decree.

The Yungas peasantry, many of whom were initiated into the market system before the agrarian reform, would prove to be a dynamic force in the developing world of Indian, cholo, and mestizo penny capitalists. There was some luck involved in this, because coca and coffee are among the more lucrative cash crops in Bolivia. The coca leaf is the most valuable Yungas product and development of *cocales* (coca plots) proliferated following the Agrarian Reform Decree as peasants sold their thrice-annual coca harvests to peripatetic middlemen for resale in the markets of Coroico, Coripata, or in distant La Paz. The

Aymara penny capitalists (*cocatakis*) from the Altiplano, who traversed the Yungas in search of small coca purchases, became large-scale middlemen controlling over 70 percent of the trade in some areas after the revolution.[69] Demand for the coca leaf remains strong, although use by Indians is said to be in decline. Cocaine hydrochloride, the refined narcotic, however, exhibits global demand and astronomical profits.

The redistribution of land in the Yungas failed to end inequality among the peasantry; the differentiation between rich and poor peasants, renters, and landless *utawawas* continued after the agrarian reform. Indeed, the Agrarian Reform Decree accelerated the process of capitalist change, catalyzing the differential between rich, poor, and landless peasants by granting peasants ownership of usufructs they had previously farmed under the colonato. Generally, "wealthy peasants are more acculturated to mestizo norms, buy and sell more in the market, and are more likely to have *compadrazgo* [fictive kinship] relations with traders and mestizos from outside the community," observed Leons in the Yungas, while "poor peasants have correspondingly less access to these economic and political advantages."[70]

Freedom from the hacienda regimen increased the time to work one's individual field and fostered the production of the emergent peasant capitalists. A noteworthy local variant of the agrarian reform process in the Yungas is the cultivation of fruits and vegetables for cash sale. Largely ignored in the pre-revolutionary era, the labor-intensive farming of tomatoes, carrots, chili peppers, and cabbage proved to be lucrative. In common with the national experience, a marketing system evolved to replace that of the finqueros. Increasingly, peasants began to reside in rural towns in the Yungas, or migrate to La Paz to seek a new life. Indeed, the comunarios who had migrated to La Paz were more adept than colonos in combatting hacienda encroachment because of their broader experience with creole-mestizo culture and society.[71]

Potosí Department

The Altiplano extends to the western provinces of Potosí Department, while the terrain to the east and southeast includes highland puna and temperate valleys. Indigenous agriculture followed the ancient practice of vertical integration of various ecological niches; ayllu comunarios cultivated quinoa and tubors (potatoes, *quinoa, oca, ulluco*) on the Altiplano, wheat, quinoa, and barley in the puna and maize and fruit in the valleys. The surplus grains and flour were exchanged for cotton, coca, *ají*, and aguardiente from sites as far away as La Paz, the Yungas, the lowlands of the Oriente, and the Pacific coast. The ayllus of Potosí Department were the preeminent producers of wheat into the mid-nineteenth century and the revenue was used to render tribute to the state. Collected annually, the tribute was a continuation of a reciprocal arrangement dating from colonial times, assuring the comunarios' rights to their lands. The data for determination of tribute, gathered periodically from a census (*revista*) of the ayllu communities, was difficult to ascertain because fields were farmed in both the highlands and valleys. The revistas often precipitated resistance and engendered boundary disputes between communities.[72]

Studies of Aymara ayllus in northern Potosí reveal a world apart from the amalgam of medieval feudalism and indigenous culture that was the colonato. The Macha and Laymi communities of Chayanta Province still hew to traditional economic practices of reciprocal exchange, barter, and money (cash). Although money was absent in the pre-Colombian economy, the native peoples quickly adopted its use following the Spanish conquest, but in a much more complex and nuanced form than simple cash transactions.[73] Cash is garnered through the sale of a variety of potatoes savored by vecinos and exchanged within the ayllu to buy, sell, and pay debts; it is also used to purchase the necessities for fiesta sponsorship and buy farm animals. Profit, credit, and debt have meanings unique to indigenous culture.[74] Barter is the preferred means of exchange for foodstuffs and maize is exchanged in lieu of money that is utilized primarily as a courtesy or convenience:

> If townspeople visit the rural areas in search of potatoes and maize they must use barter; if ayllu members to go town, however, they prefer to sell for money. . . . The little cash that is needed in the remote valleys is accepted almost as a favor from close kin who find it more convenient than transporting loads of produce to exchange. There are no products that are exclusively exchanged for cash; conversely, everything that is obtained with cash may also be acquired without it.[75]

The remote Potosí ayllus were not immune to the developing world economic system embraced by the creole-mestizo oligarchs. Free trade policies adopted in the latter half of the nineteenth century led to imports of cheaper wheat and flour, resulting in the impoverishment of the once wealthy comunarios. Yet the state continued to rely on tax and tribute levied on the comunarios, while the Altiplano mining elite coveted ayllu lands as a source of food to supply their labor force. The upshot was President Mariano Melgarejo's 1866 confiscation decree declaring that all ayllu lands were state property. Ayllu comunarios were given 60 days to purchase *individual* land titles before they were put up for auction. Comunario resistance to the decree has been interpreted as a violation of an implicit "reciprocal pact," whereby tribute was paid to the state in exchange for recognition of ayllu territory. A more recent interpretation considers this relationship as an "understood truce" in the unending "battle between colonized and colonizers, with partial and temporary agreements—among them the payment of tributes—as a means of defending the status quo of territorial occupation."[76] The violent resistance that followed the decree resulted in the return of most of the confiscated lands after Melgarejo's death.[77]

Creole-mestizo designs on ayllu lands persisted, justified by the belief that for the nation to become modern, it was imperative that Indians be "civilized" and

222 Agrarian Reform

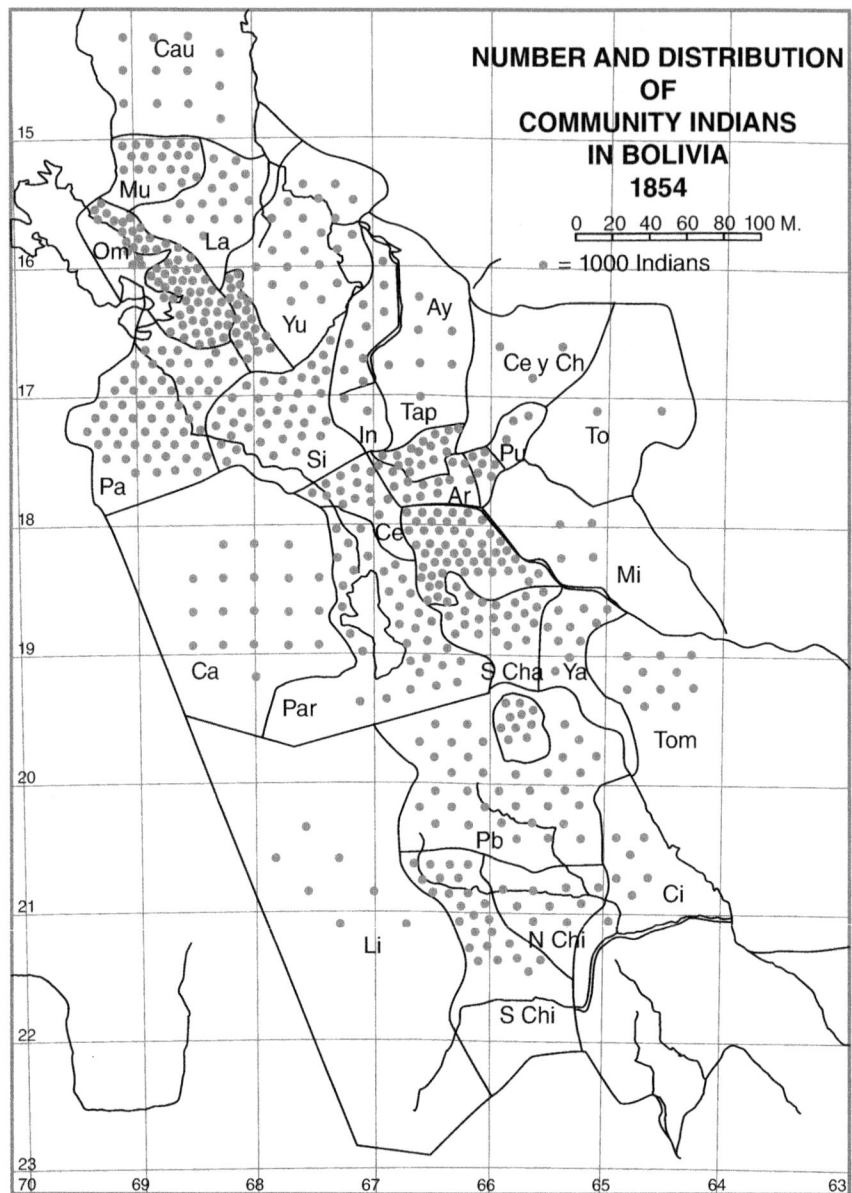

MAP 6.2 Number and Distribution of Community Indians in Bolivia, 1854

Legend for Maps 6.2 and 6.3: Department of La Paz: Cau, Caupolican; Mu, Muñecas; La, Larecaja; Yu, Yungas; Om, Omasuyos; Ce, Cercado (of La Paz); Pa, Pacajes; Si, Sicasica; In, Inquisivi; Department of Oruro: Ca, Carangas; Ce, Cercado (of Oruro); Par, Paria; Department of Cochabamba: Ay, Ayopaya; Tap, Tapacarí; Ar, Arque; Cl, Cliza; Pu, Punata; Ce y Ch, Cercado (of Cochabamba) y Chapare [Ch, Chapare]; To, Totora; Mi, Mizque; Department of Potosí: N Cha, Nor Chayanta [Char, Charcas]; S Cha, Sur Chayanta; [Cha, Chayanta]; Po, Porco; [Lin, Linares]; Ce, Cercado (of Potosí); [Fr, Frias]; Li, Lipez; Se Chi, Sur Chicas; N Chi, Nor Chicas; Department of Chuquisaca: Ci, Cinti; Tom, Tomina; [Az, Azero]; Ya, Yamparaez.

Source: Courtesy of the American Geographical Society.

rid of "the imbecility which is characteristic, their instinctive cruelty . . . that make this group of men savage and inhuman beasts." Thus, in order to civilize the Indian, the Minister of Finance argued in 1899, that it was necessary to abolish the "pernicious system of the communities."[78] As Tristan Platt anatomizes in fascinating detail, the 1874 Disentailment Law—the creole-mestizo embrace of liberal ideology—constituted a dire threat to the very existence of the ayllu communities. This attempt to eradicate traditional indigenous culture, ostensibly transforming comunarios into yeoman farmers, provoked concerted legal resistance as evidenced in the subsequent avalanche of legislative measures.[79] Platt refers to this as the "first agrarian reform" and recounts the history of ayllu resistance to the creole-mestizo state's persistent attempts to collect tribute and taxes from the comunarios of Chayanta Province, noting that because the census officials were often accompanied by government troops, "it appeared more like a military campaign than a bureaucratic process."[80] The ayllus of Northern Potosí rebelled against the Revista of 1882–1903, contrived to collect data for implementation of the 1874 Disentailment Law, "abolishing the ayllus, measuring each household plot, issuing individual titles, and recalculating the tribute as a tax on annual production. Its further aim was to create a national market in land, in order to pave the way for expansion of the hacienda."[81]

The incursion of the colonato in Potosí Department was less pronounced than in the Altiplano: only 12 percent of the 18,000 Indians residing in Potosí Department in 1877 were hacienda colonos. Most landowners in Charcas and Chayanta Provinces owned less than 1,000 hectares in 1903, although 239 properties of over 1,000 hectares were recorded. The loss of ayllu lands in Potosí Department, which increased fourfold in the first two decades of the twentieth century, led to a violent rebellion in Chayanta Province in 1927.[82] When agrarian reform was decreed in 1953, virtually every ayllu in Chayanta's Toracari valley had suffered loss of land.

The mestizo smallholders, who gained title to ayllu parcels in the nineteenth century, had once made common cause with the comunarios resisting disentailment; however, after engaging in commercial pursuits in the provincial towns, their interests had become aligned with the creole mining and hacienda oligarchs.[83] After the onset of the National Revolution, many of these mestizo vecinos joined the MNR, assuming bureaucratic positions in towns and in the nationalized tin mines, which put them further at odds with the ayllu comunarios struggling to both maintain and reclaim lost lands.[84] The turbulent relationship of comunarios and vecinos is discussed in Chapter 8.

The "second Agrarian Reform" introduced in 1953 by the MNR creole-mestizos was yet another attempt to forge capitalists from Indians by fiat (viz., Article 57: "The indigenous communities are private proprietors of the lands which they possess in common"). Regarding the question of usurped ayllu lands, the decree augured a confrontation between comunarios and hacienda colonos: "The colonos of the fincas held by communities and exploited by feudal systems have the same rights of endowment as the colonos of particular properties."[85] As was the case with the nineteenth-century laws, the MNR decree occasioned litigation over inheritance, boundaries, taxes, and tribute, but with the added complications of sindicatos, dirigentes, and creole-mestizo electoral machinations to capture the votes of the enfranchised majority.[86]

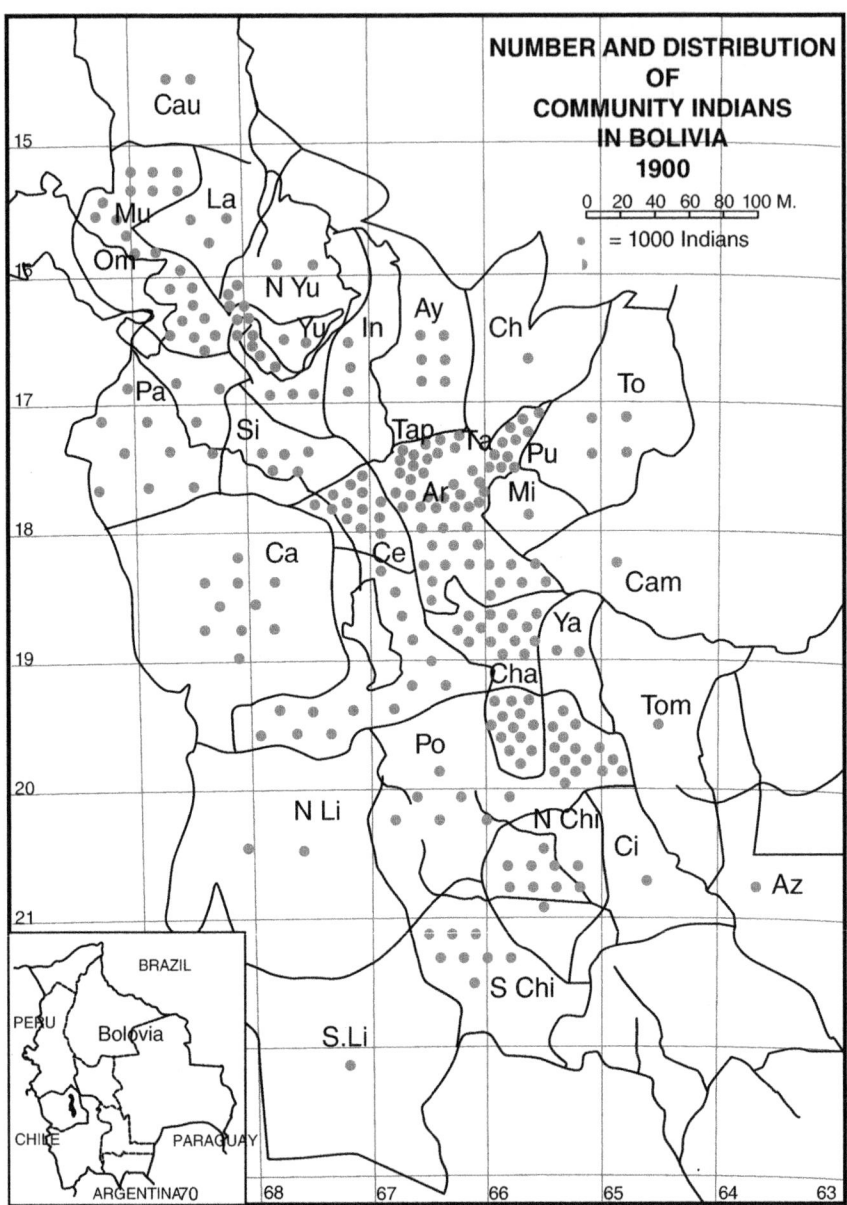

MAP 6.3 Number and Distribution of Community Indians in Bolivia, 1900

Source: Courtesy of the American Geographical Society.

Cochabamba Department

The intermontane region east of the Altiplano comprises the Department of Cochabamba, populated by Quechua comunarios in the *serranía* (highlands) and hacienda colonos and small farmers (*piqueros*) interspersed in the valleys where the temperate climate allows for two to three harvests a year. The region supplied the city of Cochabamba and the mines of Potosí and Oruro with food for centuries. Under the ancien régime, landlords in the Cochabamba valleys, constituting some 5 percent of the population reaped 80 percent of agricultural income. The peasantry, 95 percent of the population, garnered 20 percent of the income.[87] *Pegujaleros* (regional term: colonos) worked hacienda lands, performed personal service, and rendered tribute to their patrón in exchange for usufruct rights to small plots of land. The colonato regimen involved four days a week working hacienda land; at least three weeks a year rendering pongueaje; two or more days a week of household service required of female peasants (mitanaje); and 10–15 days per annum required of colonos tending livestock and gathering and transporting firewood. Payments of 10–20 percent of a family's personal livestock were to be made to the patrón (with the patrón also granted the pick of the litter) in addition to delivering poultry and eggs to the patrón from the pegujalero family's stock. Cash was used to entice peons to work on haciendas in the valleys.[88]

The Cochabamba valleys were notable for the large numbers of small landowners (*piqueros*) who had managed to accumulate sufficient cash to purchase land.[89] In 1929, 72 percent of the properties in the valleys of 1 hectare or less were owned by piqueros.[90] A number of factors had led to the reduced size of hacienda landholdings and the proliferation of smallholders in the Cochabamba valleys. Free trade policies in the later nineteenth century opened the door to Chilean wheat imports, which negatively impacted the region's once thriving commerce. The post–World War I depression in the tin market reduced the demand for foodstuffs in the Altiplano mines and the cities of Oruro and La Paz, and periodic droughts diminished harvests: inheritance, and loan defaults also led to the parcelization of haciendas. The result was a significant increase in the number of peasant sharecroppers and piqueros. In the Sacaba Valley, hacienda fragmentation had increased from 1,045 private properties in 1846 to 44,904 in 1912 and to 68,250 by 1940.[91] The parcelization of hacienda properties mandated by the 1953 agrarian reform decree was but the continuation of a process ongoing since the mid-nineteenth century. The haciendas in the Lower Valley were smaller than in the serranía and hacendados more likely to reside on or near their estates. Consequently, these haciendas were often classified as "medium-sized" properties or "agricultural enterprises" and hence their owners eluded expropriation.[92]

In the *serranía*, high above the more densely populated valleys, peasants toiled in a different world, wresting crops from rocky soil, bereft of irrigation. The colonato assumed a different form in the serranía with larger parcels to farm because of the poverty of the soil and two days' work a week required on the patrón's land (one-half to one-third the days worked in the valley colonato).[93] Over 80 percent of the 561 haciendas with 500 or more hectares in Cochabamba Department were concentrated in the provinces of Ayopaya, Mizque, and Campero; land in the latter two provinces was the exclusive preserve of 1,178 hacendados.[94] The serranía peasants bartered oca, potatoes, *chuño* (freeze dried potatoes), quinoa, and occasional livestock for lowland vegetables, flour, peppers, and other provisions. Poor to nonexistent roads and a paucity of pack animals meant as much as five days round-trip delivering goods to distant markets in the valleys below. Referred to as *estancia runas*, the Indians of the serranía were among the poorest, most isolated, and least acculturated to creole-mestizo norms.

The agrarian reform removed the yoke of hacienda labor, personal servitude, tax, and tribute from the peasantry. Revolutionary changes in transportation, marketing, and social relations unfolded after the dead hand of the manorial system was removed by fiat and enforced by a burgeoning sindicato movement. However, the estancia runas were latecomers to the developing market economy. The isolation and lack of sophistication of the serranía Quechua made for their continued inequality and exploitation by truckers, middlemen, sindicato dirigentes, and assorted hustlers of the post-colonato world, "they have floated among the currents of change and marginalized from political power . . . utilized as masses of pressure in the political maneuvers of the directives of the agrarian sindicatos."[95]

Agitation for revolutionary change in the Cochabamba valleys antedated the Agrarian Reform Decree of August 1953. Resistance to the colonato, revendicationist struggles over usurped ayullu lands, and boundary disputes between comunarios, hacendados, and colonos had often erupted in violence in the first decades of the twentieth century.[96] After the Chaco War, politicized peasant and miner war veterans organized a sindicato in the Upper Valley outside the town of Cliza in 1936 and successfully managed to lease hacienda land owned by the Monastery of Santa Clara. The sindicato was a harbinger of a peasant awakening as sindicatos were formed in Cochabamba and Tarija Departments in 1937. Although suppressed in 1939, and subsequently evicted from the Monastery land, the militant colonos remained a latent force (see Chapter 1). After the victory of the National Revolution, the colonos demanded the expropriation of all 799 hectares of the land owned by the Monastery in 1937—of which 518 hectares had been previously sold to creole-mestizo hacendados. Their claim was withheld despite the concerted action of both the Catholic Church (a pillar of the oligarchy) and the hacendados who had purchased land from the Monastery. Their success emboldened colonos elsewhere to demand the expropriation of their usufructs.[97]

The vacuum resulting from the hacendados' abdication of the marketing and transportation of foodstuffs was soon filled by cholo and mestizo entrepreneurs, as well as enterprising peasant capitalists who incurred debt and purchased trucks to become part of an emergent transportation system. The more ambitious of the *transportistas* (truckers) soon became *rescatadores* (middlemen), traversing the countryside, buying directly from campesino farmers, and reselling at a profit in urban markets.[98] Other post-1953 developments in the Cochabamba valleys included an increase in the number of *tambos*, the commercial roadhouses frequented by itinerant peasants with their goods, and *chicherías* (bars) purveying *chicha* (maize beer), the popular libation.[99] Control of the tax on chicha sales was a perquisite vigorously contested by Indian sindicato dirigentes and creole-mestizo MNR functionaries. The struggle among Cochabamba peasant sindicatos for control of the lucrative chicha tax is discussed in Chapter 7.

As with all farmers, the vicissitudes of weather, pests, disease and market forces often necessitate loans and the resultant danger of foreclosure for indebted farmers. Under the colonato, peasants hedged their need for economic and social security through compadrazgo ties with their patrons; after the revolution, peasants began to seek compadrazgo ties with middlemen, truckers, tambo owners, and influential townspeople to gain advantage marketing their products. The use of compadrazgo for manipulation and domination of peasants by shrewd truckers, middlemen, and tambo owners—and the use of chicha by middlemen to lubricate negotiations with hapless peasants during harvests—is revealed in interviews with peasants in an official SNRA study.[100]

The densely populated Lower Valley (twice that of the Upper Valley), a wide and fertile expanse of irrigable fields, underwent epic changes as a result of the revolution. The dimensions of this transformation are evident in land tenure demographics compiled in 1973, indicating that 55 percent of the landholders in the Lower Valley were ex-colonos; 30 percent of landowners were piqueros (who had purchased land before the Agrarian Reform); 10 percent were landless (jornaleros); ex-miners and hacendados constituted the remaining 5 percent of landowners.[101] The fact that over one-half of the land in the Lower Valley was in the hands of ex-colonos by 1972 demonstrates that the potential of the market, once envisaged by only the more prescient ex-colonos, had become evident to all.[102]

The transition of ex-colonos to the highest levels of rural income in the country is a remarkable example of the power of the market. Indeed, by 1967, the production (per hectare) of campesino land was four to five times greater than that of the pre-reform haciendas.[103] The most successful of the emergent small landowners were those who became truck farmers. Vertical integration, accomplished through production and transport of specialized crops (onions, carrots) without a trucker or middleman, maximized profit for entrepreneurial ex-colonos whose success was dependent upon their facility to operate in the world of the acculturated cholos.

Ex-miners were among the most aggressive of the agrarian reform beneficiaries in the Cochabamba valleys. More cosmopolitan than the ex-colonos, the ex-miners knew of a reality beyond the valleys, and had been exposed to the revolutionary class consciousness of the mines. Thus, an influx of 50 ex-miners provided the impetus for sindicato formation at the Hacienda Paratoni in the Lower Valley where they became a powerful force in pursuit of land and political influence. The upshot was a patrón left with a mere 3 hectares of land, a toady local corregidor enforcing sindicato sanctions against perceived miscreants, and the eventual split between compliant ex-colonos and the radical ex-miners into two separate sindicatos. The ex-miners appear to have taken advantage of whatever means necessary to enhance their position, whereas the ex-colonos were more constrained in their approach.[104]

In contradistinction to Paratoni is the case of Hacienda Caramarca in the Lower Valley where peasants remained unorganized until a small contingent of ex-miners arrived to organize a sindicto. However, the ex-colonos pursued a moderate course under the influence of MNR vecinos who controlled the provincial sindicato central in nearby Quillacollo. The pitfalls of timidity and moderation are evident in the history of the Caramarca sindicato: continued negotiation with the patrón, together with the failure of a cooperative on expropriated hacienda property, eventuated in the reclassification of the hacienda as an agricultural enterprise, occasioning the return of the patrón who then sold his ex-colonos tiny plots of land at inflated prices. The ex-colonos eventually received only one-half of the land available for redistribution under the Agrarian Reform Decree. In the Lower Valley, responses to the Agrarian Reform Decree varied from the militant Paratoni ex-colonos to the moderate and accomodationist ex-colonos of Caramarca, as well as the piqueros of Itapaya who identified with vecinos and not the lower status colonos or ex-colonos. Victims of their self-perceived superiority, the piqueros failed to form a sindicato and thus opted out of the potential fruits of the agrarian reform.[105]

Land scarcity amid the dense population of the Lower Valley (for example, plots averaging 1 hectare in Paratoni; one-third hectare plots in Caramarca) allowed the continuation of various forms of exploitative land tenure relationships involving the exchange of labor for the right to land use. Sharecropping (*compañía*), the pawning of land (*anticresis*), and various forms of debt peonage were common practices. A decade after the Agrarian Reform Decree, one-tenth of the peasantry remained landless jornaleros. Other continuations of pre-revolutionary land tenure arrangements involved the use of wage labor for production of labor-intensive crops and labor exchanges through traditional reciprocal agreements (ayni).[106] The agrarian reform process in Cochabamba transformed the rural sector and ushered the peasantry into the market economy as envisaged by the MNR. Entrance into the evolving capitalist system initiated by the agrarian reform decree entailed both the production of more lucrative cash crops and the means to maximize profit in the marketing and transportation of goods. The results were evident in the post-reform improvements: an 80 percent boom in house construction with metal roofs, concrete floors, and windows and the appearance of bicycles, sewing machines, transistor radios, and store-bought clothes and dishware.[107]

Chuquisaca and Tarija Departments

The highlands and valleys of northern Chuquisaca are populated by Quecha peoples descended from Inca colonists (*mitimaes*) sent to guard the imperial marches from the warlike tribes of the eastern lowlands. Quechua ayllus were also relocated during the administration of the Spanish Viceroy Francisco de Toledo in the sixteenth century. In accord with the Andean practice of hedging against crop failure by diversification of land tenure, ayllu members colonized and farmed the temperate and tropical valleys to the east. These ecological niches ("archipélagos") were also common to the Altiplano-Yungas and Cochabamba-Chapare zones.[108] Traditional indigenous crops were cultivated: oca, yucca, potatoes, and broad beans in the highlands, as well as wheat, barley, and alfalfa introduced after the Spanish conquest. Maize and fruit grown by ayllu comunarios in the temperate and tropical lowland valleys augmented the highland crops. Further south, expanses of puna reach altitudes 4,000 meters above sea level. The terrain begins a transition in southernmost Chuquisaca in the Provinces of Nor and Sud Cinti and the Department of Tarija, where the fertile valleys are cut by streams and rivers. This irrigable land produces wheat, maize, sugarcane, and grapes often converted to *aguardiente* and *singani* wine; livestock is marketed as far away as Potosí, Sucre, Cochabamba, Oruro, and La Paz.

Ayllu lands that escaped seizure by the Spaniards were later usurped by their offspring. The Disentailment Law of 1874 and later pressure to develop haciendas after the collapse of the mining economy in the first decades of the twentieth century devastated ayllu landholdings. Furthermore, the specter of debt haunted the peasantry. The danger of debt and litigation, as revealed in Eric Langer's history of *Economic Change and Rural Resistance in Southern Bolivia, 1880–1930*, found that during the ancien régime, over 50 percent of the Indians had lost their land because of debts and another 34 percent were forced to sell land to pay for legal expenses. Resistance to hacienda land depredations, injustices to Indian workers, and violations of traditional cultural norms regarding reciprocal exchange by peasant and patrón, as noted by Langer, resulted in litigation, work slowdowns, strikes, social banditry, murder, riots and rebellion, and emigration.[109]

Agrarian reform came late to the puna and valleys of southeastern Bolivia where hacendados in Chuquisaca and Tarija, far from the influences of radical syndicalism in Cochabamba and La Paz Departments, were relatively successful in mitigating the full potential of the decree. The sindicato movement was in some instances organized by militants from outside the region.[110] An example is Juan Chumacero Poveda who arrived in Nor Cinti Province (Chuquisaca Department) after the MNR granted amnesty to Indian prisoners in 1952. Chumacero was a militant mine leader at Catavi, imprisoned for the murder of two U.S. technicians. Released from prison, he reinvented himself as an agrarian revolutionary and arose as a regional caudillo backed by armed militiamen on horseback who seized haciendas and invaded towns. Landlords were expelled from their estates, hacienda houses burned, peasants freed from personal service, and lands redistributed to them before Chumacero's assassination in 1956.[111]

A sample of 335 fields reform expedients compiled in 1963 reveals 45 properties declared latifundia with an average size of over 1,350 hectares; 188 medium-size properties averaging 950 hectares; and 102 small properties with an average size of 100 hectares. Only 15 percent of the latifundia lands were cultivated, while the other 85 percent of the properties were used for grazing or tilled by *arrenderos* (regional term for colono) under contractual agreements with the hacendados who rented two-thirds to four-fifths of their least productive lands in exchange for labor to work their more productive land. Here, as elsewhere, intensity of cultivation declined in inverse proportion to increased size of landholdings.[112]

Labor requirements under the colonato in southern Bolivia were similar to the regimen found throughout the Andean highlands. In exchange for the right to farm a parcel of hacienda land, the arrendero rendered payment in fieldwork, rent in the form of cash and/or a percentage of a crop (*catastro*), and payment in livestock (*diezmo*) for grazing rights on hacienda lands. Additionally, pongueaje and mitanaje were required of men, women, and children. Female members of the arrendero family in addition to housework (mitanaje), spun wool, wove cloth and in some cases masticated maize (*muqueo*) preparatory to production of chicha, besides tending to family needs. Two-thirds of the male arrenderos worked between 100 and 200 days a year for the patrón, in the hacienda house (pongueaje), tending livestock, delivering messages (*runacacha*), gathering and delivering firewood to the manor, and transporting hacienda goods to market (*cacha*). Other work obligations included the exchange of labor for seeds necessary for planting the arrendero's plot (*yanapacu*) and the *quincena*, a biweekly division of arrenderos into alternating work details on the hacienda.[113]

For the ambitious or the destitute in southern Chuquisca, there was possibility of work in the Argentine sugar plantations of Salta and Jujuy at much higher wages than paid for work in Bolivia. Landowning peasants could also maximize their earnings by alternating farm work between the sugarcane harvest and the planting and harvest seasons on their home plots. Migrant workers from southern Bolivia often lingered in Argentine cities to work as domestics and laborers in Salta, Jujuy, or smaller regional towns. A study of Bolivian migrant workers in Argentina conveys the magnitude of the adjustment faced by seasonal workers:

> The precarious efforts to maximize security in an effort to survive, a goal for which migrant workers struggle, is part of a way of life more perilous than many hunters and gatherers faced in an earlier period. Seasonal agricultural laborers are the rural gatherers of the industrial era, for whom settlement within a single generation may require as profound a change and innovation as domestication required over many generations, thousands of years ago.[114]

Implementation of agrarian reform in Chuquisaca and Tarija was affected by geographic isolation and a primitive transportation and information infrastructure that further isolated the population.[115] This, together with manipulations by capricious patrones, minimized hacienda expropriations. The domination of Chuquisaca hacendados over their arrenderos is illustrated by the belated formation of sindicatos and the inordinate length of the expropriative process. Moreover, topographers were loath to make the arduous trek to the isolated region where, 25 years after the Agrarian Reform Decree, only 865 persons had received land titles in the provinces of Hernando Siles and Luis Calvo.[116] Ninety-five percent of the peasants in Entre Rios (Tarija Department) did not hold title to the land they farmed; as in Chuquisaca, surveyors in Tarija Department were disinclined to make the arduous and lengthy trip to visit remote haciendas because of the difficulty in collecting money from arrenderos to pay the cost of a property survey necessary to begin the expediente process. Consequently, graft came into play: measuring extraneous pasture plots to collect extra fees, collecting fees from landlords to diminish the size of a survey, charging survey fees and then never producing the result. And, as elsewhere, crooks masquerading as surveyors bamboozled innocents with fake measurements.[117]

Landlords utilized threats and occasional violence to impede the agrarian reform process, as well as legal obstructions enjoined at every stage of the process and control of information regarding the specifics of the decree. A common hacendado gambit involved the sale of land after which the property, now diminished in size, fell into the medium-size category, thereby eluding confiscation. Some landlords joined the MNR party in order to maintain control under the new order.[118] Sindicatos were often suborned by dirigentes: overcharging members for dues, misappropriating sindicato funds, dividing hacienda lands for themselves, and tricking other peasants to work their lands.[119]

While not exclusive to Chuquisaca, or unique to the national sindicato experience, the aberrant dirigente behavior noted previously is indicative of an evolving pattern of rural domination within the revolution as new creole-mestizo elites replaced the hacienda patrón. José Havet has defined the control of money, goods, and services by these elites as "indirect domination."[120] Examples abound: priests pilfering clothes (sent by aid agencies) to Indians; doctors exploiting Indians for sex and money; public health funds co-opted and used for school construction in the provincial capital; milk (provided by charitable contribution) sold for personal profit by a regional school director; the continuation of the age-old practice of Indians dragooned by local authorities into unremunerated labor for hospital and road construction, or forced to clean town plazas and streets.[121]

Although stalled and often thwarted in southeastern Bolivia, the revolution nevertheless delivered freedom from personal servitude, citizenship, and the legal right to acquire lands previously worked in usufruct by the peasantry and consequently sowed the seeds of change. Under the agrarian reform, some large landholdings remained, and class differentiation within the peasantry continued as arrenderos held legal claim to lands worked under the colonato, yet others were ignored in the decree and (in a continuation of pre-revolutionary tradition) remained dependent workers for landowning arrenderos.[122] Another consequence of the agrarian reform process in Chuquisaca (presumably unintended) was the demise of the medium and small landowners. While the terratenientes were adroit in the art of manipulating the SNRA bureaucracy, presenting legal obstacles throughout the expediente process; the small and medium-sized landowners were less successful defending their properties against aggressive arrenderos seeking valuable farmland. Lacking sufficient financial resources, political connections, and bureaucratic savvy, the small and medium-size landowners were devastated by the expropriation of their properties.[123]

The agrarian reform process in Chuquisaca and Tarija, compared with neighboring Cochabamba, reveals the effects of a welter of factors precluding more rapid and widespread implementation. Most peasants awaiting legal title to their parcels lived and worked on their sought-after land without title. Without a strong sindicato, there was no assurance that the hacendados would not return. Isolation and poor infrastructure in the countryside inhibited communication and necessitated arduous and expensive trips to entreat with the agrarian reform bureaucracy. In the province of Belisario Boeto, there were two telephones, only 15 percent of the population had a radio in 1970, and written communication often arrived via an individual's truck or automobile.[124] Isolation limited peasant participation in the distant market economy; only 27 percent of harvests were sold for cash, fostering the continuation of barter as a means of exchange.[125]

The expenditure of surplus funds continued with the individual sponsorship of fiestas: the ritual redistribution of surplus wealth exchanged for status and leadership in the community hierarchy referred to by anthropologists as the cargo (office) system.[126] The elected elder (hilacata/jilakata), whose status derived from ascension in the cargo hierarchy, adjudicated conflicts, rights of inheritance, the distribution of land within the ayllu, as well as the defense of community land rights against outsiders. The hereditary leaders (Aymara *mallku*; Quechua, *kuraka*) descended from the pre-Colombian elite had once exercised influence over multi-ayllu associations, but following the "reforms" of the later nineteenth century, their powers were diminished.

Sponsorship of fiestas served to dissipate the envy, jealousy, and hostility attendant to a bountiful harvest or material success, validating leadership in the ayllu community. The cargo system, a classic example of cultural syncretism between indigenous and Catholic traditions, has been affected by Protestant missionaries preaching capital accumulation as a route to individual salvation: on the Altiplano, Methodist converts who avoided fiestas, dancing and drinking, abandoned the traditional rituals of peasant solidarity.[127] However, a survey conducted by the anthropologist Charles Erasmus found fiesta sponsorship and "festive consumption patterns" alive and well among Quechua peasants in the more remote regions.[128] The continuation of fiesta sponsorship at the expense of capital accumulation is taken as irrational by the apostles of Protestantism as well as modernization technocrats who consider the practice an obstacle to rural development.

Although a tortuous process in southeastern Bolivia, the benefits of agrarian reform could not be denied: mud floors replaced by cement, windows in houses, the construction of larger two-story buildings, and families sleeping on beds, eating with metal instead of wooden spoons, listening to radios, and sending their children to school.[129] But the agrarian reform also increased the inequality between originarios and the poor and landless *utuwawa* squatters living literally and figuratively on the margins of the land. Because the Agrarian Reform Decree included the caveat that expropriated lands could not be sold, the subdivision of land among succeeding heirs led inexorably to smaller and smaller parcels. The resultant minifundisimo often precluded a marketable surplus, rendering subsistence increasingly problematic, and following a poor harvest, forcing the unfortunate peasant to seek temporary work elsewhere.

Cooperatives

The Agrarian Reform Decree (Articles 133–134) mandated the formation of agrarian cooperatives. Whereas the salient vision of the MNR was the metamorphosis of colonos into capitalist farmers, the decree's cooperative provision harkened back to the fabled days of Andean communal ayllus. Minister of Peasant Affairs Ñuflo Chávez expressed this vision: "We distributed land collectively, on the one hand, because of the tradition still present in many areas of the country of the ancient commune which dates from the time of the Incas, and on the other, because of the thesis that communal work, in regard to land, gives a much larger yield."[130] The decree offered no specifics regarding agrarian cooperatives. A later "General Law of Cooperative Societies" in 1958 suggests that the cooperatives were intended to be an agrarian panacea: replacing the latifundia, overcoming the "techniques and relations of production of the hacienda"; "modernizing the ancient indigenous communities"; and "regrouping the small property owners in areas where minifundias predominate."[131]

The history of the agrarian cooperatives is rife with errors in conception and execution, compounded by a willful lack of government commitment and financial support. The presumed enthusiasm of ex-colonos working harmoniously together is absent in the cooperative experience. In Cochabamba Department, as a reward for their vanguard role in the revolutionary struggle led by Juan Lechín and Mario Torres, the MNR leftists granted land parcels to miners from Catavi, Siglo XX, and Colquiri. The miners were given 2 to 8 hectares parcels to work cooperatively with ex-colonos from 25 expropriated haciendas in the Cochabamba valleys, two in Sucre, and another in Potosí.[132] A total of 554 miners' families and over 600 ex-colonos worked the cooperatives in the Cochabamba valleys. But the cooperatives were fatally flawed. Jointly owned and operated by ex-colonos and miners who were awarded individual land parcels, the cooperatives operated as quasi-haciendas with miners in control of the administrative hierarchy and the ex-colonos continuing as they had under the colonato, but without the demands of personal service. After a visit to the cooperative at the expropriated El Convento hacienda, the Cochabamba sindicato cacique Sinforoso Rivas found: "The miners immediately converted themselves into the new hacienda patrones . . . and in the course of four years the finca [hacienda] fell into ruin: all the eucalyptus cut down, the machinery, trucks, carts, cattle, horses, birds disappeared. Three miners were the only ones that stayed, as if they were the owners, making the same ex-colonos work the land in a system of share cropping."[133]

After observing the dysfunctional operations at El Convento, Novillero and other Cochabamba haciendas that had been converted into cooperatives, Rivas concluded that the cooperative decree was a failure, "many of the properties had been left deforested, some had lands sold without any right [illegally]; everything was a disaster."[134] Peasants tended to view the cooperative as a vestigial form of colonato rather than a pre-Columbian utopia. Two to three days a week were generally required for labor on the cooperatives, and failure to perform work obligations was punished by fine or imprisonment: "When a man is working for the Cooperative he is said to be 'working for the hacienda' and in the work situation syndicate officials are commonly referred to by names applicable to supervisory personnel of the hacienda."[135]

As with most communal experience, the cooperative members unevenly embraced a commitment to the common cause: the harvest, shared equally, created resentment toward the venture.[136] This is far from the Marxist dictum, "From each according to his abilities, to each according to his needs," ostensibly embraced by MNR left-wing ideologues. Incompetence, corruption, and inefficient administration plagued the ill-fated cooperative experiment since inception. The administrative hierarchy, a recapitulation of the peasant sindicato, echoed the personality and character of the local dirigentes, affording sinecures and perquisites for the ambitious and dishonest dirigentes who capitalized on the MNR's import quotas granted to the cooperatives; products were available at the official rate of 180 bolivianos per dollar and then sold at black market rates of 12,000 per dollar, offering tantalizing opportunities to unscrupulous dirigentes.[137] Dwight Heath concluded in a study of the Yungas that the administrators of the cooperatives were untrustworthy cheats and thieves, and all five cooperatives were failures.[138]

The MNR failed to adequately support the cooperatives, thereby condemning the enterprise to a slow death. The agricultural cooperatives once touted by President Paz and later mandated by decree were far from Antonio Mamani Álvarez's vision of indigenous cooperatives (see Chapter 4). The potential for an imaginative utilization of Andean cultural norms of communal labor and mutual aid in southeastern Bolivia were unrealized, as Antonio García notes in a critique of the cooperatives: "None of the experiments has helped to develop a technique for the projection of new cooperative structures, nor to promote integration at different levels, or to create a link between agrarian cooperativism and the different institutions for credit, promotion, rural extension, experimentation, industrialization and farm marketing."[139] Beyond government rhetoric, one finds in the ledgers of the Central Bank, the Agricultural Bank, and the Supervised Credit Service, the realities of the MNR commitment to the cooperative venture. In December 1956, the fixed assets of 30 agricultural cooperatives in Ingavi Province (La Paz Department) totaled some US$21, amounting to 2 percent of the debts incurred by their dirigentes.[140] As with the ejido, an analogous program of the Mexican Revolution, insufficient financial commitment by the MNR doomed the venture. The focus of the National Revolution was directed to large-scale commercial agricultural enterprises oriented toward the export sector.[141] In both countries, reliance on traditional banking practices prevented a meaningful commitment to the cooperative enterprise. The inalienability of cooperative and ejido lands precluded their use as collateral, thus condemning the experiment to undercapitalization and short-term loans at exorbitant rates.

Undercapitalized and mismanaged, the failed cooperatives had a similar history throughout the Andean highlands: under the direction of sindicato dirigentes and without adequate supervision, technical, and financial support, the cooperative experiment was doomed. The ideal of Andean communal labor could not be resurrected by decree. Indeed, the native practice of reciprocal exchange of labor was soon to become an anachronism among a peasantry subsumed into the capitalist world system of private property, individualism, competition, and consumption.

Colonization

Article 91 of the Agrarian Reform Decree addressed the dichotomy between the densely populated Andean highlands and the vast lowlands of the Oriente, sparsely populated by tribal peoples. Because arable parcels of land in the highlands decreased in size with each generation, and because minifundismo led to increasing numbers of squatters and landless Indian migrants to cities, the MNR viewed colonization of the lowlands of Santa Cruz, Chapare, and Beni as a revolutionary opportunity to resettle impoverished highland peasants on 50-hectare plots, increase food production, and promote national unity in a region known for the separatist inclination of its creole-mestizo populace. The colonization decree offered the incentive of free land for Indian colonists as well as thousands of hectares for creole-mestizo commercial farmers and cattle ranchers.

Colonization of the tropical lowlands, while considered revolutionary in the 1950s, had been envisioned in an earlier eighteenth century developmental scheme by the Spanish Intendant Francisco de Viedma. The historian Brooke Larson informs us of past as present in a classic study of Cochabamba: "Like Viedma's plan, state-directed colonization in the middle of the twentieth century was designed to shift peasant population from Cliza and the Valle Bajo to the sparsely populated tropics. . . . [C]olonization was not only a commercial opportunity but also a safety valve for restless peasants beset by the uncertainties of subsistence agriculture. Harvesting the jungle to commercial enterprise was a solution to widespread poverty, vagrancy, and threats to the public order."[142]

Two centuries later, the 1942 Bohan Plan contrived by a U.S. Mission comprised of representatives of the departments of state, agriculture, and mines, and the Public Highway Administration proposed construction of a highway network connecting the lowlands with the Andean highlands and development of large-scale farming (rice, wheat, sugar, cotton), as well as mining and petroleum industries in the Oriente. The MNR initiated implementation of the Bohan Plan in 1954 with the completion of the Cochabamba–Santa Cruz highway that fostered development and colonization of the Oriente.

Settlement of the Oriente took two forms: spontaneous, and government directed with financial aid and technical assistance. Surprisingly, all four spontaneous settlements (50 hectares; without aid or assistance) begun before 1962 were successful as were three settlements by Japanese, Okinawans, and Mennonites; two government-directed settlements by Potosí miners were failures with less than half of the settlers remaining in 1963. Spontaneous settlements appeared where new roads were constructed. They were doomed to failure: their location was too isolated and markets too difficult to access. Compounding the difficulty of resettlement in a tropical environment for the highland Quechua and Aymara were a change in diet, the shift from communal Andean life and culture to individualism, isolation, and difficulty in communication with the local Spanish-speaking mestizos with racist attitudes toward indigenous peoples.[143]

Two decades after the Agrarian Reform Decree, over 250,000 migrants had settled in the region and the population of Santa Cruz de la Sierra, the capitol of Santa Cruz Department, increased sixfold.[144] The country also experienced a shift in wealth and power toward the Department of Santa Cruz. The Bohan Plan was visionary, but the financial and administrative constraints of the MNR regime hampered implementation and foreign aid and assistance by agencies of the U.S. government were required to facilitate its implementation. U.S. economic aid was forthcoming after Milton Eisenhower (President Dwight Eisenhower's brother) recommended assistance as part of a strategy to combat leftist and communist influence. The rise of Castroism, perceived as a strategic threat to North American hegemony in Latin America, drew attention to Bolivia in the 1960s and 1970s. Consequently, per capita economic aid to Bolivia exceeded that given by any other Latin American country during this period.[145]

The dependence of the National Revolution on U.S. economic and technical assistance—finance, credit, education, social services, colonization schemes—brought the revolution firmly within the orbit of North American suzerainty. North American aid was to prove revolutionary, but not in ameliorating the economic and social conditions that make rural Bolivians among the most wretched of the earth. U.S. aid and technical assistance were committed to a shift in the focus of the revolution toward the lowlands and away from the indigenous demographic center in the highlands. The North American program (USAID) prioritized credit, loans, and technical assistance to development of commercial agricultural enterprises in the Oriente, to the detriment of the indigenous highland majority.[146] Ex-colonos were prohibited from selling land acquired under the Agrarian Reform Law; because the land could not be used as collateral, the ex-colonos were ineligible for bank loans.[147] The Andean highlands, perceived as economically unproductive and populated by a hidebound peasantry, were effectively abandoned in favor of plans for development of the Oriente: 80 percent of domestic agricultural credit and virtually all foreign credit were directed to the eastern lowlands. A pittance remained for the highland peasants scratching out an existence in the demographic center of the country.

The political ramifications of the MNR's vision of agricultural development became manifest with General Hugo Banzer Suárez's 1971 coup that signaled a power shift: the rise of the *camba* (Santa Cruz) agricultural elite to national power.[148] The nexus of U.S. aid and the burgeoning agro-business of the Oriente (including cocaine) are discussed in the Epilogue.

Conclusions

Agrarian reform remains a touchstone of the Bolivian National Revolution. Unlike the MNR government that bequeathed the Decree in 1953, only to fall prey to a military coup in 1964, the decree remains inviolate. The process of expropriation and redistribution of hacienda lands, while imperfect, nevertheless allowed peasants to enter the market economy. The protracted struggle of ex-colonos to own land taxed the financial resources of the indigenous litigants. Implementation of the land reform drew only meager resources and commitment—fiscal, judicial, bureaucratic—from successive MNR administrations. Indeed, by mid-1955, there were only 189 rural juntas working to gather data relevant to expropriation in the entire country and only 87 agrarian judges had been assigned to render decisions.[149] At the end of the revolution in 1964, less than one-third of the ex-colonos had received land and 72 percent of those with land held less than 5 acres.[150]

Subsequent attempts to expedite the implementation process included mobile brigades (streamlined teams of agronomists, topographers, and judges) initiated in 1968 and an IBM computer to process data. The addition of digital computation, through the assistance of the University of Wisconsin's Land Tenure Center, proved an antidote to the tedious workings of a sclerotic bureaucracy, producing an average of 36 land titles per day (awaiting a presidential signature), before a computer was enlisted to process some 400 titles per hour.[151]

Ultimately, the MNR failed to maximize the historic opportunity for revolutionary change in the countryside. Instead of redistributing sufficient land to

TABLE 6.7 Agrarian Structure in Bolivia After 10 Years of Agrarian Reform

Scale of Tenancy (in Hectares)	Units		Area		Plots	Average in Hectare per Plot
	Thousands of Hectares	Percentage	Thousands of Hectares	Percentage	(in Thousands of Hectares)	
Less than 1	55.0	12,2	25	0.32	150	0.16
1 to less than 5	266.0	59.8	621	7.91	1,125	0.54
5 to less than 19	114.0	25.6	930	11.87	699	1.30
20 to less than 200	7.5	1.7	332	4.87	50	6.60
200 to less than 500	0.75	0.17	187	2.38	19	9.80
500 to less than 2,500	1.0	0.21	1.050	13.46	38	27.50
2.500 and more	1.0	0.22	4.700	58.81	1.5	3.200

Source: Courtesy of Latin American Perspectives. Uri Mendelberg, "Impact of the Bolivian Agrarian Reform on Class Formation," *Latin American Perspectives*, 12.3 (Summer 1985), 47.

create a nation of Indian farmers, the MNR focused primarily on redistribution of the small plots previously worked in usufruct under the colonato. This, as well as the manifest failure to invest the financial and technical commitment necessary for development of the highlands, elicited the following judgment: "The Bolivian experience of agrarian reform is one of the most pathetic lessons in the sense that it is not enough to apply the revindicationist principle of *giving the land to who works it* . . . if this operation does not function within the framework of a global strategy of integration and development."[152]

The agrarian reform decree was flawed in conception and imperfect in its execution. The product of a Nationalist Revolutionary Movement and not a homogeneous party, the result was a compromise of competing visions contrived amid a mounting agrarian revolution in the countryside. Hindsight reveals egregious errors: the continuation of latifundio properties in disguised form via legal subterfuge; the lack of sufficient attention to revindication of usurped ayllu lands; the failure to address the question of inequality among the peasant subclasses, resulting in continued sub-tenancy and sharecropping; the failure to adequately support the cooperatives planned for expropriated latifundia lands; the deleterious effects of the decree on many medium and small farms; and the failure of government financial and technical assistance to the emerging peasant landholders. The priorities of the creole-mestizo agenda suggest the MNR was more concerned with reducing the power of the landed oligarchy than in modernizing agriculture.[153]

Despite its manifest imperfections, agrarian reform succeeded in destroying the underpinnings of the landed oligarchy. Personal service and tribute would become relics of a feudal past replaced by a new regimen of wage labor and participation in a market economy. The peasant was drawn from the insular world of subsistence, outward toward a nexus of regional and national markets. But while the MNR creole-mestizos sought to integrate the campesino (read: Indian) into the capitalist cash economy to "modernize" the nation, the ancient tradition of barter and reciprocal exchange of goods continues, "to equalize exchange relations, buffering each trading partner from price fluctuations in the larger market, while marginalizing the role of commercial intermediaries."[154]

The great evasion of the agrarian reform was its singular inattention to the class structure within the peasantry. "But the land reform was never designed to merely benefit the peasants," the sociologist Susan Eckstein reminds us, "The intent was also to encourage agrarian capitalism."[155] The plot sizes worked under the colonato continued, as did the disparities in wealth accrued by peasants because of plot size and land quality.[156] Social stratification continued among the peasantry because the Agrarian Reform Decree mandated redistribution of land to ex-colonos, but ignored the subclass working for them. For these renters and squatters, little remained unchanged with regard to their status, but the landless utawawa was ignored, "left suspended in a vacuum—as a pariah on the land."[157]

For comunarios, the revolution presented the possibility of regaining usurped ayllu territory despite the 1953 Agrarian Reform Law's initial restriction of land claims to post-1900 losses. The MNR intended to limit comunario land claims because of the likelihood of conflicts with colonos who sought land via expropriation of hacienda properties. Furthermore, the government's mission to modernize the rural economy through creation of small property owners was incompatible with the augmentation of ayllu communal territory. After an upwelling of comunario claims for revendication of ayllu lands lost before and after 1900, President Paz Estenssoro decreed in May 1954 that "all communal land turned into individual property after January 1, 1900, will be subject to restitution, without economic compensation."[158] Increasing population pressure aggravated conflicts between comunarios and emancipated colonos who laid claim to hacienda usufructs—lands that had once belonged to ayllu comunarios.

Minifundismo was an inevitable result of the agrarian reform. Under the right of primogeniture, the land inherited by each generation becomes progressively subdivided and subsistence becomes more difficult. Because the decree focused on redistribution of lands farmed in usufruct under the colonato, the ex-colonos benefiting from the agrarian reform gained only 2 percent more cultivable land than they had worked before the decree.[159] Forty-four percent of properties redistributed between 1953 and 1967 in the Altiplano and highland valleys were less than 3 hectares.[160]

Options to this grim metric include working for wages, sharecropping on the lands of rich peasants and landlords, participation in a local cottage industry, working as a middleman, or migration to the Oriente. "All these population movements testify to a continuous, large scale 'milling around' of poor farm people in the hemisphere—no doubt the greatest migratory movement in all history."[161] Bolivian cities teem with unemployed and underemployed Indian migrants in search of work. The absence of a significant industrial base and lack of public services contribute to the misery of urban migrants. The demographic effects of the transformative decree became most evident a half-century later as El Alto, the once barren Altiplano zone in the heights above the city of La Paz, had become home to well over a million Aymara residents.

The education of the rural population remains a salient gift of the revolution to the nation. Illiteracy and ignorance, forced upon Indians under the colonato, facilitated centuries of domination by creole-mestizo oligarchs. Attempts to educate Indian children were anathema to the lords of the land: schools were burned, teachers persecuted and murdered. From the earliest days of the revolution, peasant delegations to La Paz agitated for education. The MNR delivered more rhetoric than investment in education, but nevertheless the demise of the Rosca ended the patrón's ability to enforce ignorance upon colonos. While the agrarian reform failed to create an egalitarian land tenure system or educational equality for Indian children, the revolution nevertheless set in motion a historic process of epic consequence.[162] By the twenty-first century, Bolivian illiteracy had fallen to 14 percent (from 69 percent in 1950), and 75 percent of the four million indigenous people were bilingual.[163] Incomprehensible as it would seem from the perspective of the era of the Nationalist Revolution, within a half-century, Indian students were graduating from universities, and an indigenous electorate would elect one of their own, Evo Morales, president of the nation.

Notes

1. Joel Migdal notes the relationship between land and power: "It was the intensity of sanctions available to the landlord because of the primacy of land that was the key to his power." Joel Migdal, *Peasants, Politics and Revolution: Pressures Toward Political and Social Change in the Third World* (Princeton, NJ, 1974), 38.
2. Thirty-six percent of Bolivian imports in 1952 were food products: Susan Eckstein, "Transformation of a 'Revolution from Below'—Bolivia and International Capital," *Comparative Studies in Society and History*, 25 (1983), 107.
3. William Manchester, *American Caesar: General Douglas MacArthur, 1880–1964* (New York, 1983), 599–600.
4. John Bodley, *Victims of Progress* (Lanham, MD, 2008), 7. In the 150 years between 1780 and 1930, the tribal peoples of North and South America, Africa and Oceania were reduced by 30–40 million as a result of the spread of industrial civilization. Bodley notes, "This process created the modern world system, but it did so at an enormous cost in ethnocide, genocide, and ecocide suffered by the peoples and territories forcibly incorporated into the new global system." Ibid., 10, 15–19.
5. The Radical Republicans who struggled to ameliorate conditions for freed slaves in the aftermath of the American Civil War would later turn to the task of forcing the indigenous plains tribes from their communal world: "It was an article of faith with the reformers that civilization was impossible without the incentive of work that came only from individual ownership of a piece of property." The Dawes Act (1887) delivered the coup de grâce to North American plains Indians. Ninety million acres of tribal lands were divided among the nomadic plains tribes as individual landholdings: within a few decades these lands were in the hands of large cattle ranchers and the tribes were left penurious. See Francis P. Prucha, *The Great Father: The United States Government and the American Indian* (Omaha, NE, 1986), 224, 227.
6. For the global pattern of these "reforms," see Joel S. Migdal, *Peasants, Politics, and Revolution*, 134–135.
7. Robert A. White, "Mexico: The Zapata Movement and the Revolution," in Henry A. Landsberger, ed., *Latin American Peasant Movements* (Ithaca, NY, 1969), 115, 227.
8. Amado Canelas, *Mito y Realidad de la Reforma Agraria en Bolivia* (La Paz, 1966), 97; Peter Dorner, *Latin American Land Reforms: In Theory and Practice* (Madison, WI, 1992), 49.
9. Tristan Platt, "The Andean Experience of Bolivian Liberalism, 1825–1900: Roots of Rebellion in 19th Century Chayanta (Potosí)," in Steve Stern, ed., *Resistance, Rebellion and Consciousness in the Andean Peasant World: 18th to 20th Centuries* (Madison, WI, 1987), 281. Luis Antezana posits an earlier "agrarian reform" instituted by President Mariano Melgarejo's 1866 order that ayllu properties be sold: see Luis Antezana E., "La reforma agrarian campesina en Bolivia (1956–1960)," *Revista Mexicana de Sociología*, 2 (April–June 1969), 309–310.
10. Joseph Bastien, *Mountain of the Condor: Metaphor and Ritual in an Andean Ayllu* (St. Paul, MN, 1978), 42. For the ayllu structure underlying this metaphor, see John Murra's seminal works, *The Economic Organization of the Inka State* (Greenwich, CT, 1980), and "Los límites y las limitaciones del 'archipiélago vertical' en los Andes," *Advances*, 1 (February 1978), 75–80.
11. Carmen Soliz, "Fields of Revolution: The Politics of Agrarian Reform in Bolivia, 1935–1971," Ph.D. dissertation, New York University, 2014, 50. Soliz argues that the

hacendados were not a hereditary elite but included middle-class landowners who leveraged the economic and social assets of landownership to advance their interests in mining and politics. Carmen Soliz, "'Land to the Original Owners': Rethinking the Indigenous Politics of the Bolivian Agrarian Reform." *Hispanic American Historical Review*, 97.2 (2017), 37.
12. Buechler, "Agrarian Reform and Migration," 37. The colono provided all draft animals used in hacienda farm work. The colonato in the north highlands also utilized a crude inventory control: for example, a predetermined ratio of maize kernels was expected to produce a given quantity of *chicha* (masticated to begin fermentation of the Andean maize beer); other variations of the practice involved an expected ratio of raw potatoes to *chuño* (the freeze dried Altiplano staple), or for *c'aya* (freeze dried *oca*). Recompense for failure to meet the given requirement could result in confiscation of a colono's livestock.
13. Wálter del Castillo Avendaño, *Compilación legal de la reforma agraria en Bolivia* (La Paz, 1955), 45–47.
14. In a cautionary note, James Wilkie points out that the 1950 Census "recorded the number of property owners and not the number of properties they owned," and in 1964, "more cultivable lands were distributed than censused in 1950." Wilkie, *Measuring Land Reform* (Los Angeles, CA, 1974), 40. See also Laurence Whitehead's insightful critique of "Basic Data in Poor Countries: The Bolivian Case," *Bulletin of the Oxford University Institute of Economics and Statistics*, 31.3 (1969), 205–227.
15. Castillo Avendaño, *Compilación*, 48.
16. Soliz, "Fields of Revolution," 256, 258–259, 264, 268, 274.
17. Castillo Avendaño, *Compilación*, 51.
18. Ibid., 51–52.
19. Ibid., 83.
20. Antonio García, "Agrarian Reform and Social Development in Bolivia," in Rodolfo Stavenhagen, ed., *Agrarian Problems and Peasant Movements in Latin America* (New York, 1970), 345.
21. E.V. Kovalev, "The Class Essence and the Significance of Agrarian Reform in Bolivia," in Robert Carlton, ed., *The Soviet Image of Contemporary Latin America*, translated by J. Gregory Oswald (Austin, TX, 1970), 196.
22. See Wilkie, *Measuring Land Reform*, 29. The SNRA shortcomings are also noted in Paul Turovsky, "Bolivian Haciendas: Before and After the Revolution," Ph.D. dissertation, University of California, Los Angeles, 1980, 211; García, "Agrarian Reform," 328; Patch, "Social Implications," 113–114; and José Havet, "Rational Domination: The Power Structure in a Bolivian Rural Zone," Ph.D. dissertation, University of Pittsburgh, 1979, who summarizes the situation: "The implementation of the Agrarian Reform has been confused, slow, and plagued by inconsistency, red tape, and corruption. This poor and arbitrary process of implementation constitutes an efficient means of control since it allows administrative agents and political incumbents to threaten peasants with an eventual loss of their property title." 101–102. Regarding problems with implementation in Chuquisaca, see Charles Erasmus in Heath, et al., *Land Reform*, 138–139.
23. William Carter, "Revolution and the Agrarian Sector," in James Malloy and Richard Thorn, eds., *Beyond the Revolution: Bolivia Since 1952* (Pittsburgh, PA, 1971), 247.
24. "In order to understand the peasants' bewildered perception of red tape, one has to remember that they have no clear knowledge of what an administrative process is. In particular, they do not grasp what is the logic inherent to a setting where secondary relationships are prevalent." Havet, "Rational Domination," 206. See also Maria Lagos, *Autonomy and Power: The Dynamics of Class and Culture in Rural Bolivia* (Philadelphia, PA, 1994), 59–60.
25. Mario Vargas Llosa, *A Fish in the Water* (New York, 1995), 32.
26. Ibid., 262; Dwight B. Heath, Charles J. Erasmus, and Hans C. Buechler, eds., *Land Reform and Social Revolution in Bolivia* (New York, 1969), 53–54. For examples of the

complexity of court cases waged by comunario litigants against ingenious landlords and determined colonos (occasionally allied), see Soliz, "Land to the Original Owners," 288–290.
27. The legal struggle for land via the Agrarian Reform process was rife with obstructions and fraught with difficulty for peasants seeking revindication. Hacendados utilized a host of maneuvers to suborn the process: for evasion through land grants to landlords, see Kevin Healy, "Power, Class and Rural Development in Southeastern Bolivia," Ph.D. dissertation, Cornell University, 1979, 53; for landlord legal machinations, see Amado Canelas, *Mito y realidad*, 195–197; Paul Turovsky, "Bolivian Haciendas Before and After the Revolution," Ph.D. dissertation, University of California, Los Angeles, 1980, 210–211; Peter Graeff, "The Effects of Continued Landlord Presence in the Bolivian Countryside During the Post-Reform Era," *Land Tenure Center Research Paper*, 103 (October 1974), 10; Havet, "Rational Domination," 94; David A. Preston, *Farmers and Towns: Rural-Urban Relations in Highland Bolivia* (Norwich, UK, 1978), 95; and Joseph F. Dorsey, "A Case Study of the Lower Cochabamba Valley: Ex-Haciendas Parotani and Caramarca," *Land Tenure Center Research Paper*, 64 (June 1975), 30–31; for bribes, see Healy, "Power, Class and Rural Development," 43, 47, Havet, "Rational Domination," 205, Heath, et al., *Land Reform*, 55–56, Preston, *Farmers and Towns*, 172–173; for co-optation of judges by landlords, see Healy, "Power, Class," 46; for landlord infiltration of the SNRA bureaucracy, see Havet, "Rational Domination," 100 and Healy, "Power, Class and Rural Development," 38; for landlord co-optation of sindicatos, see Healy, "Power Class and Rural Development," 36, 50–51, Havet, "Rational Domination," 95 and McEwen et al., *Changing Rural Society*, 49–50; for underreporting of land to avoid expropriation, see Healy, "Power, Class and Rural Development," 44, 47; for landlord resistance through threats and violence, see Havet, "Rational Domination," 187 and Healy, "Power, Class and Rural Development," 37–38; for landlord–colono alliances to thwart comunario land restitution claims, see Soliz, "Land to the Original Owners," 288–290.
28. Jorge Dandler, "Peasant Sindicatos and the Process of Cooptation in Bolivian Politics," in June Nash, Jorge Dandler, and Nicholas Hopkins, eds., *Popular Participation in Social Change* (The Hague, 1976), 347.
29. Soliz, "Fields of Revolution," 226.
30. Ibid., 207–216.
31. Ronald J. Clark, "Problems and Conflicts Over Land Ownership in Bolivia," *Inter-American Economic Affairs*, 22.4 (Spring 1969), 6–8, 17.
32. Turovsky, "Bolivian Haciendas," 220.
33. Ibid., 220–221.
34. Lagos, *Autonomy and Power*, 53–54. José Havet observed that in northern Chuquisaca, "the hearings have generally been held in Villa Serrano, in rare instances in the capital of the canton, never in the landholding. Hence, the peasant is in 'foreign territory,' which obviously weakens his position . . . when the Agrarian Reform officials arrive in Villa Serrano they are wined and dined by the local elites, especially by the landholders. The Agrarian Judges and the topographers are systematically bribed. Before the official hearing takes place, an extra-legal one is often organized outside of any peasants' presence; it 'prepares' the results of the official hearing." Havet, "Rational Domination," 205; see also 54, 187.
35. Turovsky, "Bolivian Haciendas," 285.
36. Ronald Clark, "Land Reform and Peasant Market Participation on the North Highlands of Bolivia," *Land Economics*, 64 (May 1968), 165; Turovsky, "Bolivian Haciendas," 230–231, 285; also see Daniel Heyduk, "Huayrapampa: Bolivian Peasants and the New Social Order," Ph.D. dissertation, Cornell University, 1971, xii–xiii.
37. Clark, "Land Reform and Peasant Market Participation on the Northern Highlands of Bolivia," 166. Significantly, Clark identified drought as a contributing factor to the decrease in agricultural production following the 1952 Revolution. Melvin Burke

found that rumors of peasant confiscation of hacienda cattle, allegedly creating meat shortages in the cities following the Revolution, were exaggerated: "This is reflected by the increased meat consumption in the city of La Paz and in the nation during 1952 and 1953." Melvin Burke, "Land Reform and Its Effect Upon Production and Productivity in the Lake Titicaca Region," *Economic Development and Cultural Change*, 18 (April 1970), 427.
38. See Clark, "Problems," 6, fn. 3; Uri Mendelberg, "The Impact of Bolivian Agrarian Reform on Class Formation," *Latin American Perspectives*, 12.3 (Summer 1985), 49; Turovsky, "Bolivian Haciendas," 286.
39. Kovalev, "The Class Essence," 193.
40. Soliz, "Fields of Revolution," 47–48, 227–229, 234–236.
41. On the relationship of ayllu comunarios to the agrarian reform, see Carmen Soliz, "Fields of Revolution," Chapter 6, and "'Land to the Original Owners': Rethinking the Indigenous Politics of the Bolivian Agrarian Reform," *Hispanic American Historical Review*, 97.2 (2017), 259–296. While Soliz's innovative research focused on ayllus in La Paz and the Sud Yungas, further research awaits, for example, Potosí Department.
42. Alma Guillermoprieto, "The Altiplano," *National Geographic* (July 2008), 74.
43. Armando Cardozo, *Estudio del Altiplano* (La Paz, 1969), 1–33.
44. Erwin P. Grieshaber, "Survival of Indian Communities in Nineteenth-Century Bolivia: A Regional Comparison," *Journal of Latin American Studies*, 12.2 (November 1980), 249.
45. Railway construction was considered essential for economic development and national integration. See "Dreams of a Railroad" by the diplomat Ignacio Calderón, excerpted in Sinchalr Thomson et al., eds., *The Bolivia Reader* (Durham, NC, 2018), translated by Alison Spedding, 193–194.
46. An examination of nineteenth-century tribute censuses found that the fate of ayllu communities "varied with regional, demographic and ecological conditions and not with relationship to haciendas." For example, disease and famine ravaged the Altiplano in the last half of the nineteenth century: an epidemic in 1856 that spread inland from the Peruvian coast killed an estimated 200,000 Indians, in La Paz Department. Grieshaber, "Survival of Indian Communities," 223, 253, 262.
47. Ibid., 106–108.
48. Rivera Cusicanqui, "La expansion del latifundio," 106–108. For the legal appeals of ayllu comunarios whose Altiplano lands were usurped during this period, see Soliz, "Fields of Revolution," 303–305.
49. La Paz and Oruro Departments experienced over 35 "uprisings" in the first two decades of the twentieth century; 16 were reported in Cochabamba Department and another half-dozen in Potosí Department. Gonzalo Flores, "Levantamientos campesinos durante el período liberal," in Fernando Calderón and Jorge Dandler, eds., *Bolivia: la fuerza histórica del campesinado* (Geneva, 1984), 129–131.
50. Silvia Rivera Cusicanqui, *Oprimidos pero no vencidos: luchas del campesinado Aymara y qhechwa de Bolivia, 1900–1980* (Geneva, 1886), 114–116.
51. Buechler cites census figures for the period 1900–1950, indicating an increase in the Indian population of nearly 100 percent (from 906,126 to 1,703,371). Buechler, "Agrarian Reform and Migration," 22; for land disputes, see Ibid., 99–102.
52. Decree 3464, 2 August 1953. Castillo Avendaño, *Compilación*, 46.
53. Decree 3732, 19 May 1954. Ibid., 157.
54. Ibid.
55. Soliz, "Land to the Original Owners," 260, 287.
56. For barter on the northern Altiplano, see Preston, *Farmers and Towns*, 117–118, 140.
57. Buechler, "Agrarian Reform and Migration," 93–94.
58. Preston, *Farmers and Towns*, 63.
59. On the appearance of the rural entrepreneur in the Cochabamba highlands, see Brooke Larson and Rosario León, "Markets, Power, and the Politics of Exchange in Tapacarí, c.

1780 and 1980," in Brooke Larson, Olivia Harris, with Enrique Tandeter, eds., *Ethnicity, Markets, and Migration in the Andes* (Durham, NC, 1995), 243.
60. David Preston, "New Towns—A Major Change in the Rural Settlement Pattern in Highland Bolivia," *Journal of Latin American Studies*, 2 (1970), 10–11.
61. Ronald Clark notes statistics from the Ministry of Defense which reveal a postrevolutionary increase in the height and weight of army recruits, "indicating either higher levels of calorie consumption or a general improvement in quality of diet, or both, during the last decade." Clark, "Land Reform," 164, fn. 14. See also, Andrew Pearse, *The Latin American Peasant*, 150.
62. Clark, "Land Reform," 161, 169.
63. Ibid., 169–170.
64. Ibid., 171. The new towns of the Altiplano, in addition to drawing women into the market economy, also attracted young men marginalized by minifundismo. David Preston's research on new towns revealed that over one-half of the dealers drawn to the new town of Batallas' lucrative pig market were "young men who had little opportunity to engage in farming." Preston, *Farmers and Towns*, 132. See also David Preston, "Life Without Landlords on the Altiplano," *Geographical Magazine*, 41 (1969), 819–827.
65. Peter Graeff, summarizing field work on the north Altiplano, found: "In the Pairumani area, campesino participation in the revolutionary process of 1952 was nonexistent and campesino pressure for land redistribution came only with prodding from outside. Most of the union organizing took place in 1953 with the direction of leaders from La Paz and the regional union offices of Huarina and Achacachi." Graeff, "The Effects," 13.
66. Madeline Barbara Leons, "Land Reform in the Bolivian yungas," *América Indígena*, 27.4 (October 1967), 692.
67. Graeff, "The Effects," 12.
68. Madeline Barbara Leons and William Leons, "Land Reform and Economic Change in the Yungas," in James M. Malloy and Richard Thorn, eds., *Beyond the Revolution: Bolivia Since 1952* (Pittsburgh, PA, 1971), 280.
69. Ibid., 294.
70. Ibid., 281.
71. Madeline Barbara Leons, "Changing Patterns of Social Stratification in an Emergent Bolivian Community," Ph.D. dissertation, University of California, Los Angeles, 1966, 100.
72. Tristan Platt, *Estado boliviano y ayllu andino: tierra y tributo en el norte de Potosí* (Lima, 1982), 38–69.
73. Olivia Harris, "The Sources and Meanings of Money: Beyond the Market Paradigm in an Ayllu of Northern Potosí," in Larson and Harris, with Tandeter, eds., *Ethnicity, Markets, and Migration in the Andes*, 305.
74. The accretion of money is seen as "giving birth." Profit, credit, and debt are considered in terms of fertility; and it is believed desirable to possess both credit and debt. Ibid., 309.
75. Ibid., 306–307. Likewise, in the Cochabamba serranía peasants simultaneously engaged in mercantile activities and non-monetary, reciprocal forms of labor and product exchange as part of their manifold strategy of subsistence and reproduction. Larson and León, "Markets, Power, and the Politics of Exchange," 227.
76. Platt, *Estado boliviano y ayllu andino*, 100 and Silvia Rivera Cusicanqui, "Liberal Democracy and *Ayllu* Democracy in Bolivia: The Case of Northern Potosí," *The Journal of Development Studies*, 26.4 (1990), 117, n. 2.
77. Herbert S. Klein, *Bolivia: The Evolution of a Multi-Ethnic Society* (New York, 1982), 140; Platt, *Estado boliviano y ayllu andino*, 118. Luis Antezana claims there were six thousand uprisings between the 1866 Melgarejo decree (the "first agrarian reform") and 1953 MNR decree (the "second agrarian reform"). Luis Antezana, "La reforma agrarian campesina en Bolivia (1956–1960)," *Revista Mexicana de Sociología*, 2 (April–June 1969), 309.

78. Platt, *Estado boliviano y ayllu andino*, 92, 74.
79. Between the 1874 Exvinculación Decree and 1900, more than 100 legal decrees were introduced to deal with the myriad issues raised by this drastic creole attempt to apply a foreign ideology to indigenous culture and society. For the legal particulars, see Miguel Bonifaz, *Legislación Agrario-Indigenal* (Cochabamba, 1953), 231–593.
80. Platt, *Estado boliviano*, 86. See chapters two and three for a superb examination of the relationship of the state and the Potosí ayllus in the nineteenth century.
81. Tristan Platt, "The Role of the Andean Ayllu in the Reproduction of the Petty Commodity Exchange in Northern Potosí," *Cambridge Studies in Social Anthropology*, 41 (1982), 36–37.
82. The increased usurpation of the ayllu lands came after the victory of the La Paz elites in the Federal War. Platt, *Estado boliviano*, 128–130, 121–127. Also see Eric Langer's insightful, "Andean Rituals of Revolt: The Chayanta Rebellion of 1927," *Ethnohistory*, 37.3 (Summer 1990), 227–253.
83. Into A. Goudsmit, "Exploiting the 1953 Agrarian Reform: Landlord Persistence in Northern Potosí, Bolivia," *The Journal of Latin American and Caribbean Anthropology*, 13.2 (November 2008), 367.
84. Ibid., 376–378; Platt, *Estado boliviano*, 124, 143.
85. See Article 62 in Castillo Avendaño, *Compilación*, 63–64.
86. For details of the confrontation of the Potosí ayllus with the 1953 "Second Agrarian Reform," see Platt, *Estado boliviano y ayllu andino*, 148–172; for La Paz Department, see Soliz, "Land to the Original Owners," 285–286.
87. Dorsey, "A Case Study," II.13–14.
88. Stephen M. Smith, "Labor Exploitation on Pre-1952 Haciendas in the Lower Valley of Cochabamba, Bolivia," *The Journal of Developing Areas*, 11.2 (January 1977), 235, 241. See also Alberto Rivera Pizarro, *Los terratenientes de Cochabamba* (Cochabamba, 1992), 108–109, 111 and Mario Carranza Fernández, "Estudio de Caso en el Valle Bajo de Cochabamba" (La Paz, 1972), 3–4.
89. The development of the Cochabamba piquería has been traced to the 1920s when affluent peasants began to outbid landlords in competition for the purchase of rural land: see Dorsey, "A Case Study," II.7; Robert H. Jackson, *Regional Markets and Agrarian Transformation in Bolivia: Cochabamba, 1539–1960* (Albuquerque, NM, 1994), 140; Brooke Larson, *Cochabamba 1550–1900: Colonialism and Agrarian Transformation in Bolivia* (Durham, NC, 1998), 301–303, 313–316; Lagos, *Autonomy and Power*, 31–32.
90. Rivera Pizarro, *Los terratenientes*, 53.
91. Robert H. Jackson, "The Decline of the Hacienda in Cochabamba, Bolivia: The Case of the Sacaba Valley, 1870–1929," *Hispanic American Historical Review*, 69.2 (1989), 263, 277.
92. Dorsey, "A Case Study," VI. 94. See also Lagos, *Autonomy and Power*, 54–55 and Simmons, *Palca and Pucara*, 18.
93. Ronald S. Clark, "Reforma agraria e integración campesina en la economía boliviana," *Estudios Andinos*, 1.1 (1970), 12.
94. Rivera Pizzaro, *Los terratenientes*, 53, 56, 82–83, 90.
95. Barnes and Torrico, "Cambios Socio-Económicos en el Valle Alto de Cochabamba Desde 1952: Los pueblos provinciales de Cliza, Punata, Arani, Sacaba, Tarata y Mizque" (La Paz, 1971), 37.
96. Rivera Pizarro, *Los terratenientes*, 106.
97. See Soliz, "Fields of Revolution," 217–225.
98. Lagos. *Autonomy and Power*, 46–47; Simmons, *Palca and Pucara*, 34–37.
99. The dynamics of these developments in the Valle Alto and the serranía are analyzed in Barnes de von Marschall, and Torrico Angulo, "Cambios socio-económicos en el Valle Alto de Cochabamba desde 1952: Los pueblos provinciales de Cliza, Punata, Arani, Sacaba, Tarata y Mizque." Utilizing questionnaires and interviews with peasants, the study reveals a keen awareness by peasants of local developments.

100. Ibid., 23. See also Simmons, *Palca and Pucara*, 89–90. On the role of compadrazgo in the northern Altiplano, see Preston, *Farmers and Towns*, 128–130.
101. Dorsey, "A Case Study," I.4.
102. Ibid., IV. 34.
103. Ibid., IV. 32. Dorsey found that because of soil fertility, a favorable climate, and available transportation to markets, the peasants of the Valle Bajo were more able to enter the cash market than peasants in the Valle Alto or Altiplano. Ibid., II.13.
104. Graeff, "The Effects," 18.
105. Thus, the unexpected result of the agrarian reform process: "As campesinos built new houses, vecino style, by the main road in an urban-type arrangement, and as they acquire all or part of their land from the former patrón by purchase, just as the piqueros had done, the erosion of these differences, which the campesinos by their own actions attempt to speed up, makes it very difficult for vecinos to maintain their former superior status." Dorsey, "A Case Study," I. 6.
106. Ibid., II. 13. Dorsey summarizes these practices: "In the 1967 LTC-CIDA case study of the Lower Valley, compañía was found to be practiced by nearly a third of the ex-miners of Paratoni compared to less than a tenth of the campesinos, ex-colonos and jornaleros; none of the ex-colonos of Caramarca gave out their land in compañía, whereas three ex-miners who had moved elsewhere left their land to campesinos to be worked in this way." Ibid., IV. 27.
107. Carranza Fernández, *Estudio en Caso en el Valle Bajo de Cochabamba*, 142–145, 152–153; Simmons, *Palca and Pucara*, 24–25; for Chuquisaca, see Charles Erasmus, "Farm Labor After the Reform," in Heath, et al., eds., *Land Reform*, 156.
108. For the "vertical archipelago" model, see John Murra, "Verticality and Complimentary," excerpted in Sinclair Thomson, et al., eds., *The Bolivia Reader*, translated by Alison Spedding, 27–33.
109. Erick D. Langer, *Economic Change and Rural Resistance in Southern Bolivia, 1880–1930* (Palo Alto, CA, 1989), 69.
110. Healy, "Power, Class and Rural Development," 61; Havet, "Rational Domination," 92, 204.
111. Luis Antezana Erguita, *Historia secreta del movimiento nacionalista revolucionario*, Vol. 8 (La Paz, 1992), 1294–1296.
112. Erasmus, "Upper Limits of Peasantry and Agrarian Reform," 350–354. The 1950 census reveals that informants with less than three hectares cultivated 55 percent of their property, while landowners with over 3 hectares cultivated an average of less than 2 percent of their land. Kohl, "The Role of the Peasant," 51.
113. Erasmus, "Upper Limits," 356.
114. John H. Whiteford, "Urbanization of Rural Proletarians: Bolivian Migrant Workers in Northwest Argentina," Ph.D. dissertation, University of Texas, Austin, 1974, 376.
115. Thus, 60 percent of peasants in 1970 were unaware of the 1970 *Impuesto Único Agropecuario*, a national tax to be levied on the peasantry. The following year these peasants failed to react to the right-wing seizure of power by General Hugo Banzer Suárez, another potential threat to their livelihood. Havet, "Rational Domination," 143–144.
116. Healy, "Power, Class and Rural Development," 57, 60. José Havet cites similar results for the province of Belisario Boeto where only 47.6 percent of the families of the province had received a property title from the SNRA by 1970. Havet, "Rational Domination," 207.
117. Instituto Boliviano de Estudio y Acción Sociales, *Entre Rios*, 74. See also Soliz, "Fields of Revolution," 288–289.
118. Havet, "Rational Domination," 94. See also McEwen, ed., *Changing Rural Society*, 49–50.
119. Erasmus, "Upper Limits," 366–367; Kevin Healy similarly notes the emergence of corrupt sindicato leaders in "Power, Class and Rural Development," 52; see also Havet, "Rational Domination," 172, 208; Simmons, *Palca and Pucara*, 39–40, 75; *Unidad*, 19 March 1960, 6.

120. Havet, "Rational Domination," 163. Havet also notes: ". . . money has become the common denominator of the siphoning off by all categories of elites. . . . the Agrarian Reform has modernized not only the power structure and the means of siphoning off of the peasants, but also of what is siphoned off." Havet, "Rational Domination," 216. For examples, see *El Diario*, 14 January 1958, 4; *La Presencia*, 8 October 1959, 5; and *Unidad*, July 1959, 6.
121. Ibid., 254. Havet underscores the cultural bias against peasants, "The *prestación vial* is a compulsory three days of work that theoretically all Bolivian male citizens have to carry out. However, the urbanites, and this includes the inhabitants of Villa Serrano, may buy their prestación vial. It costs $10 bol. and can be bought in any store." Ibid., 146. David Preston found similar use of Indians (and not townspeople) providing labor for public works projects in the northern Altiplano. See Preston, *Farmers and Towns*, 174.
122. Heyduk, "Huayrapampa," 55. Heyduk also observed "the arrimantes and vivientes who officially were their dependents, remain as much in that status today as they were prior to the agrarian reform. A significant proportion of the rural population, then, remains virtually unaffected by the reform program." Ibid. The continuation of inequality among the Chuquisaca peasantry is noted in Heyduk, 50, 276, 281, 290, and Turovsky, "Bolivian Haciendas," 88.
123. José Havet's research reveals the paradoxical results of the agrarian reform: "The Agrarian Reform impoverished [sic] the small and medium-sized landowners, but did not significantly affect the biggest landholdings. Consequently, it increased the dichotomy existing within the rural society." Havet, "Rational Domination," 101. But, David Preston found quite the opposite for the northern Altiplano where the smaller estate owners lived in the nearby towns and used their influence to effect: because their income was more directly related to agricultural production, they were more aggressive in defending their patrimony than were the largely absentee owners, many of whom derived more status than income from their estates. See Preston, *Farmers and Towns*, 95
124. Havet, "Rational Domination," 133–135.
125. This differential in exchange is illustrated in examples observed in 1967: 3 pounds [1.3 kilos] of potatoes with a value of $bolivinos 2.4–3.0 to be exchanged for 8–9 onions valued at $bolivianos 1.0; or for three boxes of matches valued at $bolivianos 0.60, or a liter of kerosene valued at $bolivianos 0.25. Barnes and Torrico, "Cambios Socio-Económicos," 17.
126. See, for example, Erasmus, "Upper Limits," 356–364; Herbert S. Klein, *Haciendas & Ayllus: Rural Society in the Bolivian Andes in the Eighteenth and Nineteenth Centuries* (Palo Alto, CA, 1993), 58–60; Havet, "Rational Domination," 115; Heyduk, "Huayrapampa," 303.
127. See Libbet Crandon-Malamud, *From the Fat of Our Souls* (Berkeley, CA, 1993), 195.102–105.
128. Erasmus, "Farm Labor After the Reform," 163.
129. See Ronald Clark, "Reforma agraria y integración campesina en la economía boliviana," *Estudios Andinos*, 3 (1970), 20; also, Charles Erasmus, "Upper Limits of Peasantry and Agrarian Reform: Bolivia, Venezuela and Mexico Compared," *Ethnology*, 6.4 (October 1967), 361–362.
130. James Wilkie, *Measuring Land Reform*, 34. Ñuflo Chavez, Minister of Peasant Affairs in the early years of the Revolution, concurred with this view. Interview with the author 2 July 1970, La Paz, Bolivia.
131. Canelas, *Mito y Realidad*, 273; Arturo Urquidi, *Bolivia y su reforma agraria* (Cochabamba, 1969), 78.
132. José Gordillo, *Campesinos revolucionarios en Bolivia: Identidad, territorio y sexualidad en el Valle Alto de Cochabamba* (La Paz, 2000), 78.
133. Sinforoso Rivas Antezana, *Los hombres de la revolución: memorias de un líder campesino* (La Paz, 2000), 98.

134. Ibid., 100.
135. Leons, "Land Reform," 705.
136. Dorsey provides an excellent summary of the problem-fraught cooperatives in "A Case Study," III.20.
137. García, "Agrarian Reform," 331.
138. Dwight B. Heath, "Land Reform in Bolivia," *Inter-American Economic Affairs*, 12 (1959), 17. The MNR government distributed tractors on the northern Altiplano to improve production, but they soon fell into disrepair because of mismanagement: "after an alarming number of cases of mismanagement, the peasants soon did not even want to hear the word cooperative anymore. Since Compeños themselves did not possess the prerequisite managerial capacity to establish a cooperative, Paceños, often relatives of the ex-colonos, stepped in to manage them, and then left with the cooperative's funds." Buechler, "Agrarian Reform and Migration," 57–58.
139. García, "Agrarian Reform," 320–321; Cesar Ayaviri Arana, *Panorama de un Proceso de Reforma Agraria: Participación del campesinado en el caso boliviano* (La Paz, 1972), 17.
140. García, "Agrarian Reform," 332–333.
141. For the development of these commercial enterprises, see Susan Eckstein, "The Impact of Revolution: A Comparative Analysis of Mexico and Bolivia," *Studies in Comparative International Development* (Fall 1975), 12–13.
142. Larson, *Cochabamba, 1550–1900*, 255.
143. Allyn M. Stearman, "Colonization in Eastern Bolivia: Problems and Prospects," *Human Organization*, 32.3 (Fall 1973), 286. Stearman's personal account of the tribulations of the Yapacaní Colony in Santa Cruz Department, his critique of its failure, and guidelines for future settlement projects are insightful and instructive.
144. Javier Albó, *¿Bodas de plata o requiem para una reforma agraria?* (La Paz, March 1969), 13, 51.
145. Cole Blasier, "The United States and the Revolution," in Malloy and Thorn, eds., *Beyond the Revolution: Bolivia*, 86. Also see James Wilkie, *The Bolivian Revolution and U.S. Aid Since 1952* (Los Angeles, CA, 1974), 8–14; Laurence Whitehead, *The United States and Bolivia: A Case in Neocolonialism* (Oxford, UK, 1969); Richard Patch, "Bolivia: U.S. Assistance in a Revolutionary Setting," in Richard N. Adams, et al., eds., *Social Change in Latin America Today* (New York, 1960). 108–176.
146. García, "Agrarian Reform," 335–336. Thus, "Credit for farming is almost nonexistent in Chuquisaca," notes Charles Erasmus, "Farm Labor After the Reform," 154.
147. Simmons, *Palca and Pucara*, 92–93, 98.
148. For the political implications of this historic development, see James Dunkerley, *Rebellion in the Veins: Political Struggle in Bolivia, 1952–1982* (London, 1984), 219–230; Laurence Whitehead, "Banzer's Bolivia," *Current History* (February 1976), 61–64, 80, and James Kohl, "Bolivia: Andean Power Shift," *The Progressive* (February 1977), 39–42.
149. *El Diario*, 11 February 1955, 8.
150. Wilkie, *Measuring Land Reform*, 50; Mendelberg, "The Impact of Bolivian Agrarian Reform on Class Formation," 47–48.
151. Carter, "Revolution and the Agrarian Sector," 246.
152. Antonio García, *Reforma agraria y dominación social en América* (Buenos Aires, 1973), 240. Because of the MNR's failure to commit adequate resources for the reform of the agrarian sector, it can be argued that this venture was "not an 'agrarian reform' in the true sense of the term. . . . It can more realistically be called a 'land reform' since little more than land redistribution was ever attempted." Graeff, "The Effects," 2.
153. Carter's judgment is apropos: "The impediments placed before the council by the MNR government testify to the essentially political nature of the agrarian reform movement." Carter, "Revolution and the Agrarian Sector," 245–246.
154. Larson and León, "Markets, Power, and the Politics of Exchange," 246.
155. Susan Eckstein, "Transformation of a 'Revolution from Below': Bolivia and International Capital," *Comparative Studies in Society and History*, 25 (1983), 108.

156. Turovsky, "Bolivian Haciendas," 288.
157. García, "Agrarian Reform and Social Development," 319.
158. Soliz, "Land to the Original Owners," 280–283.
159. Ibid., 226.
160. José Havet, "Rational Domination: The Power Structure in a Bolivian Rural Zone," Ph.D. dissertation, University of Pittsburgh, 1979, 72. William E. Carter, "Revolution in the Agrarian Sector," Malloy and Thorn, eds., *Beyond the Revolution*, 146, 252.
161. Ernst Feder, *The Rape of the Peasantry* (New York, 1971), 38. On minifundismo, see James Wilkie's cautionary remarks in *Measuring Land Reform*, 57.
162. Kelly and Klein, *Revolution and the Rebirth of Inequality*, 9. For a critical assessment of the MNR's commitment to education, see Manuel E. Contreras, "A Comparative Perspective on Education Reforms in Bolivia, 1950–2000," in Merilee S. Grindle and Pilar Domingo, eds., *Proclaiming Revolution: Bolivia in Comparative Perspective* (London, 2003), 259–286.
163. Herbert Klein, "Social Change in Bolivia Since 1952," in Grindle and Domingo, eds., *Proclaiming Revolution*, 248–250.

7

SINDICATO AND REVOLUTION

They began their descent from the heights of the serranía toward the verdant valleys below. Wielding rifles, pistols, knives, staves, pitchforks, hoes, and shovels, the three columns marched under red flags emblazoned with their identity: "Ayllu Comunarios." Each column moved toward its objective: the Challa comunarios followed the Oruro–Cochabamba road toward Cochabamba; a second column descended along the banks of the Río Tapacarí toward the town of Paratoni; the third column of comunarios from the ayllu Totora Pampa descended on the pueblo of Pairumani, where they pilfered houses, abused vecinos, and tortured those suspected of witchcraft. One victim, hoisted by his feet on a rope, was left hanging in the plaza for all to see, terrorizing the residents.[1] The comunario rebellion followed the 19 May 1954 addendum to the Agrarian Reform Decree (3732) prohibiting restitution of ayllu lands lost before the twentieth century. The ayllu farmlands in the valleys, usurped following the 1874 Law of Expropriation, were decreed irrecoverable; the lands were now to pass from the hacendados to their ex-colonos. Resentment over this provision in the Agrarian Reform Decree had turned to rage vented on the vecinos.[2]

The public display of force by the comunarios was a reminder of the power of the indigenous majority and the tenuous hegemony of their vecino antagonists. Towns remained a hostile environment where use of a sidewalk constituted trespassing, and transgressors could be forced into such indignities as cleaning the town plaza or sweeping streets. As the British sociologist Andrew Pearse put it: "The town (or village) is the point of contact between the peasant . . . and the rest of society, it is the cork in the bottle for the communities, the administrative centre where servile *postillonaje* [postal delivery] had to be rendered, where taxes were paid, where commercial transactions were carried out."[3] In addition to public degradations, comunarios were routinely cheated in urban market transactions and the scales used for weighing products were known to be rigged against them. Vecino businessmen routinely plied comunarios with alcohol to bilk them during harvest negotiations.[4] The accusation of witchcraft was a symbolic reminder of comunario resentment against double-dealing vecino merchants, haughty government functionaries, and grasping tinterello paper pushers.

Sinforoso Rivas, the dirigente of the Valle Bajo cuartels at Bella Vista and Quillacollo (comprised of ex-colonos), launched an offensive against the rebellious serranía comunarios, transforming the comunario rebellion into an intra-ethnic confrontation. Rivas's counterinsurgency strategy involved encirclement of the comunario columns followed by a display of overwhelming firepower unleashed from machine guns—fired into the air to intimidate the comunarios and induce them to negotiate. Rivas had compromised the revolutionary potential of the sindicato by pitting colonos against the comunarios.

Rivas began negotiations with a critique of the fruitless comunario pursuit for legal redress of historic grievances as well as the fatal inability of the Indian masses to organize and struggle in concert: "I am certain that you are never going to obtain that which you desire . . . [you] have walked many years behind the lawyers seeking justice, spending . . . [your] meagre income on paperwork, leaving only a mountain of papers that have been converted into files." He counseled, "Compañeros, I will not reproach you for this uprising, but this is not the route that you should take because, as has been seen for many years, all the rebellions have failed for lack of organization and unity." Rivas then argued for a united peasantry organized nationwide. The irony of his reproach to the captured comunarios regarding the need for indigenous unity escaped him. When asked by Rivas what to do with the captured comunario leaders, the Cochabamba prefect replied, "Send them to the Chapare" [penal colony].[5]

A Divided Nation: Indians and Vecinos, Town and Countryside

The hacendados who abandoned their estates following the 1952 Revolution found that the hostility of their former colonos followed them to their urban sanctuaries. Two months after the proclamation of the Agrarian Reform Decree, a force of 2,000 peasants responding to the murder of a friendly *alcalde* (mayor) invaded the town of Santivañez in Cochabamba Department (Capinota Province) where they publicly executed the perpetrator before horrified vecinos assembled in the town plaza. An editorial in *El Diario* is suggestive of the vecino racism that elicited the violence.[6] "The event in Santivañez has served to greatly encourage the barbaric and criminal spirit of the campesino." Nowhere was the confrontation between Indian and vecino as contentious as in Cochabamba: "it was the most conflictive place in Bolivia," and according to the Minister of Peasant Affairs, "the center of the latifundista counterrevolution."[7]

Cochabamba city was the epicenter of a Falangist uprising that began the morning of 9 November 1953 in the departmental capitols of Cochabamba, La Paz, Potosí, Sucre, and Santa Cruz. The revolutionary syndicalism of peasants and workers together with hacienda invasions, land seizures, attacks on landlords, assaults on towns, and threats to cities by miner, factory worker, and peasant sindicato militias were perceived by the FSB as indications of a communist takeover under the guise of the National Revolution. The Falange included hacendados, middle-class vecinos (buffeted by rampant inflation and threatened by the prospect of food shortages resulting from agrarian unrest) and displaced government bureaucrats, military officers and cadets purged by the MNR. Avowedly racist, the FSB constituency was unambiguous regarding the Indian. As a Falangista put it, "Víctor Paz Estenssoro wanted to demonstrate to international opinion, that the Movimiento Nacionalista Revolucionario had the support of the Indian, that is, with 80 percent of the population of the Republic, but failing to inform abroad that this element is illiterate, of extreme ignorance, with a mental age lower than a child of six years old raised in whatever civilized medium."[8]

The November 1953 Falangista revolt reveals similarities with the MNR plans of 1949 and 1952: simultaneous revolts in the departmental capitols of La Paz, Cochabamba, Potosí, Sucre, and Santa Cruz carried out by carabineros, military officers, cadets, FSB militants and supporters. Cochabamba constituted the center of the uprising with railroad and highway connections to Oruro and Santa Cruz, a supply route from Puerto Suárez, and the 18 aircraft of the Lloyd Aéreo Boliviano fleet; an arms cache in Sucre (10,000 rifles and 20,000 rounds of ammunition), together with stashes secreted in other towns, provided weaponry for the Falangistas. Militants in Oruro were to impede the movement of mine worker militias from reaching Cochabamba or Sucre, and militants in Santa Cruz were tasked with the seizure and occupation of the Camiri oil fields.

In the event of failure to accomplish a coup d'etat, the Falangistas planned a "civil war" in the departments of Cochabamba, Sucre, and Santa Cruz.[9] But when anticipated military defectors failed to appear and, following a botched attempt to capture President Paz Estenssoro, the insurrection in La Paz fizzled. Revolts in Sucre and Santa Cruz failed to materialize. The Cochabamba uprising initially fared better. The telephone switchboard, Lloyd Aéreo installations, Military Air Base, Carabinero Headquarters, Radio Popular, and the railroad station were seized. The Commandant of the Escuela de Clases, Colonel Felsi Luna Pizarro (a Radepista), was captured as was the COB leader Juan Lechín.[10] But, when informed of the mobilization of peasant militias, the leaders of the *Comando Revolucionario* boarded three Lloyd Aéreo aircraft and fled the country. The FSB Jefe Unzaga de la Vega escaped to the safety of the Uruguayan Embassy in La Paz.[11] The FSB revolt prompted President Víctor Paz's fateful decision to form *Control Politico*, the state security force that would become notorious for its brutality.

The MNR decision to purge the armed forces of disloyal officers and military academy cadets created resentment and opposition. But had the military not been purged, perfidious officers within the institution would have posed a threat to the revolution. The balance of power shifted from the creole-mestizo military institution to the indigenous peasant, miner, and worker sindicatos. The sindicato militias were a counterpoise to the military and a foil against counterrevolutionaries, but the MNR creole-mestizos also sought to control the sindicatos and deny an autonomous indigenous agency within the National Revolution. Thus, the repeated use of military forces to relieve towns besieged by sindicato militias, as when a detachment of carabaneros was dispatched to disperse hostile campesinos at the canton of Acchilla in Nor Cinti Province (Chuquisaca Department).[12]

Attacks by peasant militias on Altiplano towns were commonplace. A peasant militia invaded the pueblo of Ilabaya in Larecaja Province (La Paz Department). The timely airlift of carabineros from La Paz relieved the town of Apolo from the threat of invasion by hostile peasants.[13] Three hundred comunarios from the Cheja community encircled Sorata, a town in Larecaja Province (La Paz Department) in late February 1954 demanding the release of their secretary general jailed by the local authorities. Only the timely intercession of the subprefect and a carabinero detachment averted violence.[14] In April 1954, a sindicato militia surrounded the town of Calamarca in Aroma Province (La Paz Department), demanding a change in local authorities: the frightened townspeople took refuge in the village church.[15]

A peasant militia invaded Achacachi, the capital of Omasuyos Province (La Paz Department), in 1955 during Carnaval; colonos and vecinos exchanged gunfire, townspeople were abused, and a house razed. An earlier incursion had occurred when Toribio Salas, a powerful Altiplano dirigente, occupied the town to enforce a favorable price on the sale of potatoes in the market.[16] Violent confrontations between peasant militias and townspeople continued in 1956. Peasants invaded Ancoraimes, on the northwest shore of Lake Titicaca, in April and looted the church. Later in the year, peasants laid siege to the Altiplano town of Escoma in Camacho Province (La Paz Department).[17]

The Agrarian Sindicato

The triumph of the National Revolution sparked a wave of syndical organization in the countryside. The dense populations of the Cochabamba valleys, the northern Altiplano region of Lake Titicaca (Omasuyos Province), and the semitropical Yungas were the initial foci of sindicato development. Communist militants had begun to focus on the peasantry in the 1930s and following the onset of the National Revolution, PORista and PIRista *entristas* (militants who "entered" the MNR), together with Movimientista cadre and ex-miners, were at work radicalizing hacienda colonos and organizing sindicatos. An interview with a peasant by the anthropologist Madeline Leons offers insight into the revolution in the Yungas, "After the revolution, a *caballero* (horseman: gentleman) lawyer from La Paz came to Santa Ana as an organizer for the P.O.R. . . . and the Santa Ana campesinos were being organized to take part in a leftist coup. They were even prepared, given the word, to attack the provincial capital of Coroico. The organizer supplied them with dynamite but not rifles."[18] The Santa Ana peasants were engaged in an ongoing dispute with colonos from the neighboring hacienda San Juan. Affiliation with the Trotskyist organizer afforded the opportunity to vanquish factional rivals and establish control over the town of Coroico in the bargain. As Leons recounts, when the MNR got wind of the plot and "sent in truckload after truckload of armed campesinos from as far away as Caranavi to overrun Santa Ana ... the invading campesinos completely sacked Santa Ana, entering every house and carting away everything movable. Men exchanged old clothes for new; they even took the guinea pigs and helped themselves to the cooking food."[19]

The MNR strategy was to subvert agrarian revolutionaries through co-optation or removal of radical dirigentes. Article 132 of the Agrarian Reform Decree defined the role of the sindicato. "The campesino sindicato organization is recognized as a means of defense of the rights of its members and the conservation of social conquests. The campesino sindicatos will take part in the execution of the Agrarian Reform. They are able to be independent or affiliated with a central organization."[20] The article legitimized what was in many instances a fait accompli—the de facto seizures of land by revolutionary peasants—and called for the organization of sindicatos "to defend their rights," "to conserve social conquests," and "participate in the execution of the Agrarian Reform." Legitimation of the agrarian sindicatos through co-optation of the grassroots movement into a state-sanctioned syndical network was eminently pragmatic and not uncommon in Latin America.[21] The sindicatos became a bulwark of the National Revolution as armed force, the ultimate arbiter of power, passed to their militias.

Following the collapse of the Old Regime, the sindicato functioned as a surrogate for governance of the rural sector. Initially, indigenous sindicatos arose as an instrument of change in the countryside, ousting landlords and disrupting the colonato. The power of peasant and proletarian militias was considered essential to the survival of the National Revolution. Between 1952 and 1956, the number of sindicato members grew to an estimated 600,000 peasants and 150,000 workers in offices, mines, and factories. One half of the nation's economically active population fell under the national leadership of the *Central Obrera Boliviano* (COB) syndical umbrella.[22] These were the heady days of *co-gobierno*. With leftist labor leaders Juan Lechín, Mario Torres, and Ñuflo Chávez in cabinet positions, this presented a historic opportunity for peasant and proletarian masses to gain political agency and assert hegemony over the National Revolution.

It would not be so. The syndicalization of peasants, miners, factory and railroad workers, artisans, and bureaucrats offered an unprecedented opportunity for a revolutionary redistribution of power within the revolution. But the creole-mestizo MNR elites were wary of radicalization of the revolution and cognizant of urban middle-class trepidation (invasions by armed miners and peasants, transportation blockades, food shortages, civil war). Moreover, the ethic bias of the creole-mestizo MNR élites precluded an imaginative and equitable role for the peasant majority. Peasant representatives in the COB were outnumbered nearly three to one by proletarians, and peasant representatives from the *Confederación Nacional de Trabajadores Campesinos de Bolivia* (CNTCP) were removed and replaced with

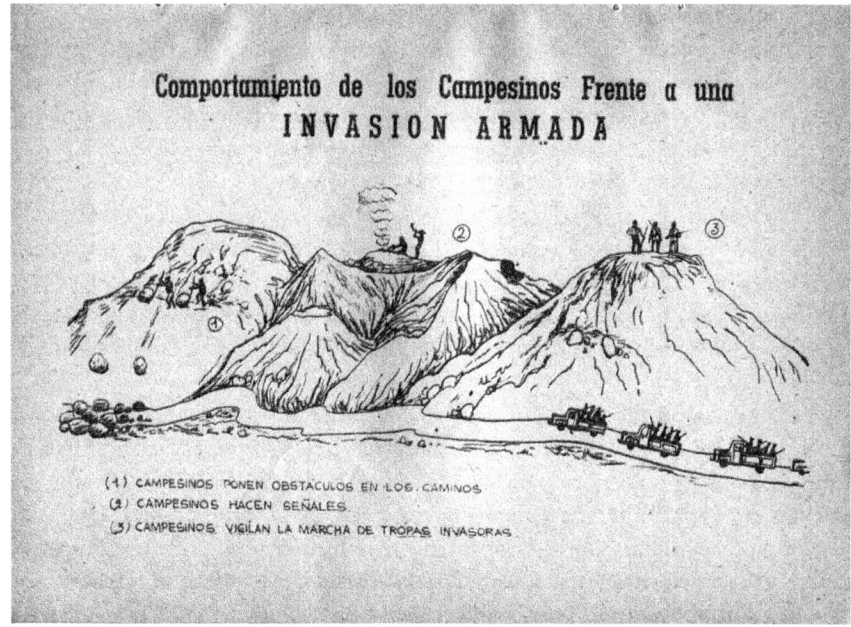

FIGURE 7.1 Peasant Comportment in the Face of an Armed Invasion

Source: Capitán Óscar Daza Barrenechea, *Sistematización Armada de la Revolución Nacional.*

government appointees.[23] MNR concerns regarding the power of Indian militias boded ill for the future of autonomous peasant sindicatos.

Syndicalization irrevocably altered indigenous society and culture. Traditional peasant societies functioned within a civil-religious hierarchy (often referred to as the cargo system), "an articulated system of posts which the various families are to occupy throughout their life cycle, in ascending order, as part of the services and duties they are to render to the collective."[24] This highly structured order often failed to meet the needs of the sindicato and was altered in favor of a system where leaders were selected on the basis of their political capabilities. The leader (*dirigente*) of the sindicato held the supreme post of Executive Secretary, Secretary General, or Secretary of Government and was assisted by subordinate officials. Local sindicato governments were organized around *sindicatos de hacienda* grouped in cantonal and provincial *centrales* to form a departmental federation. At the national level, delegates to the CNTCP represented the peasantry in the COB.

The sindicato organization, following William Carter's example for the Altiplano, includes the following positions. *Secretary General:* calls together meetings of householders; makes periodic trips to central peasant labor organization in county seat to make reports and bring back instructions; arranges hospitality for visitors to the ex-hacienda; deals with all supra-community legal proceedings (such as land reform briefs and appeals). *Secretary of Relations:* works as assistant to the general secretary; in his absence, announces and directs meetings. *Secretary of Finance:* collects quotas to cover expenses of members' trips to La Paz and costs of securing land titles. *Secretary of Justice:* In conjunction with other members of sindicato, conducts hearings on misdemeanors and minor lawsuits and imposes fines. *Secretary of Agriculture:* helps select *camana* and supervises his labor. *Secretary of Livestock:* takes annual census of animals within the community. *Secretary of Roads:* directs labor for local road repair and construction. *Secretary of Sports:* organizes soccer teams; collects fees to pay for sports equipment. *Secretary of Recording:* keeps minutes of meetings. *Secretary of Education:* takes school attendance; supervises teacher. *Secretary of Health:* arranges for visits of *yatiri* (native religious specialist) or medical doctor. *Secretary of Culture:* maintains order in meetings. *Member at Large:* attends meetings and has a vote.[25]

As illustrated in the preceding schema, the sindicato provided administration of the land group, obviating the potential power vacuum inherent in the agrarian reform process by replacing the pre-revolutionary hierarchy of patrón, mayordomo, and jilikata with a sindicato secretary general and subordinate officers. However ideal the organization might appear in conception, execution presented a host of unforeseen consequences, including factional conflicts, turf wars, and racketeering. The position of Secretary General offered the opportunity for graft, as evidenced in the following list of improprieties common to the office, compiled by Andrew Pearse: "The actual pillage of estate property in furniture, installations and stock, collection of municipal dues, the charging of fees in connection with land transactions, benefits from lands worked collectively by union members, usufruct of demesne lands in dispute with governmental machinery, use of union transport for commercialization of estate products, sale of arms allocated for distribution and even the manufacture of cocaine."[26] The possibilities for corruption were limited only by one's imagination.

The MNR dispatched organizers to accelerate sindicato formation and instruct constituents regarding initiation of the agrarian reform process. Because the sindicatos offered the potential to deliver land to their members, they spread throughout the countryside. This is of a piece with comparative developments on a global level where the offer of a tangible reward, rather than an ideology or political aspirations, attracts peasant participation in land-group unions.[27] The power of the sindicato movement rested upon the armed militias to provide and guarantee land and "coerce with violence and the threat of violence, in a country where the rule of law had never been established."[28]

The agrarian reform process engendered a transition in indigenous leadership as status and authority depended on the ability of the sindicato dirigente to manipulate the Spanish-speaking bureaucracy of the regime.[29] Those dirigentes most successful in wringing patronage (e.g., roads, schools, potable water, electricity, favorable adjudication of boundary disputes) were associated with the MNR. Those who pursued an agenda beyond the pale were marginalized. Branded as "extremists," "agitators," and "communists," they faded from power in the early years of the revolution. Sindicato development occurred sporadically throughout the countryside, dependent on local and provincial dynamics, and resulted in the development of a syndical bureaucracy of dirigentes faithful to the MNR leadership.

The rural sociologist Andrew Pearse observed that sindicato structure was conducive to prebendalismo, "a situation in which the licit and illicit perquisites of office become the major concern of the officeholder, to the detriment of the performance of the office" and notes the appearance of the sindicato chieftain (cacique) as an agrarian prebendal position.[30] The MNR promoted the sindicato movement in the unorganized areas of the country and attempted to control or neutralize the more militant leaders. Consequently, the process of ending the colonato and distributing land to the colonos who worked it was slow and tedious. The agrarian sindicatos lost their power as they surrendered their autonomy to authoritarian leaders linked to the MNR regime.[31]

The Gordian Knot

Prebendalismo was not confined to the agrarian sindicatos. By 1964, the Ministry of Labor reported there were 51,000 dirigentes for the 150,000 workers organized in 5,100 non-campesino sindicatos: a ratio of one dirigente per every three workers and ten dirigentes per sindicato![32] The MNR *empleocracía* ensconced in state enterprises demonstrated a proclivity for the perquisites of government employment as well as the genius of bureaucrats to optimize the spoils of an unofficial economy rooted in graft. Differential exchange rates allowed party insiders the opportunity to make huge profit by buying and selling dollars and bolivianos in an inflationary environment.[33] Inflation soared to historically unprecedented levels as the MNR doled out rewards to powerful sectors within the party elite and influential constituents concocted schemes to profit from what was economically disastrous for others. Bolivia emerged as a smuggling entrepôt, the spoils system within the regime was exposed, and the "pristine revolutionary image of the party" destroyed.[34]

Government corruption was widely known by the urban populace who bore the brunt of inflation and food shortages. The urban middle class and factory worker sectors within the regime were sacrificed to party apparatchiks and laborers in the nationalized mines who profited from inflation through resale of official *cupos* (coupons) for subsidized purchases at the *pulperías* (company stores) as well as outside the mines. By 1955, pulpería subsidies accounted for one-third of labor expenses in the mines.[35] The number of bureaucrats employed above ground ("Outside the Mine") multiplied during President Paz Estenssoro's administration (1952–1956), reaching a total of 35,600 in 1956, the zenith of the bureaucratization of COMIBOL during the National Revolution. The percentage of workers engaged in the extractive labor below ground ("Inside the Mine") decreased relative to the percentage of bureaucrats ("Outside the Mines"): by 1956, the number of those employed "outside" (24,222) doubled that of those "inside" (11,438). This trend continued during the revolution. Seventy percent of COMIBOL employees were office workers in 1962.[36]

The tin content of ore mined by COMIBOL decreased by 50 percent (1.06–0.54 percent) during the revolution (1953–1964). This was the continuation of a 40-year decline for the Catavi Mine. By 1964, the tin content of Catavi ore constituted an infinitesimal *one-half of 1 percent*. The mines were operated with minimal capital outlay for modernization of machinery. The exodus of nearly 90 percent of foreign engineers and managers from the nationalized mines added to the inefficiency of the enterprise.[37] The MNR had expropriated the tin mines for reasons of sovereignty and resource nationalism, but as Wálter Guevara argued, they were no economic bargain. Indeed, the MNR expropriated a white elephant—worked with outdated equipment, extracting ore of miniscule tin content, overstaffed by bureaucrats above ground, and a proletarian vanguard in the veins below, the mines were economically unsustainable. The mining superestado had been profitable only because of low wages, inhuman working conditions, and brutal repression.

All did not bode well for those sectors unable to profit from inflation. Factory workers lost an estimated 15 percent of their purchasing power in the first four years of the revolution. Middle-class workers experienced a 50 percent drop in real wages and the cost of living in La Paz nearly doubled from 1952 to 1954. In 1964, the cost of living was 80 times what it had been at the onset of the National Revolution in 1952. A civil servant's wage in 1955 was half of what it was in 1950, and factory workers wages dropped below pre-revolution levels.[38]

The handwriting was on the wall. The deleterious impact of the economy on the National Revolution was confirmed in the 1956 election when over 40 percent of the voters in La Paz cast a ballot for the counterrevolutionary FSB. In the other major cities, the vote was closely divided between the MNR and FSB.[39] An ominously high percentage of the middle-class and factory workers (two sectors crucial to the victory of the revolution) afflicted by the spiraling inflation had repudiated the party and voted for counterrevolution.

A Deadly Embrace: The MNR, the United States, and Neocolonialism

Faced with crippling inflation, the disaggregation of its sectoral components, and the imminent disintegration of the revolution, the MNR was forced to seek foreign assistance to stave off the inevitable. Reduced to supplicants, the MNR nationalists sought salvation from their bête noire, the Yankee imperialists—once excoriated for their sordid history of support for the ancien régime and implacable opposition to resource nationalism. In October 1953, President Paz Estenssoro penned a letter to President Dwight Eisenhower pleading the case for economic assistance and pledging obeisance: "In this circumstance I direct myself to Your Excellency, to ask that . . . food and other essential articles . . . be urgently considered. . . . This is a case of giving aid to a people sincerely engaged in improving the democratic institutions peculiar to the free world. . . . [The Bolivian people also declare] solidarity with the principles of Mutual Security which regulate the nations of the Western Hemisphere."[40]

The U.S. government, busy concocting stratagems for the overthrow of nationalist governments in Iran and Guatemala, opted to bail out the Bolivian revolution to preclude its collapse into chaos. Strategic concerns regarding the breakdown of the National Revolution and its effects on regional stability influenced the North American decision to provide financial aid, food imports, and technical assistance to mitigate the crisis and avert the collapse of the MNR regime. In November 1953, the United States announced it would provide $9 million in food to aid the beleaguered revolution, the highest per capita rate of food aid in the world. By 1958, U.S. financial assistance accounted for a third of the Bolivian budget.[41]

The aid and assistance came with strings attached. The MNR was forced to accede to the Hull Doctrine of "prompt, adequate and effective compensation"—a highly unpopular measure earlier contested by Bolivian nationalists as an infringement of national sovereignty—and agree to compensate the Tin Barons and the American stockholders of the Patiño mines.[42] As a quid pro quo, the United States agreed to purchase Bolivian tin for an initial year, although it was later extended until 1957.

An additional grant of $3 million in food followed the Bolivian quid pro quo: in March 1954, the MNR voted "to eradicate the danger which the subversive activities of international communism pose for the American States" at the Ninth International Conference of the Organization of American States at Caracas.[43] The "Caracas Declaration" was a masterful diplomatic stroke by Secretary of State John Foster Dulles. The OAS voted to reiterate the Monroe Doctrine—with a subtle twist by Dulles. Whereas in 1823 President Monroe proclaimed the New World off limits to intervention from the Old World, Dulles broadened the doctrine to include the intervention of Old World ideologies. In a Cold War touch, Dulles conflated nationalism with communism. The United States previously conflated nationalism with fascism to smear the Villarroel-MNR regime, debilitating the fledgling revolution (1943–1946) and abetting a counterrevolution. The MNR now supported the overthrow of Guatemala's attempt to regain sovereignty of its land and economy.

While the OAS was in session, CIA preparations were underway for the overthrow of Jacobo Árbenz, the democratically elected president of Guatemala who intended to expropriate plantations and nationalize the railroad, electrical, and port facilities owned by the United Fruit Company. On the board of directors were Secretary of State John Foster Dulles and his brother Alan Dulles, the Director of the CIA: a deadly combination. When the Guatemalan foreign minister addressed the OAS and decried the impending overthrow of his country for attempting "to put an end to feudalism, colonialism, and the unjust exploitation of its poorest citizens," the words could have been written by the MNR summarizing the objectives of the National Revolution.[44] Among the co-signers at Caracas voting "to take the necessary measures to protect their political independence against the intervention of international communism" were foreign ministers representing seven of the most infamous dictatorships in the hemisphere.[45] The United States then invaded and averted a social revolution in Guatemala. The horrific results included ethnocide of the indigenous populace, death squads supported by the United States, and a diaspora to safety in the Colossus of the North.

The MNR kowtowed to North American hegemony, compromised its principles, condoned the overthrow of the Árbenz regime, and betrayed a kindred revolution at Caracas to ensure the continuation of U.S. financial aid.[46] In the throes of a social revolution, the MNR was now ensnared in a deadly embrace that would eventuate in the undoing of the National Revolution. President Paz Estenssoro set the stage for the denouement when he resuscitated the military institution, acquiesced to North American suzerainty at Caracas, and formed the Control Politico. He would next surrender Bolivian economic sovereignty.

The Petroleum Code

The Petroleum Code decreed by President Paz in 1955 was a prelude to the United States takeover of the Bolivian economy. The document contravened the victory of President Toro's expropriation of Standard Oil in 1937 and capitulated to the Hull Doctrine regarding compensation to the Standard Oil behemoth. The Petroleum Code rescinded a provision in Bolivian law for retention of national reserves and assessed royalties at 11 percent of the value of production, set a tax rate of 30 percent of *net profits*, included a depletion allowance of 27 percent of the total value of production as tax exempt, specified exemptions from all other taxes (including dividends) for the duration of the contract, and in the event of a change in Bolivian law guaranteed the previous contract. Article 100 of the code declared the tax provisions as "independent and autonomous of the general fiscal system of the Nation."[47]

The Bolivian state oil and gas entity *Yacimientos Petrolíferos Fiscales Bolivianos* (YPFB) had been a success, increasing production by 500 percent in three years (1952–1955) and refining gasoline and diesel fuel. The Petroleum Code slashed YPFB's budget and confined its operation to a small zone in southeast Santa Cruz Department where the oil reserves dwindled and production declined. U.S. oil companies successfully exploited a wide expanse of the zone. The Shell Oil Company (a U.S. subsidiary of Royal Dutch Shell) received a contract for some 2 million hectares and Gulf Oil (a U.S. corporation) signed a contract for 2 million hectares—together with another million and a half hectares within the YPFB zone.[48] Within a decade, the revenue of Gulf Oil mushroomed to nearly 10 times the Bolivian national income and 100 times the income from COMIBOL.[49]

The Monetary Stabilization Plan

U.S. aid and assistance to Bolivia, totaling over $50 million between 1952 and 1955, averted the collapse of the National Revolution. Nevertheless, with foreign reserves depleted to $2,000,000, Paz Estenssoro's nearly bankrupt government was on the verge of a collapse. Foreign exchange earnings had declined because of the drop in the price of tin; increased food consumption and the disruption in the countryside led to food shortages in the cities; government revenue was insufficient to purchase and import foodstuffs; and inflation was rampant.[50] An American advisory team led by George Jackson Eder, a strict monetarist, was dispatched to access the situation and provide a remedy.

Eder functioned as Executive Director of a newly created National Monetary Stabilization Council and together with the U.S. Embassy controlled Bolivian appointments to the Council and administered the economy. Eder's diagnosis of the MNR's malady was straightforward: "There were no doubts in my mind about the prime cause of the inflation—briefly, spending by the government and government enterprises in excess of their means, with deficits financed by the Central Bank through the issuance of additional paper currency." He proposed transition to a free market economy. "The obvious remedy for this situation was simple, but, of course, it meant the repudiation, at least tacitly, of virtually everything that the Revolutionary Government had done over the previous four years."[51]

The 50-point Monetary Stabilization Plan, drawn up by Eder in the last year of the Paz administration—supported by an initial $25 million in loans and grants from the United States and the International Monetary Fund (IMF)—called for the reduction of government expenditures, elimination of state subsidies, including those to pulperías, price controls, an increase in taxes, tariffs, and bank reserves, a uniform exchange rate, and, after initial cost of living increases, a freeze in workers' wages.[52] The continuation of U.S. aid was contingent on implementation of Eder's plan that also required financial compensation to the Tin Barons for their expropriated mines.[53] Although the Stabilization Plan offered a respite from the collapse of the National Revolution, it portended ill for its future.

In an early critique of the Stabilization Plan, Laurence Whitehead defined the relationship between the United States and Bolivia as neocolonialism: "A situation, in other words, closely resembling colonial rule in its allocation of power, but quite different in its allocation of formal responsibility—quite different, we might say, in its 'transparency'."[54] Subsequent discussions of the topic by North American scholars note the collusion of the MNR right-wing with U.S. diplomats in the imposition of the Stabilization and Triangular plans. Their objectives included breaking the power of the MNR leftists (Juan Lechín, Germán Butrón) and the militant mine and factory unions; layoffs and reduction of miners' wages and benefits; promotion of private investment; subversion of foreign (Soviet and Czech) offers of financial aid for construction of tin and antimony smelters, road and railway modernization; and averting the specter of another Cuba.[55]

Implementation of the Stabilization Plan began in 1956 following the election of MNR President Hernán Siles Zuazo and Vice President Ñuflo Chávez Ortíz. Eder minced no words in his assessment of the task at hand:

> It was the first time I had ever attempted to borrow money on behalf of a borrower whose record was a history of bad faith and broken promises and

whose credit, if any, must be based solely on the hope that a single man, President Hernán Siles Zuazo, not immune to bullets, would have the courage and ability to impose standards of good faith and responsibility on what was perhaps the most corrupt, incompetent, and opportunistic group of politicians that had ever ruled the destinies of the nation.[56]

Winners and Losers

Execution of the stabilization plan deepened the divide among the middle class, peasant, and worker sectors within the National Revolution. Although rescued from economic ruin, the MNR surrendered the nation's economic sovereignty to the United States.[57] The Tin Barons were replaced by the U.S. Agency for International Development (USAID). An early study of U.S. aid to the Bolivian revolution found, "Political considerations obviously weighed more heavily on policy than economic planning, for the U.S. was concerned with keeping non-Communist Marxists in power to prevent the rise of a Communist government."[58] But a recent study argues that combating resource nationalism, re-privatization of oil and tin industries, taming the leftist mine workers' union, and maintaining MNR moderates in power were the primary concerns of U.S. policy rather than prevention of a communist government.[59]

Critical to an assessment of the strategy employed by President Siles (supported by U.S. aid, assistance, and direction) to enforce the stabilization measures is Laurence Whitehead's perception that neocolonialism offers the metropolitan power advantages of both flexibility and opaqueness "because it can so often transmute a conflict between metropolis and colony into a domestic dispute among the dominated."[60] The Stabilization Plan was contingent on a political agenda that shattered the MNR multigroup alliance: a middle-class (creole-mestizo) sector of merchants, teachers, bank workers, journalists, attorneys, and government bureaucrats at national, provincial, and municipal offices; an indigenous proletarian sector of miners, oil field roustabouts, railroad, factory, and construction workers; and an indigenous sector of peasants and small farmers.

There would be fewer winners than losers within this diverse and increasingly discordant assemblage. The monetary stabilization measures adversely affected those entities and groups previously privileged by the differential exchange rate system.[61] Miners who had profitably resold their subsidized *pulpería* purchases on the black market—sugar at 24 times cost, meat at 33 times cost, rice at 38 times cost, flour at 85 times cost—were particularly hard hit by the imposition of stabilization controls, as was the clique of Movimientista insiders who would later shift their black market profiteering to other sources of lucre.[62]

As the consequences of Eder's plan became obvious, the MNR sectoral alliance began to break down, leading to factional conflicts. Adherents of the plan led by Hernán Siles, Víctor Paz, Wálter Guevara Arze, and José Quadros Quiroga were opposed by Juan Lechín and Ñuflo Chávez who represented the indigenous miner and peasant sectors. The COB *co-gobierno* of workers and peasants, hostile to Eder's free enterprise agenda, was to be reined in and their leftist leaders brought to heel. Defiant and divided, the COB voted (439 to 260) to strike. The result was tumultuous. President Siles claimed communists and Falangistas instigated the strike and threatened a hunger strike and/or resignation if the COB followed through with its strike. Vice President Ñuflo Chávez resigned and Wálter Guevara Arze relinquished his position as Minister of Foreign Affairs. The mining bloc splintered into feuding factions. Finally, the weakened COB (split between a miners' faction led by Lechín and a railway and factory workers faction) called off the strike.

Yet violent confrontations ensued. MNR *commandos* together with militia from Huanuni—opposed by dynamite-wielding miners from Colquiri—attacked delegates en route to a FSTMB meeting at Siglo XX.[63] Rifts opened between workers inside the mineshafts and those working outside the mines at Siglo XX (although both factions experienced a drastic drop in their standard of living with the end of the pulpería subsidy). Miners at Huanuni and Colquiri, who had benefitted less from the pulpería bonanza, were less affected. Sectarian Trotskyist and Stalinist labor militants rejected the stabilization mandate. Resistance to the austerity measures snowballed (220 labor strikes in 1956; 310 in 1957; 1,570 in 1958; 1,272 in 1959), exacerbating strife within the MNR sectoral coalition. Teachers and government workers were also hard hit by inflation. Reduction of government revenue from declining tin prices resulted in stagnant wages, an exodus of skilled workers seeking higher wages outside the country, and a decline in bureaucratic efficiency.[64]

President Siles, the point man for implementation of the stabilization dictates, saved the National Revolution from economic collapse, but sowed the seeds of its eventual downfall. The manipulation of factional conflicts to weaken opposition to his mandate resulted in the ruinous fracturing of the MNR sectoral coalition and the demise of co-gobierno. Food from the United States to avert famine in Bolivia's cities was a mixed blessing: the urban population, miners, and black market speculators enjoyed the benefits of subsidized food imports, while others, such as workers in the milling industry, suffered. Moreover, U.S. food aid inhibited economic diversification and stifled domestic production.[65] The peasantry benefited from the freedom to market their crops at higher prices resulting from food shortages and the disruption of the hacienda distribution system. But this was to change with the advent of the Stabilization Plan as U.S. policy makers sought to undermine the latent power of the Indian sindicatos, and USAID technocrats worked to shift the agricultural locus of the country away from the Andean highlands, toward the lowlands of the *Oriente*.

The MNR's 1956 electoral victory (83 percent of the vote) was a gift from the newly enfranchised Indians laboring in mines, factories, and fields. But the Stabilization Plan was not contrived to benefit the indigenous proletarian and peasant masses. The subaltern peasants were manipulated by MNR creole-mestizos and their leaders co-opted or marginalized. Unable to unite in a nationwide organization, the indigenous majority failed to capitalize on the historic opportunity to seize power and create an autonomous destiny. Despite overwhelming numerical superiority, the native people still remained under the dominion of creole-mestizo overlords: unable to achieve political agency, they voted for the MNR as an act of eternal gratitude to the MNR elites and their revolution. In a telling indication of the MNR's lack of commitment to the indigenous majority, President Siles slashed funding for the Ministry of Peasant Affairs in 1957 from 8.5 to 3.6 percent of the national budget.[66]

The Agrarian Sector

President Siles' divide and conquer strategy, devised to overcome proletarian resistance to Eder's stabilization measures, was also used to fragment the agrarian sector of the COB. Paz's administration had wrested command of the Quillacollo Central from Sinforoso Rivas, rendering the sindiatos of the Cochabamba Valle Bajo obedient to the MNR. Rivas's replacement, Alejandro Galarza, immediately pledged the support of the Central to Siles' stabilization plan. But José Rojas and the agrarian revolutionaries of the Ucureña Central in the Valle Alto were yet another matter. Siles accordingly focused on bolstering urban resistance to the agrarian revolutionaries. Right-wing Movimientistas were appointed departmental prefects (who commanded the carabineros), provincial subprefects and local MNR commandos given control of town militias, compliant divisional army officers posted, and a propaganda campaign mounted against autonomous indigenous revolutionaries. This resulted in the bureaucratization and division of the party into a multitude of competing sectors. While not without short-term success, the strategy was ultimately disastrous.

The MNR scheme to constrain the Cochabamba peasant movement centered at Cliza, a town that epitomized the rift between town and country. Populated by creole-mestizo businessmen, refugee landlords, petty bureaucrats, artisans, shopkeepers, and cholos, Cliza was, "a town of nimble-fingered persons with an art for appropriating articles that do not always belong to them. The villagers are *muy vivo*—picaresque characters who always manage to gain the advantage over a person from any less fortunate place. It is apparently true—certainly often repeated—that some thirty years ago a townsman purloined the hat of President Salamanca while he was making a speech in Cliza."[67] The town is also known for the quality and quantity of chicha (maize beer) consumed at the Wednesday and Saturday market, attracting peasants as well as city folk from Cochabamba.

An occasional stream known as the Rio Retama divides Cliza from the ranchería of Ucureña: the epicenter of revolutionary agrarian syndicalism. The Ucureña sindicato antedated the revolution by 15 years, and Ucureña was chosen as the emblematic site for proclamation of the Agrarian Reform Decree of 2 August 1953. The densely populated Valle Alto surrounding Cliza and Ucureña was a rural anomaly because of its pronounced pattern of subdivided landholdings held by vecinos and Indians as well. The division and sale of hacienda land that began in the nineteenth century made for a variegated populace of hacendados,

FIGURE 7.2 Ucureña Campesino Central
Source: Photo by author

colonos, small farmers, and renters. The Ucureña chieftain, appealed to the poorest campesinos, as José Rojas reckoned: "The *piqueros* [small peasant landholders] were satisfied people . . . [those] who wanted to become organized now were colonos who had no land."[68]

With the revolution came the threat to Cliceño domination of the peasantry— a dramatic reversal with the perquisites of power now gravitating to the Ucureña Central as the Rojas organization began to incorporate local officials in a regional network of loyal sindicatos rooted in the Cochabamba valleys.[69] Control of the tax on chicha (some 4,900 bottles quaffed per day in Cliza) supported the Ucureña Central.[70] Sale of the brew (advertised by white flags flying from cane poles atop purveyors' houses) constitutes a significant cottage industry in the Cochabamba Department where 58,000,000 bottles were consumed per annum. "Enough to fill more than half the water in the Laguna de Alalay."[71]

The onerous tax was a source of widespread bitterness during the Old Regime. Indian women on haciendas (colonas) spent untold hours daily masticating kernels of corn (*muko*) to be spat into jars for fermentation. Villagers who failed to pay the chicha tax were forced to pawn their valuables. During the 1947 Ayopaya Rebellion, colonos stormed the offices of tax collectors and retrieved personal items confiscated for failure to pay the chicha tax.[72] The tax survived the revolution and collection remained an invaluable source of government revenue. As the Cliza cacique Miguel Veizaga recalled in a conversation with the author, "The campesinos hated the townspeople, but not all, only a few: the authorities. They took away clothes. They took away earings and womens' jewelry. The *visitador* [collector] of the chicha tax had his employees. Because the campesinos weren't able to pay easily they pawned *polleras* [skirts], a *manta* [shawl], whatever thing. They gave him a prize as a guarantee, then after thirty days or two months, when the term was over, he would grab everything."[73]

The campaign by President Siles and the MNR right-wing against the Ucureña agrarian revolutionaries featured a propaganda attack by journalists in the urban newspapers. "The situation in the Cochabamba valley could not be worse, since certain 'dirigentes' have made a daily practice of bullying, imposing their dictatorship to the peasantry. . . . Thus, in Tarata, Punata and Arani there are the lords and masters of pitch-fork and knife, the 'interventors' appointed by [José] Rojas and [Salvador] Vásquez], who by force of arms impose their will on the peasantry."[74] Editorial diatribes against the agrarian revolutionaries avoided the underlying causes of colono land seizures, choosing instead to obfuscate the issue as a clash between loyal and disloyal peasant dirigentes. José Gordillo's perusal of the "rhetoric of the National Revolution" reveals a dual focus: demonization of the Ucureña Central as a hotbed of communist syndicalism, disloyal to the National Revolution, and a paternalistic glorification of the Indian during the bygone days of the Inca. An editorial from the Cochabamba daily *El Pueblo* is exemplary:

> It [Ucureña] has inculcated in the naïve and ignorant mentality of the Bolivian campesino, the idea that all extensive property corresponded to them in fact and right. . . . This fallacious prediction distorts the postulates of the Agrarian Reform. . . . When we spoke to them with frankness and clarity . . . stupor, doubt, and uncertainty was noted in the campesino physiognomy, which demonstrates that the demagogic propaganda had changed the autochthonous mentality, who from the paternal Inca era practiced the virtues of work, truth, discipline and lived by following moral and legal norms.[75]

Agrarian Reform Versus Agrarian Revolution

The MNR's assault against indigenous revolutionaries transcended rhetorical volleys in the press. The Ucureña colonos remained steadfast in opposition to an agrarian reform that allowed hacendados to retain ownership of usurped lands through bribery and chicanery. In his memoir, *Los hombres de la revolución*, Sinforoso Rivas recalls a telling example of the politics and pitfalls of hacienda expropriation. Ousted from leadership of the Quillacollo Central during the Paz Estenssoro presidency, Rivas was given a sinecure at the National Agrarian Reform Council (*Consejo Nacional de Reforma Agraria*: CNRA). The position was short-lived. Unknown to Rivas, among the latifundia he approved for expropriation in Quillacollo Province (Cochabamba Department) was the Hacienda Mallcochapi, the property of President Hernán Siles' mother. Rivas was summarily removed from the CNRA by the outraged president. Other prominent Movimientistas, including Edmundo

Nogales, Vicente Álvarez Plata, and Roberto Pérez Patón, were accused of sheltering their haciendas from expropriation.[76]

The selection of army Colonel Moreira Mostajo as prefect reinforced the MNR's bellicose position toward governance of Cochabamba Department. The choice of a militant from the MNR Departmental Command, Hugo Yañez Barrero, as Alcalde of Cliza without the consultation of the Ucureña Central was taken as a provocation. On 5 October 1957, during the alcalde's inauguration fiesta in Cliza, 400 Ucureños shouting "Viva Ñuflo Chávez" attacked the town, hurling dynamite and sparking a firefight with the Cliceños.[77]

An official visitation by the MNR right-wing ministers of government and peasant affairs, José Quadros Quiroga and Vicente Álvarez Plata, did little to assuage the Ucureña revolutionaries. Quadros Quiroga incensed the Ucureña colonos when he stated in a speech at Cliza that the MNR Departmental Command had selected their alcalde "to guarantee the security of the inhabitants of the pueblo of Cliza and of all those *owners of small and medium-sized land*" who are engaged in agricultural work (emphasis added).[78] The reactionary Rural Society and Pro-Cochabamba Committee continued their harangues against the agrarian revolutionaries with the familiar arguments that land belonged to those who owned it and would be defended against "communist" agitators bent on illegal seizure.

To the chagrin of the Cochabamba prefect, the Ucureña militia routed a detachment of carabineros sent to assert government control, suggesting that the balance of power had tilted toward the colonos of the Valle Alto. Further complicating matters, the Ucureña Central and the Catavi Miners' Sindicato announced a "Worker-Peasant Pact of Alliance." Every move by the MNR authorities against the Ucureña revolutionaries incited more resistance. Siles' strategy to divide and conquer the proletarian and peasant sectors of the leftist COB had united the Ucureña peasants and Oruro miners. Their Pact of Alliance was a milestone for the revolutionary peasant and miner sectors whose sindicato militias possessed numerical superiority over the emasculated armed forces.[79]

Caciquismo

The responsibilities of the sindicato secretary general included service as a broker between ex-colonos and the MNR hierarchy. These asymmetrical relationships, referred to as patron–client relationships, ascend from the local level to clients at a higher level within the government hierarchy.[80] In a seminal essay on the topic of peasant brokerage, the anthropologist Eric Wolf noted the complexity of the power broker's position, "since Janus-like, they face in two directions at once. They must serve some of the interests of groups operating on both the community and the national level, and they must cope with the conflicts raised by the collision of these interests."[81] The sindicato replicated functions common to pre-revolutionary indigenous society; thus, the secretary general assumed the role of the hacienda mayordomo when overseeing work (*faena*) on ayllu community property.[82] The dirigente level of sindicato leadership, based on patronage and local control by the secretary general, was in some instances superseded by power brokers (caciques/caudillos) at the provincial, departmental, and national levels.

National politics could hardly avoid an armed, organized, and enfranchised peasantry. Dirigentes controlled local sindicatos and a handful of *caciques* extended their influence beyond the local level to a wider geographical region in the areas of greatest demographic concentration: the Provinces of Quillacollo, Jordan and Punata in the Cochabamba valleys, Omasuyos Province in La Paz Department, and Charcas Province in Potosí Department. Competition for hegemony in these areas was marked by endemic violence as armed force became the arbiter of syndical politics. Because the interests of the sindicto members are not necessarily those of their leader, the cacique phenomenon (caciquismo) has been considered detrimental to peasant movements: "it is clearer that José Rojas the peasant leader in Ucureña, and Narcisco Torrico (who took over San Pedro de Buenavista) benefited [more] personally from these activities than the peasantry as a whole benefited from them in other than an ephemeral way."[83] But this argument fails to consider that these caciques were leading an agrarian revolution whose objective was "Tierra y Libertad" for their followers and, as is generally the case with political leaders, Rojas profited materially from his position. Yet to focus on prebendalismo is to ignore the dynamics of the social revolution inspired and led by caciques in Cochabamba, Potosí, and La Paz Departments.

Cochabamba Department

José Rojas was profoundly influenced by the PIRista militant and teacher Juan Guerra who assisted in the genesis of what was to become the Ucureña sindicato. Guerra infused Rojas with a sense of class consciousness and the necessity for proselytization beyond the local confines of Ucureña.[84] Leading by example, José Rojas and the Ucureños expelled hacendados and seized land—taking what they wanted rather than waiting to take what they were given. Ucureña became the preponderant force in the regional Sindicato del Valle, composed of the rancherías of Ucureña, Ana Rancho, Kekoma, Rumi Rumi, Punata, Ansaldo, and Pili Coccha.[85] A firebrand who minced no words, José Rojas inspired and cajoled the timid and dispirited to fear not, seize the moment, and make the revolution. Power was no longer the monopoly of the *gente decente*. It now rested with those peasants willing to organize themselves and seize the land, rather than begging for a pittance under an agrarian reform law contrived by creole-mestizos.

The Mexican revolutionary most comparable to José Rojas was Emiliano Zapata, the caudillo of Morelos whose influence extended into the neighboring states of Guerrero, Puebla and the southern lands of the Federal District. As with José Rojas, "in the mind of the middle-class reformers . . . Zapata's major crime, [was] not simply to have been born a country hick, but to have endangered the private property upon which their world rested."[86] Zapata had little patience for the bigwigs in Mexico City, dramatically evidenced in his response to President Francisco Madero's order to disband his troops. In John Womack's words:

> Zapata stood up and, carrying his carbine, walked over to where Madero sat. He pointed at the gold watch chain Madero sported on his vest. "Look Señor Madero," he said, "if I take advantage of the fact that I'm armed and take away your watch and keep it, and after a while we meet, both of us armed the same, would you have the right to demand that I give it back?" Certainly Madero told him; he would even ask for an indemnity. "Well," Zapata concluded, "that's exactly what has happened to us in Morelos, where a few planters have taken over by force the villages' lands. My soldiers—the armed farmers and all the people in the villages—demand that I tell you, with full respect, that they want the restitution of their lands to be got underway right now."[87]

The differences between the two agrarian leaders are noteworthy. Rojas was a peasant expelled from his plot by vengeful landlords and forced to flee to northern Argentina. Zapata's father was a peasant, but Emiliano was orphaned at 15 and never worked on a hacienda. Imbued with an entrepreneurial bent, business was his calling: a horse trainer, trader, and muleteer whose travels far beyond Morelos set him apart from his parochial campesino compatriots. Unlike José Rojas, who advocated outright hacienda expropriation with no compensation, Zapata the businessman respected the right of private property. There was to be no land seizure without payment. His Plan de Ayala proposed the expropriation of but one-third of hacienda lands and then only after prior indemnification. Haciendas and Indian villages would coexist in Zapata's agrarian world.[88]

The Zapatistas offered cash payments to entice recruits to the revolutionary cause and sold protection to hacendados to avoid destruction of their estates. José Rojas would brook no bargain with hacendados, nor would he countenance the coexistence of haciendas and Indian villages, or pay for recruits: the incentive was syndical organization, the seizure of haciendas, and distribution of land to those who worked it. Payment for land stolen from Indians was incomprehensible to Rojas and the Ucureña revolutionaries. The tentacles of agrarian revolution spread from epicenters, home to Rojas and Zapata, to distant haciendas and villages far beyond.[89]

Both men came of age in a time of heightened tensions between indigenous communities and neighboring haciendas. The agrarian revolutions began in areas of traditional discontent, noteworthy for their histories of brutal government repression.[90] Zapata demanded that the government in Mexico City accede to the principles of the Plan of Ayala. His steadfast refusal to compromise and subsequent assassination have enshrined him as the iconic symbol of the Mexican Revolution. But José Rojas chose to be co-opted: twice serving as Minister of Peasant Affairs, chauffeured about while doing the bidding of the MNR elite, occasionally dispatching peasant militias to suppress strikes by unruly mine workers.

Northern Potosí Department

Chayanta and Bustillo provinces in northern Potosí Department were home to the largest number of Aymara ayllu communities remaining in the Andean highlands. The region is a mixture of high plateaus (puna) and temperate valleys that provide the communities access to a wide range of crops, including fruits, wheat,

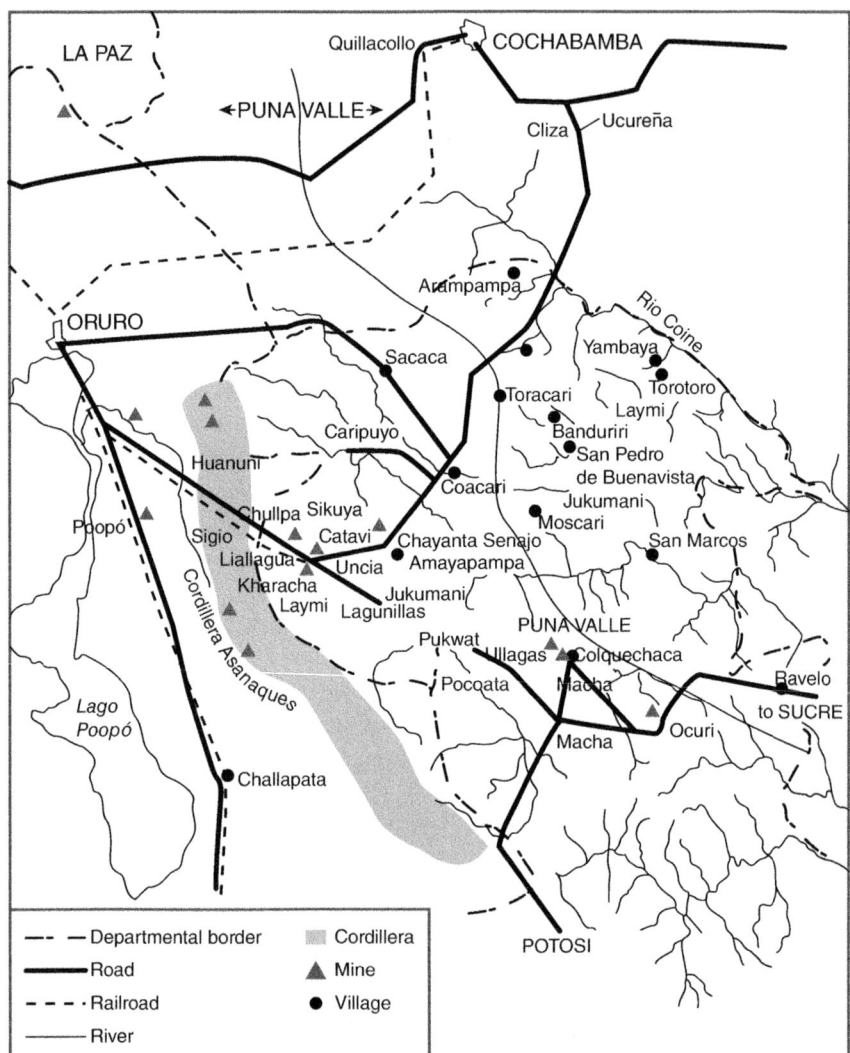

MAP 7.1 Northern Potosí

Source: Courtesy of Cambridge University Press. Olivia Harris, "Sources and Meanings of Money: Beyond the Market Paradigm in an Ayllu in Northern Potosi," in Brooke Larson and Olivia Harris, eds., *Ethnicity and Migration in the Andes*, 1995, 298.

maize, and vegetables at lower elevations. Isolated ayllu communities in the remote highlands of the puna survived the hacienda encroachments that devastated ayllu landholdings in the fertile riverine valleys. After the 1953 Agrarian Reform decree, hacendados laid claim to virtually all lands of the valley ayllus.[91]

Northern Potosí was fabled for its silver mines in the colonial period, and in the twentieth century renowned for the tin deposits of the Catavi-Siglo XX mining complex that yielded a fortune for the "Tin King" Simón Patiño and misery for the Indian miners drawn into the shafts to exchange their labor for a pittance. Primitive working conditions often led to injury and silicosis ("Black Lung" disease). Less predictable were the exigencies of the world metals market and boom-bust cycles of layoffs, labor agitation, strikes, repression, and government massacres.

The mines were home to the most class-conscious and combative labor movement in South America, where the grim dialectic of strikes and draconian government responses—massacres of miners at Uncia in 1923, Catavi in 1942, Siglo XX in 1949—underscored the violent relationship of mine workers to those who owned the means of production.[92] Militants from the POR, PIR, and MNR spearheaded union organization and the miners played a crucial role in the defeat of the Old Order during the 1952 MNR insurrections in La Paz and Oruro. Under the leadership of Juan Lechín, the mine worker sindicatos were a powerful sector in the COB; their militias provided a counterpoise to counter-revolutionaries, most notably the Falangistas who found themselves awash in a social revolution loathsome to the party's racist dogma of white supremacy. Indians returning from the mines brought a Marxist class perspective to their communities. This influence was strongest in, but not exclusive to, Cochabamba Department where demographic pressure in the valleys provided the impetus for long-term work in the mines; whereas the comunarios of northern Potosí were drawn to the nearby mines, generally for short-term work when pressured by necessity.[93]

The tin boom at the turn of the twentieth century and the development of mines near Llallagua incentivized regional hacienda expansion to meet demand for pulpería foodstuffs. Research in the vicinity of Toracari, a town nestled in a valley northeast of the municipality of before San Pedro de Buena Vista, reveals a complex land tenure pattern resulting from hacienda encroachment on ayllu communities.[94] The usurpation of comunario lands followed a regional form of loan sharking by crafty landowners. A peasant in need of cash could secure a loan (*prenda*) with land as collateral. If the loan was not repaid on time, the land became the property of the hacendado and the comunario obliged to work as a sharecropper on what was once his land. Sharecropping in northern Potosí was more commonplace than in other highland regions. The sharecropping relationship (a 50–50 division between peasant and patrón), together with the continued presence of ayllu communities and the absence of pongueaje on some haciendas, resulted in a less exploitative system than elsewhere.[95] Interspersed within the ayllus were the intermittent fields held by hacendado interlopers—constant reminders of a corrupt bargain—whose existence festered resentment among comunarios. The colonato in northern Potosí entailed the obligations common to the highlands: ponguaeje, mitanaje, animal herding and shepherding, wood gathering, preparation of chicha, and work on construction projects.

The history of the region is one of endless resistance to injustice and abuse of authority. Northern Potosí was the epicenter of the 1780 rebellion, considered by historians as the greatest challenge to colonial rule since the Spanish conquest. The sieges of Cuzco by Tupac Amaru and of La Paz by Tupac Katari and Bartolina Sisa are well known, but there was a third locus of rebellion in northern Potosí led by Tomás Katari and his brothers Dámaso and Nicolás. Indigenous resistance to royal and clerical abuses began with a litany of legal appeals at ascending levels of the colonial bureaucracy from the Audencia of Charcas to the Viceroyalty of the Rio de la Plata in Buenos Aires. Only after pursuing legal resolution of his entreaties (traveling by foot to the distant Audencia in Sucre and Viceroyalty in Buenos Aires), his patience exhausted, did Tomás Katari's frustration eventuate in rebellion.

Indians from Chayanta served under Zarate "El Temible Willka," the fabled Indian leader who joined the forces in the 1899 civil war. As Ramiro Condarco Morales points out in a classic history of the rebellion, Willka sought a drastic reordering of the country and hence ordered "fincas converted to communities", "declared a war of elimination against 'whites' and 'mestizos'", proclaimed that government "authorities should be Indians", and mandated the "universal imposition of *bayeta* (homespun) clothes" to be worn by townspeople.[96]

In 1927, a massive massive rebellion swept the province of Chayanta. A combined force of 5,000 colonos and comunarios attacked the hacienda of Don Julio Berdeja on 1 August, burned buildings, captured Don Julio, and cannibalized his body before burning his corpse. The deed that elicited such ritualized hatred is unimaginable: infantry troops arrived to find "a mountain of burned bones and pieces of dispersed meat." The government response was even more brutal. "Hundreds of Indians were assassinated, their fields burned, the women violated without consideration of age."[97] Twenty years after the Chayanta rebellion, during the Sexenio years of repression, neighboring Charcas Province was the scene of another rebellion. Thousands of Indians led by dynamite-wielding miners from Llallagua sent a tremor of fear throughout the region.[98] During the National Revolution, the vecinos of San Pedro de Buena Vista and the neighboring pueblos of Moscari and Toracari were recurrently assaulted by indigenous insurgents.

San Pedro de Buena Vista

San Pedro de Buena Vista is the largest town in northern Potosí and the seat of provincial governance for Charcas Province. Its origins are traced to the policy of *reducciones*, the forced resettlement instituted in the sixteenth century by the Spanish Viceroy Francisco de Toledo to centralize control of the Andean peoples, facilitating imperial levies of mine labor (*mita*) and tribute. "A strong factor motivating Indians to participate in the mita was the monetization of tribute. To earn that coin, Indians would be forced to labor for wages . . . part of a more thoroughgoing program to 'civilize' Indians . . . so that they might pull themselves up by their own (store bought) bootstraps into the capitalist world. They were to learn, in other words, how to conduct social relations and construct social position and obedience to the laws of god and king through the medium of money."[99]

The liberal "reforms" of the late nineteenth century enacted to encourage capitalism and transform comunarios into independent farmers through the forced sale of ayllu lands, spurred ayllu usurpations, and increased tensions between Indians and hacendados.[100] San Pedro de Buena Vista remained a creole-mestizo enclave of absentee landlords, merchants, petty bureaucrats, and clergy. True to its history, San Pedro was the most abusive pueblo in the region.[101] Recognition of the Indian as a legitimate member of society, including the legal rights of citizenship and union organization (to facilitate implementation of the agrarian reform law), was ill received in San Pedro. Implacably hostile to the Indian masses, the vecinos found themselves subsumed in a social revolution amidst a subaltern people committed to combating their domination.

Checkered with ayllus and haciendas, northern Potosí is geographically an extension of the Cochabamba serranía. Syndical organization among the ayllu comunarios, in contradistinction to the radical agitation of the miners, was slow to develop in the remote Potosí highlands. The hacendados, vecinos, and right-sector MNR administrators in the valleys were quick to co-opt syndicalism and turn the agrarian reform to their advantage. Thus, for the comunarios of the puna, the agrarian reform was but another creole-mestizo liberal attack aimed at the heart of the ayllu itself. The comunarios were beset yet again with an attempt to destroy their communal existence and remake them in the alien image of creole-mestizos.[102]

The revolutionary violence that was to engulf San Pedro and surrounding towns in northern Potosí should not obscure the non-violent legal pursuit of indigenous land revendication through the agrarian reform process. In northern Potosí, as elsewhere, the majority of peasants demonstrated a centuries-old adherence to the legal conventions of creole-mestizo rule before embarking on the road less traveled, to violence and rebellion. The problematics of law and justice, reform and revolution, for a subaltern people are nicely summarized by the historian Steve Stern: "to the extent that reliance on a juridical system becomes a dominant strategy of protection for an oppressed class, or social group, it may undermine the possibility of organizing a more ambitious assault aimed at toppling the exploitive structure itself. When this happens, a functioning system of justice contributes to the hegemony of the ruling class."[103]

Caciquismo in Northern Potosí

The indigenous assault on the regional power structure in northern Potosí, precipitated by the agrarian reform process, was incited by ex-miner Narciso Torrico. Together with his two brothers, Narciso had traveled from Cochabamba to work in the mines during the Sexenio. Radicalized by the miners' struggle, Torrico became a militant Movimientista. He carried his militancy with him when he departed the mines for the Potosí countryside. At the canton of Choroma (Charcas Province) in the heights above San Pedro de Buena Vista—assisted by sindicato revolutionaries from the Ucureña Central—Narciso Torrico organized the *Federación Campesina del Norte de Potosí* (Peasant Federation of Northern Potosí). The Choroma Central included peasants as well as ex-miners, waiters, and "resentful cholos" (*cholos resentidos*) from San Pedro de Buena Vista.[104] Torrico's violent opposition to the hacendados, vecinos, and recalcitrant officials obstructing implementation of the agrarian reform law threatened creole-mestizo suzerainty throughout Charcas, Bernardino Bilbao, and Alonzo de Abáñez Provinces.[105]

In late April 1957, vecino vigilantes from Acacio, a small town to the north of San Pedro, captured Narciso Torrico. Freed by Indian partisans the following day, Torrico unleashed the fury of personal retribution. Militias under his command assaulted Acacio and the towns of Arampampa and Toracari to the northeast where they blockaded roads, levied taxes, administered beatings to vecinos, and seized hacendia lands and livestock for cash to purchase weapons at the tin mines.[106] Towns were sacked and local authorities, particularly the agrarian judges responsible for aiding and abetting hacendado subversion of the Agrarian Reform Law, replaced with sindicato representatives.[107]

The hacendados found support among vecinos in Potosí, Cochabamba, and Oruro Departments where the press sensationalized the conflict as a confrontation between gente decente and primitive "aborigines" given to bestial savagery. The Centro de Acción Charcas fed the press stories of "communist vandalism," "delinquents," and "pseudo-dirigentes" of the Choroma Federación Campesina.[108] The demonization of the indigenous dirigentes as mentally inferior, uncivilized, barbarous, and criminal miscreants was used to justify vecino retribution. Thus, the dirigente Carlos Condori was hanged in 1948 by vecinos because they believed he was a danger to "civilized citizens."[109]

Ironically, the bourgeois MNR reformers had decreed an Agrarian Reform Law to end the colonato, only to have hacendado oligarchs, government officials, army, carabinero, and police officers subvert the mandate. As elsewhere in the hinterland, the agrarian reform issue exacerbated the underlying conflict between Indians, hacendados, and vecinos. In late January 1958, the Minister of Peasant Affairs instructed the prefect of Cochabamba Department, Gabriel Arze Quiroga, to send a joint "commission" of Ucureña militia and army soldiers to "pacify" the conflict at San Pedro de Buena Vista. The prefect telegraphed his objections to the inclusion of a peasant contingent from Ucureña "because of the painful previous experiences in which they committed serious disorder and abused populations. I must state that such pacifying powers that would be conferred on Ucureña dirigentes would be in disagreement with a policy initiated to restrict powers to that Central and might lead to further complications." José Gordillo points out the bias evidenced in the prefect's remarks: the a priori assumption that peasants are the cause of the conflict (ignoring the "despicable role of the vecinos"), thereby creating the image of an unarmed village, besieged by Indians, and in need of assistance ("The idea of assistance is [unquestionably] linked to that of armed repression which must be carried out by regular forces and by the vecinos.")[110] The rule of the urban elite—whether during the Old Regime, under the military nationalists, or the nationalist revolutionaries—continued uninterrupted, the indigenous countryside ruled as a conquered domain of the creole-mestizo state.

On 28 January 1958, vecino vigilantes from San Pedro commanded by an MNR militant ambushed Narciso Torrico at the pueblo of Cuchira. In the ensuing firefight, the MNR militant was killed after throwing dynamite at Torrico, who died of wounds from the blast.[111] The Choroma Central survived Torrico's death and endured the opposition of the San Pedro vecinos. Newspapers inflamed urban public opinion with sensational press accounts of the cacique's death and castigated him for instigating a "wave of terror." Ignored were the underlying causes of the indigenous uprising and the violence of the creole-mestizos: "After having killed him the q'aras [creole-mestizos] cut off his head, his penis and his testicles, which his wife had been made to carry to San Pedro, where they hung him in the church tower, for all the people to see; he was hanged for a long time."[112]

The ritualized emasculation and decapitation of Torrico, the cruel degradation of his widow forced to carry her husband's severed head in a penitential trek to San Pedro de Buena Vista—where the cacique's head was kicked about the plaza in a grotesque football pantomime—together with the vengeful mutilation and display of other desecrated Indian bodies in the town church, symbolized the reassertion of vecino domination. This spectacular display of violence echoes the earlier fate of the colonial cacique Tomás Katari, condemned by Spanish overlords to be drawn, quartered and beheaded, as an example of the perils of resistance.[113]

The hidden history of this town, with its colonial plaza and church nestled in a valley along the Rio San Pedro, lies dormant. Indians had invaded San Pedro de Buena Vista nearly two centuries before Narciso Torrico's decapitated and castrated corpse provided a macabre spectacle for onlookers. It was the second week of Lent, March 1780, when vecinos were overwhelmed in a massive assault on the town from the surrounding highlands. The vecinos retreated to safety behind the walls of the church, but alas, the Indians stormed the church and killed everyone. "The killing of hundreds of people inside the church was accompanied by symbolic gestures that underscored the radical rejection of what the church represented both spiritually and politically." Amidst the carnage, "The Indians made a point of using *vasos sagrados* (holy vessels) for their libation of chicha; destroyed and profaned sacred images; made banners and clothes out of the clergy vestments; 'began to dance the dances of carnival [*Carnestolendas*] over that pond of blood in which the beheaded corpses swam'; and then looted silver cups and other objects."[114]

The Choroma Cuartel General withstood the death of Narciso Torrico; yet the dirigentes Rosendo Caguasiri, Denne Moscoso, Benedicto Paredes, Telesforo Medrano, Rodolfo Lafuente, Octavio Torrico, and Pedro Carita continued the struggle for land revendication.[115] The post of Secretary General of the Choroma Central was initially assumed by Rufino Vargas, an ambitious ex-miner, who also was appointed to the influential position of subprefect of Charcas Province. Vargas's brief tenure as both government official and dirigente of the Choroma Central illustrates the possibilities and pitfalls of prebendalismo. Outraged because of his collusion with hacendados to obstruct their land claims, Rufino Vargas was executed by aggrieved peasants together with the corrupt agrarian reform judges Esteban and Francisco Pérez.[116]

A vivid reminder of the continued conflict in northern Potosí occurred at Toro Toro, a pueblo northeast of San Pedro de Buena Vista, when in June 1958 the town was surrounded and communication and water services cut by a sindicato militia.[117] The town was again besieged in August by 2,000 peasants from northern Potosí, later reinforced by a Cochabamba contingent of 70 militiamen from the Ucureña Central under the command of Jorge Solis and Salvador Vásquez. The vecinos had prepared for the inevitable and purchased weapons. After a ten-hour battle, the attack was repulsed.[118] Nevertheless, the vecinos lived in fear, the town remained isolated, surrounded by hostile Indians, its communications severed.

Amid rumors of impending attacks on remote towns in northern Potosí, a number of government fact-finding commissions were dispatched to the region to contrive an end to the violence. The Cochabamba prefect sent a commission led by a police lieutenant to investigate the situation. But the prefect's attempt to dispatch the compliant dirigente Alejandro Galarza as a representative of the Quillacollo Central was squelched by José Rojas (a newly elected legislative deputy) who led 50 militiamen from the Ucureña Central to the "pacification zone." The Oruro deputy Zenón Barrientos Mamani, a MNR veteran of the 1949 Civil War and the 1952 Revolution, arrived to find the town besieged by 4,000 peasants from the Choroma Central commanded by the dirigente Demetrio Moscoso. The government found the vecinos to be victims and the peasants guilty of subverting the established order.[119]

Northern Potosí had become a cockpit of confrontation between peasants seeking revolutionary change as promised in the MNR Agrarian Reform Law and creole-mestizo opponents supported by the MNR regime. This predicament did not sit well with the peasantry who found themselves under attack after the prefects of Potosí, Cochabamba, Oruro, and La Paz ordered police, carabinero, and army units to the conflicted zone. Despite the MNR reforms, the Old Order prevailed in the countryside under the National Revolution. Hence, the appearances of dual power between contentious Indian sindicatos and the creole-mestizo government as, for example, when captured vecinos were delivered by militiamen from the Choroma Central and the Anzaldo sindicato for trial at Ucureña in June 1958. The ensuing confrontation between race and class is captured in an episode involving the caudillo José Rojas and a police lieutenant ordered by the prefect to retrieve and deliver the vecino prisoners to the city of Cochabamba. Accompanied by the alcalde of Cliza, Wálter Revuelta Padilla, the lieutenant sought Rojas' assistance in the matter:

> Once in Ucureña we encountered José Rojas. . . . [U]pon my arrival I saw that he was upset and [Walter] Revuelta told him: "He is the Lieutenant

that is going to Anzaldo and wants you to accompany him." Rojas with the tone of a mayordomo and irritable, said: "Ja!! . . . my lieutenant. You're the commission? That commission that I don't know of? . . . Who am I? Pongo, slave, mitani, no carajo" . . . Rojas ended his rant with a threat. "Because when they [vecinos] cut off the head of Narciso Torrico and made his widow carry his head for leagues and leagues. . . . There will be vengeance from the campesinos."[120]

The Prefect of Potosí also visited the embattled vecinos of San Pedro de Buena Vista. His observations, sent to the Prefect of Cochabamba, underscore the inherent racism of MNR officials: "I beg you to take your most energetic measures to impose sanity on those that are called dirigentes, and that have lost the last iota of good sense."[121]

After the deaths of Narciso Torrico and Rufino Vargas, the Choroma Central fell into internecine feuding. Opportunistic dirigentes turned upon each other in an orgy of syndical gangsterism: the ex-waiter, Rosendo Cawasiri gunned down by rivals from Torotoro; Cipriano Calatayud, a dirigente from the vicinity of Toracari, killed and mutilated by Vicente Colque, a rival campesino from a pueblo near San Pedro de Buena Vista; Telésforo Medrano, a dirigente associated with Calatayud, escaped Colque's wrath, only to later visit revenge on Colque by stoning him to death.[122] The ex-colono Pedro Carita Chacmi emerged from the violence of the Choroma Central to become the most enduring cacique in northern Potosí. A man whose militancy antedated the National Revolution, Pedro Carita's life story, as traced by the anthropologists Olivia Harris and Javier Albó, reminds one of the archetypical revolutionary corrupted by power in *The Death of Artemio Cruz*, Carlos Fuentes' morality tale of the Mexican Revolution.[123]

Pedro Carita had labored as a colono on the Hacienda Cochu in the years before the National Revolution, emerging as a community leader when the colonos, in an act that defied convention, selected him as mayordomo. Illiterate, with rudimentary Spanish, yet nonetheless an astute politician, Carita became an agrarian cacique seizing hacienda land and then converting it into a sindicato central with himself as secretary general. Because of his relentless opposition to the landlords, Carita enjoyed the widespread support of the peasantry even as he used his position to enrich himself through prebendalismo. He continued his militancy toward hacendados while associating with an emerging group of *ponchudos*, villagers who had manipulated the agrarian reform to make themselves landowners. Carita managed to appeal to peasants for mass support while representing the ponchudos' interests in regional politics. He later emerged as a politico on the national level, serving as a legislator in La Paz after the military coup of 1964, where he became known for strident denunciations of "communist" activity in the countryside.[124] Carita's metamorphosis from peasant dirigente to sindicato profiteer epitomizes the devolution of the National Revolution into personalismo and prebendalismo.

The brief career of Eugenio Vargas, an ex-colono from the vicinity of Moscari southeast of San Pedro de Buena Vista, is another example of prebendalismo.

Vargas utilized his position as a caudillo to engage in social banditry, enriching himself through extortion, cattle rustling, and robbery.[125] Captured and under police escort to jail in Uncia, the renegade dirigente was stabbed to death by the son of one of his victims.

Intra-ethnic Factionalism: The Jukumani–Laymi Blood Feud

Northern Potosí, notorious for Indian-vecino violence, was also wracked by intra-ethnic strife among feuding Aymara ayllus. As we have seen, episodic conflict born of boundary disputes predates the National Revolution. Traceable to the pre-Colombian past, factional quarrels among and between ayllus continued into the twentieth century and beyond. Underlying the ayllu is a dualism: the "double face of the Aymara coin," posits Xavier Albó, "solidarity, but factionalist." Members of an ayllu community identify themselves with their birthplace and those born elsewhere are considered "the other." And while everyday difficulties might arise among themselves, these inherent annoyances do not hinder the internal solidarity of the ayllu. And thus, "In effect, the solidarity shown by the community group could be defined as a synchronization of individualisms, and its result, as an individualism of group." The other side of the coin is factionalism, whether latent "or of mutual distrust and tensions, or also in form of open hostilities" between oppositional groups, "the others."[126]

The vagaries of the agrarian reform process exacerbated the episodic factional conflicts between ayllus over land, water, and other resources. In the latter years of the revolution, a crescendo of violence swept the Laymi and Jukumani ayllus. Between 1958 and 1964, death and destruction reigned: 500 comunarios were killed and over 700 houses razed as a blood feud raged in the Potosí highlands.[127] The roots of the violence lie in Jukumani history and a complex interplay of disease and demographics, mining and deforestation, taxation and politics. Northern Potosí was ravaged in the mid-nineteenth century by an epidemic that decimated one-fifth of the population, thus reducing the number of Jukumani taxpayers (taxes were paid at a fixed rate and not per capita).[128] The Jukumani response to the demographic catastrophe and resultant increase in taxation was to encourage settlement of their lands by outsiders. The anthropologist Ricardo Godoy traced the sevenfold increase of *katun runas* ("people of the margin") from 1858 to 1958 and discovered the drastic decline of Jukumani *originarios* (descendants of original taxpayers) during the period (from 86 percent to 54 percent). Godoy also documented a phenomenal increase in population: "In density terms, the highlands would have had in the first quarter of the last century [1800] about three persons per km^2; toward the end of the century, about five. Today the Jukumani highlands have 28 persons per km^2, or more than twice the figure for rural Cochabamba, the densest area of the nation."[129]

The unfolding of this Malthusian disaster led to increased pressure on farm land and natural resources with the effects most pronounced within the Jukumani ayllus and between the Jukumani and contiguous ayllus, most notably the Laymi and

Kakachaka. The situation was further exacerbated by the development of antimony mining in the region. Land was usurped and waters contaminated to the detriment of resources available to the Jukumanis. The response was to intensify agricultural production; but because of the resultant erosion, new land was required for cultivation.[130] This vicious circle became a zero-sum game for the Jukumani.

The quest for land led outward, toward soils of marginal utility, and inward to the ayllu commons where landless katun runas usurped virtually all the land once controlled by the *jilanqus*, the authorities elected by ayllu originarios.[131] The relentless pressure for land and sustenance, besides affecting the internal order of Jukumani society, led to the intensification of traditional boundary conflicts (viz., tinku ritual combat) with neighboring ayllus.[132] However, the nineteenth-century attempts to transform the "free communities" into individual landholders created a disjuncture with past resolution of boundary conflicts. Consequently, disputes were no longer resolved locally, but were subject to the decisions of the state courts. The legal process observable in court records from the early years of the twentieth century is suggestive of the litigious chicanery to follow 50 years later in the agrarian reform process. In northern Potosí, careers were made defending the interests of hacendados and merchants, "nurturing and resolving land disputes," and acting "simultaneously for defendant and plaintiff for Jukumanis and Laymis."[133] The result was a bonanza for the creole-mestizos at the expense of the destitute comunarios. The exploitation of land within Jukumani ayllus and the violent usurpation of the lands of neighboring ayllus, particularly those of the Laymis, intensified during the later years of the National Revolution.

Summary and Conclusions

President Hernán Siles (1956–1960) inherited a revolution afflicted by inflation, declining revenue from the tin mines, a bloated bureaucracy, and a countryside beset with indigenous factionalism and interracial conflict. President Paz Estenssoro, in a desperate move to avert insolvency, had begged President Dwight Eisenhower to rescue the revolution. The U.S. bailout came at a price: the MNR abandoned its core principles of national sovereignty and resource nationalism. U.S. funds ($50,000,000 during the Paz administration) were contingent on payment of the tin magnates for their expropriated mines. The MNR again betrayed its commitment to national sovereignty at the March 1964 OAS meeting in Caracas and supported the U.S. overthrow of Guatemala's revolutionary struggle for resource nationalism. Bolivia's vote was rewarded with $3,000,000 from the United States.

Rather than overthrow the revolution, the Colossus of the North adopted Bolivia as a client state. The MNR descent into neocolonialism began with the 1955 Petroleum Code that privatized the nation's oil resources and marginalized COMIBOL, the state petroleum entity. Within a few years, Gulf Oil's revenue would grow to 100 times COMIBOL's. In 1956, the MNR agreed to a

$25,000,000 monetary Stabilization Plan to combat rampant inflation and avert government insolvency. The draconian measures—reduction of government expenditures through price controls, elimination of state subsidies, reduction of wages, and layoffs of mine workers—escalated labor resistance from 220 strikes in 1956 to 1,272 in 1959.

President Siles opted for a divide and conquer strategy to disrupt and weaken opposition to his mandate. The COB worker and peasant sectors, splintered into competing factions, were no longer a threat to the MNR. But the factionalism fanned by Siles to disrupt his opponents, while successful in the short term, created dangerous divisions within the Movimientista elites.

The ambiguity of the agrarian reform process compounded the problem of rural order, exacerbating tensions between colonos and hacendados and aggravating factionalism among and between ayllu comunarios, comunarios and ex-colonos, comunarios and vecinos, ex-colonos and miners, ex-colonos and vecinos, and clashes between Catholic and Protestant colonos. The peasant sindicato arose from the need to replace the colonato with a substitute form of governance. The sindicato dirigente supplanted the landlord in the land-group unions, sindicato dirigente assumed a role similar to that previously played by the hacendado patrón.[134] Under the ancien régime, the landlord controlled the relationship of the Indian to the national political structure, a role assumed by the sindicato dirigente following the MNR victory. The sindicato was to serve as a vehicle for revolutionary change in the countryside, by providing the organization necessary to negotiate the agrarian reform process, as well as the requisite force to expel recalcitrant landlords and thwart counterrevolutionary uprisings.

In the MNR scheme of government, the peasant sindicato constituted one sector of a syndical organization that also included the factory and mining proletariat, artisans, and the urban middle class. Because the sectors were also militarized, their militias constituted a bulwark for defense against the resurgence of the Old Order: yet an unforeseen consequence was the confrontation of peasant dirigentes with the vestiges of traditional rule exercised by MNR rightists controlling local and regional government. In the early years of the revolution, syndicalism was propagated by politicized peasants, miners, ex-miners, and urban militants. By 1956, the number of agrarian sindicatos was estimated at 20,000 with the local land-group unions linked to provincial and departmental federations in a national confederation represented within the umbrella COB.[135]

The MNR regime rewarded the fealty of provincial, regional, and national level peasant caciques with government largesse (prebendalismo): money, *cupos* (government subsidized food coupons), and political sinecures. The sindicato dirigentes curried favor with their followers through their ability to deliver land as well as these perquisites. Thus, competition for official MNR support became the sine qua non of rural syndicalism.

President Paz Estenssoro's use of rural sindicatos to support the MNR regime led to an increase in factionalism within and between sindicatos, as prebendalismo became the objective for opportunistic leaders. Government aid for public works projects (roads, irrigation projects, schools, clinics), as well as sindicato membership dues, bribes, and kickbacks for assistance in the agrarian reform process, and payoffs from landlords were among the perquisites of sindicato leadership.[136]

The emergence of caciques, indigenous power brokers less interested in reform than in the perquisites of power, further complicated the situation in the countryside. The emergence of caciques further complicated the mobilization of sindicato militias on a regional level in the Cochabamba valleys and northern Potosí led to widespread violence. The Ucureña Central played a vanguard role in confronting the power of hacendados, vecinos, and rightist MNR officials. Under the aegis of the sindicato caudillo José Rojas and his lieutenants, the Ucureños spearheaded an agrarian revolution throughout the Valle Alto, into outlying provinces, and beyond to Chuquisaca and northern Potosí Department.

Land disputes between the Jukumani and Laymi ayllus devolved into a disastrous blood feud. As Sylvia Rivera Cusicanqui put it, "In the puna of the north of Potosí, is it easy to see that the peasant sindicato apparatus could never function, but as a device imposed from afar and above," and in the valleys "we are only metaphorically able to speak of a syndical movement . . . [but rather] the momentary recruitment of an armed band of followers."[137]

The MNR failed to utilize the extensive peasant syndical organization as an effective tool for rural social and economic development, opting instead to use the regional militias as a political instrument. The factional struggles among Hernán Siles, Wálter Guevara, Víctor Paz, Juan Lechín, and their cacique supporters revealed the distortion of the syndical movement from grassroots organizations to political pawns, as illustrated by the intercession of Sinforoso Rivas's Quillacollo militia of ex-colonos against revolutionary serranía ayllus and José Rojas' use of the Ucureña militia to intimidate rebellious miners. Thus, "The active participation of the masses was replaced by bureaucratic structures, revolutionary leadership by artificial caudillismo, [and] internal democracy by the centralization of power in the highest level of the pyramid."[138] The sindicato militias had the potential to deliver the indigenous majority the political agency historically denied them. But the MNR creole-mestizos neutralized the peasant sindicato leaders and eradicated an agrarian revolution.

Notes

1. Sinforoso Rivas Antezana, *Los hombres de la revolución: memoria de un líder campesino* (La Paz, 2000), 106.
2. Carmen Soliz has made the case that comunarios, particularly in La Paz Department, were often successful in regaining lost ayllu land despite the decree's exclusion of pre-1900 usurpations. More is yet to be learned regarding other highland departments, including Cochabamba, the site of this comunario rebellion. Carmen Soliz, "Land to the Original Owners': Rethinking the Indigenous Politics of the Bolivian Agrarian Reform," *Hispanic American Historical Review*, 97.2 (2017), 259–296.

3. Andrew Pearse, *The Latin American Peasant* (London, 1975), 134–135.
4. José Gordillo, *Campesinos revolucionarios en Bolivia: Identidad, territorio y sexualidad en el Valle Alto de Cochabamba, 1952–1964* (La Paz, 2000), 87.
5. Rivas Antezana, *Los hombres*, 107–109.
6. *El Diario*, 24 October 1953, 5.
7. Ñuflo Chávez Ortiz, *Recuerdos* (La Paz, 1988), 86–87.
8. Hernán Barriaga Antelo, *Laureles de un Tirano* (La Paz, 1965), 57.
9. On the FSB insurrection, see Enrique Achá Alvarez and Mario H. Ramos y Ramos, *Unzaga: Mártir de América* (Buenos Aires, 1960), 51–61.
10. *El Diario*, 12 November 1953, 6–7, 13 November 1953, 6–7, 15 December 1953, 7.
11. Achá Alvarez and Ramos y Ramos, *Unzaga: Mártir de America*, 66. The authors also note that Major Elías Belmonte Pabón, a founder of the RADEPA military lodge, was a member of the FSB National Military Committee.
12. *El Diario*, 22 October 1953, 5. In the later invasion of Culpina in Sud Cinti Province, four townspeople were dragged off behind horses to the sindicato headquarters, where they were executed. *El Diario*, 18 April 1956, 5.
13. *El Diario*, 28 September 1954, 7; 29 September 1954, 7; 1 October 1954, 5.
14. *El Diario*, 26 February 1954, 7.
15. *El Diario*, 20 April 1954, 5.
16. *El Diario*, 25 February 1955, 5.
17. *El Diario*, 24 October 1956, 6.
18. Madeleine B. Leons, "Changing Patterns of Social Stratification in an Emergent Bolivian Community," Ph.D. dissertation, University of California, Los Angeles, 1966, 64–65.
19. Ibid., 65.
20. Wálter Castillo Avendaño, *Compilación Legal de la Reforma Agraria en Bolivia* (La Paz, 1955), 83.
21. See Peter Lord, "The Peasantry as an Emerging Political Factor in Mexico, Bolivia, and Venezuela," University of Wisconsin, *Land Tenure Research Paper*, No. 35 (May 1965), as quoted in Joel Migdal, *Peasants, Politics, and Revolution* (Princeton, 1974), 209.
22. Antonio García, "Los Sindicatos en el Esquema de Revolución Nacional," *Trimestre Económico*, 33.4 (October–December 1966), 608.
23. Kevin Young, *Blood of the Earth: Resource Nationalism, Revolution, and Empire in Bolivia* (Austin, TX, 2017), 137.
24. Sylvia Rivera Cusicanqui, "Liberal Democracy and Ayllu Democracy in Bolivia: The Case of Northern Potosí," *The Journal of Development Studies*, 26, 4 (1990), 101.
25. William E. Carter, *Aymara Communities and the Bolivian Agrarian Reform* (Gainesville, 1964), 58. For the organization and history of a sindicato in the Upper Valley of Cochabamba Department, see Roger A. Simmons, *Palca and Pucara: A Study of the Effects of Revolution on Two Bolivian Haciendas* (Berkeley, CA, 1971), 126–149.
26. Ibid.
27. Migdal, *Peasants, Politics, and Revolution*, 212.
28. Pearse, *The Latin American Peasant*, 157.
29. In general, the agrarian revolution allowed for the rise of a new style of leadership. For observations regarding the altiplano, see William Carter, "Revolution in the Agrarian Sector," in Malloy and Thorn, eds., *Beyond the Revolution*, 237, and Hans Buechler, "Agrarian Reform and Migration on the Bolivian Altiplano," Ph.D. dissertation, Columbia University, 1966, 65, 155; for the Yungas, see Dwight B. Heath, "Bolivia: Peasant Syndicates among the Aymara of the Yungas—A View from the Grass Roots," in Henry Landsberger, ed., *Latin American Peasant Movements* (Ithaca, 1969), 195–198. Madeline Leons discusses the jilikata–sindicato nexus and the emergence of younger, Spanish-speaking dirigentes in "Changing Patterns of Social Stratification," 53–54. There are exceptions, however; Roger Simmons notes that at the ex-hacienda Palca in the Upper Cochabamba Valley, although a local dirigente was selected because he spoke Spanish, the "skill turned out to be a minor consideration," and the dirigente "fails

totally as a modernizing 'cultural broker,' in dealing with the outside." Simmons, *Palca and Pucara*, 135.
30. Pearse, *The Latin American Peasant*, 157–159.
31. Turovsky, "Bolivian Haciendas: Before and After the Revolution," Ph.D. dissertation, UCLA, 1980, 214, and Antonio García, "Agrarian Reform and Social Development in Bolivia," in Rodolfo Stavenhagen, ed., *Agrarian Problems and Peasant Movements in Bolivia* (New York, 1970), 31–32.
32. Garcia, "Los Sindicatos," 607.
33. Christopher Mitchell, *The Legacy of Populism in Bolivia: From the MNR to Military Rule* (New York, 1977), 53–54. The government bureaucracy's share of the domestic gross national product increased from $62 million in 1956 to $88 million in 1964; the income of government bureaucrats rose to 50 times the national average. Fernando Garcia Arganaras, "Bolivia's Transformist Revolution," *Latin American Perspectives*, 19.2 (Spring 1992), 66.
34. Richard Thorn, "The Economic Transformation," in James Malloy and Richard Thorn, eds., *Beyond the Revolution: Bolivia Since 1952* (Pittsburgh, PA, 1971), 179.
35. Mitchell, *The Legacy of Populism*, 54.
36. Thorn, "The Economic Transformation," Malloy and Thorn eds., *Beyond the Revolution*, 193.
37. Ibid., 170.
38. Mitchell, *The Legacy of Populism*, 54.
39. *El Diario*, 19 June 1956, 4; *La Nación*, 26 June 1956, 5.
40. Mitchell, *The Legacy of Populism*, 55–56.
41. James Dunkerley, *Rebellion in the Veins: Political Struggle in Bolivia, 1952–1982* (London, 1984), 82.
42. Examples of the use of food by the U.S. government to influence the revolution are evident in State Department memoranda, for example, "we may . . . want to exact some quid pro quo from the Bolivians—such as disassociation from Communist influences and progress toward agreement on the value of expropriated American mining properties"; "the Embassy is under the definite impression that the action of the United States Government in furnishing food grants to Bolivia has begun to pay dividends"; "We believe that our aid is helping to rid the Bolivian Government of pro-Communist influences now present." Stephen Zunes notes, "As a result of subsequent U.S. aid and the tolerant U.S. attitude toward the regime . . . the MNR has become increasingly pro-U.S. in its outlook and has taken the position that Bolivia's interest will be best served by cooperating with the U.S." Stephen Zunes, "The United States and Bolivia: The Taming of a Revolution, 1952–1957," *Latin American Perspectives*, 28.5 (September 2001), 41–43.
43. *The Avalon Project*, "Caracas Declaration of Solidarity; 28 March 1954," Yale Law School, http://avalon.law.yale.edu/20th_century/intam10.asp. Regarding North American food aid, see James F. Siekmeier, *The Bolivian Revolution and the United States, 1952 to the Present* (University Park, PA, 2011), 118–119.
44. Stephen Kinzer, *The Brothers: John Foster Dulles, Allen Dulles, and Their Secret World War* (New York, 2013), 166, 174.
45. Among the more notable dictators were Marcos Pérez Jiménez (Venezuela), Anastasio Somoza (Nicaragua), Fulgencio Batista (Cuba), Rafael Trujillo (Dominican Republic), Alfredo Stroessner (Paraguay), Gustavo Rojas Pinella (Colombia), and Manuel Odría (Peru). See John Gerassi, *The Great Fear in Latin America* (New York, 1963), 240–242.
46. Kenneth D. Lehman, *Bolivia and the United States* (Athens, GA, 1999), 116. Juan Lechín, the proletarian jefe of co-gobierno, bowed to necessity as documented in a State Department memorandum of a conversation unearthed by Lehman: "Understand, I'm an anti-imperialist. Naturally, because I'm Bolivian. But when it comes to a choice between Russia and the United States, I'm with the United States. Who do we think we are—a small and impoverished country—that we can afford to disregard the fact that we are a part of the American Orbit?" Ibid., 117.

47. The Petroleum Code (over 130 articles) is deciphered in Laurence Whitehead, *The United States and Bolivia; A Case Study in Neo-Colonialism* (London, 1969), Appendix 2, 28–34. See also Young, *Blood of the Earth*, 61–66; Siekmeier, *The Bolivian Revolution*, 51–52; Thorn, "The Economic Transformation," 191–192; and Cole Blasier, "The United States and the Revolution," in Malloy and Thorn, eds., *Beyond the Revolution: Bolivia Since 1952*, 78–79.
48. Young, *Blood of the Earth*, 65–66.
49. Whitehead, *The United States and Bolivia*, 33.
50. Thorn, "The Economic Transformation," 179.
51. George Jackson Eder, *Inflation and Development in Latin America: A Case History of Inflation and Stabilization in Bolivia* (Ann Arbor, MI, 1986), 87–88.
52. Ibid., 626–647.
53. See Young, *Blood of the Earth*, 67–68, 211, fn. 40.
54. Whitehead, *The United States and Bolivia*, 3.
55. James Siekmeier, *The Bolivian Revolution*, Kenneth Lehman, *Bolivia and the United States*, and Kevin Young, *Blood of the Earth*, avoid the term "neo-colonialism," opting instead for the labels "asymmetrical power relations," "unequal partnership," "limited partnership," "patron–client," "dependent," and "clientelist state."
56. Eder, *Inflation and Development in Latin America*, 241.
57. Thorn, "The Economic Transformation," 184.
58. James W. Wilkie, *The Bolivian Revolution and U.S. Aid Since 1952* (Los Angeles, 1969), 32.
59. Young, *Blood of the Earth*, 60–65, 68–69, 71.
60. Whitehead, *The United States and Bolivia*, 3.
61. Cornelius Zondag, *The Bolivian Economy, 1952–1965* (New York, 1966), 57, 61.
62. Dunkerley, *Rebellion in the Veins*, 88.
63. Ibid., 90–93; Young, *Blood of the Earth*, 67–74, 122–134; James Malloy, *Bolivia: The Uncompleted Revolution* (Pittsburgh, PA, 1970), 236–240; Garcia, "Los Sindicatos," 611–623.
64. Thorn, "The Economic Transformation," 186–187.
65. Siekmeier, *The Bolivian Revolution*, 52.
66. Wilkie, *The Bolivian Revolution and U.S. Aid*, 24.
67. Richard Patch, "Bolivia: The Seventh Year," *American Universities Field Staff*, 6 (February 1959), 12.
68. Dandler, "Politics of Leadership," 40.
69. Richard Patch was an early academic observer of the Rojas organization, see "Bolivia Today: An Assessment Nine Years After the Revolution," *American Universities Field Staff: West Coast South America Series*, 8.4 (17 March 1961) and "Bolivia: The Seventh Year: An Assessment Nine Years After the Revolution," *American University Field Staff: West Coast South America Series* 6.1 (3 February 1959). Roger Simmons found, "There is some indication, for example, that the Punata Central collects a rake-off on taxes collected from peasants in the market." Simmons, *Palca and Pucara*, 139–143.
70. An editorial in *Unidad*, 31 December 1960, 3 on the "Fifth Campesino Conference of Santivañez," noted, "Ucureña, the bastion of the Reform, was converted into a redoubt of caudillismo." Control of the Punata chicha taxes was included among other accusations of prebendalismo.
71. The government tax on chicha (per Supreme Decree 3796, July 1954) assigned revenue collection to the municipalities. See *Revista de Hacienda*, 1.2 (May 1955), 13–14, 33–34. The funds were to be dispersed among local and national government offices and departmental universities. The potential rake-off in chicha tax collection is apparent in the consumption rate. Figures for the year 1954 in the Cochabamba valleys show the phenomenal consumption in the valleys (e.g., Tarata, 2000 bottles per day, Punata, 8,000, Tiraque, 1500, Arani, 2000, Totora, 5,000, Pojo, 1300, Quillacollo, 10,00,

Capinota, 3000). *El Diario*, 1 January 1955, 7; 25 January 1955, 6. Alberto Rivera Pizarro, *Los terratenientes de Cochabamba* (Cochabamba, 1992), 64.
72. Laura Gotkowitz, *A Revolution for Our Rights* (Durham, 2007), 237. Gotkowitz also points to Juan Lechín's claim that an increase in the chicha tax was among the causes precipitating the Ayopaya rebellion. Ibid., fn. 10, 347.
73. Interview with Miguel Veizaga by the author in Cochabamba, 23 August 1970.
74. Gordillo, *Campesinos revolucionarios*, 97.
75. Ibid., 171.
76. Rivas Antezana, *Los hombres*, 116–119; *Unidad*, September 1958, 6.
77. *El Diario*, 5 October 1957, 2. Gordillo, *Campesinos revolucionarios*, 98.
78. Gordillo, *Campesinos revolucionarios*, 99.
79. On 8 April 1958, the La Paz Departmental Campesino Federation announced that 11,000 militiamen from sindicato regiments in Omasuyos Province would march to La Paz the following day to commemorate the National Revolution of 9 April 1952. In 1953, the number of peasants in 16 altiplano militia ("regiments") was estimated at 110,000. *El Diario*, 8 April 1958, 6. Although the certitude of these numbers may be problematic, they greatly exceeded those of the armed forces, 80 percent of whom were purged following the onset of the 1952 revolution: "In a matter of months the civilian militias were the strongest military forces in the country." Foreign Areas Studies Division, Special Operations Research Office, *U.S. Army: Area Handbook for Bolivia* (Washington, DC, 1963), 660; see also 661–662, 688–689.
80. Madeline Barbara Leons, "The Economic Networks of Bolivian Political Brokers: Revolutionary Road to Fame and Fortune," in Rhoda Halperin and James Dow, eds., *Peasant Livelihood: Studies in Economic Anthropology and Cultural Ecology* (New York, 1977), 105.
81. Of particular interest is Wolf's observation that the broker cannot settle conflicts because to do so would "abolish their own usefulness to others," and "Thus they often act as buffers between groups, maintaining the tensions which provide the dynamic of their actions . . . [they] would have no *raison d'etre* but for the tensions between community-oriented groups and nation-oriented groups." Eric Wolf, "Aspects of Group Relations in a Complex Society: Mexico," *American Anthropologist*, 58.6 (December 1956), 1076.
82. Dwight B. Heath, "New Patrons for Old: Changing Patron–Client Relationships in the Bolivian Yungas," *Ethnology*, 12.1 (January 1973), 88. See also Dwight B. Heath, "Hacendados with Bad Table Manners: Campesino Syndicates as Surrogate Landlords in Bolivia," *Inter-American Economic Affairs*, 24 (1970), 3–13.
83. Henry Landsberger and Cynthia N. Hewitt, "Ten Sources of Weakness and Cleavage in Latin American Peasant Movements," in Stavenhagen, ed., *Agrarian Problems and Peasant Movements*, 569–570.
84. By 1946, there were 41 schools linked to the Ucureña nuclear school for a total of 2,100 students. Gerrit Huizer, *The Revolutionary Potential of Peasants in Latin America* (Lexington, MA, 1972), 90.
85. *La Nación*, 25 April 1959, 4.
86. Ramón Eduardo Ruíz, *The Great Rebellion: Mexico, 1905–1924* (New York, 1980), 212.
87. John Womack, Jr., *Zapata and the Mexican Revolution* (New York, 1968), 96.
88. Ruíz, *The Great Rebellion*, 204; Womack, Jr., *Zapata*, 131.
89. A sindicato militia dispatched from the Ucureña Central invaded neighboring Chuquisaca Department in April 1956 and occupied haciendas along the Rio Chico near the pueblos of Poroma and Copavilque (a region noteworthy for the isolation of its hacienda communities and the persistence of landlord domination). Ucureña militiamen also marched southeast to Presto and then pressed south to Yamparéz Province in Chuquisaca Department, urging reluctant peasants to rise up against their patrones. *El Diario*, 6 May 1956, 5.
90. Womack, Jr., *Zapata*, 61.

91. Into A. Goudsmit, "Exploiting the 1953 Agrarian Reform: Landlord Persistence in Northern Potosí, Bolivia," *Journal of Latin American and Caribbean Anthropology*, 13.2 (November 2008), 367.
92. For the rise of the Bolivian labor movement, see Robert L. Smale, *"I Sweat the Flavor of Tin": Labor Activism in Early Twentieth-Century Bolivia* (Pittsburgh, PA, 2010).
93. Olivia Harris and Javier Albó, *Monteras y guardatojos, campesinos y mineros en el norte de Potosí* (La Paz, 1976).
94. Goudsmit, "Exploring the 1953 Agrarian Reform," 363–365.
95. Ibid., 370.
96. Willka's last order is noteworthy because it echoes Tupac Katari's earlier instance of forcing creole-mestizos to abandon Spanish clothing and parade around captured towns clothed in homespun bayeta cloth: a cultural statement against the class essence associated with creole fashion, symbolic of domination. Ramiro Condarco Morales, *Zarate 'El Temible' Willka* (La Paz, 1965), 289–290.
97. Augustin Barcelli S., *Medio Siglo de Luchas Sindicales Revolucionarias en Bolivia* (La Paz, 1956), 117.
98. Harris and Albó, *Monteras y guardatojos*, 36–37.
99. Thomas Abercrombie, *Pathways of Memory and Power: Ethnography and History Among an Andean People* (Madison, WI, 1998), 225.
100. Rivera Cusicanqui, "Liberal Democracy and Ayllu Democracy," 103.
101. Harris and Albó, *Monteras y guardatojos*, 41; Silvia Rivera Cusicanqui, *Oprimidos pero no vencidos. Luchas del campesinado aymara y qhechwa de Bolivia, 1900–1980* (Geneva, 1986), 92–99. See also David Preston, *Farmers and Towns: Rural–urban Relations in Highland Bolivia* (Norwich, England, 1978), 15.
102. The history of northern Potosí ayllus owes much to the erudition of the British anthropologist Tristan Platt: see in particular *Estado boliviano y ayllu andino: tierra y tributo en el norte de Potosí* (Lima, 1982), chapters 3, 5.
103. Steve Stern, *Peru's Indian Peoples and the Challenge of Spanish Conquest: Huamanaga to 1640* (Madison, WI, 1982), 137.
104. Harris and Albó, *Monteras y guardatojos*, 38. The authors note the "resentful cholos" who threw in their lot with Torrico included Rosendo Cawasiri, Telesforo Medrano, and Demetrio Moscoso, the ex-miner Rufino Vargas, and Pedro Carita Chacmi, an ex-colono from Hacienda Qochu, in the Choroma area. See also *El Diario*, 5 January 1958, 4, 6.
105. *El Diario*, 25 May 1957, 7. Narciso Torrico's relationship with Cochabamba dirigentes is discussed in Simmons, *Palca and Pucara*, 198.
106. *El Diario*, 28 April 1957, 5. Torrico is referred to as a "common delinquent . . . pursued by the law of Catavi." These allegations, including claims that Torrico led a force of 30,000 campesinos (and that his reluctant followers had been abducted and tortured at the Choroma Central), were attributed to vecinos from San Pedro de Buena Vista, reported as factual by *El Pueblo*, and repeated in *El Diario* begs the question: how could a "common delinquent" attract 30,000 followers? The question of ultimate causation for indigenous unrest is ignored in the press accounts derived from vecino informants seeking "pacification" (viz., military control) of the Indians.
107. *El Diario*, 5 January 1958, 6. This article includes a petition ostensibly signed by "over a hundred vecinos and sindicato representatives" at a *cabildo abierto* (town meeting) that refers to the cacique Narciso Torrico and his dirigentes Rosendo Caguasiri (Cawasiri), Demetrio Moscoso, Telesforo Medrano, Rodolfo Lafuente, Eugenio Vargas, Manual Buitrago, and Cristobal Villanueva as "communist vandals" and asks President Hernan Siles to guarantee the safety of the populace. Also see *El Diario*, 7 October 1958, 4.
108. Gordillo, *Campesinos revolucionarios*, 104–105; *El Diario*, 5 August 1958, 6; 10 August 1958, 7.
109. Waskar Ari Chachaki, *Earth Politics: Religion, Decolonization, and Bolivia's Indigenous Intellectuals* (Durham, NC, 2014), 116.

110. Gordillo, *Campesinos revolucionarios*, 105–106
111. *El Diario*, 30 January 1958, 4; *El Pueblo*, 4 March 1958, 4. Harris and Albó, citing an unpublished manuscript by Herbert Villegas, allude to a shootout between Torrico and a force of 30 men led by Lieutenant Jaime Cava at Cuchira. See Harris and Albó, *Monteras y guaradatajos*, 39.
112. Harris and Albó, *Monteras y guardatojos*, 40; see also Fausto Reinaga, *La Revolución India* (La Paz, 1969), 84.
113. Serulnikov, *Subverting Colonial Authority*, 214. A similar fate befell Katari's fellow insurrectionist, Tupac Amaru—drawn and quartered in the Cuzco public square after the failed colonial rebellion.
114. Ibid., 204–205. This was not a singular occurrence: the cross accompanied the sword in the Spanish conquest of the Americas and their churches represent the sacred power of the dominant elites. Noteworthy in the pageant of violence within the confines of the church is the *Noche Triste de Mohoza*, the creole-mestizo "sad night" of 1 March 1899 when 120 creole cavalrymen were slaughtered in the church at the pueblo of Mohoza by Indian partisans of "Temible Willka" aligned with the Liberals' General Pando. See Ramiro Condarco Morales, *Zarate*, 280–291.
115. *El Diario*, 8 August 1958, 6.
116. Harris and Albó, *Monteras y guardatojos*, 41, *El Diario*, 8 March 1958, 4.
117. *El Diario*, 10 August 1958, 7 and Harris and Albó, *Monteras y guardatojos*, 41.
118. *El Diario*, 10 August, 1958, 7; 11 August 1958, 5, Harris and Albó, *Monteras y guardatojos*, 41, David Preston, "New Towns: A Major Change in the rural Settlement Pattern in Highland Bolivia," *Journal of Latin American Studies*, 2 (1970), 15.
119. Gordillo, *Campesinos revolucinarios*, 106–108.
120. Ibid., 110.
121. Ibid., 112. Vecino abuses included assault, robbery of animals, garments, and household property. Ibid., 111.
122. Harris and Albó, *Monteras y guardatojos*, 44–45.
123. Ibid., 45–46. The authors credit much of their information to an unpublished manuscript by Herbert Villegas, *Solidaridad y divisionismo en la region de San Pedro de Buena Vista*, 1974.
124. This characterization of the cacique Pedro Carita is drawn from Harris and Albó, *Monteras y guardatojos*, 46–47; see also Goudsmit, "Exploiting the 1953 Agrarian Reform," 378.
125. Rivera Cusicanqui, *Oprimidos pero no vencidos*, 95.
126. Xavier Albó, "¿Khitipxtansa? ¿Quines Somos? Identidad localista, étnica y clasista en los aymaras de hoy," *America Indígena*, 39.3 (July–September 1979), 482. This is the second of a pair of seminal articles penned by the Jesuit savant (anthropologist, linguist, ethno-historian, indigenous activist, and co-founder of the CIPCA research institute) after years of study among the Altiplano Aymara. See also Xavier Albó, "Achacachi: Rebeldes pero conservadores," in *Actas du XLII Congres International des Americanistas* (Paris 1976), 3, 9–36.
127. Harris and Albó, *Monteras y guardatojos*, 50. The authors (based on police records) estimate the death toll at 654. Óscar A. Bustillos Hernanz presents the figure (without benefit of source) as 81 dead and 708 houses burned. Óscar A. Bustillos Hernanz, "Los Laimes y Jucumanis," *America Indígena*, 33.2 (July–September 1972), 828. The blood feud was extensively reported by the press. See *La Presencia*, 1 September 1959, 6; 13 January 1960, 4; 15 January 1960, 4; 30 January 1960, 4; 24 August 1960, 5; 26 August 1960, 5; 15 September 1960, 5; 29 September 1960, 4; 14 October 1960, 4; 8 December 1960, 5; 29 December 1962, 6; 5 February 1961, 6; 29 January 1963, 6; 14 May 1963, 4; 12 October 1964, 5; 10 December 1964, 5; *El Diario*, 5 May 1959, 4; 21 August 1959, 4; 4 September 1961, 5; *La Tarde*, 22 January 1960; 28 January 1960, 6; 30 January 1960, 4; 6 April, 1960, 4; 16 September 1960, 4; 3 November 1960, 4; 7 January 1961, 4; 9 January 1961, 4; 4 May 1961, 4; 16 May 1961, 4; 21 June 1961,

1; 23 June 1961, 5; 28 July 1961, 3; 1 December 1961, 5; *Unidad*, 11 January 1962, 3; 1 May 1962, 7.
128. Ricardo A. Godoy, *Mining and Agriculture in Highland Bolivia: Ecology, History, and Commerce Among the Jukumanis* (Tucson, AZ, 1990), 34.
129. Ibid., 33, 35.
130. Ibid., 34.
131. Ibid., 45.
132. The tinku ritual, essential for maintaining solidarity within the ayllu, is traceable to Andean prehistory as evident in ancient iconography. "Social fission was continually mediated by rituals of unity best labeled by the Quechua term *tinku*, which refers to the joining of two to form one. A pair of streams united in *tinku* to form one. Yet people are more fluid, because they can converge to form a social whole, only to diverge again into discrete moieties and descent groups. Therefore, uniting the dual divisions of society has long been the focus of elaborate rituals. . . . Historically, tinku rituals can also unite people by releasing tensions through fierce competition or bloody ritual battles. Combative tinku often involves an equal number of participants from each social division, and in some cases there are but two combatants who duel hand to hand, each armed with a large stone." Michael E. Moseley, *The Inca and Their Ancestors: The Archaeology of Peru* (London, 2001), 66–67. For insight into the role of the tinku ritual in contemporary northern Potosí, see Tristan Platt, "Pensamiento politico Aymara," in Xavier Albó, ed., *Raíces de América* (Madrid, 1988), 390–403.
133. Godoy, *Mining and Agriculture*, 47.
134. Dwight Heath essays the recincarnation of the patrón as peasant dirigente in "New Patrons for Old: Changing Patron–Client Relationships in the Bolivian Yungas," 46–66.
135. Jorge Dandler, "Peasant Sindicatos and the Process of Cooptation in Bolivian Politics," in June Nash, Jorge Dandler, and Nicholas Hopkins, eds., *Popular Participation in Social Change* (The Hague, 1976), 342.
136. For examples of dirigente corruption, see Turovsky, "Bolivian Haciendas Before and After the Revolution," 221; Havet, "Rational Domination," 95; Buechler, "Agrarian Reform and Migration on the Bolivian Altiplano," 158; Simmons, *Palca and Pucara*, 134, 145. On clientalism and the co-optation of the peasant syndical movement, see Dandler, "Peasant Sindicatos and the Process of Cooptation in Bolivian Politics," 343–346; Simmons, *Palca and Pucara*, 140–142; Lord, "The Peasantry as an Emergent Political Factor," 54; and *Unidad*, December 1958, 6.
137. Rivera Cusicanqui, *Oprimidos pero no vencidos*, 95–97.
138. Antonio Garcia, "Los Sindicatos," 624.

8

THE "REVOLUTION OF RESTORATION"

On 4 November 1964, Generals René Barrientos and Alfredo Ovando executed a bloodless coup d'état. The revolution had run its course. The overthrow of the National Revolution was the result of a complex web of internal and international intrigue. To an American journalist, U.S. hegemonic interests were obvious: "our influence is greater in Bolivia than it has been in any foreign country I have seen except occupied Japan and South Korea in wartime. (I haven't seen Vietnam recently) . . . Bolivia is very much a client state of ours."[1] Less obvious were the particulars of the military's return to power.

In the final years of the National Revolution, factional conflicts within the MNR degenerated into extreme polarization, internecine violence, and authoritarian rule. Adding to this domestic mélange was the Cuban Revolution. Fidel Castro's defiance of North American hegemony and the expropriation of Exxon, Texaco, IT&T, Coca Cola, U.S. mines, tobacco, and sugar plantations outraged Yankee sensibilities. The upshot was a crescendo of escalation—a U.S. embargo, the Bay of Pigs invasion, CIA-sponsored terrorism by Cuban exiles, serial assassination attempts on Fidel Castro, and a crisis that nearly resulted in nuclear war between the U.S. and the Soviet Union.

The Cold War confrontation between the United States, the Soviet Union, and Cuba profoundly influenced the Bolivian revolution. The earlier iteration of the National Revolution (1943–1946) had drawn the attention of the Anglo-American powers who abetted the overthrow of President Gualberto Villarroel: its redux (1952–1964) again drew the concern of the United States. Intent on countering social revolutions in the Third World, President Dwight Eisenhower overthrew nationalist governments in Guatemala and Iran, but opted to save the Bolivian revolution by granting millions in military, financial, and technical aid and assistance to prevent resource nationalism, avert a revolution of indigenous peasants and workers, and ensure the continuation of the MNR regime.

In response to the revolutionary challenge of the 1960s, posed by national liberation threats to American hegemony in the Third World, President John F. Kennedy countered with the policy of flexible response. Whereas postwar strategy had embraced the idea of collective security against an external Soviet threat, Kennedy's national security policy focused on the suppression of indigenous revolutionary movements. Nationalist revolutions in Cuba and Vietnam elicited a robust counterinsurgency effort to avoid their recurrence elsewhere.[2] Thus, Bolivia became the South American centerpiece of a grandiose imperial counterpoise launched in 1961 and subsumed under the Orwellian alias: "The Alliance for Progress." The grand design was ambitious—a preventive program to deter revolution through modernization of the Latin American nations—to promote economic development, alleviate the socioeconomic conditions breeding discontent, and win the "hearts and minds" of the population. Loans and technical assistance experts from the United States Agency for International Development (USAID) and AIFLD (American Institute for Free Labor Development) were deployed, Peace Corps volunteers dispatched, and "Civic Action" projects undertaken by U.S.-trained military officers to endear themselves to the peasantry via construction of public works projects popularized by United States Information Service (USIS) propaganda.[3]

Beneath the velvet glove of the Alliance for Progress was the mailed fist of repression—CIA agents, Defense Intelligence (DI) officers, U.S. Army, Navy and Air Force attaches, Green Berets, USAID "Special Group on Counterinsurgency" personnel, and "Office of Public Safety" operatives who specialized in training Latin American military and police officers in the "Black ops" of counterinsurgency—including refined "advanced interrogation" (viz., torture) techniques.[4] Since the revolutionary thrust of the 1960s sprang from attempts to replicate the Cuban rural *foco* experience, counterinsurgency focused on the necessities for domination of the countryside. U.S. Air Force planes mapped the rural terrain, and U2 reconnaissance aircraft overflew the countryside[5]; social scientists studied the peculiarities of peasant society[6]; USAID technocrats contrived rural development schemes; U.S. military officers promoted "Civic Action" projects; Peace Corps volunteers assisted in public works ventures, dispensed American goodwill, and accumulated local knowledge. When these measures failed to accomplish their objective, the response was repression, applied with sophistication and to deadly effect.

During the second Paz Estenssoro regime (1960–1964), the National Revolution morphed into an authoritarian police state supported by the Alliance for Progress. This chapter will examine the downfall of the National Revolution with a focus on indigenous factionalism in the Cochabamba Valleys, the Altiplano, and Northern Potosí—and the nexus of creole factionalism and North American statecraft with the return of praetorian rule.

Factionalism and the National Revolution

Factionalism is a deeply rooted undercurrent in Andean indigenous society, and ingrained in the creole state notorious for its coups d'état, *cuartelazos*,

FIGURE 8.1 Repurposed USAID Tear Gas Containers, La Paz
Source: Photo by author.

rebellions, and civil wars since independence in 1825. Indigenous resistance to Spanish viceroys and their republican successors was compromised by factional divisions: thus, the 500-year domination of the subaltern indigenous population, numbering in millions, by a miniscule creole caste. The National Revolution presented the unprecedented possibility for indigenous peasants and workers to create an autonomous political agency. The factors underlying the indigenous majority's failure to seize the historic opportunity for an agrarian revolution—the machinations of the criollo elite, indigenous factionalism, and fratricidal divisions among peasant chieftains—are examined in the following section.

Creole Factionalism

Wary of the revolutionary potential of the COB militias, President Siles undertook a systematic campaign to bolster the Movimientista right-wing sector and centralize power. The Jefes of the MNR *Comandos Departmentales* were staffed with administrators loyal to the president and cabinet positions shuffled to insure the support of ministers amenable to the Stabilization Plan.[7] Siles also introduced *Bloques Reestructuradores* designed to drive a wedge in the COB between revolutionary and reformist labor unions, thereby blunting the power of the proletariat to resist the MNR rightist sector. Juan Lechín was brought into line (publicly renouncing a planned general strike), and fellow leftist Ñuflo Chávez driven to resign the vice presidency. Siles's strategy to fracture the unity of the COB's indigenous proletarian and peasant sectors created irreparable fissures. The appointment of José Rojas as Minister of Peasant Affairs removed him from direct control of the Ucureña Central, minimizing the danger of a peasant–miner alliance forged by the Ucureña caudillo, as well as obviating a potential threat to the MNR creole-mestizos.[8] Thus, the co-opted caudillo mobilized the Ucureña militias to intimidate unruly miners and crush Falangista revolts.[9]

Despite the pretense of democratic elections, a clique within the MNR party determined presidential succession. The centrist Paz Estenssoro had yielded power to the rightist President Siles Zuazo in 1956, but the 1960 election was a different matter. Paz Estenssoro's decision to run for a second term thwarted the presidential expectations of presumed heirs-apparent Juan Lechín and Wálter Guevara Arze. Critical of Paz's control of the National Revolution, Guevara Arze was expelled from the party. He then formed the "Authentic Party of the Nationalist Revolutionary Movement" (*Partido del Movimiento Nacionalista Revolucionario Auténtico*: PMNRA) that appealed to those whose ambitions were stifled by the bureaucratization of the revolution: "The MNR has become an organization of subsidized functionaries, jealous of their prerogatives and their advantages, extraneous to the profound political happenings of the country. Only one condition is required to keep them above in their positions: their unconditional loyalty, sincere or feigned, to the Jefe of the Party [Víctor Paz Estenssoro]." Guevara Arze denounced Paz and Lechín as dictatorial caudillos operating "from above by a system of syndical dictatorship, bribery, and intimidation." He also decried the political role played by the army and police ("as if a totalitarian regime were in force") and the "persecution of anyone who was not a submissive supporter of the government."[10]

The Cochabamba Valleys

Garnering the votes of Indians who identified Don Víctor as their patrón was an uphill struggle for Guevara Arze and the Auténticos. As Guevara Arze averred, "By their number the campesinos are able to determine the course of Bolivian politics . . . manipulated, directed or intimidated by local political machines," but the National Revolution had "legally liquidated the semi-feudalism prevailing in the campo . . . [only to be] replaced by a new syndical feudalism."[11] The Ucureña caudillo José Rojas epitomized the "syndical feudalism" assailed by the Auténticos. Rojas's political machine dominated sindicato politics in the Valle Alto, controlled the departmental *Federación Sindical de Trabajadores Campesinos Cochabambinos* (FSTCC), and influenced syndical developments in distant Chuquisaca and Potosí Departments. Auténtico strategy for the votes of Cochabamba campesinos in the 1960 presidential election focused on undermining Rojas's hold on the FSTCC. Latent tensions in the Valle Alto between the Ucureña ex-colonos and *piqueros* (small land owners), together with the opposition of Cliceño vecinos to an agrarian revolution, made for an explosive situation.

In the early years of the revolution, Rojas had wrested control of the FSTCC from the Quillacollo Central led by his rival Sinforoso Rivas. Yet the sindicatos of the Valle Bajo remained loyal to Quillacollo and hostile to Rojas's Ucureña Central. For Guevara Arze to secure a significant number of votes in Cochabamba Department, it was imperative to diminish Ucureña's control of the departmental federation. But this was difficult because the MNR Jefe Víctor Paz and José Rojas (appointed Minister of Peasant Affairs) interjected loyalists into the Cochabamba prefecture, the MNR Comando Departamental, and the Quillacollo Central where the Ucureña dirigente Jorge Soliz "intervened," inserting a "Special Tribunal" to unseat the sindicato secretary general through a rigged election.[12]

President Siles had attempted to mitigate Paz's intervention in Cochabamba syndical politics by first offering the Ministry of Peasant Affairs to the Ucureña dirigente Salvador Vásquez as a replacement for José Rojas, and when Vásquez refused to be co-opted, employing a second tactic. Faced with an impending strike by miners, railway, and petroleum workers protesting stabilization, Siles induced Rojas to mobilize Cochabamba campesinos to repress the strike. And then, negotiating from a position of strength in Oruro, Rojas and Colonel Eduardo Rivas Ugalde, the Jefe of the Cochabamba Departmental Comando, negotiated an "Inter-syndical Pact" for the defense of the Siles regime: signatories included the mine workers' sindicatos of Huanuni, Colquiri, Morococala, and Japo and the campesino centrales of Ucureña, Sacaba, and Quillacollo.[13] Superficially, President Siles had dampened tensions among the peasant and miner sindicatos: a ploy too clever by half.

The factional rift over leadership of the FSTCC proved fortuitous for Guevara Arze's Cochabamba campaign when Miguel Veizaga, a rising star in the Ucureña Central, was elected Secretary General of the FSTCC at the Fourth Departmental Congress in April 1959. Rojas perceived Veizaga as a Young Turk and had him unseated and replaced by Crisóstomo Inturias, a Rojas loyalist.[14] Miguel Veizaga then joined the PMNRA campaign against the MNR, fracturing the FSTCC. The anthropologist Richard Patch, who penned field reports at the time, noted:

> Veizaga is a different person from José Rojas. He is articulate, enjoys playing chess, and for a time was an "evangelist," a convert to a fundamentalist

Protestant sect active in the valley. He resides in an indeterminate area on the fringe of Cliza which is not identified as either "town" or "rural." This is part of his philosophy of working with campesinos closely surrounding the towns and the city of Cochabamba, those who have been least happy with Rojas' forceful and sometimes brutal methods. He has the support of many of the townspeople of Cochabamba.[15]

In September 1959, presidential candidates Paz Estenssoro and Guevara Arze campaigned in Cochabamba. Their verbal barbs inflamed tensions between ex-colonos and piqueros in Cliza and Ucureña, escalating the conflict between the Ucureña sindicato supported by the MNR and Cliceño campesinos aligned with the PMNRA and led by Miguel Veizaga.[16] The ensuing clash of factions within the creole elite and their Indian surrogates was to become the bloodiest indigenous conflict in the nation's history.

The Cliza and Ucureña War

One of the Cliceños who did not support Miguel Veizaga was Wálter Revuelta Padilla. MNR deputy and President of the Cochabamba Rural Society, Wálter Revuelta was distinguished from other members of the Cochabamba gentry because of his long-standing friendship with José Rojas. As subprefect of Cliza, Revuelta had backed José Rojas in his struggle with Sinforoso Rivas and once had intervened to prevent Rojas from invading the city of Cochabamba to force local officials to enforce agrarian reform laws. The immediate event that plunged the Cochabamba valleys into civil war involved both Revuelta and Cliza. During an evening in late October 1959, Revuelta was passing the night in Cliza with "friends and some señoras, a copita it's called," when sometime before midnight the party was interrupted by the sound of gunfire.[17] When he stepped out to investigate the disturbance, a fracas ensued with a group of Veizaguistas after he refused to give *Vivas!* for Wálter Guevara Arze, but instead cheered Víctor Paz as his Jefe. His fealty cost Revuelta a severe beating and a fractured skull. It was also an affront to his honor, to his Jefe, and to his party.

On 31 October 1959, José Rojas's Ucureña militia attacked Cliza to avenge the "damaging affront" suffered by Wálter Revuelta. Six casualties were reported in four days of skirmishing between the militias. The Ministry of Government issued a communiqué stating that because of "violence between the campesino centrales of Ucureña and Punata on the one hand, and those of Cliza and Quillacollo on the other hand," government troops were dispatched to restore order.[18] Noteworthy is the reliance of the MNR on the army to control the peasantry as well as the appearance of Colonel Alfredo Ovando Candía, an influential officer in the resurgent military institution, to take charge of the situation. Implicit are the deleterious effects of factional divisions among the peasant sindicatos whose political agency was becoming subordinated to the control of the creole MNR elite and the armed forces.

The Tangled Web of Ultimate Causation

Underlying the conflict between Ucureña Movimientistas and Cliceño Auténticos were significant socioeconomic differences among the Cochabamba peasantry. These differences provide a key to understanding the political disposition of the conflicting sindicatos of the Valle Alto and Valle Bajo. The primary goal of colonos emerging from servitude was procurement of land. In the complex socially differentiated realm of the Cochabamba valleys, the National Revolution held different meanings within the variegated peasant population. By the eve of the 1952 Revolution, one-third of the peasantry of the Upper and Lower Valleys had gained title to land. These piqueros tilled small plots (*picos*) of generally less than 3 hectares and capitalized on the economic opportunities afforded by the collapse of hacendado control of the markets for agricultural foodstuffs sold at the weekly fairs in the city of Cochabamba and the towns of Cliza, Quillacollo, Capinota, and Punata. Meanwhile, colonos and ex-colonos struggled to reap a harvest for family subsistence with hopes of producing the surplus necessary for participation in the market economy.

The eclipse of hacendado control of the regional agricultural markets was a boon to the small farmers and petty capitalist ex-colonos participating in regional markets. The more enterprising of the indigenous entrepreneurs opened profitable *chicherías*; some began the business of trucking foodstuffs to towns in the valleys and the mines in Oruro; others entered the commodities market buying, transporting, and selling goods while capitalizing on regional and departmental price differentials. Cliza and Punata emerged as the dominant commercial entrepôts of the Valle Alto. A study of socioeconomic changes during the National Revolution in the Valle Alto towns of Cliza, Punata, Arani, Sacaba, and Mizque analyzed "the new social panorama" that arose: the "socio-political freedom of the peasantry" following the demise of the hacendado-vecino monopoly of agricultural markets, the transformation in marketing patterns with increased peasant participation, the "new political power of these [campesino] merchants," the rise in the volume of goods transported because of increased road construction, and the surge in campesino consumption and competition for the sale of chicha.[19]

With the onset of the revolution and the peasant awakening, Movimientista vecinos were forced to share political control with the powerful Ucureña Central. Most important was the tax revenue levied on the sale of chicha, foodstuffs, and livestock sold at the weekly fairs. To obtain a tax license, the interested party now had to enter into an agreement with the municipal authorities as well as the peasant sindicato authorities.[20] Considerable wealth could be gained by those with the power to levy and collect taxes on the burgeoning agricultural commodities market of the Cochabamba valleys. José Rojas's Ucureña Central collected a share of the taxes on chicherías, livestock sales, trucking permits, resale of government divisas, and whatnot picked from the pockets of campesino farmers, chicha vendors, middlemen, and truckers capitalizing on opportunities created by the revolution.

The Áutentico agenda resonated with the piquero small farmers: technical assistance, fertilizer, development of roads to facilitate transportation of goods to market, schools, and improved health care. The anthropologists Katherine Barnes and Juan Torrico note, "It is the sphere of marketing where the positive effects of the 1952 Revolution are most noticeable, and . . . future changes . . . will be essentially linked to the extension of the road network, to the expansion of internal markets, thus producing greater national integration . . . in the infrastructure for the liberation of the potential of campesino groups that are isolated, and as yet have only very limited alternatives and resources."[21] Land reform was necessary "only as a first step," argued Guevara Arze, without the "integration of the great peasant mass into western civilization," the National Revolution would "betray its historic destiny."[22] Yet the Áutentico vision of Bolivia's "historic destiny" was at odds with indigenous culture which was to be transformed into the "civilized" nation. Silvia Rivera Cusicanqui notes:

> The incompatibility between the claims of the [indigenous] community movement and the projected reforms of the nationalist movement was already obvious. The community plan was diametrically opposed to the plans of civilizing the Indian by means of Creole racial amalgamation, Hispanicization, the sub-division of the land and the commercialization of agricultural production associated with the MNR, which was summed up in the phrase "integrating the Indian into the nation." Consequently, the successful April [1952] insurrection was met in the Altiplano with a wait-and-see attitude tinged with distrust.[23]

The Auténticos would salvage the revolution and rescue a people betrayed by corrupt and complacent leaders. The contest between the Auténticos (Wálter Guevara and Miguel Veizaga) and the Movimientistas (Víctor Paz and José Rojas) was both political and personal. Guevara Arze's expectation of a turn at the helm of the National Revolution—rebuffed by Paz Estenssoro's predilection for power—obliged him to found the Áutentico party. Summoned from exile in Argentina by Víctor Paz Estenssoro to influence the Quillacollo Central on his behalf, Sinforoso Rivas noted the state of affairs in the region: "Of all that unprecedented chaos the winners were the ex-gamonales [hacendados] because from the beginning they worked within the MNR itself, through their families or social circles that were incrusted in the party. . . . That which interested the *latifundistas* of the MNR was to climb to the cusp of power by whatever means necessary in order accomplish the objective of rescinding the emancipation of the Bolivian peasantry."[24]

The frustration and antipathy shared by Miguel Veizaga and Wálter Guevara toward the MNR power brokers Víctor Paz and José Rojas were determining factors in the genesis of the PMNRA and an underlying cause of peasant conflict in the Cochabamba valleys. In a conversation with the author, Miguel Veizaga recalled his expulsion as Secretary General of the FSTCC as well as the initial cause of the internecine conflict. "They attacked us, assaulting our houses—Pajpani, then

Lindo Mundo Redondo, Jinchupampa—the three have been attacked and all their food and cattle taken, and this led by José Rojas, Salvador Vásquez, Jorge Soliz . . . that is the point." Veizaga claimed that Rojas was "good for nothing," a "bandit who mobilized ignorant people like little sheep," and through his position as Minister of Peasant Affairs and connections with the MNR officials in Cochabamba, enriched himself by control of the chicha tax and other perquisites of office. "The MNR had an import cell. All the Movimientistas were capos. . . . They formed a group of importers which gave them divisas. As a [government] minister, José Rojas was a dealer. He led and sold the peasants. He had a suitcase full of money, about 200 million [Bolivianos] from transactions."[25]

Veizaga's criticism also included Paz Estenssoro "because Dr. Paz had done nothing to unify the peasants. . . . [W]e invited Dr. Paz to Cliza to speak to a gathering. . . . He left after an hour, escaping to Cochabamba. . . . [H]e is not going to fix things. Because of this Wálter Guevara Arze was chosen."[26] Speaking at Capinota, Guevara Arze noted that "some dirigentes had been converted into substitutes of the gamonales [hacendados]," while the dirigente Jorge Campos endorsed the Auténtico candidate, stressing his history as an advocate of agrarian reform. Yet, to the nation's newly enfranchised ex-colonos, Guevara Arze's identification with the MNR right-wing was a liability.[27]

A Conflicted Terrain

Pazestenssoristas rose to the Auténtico challenge. José Rojas took leave of his cabinet position to assume personal control of the Ucureña Central. The Ucureña Central enforced an economic blockade of Cliza to pressure the piqueros. Beginning in late November and continuing into December 1959, campesinos traveling to Cliza from Arani, San Benito, and surrounding areas were forcibly detained in Punata by sindicato militia loyal to José Rojas. The Ucureños lodged boulders on the railway tracks between Cliza and Arani to deny peasants access to the Cliza market. This would lead to the decline of Cliza and the rise of Punata as the preeminent market in the Valle Alto. In late November 1959, militiamen from the Ucureña barracks were reportedly training sindicato militias in the departments of Potosí, Sucre, and Tarija. In December, the Ucureña Central dispatched 50 militiamen to mobilize the Tiraque militia. Faced with an escalation of regional dimensions, the Cliza "August 2nd" Central announced itself "armed and prepared to repel any aggression."[28]

A government commission sent to investigate the situation in the Valle found the opposing militia entrenched along a "frontier" following the course of the Rio Retama where they questioned the principals. José Rojas stated that the conflict stemmed from "factors derived from the incorporation of the peasantry into national life"; the Rojas lieutenant Salvador Vásquez accused Wálter Guevara Arze of "intellectual authorship" of the conflict; Guevara Arze suggested communist instigators as the source of the problem. Miguel Veizaga said the feud was the result of the "deepening of the Revolution" and accused José Rojas of exploiting campesinos through monopoly of the regional patronage system (control over local government officials and the taxes that supported them). Veizaga claimed the battle was for "syndical democracy, against bad dirigentes—against the syndical caudillos and the massacres they commit."[29] A Cliceño peasant put it simply: "They attacked us in our houses in the early hours of 29 October and we had to defend ourselves."[30]

Paz confronted the Auténtico challenge on multiple fronts. In La Paz, MNR militants forcibly broke up a "National Conference of Peasants" organized as a counterpoise to the Movimientista-controlled sindicatos. On the Altiplano, Paz-estenssorista campesinos attacked a number of ayllu communities "inclined toward the Auténtico party," resulting in 36 deaths. Another deadly attack by campesinos (reinforced with militants from the Matilda Mine) in the vicinity of Puerto Escoma led to more deaths, houses sacked, livestock stolen, and allegations of cannibalism.[31] In Cochabamba, the Ucureña-dominated FSTCC called for the expulsion of Miguel Veizaga, Alejandro Galarza, Jorge Campos, and Agapito Vallejos. Miguel Veizaga's responded with a defensive pact that included the Quillacollo, Capinota, and Tarata sindicatos. The Ucureña Central countered with an inter-sindicato pact with the miners' sindicatos of Colquiri, Japo, and Morocoala, and Miguel Veizaga concluded a "mutual defense pact" with the miners' sindicato at Huanuni.[32] The dispute between the Cliza (MNRA) and Ucureña (MNR) peasant chieftains made for a dangerous escalation of the conflict. Born of the Cliza-Ucureña feud, a new phase of syndical politics had emerged in the National Revolution.

The press referred to the situation as a "cold war" as representatives of the factions were busy purchasing arms and ammunition in the mining centers of Oruro and Potosí. The cold war turned violent in late January 1960 when Rojas partisans hanged a Veizaguista at the Huanuni mining district.[33] Miguel Veizaga mobilized the militias at his disposal, occupied the towns of Torata and Tolata, and seized control of the La Angostura Dam, crucial to the region's water supply. Rumors had Veizaga preparing to invade Ucureña and Punata, and Rojas planning to besiege the city of Cochabamba. The capture of the Veizaguista dirigente, Jorge Campos of Quillacollo, and his detention at the Ucureña sindicato subcentral at Mallco Rancho exacerbated an already explosive situation. A second government commission was dispatched. Víctor Paz and Wálter Guevara arrived in Cochabamba on separate airplanes and proceeded to the zones of their supporters: Paz to Ucureña and Punata, Guevara to Cliza. A revealing incident, apropos of the peasants' alleged reverence of "Don Víctor," marred his visit to Cochabamba. When the "Jefe Máximo" arrived at the Angostura Dam, controlled by Veizaguistas, armed militiamen stopped his auto and relieved him and the other passengers of their money, watches, and pistols.[34]

An uneasy truce, occasionally broken by skirmishes, was imposed on the region for the next few months. Jordan and Punata provinces were declared military zones and the army enforced a "dry law" prohibiting the sale of alcohol, forbade campesinos to bear arms, and refused admittance to MNR and MNRA politicians. Wálter Guevara Arze interpreted the imposition of a military zone and the prohibition of political activity as an MNR scheme to deny votes to the MNRA and in a spate of public announcements accused the Siles administration of siding with the Rojas bloc, citing incidents in which government officials ignored abuses perpetrated by Rojistas.[35] He also noted the penchant of the MNR regime to rely on the army to intimidate miners, break strikes, and repress peasants. Guevara Arze denounced the MNR's utilization of the military as a "political instrument" (as under the Old Regime), and pointed out that Colonel Eduardo Rivas Ugalde, a former RADEPA officer, served multiple functions: as a member of the MNR Comando Político, Commandant of the armed forces' advanced training school at Cochabamba (*Escuela de Clases*), Commander of the Army's Seventh Division, Prefect of Cochabamba, Minister of Government, and Secretary General of the MNR.

The colonel denied Wálter Guevara access to the military zone, but allowed Víctor Paz to enter and garner campesino support (i.e., votes) for his presidential campaign. "The Pazestenssorista sector," Guevara Arze averred, "seems to be using the systems of the oligarchy in a way that Señor Urriolagoitia [the last president of the Old Order] himself would be unable to better."[36] Indeed, the militarization of the regime, including the appointment of General Alfredo Pacheco Iturri as José Rojas's replacement as Minister of Peasant Affairs, signaled the return of the military institution—once dreaded by the Movimientistas—in a political role.

The truce imposed by the Army's Seventh Division in Cochabamba was untenable.[37] Whereas the Cliza-Ucureña conflict previously involved roadblocks, disruption of railway traffic, besieging of towns, and attacks on military posts, the confrontation now assumed a new dimension. A line of fixed fortifications extended along a "frontier" following the course of the Rio Retama. Beyond these lines of entrenchments, peasant marauders roamed the countryside terrorizing the inhabitants. When José Rojas threatened to sack the city of Cochabamba, women and children from Cliza marched to Cochabamba carrying placards ("We Demand Guarantees in Order to Live," "Cliza Asks Liberty"). Efforts to enlist mediation by the Papal Nuncio and the good offices of foreign diplomats to settle the imbroglio came to naught as the situation worsened.[38]

Entrenchments manned by militiamen equipped with mortars, machine guns, automatic rifles, and homemade explosives extended for ten kilometers on each side of the Rio Retama. Machinegun nests covered the no-man's-land between the trenches. Passage was impossible and the economic consequences severe. Gunfire from both sides of the frontier devastated livestock; martial obligations drew campesinos from their fields, resulting in an estimated 60 percent decline of harvests. The Cliza weekly market suffered as farmers and merchants chose to frequent the Punata market controlled by the Rojas organization. Newspaper reporters predicted that with over 8,000 peasants mobilized in the region, any attempt to assault the entrenchments would end in bloodshed of proportions unprecedented in Bolivian history. "We are able to see in different houses . . . light and heavy machine guns, different kinds of mortars . . . boys of 8, 10, and 12 years of age dedicated to cleaning guns and lubricating their mechanisms. Some of these boys arm and disarm a heavy machine gun with incredible speed . . . those same kids, obeying orders from their combatant fathers, are those that carry ammunition and provisions to the front. . . . We come to the conviction that they have embarked on a true arms race unprecedented in national history."[39]

President Siles dispatched another pacification commission to forestall the prospect of civil war. The commission led by General Alfredo Ovando visited first Punata and then Cliza where the Veizagista dirigente Ramón Torrico stated that the conflict began at the Peasant Congress at Sacaba where Miguel Veizaga had challenged José Rojas's suzerainty. José Rojas accused Wálter Guevara Arze of intervention in sindicato affairs, inciting the peasantry, and distributing arms and munitions to his partisans to destroy Ucureña in a bloody quest for votes. Miguel Veizaga asked for an agrarian reform of "construction and not destruction and death."[40]

The warring caciques agreed to a pacification pact with the following guarantees: exclusion of politicians from the zone, respect for the authority of the army, freedom of traffic on the Cochabamba–Santa Cruz highway, free entrance to the provincial markets, and prohibition of the sale of liquor before 6:00 p.m. The accord specified an exchange of prisoners and the surrender of weapons to the army, and was signed by the two caciques and their dirigentes: Constantino Inturias, Jorge Solíz, Fermín Delgadillo, and Gregorio López for Ucureña; and Ramón Torrico, Macedonio Pérez, Manuel Pedrazo, Basilio Grágeda, Julian Chávez, Sixto Soto, Ignacio Guevara, and Froilán Escobar for Cliza.[41] The pact sought to settle the Cliza–Ucureña war through prohibitions, but avoided the underlying causes of the conflict. The caciques were locked in a power struggle for syndical leadership of the Cochabamba peasantry, and any attempt to resolve the problem that ignored this reality was doomed to failure. José Rojas and the MNR government officials were not about to surrender political control and the perquisites of office to the MNRA upstarts Miguel Veizaga and Wálter Guevara.

In late May 1960, the caciques were again at war. Battalions of well-armed campesinos broke out of the military zone and into northern Potosí Department. Units of up to 200 militiamen operated along the Cochabamba–Potosí border using explosives and modern weapons to expand the theater of operations. Veizagistas controlled the pueblos of Yambata, Tunasani, and Taconi; Rojistas dominated the pueblos of Choroma, Huacahuatana, and Laguna. The military zone was then extended from the Cochabamba provinces of Punata and Jordán into northern Potosí Department.[42] A number of pitched battles were fought and at the pueblo of Vila Vila, a common grave was discovered with the bodies of 17 militiamen. The Vila Vila atrocity aroused national interest.[43] Miguel Veizaga denied complicity, Walter Guevara opined that the Vila Vila affair was a maneuver to liquidate the Auténtico cacique, and Juan Lechín accused Guevara Arze of "arming and paying the militias . . . in order to sow hatred and divide Bolivians." After an official inquiry determined that the victims were Rojistas, Miguel Veizaga proposed a duel between the rivals to settle the matter. José Rojas ignored the challenge.[44]

Oruro Department

Although synonymous with agrarian revolution, Cochabamba Department was but one locus of indigenous struggle. The Department of Oruro had long been a center of resistance to creole rule. The great mines of the southern Altiplano were incubators of revolutionary trade unionism. Trostkyist, Stalinist, and Movimientista revolutionaries vied for the support of Indian miners, colonos, and comunarios. It was in these mines that the Aymara revolutionary Zenón Barrientos Mamani came of age. Born in the remote community of Salinas de Garci Mendoza (Ladislao Cabrera Province) in Oruro Department, Barrientos Mamani worked in the mines at Pulacayo and Siete Suyos (Sud Chichas Province) in Potosí Department where he was initiated as an MNR militant.

Luis Peñaloza notes Zenón Barrientos Mamani's role in the 1949 MNR scheme to seize the border town of Villazón as the lynchpin of an insurrection to take control of southern Bolivia. Barrientos Mamani was able to cross the Bolivian–Argentine border at La Quiaca with impunity, while the authorities questioned creole-mestizos suspected of resistance to the Rosca.[45] He later distinguished himself as an MNR leader in the pivotal battle of Oruro during the insurrectionary phase of the 1952 National Revolution. Zenón Barrientos Mamani was a signatory to the MNR's landmark Agrarian Reform Decree of 2 August 1953.

The Aymara MNR veteran was expelled from the FSTMB at the Third National Congress of Bolivian Workers in May 1957. Barrientos Mamani's public condemnation of the bureaucratization of the MNR regime following his expulsion by an assortment of urban creole-mestizos is noteworthy: "As an Indian I will remain irreducible; nor will the threats of assassination be able to silence this voice of the Aymara struggle." He let it be known that voting for his expulsion were nine attorneys, two functionaries of the Ministry of Peasant Affairs, two merchants, an assortment of bureaucrats, and that the "pantomime" of his expulsion resulted from participation in the Izquierda sector of the MNR and his interest in "sweeping out the corruption and irresponsibility that prejudiced the Agrarian Reform." The self-described "MNR leftist, but not Lechinista" defined the MNR as a party of "subsidized functionaries" controlled by their Jefe Paz Estenssoro to whom they owed "unconditional loyalty." He characterized Juan Lechín's control of the COB as a "machine of similar characteristics . . . managed from above by a system of syndical dictatorship, bribery, and intimidation."[46] This criticism, not unlike that of the Cochabamba cacique Miguel Veizaga, resonated in Walter Guevara Arze's opposition to Paz Estenssoro's stewardship of the National Revolution.

Barrientos Mamani became entangled in a factional struggle within the Oruro Departmental Peasant Federation after his election as Secretary General in October 1959 when it was rumored that the Oruro Federation might support Walter Guevara Arze's presidential bid. Meanwhile, Guevara Arze continued his criticism of the Agrarian Reform process, citing difficulties related to determination of land boundaries in the title process, insufficient technical assistance to smallholders, and the predicament of minifundismo, the division and subdivision of plots insufficient for participation in the market economy.[47]

Syndical politics was a precarious venture. Zenón Barrientos was among those beaten by a mob that attacked the Fifth Congress of the National Confederation of Bolivian Campesino Workers (Confederación Nacional de Trabajadores Campesinos de Bolivia: CNTCB) in La Paz on 10 January 1960. Reconvening the following day, the assembly chose, among others, Alejandro Galarza (Secretary General), Zenón Barrientos (Executive Secretary), Angel Mariño (Secretary of Relations), and Miguel Veizaga (Militia Secretary) and endorsed Walter Guevara Arze's bid for the presidency. Afterward the CNTCB became mired in factionalism, most notably a public spat between Zénon Barrientos and Walter Guevara in which the Aymara dirigente emphasized that the Confederation was not a "Cell of the MNRA" and that

> Veizaga, Mariño, Juarez and the others likewise have rejected the bureaucratic leadership of the extremists, we demand to be treated as equals; we are not followers, we have left behind the time when Indians were managed as mere appendages of the political apparatus.[48]

Two weeks later Zenón Barrientos Mamani was declared a traitor to the peasant class and expelled from the CNTCB—under a resolution signed by Angel Mariño.[49]

The Election of 1960

Guevara Arze's 1960 presidential campaign presented little threat to Paz Estenssoro; nevertheless, it exposed the failings of his MNR regime. The MNR had overwhelmingly carried the rural vote in the 1956 presidential election, but won by a narrow margin over the reactionary FSB in the major cities.[50] Given the preponderance of the enfranchised Indians, the MNR victory was a foregone conclusion. Agrarian reform and universal suffrage, the basis of the party's claim to have given the Indian "land and liberty," deprived the leftist opposition of a decisive issue. The use of colored ballots differentiated the choices for the largely illiterate peasantry and also facilitated supervision of the vote by their dirigentes. In many areas, only MNR ballots were distributed and in others coercion and fraudulent practices resulted in more votes than voters: all of which made for the MNR victory of 1956.[51]

Leadership of the National Revolution was to be rotated among the MNR inner circle: Hernán Siles, Víctor Paz, Walter Guevara, and Juan Lechín. Although Siles managed a stint in the Palacio Quemado, Guevara and Lechín found the presidency an elusive goal because of Paz's thirst for power and his support from the United States. Spurned, Guevara Arze created the Auténtico MNR party (MNRA) and sought the votes of the Quechua campesinos of the Cochabamba valleys and the Altiplano Aymara.[52] The leftist stalwart Lechín, anathema to the mandarins of the

Alliance for Progress and consequently thwarted by Paz's party machine, accepted the palliative of the Vice Presidency.

Lechín aggressively pursued a leftist agenda while serving as Paz's Vice President. His opposition was formalized in the Revolutionary Party of the Nationalist Left (*Partido Revolucionario de la Izquierda Nacionalista*: PRIN) whose objective was a return to the early revolutionary ideals of *co-gobierno* shared by worker-peasant sectors. The PRIN manifesto presented an exhaustive critique of the failures of the National Revolution as well as a detailed program for "National Emancipation" from the "retrocession and treason" of the MNR:

> In all aspects of Bolivian life we are able to evidence the magnitude of the national disaster, attributable to the errors and treason of the government coterie. The anti-worker politics, anti-national and *entreguista* direction of the MNR, no longer has anything in common with the interests of the majority, constituting, certainly, a mockery of the liberating ideals of the 9th of April. Such is the itinerary of the treason consummated by the rightist inner circle of the MNR. In place of a true nationalization of the mineral riches, alienation; in place of an agrarian reform planned in benefit of the campesinos . . . hunger; in place of an independent and prosperous national economy, the conversion of the country into a dismantled territory in which it is only permissible to produce cheap tin; instead of the elimination of unemployment and the flight of human capital, an alarming increase of these; in place of integrated Indian people, pariahs; in place of democratic universal suffrage, paper citizens; in place of a popular regime, dictatorship; in place of national independence, a colonized country.[53]

Lechín's PRIN courted the votes of the indigenous majority and curried some favor with the Aymara sindicatos of the Altiplano and the fractious Cochabamba peasantry. The 1960 election confirmed the obvious. Factionalism and disunity infected the revolution. One-fifth of the electorate cast a ballot for the MNRA and FSB candidates. The results in the major cities revealed the deterioration of urban support for the MNR: voters in Cochabamba, Sucre, Oruro, and Potosí gave the combined opposition parties a majority. In La Paz, the seat of MNR power, 45 percent of the voters cast ballots for the opposition. The Auténtico campaign exposed divisions in the revolutionary leadership as well as the nation's urban–rural divide. The Auténtico schism was but the first obvious fissure in the disintegration of a revolution whose greatest threat was to come from within.[54]

A number of public recantations followed the election. Auténtico chieftains renounced membership in the MNRA, lamenting the "hatred and violence, corruption and immorality" caused by the sectarian rift among the peasantry. In an open letter to President-elect Víctor Paz Estenssoro, Miguel Veizaga announced that although he had delivered 5,000 votes to the MNRA, he wished to return to the MNR and see the Cochabamba valleys pacified with free elections in the FSTCC. Veizaga stated that the Cliza–Ucureña war had resulted from syndical bullying by José Rojas while noting the marked decrease in agricultural production caused by the conflict.[55] In its last cabinet meeting, the Siles government lifted the military zone in the Cochabamba region.

José Rojas seized the initiative and redoubled his campaign against Miguel Veizaga, announcing on 29 August 1960 his intention to blockade the city of Cochabamba and cut off the city's electricity, communications, and water supply as a protest against the failure of the government to bring Veizaga to trial for the Vila Vila massacre. The CNTCB, responding to a telegram from Rojas, petitioned the minister of justice to "castigate" Miguel Veizaga and his dirigentes for "acts of genocide committed in Vila Vila against more than a hundred peasants." On the morning of 30 August, machine gun and mortar fire were reported along the Rio Retama frontier by the commander of the army's Seventh Division who immediately deployed troops along the road from Cochabamba to Cliza, and at the Angostura Dam to prevent sabotage. The Rojista dirigente Salvador Vásquez reiterated the threat to Cochabamba, "We will block the roads, the railway lines and be forced to occupy Cliza to apprehend the leaders of the bloody acts." The Chiriria Central of Chayanta Province (Potosí Department) let it be known that it was prepared to send 60,000 militiamen from its 80 sindicatos "to end once and for all the arrogance of traitorous elements like Miguel Veizaga."[56]

Rojas's grand strategy called for mobilization of his satrapies in the Cochabamba valleys as well as alliances with peasants and miners outside the region. In northern Potosí Augustín Arancibia, the Secretary General of the Chiriria Central alerted his militias to prepare "to end once and for all the power of traitorous elements such as Miguel Veizaga, guilty of dividing the Cochabamba campesinos." The miners' militias of Catavi, Siglo XX, San José, and Huanuni (previously allied with Veizaga) announced if "the problem does not come to an opportune and favorable solution," they would drive the enemy from Cliza. Aghast at the prospect of a peasant invasion, the Legion of Ex-Combatants mobilized 6,000 Chaco War veterans for the city's defense. The vecinos of Cochabamba—the Rotary and Lions Clubs, Red Cross, Catholic Women's Club, Lawyers College, Pro-Cochabamba Committee, Catholic Action—deluged President Paz with petitions for defense of the city.[57]

Zenón Barrientos Mamani attributed the Rojas-Veizaga imbroglio to "trotskolechinista" influences concocted to sow "anarchy, division, and terror" within the revolution. In a *Presencia* interview, he observed that Paz Estenssoro's reliance on military force to enforce his will exposed him to accusations of "peasant massacres, of subservience to the gamonales and latifundistas, and of being incapable of solving the problems."[58]

José Rojas's strategy was a success. On 6 September 1960, the Ucureña dirigente Salvador Vásquez cancelled the planned blockade. The MNR government initiated legal action against Miguel Veizaga and nine dirigentes for the Vila Vila massacre and for an attack on the subprefect and a carabinero major stationed at the pueblo of Tarata. One hundred carabineros were sent to apprehend Veizaga, but the cacique faded into the fastness of the serranía. In November, he was back in Cliza directing syndical affairs.

Skirmishing resumed between the hostile sindicatos.[59] President Paz Estenssoro sent 50 Ucureña militiamen disguised as carabineros to invade Cliza and apprehend the troublesome cacique and his lieutenants. The "Battle of Cliza" erupted when the sindicato headquarters and the houses of the dirigentes César Román and Octavio Cedeño were attacked. The assailants were repulsed, but intense fighting erupted when Rojista militias approached the outskirts of town. Over 50 lives were lost before a semblance of order returned to Cliza. To forestall further bloodshed, the Bolivian air force began reconnaissance flights over the region, 300 troops from the "Waldo Ballivián" Regiment were sent from La Paz to occupy the zone, and another state of siege was imposed amid sporadic violence—including assaults on army patrols and an attack on the Cochabamba air base.[60]

The Fifth Cochabamba Peasant Conference

Military occupation and a state of siege restored order to the Cochabamba valleys. After conferring with Vice President Juan Lechín, Miguel Veizaga agreed to hold free elections in the valley sindicatos and to the selection of new local authorities by the Cliceños. A pacification conference was convened on 17 December 1960 to formally terminate hostilities. Representatives of the sindicatos were to meet, elect new officers, and draw up a code of rules and regulations prohibiting sectarianism.[61] The conference convened at the El Convento hacienda near the town of Santivánez is surrounded by controversy. It opened with a stacked deck when the 19 Veizaguista delegates arrived to face over 500 Rojista militants. When the Ucureña delegate Jorge Solís announced, "Those guilty of dividing the peasantry should be shot," the threatened Cliceños retreated from Santivañez.[62] Days after the conference, representatives of the Cliza and Ucureña Centrals agreed to a truce and Miguel Veizaga tearfully announced:

> The Revolution of April 9 promised a resurgence of the peasant class and offered a flourishing future for the pueblos; it offered to the campesinos schools, hospitals, plows, seeds, discounts, loans and many other things for the progress of the country; but, where are those promises of the National Revolution? Where are the schools, hospitals, and the progress? And where is the collaboration of the peasant in his cultural and economic resurgence? Until now, we see only death and misery in our towns and the countryside.

Veizaga concluded, "Now that we are in the stage of gaining pacification and unity, I will shortly return to work in my *chacra* [plot], withdrawing from syndical life." Despite Miguel Veizaga's claim to relinquish politics and President Paz Estenssoro's demand for "pacification at any price," the Cliza and Ucureña war reignited in episodic feuding.[63]

The Altiplano

The Aymara of Omasuyos Province (La Paz Department) are most populous in the fertile, well-watered lands along the littoral of Lake Titicaca. The ancient archaeological site of Tiwanaku attests to the past accomplishments of a united Quolla people. Since the decline of Tiwanaku, the Aymara have served foreign lords—Inca, Spanish, creole—while retaining much of their ethnic identity. In doing so, they have paid a price in the eyes of others. Thus, their most astute observer refers to the "Black Legend" of Aymara hostility toward outsiders who have "marginalized and exploited them for centuries."[64] One finds in the urban folklore of La Paz, as well as in academic treatises, a veritable lexicon of opprobrium compiled by outside observers. Writing in 1966, the behavioral psychologist John Plummer observed:

> "Over the years, they [Aymara] have been described as hostile, apprehensive, negative, depressed, pessimistic, unimaginative, sullen, cruel, suspicious, brutal, ignorant, irresponsible, unsmiling, dull, stolid, malevolent, thieving, treacherous, melancholic, drunken, untrustworthy, violent, insecure, careless, rancorous, morose, jealous, quarrelsome, malicious, reticent, silent, uncommunicative, tense, distrustful, sad, dishonest, fearful, anxious, doubtful, gloomy, slovenly, and filthy."[65]

These observers, of course, were indistinguishable to the Aymara from local oppressors, and hence "these attitudes were recorded as part of the innate personality of the Aymara." Summing up this Black Legend of Aymara behavior, Plummer noted: "What many, but certainly not all, Aymara share and have shared is brutal domination by other societies and the pressures of a harsh environment. The result of this long history of socio-economic domination by Inca, Spanish, and then mestizo society has been the development of an attitude of hostility, sullenness, and suspicion toward mestizos and those whom they have classified as being associated with mestizos."[66]

The National Revolution intensified the complex sociopolitical relationships among Altiplano comunarios, hacienda colonos, and creole-mestizo hacendados. Tensions between Indians and townspeople heightened as the subaltern majority became politically organized and active in defense of their rights to land and liberty. In search of political advantage, creole-mestizo townspeople and hacendados looked to the MNR for the means to continue their dominion. Vecinos joined the MNR and formed networks of political patronage to continue domination of the peasantry through penetration of the agrarian sindicato structure.[67]

Aymara Factionalism

Prior to the 1952 Revolution, the highland Aymara, whether comunarios or hacienda colonos, lived within the kin-based ayllu community and, as Xavier Albó notes, "In some places, above all in the Yungas of La Paz and the vicinity of the shore of Titicaca . . . haciendas had gone as far as *virtually borrowing* [original emphasis] the Aymara organizational system."[68] It should be remembered that although the sindicato was introduced during the National Revolution, much of the political behavior (e.g., sindicato factionalism and conflict) can ultimately be related to the workings of Aymara and Quechua kindreds. Factional politics among the urban elites, such as the internecine squabbles of the MNR regime, as well as implementation of the agrarian reform decree, would have local and regional reverberations among a backdrop of indigenous kin conflict. Disputes between ayllus may be traced for centuries in colonial and republican legal records and the practice of *tinku*, the ritual combat between ayllus, is discernable in the Andean iconographic record as far back as 500 AD.[69]

It has been observed that the underlying cause of Aymara factionalism is access to land and water. The resource most frequently in dispute is land, and boundary conflicts are a frequent cause of litigation. Factionalism is also influenced by demographic pressure. A study of 60 highland cases found conflicts over natural resources were most frequent in areas of high population density, and the ayllus most marginal to urban influences best maintained their equilibrium, albeit "a static and cyclical one."[70] Factional conflicts among ayllus in the Altiplano Department of La Paz and northern Potosí Department were, in turn, subsumed by the factionalism of the Movimientista elites during the latter years of the National Revolution. Two regions experienced particularly virulent syndical rivalries: the Achacachi–Warisata area of Omasuyos Province (La Paz Department) and the Laymi–Jukumani territory in Bustillo Province (Potosí Department). Achacachi is influenced by metropolitan La Paz and Bustillo by the great mines at nearby Catavi-Siglo XX. Increased communication, greater population density, and differential access to limited natural resources made for heightened factionalism in both areas.[71]

Achacachi–Warisata Conflicts

The conflict between the ayllu community of Warisata and the neighboring town of Achacachi affords a look into the workings of Altiplano syndicalism and the nexus of local, regional, and national-level politics. Underlying the syndical struggle were historical forces, including hostility between peasants and townspeople, the pressures of hacienda encroachment on ayllu communities due to increasing demand for foodstuffs to supply the mines, and the resultant expansion in numbers and size of haciendas to supply this increased demand. By the eve of the 1952 Revolution, Warisata remained one of the few ayllu communities that had escaped hacienda expansion.

Achacachi lies 90 kilometers northwest of La Paz near the shore of Lake Titicaca. It is the provincial capital and the largest town (3,600 inhabitants in 1969) in the most densely inhabited (60 inhabitants per square kilometer) rural region of La Paz Department. The seat of a biweekly market, it is visited by campesinos from the surrounding countryside who sell their goods to Achacachi middlemen. As the teacher Elizardo Pérez noted in his memoir, the town is rife with small-town hustlers: "The fauna of exploiters includes all the pettifoggers, judges, secretaries, auxiliaries, agents, subprefects, intendents, corregidores, priests, and even gendarmes whose imagination makes them conceive of all kinds of swindles with the appearances of legality. . . . [I]n Achacachi all are shysters." Achacacheños were widely known for rapaciousness and the town was symbolic of "social dominance of hispano-criollo orientation."[72] In common with other provincial capitals, hacendados were numerous among the townspeople, and within the realm of their influence was the Warisata ayllu community.

When Elizardo Pérez was searching for a location for his Indian school, he was drawn to Warisata. Sometime before his arrival, the community had been afflicted by encroaching Achacachi landlords, "who had been gradually despoiling the Indians until they had converted themselves into owners of nearly the entire zone."[73] Resistance to this invasion, together with the cumulative effects of Pérez's ayllu school and earlier messianic movements on the ayllu in the 1920s, fostered the community's synergy—"the peculiarity of being *the comunidad originaria* of the region."[74] The Warisata ayllu was singularly adept in defense of its interests. Threats to Warisata came from neighboring sindicatos comprised of hacienda ex-colonos—a continuation of ancient boundary feuds now aggravated by the ambiguities of the agrarian reform process.

Conflict over access to land and water rights remained a source of contention between the ayllu comunarios, ex-colonos, and hacendados. Only weeks after the Agrarian Reform Decree, a boundary dispute between Mirq'i Achacachi comunarios (under the sway of Hacienda Belén ex-colonos) and Warisata comunarios escalated from a boundary dispute into a wider confrontation. Thousands of peasants were mobilized after the Warisata dirigente Samuel Marcos Mamani was beaten and taken captive at Mirq'i Achacachi.[75]

Factionalism often led to rivalry between sindicato dirigentes competing for power. Luciano Quispe, a cholo schoolteacher from Achacachi and dirigente of the Belén sindicato, was overthrown by another Achacachi cholo, Toribio Salas.[76] A shoemaker by trade and politico by temperament, Salas was an early syndical organizer whose activities predated the revolution. The British geographer David Preston found that at the newly formed town of Umacha: "The local political agent, Toribio Salas, had waited secretly nearby and sent an envoy to approach several of the known sympathizers from among the community leaders. He said they should form a union that would educate the workers to unite against their landowner, give him only his due and take over his land when the new government came to power."[77]

From 1955 to 1963, the Salas political machine dominated both the La Paz Departmental Peasant Federation and the Achacachi vecinos and hacendados.[78] A study of the lakeside community of Compi notes, "Achacachi and Compi mutually fear and detest each other," and "Toribio Salas . . . who terrorized the province for many years during the last governmental term was especially despised. For the women and children the mention of his name was like that of the Roman 'Hanibal ad portas.' When he finally came, everyone packed his valuables and fled until the menace was over." Salas controlled the regional political offices vital to local development: "Salas appeared twice in Compi; once when he replaced the secretary-general for working too closely with the patron and once when the school was being built. His inquiry as to why the people were accepting assistance from a Catholic institution, one which was believed to support the main opposition party, was enough to stop school construction from some time."[79] This, in itself, would not have led the cacique afoul of the MNR: it was his support of Juan Lechín's presidential bid that led to his undoing.

Incident at Atahuallpani

In the afternoon of 15 November 1959, Aymara Indians assassinated a white man. The rare breach of taboo occurred on the outskirts of Atahuallpani, a village in northern La Paz Department. The victim was Vicente Álvarez Plata, a hacendado, right-wing Movimientista, and an ex-Minister of Peasant Affairs in the Siles government. The incident illustrates syndical politics at the cacique level as well as the MNR's precarious control over the Altiplano sindicatos. President Siles had found it expedient to mobilize peasant militias to intimidate miners, but ushering peasant militias into politics on the national level was a two-edged sword.[80]

The president's decision to utilize peasant militias involved subsuming the La Paz Peasant Federation within the Ministry of Peasant Affairs—a move tantamount to a creole usurpation of the Indian federation. The choice of Vicente Álvarez Plata, an MNR insider from a Yungas landowning family, as the agent for the maneuver occasioned a storm of anger among the La Paz peasantry. Delegates from 16 provinces declared the Minister their enemy, accused him of fomenting divisions among them, and petitioned the president for Álvarez Plata's resignation.[81] Siles was forced to acquiesce and Álvarez Plata resigned his position. Yet the ex-minister continued to meddle in campesino politics. This was a dangerous move, as was his decision to attend a provincial sindicato meeting at Sorata that included peasants from Atahuallpani, a village with a reputation for militant politics, and their rivals from the Millipaya sindicato aligned with the Izquierdista faction led by the cacique Toribio Salas.

Vicente Álvarez Plata's fate is recounted in a study by the Research Institute for the Study of Man: "Late in the afternoon Álvarez Plata set out by car for La Paz, accompanied by two of his machinegun carrying bodyguards, by Carlos Palacios, a prominent Sorata vecino who was also a prominent politician, and one or two other MNR politicians. When the group reached the campesino village of Atahuallpani, on the hillside almost directly opposite Sorata, they found the road blocked by a truck loaded with armed campesinos, including some from Atahuallpani. The campesinos attempted to seize [Álvarez] Plata, but he resisted and was shot to death."[82]

The convicted assassin was Paulino Quispe, a trusted Salas lieutenant known as the *Wila Saco* (Aymara: "bloody shirt").[83] Toribio Salas's involvement in the assassination was based on circumstantial evidence as the "intellectual author" of the murder. Salas steadfastly denied complicity, pointing out his compadrazgo relationship with the dead man's brother, Federico Álvarez Plata, and hinted at sinister forces at work: "I refer to the politics of the government that had an interest in eliminating me as a dirigente. . . . I was of the Sector de Izquierda with Don Juan Lechín and others."[84] Salas regarded Lechín as the defender of the National Revolution and, "because there was bad between them (Siles and Lechín) they looked for a motive to eliminate me as a leader because I was the hope of all Bolivia, of the peasantry. My plans were immense and because of this they didn't like me, *los señores políticos*."[85] In an interview with the author, Ñuflo Chávez attributed Álvarez Plata's demise to the designs of Toribio Salas for control of the La Paz departmental sindicato federation. Adding credence to Chávez's point is the fact that following the assassination, the secretary of the Sorata Central (an Álvarez Plata supporter) was murdered.[86]

The assassination of a member of the MNR elite by an Indian elicited sensational media attention. Toribio Salas was labeled "Assassin and Scourge of Belén," at the service of "Red Extremism" and Achacachi was said to be "Under the Terror of Toribio Salas." Lurid stories of indigenous violence, replete with references to drunken peasant hordes, murders, the "bloody shirt" (and a visit by a Cuban diplomat to Achacachi to confer with Salas and distribute photos of Fidel Castro), obscured the underlying conflict among the creole leaders of the National Revolution. The Altiplano sindicatos remained under the sway of the intractable Achacachi cacique whose fealty was to Vice President Lechín, "who we call 'El Viejo' . . . a man sacrificed for the workers. The situation escalated and we went on the side of Lechín."[87]

Toribio Salas' expulsion from the Omasuyos federation failed to deter him from further violence. On 3 February 1960, Salas and Paulino Quispe allegedly killed a campesino and wounded two others near Belén.[88] Again, accusations of murder failed to tarnish the cacique's reputation among his followers. Two months later, the National Campesino Federation expressed support for Salas and the Huila Saco over the objections of the La Paz Departmental Federation now under the leadership of Felipe Flores, an *evangelista* (Protestant missionary) schoolteacher from Huarina. Toribio Salas was accused of misappropriation of sindicato funds and the bloody shirt of the Álvarez Plata affair waved in a campaign to neutralize the Izquierdista strongman. Undeterred by an impending government investigation of the Atahuallpani assassination, related murders, and opposition to his leadership sponsored by the Paz regime—voiced in the denunciations of provincial and departmental campesino sindicatos—Toribio Salas announced the formation of a new militia, the "Colorados of Bolivia," who would wear the red uniform of the Bolivian army in the War of the Pacific (1879–1880). Two months later, at a departmental congress at Pucurani, delegates voted "to defend the innocence" of the cacique and, if necessary, declare a national strike on his behalf.[89]

Factional Storm: The Downfall of the Izquierdista Caciques

Accounts of the peasantry in the twilight of the National Revolution tend to focus on the syndical gangsterism highlighted by the sensational murder of Vicente Álvarez Plata.⁹⁰ Yet also at work was a reign of terror unleashed by the Paz Estenssoro regime against Vice President Lechín's Izquierdista supporters in Cochabamba Department—Facundo Olmos (Sacaba), Miguel Veizaga (Cliza), Sinforoso Rivas, and Enrique Encinas (Quillacollo)—resulting in their elimination as a threat to the dictates of the MNR jefe.⁹¹ Behind Víctor Paz loomed the Control Político secret police and the renascent military, resuscitated by the president for use in factional schemes against a rising tide of opposition.

The venue for determination of peasant syndical alliances was the Second National Congress held in Santa Cruz in mid-March 1963 where Toribio Salas's Altiplano contingent planned to combine forces with the Cochabamba Izquierdistas Rivas, Veizaga, and Olmos. According to Salas, the Congress was to be a forum for debate of sindicato leadership and the subsequent determination of whom to support. However, the road to Santa Cruz was perilous. "The route was barred to us; armed with machine guns they [Control Político agents] reviled us, hitting and insulting us. . . . [T]hey treated us like delinquents."⁹² The Salas delegation traveling in rented taxis could not afford to dally. MNR thugs in Cochabamba assaulted the dirigente Marcos Rojas of Pucarani. As Salas recalls, "We were unable to walk the streets." Once in Santa Cruz, the delegates found the prefect unwilling to guarantee their safety unless they switched their allegiance to President Paz Estenssoro. Worse, they learned that Colonel Claudio San Román, the infamous master of Control Político, was in town for the affair.⁹³ Outnumbered, isolated, and intimidated, the Iziquerdistas withdrew after a stormy opening session where the Congress elected the Pazestenssorista Felipe Flores Executive Secretary. Salas and the other Izquierdistas fled to the local COB headquarters—with army troops, bayonets drawn, in hot pursuit—and then to the Quillacollo Central where a hastily convened National Peasant Congress elected Pedro Rivera Executive Secretary, and Sinforoso Rivas, Facundo Olmos, and Toribio Salas to other leadership positions.⁹⁴

Trouble awaited the Achacachi cacique's return to the Altiplano. Salas and his militiamen were shot at in La Paz while celebrating the annual "March of the Revolution" on 9 April 1963. The attackers were Pazestenssoristas under the command of Salas's enemies Felipe Flores of Huarina and Eliseo Gutiérrez of Warisata. After sacking the houses of Salas and Paulino Quispe, the Achacachi Central delivered the coup de grâce—ousting Toribio Salas and replacing him with Felipe Flores as Executive Secretary. Salas's ouster was the finishing touch of a web spun by senior military officers. Preparatory to the sindicato coup, Air force planes had circled Achacachi dropping leaflets stating that Salas was a communist and calling for support of Felipe Flores. After the coup, army troops occupied the area and Flores's militiamen took control of Achacachi and Huarina. The deposed cacique called a press conference in La Paz where he claimed his overthrow was the work of the MNR regime, but also added that to avoid further strife, he would desist from political activity. Toribio Salas was "ignominiously expelled from the peasant family" at the Izquierda's National Congress of Campesino Workers in May 1963 for the alleged sale of the Achacachi vote to the MNR in the forthcoming election.[95]

The military's interest in controlling the Achacachi sindicato continued with a Civic Action program to provide a water tower for the town to endear the locals to their military benefactors and woo them away from supporting Juan Lechín. The project was the brainchild of the army's senior engineer, Colonel Julio Sanjinéz Goitia, the son of an Altiplano hacendado, director of *El Diario*, and a well-connected West Point graduate with influence at the U.S. Embassy where he initiated Alliance for Progress civic action projects. Construction of the water tower, however, failed to accomplish its political objective. Instead it backfired, incurring the wrath of the populace (an attempt was made to bomb the installation) who objected to the notion that they should pay for the project. Despite the artifice of Civic Action, hearts and minds were not easily won among the Altiplano Aymara.[96] Meanwhile, the conflict between Achacachi Lechinistas and Warisata Pazestenssoristas continued despite the expulsion of Toribio Salas from the peasant federation. In mid-June 1963, *El Diario* reported an outbreak of violence at Achacachi where two Lechinistas were murdered by Warisata Pazestenssoristas commanded by Felipe Flores, "the new cacique of that region."[97] As Víctor Paz asserted control over the Altiplano peasantry, hegemony in Omasuyos Province passed to the Warisata dirigente Felipe Flores.

In Cochabmba Department, the Izquierdista dirigente Facundo Olmos of the Quillacollo Central (who had boasted after Salas's defeat that nothing similar could happen at Quillacollo) found himself the target of campesinos loyal to President Paz.[98] Meanwhile, Air Force General René Barrientos planned to enter the Cochabamba political fray amidst the factional conflicts of the Quillacollo Central and the Cliza–Ucureña vendetta between José Rojas and Miguel Veizaga. The drama was orchestrated against a cacophony of violence between August and October 1963. After the grisly death of a Cliceño peasant, the Quillacollo sindicato asked for government intervention to halt the violence and denounced José Rojas, "once a symbol of liberation" and now "converted into a symbol of terror." Amidst a wave of assaults and beatings, Facundo Olmos, "maximum leader" of the Quillacollo federation and a parliamentary deputy, was machine-gunned in an ambush at Sacaba. Other dirigentes were shot, and houses including Miguel Veizaga's were sacked and burned.[99]

Juan Lechín's influence in the Cochabamba valleys evaporated. In the aftermath of the Olmos assassination, a coup at the Quillacollo Central by sindicato militia from the area expelled the remaining Izquierdista dirigentes and new leaders were "elected" under the direction of the Ucureña militia. As with Achacachi-Huarina, the region was then declared a military zone. Curiously, the military zone in Quillacollo was declared days before the coup and a motorized battalion from Oruro was dispatched to control the fait accompli. The Trotskyist publication *Masas* presciently argued that "the campesino Facundo Olmos, beastly assassinated by the

[MNR]counterrevolutionary officialdom," was part of a Pentagon-backed scheme that included civic action projects as part of General René Barrientos' strategy to ingratiate himself with the peasantry, become Vice President, and then President of a military dictatorship.[100]

Following the Quillacollo coup, 35 dirigentes from the Cochabamba valleys (including José Rojas, Jorge Soliz, Ramon Torrico, and Macedonio Juárez) were flown with Generals Barrientos and Rivas Ugalde to La Paz where General Barrientos discussed pacification of the Cochabamba valleys with the dirigentes over champagne and caviar at his home.[101] A military zone imposed in September 1963 was followed by the report of a government commission recommending the removal of Miguel Veizaga from Cochabamba to La Paz where he was to remain following his arrest. The commission recommended measures to augment military influence over the peasant sindicatos through the U.S.-sponsored Civic Action program of rural school construction, irrigation projects, and technical assistance to win the allegiance of the campesinos. Army General Alfredo Ovando Candia, later to be revealed as a conspirator in a military *golpe de estado* against the MNR, was a prominent member of the commission.[102] The appointment of General Eduardo Rivas Ugalde (who earlier had enforced "pacification" of the Cochabamba peasantry) as Minister of Peasant Affairs tightened the military's control over the peasant militias.

Northern Potosí: Peasants, Miners, and the Alliance for Progress

The emergence of peasant sindicatos in the Chayanta and Bustillo provinces of Northern Potosí incurred the concerted opposition of hacendados and vecinos centered in the creole-mestizo stronghold of San Pedro de Buena Vista. The Agrarian Reform Law excluded claims to lands lost before the year 1900, but the law nevertheless sparked indigenous attempts to reclaim usurped lands and occasioned boundary disputes between ayllu communities. The comunarios and colonos of northern Potosí, denizens of a remote mountainous world, were influenced by the tin mines that drew upon indigenous laborers to extract the *Metal del Diablo*. Army massacres of mine workers protesting their abysmal lot is a recurrent chapter in Bolivian history. Led by the Inquierdista Juan Lechín, the miners' unions were anathema to the modernization strategy formulated by the Kennedy administration to counter the influence of Cuban inspired anti-imperialism. Indeed, U.S. insistence that Paz—and not Lechín—assume the presidency prompted Paz Estenssoro's decision to seek a third term in office.

The North American assessment of the "Situation in Bolivia," prepared for the CIA Directorate of Intelligence, summarized the Agency's views regarding Juan Lechín and the miners: "The miners' unions are organized under the Mine Workers Federation (FSTMB) which is headed by pro-Communist Juan Lechín Oquendo. Most of the mine leaders are extreme leftists and Communists whose purposes are not to assist in the nationalization of the industry but to obstruct it." The report concluded that the miner and peasant militias, once used as a counterweight by Paz against the armed forces, had now become a formidable military force.[103] Hence, if Bolivia was to become a Latin American prototype for modernization of an underdeveloped country, it was imperative that the recalcitrant miners be repressed.

The bailout of the insolvent Bolivian economy depended on implementation of the Triangular Plan to fund the rehabilitation of COMIBOL, the state mining entity destined to receive some $45 million in aid from USAID, the Inter-American Development Bank, and West Germany. COMIBOL employed 28,000 workers, the majority comprising the bloated above ground MNR bureaucracy. Tin production had fallen by 50 percent in the first six years of the National Revolution and, despite the enforced layoffs and reduction of miners' perquisites in accordance with the Stabilization Plan, production in 1963 was two-thirds of prerevolutionary output, and earnings in the decade 1953–1963 had decreased by 22 percent.[104]

The Triangular Plan, introduced to salvage the Paz Estenssoro government, mirrored the draconian stabilization measures implemented under the Siles administration. President Paz was to enforce the Triangular Plan administered by USAID technocrats under the aegis of the Alliance for Progress. The plan stipulated a reduction in the number of miners (i.e., layoffs), elimination of the leaders of the mine workers' union (a violation of the *fuero sindical*), and reprivatization of state-owned mines (i.e., COMIBOL). In the estimation of the CIA, the most serious obstacles to the plan were labor obstruction and Paz Estenssoro's probable failure to implement the decree because of miners' strikes and the possible kidnapping of COMIBOL administrators and foreign technicians.[105] The Triangular Plan's debt trap required COMIBOL to use one-half of the loans to purchase U.S. manufactured products.[106] The COB suggested an entirely different approach, including higher taxes on private capital, price controls, wage increases for workers, acceptance of Soviet aid for construction of a tin smelter, road and railway construction. As had been the case with the earlier Stabilization Plan, the Triangular Plan met with the strident opposition of the mine workers. Over 150,000 work days were lost to strikes in 1960 and another 490,000 to strikes in 1961.[107]

Within this scenario emerged the ex-miner and right-wing MNR fanatic Wilge Nery, a municipal official and parliamentary deputy from the northern Potosí town of Uncia near the Catavi-Siglo XX mines. A fanatical anti-communist, Nery enlisted the support of comunarios from the Jukumani ayllus in an effort to forestall the possibility of an alliance between Marxist miners and Laymi comunarios. Stoking fear of communist land expropriation, Nery utilized his government connections to obtain and distribute guns and ammunition to the Jukumani comunarios. He used the Jukumani–Laymi feud to his advantage against the miners, supplying arms to the Jukumanis, while walking about accompanied by Jukumani bodyguards armed with machine guns.[108]

Northern Potosí was fertile ground for trafficking in guns and ammunition. As reported in *La Presencia*, "The dispute over boundaries between Laymis and Jucumanis has degenerated into a war to the death owing to the intense activity conducted by unscrupulous merchants selling arms and ammunition to campesinos, selling machine guns for Bs. 3,000,000 each and bullets Bs. 1,500."[109] The Jukumanis used weapons acquired from Nery to pillage neighboring ayllus. Marauding Jukumanis plundered Laymi ayllus to their northwest and Kakachaka ayllus to the southwest, razing houses and killing scores of comunarios. The horrors of this blood feud are graphically portrayed in Néstor Taboada Terán's, *Indios en Rebelión*:

> And there were over seven hundred plotters who attacked at the [Laymi] ranchos at three in the morning. . . . [T]hey entered with stealth . . . carrying torches . . . quickly thrown to the thatched roofs of the cabins. Instantly confusion reigned. The Indians, Laymi women and children who tried to flee were cornered by rifle shots from strategically positioned sharpshooters. . . . Some of the Laime families . . . fled like torches illuminating the tragedy, others perished, charred. The young girls that escaped the gunshots and the flames . . . soon fell into the hands of hundreds of assailants who raped them mercilessly. The infants, witnesses to the violence were hacked to death with an axe . . . [others] had their tongue cut so they could not speak of their experience.[110]

Unknown to those at the time (including the Jukumani, Laymi, and Kakachaka peasants), was a gambit played by President Paz Estenssoro and orchestrated by North American agents under the cover of the Alliance for Progress. As the diplomatic historian Thomas Field Jr. found, "In mid-1963, the economists' demands dovetailed with the growing militarization of Washington's larger aid program, as well as a burgeoning CIA role in support of President Paz's repressive apparatus. This culminated in a covert, US-funded Indian militia operation against the Siglo XX mining camp, approved by the Kennedy White House under the official aegis of the Alliance for Progress."[111] How one of the most remote regions in the heart of the Andes became a cockpit of Cold War geopolitics provides a telling example of the impact of neocolonialism on an indigenous people, unaware of their circumstances, within a Machiavellian scheme spun from afar.

The Laymi responded to Jukumani depredations by allying with the miners of Siglo XX. The alliance was the handiwork of Federico Escobar, a member of the Bolivian Communist Party (PCB) renowned for his indefatigable union leadership at Siglo XX.[112] Escobar promoted literacy among the Laymi to raise their political consciousness, and arms and ammunition flowed from the mines to the Laymi communities as a quid pro quo for their pledge to defend the miners in the event of government repression: in return the Laymi were granted pulpería foodstuffs at a favorable price. Unfortunately, the effort proved counterproductive, drawing the ire of Wilge Nery and resentful Jukumanis who responded by assaulting Laymi settlements, murdering, plundering, and burning houses.[113] Unknown to the Laymi comunarios, Federico Escobar, and the miners, a plan was afoot and they were its target. The U.S. ambassador's "Contingency Plan" was approved by the Alliance for Progress administrator who gave the go-ahead to USAID Office of Public Safety agents to "force a show-down" at Siglo XX, and "arm an Indian paramilitary force to attack the mining camp."[114]

The Indian paramilitaries would be Jukumanis led by Wilge Nery with weapons surreptitiously provided by the Alliance for Progress. Thomas Field Jr. notes, "The CIA reported that Paz planned to employ this paramilitary force in order 'to avoid using the army as a repressive force against the miners, to create a climate for army occupation to pacify the area, and to create a climate for elimination of extremist labor leaders.'"[115] Considered a subversive threat to the security of the Paz regime and the national security of the United States, the tin miners were to be provoked and then crushed in a counterinsurgency scheme concocted and orchestrated by Ambassador Ben Stephansky, financed by USAID, and coordinated by Office of Public Safety operatives, with the backing of the Kennedy White House. Pressured by the threat of a halt in Alliance for Progress loans should he fail to implement the Triangular Plan's labor strictures, President Paz acquiesced to the showdown at Catavi-Siglo XX. Faced with a failing economy, the defection of the middle class, the opposition of the entire spectrum of political parties, as well as the specter of military intervention, Paz was understandably reluctant to confront the mine workers. Hence, he requested $1,000,000 in military funds to finance a covert operation organized by his National Chief of Political Control. As reported by the CIA, "Colonel Claudio San Román, head of . . . the government's covert action arm . . . has organized a 200-man battalion of civilians armed with 170 rifles and 30 machine guns and disguised as Indians for deployment in the Catavi area. This battalion will descend on Catavi . . . kill as many of the extremist leaders as possible, and force the miners into a defensive situation."[116]

The expectation was that the miners would respond with a strike and Paz would then send in the army to repress the miners and rid the union of communists, eliminating Juan Lechín's political base. General René Barrientos confided to U.S. Air Force Attaché Colonel Edward Fox that a state of siege would likely be imposed on the country to lessen the possibility of a civil war and suggested that U.S. Special Forces might be necessary to assist the Bolivian armed forces in the event of an uprising by the populace. Contingency plans were laid. The State Department informed the White House of its intention to involve the Organization of American States should armed intervention be necessary to support the Paz regime. Failing multilateral intervention by the OAS, the Pentagon would act unilaterally. Ambassador Stephansky prepared for the mass evacuation of embassy personnel, and Secretary of State Dean Rusk approved the shipment of arms and ammunition to the La Paz USAID office. On 26 July 1963, Office of Public Safety operatives took possession of the Alliance for Progress weapons and munitions to enforce implementation of the Triangular Plan, deemed essential to the survival of Paz Estenssoro's regime: 4,500 tear gas grenades, 200 semiautomatic M-1 carbines, 200,000 rounds of machine gun ammunition, 50,000 rounds of .38 Special ammunition, and 12,500 shotgun shells. "The following day, the US military mission chief in La Paz submitted an 'urgent request for 408 3.5-inch high explosive rockets'."[117]

Much of the weaponry was handed over to Paz's presidential guards who were instructed to deliver their cargo to Nery; regional authorities and transit police were ordered to allow Nery's shipment free passage en route to northern Potosí. The logistics of the operation were successful; Paz's presidential guards, disguised as peasants and with two truckloads of USAID armaments, rendezvoused with Nery's militia at the town of Irupata. The stage was set for implementation of the ruse beginning with an attack by Nery's Jukumani militiamen together with Paz's presidential guards on the miners of Siglo XX.

At this point, the scheme went awry. Nery's militia failed to operate clandestinely, villagers became aware of the strangers in their midst, and word of their presence quickly reached Siglo XX. Before dawn on 29 July 1963, Wilge Nery and his militiamen were surrounded by the miners' militia. When Nery refused to surrender, the miners dynamited his hideout. Under the pretense of surrender, Nery's militiamen gunned down the approaching miners: among the victims was MNR militant Octavio Torrico, the leader of the Siglo XX militia. Nery's duplicity was answered with a barrage of dynamite and rifle fire, wounding Nery's wife, prompting the exit of the Jukumani paramilitaries, and resulting in Nery's capture and execution. The USAID weapons cache fell into the hands of the Siglo XX miners' militia.[118]

Paz Estenssoro's covert action operation failed to accomplish its objective. The miners continued their intransigence, Juan Lechín's influence remained intact, and completion of the Triangular Plan awaited another solution. Following a visit to Washington and a meeting with President Kennedy, Paz upped the ante over Siglo XX. Scores of communist miners were fired and warrants issued for the arrest of their leaders. Predictably, the intractable miners responded with a walkout and a hunger strike by their families. Paz retaliated. Two key PCB leaders were captured and imprisoned by Control Político agents. The miners responded with a sensational gambit. Four North American technicians at nearby Catavi were captured and held hostage. The ensuing "hostage crisis" embarrassed and incensed the Paz and Kennedy governments. White House plans for covert action to eradicate Paz's opposition within worker and peasant sindicatos were authorized and military preparations initiated. Bolivian infantry, a motorized battalion, airborne troops, carabineros, and militias from Ucureña and Achacachi were mobilized to crush the miners. Only after Juan Lechín negotiated the release of the hostages were the military and peasant detachments ordered to stand down.

Overthrow

By late 1963, it was evident that the armed forces had returned to prominence as a political force. Beginning with an infusion of U.S. Military Assistance Program (MAP) funds in 1958, the percentage of MNR government expenditures apportioned to the armed forces expanded, accounting for 14 percent of the national budget in 1964.[119] North American military advisors had recommended expansion of the armed forces to enforce the Stabilization Plan during the Siles administration as a counterpoise to the indigenous militia forces, particularly the miners who were considered the cause of political instability. U.S. Army Attaché Paul Wimert warned of the dangers posed by militias in a 1960 memo: "The civilian militias, with arms and weapons, are large in number, spread throughout the country . . . able to appear on the scene without formal orders . . . and their logistical problems are few. With what the Bolivian Army has at hand today, it would be like 'killing ants at a picnic' to eliminate the civilian militia."[120]

The military buildup continued under the second Paz Estenssoro government, increasing in size and influence: 659 officers were trained at the School of the Americas in Panama in 1962–1963. The entire class of senior cadets was schooled at the jungle warfare facility in Panama, and 20 of the 23 senior officers attended the School of the Americas during 1963–1964.[121] A contingent of U.S. Green Berets arrived in 1962 to instruct the Bolivian army in counterinsurgency operations. The Méndez Arcos Ranger regiment, replete with modern armaments, was installed at Challapata (Oruro Department) and the "Max Toledo" Regiment, barracked at the Viacha railway junction outside La Paz, was motorized and rearmed. The "Waldo Ballivián" presidential guards, the "Ingavi" Regiment, and the cadets of the Escuela Militar de Clases in La Paz were equipped with semiautomatic rifles, machine guns, bazookas, and morters. The miners' militias of Oruro were now outgunned by a modernized army as were the peasant and worker militias near La Paz, courtesy of U.S. As a foreign journalist observed, "General Barrientos himself has a rather 'made in USA' appearance, as have the armed forces generally, with their United States equipment, United States-style uniforms, and United States trained officers."[122]

Civic Action

The State Department's Bureau of Intelligence and Research advocated deploying the armed forces to the countryside to combat the hostility and resentment of a peasantry that associated the military with repression and violence. The mission was to initiate Civic Action projects to improve the rural standard of living and foster respect for the military, engendering an image of soldiers as friends, not foes. Eighty percent of the Bolivian military budget went to Civic Action projects, noted Ambassador Stephansky.[123] The military institution was now the proverbial 800-pound gorilla in the Palacio Quemado. Paz Estenssoro's use of the military for Civic Action drew praise from Teodoro Moscosco, the coordinator of the Alliance for Progress: "I was in Bolivia several months ago, and what I saw the armed forces doing in the name of the betterment of their country and the lives of their people was something incredible. Roads are being built and repaired, virgin lands are being colonized, maps of the country are being drawn up, rural schools are being built, potable water is being provided to tiny communities, and medical services are being given to people who live in remote areas."[124]

General René Barrientos Ortuño

General Barrientos quickly grasped the political opportunities of rural development. Bankrolled by civic action funds, the general flew about the Cochabamba countryside personally inaugurating public works projects, as he decried the "sterile struggle" between peasant factions. The General's efforts to endear himself to the indigenous populace were herculean: "Barrientos had flown the equivalent of two and a half times around the earth, at a cost to the government of $800,000 U.S. dollars, he barnstormed among the *campesinos*, listening to their complaints, promising them favors, and generally showing himself to be at home in their company—breaking through the barrier of their illiteracy by personal contact."[125] Addressing the campesinos in Quechua while identifying himself as a Cochabambino, the General recalled his year's sojourn among the peasantry after the failed MNR Civil War, when "the peasants were like brothers to me." The heroic Movimientista aviator presented himself as patrón and heir apparent to another Cochabambino, the martyred benefactor of the National Revolution, Gualberto Villarroel. But the general's intentions extended far beyond Cochabamba Department.

Described in the press as "handsome," "impetuous," and "high-living," the General exemplified the military ideal: courageous, audacious, dynamic. An inveterate philanderer, René Barrientos was the quintessential macho: one wonders how he found time for politics. Born in the pueblo of Tarata in the Cochabamba Valle Alto, Barrientos elicited analogies with a fellow Tarateño, the nineteenth-century tyrant Mariano Melgarejo, a general similarly famous for his excesses. Barrientos demonstrated a flair for the dramatic and a knack for publicity. After three airmen died when their parachutes failed to deploy, the general fastened a parachute and made the jump himself.[126] This demonstration of unabashed bravery brought public adulation and the military's highest honor, the "Condor of the Andes" medal.

Barrientos had piloted Víctor Paz home from exile in April 1952 and because of his history of fealty to Paz, the general was called upon to tame the feuding Cochabamba peasantry.[127] Barrientos' designs among the Cochabamba peasantry were advanced with the "pacification" of the valleys following the assassination of Facundo Olmos, and the subsequent golpe against Juan Lechín's Quillacollo stronghold. The military zone imposed on the region and the arrest of Miguel Veizaga furthered the General's political ambitions. In January 1964, the Cochabamba peasant federation announced its support of a Paz-Barrientos ticket in the upcoming presidential election scheduled for May.[128]

Paz's chose a crony, Federico Fortún Sanjinés, as his vice-presidential running mate. The news was greeted in Cocahabamba with a mass protest by peasants loyal to General Barrientos. Moreover, a clique of junior air force officers took Paz's autocratic move as a snub to Barrientos and began to entertain alternate scenarios for the general's accession to power. The rigged MNR national convention that nominated Fortún also refused to seat the Izquierda delegates. Víctor Paz had accomplished the impossible, uniting the fractious Bolivian body politic (unfortunately in opposition to his rule)—Lechín's PRIN, Wálter Guevara Arze's Auténticos, Ñuflo Chávez's Intransigentes, Falangistas, PIRistas, the *Partido de la Unión Republicana Socialista, Partido Liberal, Partido Social Demócratica, Partido Social Cristiano*, and Hernán Siles's *Bloque de la Revolución*. Also included in the opposition were university students, miners, workers, and the *Comité Pro Santa Cruz* representing the conservative agro-export sector of the Oriente. To this disparate group, the military allied itself.

General Barrientos and Army Chief of Staff General Alfredo Ovando were obliged to attend the clandestine meetings of junior officers, disaffected Young Turks incensed by Paz's authoritarian regime and determined to put an end to it.[129] Barrientos later claimed it was Paz's rejection of his vice-presidential aspirations that drove him to conspiracy. His target was the presidency, and his strategy involved building grassroots support among the nation's largest constituency, the indigenous populace. When Víctor Paz picked a less charismatic running mate, Barrientos directed his focus on the traditional pastime of Bolivian generals, concocting a coup d'état. In this context, two events were crucial to the developing scenario. The first, staged in late February, was a tactical gem, the curious "Magic Bullet" episode involving an alleged assassination attempt against General Barrientos. The second was a masterpiece: the Military-Campesino Anti-Communist Pact (*Pacto Militar-Campesino Anticomunista*).

The "Magic Bullet" Episode

General Barrientos was allegedly shot in the chest by an assassin. Miraculously, a set of U.S. Air Force wings pinned to the general's chest deflected the assassin's bullet. The chain of events surrounding the "Magic Bullet" episode captured the sympathy as well as the suspicion of an urban populace subjected to a regime that had become notorious for repression, murder, and torture.[130] After all, folks wondered, who had the most to gain by killing the general? Failing to gain Paz's nod for the vice-presidency, the general was offered the post of Ambassador to the Court of St. James in an attempt to rid the country of his audacious rival.

The timing of the episode is suggestive. Barrientos was *shot* at 2:00 a.m., hours before his scheduled flight to London; the General's bodyguards informed police investigators that he was being attended to at a clinic near the scene of the alleged crime. At 3:00 a.m., U.S. Air Force Attaché Colonel Edward Fox called the U.S. Ambassador, notifying him that a flight was needed to airlift the General to a hospital in the Panama Canal Zone. At 3:30 a.m., Ambassador Douglas Henderson cabled Secretary of State Dean Rusk (cc: the White House, Pentagon, and CIA) requesting the airlift; the Pentagon ordered the airlift at 5:00 a.m. and at 8:00 a.m. Barrientos left Bolivia's El Alto air base bound for a military hospital in the Panama Canal Zone. Three weeks later, the General Barrientos returned to Bolivia—celebrated as a hero.[131]

The veracity of the alleged assassination attempt remains doubtful. Barrientos was never examined by a Bolivian physician, but instead was spirited away aboard a U.S. Air Force plane to a U.S. military hospital in the Panama Canal Zone. The Magic Bullet doubters include friends and military insiders. General Alberto Guzmán claimed that Barrientos shot himself. Alberto Iriarte, another friend, stated. "It was a staged assassination attempt, planned by Arguedas [Bolivian Air Force Colonel Antonio Arguedas]." Arguedas claimed that he and another officer had proposed the idea to Barrientos, who agreed to it. Ambassador Henderson, Air Force Attaché Fox, and the CIA Station Chief believed the Magic Bullet may well have been a ruse. Ambassador Henderson opined, "Without the 'Magic Bullet,' Barrientos would certainly not have become the MNR candidate, as the general himself admitted."[132]

If not a spectacular contrivance, the incident was nonetheless fortuitous. Amid a wave of public support for the wounded general, President Paz was forced to accept Barrientos as a vice presidential running mate to dispel the appearance of wrongdoing. Yet another scenario is also probable. Given the role of Claudio San Román's infamous Control Político, the Magic Bullet could well have been an assassination attempt. After all, the charismatic General posed a threat to Paz's suzerainty. Perhaps Barrientos' flight to the U.S. Panama Canal Zone was imperative for his safety and recovery—affording the wounded hero an opportunity to rally popular support—while safe from Paz's murderous secret police?

Víctor Paz Estenssoro: A Wolf in Sheep's Clothing

Seemingly mild-mannered, the bespectacled Víctor Paz Estenssoro hardly evidenced the Machiavellian persona beneath his scholarly demeanor, "An unforewarned visitor would never have guessed what depths of calculation, ambition, love of power, jealousy, cruelty, and sly vindictiveness lurked behind this unpretentious façade."[133] Walter Guevara Arze knew him well: "Víctor Paz Estenssoro, masks his intentions and his soul, he needs illusions of piety and sincerity, and sees in each man a competitor, an obstacle, a danger. Everything is artifice, distrust and obstruction. This obsession has no respite. . . . The Revolution, the government, the party, are for nothing other than means for domination; instruments to ensure revenge in the dark."[134] Frustrated by his inability to persuade the reluctant Villarroel of the need to unleash his armed forces to save the Revolution in 1946, Paz allegedly ordered a subordinate to cut the telephone line to the Palacio Quemado, isolating and endangering the president and his aides. Questioned by hesitant subordinates aware of the consequences, Víctor Paz's alleged response was "I don't care. Fuck 'em. Let's go." ("No importa. Que se jodan. Vámanos").[135] The hapless Villarroel then met his horrific end at the hands of a raging mob. Years later, Paz would invoke the symbol of the martyred Villarroel.

The CIA station chief did not mince words: "Paz Estenssoro *was* a Nazi. Most of those around him were Nazis. Same jails, same brutality." Paz's son noted that his father's intelligence team was comprised of "ex-Nazis, old Gestapos he had met in Argentina. . . . They put together this massive cardex . . . of everyone in the country . . . and they worked closely with San Román."[136] Klaus Barbie, the infamous "Butcher of Lyon," part of a Nazi network prized for their experience in repression, arrived in Bolivia in 1951 and was granted Bolivian citizenship under the alias Klaus Altmann. "Paz Estenssoro," observed an exiled Bolivian newspaper editor in 1954, "has hired a number of totalitarian experts . . . to achieve control of the masses and perfect his methods of repression."[137]

Paz ordered Colonel San Román to have his secret police brutalize Vice President Juan Lechín: "Don't kill him, just leave him paralyzed." Lechín urinated blood for a week because of kidney damage resulting from a severe beating administered by Paz's Control Político agents.[138] Referring to the sadistic Claudio San Román during a press conference, Paz pointed to a book on the Nazi Gestapo and quipped "This one is for San Román."[139] After numerous attempts on his life, including bombs detonated on the adjoining Barrientos and Lechín residences in La Paz, Barrientos' house in Cochabamba, and quite possibly the "Magic Bullet" assassination episode—General Barrientos stated that he "had more enemies within the MNR than in the ranks of the opposition." In an interview with William Brill, "the general flatly stated that he was convinced Paz was behind the assassination attempts."[140]

The Pacto Militar-Campesino Anticomunista

On 9 April 1964, exactly 12 years after the MNR launched a revolution and defeated the Rosca's armed forces, peasant dirigentes pledged allegiance to the military at Ucureña. The Pacto Militar-Campesino Anticomunista assured the peasantry the gains of the National Revolution and acknowledged the preeminence of the military institution: "The Armed Forces will make sure that the conquests achieved by the majority classes are respected, such as the Agrarian Reform, basic education, union rights, and others. . . . [T]he peasants will support and defend, firmly and loyally, the military institution in all circumstances. They will put themselves under military orders, against the subversive maneuvers of the left.[141]

Víctor Paz now faced a resurgent military institution of his own making. The powerful Cochabamba peasant militias could no longer be counted upon to defend the beleaguered president. Asked by reporters for a comment on the Pact, the Ucureña chieftain José Rojas smiled and replied, "I'm still unable to speak."[142] A month later the results were evident. "It has been argued that civil-action campaigns of the type in which the armed forces are actively engaged are likely to lessen their taste for political adventures. However, General Barrientos's rise to prominence, within ten years of the reconstitution of the army gives pause for thought. The armed forces must now be considered an integral part of Paz's Revolution."[143]

The "institutionalist" faction represented by Army Chief of Staff General Alfredo Ovando, ostensibly comprised of officers more interested in the dignity of the military institution than in General Barrientos' political ambitions, was crucial to Paz Estenssoro's survival.[144] The "Magic Bullet" forced the institutionalists to support Barrientos, the man in uniform, against Paz Estenssoro's authoritarian MNR regime. As Richard Patch observed, "He has an uncanny ability, even in the weakest of positions, to play off two attacking groups, ruin the positions of both, and emerge unscathed and even stronger." Patch also sensed something else about Paz, his ruthlessness, "at selected times, he must politically decapitate potential rivals to leave himself as the only alternative."[145]

A crescendo of opposition from a discordant populace befell the president: Falangista guerrilla insurgency in Santa Cruz, strikes and demonstrations by miners, factory workers, students and teachers, bombings and riots in the cities. Paz answered with states of siege, press censorship, mass arrests and torture by Control Político, and the expulsion from the MNR of party founders Juan Lechín, Walter Guevara, and Hernán Siles. The president's descent into despotism drew the concern of Secretary of State Dean Rusk who noted in July 1962 that repression "encourages violence," and when it remained the sole recourse by which the opposition could express its views, violence pushed dissidents into the "extreme left" (i.e., communism). Yet *Time* magazine heralded Paz as "Latin America's ablest President when it comes to anticipating and disarming trouble before it starts."[146]

The Alliance for Progress supported Paz's authoritarian regime. Control Político, directed by San Román (with the assistance of ex-Gestapo officers and CIA agents) tapped telephones, operated an extensive network of informants to spy on their neighbors, and created a massive data file on citizens. San Román's victims were intimidated, extorted, imprisoned, and tortured as Control Político extended its focus from political repression to criminal racketeering. San Román turned Control Político into a lucrative business and himself into a millionaire.[147] Questioned about Paz's tyrannical rule, the CIA Station Chief in La Paz stated, "I have served in six countries, and the last days of the Paz regime were the most repressive I ever saw. Claudio San Román, with whom I worked on a daily basis [!], was the most brutal Latin American I ever met." After visiting San Román's torture chambers, the CIA agent declared: "They were the bloodiest things I've ever seen. Skin, blood, arms, legs. Blood on the walls."[148]

Among the most persecuted opponents of the MNR revolution were the Falangistas who time and again attempted coups against the National Revolution. In May 1958, 10,000 campesino militiamen led by José Rojas invaded and occupied the city of Santa Cruz after a Falange revolt. In what became known as the Massacre of Terebinto, the Falangista rebels were hunted down and ten were captured, tortured, and executed at an estate outside the city. The Paz regime then added the infamous Ñanderoga jail in Santa Cruz to its assorted concentration camps, prisons, and Control Político torture chambers.[149] Oscar Unzaga de la Vega, the irrepressible Jefe of the Falange died in suspicious circumstances (viz., execution) during an aborted coup in La Paz in April 1959. Once persecuted by the Old Regime, the MNR had retrogressed to the sins of its predecessors.

Endgame: The "Revolution of Restoration"

The survival of the National Revolution depended on the support of U.S. government, the loyalty of Paz's presidential guards, Control Político, MNR urban militias, and whatever peasant sindicatos Paz could muster for his defense. All did not bode well. On the Altiplano, the Pazestenssorista jefe Felipe Flores of Huarina was engaged in a bitter conflict; 40 combatants were killed in battles between Flores' militia and Barrientistas led by Samuel Marcos Mamani and Eliseo Gutiérrez of Warisata.[150] The warring campesinos occupied Achacachi and sacked houses before truckloads of carabineros arrived to squelch the conflict. Víctor Paz's remaining support among the Altiplano peasantry was dealt a fatal blow when Felipe Flores died in a shootout on the steps of the Ministry of Peasant Affairs in La Paz. Warplanes buzzed the dirigente's funeral, Barrientista peasants from Warisata commanded by Samuel Marcos Mamani and Eliseo Gutierrez occupied Achacachi, and a detachment of carabineros arrested Flores' successor, Francisco Viscarra.[151]

In a final paroxysm, the Omasuyos federation initiated a strike and enforced a roadblock in the Lake region, briefly paralyzing transportation and commerce outside the capital city.[152] Military occupation of the zone by army troops and warplane overflights finalized Barrientos' takeover. Paz lost control of the only Altiplano peasant militia capable of providing a counterpoise to an open secret: General René Barrientos's preparations for a military coup d'état. Infantry troops controlled the department of Cochabamba. Although residual rivalries among caciques in the Upper and Lower Valleys persisted, including conflicts over the leadership of the Quillacollo Central, competition between José Rojas and Gregorio López of Punata, and strife among dirigentes in Apopaya Province.[153]

Miners and students occupied Oruro on 21 October 1964. After 60 miners sent to reinforce the uprising were killed in a firefight with a Ranger battalion, infantry troops occupied the San José mine and warplanes bombed rebellious miners at Huanuni. Anti-government riots erupted in Santa Cruz, Cochabamba, Sucre, and La Paz where 30 trucks of Altiplano peasant militia arrived to intimidate "March for Liberty" demonstrators. Paz requested 500,000 rounds of M1 ammunition to bolster his position. Ambassador Henderson requisitioned immediate delivery of 95,000 rounds of M-1 ammo 2,000 long-range (armor piercing) projectiles; 2,000 M7A2 CS (riot control) grenades, and 300 gas masks from the U.S. Panama Canal Zone. The Embassy Country Team believed, "Paz [is] in control, and remains determined in face of difficult situation. He controls his militia and party and can count on support of carabineros." But accompanying this assessment was doubt regarding the loyalty of the armed forces in the event of a serious insurrection.[154]

The contours of the expected military coup remained unclear amidst a rising wave of resistance to the Paz Estenssoro regime. The U.S. Embassy, in anticipation of a confrontation between armed forces, estimated Paz's support in the capital at "500 Presidential Guards of the Waldo Ballivián Regiment, 3,000 carabineros, 1,500 MNR militia, 2,000 campesino militia, and perhaps 500 other[s] in miscellaneous units."[155] The President's fatal error, asserts former Bolivian air force officer Jaime Calderón, was neglect of the Altiplano campesino sindicatos, "If only because they could easily defend La Paz due to their proximity."[156] Colonel Sanjinéz Goitia's civic action attempt at Achacachi had failed to secure campesino support for the regime. Moreover, the 30 truckloads of Achacachi militiamen who only days earlier helped quell a demonstration in La Paz had withdrawn to the Altiplano to celebrate the Feast of Todos Santos. Assured of the incapacity of the inebriated militia to defend President Paz, General Barrientos prepared to strike.

The Ambassador

U.S. Ambassador Henderson reported "calm throughout country" on 2 November 1964 and stated that Paz attributed the unrest to "communist-led student activists trained in Cuba and Czechoslovakia" and General Barrientos' public opposition to his actions. Henderson noted that while uncertain regarding the solution to his problem with General Barrientos, Paz "has suppressed the recent disturbances in due course, without drawing on his reserve strength, and appears willing and able to do so for the foreseeable [sic] future."[157] The following day Henderson sent a telegram to the Secretary of State, requesting 1,000,000 rounds of 30 caliber ammunition and five side-band radios from the Panama Canal Zone. That evening the Embassy's Country Team Assessment noted that Paz was "not so firmly in control as in past" because of his appointment of "political hacks" to cabinet positions, impositions of "state[s] of siege unnecessary to deal with various opposition activities and plots," press censorship that alienated the middle class, and the emergence of active communist leadership among students. The Country Team concluded that Paz's most serious threat was his public rift with General Barrientos that "gave rise to speculation that [the] military could be persuaded [to] oppose Paz."[158]

On the evening of 3 November, Ambassador Henderson informed the Secretary of State of a conversation with Vice President Barrientos during which Barrientos "had flaunted [the] High Command's agreement to a coup," and General Ovando "confronted with this information," did not deny it. The ambassador noted that the "Bolivian High Command had tested us on idea of coup and found us completely unsympathetic" and concluded, "Present evidence is that military generally supporting government . . . although questionable should they be called upon [to] carry out highly unpopular tasks in defense [of] Paz government." Paz stated his intention to reorganize his campesino militias near La Paz under military leadership as a "counter-poise to and check on the armed forces." Paz also reported that General Ovando intended to use peasant militias to intimidate the miners. Henderson estimated there were between 4,000 and 5,000 members and 25,000 sympathizers in the Bolivian communist party, and cautioned, "Paz will need all his political power and skill to resolve [the] continuing problems still facing him (miners, Barrientos, inevitable plotting, and internal MNR friction)."[159] Unbeknownst to the Ambassador, General Ovando and General Barrientos had meticulously developed a scheme to overthrow President Paz's National Revolution.[160]

Just before midnight, Ambassador Henderson notified the State Department, the White House, and the CIA that revolts had broken out in Cochabamba, Santa Cruz, Oruro, and Potosí "in favor of armed forces or Barrientos." He reported that

La Paz remained quiet; MNR militia were patrolling the streets, the El Alto air base had been reinforced by MNR militia, and 2,000 campesinos from Achacachi were expected to arrive in the city. In the early hours of 4 November, Henderson telegraphed the State Department, White House, and CIA that Paz had requested a "full arms and munitions shipment" and urged compliance because failure to do so "would signal US withdrawal [of] support of present government and would be significant unbalancing present odds." Henderson estimated Paz's chances of survival at "better than even," but warned that a "Barrientos-led military overthrow of [the] Paz government provides communists opportunity [to] infiltrate successor government with chance [to] eventually take over, especially since Barrientos has repeatedly demonstrated his inability [to] discern communists and crypto-communists among his advisors."[161]

But the die was cast. On 4 November 1964, rebellious military forces occupied the city of Cochabamba. In La Paz, the Ingavi Regiment joined the rebellion as Víctor Paz, unwittingly relying on his unknown enemy, dispatched co-conspirator General Ovando to negotiate with the rebels. Meanwhile, by day's end, General Barrientos' forces had seized control of Oruro, Potosí, Sucre, and Santa Cruz. The 120,000 militiamen from the Potosí peasant federation and 1,500 Ucureña militiamen expected to defend Paz failed to materialize. The Altiplano militia had been rendered ineffective by the excesses of their Todos Santos festivities. Of the 50 truckloads of Achacachi militia expected to save the day for Paz Estenssoro, only three trucks of militiamen were sober enough to rise to Don Víctor's defense.[162] Other support, most notably in the Cochabamba valleys, had been neutralized by the Pacto Militar Campesino.

On the morning of 4 November, Ambassador Douglas Henderson notified the State Department that Paz had informed him of his intention to abdicate the presidency, expressed his appreciation of U.S. support, and stated that the requested ammunition shipment was now unnecessary.[163]

Despite the embassy's critical assessments of the Paz regime as administered by "political hacks," enforced by states of siege, press censorship, and imprisonment of opposition leaders, Ambassador Henderson and the State Department perceived the survival of the National Revolution as an armed contest to be decided by "rate of fire." Víctor Paz, Ambassador Henderson, and the U.S. Department of State were willing to drown the regime's opponents in blood. Paz had considered the October 1963 uprising in Oruro as an opportunity to crush the miners' resistance and General Ovando proposed the use of peasant militias "to lend credence" to the repression.

Noteworthy in the diplomatic cables from La Paz to Washington were embassy concerns about the specter of communism in the event of the regime's collapse. Thus, the decision was made to bolster Paz Estenssoro's rule. The U.S. had invested some $368,000,000 in the National Revolution: the $35,000,000 per annum (1953–1964) was estimated to represent 20 percent of Bolivian GDP and 40 percent of public expenditures.[164] Yet, despite the concerted efforts of his Control Político enforcers, the State Department's Alliance for Progress mandarins, U.S.

dollars, USIS propaganda, CIA and DIN agents, USAID operatives, armaments and tear gas, President Víctor Paz Estenssoro was overthrown. After a dozen years of life in the barracks, the Bolivian armed forces were back in the Palacio Quemado. They evidenced no interest in returning the nation to civilian rule.

The MNR reliance on the armed forces for resolution of political problems invited military involvement in the regime's factional politics. The result was the obverse of political scientist William Brill's notion that "civil action may have also reduced the military's incentive for active political involvement, because it provided it with an alternative means of achieving such basic institutional objectives as prestige, a feeling of self-worth, and financing."[165] As we have seen, this only whetted the appetite of the Bolivian military for political intervention in the political fray, a theater to which it was accustomed under the Old Regime. The armed forces enforced the Stabilization and Triangular plans in the tin mines and subdued feuding peasant caciques in the countryside. In the estimation of the U.S. Army Special Operations Research Office, "The civilian militias are considerably more dangerous and effective than appearances indicate. What they lack in professional polish they more than make up for in reckless abandon. The record shows that on every occasion when their services were required to protect internal security, they performed successfully and well."[166] General Barrientos neutralized the peasant militias with a Civic Action campaign, the Pacto Militar Campesino, and Barrientista sindicatos in the Altiplano. The modern arms, equipment, and training under the aegis of U.S. military advisers assured the supremacy of the Bolivian armed forces over peasant and worker sindicato militias.

The November 1964 "Revolution of Restoration" returned the military institution to power after its disastrous defeat by civilian insurgents in April 1952. The Kennedy administration's obsession with communism, the Cuban Revolution, counterinsurgency strategy, and Civic Action inadvertently set the stage for the return of the military to the Palacio Quemado. Yet the ultimate cause of the downfall of the National Revolution was its mutation by Víctor Paz and the Alliance for Progress into an autocratic state. In its final hours—when confronted with overwhelming opposition to Paz's rule—the American Ambassador's response was to order one million rounds of ammunition to perpetuate the regime.

The North American Nexus

The military overthrow of the National Revolution occurred amidst a profound shift in U.S. foreign policy. Adamantly opposed to the appearance of another Cuba, President John F. Kennedy mounted a campaign to subvert leftist political movements and overthrow nationalist governments considered breeding grounds for communism. The campaign was launched in 1961 after the failed Bay of Pigs invasion of Cuba under the Madison Avenue slogan "Alliance for Progress."[167] President Kennedy, an inveterate Cold War protagonist obsessed with the topics of revolution and counterinsurgency, mobilized the assets of the State Department, Pentagon, USAID, intelligence agencies, financial institutions, and the media as

Alliance for Progress assets in what he believed was "the most dangerous area in the world." President Lyndon Johnson continued the policy: "We must protect the Alliance against the efforts of communism . . . the full power of the United States is ready to assist any country whose freedom is threatened by forces dictated from beyond the shores of the continent."[168] As the CIA field officer in charge of the 1954 overthrow of the Guatemalan government had it, "the U.S. cannot afford the moral luxury of helping only those regimes in the free world that meet our ideals of self-government. Eliminate all the absolute monarchies, dictatorships and juntas from the free world and count those that are left and it should be readily apparent that the U.S. would be well on its way to isolation."[169]

The Mann Doctrine

On 19 March 1964, Assistant Secretary of State for Inter-American Affairs Thomas Mann terminated the policy of U.S. sanctions against dictatorial regimes that seized power through the overthrow of democratically elected governments. The "Mann Doctrine" was a reaffirmation of the Olney and Roosevelt corollaries to the Monroe Doctrine: a statement of Yankee realpolitik fashioned to safeguard North American hegemony threatened by Cuban influence in the Americas and a green light to despotic Latin American generals.[170] Under the benign image of the Alliance for Progress, the Kennedy and Johnson administrations facilitated the overthrow of ten Latin American governments and replaced them with military dictatorships amenable to the American empire.[171]

Implementation of the policy rested on the Pentagon's counterinsurgency and Civic Action programs to counter communist threats and indigenous revolutions. President Kennedy adopted the strategy (National Security Action Memorandum 119) and in an address to Latin American military officers affirmed that "armies can play constructive roles in defending the aims of the Alliance for Progress by striking at the roots of economic and social distress."[172] Over 16,000 Latin American military officers were trained in counterinsurgency and civic action at the School of the Americas in the Panama Canal Zone between 1961 and 1964. Additionally, the Inter-American Police Academy in the Canal Zone specialized in teaching counterinsurgency strategy and tactics.[173] The State Department, United States Agency for International Development (USAID), the Pentagon, the Central Intelligence Agency, and the Inter-American Development Bank were to coordinate implementation of the strategic and tactical details of the doctrine. Indeed, the Inter-American Development Bank (IDB) had posited a plan to use Alliance for Progress funds for political ends—most particularly to neutralize the powerful miners' sindicatos opposed to implementation of the Stabilization and Triangular Plans.[174]

The case for counterinsurgency is presented in a paean by Lt. Colonel Jonathan Ladd in the *Military Review*: "Counterinsurgency is by definition geared to military, political, economic, and civic action. . . . The major problem before us is to learn to orchestrate the magnificent counterinsurgency resources we have into a single *symphony* [emphasis added] and to persuade the governments we help to apply their energies and resources against threats that confront them."[175] This *symphony* was first performed by the Brazilian military, abetted by the United States, on 31 March 1964—two weeks after proclamation of the Mann Doctrine.

The Barrientos coup followed eight months later. In each instance the workings of the Pentagon and the White House were evident. Lt. Colonel Vernon Walters, the U.S. military attaché (later Deputy Director of the CIA) and a close friend of Brazilian co-conspirator General Castelo Branco, wired the details of the forthcoming coup to Washington a week before the event.[176] Likewise, General René Barrientos was close to Lt. Colonel Edward Fox, the U.S. Air Force Attaché and DIA operative, a man widely believed by Bolivians to be a supporter of the overthrow of the MNR regime.

Fox of the Andes

Colonel Fox first met then Captain Barrientos in the early 1950s when Fox was in charge of training Bolivian air force officers. A close friendship followed. Colonel Fox returned as Air Force attaché in 1962, following a request by General Barrientos to the Pentagon that corresponded with the General's political aspirations. Fox's arrival has been interpreted as evidence of a scheme that resulted in the coup d'état against President Paz. Known by Bolivian officers as the "Zorro of the Andes," Colonel Fox is often vilified as a co-conspirator, if not the architect of the overthrow of the MNR regime. "Those who know Latin American temperaments will understand the esteem associated with Zorro [fox in Spanish]," remarked Edward Lansdale, the storied CIA counterinsurgency expert.[177] Barrientos informed Fox of his interest in serving as Paz's vice-presidential candidate in the 1964 election and stated that the military would not accept Juan Lechín as a presidential successor to Paz Estenssoro and, if need be, a coup against Lechín was in preparation. The General often spoke of the military's commitment to the goals and accomplishments of the National Revolution and pledged "the armed forces will never divest themselves of the beautiful treasure of constitutionality, nor will they permit Bolivia to lose this amazing reward won by blood and agony."[178]

Revisionist accounts of the coup based on declassified confidential memoranda from the U.S. State Department, National Security Files, Defense Intelligence Agency reports, and interviews with Colonel Fox, Ambassador Douglas Henderson, and former CIA agents indicate official support for President Paz and attempts to dissuade General Barrientos from attempting a coup against the president.[179] After interviews with Colonel Fox and examination of declassified State Department and military intelligence documents, the military historian Colonel Robert Kirkland, failed to find a "smoking gun" proving Fox's complicity in the coup: "While Fox's true role in the November 1964 coup may never be known his actions reinforced a cynical view of U.S. involvement in that region during the Cold War."[180] This undermines the circumstantial allegations of scholars as well as anecdotal Bolivian lore regarding Fox's involvement in the coup. Yet it was this relationship with his asset (Barrientos) that allowed the U.S. Air Force Attaché and

DIN agent to maintain influence with the politically ambitious General. And the man called "Zorro" by Bolivian officers would be undeserving of the title if he were to completely reveal his relationship with General Barrientos. The "cynical view of U.S. involvement in the region" noted by Kirkland, might be better characterized as hegemonic realpolitik.

What the documentary evidence indisputably reveals is the pervasive influence of the Pentagon, CIA, White House, State Department, and the U.S. Embassy in Bolivian politics. Whatever the outcome, the hegemon had hedged its bets. The CIA secretly funneled $1,000,000 to fund General Barrientos' rise to power "to encourage a stable government favorably inclined toward the United States . . . in support of the ruling Junta's plans to pacify the country." The investigative journalist Tim Weiner notes that the CIA file was forwarded to the White House before President Johnson's meeting with then president, René Barrientos, in 1966: "National security advisor Walt Rostow handed it to the president and said, 'This is to explain why General Barrientos may say thank you when you have lunch with him next Wednesday.'"[181]

Ambassador Douglas Henderson underestimated General René Barrientos. A victim of his arrogance, the Ambassador failed to take the correct measure of the man. Henderson's memoranda are rife with pejoratives deriding Barrientos for perceived personal, cultural, and political shortcomings: "ineptitude," "unpredictability," "egocentrism," "naiveté," and "lacking the capacity to handle the deviousness, immorality, and byzantine complexity of Bolivian politics," as well as "the innocent belief that he is being Machiavellian."[182] Meanwhile, the cunning General staged theatrical events to dramatize his machismo, absented himself when necessary to create an aura of anticipation among the populace, co-opted the peasantry, and curried favor among U.S. military attachés. His periodic press releases criticized the Paz regime, eroding public confidence in the MNR president, while creating the image of a viable alternative to the embattled autocrat.

In retrospect, Ambassador Henderson admitted that General Barrientos "sandbagged a lot of people who thought he was a clown. They underestimated him and he played up to their underestimation of him. And in a way he sandbagged Paz, too."[183] The Ambassador failed to include himself among those "sandbagged" by Barrientos. William Brill, who was in La Paz at this time researching the Bolivian military, had the true measure of the general: "His popular appeal derived from the qualities of the man himself—from the simple fact that he is the kind of man people follow. He displayed charm, personal courage, and a *macho* image. To the peasants, he represented an interested, exciting *patrón*; to the people in the cities, he meant order and discipline."[184]

The U.S. Embassy in La Paz was likewise deceived by the duplicitous General Alfredo Ovando. Six months before the November coup, Ovando had pledged to defend President Paz in the event of a "showdown between Paz and Barrientos." A month before the coup, he swore "on the Cross of my Sword my absolute loyalty to the President." Duped yet again, Ambassador Henderson informed Secretary of

State Rusk of General Ovando's "completely unqualified" loyalty to President Paz Estenssoro a week before the coup.[185]

Conclusions

Víctor Paz Estenssoro's decision to retain the military institution after its defeat in April 1952 (against the protests of Juan Lechín and the MNR left sector) proved to be a monumental mistake. The later decision to rearm and modernize the armed forces, to neutralize opposition to his rule by indigenous mine workers and peasants, was fatal. In accordance with the objectives of the Mann Doctrine, the goal in Bolivia was to suborn the presidential aspirations of Juan Lechín, the leftist labor leader, an avowed enemy of U.S. hegemony. The full panoply of State Department functionaries, CIA and Pentagon operatives, and USAID agents and technocrats were employed to enforce the strategy. U.S. military assistance in the last two years of the National Revolution (1962–1964) totaled ten times the funding for the previous decade as Paz Estenssoro and the Alliance for Progress resorted to military force to overcome political opposition.[186] As the economic historian James Wilkie concludes, the National Revolution was doomed when it embraced the International Monetary Fund and the Triangular Plan that polarized the MNR right- and left-wing elites: "With the MNR disintegrating, the U.S. Embassy saw the military as the only non-Communist force with the necessary power and experience to control the country."[187]

General Barrientos justified the military coup d'état as motivated by the best of intentions: "If the high nationalist ideals of 1952 had been fulfilled, when the M.N.R. seized the government, surely the Army would have continued in their barracks. But in carrying out their grand objectives of revindication and economic reordering, towards unbridled mismanagement and hunger, the people, headed by the Armed Forces, determined to end this despotic regime that had devastated human dignity and led to the ruin of the country."[188] Following the overthrow of the National Revolution, President René Barrientos was quick to adapt to the perquisites of office—inviting North American corporate investment, flying about in a helicopter gifted by Gulf Oil, thanks to a lucrative petroleum concession, collecting payoffs from Nazi war criminals engaged in drug and arms trafficking, and accumulating vast acreage in the Santa Cruz Oriente—the locus of USAID agricultural development plans to shift the nation's economic focus away from the Andean highlands—home to the nation's indigenous majority.

Two puzzles remain: the first involves the "Magic Bullet" episode, the alleged assassination attempt against General René Barrientos and his sudden airlift to a military hospital in the U.S. Panama Canal Zone. Who was behind the alleged episode: Víctor Paz, who would be rid of a dangerous rival? Or General Barrientos, who became a national hero? A second puzzle involves the relationship of the general with the U.S. military attaché Colonel Edward Fox. Did the "Fox of the Andes" collude with his close friend General Barrientos in the plan to overthrow President Paz (against the wishes of the State Department) and "restore" the National Revolution?

Notes

1. Christopher Rand, "Letter from La Paz," *The New Yorker*, 31 December 1966, 47.
2. Michael Klare, *War Without End: America's Planning for the Next Vietnams* (New York, 1972), 31–68; James Kohl and John Litt, *Urban Guerrilla Warfare in Latin America* (Boston, 1974), 2–14.
3. Edwin Lieuwen, "The Military: A Revolutionary Force," *Annals of the American Academy of Political and Social Science*, 334 (March 1961), 30–40. See also Thomas C. Field Jr., *From Development to Dictatorship: Bolivia and the Alliance for Progress in the Kennedy Era* (Ithaca, NY, 2014), 49–50, 109–110, 141, 177; Stephen Zunes, "The United States and Bolivia: The Taming of a Revolution," *Latin American Perspectives*, 28.5 (September 2001), 34, 43. Kevin Young, *Blood of the Earth* (Austin, TX, 2017), 96–110.
4. See, for example, "AID Police Programs for Latin America, 1971–1972," *North American Congress on Latin America* (July–August 1971), 3, "Document: AID Police Plan for 1971–1972," 13–14; A.J. Langguth, *Hidden Terrors: The Truth About U.S. Police Operations in Latin America* (New York, 1978), 92–93, 115, 124–125, 232–233; Klare, *War Without End*, 241–269; Philip Agee, *Inside the Company* (New York, 1975); Kohl and Litt, *Urban Guerrilla Warfare*, 40, 266–267, 272–273, 301; William Blum, *Killing Hope: US. Military and CIA Interventions Since World War II* (Monroe, Maine, 1995), 168, 212, 234–235; "State of Siege" directed by Costa-Gavras and Franco Solanas.
5. Che Guevara's presence in Bolivia was discovered in aerial photographs taken in a U2 overflight. The results of Pentagon aerial mapping may be seen by an Internet search where longitude and latitude coordinates of even the most remote hamlet and canton are published from data supplied by the national Geospatial-Intelligence Agency, a member of the Intelligence community of the United States of America, and Department of Defense (DoD) Combat Support Agency.
6. For the bungled attempt of U.S. social scientists to infiltrate the Chilean intellectual community and gather intelligence data, see Eric Wolf and Joseph Jorgenson, "Anthropology on the Warpath in Thailand," *New York Review of Books*, 19 November 1970, 26–35, and Irving Louis Horowitz, ed., *The Rise and Fall of Project Camelot* (Cambridge, MA, 1967). Illustrative of the relationship of cold war scholars with the "military industrial complex" is a revealing footnote in Jan Kippers Black's *United States Penetration of Brazil*: "At a military and academic conference on Latin America at West Point in the fall of 1964, David Rockefeller of the Chase Manhattan Bank told a discussion group that it had been decided quite early that Goulart [President of Brazil] *was not acceptable to the U.S. banking community, and that he would have to go* (emphasis added)." Indeed, the Brazilian military overthrew Goulart in April 1964. The author notes, "Professor Edwin Lieuwen had been present when the remarks were made." Jan Kippers Black, *United States Penetration of Brazil* (Philadelphia, PA, 1977), 78.
7. Vicente Álvarez Plata, a founding member of the MNR, was also a hacendado as was the case with numerous prominent Movimientistas, including Walter Guevara Arze, and the family of Hernán Siles. *La Tarde*, 21 June 1969, 4.
8. For further discussion of José Rojas as Minister of Peasant Affairs, see Richard Patch, "Bolivia: Decision or Debacle? An Analysis of Bolivia's Economic and Political Plight," *American Universities Field Staff: West Coast South America Series*, 6.3 (18 April 1959), 10–11.
9. For a detailed discussion of the Siles presidency (1956–1960), see Christopher Mitchell, *The Legacy of Populism in Bolivia: From the MNR to Military Rule* (New York, 1977), 64–83; and José Gordillo, *Campesinos revolucionarios en Bolivia* (La Paz, 2000), 117–125.
10. Mitchell, *The Legacy of Populism*, 55, 59, 112, 114.

11. Ibid., 66, 69.
12. Gordillo, *Campesinos revolucionarios*, 117–118.
13. Ibid., 119 and also *El Diario*, 19 March 1959, 7; 17 April 1959, 6.
14. Gordillo, *Campesinos revolucionarios*, 117.
15. Richard Patch, "Bolivia Today: An Assessment Nine Years After the Revolution," *American Universities Field Staff: West Coast South America Series*, 8.4 (17 March 1961), 15–16.
16. This and other allegations of MNR human rights violations are to be found in a report compiled by the FSB and presented to the Bolivian government on 12 April 2001 entitled, "Informe resumen sobre las violaciones a los derechos humanos durante los gobiernos de Víctor Paz Estenssoro y Hernán Siles Zuazo," *Wikisource*, Parts 1–3, June 2001. See also *El Pueblo*, 16 May 1958, 4; *El Diario*, 27 May 1958, 4; *La Presencia*, 25 November 1960, 4; also Gary Prado Salmón, *Poder y fuerzas armadas, 1949–1984* (Cochabamba, 1984), 85–87, Jorge Dandler, "La 'Ch'ampa Guerra' de Cochabamba: Un proceso de disgregación política," in F. Calderón and Jorge Dandler, eds., *Bolivia: La fuerza histórica del campesinado* (La Paz, 1984), 159, and Mitchell, *The Legacy of Populism*, 71.
17. Interview by the author with José Rojas and Wálter Revuelta, Cochabamba, 25 August 1970.
18. Leftist senators Juan Lechín and Leónidas Sánchez accused Eduardo Cámara, the rightwing mayor of Cochabamba, of intervention "in favor of one of the bands [Ucureña] in the conflict sending instructions, arms and combatants expressly to the place of the events, putting in danger hundreds of lives." *El Diario*, 5 November 1959, 7; 1 November 1959, 7; 4 November 1959, 7; 6 November 1959, 6; *La Presencia*, 4 November 1959, 5.
19. Katherine Barnes de von Marshall and Juan Torrico Angulo, *Cambios Socio-economicos en el Valle de Cochabamba Desde 1952: Los pueblos provincials de Cliza, Punata, Arani, Sacaba, Tarata y Mizque* (Mimeograph. La Paz, 1971), 29. The transformation of regional markets not only increased the number of chicherías but also sparked a dramatic rise in campesino trucking entrepreneurs, middlemen (*rescatistas*), town lodgings (*tambos*), and expansion of *compadrazgo* relationships (fictive kinship of mutual benefit to the parties), e.g., food and/or lodging provided to campesino merchants in exchange for money or other commodity. Ibid., 19–29.
20. Ibid., 40 also 34, 41.
21. Ibid., 45–46.
22. Wálter Guevara Arze, *P.M.N.R.A.*, 106, 103.
23. Silvia Rivera Cusicanqui, *Oprimidos pero no vencidos: luchas del campesinado aymara y qhechwa de Bolivia, 1900–1980* (Geneva, 1986), 83.
24. Rivas Antezana, *Los hombres de la revolución*, 133–134.
25. Interview by the author with Miguel Veizaga, 23 August 1970, Cochabamba.
26. Ibid.
27. Gordillo, *Campesinos revolucionarios*, 122–123.
28. *El Diario*, 24 November 1959, 6; 25 November 1959, 6; 10 December 1959, 7; *El Mundo*, 26 November 1959, 1; 27 November 1959, 1. See also *Libertad*, week 2, November 1959, 1.
29. Interview by the author with Miguel Veizaga, 23 August 1970, Cochabamba. *La Presencia*, 9 January 1960, 4.
30. *La Presencia*, 16 December 1959, 4, *El Diario*, 16 December 1959, 7.
31. *La Presencia*, 3 July 1960, 5, also 30 June 1960, 5.
32. *El Diario*, 19 March 1959, 7; *La Presencia*, 7 January 1960, 4; 9 January 1960, 4; 27 January 1960, 5; *La Tarde*, 23 January 1960, 5; 25 January 1960, 4; 26 January 1960, 5; 27 January 1960, 4. Gordillo, *Campesinos revolucionarios*, 123.
33. *La Presencia*, 27 January 1960, 5; *La Tarde*, 22 January 1960, 5; 25 January 1960, 4; 26 1960, 5; 27 January 1960, 4.
34. Ucureña militia were also accused of other depredations, including murder, rape, sacking of houses, and livestock theft. *La Presencia*, 28 January 1960, 5,7, 30 January 1960,

6; *El Diario*, 26 January 1960, 6; 27 January 1960, 5; *La Tarde*, 27 January 1960, 5; 28 January 1960, 1, 5.
35. *El Diario*, 8 March 1960, 4, 6–7, 9; *La Presencia*, 6 March 1960, 5. Earlier, the Fourth Campesino Congress at Cochabamba claimed that as Minister of Government, Walter Guevara Arze had given Miguel Veizaga 5,000,000 bolivianos for the purchase of weapons and ammunition. *Unidad*, 6 February 1960, 6; *La Presencia*, 7 January 1960, 4.
36. *El Diario*, 8 March 1960, 7. See also Prado, *Poder y fuerzas armadas*, 94–96.
37. The Seventh Division has played an important role in Bolivian history: it was commanded for a time by General Alfredo Ovando Candia, one of the coconspirators of the November 1964 "Revolution of Restoration," who later played a major part in the army's counterinsurgency operation against Che Guevara's 1967–1968 guerrilla *foco*.
38. *Presencia*, 14 April 1960, 4; *El Diario*, 27 March 1960, 5.
39. *El Diario*, 2 July 1960, 4; 3 July 1960, 4; 12 May 1960, 6.
40. *El Diario*, 14 May 1960, 6; *La Presencia*, 16 May 1960, 4.
41. *El Diario*, 8 March 1960, 4, 6; *La Presencia*, 14 April 1960, 4.
42. Originally reported in the Cochabamba newspapers *El Mundo* and *Crítica*, the stories were repeated in *El Diario*, 25 May 1960, 5.
43. This was also known as the Mulofalda Massacre, after the street in Vila Vila where the bodies were discovered. See Gordillo, *Campesinos revolucionarios*, 125 and Benjamin I. Cordeiro, *Tragedía en Indoamerica* (Cordoba, 1964), 189–190; also *El Diario*, 15 June 1960, 7; 16 June 1960, 7; 17 June 1960, 4; 29 June 1960, 5, 7; *La Presencia*, 20 June 1960, 5; 22 June 1960, 5; 29 June 1960, 4; *La Tarde*, 15 June 1960, 5; 18 June 1960, 5; 21 June 1960, 4,5, 22 June 1960, 4,5, 23 June 1960, 4,5, 24 June 1960, 4,5, 25 June 1960, 5; 28 June 1960, 5; 29 June 1960, 4, 5.
44. Veizaga would champion the good fight: "One Cliceño is enough for ten Rojistas, because our people fight to defend their homes, wives, and children, while the Rojas people do not defend themselves from anyone and are moved by imposition and force." *El Diario*, 29 June 1960, 5. Months later Veizaga again challenged Rojas to a duel as a solution to their conflict, *La Presencia*, 27 November 1960, 5; 16 September 1960, 4.
45. Luis Peñaloza, *Historia del Movimiento Nacionalista Revolucionario, 1941–1952* (La Paz, 1963), 189.
46. *El Diario*, 18 May 1957, 6.
47. *La Presencia*, 19 October 1959, 5; *La Nación*, 10 January 1960, 5; 11 January 1960, 4.
48. *La Presencia*, 27 July 1960, 4. Interviewed by the author at the *Panóptico Nacional* in La Paz, 27 August 1970, Zénon Barrientos averred that he was "of the MNR Left, but not a Lechinista": an "Auténtico along with Miguel Veizaga." The Aymara Movimientista was freed from one of Colonel San Román's torture chambers in La Paz after the 4 November 1964 overthrow of Paz Estenssoro's regime. Our interview came days after his imprisonment by the dictator General Hugo Banzer Suárez. Zenón Barrientos Mamani would later serve as Minister of Agriculture and Peasant Affairs in 1982 government of Hernán Siles Zuazo. He was also a (MNRV) vice-presidential candidate in the 1985 presidential campaign of Carlos Serrate Reich.
49. *La Presencia*, and 9 August 1960, 5.
50. For the national election results, see *La Nación*, 20 June 1960, 5 and 7 July 1960, 5 for the Department of La Paz.
51. See Dwight B. Heath, "The Aymara Indians and Bolivia's Revolutions," *Inter-American Economic Affairs*, 18 (Spring 1966), 36.
52. Isolated examples of PMNRA influence are noted in Omasuyos, Los Andes, Ingavi, Larecaja, and Elodoro Camacho provinces (La Paz Department): *La Tarde*, 14 January 1960, 6; 1 February 1960, 6; 20 February 1960, 4; 8 March 1960, 6; 11 March 1960, 4, 6; 14 March 1960, 6; 16 March 1960, 4; 18 May 1960, 5; 1 June 1960, 6.
53. Mario Rolon Anaya, *Política y Partidos en Bolivia* (La Paz, 1966), 335.
54. In the city of La Paz, the combined opposition parties tallied 44,449 votes to the MNR's 55,766. Opposition to the MNR was evident in the nation's major cities: in Sucre

the opposition tallied 5,501 votes to the MNR's 3,933; Cochabamba 16,311 versus 3,933 for the MNR; Oruro 6,796 to 3,582; Potosí 8,667 to 5,001. The results in the Cochabamba valleys confirmed José Rojas's hegemony over much of the region: Aiquile, Chilche, Punata, Tiraque, Machaca, Villa Grande, Ramadas, Arani, Colpaciaco, Pocoata, Ventilla, Morochata, Villa Tunari, and Vacas gave the MNR every vote cast; in Mizque and Pocana, the MNR lost a total of 28 votes to the MNRA, while polling nearly 4,400 votes. *La Nación*, 6 June 1960, 5.
55. *El Diario*, 26 July 1960, 6; 29 July 1960, 6; 20 August 1960, 7; *La Presencia*, 26 July 1960, 4; 20 August 1960, 4; *La Tarde*, 26 July 1960, 4; 27 July 1960, 5; 2 August 1960, 5;18 August 1960, 4; 19 August 1960, 5.
56. *El Diario*, 30 August 1960, 4; 31 August 1960, 5; 1 September 1960, 5; *La Presencia*, 30 August 1960, 4; 31 August 1960, 5; 1 September 1960, 5; 2 September 1960, 5; 3 September 1960, 4; 4 September 1960, 5.
57. *La Presencia*, 1 September 1960, 5; 2 September 1960, 5; 3 September 1960, 4; *El Diario*, 1 September 1960, 5; 4 September 1960, 6; 5 September 1960, 5.
58. *La Presencia*, 7 September 1960, 5.
59. *El Diario*, 6 September 1960, 5; *La Presencia*, 9 September 1960, 5; 22 September 1960, 5.
60. *El Diario*, 14 November 1960, 5; 15 November 1960, 7, 9; 16 November 1960, 6, 9; 18 November 1960, 7; *La Presencia*, 14 November 1960, 5; 15 November 1960, 4, 5; 16 November 1960, 5; 19 November 1960, 7. See also, Rivas Antezana, *Los hombres de la revolución*, 137–140 and Prado, *Poder y fuerzas armadas*, 96–97.
61. *La Presencia*, 27 November 1960, 5, *El Diario*, 30 November 1960, 7; 19 December 1960, 4.
62. *El Diario*, 18 December 1960, 7; *Unidad*, 24 December 1960, 5; 31 December 1960, 3. Also see Rivas Antezana, *Los hombres de la revolución*, 135–136.
63. *El Diario*, 22 December 1960, 7; *La Presencia*, 22 December 1960, 5. President Paz announced that the government would indemnify wounded campesinos and carabineros as well as families of those killed in the conflict. *La Presencia*, 27 December 1960, 5.
64. Xavier Albó, "La Paradoja Aymara: Solidaridad y Faccionalismo?" *Estudios Andinos*, 4.2 (1974–1976), 9.
65. John F. Plummer, "Another Look at Aymara Personality," *Behavioral Science Notes*, 1 (1966), 57.
66. Ibid., 59. Similar observations were made regarding Afro-American slaves in the antebellum South. See Stanley Elkins, *Slavery: A Problem in American Institutional and Intellectual Life*, 2nd ed. (Chicago, 1969), 81–88.
67. Rivera Cusicanqui, *Oprimidos pero no vencidos*, 82–83.
68. Albó, "La Paradoja Aymara," 97.
69. Tristan Platt examines the ritual at its various levels: "as a fertility rite, as a reaffirmation of the political structure of society, as a reaffirmation of the rights of the individual and of the group to the land," in *Espejos y maiz: temas de la structura simbolica andina* (La Paz, 1976), 18. See also, Albó, "La Paradoja Aymara," 89.
70. Albó, "La Paradoja Aymara," 84, 86, 101. For example, troops from the Camacho Regiment were dispatched to quell a boundary dispute in Oruro between comunarios from the Condiqueña, Payachita, Cotala and Tengalla communities. *La Presencia*, 1 February 1960, 4.
71. Albo, La Paradoja Aymara 100. Factionalism is most pronounced, observed Xavier Albó, among the Aymara communities of the Altiplano. Albó, "¿Khitipxtansa? ¿Quines somos? Identidad localista, étnica y clasista en los aymaras de hoy," *América Indígena* (July–September 1979), 39.3, 482.
72. Elizardo Pérez, *Warisata: La escuela ayllu* (La Paz, 1963), 129; Albó, "La Paradoja Aymara," 98. The peasant narrator of Paul Ezell's history of the Hacienda Orurillo was but one of many who had served time in the Achacachi jail. Paul Ezell, ""Man and Land in Bolivia: The Hacienda Orurillo Case," *Ethnohistory*, 13 (1966), 137.

73. Pérez, *Warisata*, 87. Don Elizardo was often visited in 1967–1968 by Warisateños at our La Paz *pensión* in Sopacachi Alto.
74. Xavier Albó, "Achacachi: Rebeldes pero conservadores," *Actas du XLII Congrès International des Américanistes*, Vol. 3 (Paris, 1976), 11. It is noteworthy that President Bautista Saavedra (1921–1925), an Achacachi landlord, sought the support of the comunidades originarias in land disputes with neighboring hacendados. Albó, "La Paradoja Aymara," 102; Albó, "Achacachi, Rebeldes pero conservadores," 12.
75. *El Diario*, 18 August 1953, 5, 7; Albó, "Achacachi: Rebeldes pero conservadores," 14; Rivera Cusicanqui, *Oprimidos pero no vencidos*, 84–85. For insight into the history and dynamics of land disputation in indigenous Andean society, see Karen Spalding, *Huarochiri: An Andean Society Under Inca and Spanish Rule* (Palo Alto, CA, 1984), 50–51.
76. Albó, "Achacachi: Rebeldes pero conservadores," 13.
77. David Preston, "Life Without Landlords on the Altiplano," *Geographical Magazine*, 41 (1969), 824; see also Albó, "Achacachi: Rebeldes pero conservadores," 15–18.
78. Rivera Cusicanqui, *Oprimidos pero no vencidos*, 85; Albó, "Achacachi: Rebeldes pero conservadores," 14.
79. Hans Buechler, "Agrarian Reform and Migration on the Bolivian Altiplano," Ph.D. dissertation, Columbia University, 1966, 89; William McEwen, et al., *Changing Rural Society: A Study of Communities in Bolivia* (New York, 1975), 263. For examples of the intrigue, extortion, and violence associated with Toribio Salas's Achacachi organization, see *El Diario*, 15 November 1959, 6; 21 November 1959, 5; and 20 December 1959, 7.
80. Mitchell, *The Legacy of Populism*, 75.
81. *El Diario*, 30 March 1958, 9; 6 January 1959, 4; 14 January 1959, 5. *El Diario*, 20 August 1959, 7.
82. McEwen, *Changing Rural Society*, 250–251. On the reputation of Atahuallpani, "Julio Martinez, campesino leader from Atahuallpani, recalls that the campesinos, who today have a formidable record for belligerence, resisted the tyranny of the patrónes before the revolution. When the patrón brought police from the town [Sorata] to enforce his authority, rebel peons occasionally sought refuge in the surrounding mountains, sometimes carrying an old firearm, forbidden to them by law." Ibid., 246.
83. Perhaps there was more to Paulino Quispe than meets the eye. Was Toribio Salas's henchman the same Paulino Quispe who signed the 1923 petition for a national inspection of land boundaries in an effort to reclaim usurped ayllu lands? See Santos Marka Tola and the Caciques-Apoderados, "The Laws of the Lands," in Sinclair Thomson, et al., eds., *The Bolivia Reader*, translated by Alison Spedding (Durham, NC, 2018), 329.
84. Interview by the author with Toribio Salas, 12 August 1970.
85. Ibid. The Achacachi cacique had also come to the attention of U.S. Army Attaché Paul Wimert: "In a dispatch to the Army filed through the embassy, Wimert stated flatly that the actions of Salas showed that given the loose conglomeration of armed peasants, any *cacique* of note could become a power in Bolivia and disrupt the government. The danger was that militias located so near to La Paz could pose a threat not only to the armed forces but to the president himself." Colonel Robert O. Kirkland, *Observing Our Hermanos en Armas: U.S. Military Attaches in Guatemala, Cuba and Bolivia, 1950–1964* (London, 2003), 107. Later posted to Chile as Army Attaché, Colonel Wimert was instrumental in the Nixon-Kissinger overthrow of the Salvador Allende government. R.C.S. Trahair, *Encyclopedia of Cold War Espionage, Spies and Secret Operations* (Westport, CT, 2004), 247.
86. Interview by the author with Ñuflo Chávez, La Paz, 22 July 1970; also, *El Diario*, 25 July 1963, 8; 8 September 1963, 4; 14 September 1963, 5.
87. Interview by the author with Toribio Salas, 12 August 1970.
88. *El Diario*, 20 November 1959, 5; 21 November 1959, 5; 23 November 1959, 4–5; 24 November 1959, 7; 1 December 1959, 7; 7 February 1960, 6; *La Presencia*, 25 December 1959, 5; 13 January 1960, 5; 21 June 1960, 5; *El Mundo*, 26 November 1959; *Libertad*, 2nd week February 1960, 1. Also Rivera Cusicanqui, *Oprimidos pero no vencidos*, 84–87.

89. *La Presencia*, 1 April 1960, 4; 16 June 1960, 4; 21 August 1960, 5.
90. *Libertad*, 2nd week February 1960, 1; 4th week March 1960, 6; 2nd week April 1960, 1; 2nd week April 1960, 1; 2nd week September 1960, 1. See also James Malloy, *Bolivia: The Uncompleted Revolution* (Pittsburgh, PA, 1970), 213; Mitchell, *The Legacy of Populism*, 76.
91. Albó, "Achacachi: Rebeldes pero conservadores," 18–19; *Achacachi: Medio siglo de la lucha campesina* (La Paz, 1979), 8; Rivera Cusicanqui, *Oprimidos pero no vencidos*, 86–87. For the Izquierdista struggle in Cochabamba Department, see Gordillo, *Campesinos revolucionarios*, 126–134, and Dandler, "La Ch'ampa Guerra," 264–268.
92. Interview by the author with Toribio Salas, La Paz, 12 August 1970.
93. *El Diario*, 14 March 1963, 6. Interview by author with Toribio Salas, La Paz, 12 August 1970; interview by author with Paulino Quispe, *Panóptico Nacional*, La Paz, 30 July 1970.
94. Interview with Toribio Salas, La Paz, 12 August 1970. *El Diario*, 12 March 1963, 3. Also, Gordillo, *Campesinos revolucionarios*, 136–139.
95. *El Diario*, 11 April 1963, 4; 16 April 1963, 5; 20 April 1963, 5; 17 May 1963, 6; 22 May 1963, 6. Also, Albó, "Achacachi: Rebeldes pero conservadores," 18.
96. Field Jr., *From Democracy to Dictatorship*, 85, 217, n 98; James Dunkerley, *Rebellion in the Veins* (London, 1984), 113–114; Sergio Almaraz Paz, *Requiem para una república* (La Paz, 1969), 24–25; William Brill, "Military Civic Action," Ph.D. dissertation, University of Pennsylvania, 1965, 191–195; René Zavaleta Mercado, *50 años de historia* (La Paz, 1992), 99–104.
97. *El Diario*, 15 June 1963, 6.
98. Ibid., 5 May 1963, 4.
99. Ibid., 21 August 1963, 6; 22 August 1963, 4; 23 August 1963, 4; 4 September 1963, 3; 6 September 1963, 4, 7; 7 September 1963, 4, 7.
100. *Masas*, 2 November 1963, 3. *El Diario*, 14 September 1963, 5.
101. *El Diario*, 27 September 1963, 5.
102. Ibid., 13 September 1963, 5.
103. Intelligence Memorandum, Central Intelligence Agency, Directorate of Intelligence, "Situation in Bolivia" (24 May 1965), 1–2. OCI No. 1806/65.
104. CIA, *Information Report*, 1. See also James W. Wilkie, *The Bolivian Revolution and U.S. Aid Since 1952* (Los Angeles, 1969), 42–43.
105. *CIA Information Report*, 3.
106. Bolivia's external debt increased 34 percent between 1960 and 1965: see Young, *Blood of the Earth*, 80–81; Dunkerley, *Rebellion*, 105–112.
107. Young, *Blood of the Earth*, 85.
108. Olivia Harris and Xavier Albó, *Monteras y guardatojos: campesinos y mineros en el norte de Potosí* (La Paz, 1976), 49; *Unidad*, 11 January 1962, 3
109. *La Presencia*, 30 January 1960, 4; 24 August 1960, 5; 26 August 1960, 5; *Unidad*, 1 May 1962, 7; *El Diario*, 20 April 1963, 3.
110. Néstor Taboada Terán, *Indos en rebelión* (La Paz, 1968), 119–120. In eight vignettes, Taboada Terán penned a multifaceted critique of the agrarian reform: the corruption of peasant and Movimientista leaders, bureaucrats, and institutions (viz., José Rojas and Movimientista commissioners portrayed as venal, chicha swilling opportunists). A vivid read, this is a work of fiction and not social science.
111. Field Jr., *From Development to Dictatorship*, 87. This meticulously researched work, indispensable to an understanding of the role of the Alliance for Progress in the final years of the National Revolution, is an excellent companion to John Gerassi's *The Great Fear in Latin America* written 50 years earlier and "dedicated pretentiously, to our Latin American policymakers."
112. See Dunkerley, *Rebellion*, 109–110; Harris and Albó, *Monteras y guardatojos*, 49.
113. Harris and Albó, *Monteras y guardatojos*, 52.
114. Field Jr., *From Development to Dictatorship*, 88. It should be noted that the USAID strategy of leveraging ethnic factional differences to further imperial designs in Bolivia was

of a piece with United States machinations in Southeast Asia, enlisting, for example, Montagnards in Vietnam and Hmong tribesmen in Laos to support the American invasion.
115. Ibid., 93.
116. Ibid., 91: the author's quotation is from *CIA Information Report*, 20 July 1963, 218 n 132.
117. Ibid., 91–93.
118. Ibid., 93–95. Harris and Albó, *Monteras y guardatojos*, 49–50.
119. The resurrection of the military institution as revealed in its budgetary trajectory is evidenced in "Table 4: Bolivian Defense Expenditures and U.S. Military Assistance," Cole Blasier, "The United States and the Revolution," in James M. Malloy and Richard S. Thorn, eds., *Beyond the Revolution: Bolivia Since 1952* (Pittsburgh, PA, 1971), 93–94.
120. Kirkland, *Observing Our Hermanos en Armas*, 107. A Research Memorandum, prepared by the State Department's Bureau of Intelligence and Research (INR) for the Secretary of State on 29 November 1963, noted: "Bolivia probably has the most heavily armed population in Latin America, except for Cuba. . . . Militia groups in Bolivia, only a few thousand of whose numbers are under the direct control of the government, are equal to or larger than the police and the army combined in terms of manpower." INR Research Memorandum, "Clandestine Arms Traffic in Latin America and the Insurgency Problem," RAR-49, 29 November 1963. Declassified copy, Lyndon Baines Johnson Presidential Library, Austin, Texas.
121. William Brill, "Military Civic Action in Bolivia," Ph.D. dissertation, 1965, 121; Dunkerley, *Rebellion*, 114.
122. Christopher Rand, "Letter from La Paz," *The New Yorker*, 31 December 1966, 47; Prado, *Poder y fuerzas armadas*, 101, 115–117.
123. Thomas C. Field, Jr., "Ideology as Strategy: Military-Led Modernization and the Origins of the Alliance for Progress in Bolivia," *Diplomatic History*, 36.1 (January 2012), 175–176; also see, Field Jr., *From Democracy to Dictatorship*, 45, 57.
124. Field Jr., *From Democracy to Dictatorship*, 81.
125. *El Diario*, 13 September 1963, 5 and Christopher Rand, "Letter from La Paz," 36.
126. Dunkerley, *Rebellion*, 115; Prado, *Poder y fuerzas armadas*, 112–113.
127. William Brill, *Military Intervention in Bolivia: The Overthrow of Paz Estenssoro and the MNR* (Washington, DC, 1967), 24.
128. Ibid.; see also *El Diario*, 13 January 1964, 4.
129. General Barrientos claimed that it was Paz's handling of the MNR Nominating Convention that drove him into the conspiracy. See Brill, *Military Intervention*, 35; Mitchell, *The Legacy of Populism*, 92–96. For the military Young Turks, see Field Jr., *From Development to Dictatorship*, 137. The classic Bolivian exposés of the military coup d'état are Sergio Almaraz Paz, *Requiem para una república*, 15–38; René Zavaleta Mercado, *La cáida del M.M.R. y la conjuración de noviembre* (La Paz, 1995); Guillermo Lora, *¡Abajo la Bota Militar!* (La Paz, 1965); and the anonymous folleto attributed to Luís Antezana, *Porqué cayó el MNR?* (Cochabamba, 1967).
130. William Brill, who coined the Magic Bullet, discusses the episode in *Military Intervention*, 27–29. See also Field Jr., *From Development to Dictatorship*, 137–138; Kirkland, *Observing Our Hermanos en Armas*, 117–118; Prado, *Poder y fuerzas armadas*, 138–139; Mitchell, *The Legacy of Populism*, 94–95; Jaime Calderón, *The Bolivian Coup of 1964: A Sociological Analysis* (Buffalo, NY, 1972), 116.
131. This chronology is derived from Field Jr., *From Development to Dictatorship*, 138.
132. Ibid., 136–139, 227 n 37–38; and William Brill, "Interview with Barrientos," 20 July 1966, in *Military Intervention*, 28 n 19.
133. This quote, in fact, a reference to Josef Stalin, is an apt description of Paz Estenssoro. The quotation is from George F. Kennan, cited in John Lewis Gaddis, *The Cold War: A New History* (New York, 2005), 11 n 4.

134. This quote from Guevara Arze is taken from Francisco Barrero, *Radepa y la Revolución Nacional* (La Paz, 1976), 264. Also insightful is José Fellman Velarde's observation: "He preferred the game of dividing and balancing forces to the exercise of authority, an indication of a subtle vein of insecurity . . . somewhat surprising for a man whose desire for power was so evident." José Fellman Velarde, *Historia de Bolivia*, Vol. 3 (La Paz, 1970), 373.
135. See Alfonso Finot, *Así Cayó Villarroel y Defensa de mi Relato Así Cayó Villarroel* (La Paz, 1966), 69–70 for a firsthand account by Paz Estenssoro's aide (and the repercussions, including his lengthy exile after his revelations regarding the telephone line incident). See also the related commentary of the RADEPA Colonel Francisco Barrero, *Radepa y la Revolución Nacional*, 263–265.
136. Field Jr., *From Development to Dictatorship*, 167.
137. Magnus Linklater, Isabel Hilton and Neal Ascherson, *The Fourth Reich: Klaus Barbie and the Neo-Fascist Connection* (London, 1984), 222. The Nazis that worked for Paz Estenssoro's Control Político continued working for the military dictatorships that began with General Barrientos. For the concentration camps and prisons mandated by Paz Estenssoro in October 1952, see *La Patria*, 31 July 2011 and *El Diario*, 4 October 2016.
138. "Lechín . . . was protected by 'a permanent squad of armed militia who live[d] at his house'; an American neighbor noted that 'the garage [of the house] cannot be used for cars as it is very well stocked with submachine guns and cases of ammunition'." Alan Knight, "The Domestic Dynamics of the Mexican and Bolivian Revolutions Compared," in Merilee S. Grindle and Pilar Domingo, eds., *Proclaiming Revolution: Bolivia in Comparative Perspective* (London, 2003), 86 n 88.
139. Field Jr., *From Development to Dictatorship*, 165, 168. The military High Command did not share Paz's enthusiasm for Colonel San Román. Prado, *Poder y fuerzas armadas*, 133–135.
140. Brill, *Military Intervention*, 37 and 37 n 17; for the bomb attack, see Prado, *Poder y fuerzas armadas*, 138.
141. Mitchell, *The Legacy of Populism*, 98. The Pact, as discussed by General Juan José Torres, is reprinted in Brian Loveman and Thomas M. Davies, Jr., eds., *The Politics of Anti-Politics: The Military in Latin America* (Lincoln, NE, 1978), 185–187. See also, Prado, *Poder y fuerzas armadas*, 128, 140–141.
142. *El Diario*, 29 February 1964, 6.
143. C.A.M. Hennessey, "Shifting Forces in the Bolivian Revolution," *World Today* (May 1964), 199.
144. For differing interpretations of the nature and timing of General Ovando's involvement in General Barrientos' machinations, see Brill, *Military Intervention*, 25, 45–48; Guillermo Bedregal, *Víctor Paz Estenssoro, El Político: Una semblanza crítica* (México, D.F., 1999), chapter XX; *¿Porque cayo el MNR?* Cochabamba, 1967 (the anonymous pamphlet attributed to Luis Antezana); Dunkerley, *Rebellion*, 114–115, 119; and Field Jr., *From Development to Dictatorship*, 135–138, 145–149, 170–171, 180–187.
145. Richard Patch, "The Last of Bolivia's MNR?" *American Universities Field Staff*, West Coast South America Series, 11.5 (June 1964), 56.
146. Field Jr., *From Development to Dictatorship*, 56, 169.
147. The most comprehensive and detailed indictment of Paz's police state is Cristóbal Kolkichuyma P'ankara, *Claudio San Román, el primero verdugo del MNR* (El Alto, 2008).
148. Ibid., 168, 189. The idea that the CIA Station Chief, an agent who stated that he worked with Colonel San Román on a "daily basis," was shocked by the butchery of the MNR Control Político defies credibility. Field Jr., *From Democracy to Dictatorship*, 134.
149. Patch, "Bolivia: Decision or Debacle," 8. Hernán Landívar Flores, *Terebinto; drama nacional* (La Paz, 1966). Hernán Bariga Antelo, *Laureles de un Tirano* (La Paz, 1965) and Enrique Achá Álvarez and Mario H. Ramos y Ramos, *Unzaga: Mártir de América*

(Buenos Aires, 1960) afford insight into the Falange mentality. Lieutenant René López Murillo recounts life inside a Control Político concentration camp of 300 prisoners (Falangistas, military officers, cadets, carabineros, university students, professors, doctors, lawyers, engineers, technicians, workers, and merchants) at Curahuara de Carangas on the frigid Altiplano. René López Murillo, *Yo Fugé de un Campo de Concentración: relato de la vida en los campos de concentaación del M.N.R.* (Santiago, Chile, 1955). See also the *Wikisource* three-part "Summary report on violations of human rights during the governments of Víctor Paz Estenssoro and Hernán Siles Zuazo, June 2001" with reference to instances of MNR repression, torture and detention centers, and government officials accused of human rights violations.

150. *El Diario,* 22 November 1963, 9; 28 November 1963, 7; 5 December 1963, 7; 28 December 1963, 1; 31 December 1963, 7.
151. *El Diario,* 4 April 1964, 7; 5 April 1964, 6; 20 April 1964, 6; 22 April 1964, 7, *Unidad,* 13 April 1964, 6. See also, Albó, *Achacachi,* 18–19. Francisco Viscarra, ex-hacendado, Achacachi vecino and *farmacía* owner was a long-standing opponent of Toribio Salas. Interviews by the owner with Francisco Viscarra's son Gregorio, Achacachi, 12 July 1970.
152. *El Diario,* 22 April 1964, 1, 7; 23 April 1964, 7.
153. *El Diario,* 7 October 1963, 4; 3 January 1964, 6; 3 April 1964, 8; 29 April 1964, 4; 12 May 1964, 3. Also see Gordillo, *Campesinos revolucionarios,* 139–145.
154. Telegrams 448, 451, 454, Ambassador Henderson to Department of State, 29 October 1964, Subject Numeric File Pol 23–9 Bol, DOS Central Files, NARA. Field Jr., *From Development to Dictatorship,* 174–175.
155. Telegram 484, Henderson to Secretary of State, 3 November 1964 (11:47 p.m.). The CIA estimate of Paz's support was somewhat more optimistic. See Field Jr., *From Development to Dictatorship,* 238 n.148.
156. Jaime Calderón, *The Bolivian Coup of 1964,* 117 and discussions by the author with Captain Calderón in Boston, Massachusetts, 1974.
157. Telegram 468, Ambassador Henderson to Department of State, 2 November 1964, Subject Numeric File Pol 23–9 Bol, DOS Central Files, NARA.
158. Telegram 474 (3:45 p.m.) and 475 (6:13 p.m.), Ambassador Henderson to Department of State, 3 November 1964, Subject Numeric File Pol 23–9 Bol, DOS Central Files, NARA.
159. Telegram 476 (9:36 p.m.), Ambassador Henderson to Department of State, 3 November 1964, Subject Numeric File Pol 23–9 Bol, DOS Central Files, NARA.
160. General Gary Prado, a junior officer at the time, provides an insightful discussion of the inner workings of the military conspirators in Prado, *Poder y fuerzas armadas,* 155–160.
161. Telegram 484, 485, Ambassador Henderson to Department of State, 4 November 1964, Subject Numeric File Pol 23–9, Bol, DOS Central Files, NARA.
162. In an interview with the author, 27 June 1970 in Lima, Peru, Víctor Paz noted the incapacitation of the Altiplano militias following the fiesta of Todos Santos. The tactical developments in the destabilization of the Paz government are intuitively obvious in a reading of the *New York Times Index,* 52 (1964), 110. For the intricacies of the military coup, see *¿Porque Cayo el MNR?*; Brill, *Military Intervention,* 18–47; Field Jr., *From Development to Dictatorship,* chapter six; Dunkerley, *Rebellion,* 103–11; Julio Mantilla C., *El Estado del 52 y la Nueva Política Económica del Gobierno del MNR* (La Paz, 1986), 10–19. Sergio Almaraz Paz's *Réquiem para una Republica* is the Bolivian touchstone on the topic.
163. Telegram 486, Ambassador Henderson to Department of State, 4 November 1964, Subject Numeric File Pol 23–9 Bol, DOS Central Files, NARA.
164. Field Jr., *From Development to Dictatorship,* 198 n 9.
165. Brill, *Military Intervention,* 31.
166. *U.S. Army Area Handbook for Bolivia* (Washington, DC, August 1963), 662.

167. Gerassi, *The Great Fear*, 263; Field, Jr., "Ideology as Strategy," 156–158, 161. Ernesto "Che" Guevara denounced the Alliance for Progress "as a new form of economic imperialism," in a pair of inspired speeches at the Organization of American States conference in August 1961. For Guevara's incisive critiques, see María del Carmen Ariet García and Javier Salado, eds., *Our America and Theirs: Kennedy and the Alliance for Progress, The Debate at Punta del Este* (New York, 2006).
168. Brian Loveman, *No Higher Law* (Chapel Hill, NC, 2010), 296.
169. Quoted in Tim Weiner, *Legacy of Ashes: The History of the CIA* (New York, 2007), 279.
170. *New York Times*, 19 March 1964, 1. As John Gerassi notes, "There could be little doubt that under Mann, the Alliance would not be between the U.S. and Latin America, but between the U.S. and U.S. businesses in Latin America." Gerassi, *The Great Fear*, 280.
171. Loveman, *No Higher Law*, 255; Jeffrey Taffet, *Foreign Aid as Foreign Policy: The Alliance for Progress in Latin America* (New York, 2007), 59–63. A CIA station chief stated that the agency maintained American influence by "becoming" their intelligence service: "They [military officers] don't know what's going on in the world. So you give them a weekly briefing—doctored to meet their sensibilities. Money definitely—that's always welcome. Procurement—toys, games, weapons. Training. And you can always take a group of officers to Fort Bragg or to Washington—a wonderful holiday." Quoted in Weiner, *Legacy of Ashes*, 280.
172. Thomas C. Field, Jr. "Ideology as Strategy," 148–149; also, Field Jr., *From Development to Dictatorship*, 79, 81.
173. Loveman, *No Higher Law*, 294.
174. Ibid. Also see, Field, Jr., "Ideology as Strategy," 161, 168–169.
175. The quotation is from an October 1964 article in *Military Review* by Lt. Colonel Jonathan Ladd, reprinted in Alfred Stepan, *The Military in Politics: Changing Patterns in Brazil* (Princeton, NJ, 1972), 362. Stepan demonstrates the immediate interest in the strategy, after its introduction during the Kennedy administration, as evidenced in the listings of the *University Index to Military Periodicals* where there are 160 entries for counterinsurgency and 33 for civic action in the years 1962–1964—and none for the previous period (1959–1961). Ibid., 361. In the 1970s and 1980s, Operation Condor was the code name for the "symphony" launched by the United States in concert with South American military fascists against domestic resistance—defined as "insurgency."
176. Philip Siekman, "When Executives Turned Revolutionaries," *Fortune*, September 1964, 216; see also *Newsweek*, 14 November 1966, 56; and United States Senate Committee on Foreign Relations, Subcommittee on American Republic Affairs, *Survey of the Alliance for Progress* (April 1969), 586. For the role of USAID in sabotaging the reformist government of Brazilian President João Goulart, see Joseph Paige, *The Revolution That Never Was* (New York, 1972), 155; Langguth, *Hidden Terrors*, 58–142; Blum, *Killing Hope*, 163–172.
177. "Secret Memorandum from General Lansdale to Secretary of Defense McNamara," 3 June 1963 cited in Kirkland, *Observing Our Hermanos en Armas*, 159, n.55; Field Jr., *From Development to Dictatorship*, 217 n 96.
178. Field Jr., *From Development to Dictatorship*, 140–158, 180–188; Kirkland, *Observing Our Hermanos en Armas*, 101–123.
179. The complex interplay among Ambassador Henderson, President Paz, and Generals Barrientos and Ovando preparatory to their coup d'état is closely traced in Field Jr., *From Development to Dictatorship*, 145–148, 165–168, 171–183; see also Bedregal, *Víctor Paz Estenssoro*, 544–549; and Prado, *Poder y fuerzas armadas*, 124–128, 138–139, 145–151.
180. The relationship between Fox and Barrientos is the focus of Colonel Kirkland's, *Observing Our Hermanos en Armas*, chapter 5. It bears noting that government documents do not necessarily reveal truths: for example, FBI Director J. Edgar Hoover removed incriminating documents when it served his purpose, as was the case with his involvement in

the Pearl Harbor disaster examined by Anthony Summers and Robbyn Swan, *Pearl Harbor: Betrayal, Blame, and a Family's Quest for Justice* (New York, 2016), 120.
181. Weiner, *Legacy of Ashes*, 281.
182. Field Jr., *From Development to Dictatorship*, 145–147.
183. Ibid., 148. For General Barrientos' skills in the effective use of force, in this case, against the MNR caudillo (and cocaine trafficker) Luis Sandoval Morón's minions in Santa Cruz, see General Gary Prado, *Poder y fuerzas armadas*, 119–120.
184. Brill, *Military Intervention*, 24–25.
185. Field Jr., *From Development to Dictatorship*, 146, 170–171; also see Prado, *Poder y fuerzas armadas*, 143.
186. Wilkie, *The Bolivian Revolution*, 24.
187. Ibid., 43.
188. Prado, *Poder y fuerzas armadas*, 153.

EPILOGUE

The military overthrow of the Paz Estenssoro regime in November 1964 terminated the National Revolution. Although General Barrientos referred to the coup as a "Revolution of Restoration" (suggesting a return of the National Revolution, without the MNR), what ensued was the restoration of military rule for 18 years, followed by the reign of creole-mestizo civilian politicians into the twenty-first century. Social revolutions are distinguished by the rapid dismantling and transformation of the political, social, and economic basis of the ancien régime. Although the Bolivian revolution came to a formal end in 1964, the process of change set in motion continues into the twenty-first century. What then is the legacy of the nation's social revolution and what are its effects on the nation's indigenous majority?

The following assessment of this process will consider (1) legacies for the indigenous people; (2) military rule and indigenous resistance (1964–1982); (3) indigenous struggle and neoliberalism (1982–2006); (4) the rise and fall of Bolivia's first Indian president Evo Morales Ayma (2006–2020).

Legacies for the Indigenous People

The revolution terminated the 500-year reign of the colonato. The freed colonos were given the right to own land (often plots previously worked in usufruct three to four days per week) and the ayllu communities were granted the right to seek restitution of lands *after* 1900.[1] Comunarios and ex-colonos were at last able to move about freely and market their goods wherever they chose without the intervention of creole-mestizo middlemen. The agrarian reform decrees enfranchised women and men, mandated land reform, universal coeducation, syndicalization of the peasantry, and colonization of the vast lowlands of the Oriente. The landmark decrees would prove to be inestimably transformative—far beyond the dozen years of the National Revolution.

Armed sindicato militias were organized by the subaltern miners, factory workers, and ex-colonos to defend the regime as a counterpoise to the praetorian proclivity of the armed forces. The syndical struggle against the creole oligarchs of the Old Regime (and the creole-mestizos of the National Revolution) remain a powerful memory in the history of the indigenous peoples (see Chapters 6–8). Their experience would resonate in the decolonization struggles waged by the subaltern populace during the twenty-first century. Indeed, the Aymara President Evo Morales Ayma was the leader of the militant coca growers (*cocaleros*) union that propelled his election to the presidency.

The Agrarian Reform Process

Less than one-third of all haciendas were totally expropriated during the National Revolution. In the majority of cases, landlords managed to retain possession of their manor houses together with a portion of contiguous land. The more militant colonos—who forcibly seized some 400,000 hectares at the onset of the revolution—remained in possession of their lands. For those colonos and comunarios who opted to secure land within the legal confines of the agrarian reform bureaucracy (as we have seen in Chapter 6), the paper chase was lengthy and complex. A decade after proclamation of the agrarian reform decree, some 200,000 ex-colono families still awaited legal title to land, the 72 percent of the peasantry with title to land parcels of under-5 hectares practiced subsistence agriculture. A sector of the peasantry with small farms of 5–20 hectare parcels grew and marketed foodstuffs for cash in the urban markets.

The inequality between rich, poor, and landless peasants persists as a legacy of the agrarian reform process that allocated land based on the particulars of pre-revolutionary hacienda usufructs. Gender inequality continues because land was distributed to men (considered heads of families). Widows were an exception. Because the decree stipulated that land acquired under the law could not be sold, it could not serve as collateral for bank loans. And because qualifications for loans required 100 percent collateral, even the smallest loans exceeded peasants' annual earnings. Improving the condition of the peasantry was not a priority of the National Revolution, given the small size of plots allocated, and the utter lack of financial and technical assistance available for improvements in horticulture, animal husbandry, the use of fertilizer, and better methods of crop storage.

The focus of MNR governments and North American advisors was not the Andean highlands and inter-montane valleys where three-fourths of the population resided on 30 percent of the country's land, but instead the lowlands of the Yungas, Chapare, and Oriente with 70 percent of the land and one-fourth of the population. Since the onset of the agrarian reform process, the population of the Andean highlands has doubled; the resultant minifundios, subsistence farming, and migration to urban shantytowns or the fields of the Oriente are salient legacies of the National Revolution. And while the revolution bequeathed land and liberty to the peasantry, the traditional differentiation between rich, poor, and landless peasants has contributed to the fragmentation of indigenous sindicatos and the hegemony of creole-mestizos.

The March to the Oriente

The potential for economic development of the Oriente, underscored by the Bohan Plan in 1942, recommended construction of highways linking highlands and lowlands, transitioning peasants from the densely populated highlands to the eastern lowlands where more land and better soil were available, fostering large-scale agricultural enterprises, and development of the region's hydrocarbon resources. This modernization schema, initiated in the 1943–1946 RADEPA–MNR revolution, resumed in the 1952–1964 MNR redux. Completion of a paved highway connecting Santa Cruz and Cochabamba in 1954 ended the isolation of the Oriente and facilitated commerce and colonization. A National Colonization Plan announced in 1963 sought to direct highland peasants to the Yungas, Chapare, and Santa Cruz where they could become small farmers or work as rural proletarians on agricultural enterprises. As will be seen, the unintended consequences of the plan far exceeded the objectives of colonizing the east with impoverished highland peasants and linking the tropical lowlands and Andean highlands to facilitate trade between east and west.

The 1953 Agrarian Reform Decree exempted large estates from expropriation if the properties utilized modern technology, employed wage labor, and evidenced capital investment. Designated "agricultural enterprises," these properties were most common in the Oriente and thus escaped the fate of latifundia associated with the colonato of the Andean highlands, which were subject to expropriation. The MNR's focus on development of the Oriente is apparent in the shift of the Bolivian Agricultural Bank (BAB) from its original mission of lending to peasants and small farmers to providing loans to large ranches and agro-businesses. Two decades after the initiation of the agrarian reform decree, highland peasants received 4 percent of BAB loans and agro-businesses in the Oriente received 90 percent of the BAB loans. Between 1961 and 1971, 60 million dollars in USAID loans and grants were allocated for colonization projects in the Beni and road construction in Santa Cruz Department.[2]

Internal Migration

Although the MNR officially promoted colonization of the Oriente to diversify agriculture, the land reform decree led to minifundismo eventuating in an exodus from the Andean highlands and valleys. Intensive farming of small plots of land in an arid environment together with the effects of drought, floods, freezing weather, erosion, soil infertility, overgrazing, and livestock diseases has made for an unsustainable existence for an ever-increasing number of impoverished Andean peasants. The doubling of the population in 50 years since initiation of the MNR land reform added to the impetus to forsake rural poverty for the lure of the city. But the curse of poverty is inescapable. After 50 years of agrarian reform, extreme rural and urban poverty continues for the indigenous populace.

At the beginning of the twenty-first century, eight of every ten peasants lived in poverty. Many departed to improve their life chances in a city. Nonetheless, poverty remains inescapable: 47 percent of the urban populace is impoverished. Yet life in the city remains a better bet than continuing immiserated in a rural existence of dreary resignation. The indigenous immigrants are not welcomed by creole-mestizo vecinos threatened by the *la indiada*, the dreaded natives with their alien language and culture. Vecino complaints of poor hygiene and the threat of contagious diseases born by indigenous arrivals ignore an underlying fact: the scourge of poverty.

Adjustment to urban society by rural emigrants necessitates adaptation of ethnic identity to existence in a hostile environment. Popularly referred to as *cholo/chola* by vecinos, the migrants have developed a distinctive subculture. "By cholo is meant a distinctive sector of the population . . . consisting of peasants, ex-peasants and descendents of peasants who have left their land group and live in the city by labour, crafts and commerce. They are Spanish speaking . . . move restrictedly, suffering social discrimination, and exhibiting strong solidarity."[3] The influx of rural emigrants to the major cities of La Paz, Cochabamba, and Santa Cruz has created metropolises of a million or more inhabitants. The Aymara city of El Alto located on the Altiplano above the city of La Paz, virtually non-existent in the 1950s, became a settlement of some 10,000 in the mid-1960s, and is now home to nearly two million residents.[4]

Education

The perceived opportunity of better education for their children is another incentive for rural families to relocate in a city. The National Revolution broke with the past when hacendados opposed education of Indian children who might use knowledge in the pursuit of freedom (see Chapter 1). The 1955 Education Reform and subsequent Education Code touted universal and free coeducation. Because of the immensity of this undertaking—the funding and construction of the thousands of schools necessary to educate the immense number of indigenous children, and the severe shortage of educated teachers required—the Education Reform has been far from revolutionary. As with the nationalization of the tin mines and implementation of agrarian reform, the devil was in the details hidden beneath grandiose platitudes.

The Education Code created a binary school structure with different curricula for urban and rural students. Rural students were taught vocational subjects in agriculture, animal husbandry, health and hygiene, echoing the agenda of the pre-revolutionary indigenista schools.[5] Rural school teachers were only required to have a primary school education and classes, taught in Spanish and not the language of the students, experienced high dropout rates. Teachers focused on memorization rather than developing skills for critical thought and analysis. Both urban and rural schools were underfunded and lacked competent teachers. The National Revolution's attempt at educational reform failed to significantly increase enrollment, nor did it change the focus of education for the indigenous majority.[6]

Yet urban migration allowed for the opportunity to attend creole-mestizo universities. Students at the Universidad Mayor de San Andres in La Paz gained access to an excellent faculty in the social sciences and began to undertake research on indigenous history and society from a perspective radically different than that found in academic works written by the creole-mestizo elite. Their revisionist studies underscored the hegemonic role of creole-mestizos in Bolivian history, reinterpreted the history of the National Revolution, and inspired an indigenous awakening among a new generation of resistance leaders.

Military Rule and Indigenous Resistance (1964–1982)

"The Revolution of Restoration"

The 18-year period of military dictatorship (1952–1964) endured far longer than the Rosca's Sexenio (1946–1952) following the first overthrow of the National Revolution. General René Barrientos and his successor, General Alfredo Ovando, honored the Pacto Militar-Campesino, left agrarian reform intact, and continued control of peasant syndicatos through patron–client relationships with local military officers. The process of land redistribution continued apace under the dictatorships of General Barrientos and his successors, Generals Ovando and Banzer: the percentage of land titles granted under the three military presidents equaled that of the MNR regime, but the percentage of total hectares granted and their size increased markedly as the land boom in the Oriente quickened.

Indigenous miners bore the brunt of violent repression. Militant miners frustrated the attempts by MNR presidents Siles Zuazo and Paz Estenssoro to implement the austerity strictures (layoffs, reduction of wages and benefits) required by foreign banks and corporations. General Barrientos had no qualms about bringing recalcitrant miners to heel; he declared the mines a military zone, abolished the COB and the miners' union, executed the militant leader of the miners' union, exiled their chieftain Juan Lechín, fired 6,000 miners, and massacred miners and their families at Llallagua, Siglo XX, and Catavi. Wages in the mines were then slashed by 40 percent and salaries doubled for military officers.

This now favorable investment climate attracted foreign banks and corporations. Within three years, Bank of America, First City National Bank, and the Banco Boliviano Americano held over 50 percent of the nation's financial deposits ($28,000,000). Lucrative contracts to exploit the nation's mineral and hydrocarbon reserves were awarded to Philips Brothers and the International Mining and Processing Corporation to extract tin, lead, zinc, cadmium, and silver on the Altiplano. Gulf Oil's concession to explore, drill, pump, and export oil from Santa Cruz was likewise extraordinary. In three years, Gulf's share of oil production grew to 80 percent and the Bolivian state enterprise (*Yacimientos Petrolíferos Fiscales Bolivianos*: YPFB) fell to 20 percent.[7] After four years of the "Revolution of Restoration," 40 percent of Bolivian imports and exports were in the hands of U.S. corporations.

President René Barrientos was quick to adapt to the perquisites of office—inviting North American corporate investment, flying about in a helicopter gifted by Gulf Oil, thanks to a lucrative petroleum concession, collecting payoffs from Nazi war criminals engaged in arms trafficking, and accumulating land in Santa Cruz. Meanwhile, unbeknownst to Barrientos, Ernesto "Che" Guevara had targeted Bolivia as the epicenter of a continental revolution in South America. Che's guerrilla *foco* (armed vanguard) operating in a remote area of Santa Cruz Department failed to attract campesinos to the revolutionary cause, but did draw the attention of the United States. CIA operatives arrived and the Pentagon dispatched a Green Beret team to train an elite force of Bolivian Rangers and then directed a counterinsurgency campaign against Che's fledgling "Army of National Liberation" (*Ejército de Liberación Nacional*: ELN). When the miners of Siglo XX declared their support for Che's guerrilla war, President Barrientos response was the infamous "Massacre of San Juan" on 24 June 1967.[8] Three months later, after suffering defeats in a number of skirmishes, Bolivian Rangers ambushed the *foco*. The wounded Che was captured, tortured, and executed at the hamlet of La Higuera.[9]

Barrientos, considered responsible for Che's execution, died in a suspicious helicopter crash in April 1969 and Vice President General Alfredo Ovando assumed the presidency.[10] Evidently influenced by the revolutionary government of the armed forces in neighboring Peru, Ovando and his successor General Juan José Torres sought to reverse the damage Barrientos had done to some of the hallmark accomplishments of the National Revolution. An advocate of resource nationalism, President Ovando's goals were to regain sovereignty over the means of production and utilize the armed forces to combat the socioeconomic conditions that give rise to armed struggle against the state. Arguing that "plows rather than bayonets" would be a better use of US aid, he requested heavy equipment for rural development, announced that the armed forces would be deployed in a literacy campaign, and criticized the U.S. mantra of "imminent communist takeover."[11]

This populist overture incited and polarized military and civilian extremists. Falangista militants backed by military fascists attacked and occupied the

University of San Andrés in La Paz after a bloody shootout with leftist students; a similar attack and occupation was carried out at a university in Santa Cruz. In July 1970, a ELN *foco* comprised primarily of university students sought to overthrow General Ovando. The *foco* began operations in the Yungas jungle north of La Paz, seized two engineers employed by a U.S. gold mining company at Teoponte, and dynamited their dredge. The fledgling guerrillas were decimated by government troops to the consternation of middle-class Paceños appalled by the slaughter. A *foco* of the Maoist *Unión de Campesinos Pobres* (UCAPO) operating in Santa Cruz Department was also defeated. Che's martyrdom may have inspired creole-mestizo revolutionaries, but after the democratization of the National Revolution and the clientelism of the Pacto Militar-Campesino, the peasantry was not ripe for revolution.[12]

Marxist guerrillas were not the only threat to Ovando whose nationalization of Gulf Oil, denunciation of the Alliance for Progress, initiation of diplomatic relations with the Soviet Bloc, and legalization of communist political parties antagonized dissident right-wing military officers and the U.S. Embassy. In a dizzying two-day turn of events beginning on 4 October 1970, President Ovando was forced to abdicate, leaving the country in the hands of a military junta, which in turn was ousted by the idiosyncratic General Juan José Torres: In one day, six presidents had ruled the nation.

General Juan José Torres and the Popular Assembly

General Torres was enigmatic. As Chief of Staff in 1967, he worked with U.S. advisors to eliminate Che Guevara's guerrilla insurgency, plotted the Ovando overthrow of 7 October 1970, gave the COB a role in government, and allowed a Popular Assembly to meet (22 June to 2 July 1971). He expelled the Peace Corps, freed the French intellectual Régis Debray (imprisoned as a supporter of Che's *foco*), accepted financial aid from the Soviet Bloc, and threatened to arm the workers. The General's nationalist view of the armed forces provoked the military's right-wing faction when he criticized, "The arch-conservatives [who] see in the armed forces an exceedingly efficient instrument to return to the night of the past while they remain allied with the foreign monopolies" and warned, "the armed forces will no longer accept the role of simple wardens of an unjust order."[13] The die was cast. As reactionaries in the military prepared to strike, leaders of the Popular Assembly frantically attempted to confront the imminent assault by the armed forces.

An exchange of words between General Torres and Juan Lechín encapsulates the nation's eternal struggle between the subaltern majority and their hegemons. "Lechín later begged Torres to arm the people, but the general reportedly replied, 'I cannot . . . if I give you the arms . . . you won't need me any more.'"[14] As was the case with the MNR in their resistance to the ancien régime, the conflict was between creole-mestizos. Their great fear then, as always, is the political agency of the conquered indigenous majority. At the eleventh-hour Torres relented and allowed the student and worker resistors 1,400 WW I Mauser bolt action rifles—a mixed blessing for those who would wield them.[15]

The "Banzerato"

The expected coup against General Torres, led by Colonel Hugo Bánzer Suárez, came on 21 August 1971. Banzer's revolt was backed by the Falange, Santa Cruz industrialists and agro-businessmen (including cocaine traffickers) and U.S. Ambassador Ernest Siracusa. Resistance to the military takeover was vicious. In a show of force, Air Force warplanes and army tanks blasted student resistors at the University of San Andres: a dozen students were killed and 25 wounded. The ensuing resistance would become the bloodiest conflict between the armed forces and civilians since the 1952 MNR revolution: 120 Paceños were killed and 700 wounded.[16] Then, to gain civilian support, General Banzer invited the FSB and MNR to join the military in a "Popular Nationalist Front" (*Frente Popular Nacionalista*: FPN). Each of the two parties was given four cabinet positions, while Banzer's military regime ("Banzerato") gained the patina of civilian participation.

General Banzer initiated a regime of state terrorism—a new form of extremely repressive governance established in Brazil, and which would soon spread throughout the Southern Cone. Banzer quickly revealed his dictatorial bona fides. After a student demonstration in the central plaza of Santa Cruz, 50 students were rounded up, shipped to the outskirts of the city, and executed. Sporadic but less dramatic executions of student leftists followed in other cities as the dictatorship tightened its grip. I lived in La Paz during the early years of the dictatorship and had experienced the Barrientos, Ovando, and Torres governments. But the Banzer dictatorship was different, more draconian: secret police suddenly appearing in restaurants and dragging customers off for enhanced interrogation, the Marquesas teenage gang murdering leftist students for money, telephones tapped, passports collected by hotels and registered with the police, and mass arrests and torture commonplace.

Outspoken journalists, labor leaders, students and professors were harshly repressed. The right of habeas corpus was suspended in June 1972. And 58 of the attorneys who argued that the denial of habeas corpus was unconstitutional were summarily imprisoned. The 1,500 political prisoners incarcerated at the Panóptico Nacional, Coati Island, Alto Madidi, Viacha, Achocalla, and private residences were routinely beaten and tortured. After the devaluation of the boliviano in late 1972, which led to skyrocketing inflation and a 40 percent increase in the cost of living—followed by a wage freeze and the removal of government subsidies that doubled the cost of foodstuffs—20 protesters in La Paz were killed by infantry bullets.

U.S. Ambassador Siracusa ardently supported General Banzer's dictatorship: "Hugo Banzer was a military officer and, I thought then, a remarkable one for

Latin America. . . . I came to know him quite well and to see in him a man of courage and principle." The ambassador viewed the dictatorship, "as providing a singular opportunity to turn things around in Bolivia to their benefit as well as our own," and urgently requested U.S. funds to support General Banzer. With the assistance of Henry Kissinger (at the NSC), Siracusa was given an initial "$10 million emergency tranche, with more to follow . . . with the help of a special team from Washington."[17] Ambassador Siracusa saw to it that Banzer received double the amount of military assistance funds than the combined total for the previous dozen years; U.S. military aid in 1973–1974 was triple the amount given to any other country in Latin America. Over $60 million in U.S. aid loans were given to the Banzer government in its first two years. With the Bolivian dictator firmly in power—and Gulf and Philips compensated for their expropriated properties—Ambassador Siracusa was posted to Montevideo, Uruguay, in 1973 to support another dictatorship.

The seven-year Banzerato (1971–1978) would be the longest period of uninterrupted rule since 1871. In November 1974, Banzer tightened his hold on the populace. Political parties were outlawed, government agents replaced labor union leaders, and strikes were prohibited. Adult men were conscripted into the army and indoctrinated by the regime. After hundreds of peasants were slaughtered during a protest outside the village of Tolata in Cochabamba Department, Banzer revoked the 1953 MNR decree that mandated indemnification for land grants. This act effectively cancelled the debts of peasant grantees. It was also a lesson in reward and punishment. Some 15,000 citizens were arrested and tortured in the first six years of the dictatorship. The walls beneath the Ministry of Interior building hid "torture chambers" where 2,000 political prisoners were kept and the dead entombed: an estimated 19,000 Bolivians fled the country.[18]

Indigenous Resistance: The Katarista Movement

Banzer's state terrorism shared some similarity with the draconian Rosca dictatorship of the Sexenio. The initial strategy of both regimes was to terrorize and destroy urban, creole-mestizo resistance and consolidate state power. Meanwhile, in the rural backlands, resistance to the dictatorships emerged among subaltern peasants in yet another struggle against creole-mestizo domination. In the dark days of the Banzerato, civic action and the co-optation of the Military-Peasant Pact had become a thing of the past. Amidst the Banzerato, a new generation of Aymara activists emerged. Evoking the long memory of Aymara resistance to creole domination, they called themselves Kataristas in honor of the heroic rebel Tupac Katari. They pointed out that they were not their fathers' generation: "We are no longer the peasants of 1952," but nevertheless were profoundly influenced by the 1952 MNR revolution's land reform process, the resultant minifundismo and urban migration to La Paz and Oruro.

The Katarista leaders shared much in common: (1) they were from Aroma Province in La Paz Department; (2) the Katarista founder Raimundo Tambo was from the hamlet of Ayo Ayo (the birthplace of Julian Apaza, the legendary Tupac Katari); another founder, Genaro Flores was from the nearby community of Antipampa; (3) many of the Karistas attended the Gualberto Villarroel school in La Paz, and some of them founded the 15 November political movement named to honor Tupac Katari's date of execution; (4) the Kataristas were part of a wave of Aymara migrants to La Paz and Oruro where they experienced the racism and social ostracism of the creole-mestizo populace; (5) those who attended a university had their political consciousness honed through exposure to the ideas of sophisticated social scientists; others were influenced by the liberation theology of Catholic clerics; (6) a few Kataristas had worked for U.S. academic researchers and USAID technocrats where they were sensitized to the racial and class biases of their supervisors.[19]

A new generation of Indian leaders had emerged, university educated harbingers of an indigenous awakening, heirs of the National Revolution's democratization and the MNR's descent into clientelism, nepotism, and the yoke of neocolonialism. They were also conscious of the decolonization struggles of the Third World. Thus, while the Kataristas were "no longer the peasants of 1952," they were privy to the collective memory of previous iterations of agrarian resistance and rebellion in Kollasuyu. Yet, could they avoid the factionalism that had divided and defeated the indigenous struggles of the past 500 years?

The Katartista founding principles appeared in the mimeographed 1973 *Manifiesto de Tiwanaku*. Signed by the Centro Campesino Tupac Katari, MINK'A, the National Association of Campesino Professors, and the Association of Bolivian Campesino Students, the document lays bare the agony of an oppressed people whose "virtues, vision of the world, life and culture are neither respected, nor comprehended." Redemption necessitated the awakening and organization of a "powerful, autonomous peasantry" to retake the lost road to greatness, "raising anew the banner and the great ideals of Tupac Katari, Bartolina Sisa, of Willka Zárate."[20] The diffusion of the Katarista Manifesto, together with the Catholic clergy's liberation theology, sparked a receptive audience among both urban and rural Aymara. The Manifesto's messages—"We are foreigners in our own country," and "I die today, but tomorrow I will return converted into thousands and thousands"—hit a collective nerve. Altiplano dirigentes organized some 10,000 adherents into a movement that soon morphed into political parties[21]

The Tiwanaku Manifesto calls to mind the earlier struggles of the 1920s to empower the subaltern populace: Santos Marca T'ula's efforts to educate the children of Altiplano migrants in La Paz, enabling them to carry on the struggle for revindication of ayllu lands usurped by creole-mestizos; Eduardo Leandro Nina Qhispi's attempt to incorporate all Indian children, rural and urban, in the *Sociedad Centro Educativo Kollasuyu*, to educate and instill self-respect, personal dignity, and commitment to the revindicationist cause in the proposed multiethnic Republic of Kollasuyu; the *Alcades Mayores Particulares* revitalization movement led by Toribio

Miranda and Gregorio Titiriku dedicated to preserving indigenous Andean culture and resisting acculturation into creole-mestizo culture and society; and the *Tesis de Caranguillas*, penned in 1947 after the defeat of an indigenous rebellion—with its detailed critique of the creole state, colonizer and colonized, capitalism and cooperativism—to awaken self-respect, and ethnic identity in a call to revolution of all Indians in Kollasuyu (see Chapter 4).

The Tiwanaku Manifesto's appeal to both rural and urban Aymara (some 50 percent of Paceños) represented a significant step in widening indigenous resistance to creole-mestizo dominion. The Katarista message could be heard in the Aymara language on radio broadcasts in Oruro and La Paz; Katarismo eroded the influence of the sindicato dirigentes tied to the Pacto Militar-Campesino as its message spread to the departments of Potosí, Cochabamba, Chuquisaca, and Santa Cruz. Genaro Flores was elected the leader of the *Confederación Nacional de Trabajadores Campesinos de Bolivia* (CNTCB) in March 1978 by representatives from the departments of La Paz, Oruro, and Potosí. This trajectory did not go unnoticed by the Banzer dictatorship. Imprisonment, torture, and assassinations forced the movement to go underground. Press and radio censors prohibited the word Katari and branded the movement as communist.

Nevertheless, two major Katarista parties were formed. The *Movimiento Indio Tupac Katari* (MITKA) founded by Luciano Tapia Quisbert in 1978 attracted urban migrants and rural peasants confronted by racial discrimination, capitalist exploitation, imperial machinations, and the failure of the National Revolution to improve their life chances. Animated by distrust of creole-mestizo politicians, MITKA refused to ally with either of the MNR parties led by Hernán Siles and Víctor Paz Estenssoro in the 1978 presidential election and ran Luciano Tapia as its own candidate. The *Tupac Katari Revolutionary Movement* (MRTK) led by Genario Flores, Macabeo Chila, and Víctor Hugo Cárdenas enjoyed widespread peasant support in La Paz and Oruro departments. Less hostile to the MNR jefes of the National Revolution, the MRTK first allied with Hernán Siles in the *Unión Democrática y Popular* (UDP), but then a faction led by Macabeo Chila broke off into the MRTK-Chila and allied with Víctor Paz.

The emergent campesino movement reconfigured as an independent trade union federation in the Single Union Confederation of Bolivian Campesino Workers (*Confederación Sindical Unica de Trabajadores Campesinos de Bolivia*: CSUTCB) in June 1979. The objectives were to foster a coordinated indigenous political agency and take direct action to confront creole-mestizo domination. A CSUTCB transportation shutdown in 1979 via well placed roadblocks in Cochabamba Department forced the military government to accept its demands—including reduced taxes on agricultural produce and co-management of the BAB—and demonstrated the potential of the indigenous majority.[22] The CSUTCB was an unequal partner in the COB: as was the case in the worker-dominated COB of the 1950s, representation of the peasants was not commensurate with their numerical majority. Unfortunately, the possibility of a unified worker peasant alliance as well as indigenous political autonomy again failed to materialize.

Power Shift

The victims targeted for repression were primarily urban. It was here that Che's ELN was reborn as a resistance strategy by urban guerrillas in La Paz, Cochabamba, Oruro, and Santa Cruz—where counterinsurgency tactics had yet to be developed and the advantages of clandestinity, initiative, and surprise could be asserted. Unfortunately, an insurrection was stillborn in the face of a lethal counterinsurgency assault. ELN actions were reduced to defense of safe houses attacked by military forces and a paramilitary Death Squadron. Over a dozen cadre were killed and 100 captured and tortured (including Mary Elizabeth Harding: a U.S. citizen and former Maryknoll nun).[23]

Banzer's state terrorism was instrumental in a power grab by Santa Cruz creole-mestizos who had long chafed at their marginalization, isolation, and underdevelopment at the hands of the preeminent La Paz elite.[24] A land boom fueled by government corruption and non-payment of millions of dollars in foreign loans made well-connected opportunists even wealthier. The profiteers included Banzer and a clique of senior military officers, displaced hacendados, cattle ranchers, loggers, industrialists, and agro-businessmen producing beef, lumber, rice, cotton, sugar cane, soybeans—and refining and exporting cocaine. Properties averaging 8,000 hectares appeared in the late 1960s and parcels of over 50,000 hectares were not uncommon in the region, known as the "Media Luna" after the half-moon crescent of eastern departments stretching from Tarija, north to Santa Cruz, Beni, and Pando. Santa Cruz Department is the heart of the Media Luna. The National Revolution's focus on development of the Oriente had set the stage for the economic ascendency of Santa Cruz based on agrobusiness, hydrocarbon, and iron exports. Money and power shifted from La Paz and the Altiplano tin mines to Santa Cruz and the burgeoning agro-industrial economy of the Oriente.

The Modus Operandi

The power shift to Santa Cruz was predicated on Banzer's totalitarian rule: this allowed a Cruceño cohort to multiply wealth through land purchases with loans from the BAB and then plant government-subsidized export crops. The loans were rarely repaid. But who within the terrorist state could object? In a masterful exercise, James Dunkerley follows the money and lays bare the details: the failure of the Santa Cruz elite to repay 69 percent of $666 million in BAB loans invested in agrobusinesses, cocaine production and trafficking, and the pernicious growth of national indebtedness to international lenders. By 1978, the foreign debt had reached $3,102 million: the interest due on the loans was 88 percent of their value.[25] The ill-gotten funds remained in Santa Cruz and the nation was left with the debt. The result was spectacular. Santa Cruz de la Sierra, the capital of the department, burgeoned from 43,000 inhabitants in 1950 to 1,450,000 in 2019 as it arose as the nation's business epicenter, a magnet for international capital, and a destination for highland peasants in search of a better life.[26]

The Confrontation Between Dictatorship and Democracy

The Mann Doctrine introduced during the Lyndon Johnson presidency succeeded in replacing politicians with generals. President Richard Nixon and Secretary of State Henry Kissinger continued the practice and abetted the overthrow of Chile's socialist President Salvador Allende in 1973. Allende's successor General Augusto Pinochet instituted a murderous regime of state terrorism against resisters to his dictatorship. President Jimmy Carter, who inherited the massive blowback of the Nixon–Kissinger years, summoned General Banzer to the White House to personally discuss the Bolivian human rights question. Banzer was prodded to allow the forthcoming election scheduled for July 1978 to give the semblance of democracy; he did so, but with a Cruceño lacky as his front man. The choice of the bland Air Force General Juan Pareda Asbún seemed a safe bet, but this gambit can be dangerous: Vladimir Putin is a noteworthy example of a front man gone rogue. Banzer also declared amnesty for political prisoners and exiles, but specifically excluded Hernán Siles, Juan Lechín, and others, including 1,000 exiled miners. Nevertheless, the news of an election energized the populace, as old and new politicos and parties emerged from the shadows.

Meanwhile, a handful of miners' wives protested the exclusion of their exiled husbands from the phony amnesty with a hunger strike in a La Paz Catholic Church. Mishandled by Banzer, the hunger strike snowballed to some 1,000 protesters before it ended on 18 January 1978. The oppressed urban populace took heart: within a week, Banzer conceded another, more robust amnesty, and relaxed control over trade union activities, further energizing those who envisioned the possibility of regime change. But to counter the half dozen political parties that arose to field presidential candidates, Banzer unleashed a media blitz, a concerted campaign of voter suppression and wholesale electoral fraud. Amidst an outpouring of protest, the electoral commission dithered, and General Banzer threatened to resolve the crisis with a military coup. Whereupon, General Pareda declared himself president, which he confirmed with a coup d'état, and announced a presidential election to be held within six months.

The incessant turmoil wrought by military coups, the machinations of 27 political parties (with conflicting agendas), and a succession of five unelected presidents exacerbated the confrontation between dictatorship and democracy. The armed forces remained an ever present threat to the pursuit of democratization. Because of its factions, the military institution was particularly dangerous. Whereas a monolithic organization under a supreme command might plan a coup d'état, each faction in this heterogenous organization could (and did) often strike. The factions came in all forms: army, air force, navy; military institutionalists concerned with the prestige and honor of the armed forces; hard-line conservatives and fascists, criminal factions (cocaine mafias, smugglers); regional factions (e.g., Cruceños); and generational cohorts (graduates of Bolivian and U.S. military schools). The most ruthless and violent faction was the emergent Santa Cruz–Beni cocaine cartel with para-military enforcers and direct ties to powerful officers. As a Bolivian senior officer pointed out, "Bringing off a successful coup in Bolivia presupposes bringing one off in the army first."[27] Civilian politicians lived precarious lives with the ever-present danger of a coup d'état, assault, arrest, torture, and death. This period is remarkable for the resistance to state terrorism by Catholic priests, human rights advocates, and indigenous activists.

The Cocaine Coup

The election promised by Generals Banzer and Pareda took place in July 1979. Hernán Siles's UDP coalition received the most votes, but not the majority needed to meet the constitutional requirement for legitimation. When the other five coalitions and 16 parties refused to join the UDP in a broad coalition, but agreed to a compromise, the president of the senate, Walter Guevara Arze, was appointed interim president until the election re-scheduled for June 1980. In the following chaotic and violent months, political leaders lambasted General Banzer for the hundreds of crimes committed during the Banzerato and called for a reduction of funds for the armed forces, alienating the military institutionalists and antagonizing the Santa Cruz criminal faction who could not abide this whiff of democratization.

On 1 November, the quixotic and homicidal General Alberto Natusch Busch, from the Oriente Department of Beni, seized power in a coup d'état. Natusch and another army captain, Luis García Meza, had arrived in La Paz as prisoners of war on 10 April 1952 in the military's defeat by MNR-led popular forces. Natusch returned as a general with a vengeance on 1 November 1979 and unleashed a 15-day reign of terror in the city, including blowing up the COB headquarters and massacring protesters with a fusillade of bullets from armored personnel carriers and a helicopter converted into a gunship.[28] Following this terrifying display of military power, the general was left to consider his position—frozen U.S. loans, the nation's impending bankruptcy, mass protests—and hastily withdrew, handing the government to the civilian politicians. Following constitutional protocol, the president of the legislature's lower house, Lydia Gueiler Tejada, was appointed to govern in the interim until the election scheduled for 29 June 1980.

When Hernán Siles won the election (once again), powerful military and criminal conspirators centered in Santa Cruz Department prepared to seize power. Siles's electoral victory threatened the Cruceño cocaine cartels and criminal military factions who feared that a civilian government would seek repayment of the purloined BAB money, prosecute Generals Banzer, Natusch, and other Cruceño military officers for human rights violations, and threaten the cartels' lucrative cocaine business.

A coup would solve these problems.

The "Cocaine Coup" occurred in the context of U.S. hegemonic interest in combatting Marxism in Latin America through aiding and abetting military dictatorships. The Chilean dictator General Augusto Pinochet, who seized power in a U.S. backed coup in 1973, masterminded "Operation Condor," a war against leftists in South America waged by a secret alliance of Chilean, Argentine, Uruguayan, Paraguayan, Brazilian, and Bolivian military dictatorships coordinated by the Pinochet regime and supported by the United States. The catalyst for Operation Condor was the discovery of a Revolutionary Coordinating Junta (*Junta Coordinadora Revolucionaria*) formed by urban guerrilla organizations in Chile, Argentina, Uruguay, and Bolivia to combat the dictatorships of the Southern Cone.[29] Operation Condor collected, shared, and centralized intelligence information among members of the alliance in a war against civilian resistance. An estimated 60,000 to 80,000 citizens were killed and 400,000 imprisoned (viz, tortured) during the Condor years of state terrorism presented in the media as a struggle between communism and the "free world."[30] In an Orwellian twist, the resisters to state terrorism were labeled "terrorists" and the terrorist regimes were portrayed by U.S. mass media (viz., *Time, Newsweek, New York Times*, etc.) as defenders of national security in a war against terrorists.

The key actors in the Bolivian coup were Roberto Suárez Gómez, the "King of Cocaine" and Godfather of the Oriente cartel ("the Corporation") who financed the venture; generals Luis García Meza Tejada and Luis Arce Gómez; U.S. government agencies (CIA, DEA, Pentagon, State Department), their agents and criminal "assets";[31] Argentine covert military operatives (responsible for the deaths of 30,000 victims in Argentina);[32] the Nazi war criminal, Gestapo Captain Klaus Barbie aka Klaus Altmann ("The Butcher of Lyon" who sent thousands of French citizens, including hundreds of Jewish schoolchildren, to death camps); and Barbie/Altmann's para-military force of neo-fascist mercenaries from Germany, Italy, South Africa, and Rhodesia who called themselves the "Fiancés of Death."[33]

The coup of 17 July 1980 was executed in a manner befitting Operation Condor. A para-military force unleashed an extended barrage of heavy weaponry at the COB building in La Paz followed by an attack on those assembled in the building. Two trade union leaders were killed, as was Marcelo Quiroga Santa Cruz, a socialist politician and prominent critic of military dictatorships; the remaining COB leaders were imprisoned and tortured. Civilian resistance was crushed in a matter of days by army, air force, and para-military forces directed by the honorary Bolivian Colonel Barbie/Altmann and abetted by a force of some 200 Argentine military operatives—leaving 50 Paceños dead and over 500 imprisoned as grist for torture. Resistance in the mining camps was crushed after an attack on the stalwart Caracoles copper miners by infantry, tanks, and warplanes, followed by a massacre and sadistic repression (beheadings, bayonettings, women and girls raped, a miner dynamited). Some 500 victims joined the tens of thousands who "disappeared" in the Southern Cone during the Condor years. Genaro Flores, the Katarista peasant leader of the MRTK political party, survived an assassination attempt, crippled by a bullet to his spine. Priests were beaten, the human rights advocate Father Luis

Espinal tortured and murdered, and the Archbishop of La Paz threatened for publicly decrying the human rights violations of the regime. Creole-mestizo politicians fled into exile, although the neighboring Condor dictatorships were not necessarily safe havens.

Media censorship and a state of siege were imposed and the universities shut down as Klaus Barbie/Altmann put his counterintelligence expertise to work rooting out suspected resistance. The Gestapo Captain found his calling in Bolivia: "All through Barbie's life, state security and political terror and organized crime revealed their fundamental identity. At the end and climax of his career, all three finally merged into the carnival of misrule that was Bolivia under military rule."[34] His underling, the notorious Italian fascist Stefano delle Chiaie (accused of the bombings of a bank and railway station in Milan), likewise found his expertise in counterterrorism a valuable asset to the García Meza dictatorship while unleashing the Fiancés of Death to terrorize the populace. Free of the threat of prosecution by a civilian government, Arce Gómez, García Meza, and a network of military criminal factions quickly expanded their cocaine trafficking, racketeering, shakedown, and/or elimination of vulnerable narcotraffickers.[35]

There is more to the Cocaine Coup than meets the eye. Most curious are the connections of Roberto Suárez Gómez with the NSA's Colonel Oliver North, the CIA, Pablo Escobar and the Medellín Cartel, French traffickers in Marseilles, the Panamanian dictator Manuel Noriega, and government figures in the Bahamas, Costa Rica, and Cuba. This topic merits an investigation beyond the scope of this epilogue, but briefly, the narrative is as follows. Colonel North met multiple times with Roberto Suárez to arrange the purchase of a vast quantity of cocaine hydrochloride to be imported and sold in the United States to finance the Reagan Administration's war against the Marxist regime in Nicaragua that was prohibited by the 1982 Boland Amendment. The cocaine was transported by Colombian narcotraffickers and Southern Air Transport (a CIA proprietary airline), using airfields in Panama, Costa Rica, the Bahamas, and Cuba, where a fee was charged per kilo or per landing in Cuba.[36]

Arce Gómez and García Meza became multi-millionaires. In a country where a general was paid $500 a month, Arce Gómez accumulated five ranches, luxury apartments in Bolivia and Argentina, and numerous airplanes; García Meza allegedly had at least $40 million deposited in Swiss banks. But their rule could not go on forever amidst internal dissention, attempted coups by military factions, dogged civilian resistance, massive debt, inflation, work stoppages by miners and truckers, international exposes of the regime's narcotrafficking, and the opposition of the U.S. government. Finally, the indomitable will of the citizenry prevailed: student activists asserted themselves by impeding motor traffic in La Paz, political parties staged protest rallies, an anti-government demonstration of 100,000 Paceños organized by the COB with a threatened general strike to follow. With the handwriting on the wall, García Meza and Arce Gómez exited the Palacio Quemado.

Indigenous Struggle and Neoliberalism (1982–2006)

On 10 October 1982, parliament met and voted to give the *Unión Democrática y Popular* (UDP) coalition candidates Hernán Siles Zuazo and Jaime Paz Zamorra the presidency and vice presidency they were denied by the cocaine coup. After 18 years of military dictatorships, the Bolivian government returned to civilian rule. The UDP coalition headed by Siles, who had led the MNR defeat of the Rosca dictatorship in 1952, was fraught with difficulty: inability to restructure the nation's massive debt ($3.8 billion) inherited from the military governments, hyperinflation of over 20,000 percent (1984–1985), incessant work stoppages and strikes (3,500 between 1982 and 1985), difficulties over control of COMIBOL involving UDP coalition members, the FSTMB miners' union and the COB, resulting in rifts within the coalition and factionalism among its component political parties.[37] The financial assets of the urban middle class evaporated and the rural sector was beset with a devastating drought in the Andean highlands and severe floods in the Oriente. Relief would not be forthcoming for the UDP's supporters—the urban middle class, miners and factory workers, peasants and small farmers—infuriated by privation, with no end in sight. Given the situation, President Siles threw in his hand, called for early elections and, as he had done in 1952, handed over the government to fellow MNR founder Víctor Paz Estenssoro.

The Neoliberal Decades (1985–2005)

It is noteworthy that in his initial years as president of the National Revolution (see Chapter 5), Paz Estenssoro implemented the resource nationalism advocated by the MNR, most notably the nationalization of the tin mines, reorganized as the state enterprise COMIBOL. When the economy foundered on the rocks of rampant inflation, Paz abandoned the MNR's precepts of state capitalism, resource nationalism, and anti-imperialism to adopt the strict monetarist doctrine agreed to in the 1956 Stabilization Plan. Hernán Siles, who succeeded Paz in 1956, was left to enforce the draconian measures: privatization of mines, except COMIBOL, mass layoffs of mine workers, price controls, wage freezes for government employees required by the plan. Paz escaped the opprobrium associated with the measures and is remembered for the National Revolution's emancipation of the peasantry, agrarian reform legislation, enfranchisement of indigenous men and women, and mandate for universal education.

Elected president again in 1986, Paz Estenssoro implemented the neoliberal economic formula mandated by the IMF and World Bank, which was reshaping the economies and societies of most Latin American countries. He was the first of seven neoliberal presidents to rule for two decades under the direction of technocrats, economists, and social scientists who were to have a profound influence on the nation's economy, society, and politics. The neoliberals redefined the contours of creole hegemony amidst an indigenous awakening led by a new generation, well-aware of the pitfalls of past resistance to creole domination and North American imperialism. The 500-year struggle between the creole minority and the indigenous majority, catalyzed by neoliberal policies, would escalate into the twenty-first century.

Paz opted to service the national debt and combat hyperinflation via the 20 August 1985 "New Economic Policy" (NEP), Decree 21060. In exchange for $57 million in credit from the IMF and the World Bank, the boliviano was pegged to the U.S. dollar, protectionist tariffs removed, and foreign investment courted. Imports of agricultural foodstuffs bankrupted small farmers in the Andean highlands, accelerating migration to cities and the eastern lowlands. Salaries of some government workers were frozen, others suffered pay cuts, 35,000 were fired, and the cost of living increased. Within a year, 100 factories were bankrupt, over 20,000 miners laid off, and real wages dropped to one-third the pre-neoliberal level. As the number of unemployed workers multiplied, strikes increased in number and intensity, followed by states of siege and arrests of protesters. In the first year of the NEP, 143 strike leaders were incarcerated in jungle prisons.[38]

Decimated by the imprisonment of its leaders, the loss of tens of thousands of unemployed members, a drastic drop in the price of tin, and internal conflicts between its constituents, the COB could no longer offer a united defense of its constituents. The once powerful bulwark of worker co-government founded at the onset of the 1952 National Revolution was neutralized by the NEP. Destitute miners joined the exodus of impoverished peasants and small farmers to find work in the cities (primarily El Alto-La Paz, Cochabamba, Santa Cruz), or become *cocaleros* (coca farmers) in the booming coca-cocaine business of the Oriente.

The architects of the NEP were Harvard economist Jeffrey Sachs and Gonzalo ("Goni") Sánchez de Losada, a creole plutocrat with a philosophy degree from the University of Chicago, and two-time president (1993–1997; 2002–2003). The plan involved wage freezes, cuts in government spending, and privatization of mismanaged state-owned enterprises (SOEs). The 1994 Law of Capitalization was instituted as a remedy, privatizing the nation's petrochemical, mining, telecommunication, aviation, and railway companies. As announced in Sánchez de Losada's "Plan de Todos," the SOEs would be auctioned off to a bidder who would pay the agreed upon price to the company, not the government. The investor would hold 51 percent: the government would hold 49 percent of the new enterprise and distribute the proceeds equally among all adult Bolivians via private management of the national pension funds. Ostensibly, private management of the funds would obviate bureaucratic corruption: but what restrictions governed the companies' use of the funds, and what sanctions were there to safeguard the minority shareholders? As analysts at the World Bank cautioned: "Bolivians were suspicious of privatization. They feared it meant a loss of jobs, a loss of the nation's patrimony, and a return to (probably Yankee) imperialism."[39]

The NEP reached its pinnacle during Sánchez de Losada's first term (1993–1997) with Vice President Dr. Víctor Hugo Cárdenas, an Aymara with a Ph.D. from the Universidad Mayor de San Andrés in La Paz and a founding member of the *Movimiento Revolucionario Tupac Katari* (MRTK). Goni's choice of Cárdenas as the nation's first indigenous Vice President garnered the creole administration the votes of the indigenous populace. Vice President Cardenas was also the President of Congress where his influence is evidenced in educational reform, the Plan de Todos, as well as in constitutional reforms: "The 1994 Constitution's aim to create 'a post-modern, multi-cultural and pluriethnic' state" recognized "indigenous cultural rights, including limited self-government, as fundamental to Bolivian citizenship." Importantly, the right of indigenous communities to administer their communities according to their cultural norms and resolve conflicts in accordance with their own customs was recognized and indigenous human rights defended by an independent office, the *Defensor del Pueblo*.[40]

The 1995 Education Reform sought to introduce a bilingual, multiethnic approach to learning, modernize teaching from memorization to active classroom participation, and develop creative thinking in the nation's public schools. Indigenous education, as we have seen, was prohibited by creole governments for centuries—and advocated by revolutionaries who believed it was the key to the freedom of a conquered race. As was the case with the National Revolution's 1955 Education Code, the 1995 reform fell far short of the objectives of combatting illiteracy and uplifting the subaltern majority. The lack of commitment by creole governments is evident in the continuation of inadequate and misallocated funding for public schools.

The Plan de Todos was a model of neoliberal policies codified in over 20 laws enacted by the Sánchez de Lozada government between 1994 and 1997. The Plan not only privatized and sold off state enterprises, cut government spending, and laid off employees, it also redefined and reorganized the relationship of the state with its citizenry. Enacted in 1994, the Law of Popular Participation (LPP) decentralized government administration to include the participation of municipal and local governments. Traditionally, government funds had been disbursed from La Paz to the departmental capital cities (particularly La Paz, Cochabamba, and Santa Cruz), with little or nothing for municipalities, hamlets, sindicatos, or ayllus. But department prefects were still appointed by the president, much to the annoyance of Santa Cruz autonomists who chafed at Paceño influence and indigenous communities who sought both autonomy and greater participation in government. The Law created *Organizaciones Territoriales de Base* (OTBs) local-level political leadership with the ability to allocate government funds (20 percent of national tax revenue) to finance public works projects through local oversight committees (*Comités de Vigilancia*).

Formal recognition of local community organizations catalyzed the political participation of indigenous residents in urban barrios, rural municipalities, agrarian sindicatos, and ayllu communities. Some 15,000 OTBs were formed, incentivized by the prospect of attaining development funds. A change in political representation introduced in the 1996 Electoral Law mandated that 50 percent of congressional representatives were to be elected from rural districts rather than be determined at the departmental level. This broke with the traditional system of creole electoral control—and legitimized the participation of indigenous rural leaders in national-level politics. The nationalist revolutionaries had enfranchised the indigenous populace in 1952. The neoliberals granted political representation in 1996. What may have been a gambit to thwart Cruceño separatists with a legislative slight-of-hand via a deluge of indigenous votes was also a tipping point: "By 1997, 11,577 campesino unions [sindictos] had petitioned departmental authorities for GTO recognition, even though, given Bolivia's history of exclusion and marginalization, they entered this new political space on clearly unequal terms."[41] After the layoffs of the combative miners and the demise of the COB, the appearance of peasant sindicatos together with municipal GTOs participating in government presented the opportunity for a revival of indigenous resistance to creole rule.

The agrarian sindicatos are a legacy of the 1953 Agrarian Reform Decree enacted by the MNR to destroy the colonato in the Andean highlands and give the freed colonos the right to own land. The indigenous peoples of the Oriente, neglected by the decree, were nonetheless affected by the invasion of impoverished miner and peasant migrants from the highlands, creole-mestizo land speculators, and the developmental plans of MNR officials and USAID technocrats.

The result was a replication of the Old Regime with some 2 percent of hacendados in control of 85 percent of agricultural properties. The National Agrarian Reform Institute (INRA) was created in 1996 ostensibly to redress this and related problems of land tenure in the Oriente. As was the case with the MNR agrarian reform, bureaucratic obstacles, a lack of government commitment, and inadequate funding stymied the potential of the reform for indigenous farmers, while provisions in the law advantaged creole-mestizos with latifundia in the lowlands usurped from tribal communities. Whereas squatters could once settle and farm vacant lands, under the INRA landowners retained legal possession of these properties by paying an annual 1 percent tax on a self-assessed valuation of their land. Titles issued after 1953 were cancelled pending government reevaluation. This did not auger well for peasants, small farmers, highland ayllu communities, and the lowland peoples of the Oriente. The MNR agrarian reform yardstick of social value ("The land to those who till it") as a property determinant was now void and land commodified per the neoliberal privatization agenda.

In 1997, General Hugo Banzer Suárez was again elected. Banzer had earlier introduced the neoliberal economist Jeffrey Sachs to Bolivia in 1985. Sachs presented "shock treatment" as a remedy for the hyperinflation that infected the country. After the general lost the 1985 election to Víctor Paz Estenssoro, as we have seen, Paz retained the services of Sachs, resulting in the neoliberal Decree 21060. Banzer's presidency (1997–2001) is noteworthy for its war against indigenous *cocaleros* (coca growers) in the Chapare region and a "Water War" fought by residents of Cochabamba City and its environs against corporate privatization of water rights. The collective experience incited popular resistance to neoliberalism, creole rule, and U.S. imperialism.

Coca, Cocaleros, and the U.S. "War on Drugs"

For miners unemployed by mine closures and peasants devastated by drought, migration to the eastern lowlands offered a chance to begin life anew. By 1988 over 200,000 Aymara and Quechua settlers were living in the El Chapare region east of Cochabamba Department farming fruit and coca. The cultivation of coca offered irresistible returns. The plant is hardy, pest resistant, and produces four to five harvests a year. On average a one-hectare plot brought US$4,000 per annum to farmers. In the 1980s, an estimated 16 percent of coca leaves were destined for the legal, internal market. The other 84 percent was processed as a paste or refined into cocaine hydrochloride destined for the international market by Cruceño narcotraffickers via Colombian cartels. By 1987, the export of semirefined coca paste and cocaine hydrochloride yielded an estimated US$1,470 million per annum to the Santa Cruz–Beni narcotraffickers.[42]

Some 300,000–400,000 Bolivians in the Chapare and Yungas valleys of La Paz Department were engaged in the coca business, perhaps one-third of whom were involved in the illegal trade.[43] The coca/cocaine industry employed a workforce of farmers, field and laboratory workers, lookouts, truckers, aircraft owners and pilots, middlemen, armed guards, police, military men, customs officers, smugglers, bookkeepers, accountants, attorneys, money launderers, etc. It was the biggest business in the country, surpassing the mining and hydrocarbon industries. A 1997 study found, "The coca/cocaine economy penetrates the totality of social and economic spheres in Bolivia and thereby affects virtually the entire population. . . . Given the low wages, limited income, and scarce opportunities available to the 'formal' [legal] sector, the coca/cocaine economy was able to absorb a great deal of the available labor and therefore became essential to the reproduction of the formal economy."[44] Cocaine made presidents Banzer and Garcia Meza multimillionaires, but low-level dealers and smugglers were targeted for arrests and seizures inside the country to demonstrate government commitment to fighting crime.[45]

Popularized in the U.S. television series "Miami Vice," the cocaine business created an economic boom in south Florida. Corruption was ubiquitous because of the fast money: at one point, every $100 bill in Miami had traces of cocaine and narcotraffickers weighed rather than counted their prodigious returns. With the end of the Cold War against communism, the United States declared war against drugs. Rather than focusing on the demand side of America's addiction to drugs, the war was directed abroad, against the supply side of the problem.[46] Loans and military assistance were an integral part of the North American intrusion of Special Operations soldiers and Drug Enforcement Agents (DEA) introduced in 1987 to eradicate coca growers (*cocaleros*) in the Chapare. Fields were either burned or sprayed with the herbicide 2,4-D, a component in Agent Orange used extensively in the U.S. war against peasants in Vietnam, Laos, and Cambodia.

FIGURE 9.1 Coca Terrace, Yungas

Source: Photo by author.

Indigenous Resistance to the "War on Drugs"

Having fled unemployment and poverty in the highlands and investing time, sweat, and money in farming a legal crop, the Chapare cocaleros were loath to surrender to creole-Yankee repression. Initial resistance took the form of individual deception, bribery, and stealthy assaults by small groups of cocaleros on eradication units. Resistance then began to involve grassroots protests, marches, demonstrations, highway blockades, and the proliferation of cocalero unions. Word of an impending (Law 1008) proposed by the Paz Estenssoro government at the behest of the United States led to a series of protests by cocalero unions in 1987. The law would prohibit coca cultivation and criminalize offences with harsh prison sentences.[47] On 27 May 1987, thousands of cocaleros assembled outside the town of Parotani, blocked the road to the Chapare, and demanded to see the government's proposed law. The protest was broken up by police: 8 protesters were killed and 500 arrested. A year later, a detachment of the Mobile Police Unit for Rural Areas (UMOPAR) massacred protesters at a highway blockade near Villa Tunari in the Chapare.[48] Among the protesters was the Aymara cocalero Evo Morales who witnessed the massacre. Morales joined the movement and a year later was severely beaten by a UMOPAR unit. Amidst a rising crescendo of repression and resistance, increasing numbers of the indigenous populace—highland and lowland peasants and farmers, urban workers, and unemployed migrants—joined the struggle against the creole state. As the number and size of subaltern political organizations grew, so did their interconnections and commitment to the common cause.

Indigenous Unions, Confederations, Parties, and Protests

In the era of the National Revolution, peasant sindicatos provided governance at the local level. Regional caudillos rarely formed alliances or confederations with sindicatos outside their departments, and political parties remained the preserve of creole politicians. The indigenous majority, co-opted by the party system, were left to vote for one or another of the creole parties. To secure political agency more was needed than the vote given by the MNR in 1952. The vote was a necessary prerequisite, but a political party was imperative for power at the national level that had eluded earlier generations.

The Kataristas understood the necessity of parties in the struggle for electoral power at the national level and fielded the MRTK, MITKA, and MITKA-1 parties in the 1980 elections. But the factionalism that had divided and defeated the peasantry during the National Revolution remained a danger to unity. Nevertheless, the nation's first indigenous vice president, Víctor Hugo Cárdenas, gained his position by allying his MRTK-L party with Gonzalo Sánchez de Losada, the MNR's creole presidential candidate. While this was considered a corrupt bargain by some, Cárdenas introduced an indigenous agenda at the national level together with important reforms, including an electoral law to increase participation in the legislature. When he stated, "We want to elect, but we also want to be elected," Cardenas encapsulated the desire of a new generation. As Brooke Larson notes, "Thus, paradoxically, the social and institutional transformations that liberalism engendered, or inspired, in the *political sphere* opened the way for the direct political participation by people who now challenge the basic precepts of neoliberal capitalism."[49]

A perusal of protests in the decade 1990–1993 reveals the consistency and breadth of indigenous opposition to neoliberalism.[50] Demonstrations, protests, mass marches, highway blockades, general strikes, occupation of government offices, and hunger strikes were met by government states of siege, beatings, murders, arrests, and imprisonment of protesters. The commitment and courage of those who dared to confront the heavily armed police and army special forces deployed to defend the creole state against "internal subversion" was truly heroic. The cost of indigenous lives was irreplaceable; the cost to business was considerable (sustained blockades of major highways could result in a loss of US$250,000 or more for business and transport companies), deprive cities of food and fuel, and undermine government control of the populace.

The Cochabamba Water War

In 1997, the World Bank offered Goni $600 million of debt relief in exchange for the privatization of Cochabamba's water. The deal was closed in September 1999 after codification of Water Law 2029. The secretly negotiated contract with *Aguas de Tunari*, a joint-venture consortium of transnationals Bechtel and Edison, gave the company a 40-year concession that included the city's water system, the rights to groundwater, well water, and irrigation water—all for $15,635![51] Other surprises followed. Water rates increased to 25–30 percent of a family's income; people without service were billed and others billed for use of what had been their own well water.[52] Resistance to *Aguas de Tunari* began in November 1999 under the direction of a *Coordinadora del Agua y Vida* coalition and continued into April 2000. The *Coordinadora* organized the strategy and tactics of the heterogeneous coalition and negotiated with the opposition.

The balance of power shifted during the five-month conflict. During an initial meeting between the *Coordinadora* and government ministers, protestors outside were tear gassed by police. A massive demonstration in February 2000, including local peasants and cocaleros from the Chapare, was repressed by 1,000 police and soldiers with tear gas and truncheons.[53] April proved to be an eventful month. Public meetings (*cabildos*) in the city's plazas drew massive crowds to listen to proposals and voice their feelings. The experience of popular participation excited and enthused the resisters, reenergizing their will to fight. A demonstration in the first week of the month drew tens of thousands of protesters: men and women, young and old from various barrios, together with peasants and cocaleros. Blockades were set up to impede the arrival of the repressive forces, neighborhoods were organized, barricades erected, and communication systems contrived to coordinate the battle from barrio to barrio. The government declared martial law and *Coordinadora* leaders were pursued by security forces. Two days after the random assassination of a young man on 8 April, an agreement was reached between government officials and the *Coordinadora*. The contract with *Aguas de Tunari* would be rejected and Cochabamba's water rights reinstated. Operation of the water system was restored to the state utility company SEMAPA with five of its seven directors chosen in a local election.⁵⁴

Indigenous Mobilization and Insurrection: The Gas War

In February 2003, Goni upped the income tax rate by13 percent. Incensed police rioted in La Paz, a shootout ensued with military police, and angry workers burned the offices of government ministries. A riot also broke out in the indigenous city of El Alto where the offices of the mayor and the electrical company were sacked. After a furious confrontation with government forces, resulting in 29 deaths and over 200 Alteños wounded, Goni rescinded the tax. Meanwhile, emboldened by their victory in Cochabamba, the *Coordinadora* leaders were determined to broaden their war against neoliberalism to the national level and "reclaim the enterprises that the government had privatized." To do so, it was decided to begin with "a march to recover the homeland . . . because it emphasized that the country had been alienated from ordinary working people and that it had been given away as a gift to foreign interests."⁵⁵ The tactic of a march created solidarity among the protesters and with members of the rural communities who supported the protesters with food and lodging. The *Coordinadora* catalyzed a political movement with a diverse indigenous constituency—peasants, miners, urban migrants and workers, cocaleros, and the peoples of the Oriente—with the potential to seize power with a ballot.

The first opportunity came with the 2002 national election and the recently formed Movement Toward Socialism (MAS) party's presidential candidate Evo Morales Ayma, the Chairman of the Committee of the Six Federations of the Tropics of Cochabamba (comprised of 935 sindicatos, and 45,539 *afiliados*, families).⁵⁶ To legally enter the election, Morales made a deal to assume the name of a registered party, the Movement Toward Socialism. The MAS party was structured similar to the Cochabamba *Coordinadora* with decentralized decision-making rather than as a hierarchal top-down organization. Morales ran against the neoliberal Goni who, seeking a second term, hired a U.S. company self-identified as "progressive," "market based," and "social democratic." The comparison between Goni's campaign with its private airplane, creole-mestizo focus groups, contrived sound bites, fixation on political polls—and Morales's grassroots campaign, heavily dependent on women members of the *Coordinadora de las Seis Federaciones del Trópica de Cochabamba* to get out the vote for the indigenous party is striking.⁵⁷ Goni got what he paid for: Evo lost by1.5 percent.

On 8 September 2003, 10,000 Aymara peasants marched to La Paz to demand the release of a comunario imprisoned at the Panóptico Nacional: as they passed through El Alto, throngs of residents joined the march. Concurrently, protests were ongoing over a variety of local issues as well as resistance to a neoliberal scheme to export Bolivian gas to the United States. This, together with the issue of the imprisoned comunario and objections to a new law that criminalized roadblocks, prompted a protest by a thousand CSUTCB militants led by the Katarista firebrand

Felipe Quispe. Students and truckers at El Alto began a hunger strike and blockades were set up on Altiplano roads as a protest against the proposed gas export.[58] Demonstrations, blockades, and violent confrontations erupted on the Altiplano after three peasants were murdered in cold blood by a military force at Warisata in Omasuyu Province; peasants were arrested in Aroma Province, and cocaleros blockaded the road from Cochabamba to Santa Cruz.[59]

A *Coordinadora* organized by the militants Oscar Olivera, Evo Morales, and the MAS party mobilized mass demonstrations in Cochabamba and La Paz to protest the export of gas. Radio broadcasts in Aymara kept listeners abreast of developments and called for the president's resignation. On 2 October, a COB demonstration in La Paz demanded the abdication of the president, as protesters clashed with government forces in El Alto. The week of 10–17 October 2003 gave rise to an Aymara insurrection in the twin cities El Alto–La Paz. On 10 September, barricades were erected in El Alto to impede government forces and an attempt was made to cut the gas supply to La Paz. The expected military attack with tanks and warplanes took the lives of 11 citizens. Historians Forrest Hylton and Sinclair Thomson, who witnessed the Gas War, note that as the uprising grew from tens of thousands to a popular insurrection of 100,000 or more, leadership slipped away from Evo Morales and Felipe Quispe: "In the climactic days of October, heterogeneous popular forces organized themselves, deliberated in open assemblies, and took action in their own spheres without waiting for orders from a political party, trade union, or other established leaders. The lack of centralized authority stymied government efforts to suppress the uprising, even by the application, in the Bolivian context, of extraordinary levels of lethal violence."[60]

Overtaken by events, Goni was in danger of losing control as the insurrection encompassed the departments of La Paz, Oruro, Potosí, Cochabamba, Chuquisaca, and Santa Cruz. Violent clashes with army troops erupted, insurgents were killed, roads blockaded, and markets closed. The country had become ungovernable. Finally, on 17 October 2003, Goni fled to a mansion in Miami, Florida.[61] His vice president, the journalist Carlos Mesa, assumed power in an untenable position between powerful national and international advocates of neoliberalism and an aroused citizenry emboldened in opposition to privatization of their patrimony. Faced with relentless indigenous resistance led by Evo Morales, MAS, Felipe Flores, and the CSUTCB, Carlos Mesa abdicated the presidency and the Chief Justice of the Supreme Court led a transitional government in preparation for a general election.

The Rise and Fall of Bolivia's First Indigenous President

On 18 December 2005, the MAS candidate Evo Morales won the presidency in a historic election. Morales, the first indigenous president in Bolivian history, was elected with 54 percent of the vote, the highest percentage ever tallied by a president. His Vice President was Álvaro García Linera, a creole intellectual, neoliberal critic, and anti-imperialist whose bona vides include membership in the Tupac Katari Guerrilla Army, and five years in prison. The synergy of García Linera's theoretical analyses of neoliberalism and commitment to indigenous struggle—fused with Evo's charisma and preternatural political sensibility—presented extraordinary possibilities for the nation. Evo Morales was one of several Latin American presidents, including Venezuela's Hugo Chávez and Brazil's Luiz Inácio Lula da Silva, who constituted the "pink tide" of reformers who rejected neoliberalism and focused on undoing its negative effects on the poor and working classes. Morales ended Bolivia's dependence on the IMF and World Bank because of their role in the neoliberal privatization of the nation's natural resources, refused to join the U.S. backed Free Trade Area of the Americas, and ended his first year in office with no fiscal debt.

Natural Resources

On May Day 2006, Evo announced Supreme Decree 28701 mandating the partial nationalization of the nation's hydrocarbons industry. The decree gave the state enterprise YPFB majority control over ownership of the foreign corporations extracting and refining oil and gas in the oil fields of Santa Cruz and Tarija. This unilateral act *reversed* the previous distribution of profits. Bolivia retained 82 percent of profits and gave the foreign lessees 18 percent. The embrace of resource nationalism yielded a fiscal bonus for Bolivia with the second largest natural gas reserves in Latin America. Renegotiation with Argentina netted an extra $110 million per month and another $32 million per month from increased profit in two extensive oil fields. Predictably, the partial nationalization rankled the transnationals involved and drew the ire of the United States, as did Evo's association with the anti-imperialist regimes in Venezuela and Cuba.[62]

Human Resources

The increased government funds were invested in social programs to improve the life chances of the populace. Under the MAS regime, poverty was reduced by over 40 percent and extreme poverty by 60 percent. Public spending was increased for health care, education, and free lunches for school children. The minimum wage was increased by 20 percent, pay for state employees raised 10 percent, and price controls instated on electricity, gasoline, potable water, and foodstuffs (flour, rice, bread, sugar). Three social programs focused on mothers, children, and the elderly in need of government assistance. One program provides financial assistance to pregnant women for consultations with physicians, including later visits of the mother and child. Another program makes biannual payments to mothers who keep their children enrolled in public schools through middle school. A third program provides retirement money (US$340–430 per annum) for seniors. The combined cost of these programs is over US$300 million a year for the 3,000,000 million beneficiaries.[63]

Agrarian Reform

The unfinished business of the National Revolution remained in the nation's agrarian backlands. As a former cocalero, President Morales was acutely aware of the problems of land and its unequal distribution between Indian small farmers and creole latifundistas. Thus, the MAS commitment to democratizing land ownership was a critical issue. The Oriente attracted highland peasants, unemployed miners, and destitute urbanites. When Evo entered office, the disparity in land ownership was reminiscent of 1952: 90 percent of all privately held land was in medium to large estates and 10 percent of the remaining land was worked by small farmers, often in plots of 1–5 hectares.[64]

Data drawn from the National Agrarian Reform Institute (INRA) indicates significant success in the distribution of land ownership during the early period of the MAS government. In the first seven years of Evo's presidency, 134 million acres were titled and distributed to peasants and indigenous communities who gained title to 88 million acres. Of the 290,000 titles granted, 25 percent were issued to women. This represents a significant contribution to the agrarian reform process, which previously omitted women recipients. By 2012, some 25 million acres of land had been seized by the MAS government from speculators who failed to put the property to use. Another 40 percent of the 262 million acres slated for redistribution awaits recipients.[65] The redistributive process has been opposed by the large landowners of the Oriente who fear the loss of their vacant properties to landless migrants (who also are attracted to the lands of tribal communities).

"Refounding" the Nation: The Plurinational State of Bolivia

Enfranchisement of the indigenous majority remains a salient legacy of the MNR revolution. Yet creole-mestizo domination continued for over half a century via monopoly of the nation's political parties. Indigenous militants have demanded changes that would give them meaningful legal representation in the party system in order to express their political objectives. The experience of popular participation and the success of the *Coordinadora* mass mobilization during the Water War was not lost on the subaltern majority. The call for a constitutional assembly by MAS in 2006 to reconfigure the electoral system was met with enthusiasm. It also revealed a good deal about the political disposition of the MAS party's class, ethnic, and regional constituencies. "When MAS unveiled its formula for the representation of delegates in March 2006, however, it rejected any form of collective representation according to ethnic criteria, trade union or neighborhood affiliation."[66] Indigenous plans for increased representation were stifled by the MAS party, presaging an elite sensibility on the part of the party's leaders and inhibiting the party's potential for truly revolutionary change. Indeed, Jeffrey Webber asserts that "the development model implemented by the Morales administration over the entire four years of its first administration (2006–2010) is best characterized as reconstituted neoliberalism."[67]

The Downfall of the Plurinational State of Bolivia

In 2009, the constitution was rewritten and the country renamed the "Plurinational State of Bolivia." The revised constitution increased state control of natural resources, gave indigenous communities the right to administer their lands, and recognized the citizenry's social rights to free health care, water, and education. Of particular note for the future of Evo and the MAS are provisions for limited regional autonomy and a two-term limit for the presidency. In the 2009 election, 64 percent of the voters cast their ballots for MAS. With a voter turnout of 90 percent, MAS won two-thirds of the seats in both the Chamber of Deputies and the Senate, and elected Evo to his second term as President of the newly renamed "Plurinational State" of Bolivia. This did not sit well with the creole-mestizo elite of the Media Luna.

In April 2009, an attempted coup by members of the reactionary Pro-Santa Cruz Committee and *Poder Democrático y Social* (PODEMOS) political party was foiled. An earlier attempt by Media Luna zealots in September 2008 involved the occupation of government buildings in the Departments of Santa Cruz, Beni, Tarija, and Pando where more than a dozen indigenous protesters were massacred in the town of El Porvenir on 11 September 2008.[68] It was imperative that the Plurinational government take a concerted stand against the white supremacist uprising, deploy police and military forces to protect indigenous citizens, and demonstrate a powerful national presence. Instead, the MAS response to the threat from the Oriente was accommodation with the enemy. This would prove to be a fatal decision.

MAS began to distribute state lands to peasants while avoiding expropriation of the latifundia held by the Cruceño elite. In 2012, the MAS government deferred verification (for five years) of the requirement that land fulfill a social function. A 2013 law exempted nearly 5 million hectares of illegally deforested land from expropriation in exchange for a fine and a promise to farm the properties. Incursions into indigenous territories by agrobusiness farmers, ranchers, and loggers continued. The most dramatic and significant example involved the conflict over highway construction in 2011 through the *Territorio Indígena y Parque Nacional Isiboro Secure* (TIPNIS) a 3,860 square-mile national park inhabited by the Moxeño-Trinitario, Yuracaré, and Chimáne peoples. Emily Achtenberg demonstrates the ways in which the highway project was

> a defining moment for the government of Evo Morales. . . . It has altered the country's political landscape, rupturing the Unity Pact, an alliance among five national social movements that brought Morales to power and refounded Bolivia as a plurinational state. It has shocked the world with the spectacle of police brutality repressing lowland indigenous marchers under a leftist indigenous government, and it has called into question Morales's status as a worldwide champion of environmental and indigenous rights.[69]

372 Epilogue

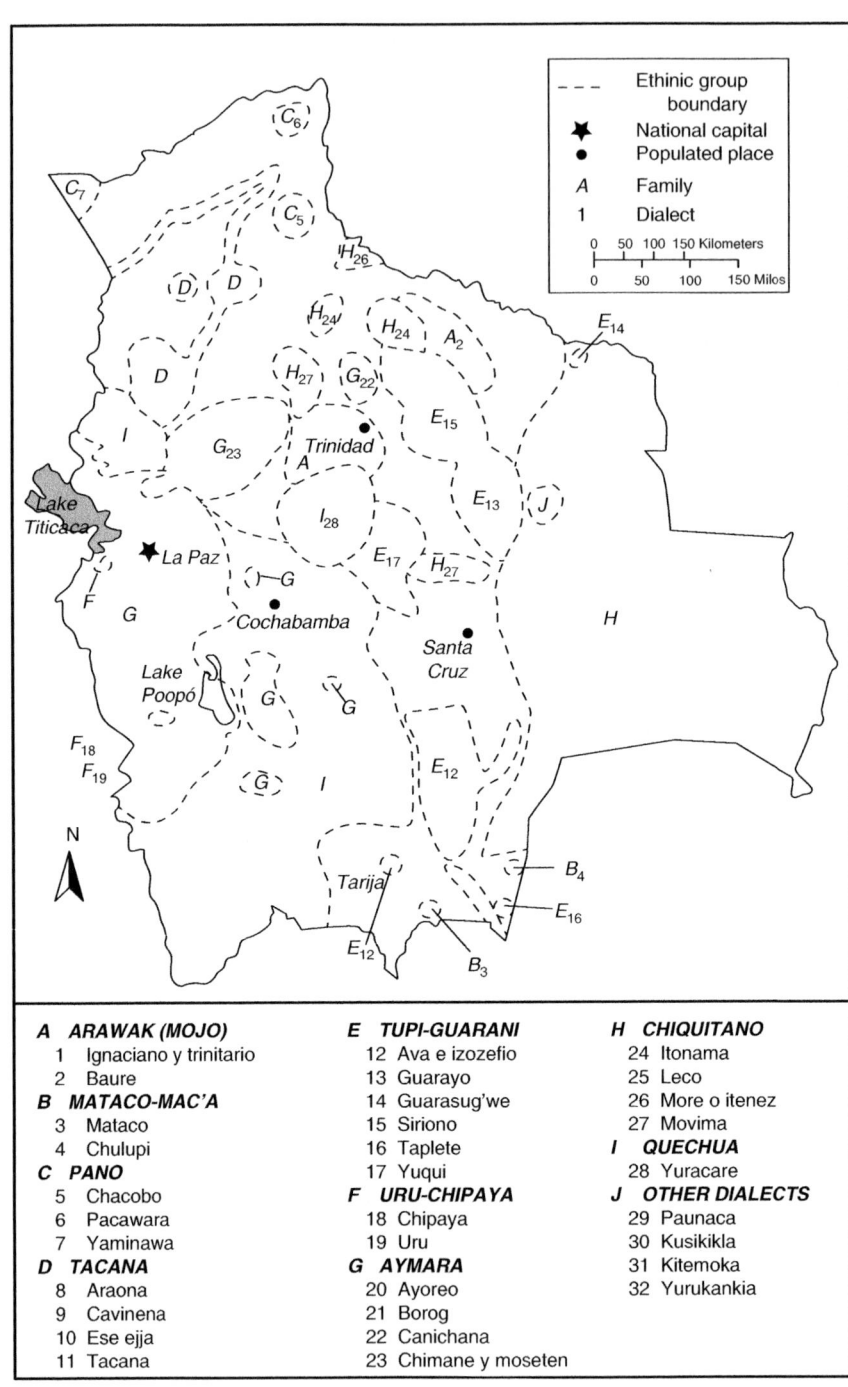

MAP 9.1 Major Ethnolinguistic Groups

Source: Courtesy of U.S. Library of Congress.

Dangerous Enemies

Evo Morales had dangerous enemies—powerful, clever, resourceful, and dedicated to his overthrow. Not the least of his enemies was the U.S. hegemon, dissatisfied with his fraternization with fellow anti-imperialists Fidel Castro and Hugo Chávez. Relations with the United States deteriorated. In 2009, after USAID was found to have subsidized separatist movements in the Oriente, Evo expelled the U.S. ambassador for fomenting separatism. The United States replied in kind and expelled the Bolivian ambassador. The hated DEA was evicted in 2008 for its forced eradication of coca (and cocaleros). Evo then expelled USAID in 2013.

Equally, if not more dangerous, were the creoles of the Media Luna, most particularly the Santa Cruz creole elite with their unsavory history of narcotrafficking, neo-fascist thuggery, and white supremacism. Petrochemical, mineral, and agro-business exports fuel the region's economic dominance and animate a drive for political power and regional autonomy. As we have seen, USAID technocrats initiated agricultural development and the colonization of the Oriente during the National Revolution. But USAID's intervention has not been confined to agriculture. There is also a hidden political component to the agency's activities.

A trove of declassified documents reveals the use of USAID to promote "decentralization" and "regional autonomy" in the Oriente to the tune of $97 million from 2002 to 2008. The documents reveal the operation of a USAID front, the Office for Transition Initiatives (OTI) introduced in 2004 to function as a "rapid response team" whose purpose is "crisis" intervention in countries of strategic interest to the United States. An OTI was introduced in Bolivia to suborn Evo Morales' 2006 presidential campaign. After the election, the OIT devoted its efforts to funding and assisting the separatist movement in Santa Cruz, including infiltration of Bolivia's indigenous communities. The OIT later merged with the "Bolivia Democracy Program" to continue the mission. In 2007, USAID/OT operatives worked with the prefects of the Media Luna to promote the separatist agenda before the 2008 referendums for regional autonomy.[70]

USAID is also involved in "Partners of the Americas," touted as originating with the Alliance for Progress and funded by U.S. corporations. The "partners" ostensibly monitor foreign elections as "independent observers." As the researcher Eva Golinger notes: "The creation of 'networks' in 'civil society' to monitor electoral processes has been a strategy utilized by Washington in countries such as Venezuela, Ecuador and Nicaragua, to later use such apparently 'independent' observers in an attempt to discredit and delegitimize elections and denounce electoral fraud when results are not favorable to US interests."[71]

Overthrow

Evo Morales was not without faults. Construction of a massive, 29-story monolith Great House of the People complete with a helipad, personal suite, including a gym, jacuzzi, sauna, and massage room—towering over the historic Palacio Quemado—did not endear him to the people who might well have preferred a modern hospital. Evo's ego was also detrimental. "A charismatic populist, he could also be arrogant and divisive," notes the journalist Jon Lee Anderson.[72] Rather than groom, appoint, and support a successor to maintain an indigenous president in office, he insisted on conniving a run for a fourth term in the 2019 presidential elections—despite his rejection by voters in a 2016 referendum to rescind the constitution to allow a fourth term. Stoked by the arrogance of office, reminiscent of President Víctor Paz Estenssoro's error and subsequent overthrow in 1964, Evo Morales was ousted by a coup d'état in November 2019 amidst phony claims of electoral fraud and weeks of violent protests organized and led by Cruceño separatists. Luis Fernando Camacho, a key figure in the coup, is president of the Pro-Santa Cruz Committee: a white supremacist and former head of the para-military *Unión Juvenil Cruceñista* noteworthy for kidnapping and torturing peasant squatters on latifundios and hate crimes against indigenous victims in Santa Cruz.[73]

Although Evo had agreed to hold a new election, protests continued before the military intervened and publicly advised the president to abdicate. As the former Ecuadorian President Rafael Correa put it: "When the police are rioting and the military 'suggest' the president resign, it's very clearly a coup d'état. Yes, President Morales did resign. But if someone holds a gun to your head and says very politely, 'give me your wallet,' and you give it to them, does this mean it wasn't robbery, but agreed by mutual consent? Clearly, what happened in Bolivia was a coup."[74] The Yale historian Greg Grandin reminds us that—at the time of his ouster—Evo Morales *was the constitutionally elected president* of Bolivia.[75]

President Morales along with Vice President Losada and a number of high-ranking MAS politicians fled the country. Unfortunately for the MAS party, because the vice president and the two senators in the line of presidential succession had abdicated, Jeanine Áñez, the Senate's Second Vice-President, declared herself President, but there was no quorum in the session in which she made the announcement. A right-wing extremist from the Media Luna's Beni Department, whose party received a scant 4 percent of the vote in the 20 October election, Áñez quickly set about consolidating control.[76] Within 48 hours, the armed forces were given immunity for the use of deadly force. Summarily, nine cocalero protesters were murdered in the Chapare and ten MAS supporters killed at El Alto. The indigenous symbols associated with the pluriethnic regime (particularly the Wiphala flags symbolizing ethnic diversity) were extirpated in a racist, anti-indigenous campaign against the ethnic and cultural inclusion that had brought MAS to power. Cuban physicians and Venezuelan diplomats were deported and journalists arrested. President Donald Trump quickly granted diplomatic recognition to Áñez who was involved in the coup, *but had not been elected*. The overthrow culminated the machinations of the United States and Santa Cruz separatists to wrest control from the nation's first indigenous president. Creole domination of the Amerindian nation that began with the Spanish conquest in 1532 would be reinstated after the 14-year interregnum of the Plurinational State of Bolivia. All does not bode well for the nation's indigenous peoples, once again under the dominion of white supremacists.

Notes

1. Recent research demonstrates that the ayllus were resourceful, persistent, and often successful in gaining revindication of lands usurped *prior* to 1900. See Carmen Soliz, "Land to the Original Owners: Rethinking the Indigenous Politics of the Bolivian Agrarian Reform," *Hispanic American Historical Review*, 97.2 (2017), 259–296.
2. On the topic of financial credit and loans in the 1960s and 1979s, I have drawn on Susan Eckstein, "Transformation of a 'Revolution from Below': Bolivia and International Capital," *Comparative Studies in Society and History*, 25 (1983), 105–135; for USAID loans and grants for colonization, see E. Boyd Wennergren, and Morris Whitaker, *The Status of Bolivian Agriculture* (New York, 1975), 227–230, and Uri Menderberg's insightful, "The Impact of Bolivian Agrarian Reform on Class Formation," *Latin American Perspectives*, 12.3 (Summer 1985), 45–58.
3. Andrew Pearse, *The Latin American Peasant* (London, 1975), 415. Because of the pejorative connotation associated with cholo/chola, Xavier Albó prefers the word "resident": for a detailed discussion of the nuances of Aymara subculture in La Paz, see Xavier Albó, "¿Khitipxtansa? ¿Quines somos? Identidad localista, étnica y clasista en los aymaras de hoy," *America Indígena*, 39.3 (July–September 1979), 477–512, and Albo, Xavier, Tomás Greaves, and Godofredo Sandoval, *Chukiyawu: La cara Aymara de La Paz*, Vol. 3 (La Paz: CIPCA), 1983.
4. Estimates of the population of the four largest cities (Santa Cruz de la Sierra, El Alto, La Paz, and Cochabamba) vary depending on sources. Nevertheless, the growth is astounding: El Alto, hardly considered a city in 1952, estimated at 2,300,000 in 2016; La Paz: 812,799; Cochabamba: 900,414; Santa Cruz de la Sierra: 1,364,389.
5. On the pre-revolutionary history of indigenous education, see Brooke Larson, "Capturing Indian Bodies, Hearths and Minds: 'El hogar campesino' and Rural School Reform in Bolivia, 1920's–1940's," in Merilee Grindle and Pilar Domingo, eds., *Proclaiming Revolution: Bolivia in Comparative Perspective* (London, 2003), 183–209.
6. "The rate of enrollment in primary schools in the revolutionary period was not greater than the growth of the decade before the revolution. Similarly, the rate of growth of rural communal schools before the revolution is very similar to that after the revolution." Manuel E. Contreras, "A Comparative Perspective of Education Reforms in Bolivia: 1950–2000," in Merilee S. Grindle and Pilar Domingo, eds., *Proclaiming Revolution* (London, 2003), 282. Importantly, research has shown that instruction in a native language before acquisition of a second language not only lowers dropout rates but also increases literacy and academic performance. Ibid., 261.
7. James Dunkerley, *Rebellion in the Veins: Political Struggle in Bolivia, 1952–1964* (London, 1984), 127–129.
8. The massacre and brutal aftermath (torture, misogyny) are narrated by the Aymara militant Domitila Barrios de Chúngara in *Let Me Speak* (New York, 1978), 115–156.
9. As Green Beret Master Sergeant Roland Milliard recalled: "It was one of the most successful SF (Special Forces) missions ever. We have different people searching for Che Guevara in different countries. First in Latin America, in Southeast Asia and down that way. But here I guess his luck ran out. And those Rangers just ate him up." Michele

Ray, "In Cold Blood: How the CIA Executed Che," *Ramparts*, March 1968. The definitive account of the Green Beret mission is Kenneth Finlayson, "Turning the Tables on Che: The Training at La Esperanza," *Veritas: The Journal of Special Operations History*, 4.4 (2008).
10. In addition to General Barrientos, two other generals involved in the military campaign against Che's foco were assassinated: General Joaquin Zenteno Anaya, assassinated in Paris on 11 May 1976, and General Juan José Torres, assassinated in Argentina on 2 June 1976.
11. Charles D. Corbett, "Military Institutional Development and Sociopolitical Change: The Bolivian Case," *Journal of Interamerican Studies and World Affairs*, 14.4 (November 1972), 419.
12. Indeed, the *foco* period of the 1960s is a chronicle of failure: defeated in Argentina, Brazil, Colombia, Ecuador, Paraguay, Peru, and the Dominican Republic. On *focismo* and the later strategy and tactics of the urban guerrilla, see James Kohl and John Litt, *Urban Guerrilla Warfare in Latin America* (Boston, 1974), 1–27.
13. Corbett, "Military Institutional Development," 418.
14. Jerry Knudson, *Bolivia's Popular Assembly of 1971 and the Overthrow of Juan José Torres* Buffalo, NY, 1974), 52. See also René Zavaleta, "Bolivia—Military Nationalism and the Popular Assembly," *New Left Review*, 73 (May–June 1972), 79–80.
15. Knudson, Bolivia's Popular Assembly, 63.
16. Ibid., 50–58.
17. Interview by Hank Zivetz with Ambassador Ernest V. Siracusa, "The Association for Diplomatic Studies and Training Foreign Affairs Oral History Project," June 1989, 65–68.
18. Andres Schipani, "Hidden Cells Reveal Bolivia's Dark Past," *BBC News*, http://news.bc.co.uk/2/hi/americas/7925694.stm. See also Dunkerley, *Rebellion in the Veins*, 208.
19. This brief survey of Katarismo is based on the essays of two extraordinary scholars, the Jesuit anthropologist, linguist, and indigenous advocate Xavier Albó and the rural sociologist Silvia Rivera Cusicanqui. See Xavier Albó, "From MNRistas to Kataristas to Katari," in Steve J. Stern, ed., *Resistance, Rebellion, and Consciousness in the Andean Peasant World, 18th to 20th Centuries* (Madison, WI, 1987), 379–419; and Silvia Rivera Cusicanqui, "Luchas campesinas contemporáneas en Bolivia: el movimiento 'Katarista': 1970–1980," in René Zavaleta, ed., *Bolivia hoy* (Mexico, D.F., 1982), 129–168.
20. Zavaleta, ed., Bolivia Hoy, 143.
21. Rivera, "Luchas campesinas contemporáneas," 142–143.
22. Earlier, opposition to General Barrientos's attempt to implement a USAID-inspired tax on peasant land plots had given rise to the resistance of the *Bloque Campesino Independiente* in the departments of La Paz and Oruro. But, faced with the general's charisma and the clientelism of the Pacto Militar-Campesino, the ephemeral organization failed to gain momentum.
23. James V. Kohl, "Bolivia Begins the Seventies," *New Politics* (Fall, 1973), 50–52. Ambassador Siracusa agreed to a final "interrogation" of Mary Harding before her deportation, discounted her claim that she was tortured, and stated she "was never abused while in custody." Interview by Hank Zivetz with Ambassador Ernest V. Siracusa, June 1989, 65.
24. A pair of documents written in the early1900s present the case against Altiplano domination: the "situation of commercial vassalage" of the Oriente under the rule of the "Altiplano rosca"; the lack of a railway to connect the region to the Atlantic, resulting in economic underdevelopment; the need to colonize "this vast and uninhabited zone"; the loss of territory to encroachment and war with Brazil and Paraguay; and the need for autonomous rule. (The fact that the "zone" was inhabited by indigenous tribes is indicative of the racism of the Crueño author) See the Geographic Society of Santa Cruz, "Integration of the Lowlands," in Sinclair Thomson et al., eds., *The Bolivia Reader*, translated by Alison Spedding (Durham, NC: Duke University Press, 2018), 189–192,

and Rafael Chávez Ortiz, "The Problem of the East," in Thomson, et al., eds., *The Bolivia Reader*, 261–267.
25. Dunkerley, *Rebellion in the Veins*, 219–227.
26. By 2001, Santa Cruz Department had the highest percentage of migrants (25 percent), primarily highland Indians, and the lowest poverty rate in the nation (38 percent). Joshua David Kirshner, "Ciudad de Anillos (City of Rings): Internal Migration and Uneven Integration in Santa Cruz, Bolivia," Ph.D. dissertation, Cornell University, 2009, 3.
27. Laurence Whitehead, "Bolivia's Failed Democratization of 1977–1980," *Working Paper of the Latin American Program of the Woodrow Wilson International Center for Scholars*, Number 100 (October 1980), 16.
28. Dunkerley, *Rebellion in the Veins*, 265–269. One can do no better than Dunkerley's detailed, incisive, and deftly written analysis of Bolivian military rule from Barrientos to the fall of the Santa Cruz cocaine cartel.
29. John Dinges, *The Condor Years: How Pinochet and His Allies Brought Terrorism to Three Continents* (New York, 2004), 51–60, 82–98.
30. teleSUR, 28 April 2019.
31. For a revealing account of the interrelationship of the CIA, DEA, Argentine secret police, Santa Cruz narcotraffickers, and the army generals who brought Operation Condor to Bolivia, see the expose by DEA agent Michael Levine, *The Big White Lie: The CIA and the Cocaine/Crack Epidemic, an Undercover Odyssey* (New York, 1993).
32. Peter Kornbluh, "Argentina Declassified," *The Nation*, 309.14 (2/9 December 2019), 20–21.
33. On Klaus Barbie/Altmann, the South American Nazi network, and the neo-fascist Fiancés of Death, see Magnus Linklatter, Isabel Hilton and Neal Ascherson, *The Fourth Reich: Klaus Barbie and the Neo-Fascist Connection* (London, 1984), 214–302.
34. Ibid., 19.
35. For the payment for protection of coca and cocaine transport, see Dunkerley, *Rebellion in the Veins*, 322.
36. Roberto Suárez's complex web of business associates and their dealings are detailed by his widow: Klaus Altmann-Barbie (Chapter 2); the D.E.A. (Chapter 3); Cocaine Coup (Chapter 4); the "Corporation" (Chapter 7); Pablo Escobar and the Medellín Cartel (Chapter 10); the Cuban connection (Chapter 11); the C.I.A. (Chapter 12); the Bahamas (Chapter 13). Ayda Levy, *El Rey de la Cocaína: Mi vida con Roberto Suárez Gómez* (New York, 2012).
37. Benjamin Kohl and Linda Farthing, *Impasse in Bolivia* (London and New York, 2006), 55–56.
38. Ibid., 71, 75–76.
39. Andrew Ewing and Susan Goldmark, "Privatization by Capitalization: A Popular Participation Recipe for Cash-Starved SOEs," *Viewpoint, The World Bank*, FDP Note No. 31, November 1994.
40. Kohl and Farthing, *Impasse*, 90–91.
41. Ibid., 133. For the complexities and complications of the LPP with respect to sindicatos and ayllus, see 133–134, 136.
42. Keith Griffin, *Studies in Globalization and Economic Transitions* (London, 1996), 200–202.
43. Ibid., 201. Official statistics related to the number, weight, and value of illicit narcotics are contrived by government agencies for bureaucratic or political purposes and should be considered as rough estimates.
44. Carlos F. Toranzo Roca, "Informal and Illicit Economies and the Role of Narcotrafficking," in Madeline Barbara Léons, and Harry Sanabria, eds., *Coca, Cocaine, and the Bolivian Reality* (New York, 1997), 195.
45. A raid on Banzer's hacienda in 1980 yielded 300 kilograms of cocaine. In 1981, the general's private secretary was arrested in Canada on cocaine charges, as was his son-in-law. Other family members were arrested in Florida for trafficking. Dunkerley, *Rebellion in the Veins*, 318–319.

46. The disastrous results remain a crime against humanity: 3,000,000 Vietnamese were afflicted with a host of birth defects and/or altered DNA resulting from exposure to the 20,000,000 gallons of Agent Orange sprayed on the countryside. U.S. military veterans suffer from numerous maladies as a result of exposure to the deadly chemical.
47. Enacted in July 1988, Law 1008 resulted in a massive increase of the prison population; 65 percent of Cochabamba Department's prison population in 2004 were from the Chapare region. *Andean Information Network,* https://ain-bolivia.org/2004/07/bolivias-prisons-and-the-impact-of-law-1008/.
48. Created, funded, equipped, trained, and advised by U.S. military officers and DEA agents, UNOPAR is identified with U.S. imperialism: see Benjamin Dangl, *The Price of Fire: Resource Wars and Social Movements in Bolivia* (Oakland, CA, 2007), 44 and Léons and Sanabria, *Coca, Cocaine,* 29, 32, 37; for UMOPAR's history of human rights violations, see Linda Farthing, "Social Impacts Associated with Antidrug Law 1008," in M. B. Léons and H. Sanabria, eds., *Coca, Cocaine, and the Bolivian Reality* (Albany, 1997), 264–266.
49. Brooke Larson, "Democratic Progress or Peril? Indigenous and Popular Mobilization in Bolivia," in Gary Bland and Cynthia J. Arnson, eds., *Democratic Deficits: Addressing Challenges to Sustainability and Consolidation Around the World* (Woodrow Wilson International Center for Scholars, Latin American Program, January 2009), 189.
50. The documentary record is available in the 13-page *Chronology for Lowland Indigenous Peoples in Bolivia,* compiled by *Refworld*: www.refworld.org/docid/469f386ble.html.
51. For insight into the behind-the-scenes negotiations between politicians and transnational corporations, see John Perkins, *Confessions of an Economic Hitman* (New York, 2006) also, John Perkins, *The Secret History of the American Empire* (New York, 2008), 99–103.
52. Kohl and Farthing, *Impasse,* 163–164.
53. The question of brutality by indigenous conscripts against their own people is analyzed in the anthropologist Leslie Gill's study of the military's socialization of recruits. Lesley Gill, *Teetering on the Rim: Global Restructuring, Daily Life, and the Armed Retreat of the Bolivian State* (New York, 2000), 104–132.
54. This synopsis of the Water War is drawn from Dangl, *The Price of Fire,* 67–69; Forrest Hylton and Sinclair Thomson, *Revolutionary Horizons: Past and Present in Bolivian Politics* (London, 2007), 102–104; Kohl and Farthing, *Impasse,* 163–167.
55. The quote is from Oscar Olivera, a prominent member of the *Coordinadora.* Oscar Olivera in collaboration with Tom Lewis, *¡Cochabamba! Water War in Bolivia* (Cambridge, MA, 2004), 142.
56. Leonidas Oikonomakis, *Political Strategies and Social Movements in Latin America: The Zapatistas and Bolivian Cocaleros* (New York, 2018), 148.
57. The contrast between the two candidates can be experienced in two documentaries: *Our Brand Is Crisis* featuring the media-savvy James Carville and company, employed by the creole candidate Sánchez, and *Cocalero* documenting the grassroots movement of the indigenous populist Morales.
58. Hylton and Thomson, *Revolutionary Horizons,* 108–111.
59. Kohl and Farthing, *Impasse,* 174.
60. Hylton and Thomson, *Revolutionary Horizons,* 114–115. The authors liken the Gas War insurrection to the 1780–1781 Aymara rebellion against Spanish rule. Yet Tupac Katari's Aymara army failed to seize La Paz and defeat the creole overlords, whereas the Aymara Alteños of 2003 chased a creole president into exile. Both insurrections remain epic events in Aymara history, equally heroic.
61. In 2004, Goni sold his holdings in the Bolivian mining company COMSUR for $220 million to the international financier Marc Rich, thus avoiding Bolivian taxes and prosecution for the human rights violations of the Gas War. President Clinton pardoned Rich (guilty of multiple counts of fraud) for a $1,000,000 donation to the Democratic Party, to help finance his wife's senate campaign. Kohl and Farthing, *Impasse,* 195, n. 1.

62. Hylton and Thomson, *Revolutionary Horizons*, 135–137.
63. Ronn Pineo, "The Decline of United States Influence and the Rise of Evo Morales," *Council on Hemispheric Affairs* (22 October 2014), 10, 15–17, www.coha.org/the-decline-of-us-influence-and-the-rise-of-evo-morales/
64. Jeffery R. Webber, *From Rebellion to Reform in Bolivia: Class Struggle, Indigenous Liberation, and the Politics of Evo Morales* (Chicago, 2011), 89.
65. Emily Achtenberg, "Bolivia: The Unfinished Business of Land Reform," *NACLA* (3 March 2013), 1–3.
66. Hylton and Thomson, *Revolutionary Horizons*, 139.
67. Webber, *From Rebellion to Reform in Bolivia*, 177. Webber supports this assertion in a trenchant analysis (chapter six: "The Economic Structures of Neoliberalism") demonstrating problems between labor and, for example, the transnational corporation Glencore that are similar to conflicts experienced under the previous neoliberal governments.
68. Ibid., 132–140.
69. Emily Achtenberg, "Contested Development: The Geopolitics of Bolivia's TIPNIS Conflict," *NACLA*, 1 August 2013, 1.
70. The information presented in this paragraph is closely drawn from the provocative summation of USAID documents obtained by Jeremy Bigwood and Eva Golinger, summarized by Eva Golinger in "USAID's Silent Invasion in Bolivia, *NACLA*, 20 May 2009, 1–3. Yet another technique of electoral chicanery appeared in the 2020 election with the use of social media (Twitter) by a Bolivian veteran of the U.S. army to spread disinformation about Evo Morales in over one million Tweets. See Igor Derysh, "Cyber Rambo": How a US Army vet aided the right-wing coup in Bolivia," *Salon*, 24 January 2020, 1–10.
71. Ibid., 3.
72. Jon Lee Anderson, "The Burnt Palace: Was Evo Morales Deposed, or Did He Flee Justice?" *The New Yorker*, 23 March 2020, 40.
73. Nicole Fabricant, "The Roots of the Right-Wing Coup in Bolivia," *Dissent*, 23 December 2019, 2, 4–6. See also Linda Farthing, "Bolivia Has Been Promised Elections. But Will They Be Fair?" *The Guardian*, 2 December 2019, 1–2.
74. Interview with Rafael Correa by Nicolas Allen, "The War on Latin America's Left," *The Tribune*, 17 November 2019, 2, https://tribunemag.co.uk/2019/11/the-war-on-latin-americas-left
75. Furthermore, allegations of electoral irregularities by OAS observers were never substantiated. Greg Grandin, "What the New York Times Got Wrong on Bolivia," *The Nation*, 18 December 2019. See Igor Derysh, "Cyber Rambo: How a US Army [Bolivian Cruceño] Vet Aided the Right-wing Coup in Bolivia," *Salon*, 24 January 2020, 1–6.
76. Angela Davis, Noam Chomsky, et al., "Repressive Violence Is Sweeping Bolivia The Añez Regime Must Be Held to Account," *The Guardian*, 24 November 2019, 1–3.

BIBLIOGRAPHY

Archival Sources

Archivo y Biblioteca Nacionales de Bolivia. Sucre, Bolivia
United States National Archives. Bethesda, Maryland.

Newspapers

Antorcha, La Paz
El Diario, La Paz
El Ex-Combatiente, Santa Cruz
Libertad
Masas, La Paz
El Mundo, Cochabamba
La Nación, La Paz
El País, Cochabamba
La Patria
El Pionero
La Presencia, La Paz
La Tarde, La Paz
Los Tiempos, Cochabamba
Ultima Hora, La Paz
Unidad

Interviews

Zenón Barrientos Mamani, Panóptico Nacional, La Paz, 29 August 1970
Ñuflo Chávez, La Paz, 2 July 1970
Antonio Mamani Alvarez, La Paz: 15 August 1970; 29 August 1970; 4 November 1971; 3 March 1972; 7 April 1972; 4 July 1972; 4 August 1972
Víctor Paz Estenssoro, Lima, Peru, 27 June 1970

Paulino Quispe, Panóptico Nacional, La Paz, 30 July 1970
José Rojas and Walter Revuelta, Cochabamba, 25 August 1970
Toribio Salas, La Paz, 12 August 1970
Miguel Veizaga, Cochabamba, 23 August 1970
Francisco Viscarra, Achacachi, 12 July 1970

Documents

Bonifaz, Miguel. *Legislación agrario-indígenal.* Cochabamba: Imprenta Universitaria, 1953.
Busch, German. *Código del Trabajo.* La Paz: Editorial Popular, 1946.
Castillo Avendaño, Wálter del. *Compilación legal de la reforma agraria en Bolivia.* La Paz: Editorial Fénix, 1955.
Central Obrera Boliviana. *Programa ideología y estatutos de la Central Obrera Boliviana.* La Paz: n.p., 1954.
Cornejo, S. Alberto, ed. *Programas políticos de Bolivia.* Cochabamba: Imprenta Universitaria, 1949.
Cuadros Quiroga, José. *Movimiento Nacionalista Revolucionario: sus bases y principios de acción inmediata.* n.p., 1942.
Flores Moncayo, José. *Derecho Agrario Boliviano.* La Paz: Editorial Don Bosco, 1956.
———. *Legislación boliviano del indio.* La Paz: Editorial Fénix, 1953.
———. *P.M.N.R.A, Exposición de Motivos y Declaración de Principios.* n.p., 1960.
Partido del Movimiento Nacionalista Revolucionario Auténtico. *P.M.N.R.A. Exposición de motives y declaración de principios.* La Paz: n.p., 1960.
Partido Obrero Revolucionario. *Programa obrero. Tesis de Pulacayo. Resolución de Colquiri-San José. Resolución política aprobada en la VIII Conferencia Nacional Minera de Catavi.* La Paz: Ediciones Masas, 1959.
United States Central Intelligence Agency, Donald N. Wilber. "Overthrow of Premier Mossadeq of Iran, November 1952-August 1953." *Clandestine Service Historical Paper* 208, March 1954. http://www2.gwu.edu/~nsarchiv/NSAEBB/NSAEBB435/
United States Department of State, Bureau of Intelligence and Research. "Clandestine Arms Traffic in Latin America and the Insurgency Problem." Research Memorandum RAR-49, November 29, 1963.
United States National Archives and Records Administration, U.S. State Department Memoranda, 1943–1946, 1952–1964.
Villarroel, Gualberto. *Mensaje a la H. Convención Nacional de 1944.* La Paz: n.p., 1944.
———. *Mensaje a la H. Convención Nacional de 1945.* La Paz: n.p., 1945.
Warachi Condorcanqui, Asto and Antonio Mamani Álvarez. *Tesis de Caranguillas*, Caranguillas Bolivia, May 10, 1945.

Published Works

Abercrombie, Thomas. *Pathways of Memory and Power: Ethnography and History Among an Andean People.* Madison, WI: University of Wisconsin Press, 1998.
Achá Alvarez, Enrique and Mario H. Ramos y Ramos. *Unzaga: Mártir de América.* Buenos Aires: Artes Gráficas Moderna, 1960.
Achtenberg, Emily. "Bolivia: The Unfinished Business of Land Reform." *NACLA*, 3 March 2013, 1–4.
———. "Contested Development: The Geopolitics of Bolivia's TIPNIS Conflict." *NACLA*, 1 August 2013, 1–9.

Agee, Philip. *Inside the Company: CIA Diary*. London: Penguin Books, 1975.
Albó, Xavier. "Achacachi: Rebeldes pero conservadores." In *Actas du XLII Congres International des Americanistes*, Vol. 3. Paris: Societe des Americanistes, 1976, 9–32.
———. *Achacachi: Medio siglo de lucha campesina*. La Paz: CIPCA, 1979.
———. "Andean People in the Twentieth Century." In Frank Saloman and Stuart Schwartz, eds., *The Cambridge History of the Native Peoples of the Americas*, Vol. 3.2. Cambridge: Cambridge University Press, 2000.
———. *Bodas de plata o réquiem para una reforma agraria*. La Paz: Centro de Investigación y Promoción del Campesinado, 17 (March 1979).
———. "Dinamica en la estructura inter-comunitaria de Jésus de Machaca." *America Indígena*, 32.3 (1972), 773–816.
———. "From MNRistas to Kataristas to Katari." In Steve J. Stern, ed., *Resistance, Rebellion, and Consciousness in the Andean Peasant World, 18th to 20th Centuries*. Madison, WI: University of Wisconsin Press, 1987, 379–419.
———. "¿Khitipxtansa? ¿Quines somos? Identidad localista, étnica y clasista en los aymaras de hoy." *America Indígena*, 39.3 (July–September 1979), 477–512.
———. "The 'Long Memory' of Ethnicity in Bolivia and Some Temporary Oscillations." In John Crabtree and Laurence Whitehead, eds., *Unresolved Tensions: Bolivia Past and Present*. Pittsburg, PA: University of Pittsburgh Press, 2008.
———. "La Paradoja Aymara: Solidaridad y Faccionalismo?" *Estudios Andinos*, 4.2 (1974–1976), 67–109.
———, ed. *Raíces de América*. Madrid: Alianza Editorial, 1988.
Albó, Xavier, Tomás Greaves, and Godofredo Sandoval. *Chukiyawu: La cara Aymara de La Paz*. La Paz: CIPCA, 1983.
Alexander, Robert J. *The Bolivian National Revolution*. New Brunswick, NJ: Rutgers University Press, 1958.
Allen, Nicolas. "The War on Latin America's Left: An Interview with Rafael Correa." *The Tribune*, 17 November 2019, 2. https://tribunemag.co.uk/2019/11/the-war-on-latin-americas-left
Almaraz Paz, Sergio. *Bolivia: requiem para una República*. La Paz: Los Amigos del Libro, 1980.
Anderson, Jon Lee. "The Burnt Palace: Was Evo Morales Deposed, or did He Flee Justice?" *The New Yorker*, 23 March 2020, 40–49.
Andrade, Víctor. *My Missions for Revolutionary Bolivia, 1944–1962*. Pittsburgh, PA: Pittsburgh University Press, 1976.
Antezana Ergueta, Luis. *Historia secreta del movimiento nacionalista revolucionario*, 9 Vols. La Paz: Librería y Editorial Juventud, 1984–2006.
———. "La reforma agrarian campesina en Bolivia (1956–1960)." *Revista Mexicana de Sociología*, 2 (April–June 1969), 245–321.
Antezana Ergueta, Luis and Hugo Romero B. *Historia de los sindicatos campesinos: un proceso de integración nacional en Bolivia*. La Paz: Consejo Nacional de Reforma Agraria, 1973.
Arce, Armando. *Los Fusiliamentos de noviembre de 1944*. La Paz: Tallares Gráficos, n.d.
Arguedas, Alcides. *Pueblo enfermo*. La Paz: Gisbert, 1979.
Ari Chachaki, Waskar. *Earth Politics: Religion, Decolonization, and Bolivia's Indigenous Intellectuals*. Durham, NC: Duke University Press, 2014.
Arze, José Antonio. *Bolivia bajo el terrorismo nazifascista; un llamado a la ciudadanía Bolivia y la consciencia democrática internacional, para reforzar la acción de la Unión Democrácia Boliviana*. Lima: Empresa Editoria Peruana, 1945.
Arze Aguirre, René. *Guerra y conflictos socials: El caso rural boliviano durante la campana del chaco*. La Paz: CERES, 1987.

Barber, Willard F. and C. Neale Ronning. *Internal Security and Military Power: Counterinsurgency and Civic Action in Latin America.* Columbus: Ohio State University Press, 1966.

Barcelli S., Agustín. *Medio siglo de luchas sindicales revolucionarias en Bolivia, 1905–1955.* La Paz: Editorial del Estado, 1957.

Barnadas, Josep M. *Apundes para una historia aymara.* La Paz: CIPCA, 1978.

Barnes de von Marshall, Katherine. "Cabildos, corregimientos y sindicatos en Bolivia despues de 1952." *Estudios Andinos*, 1 (1970), 61–78.

———. "La formación de nuevos pueblos en Bolivia: Proceso e implicaciones." *Estudios Andinos*, 1 (1970), 23–37.

Barnes de von Marschall, Katherine and Juan Torrico Angulo. "Cambios socio-económicos en el Valle Alto de Cochabamba desde 1952: Los pueblos provinciales de Cliza, Punata, Arani, Sacaba, Tarata y Mizque." La Paz: Servicio Nacional de Reforma Agraria, mimeographed, 1971.

Barrero, Francisco. *Radepa y la Revolución Nacional.* La Paz: Empresa Editora Urquizo, 1976.

Barriaga Antelo, Hernán. *Laureles de un Tirano.* La Paz: E. Burillo, 1965.

Barrientos, René. *Significado de la Revolución de Noviembre.* La Paz: Dirección Nacional de Informaciones, 1964.

Barrios de Chúngara, Domitila. *Let Me Speak.* New York: Monthly Review Press, 1978.

Bastien, Joseph. *Mountain of the Condor: Metaphor and Ritual in an Ayllu Community.* St. Paul, MN: West Publishing Company, 1978.

Beardsell, Peter. *Europe and Latin America: returning the gaze.* Manchester, UK: Manchester, University Press, 2000.

Bedregal, Guillermo. *Víctor Paz Estenssoro, El Político: Una Semblanza Crítica.* México, D.F.: Fondo de Cultura Económica, 1999.

Belmonte Pabón, Elías. *RADEPA: sombras y refulgencias del pasado.* La Paz: Multiservice ALE, 1994.

Bodley, John H. *Victims of Progress.* Lanham, MD: AltaMira Press, 2008.

Black, Jan Kippers. *United States Penetration of Brazil.* Philadelphia, PA: University of Pennsylvania Press, 1977.

Blanco, J. *Antonio Álvarez Mamani: Historia de un dirigente campesino.* n.p., 1969.

Blasier, Cole. *The Hovering Giant: U.S. Responses to Revolutionary Change in Latin America.* Pittsburgh, PA: University of Pittsburgh Press, 1976

———. "Studies of Social Revolution: Origins in Mexico, Bolivia and Cuba." *Latin American Research Review*, 2 (Summer 1967), 28–64.

———. "The United States, Germany, and the Bolivian Revolutionaries, 1941–1946." *Hispanic American Historical Review*, 52.1 (February 1972), 26–54.

———. "The United States and Madero." *Journal of Latin American Studies*, 4.2 (November 1972), 207–231.

Blum, William. *Killing Hope: U.S. Military and C.I.A. Interventions Since World War II.* Monroe, ME: Common Courage Press, 1995.

Bolloten, Burnett. *The Spanish Civil War: Revolution and Counterrevolution.* Chapel Hill, NC: University of North Carolina Press, 1991.

Botelho Gosálvez, Raúl. *Altiplano.* Lima: Ediciones Nuevo Mundo, 1967.

Breuer, William. *Deceptions of World War II.* New York: John Wiley and Sons, 2001.

Brill, William. "Military-Civic Action in Bolivia." Ph.D. dissertation, University of Pennsylvania, 1965.

———. *Military Intervention in Bolivia: The Overthrow of Paz Estenssoro and the MNR.* Washington, DC: Institute for the Comparative Study of Political Systems, 1967.

Brinton, Crane. *Anatomy of Revolution.* New York, Vintage Books, 1965.

Buechler, Hans. "Agrarian Reform and Migration on the Bolivian Altiplano." Ph.D. dissertation, Columbia University, 1966.
———. "The Reorganization of Counties in the Bolivian Highlands: An Analysis of Rural-Urban Networks and Hierarchies." In Elizabeth Eddy, ed., *Urban Anthropology*. Athens, GA: University of Georgia Press, 1968, 48–57.
Buechler, Hans and Judith Maria Buechler. "El Aymara y el cambio social: Reevaluación del concepto de 'Intermediario Cultural'." *Estudios Andinos*, 2 (1971–1972), 131–147.
———. *The Bolivian Aymara*. New York: Holt, Rinehart and Winston, 1971.
———. "Conduct and Code: An Analysis of Market Syndicates and Social Revolution in La Paz, Bolivia." In June Nash, Juan Corradi, and Hobart Spalding Jr., eds., *Ideology and Social Change in Latin America*. New York: Gordon and Breach, 1977, 174–184.
Buechler, Judith Maria. "The Dynamics of the Markets in La Paz, Bolivia." *Urban Anthropology*, 7 (Winter 1978), 343–359.
Burke, Melvin. "Land Reform in the Lake Titicaca Region." In James Malloy and Richard Thorn, eds., *Beyond the Revolution: Bolivia Since 1952*. Pittsburgh, PA: Pittsburgh University Press, 301–339.
Bustillos Hernanz, Óscar A. "Los Laimes y Jucumanis." *America Indígena*, 32.3 (July–September 1972), 817–829.
Calderón, Fernando and Jorge Dandler, eds. *Bolivia: La fuerza historica del campesinado*. Geneva: Instituto de Investigaciones de Las Naciones Unidas para el Desarrollo Social, 1984.
Calderón, Ignacio. "Dreams of a Railroad." In Sinchalr Thomson et al., eds., *The Bolivia Reader*, translated by Alison Spedding. Durham, NC: Duke University Press, 2018, 193–194.
Calderón, Jaime. *The Bolivian Coup of 1964: A Sociological Analysis*. Buffalo, NY: Council on International Studies, State University at Buffalo, 1972.
Camacho Saa, Carlos. "Minifundia, Productivity and Land Reform in Cochabamba." Ph.D. dissertation, University of Wisconsin, 1966.
Candia Almaraz, Alberto. *Razón de Patria ante la historia*. Cochabamba: Pelikan, 1957.
Canessa, Andrew. "Forgetting the Revolution and Remembering the War: Memory and Violence in Highland Bolivia." *History Workshop Journal*, 68 (Autumn 2009), 173–198.
Cardenas, Víctor Hugo. "La lucha de un pueblo." In Xavier Albó, ed., *Raíces de América: el mundo aymara*. Madrid: Alianza Editorial, 1988.
Cardozo, Armando. *Estudio del Altiplano* (La Paz, 1969), 1–33.
Carranza Fernández, Mario. *Estudio de caso en el Valle Bajo de Cochabamba: Camarca, Parotani y Itapaya* (La Paz, 1972).
Carter, William. *Aymara Communities and the Bolivian Agrarian Reform*. Gainesville, FL: University of Florida Monographs, no. 24, 1964.
———. "Revolution and the Agrarian Sector." In James Malloy and Richard Thorn, eds., *Beyond the Revolution: Bolivia Since 1952*. Pittsburgh, PA: Pittsburgh University Press, 1971, 233–268.
Cerruto, Óscar. *Aluvión de Fuego*. Santiago, Chile: Ediciones Ercilla, 1935.
Céspedes, Augusto. *El presidente colgado*. Buenos Aires: Editorial Jorge Alvarez, 1966.
———. *Sangre de mestizos*. La Paz: Empresa Industrial Gráfica E. Burillo, 1962.
Chávez Ortiz, Ñuflo. *Recuerdos de un revolucionario boliviano*. La Paz: Centro de Estudios Bolivianos, 1988.
Chávez Ortiz, Rafael. "The Problem of the East." In Sinclair Thomson, et al., eds., *The Bolivia Reader*, translated by Alison Spedding. Durham, NC: Duke University Press, 2018, 261–267.

Chipana Ramos, Francisco. "The Death of Servitude." In Sinclair Thomson, et al., eds., *The Bolivia Reader*, translated by Alison Spedding. Durham, NC: Duke University Press, 2018, 365–370.

Chomsky, Noam. *American Power and the New Mandarins.* New York: Pantheon, 1969.

Choque Canqui, Roberto. *Líderes indígenas aymaras: lucha por la defense de tierras comunitarias de origen.* La Paz: UNIH-PAKAXA, 2010.

———. *La massacre de Jésus de Machaca.* La Paz: Ediciones Chitakolla, 1987.

Choque Canqui, Roberto and Cristina Quisbert Quispe. *Educación indígenal en Bolivia: Un siglo de ensayos educativos y resistencias patronales.* La Paz: UNIH-PAKAXA, 2006.

Choque Canqui, Roberto, Vitaliano Soria Choque, Humberto Mamani, Esteban Ticona, and Ramón Conde. *Educación indígena: ¿ciudadanía o colonización?* La Paz: Ediciones Aruwiyiri, 1992.

Choque Canqui, Roberto and Esteban Ticona. *Historia de una lucha desigual: los contenidos ideológicos y políticos de las rebeliones indígenas.* La Paz: UNIH-PAKAXA, 2005.

Clark, Evelyn. "Agrarian Reform and Developmental Change in Parotani, Bolivia." Ph.D. dissertation, Indiana University, 1970.

Clark, Ronald. "Land Reform and Peasant Market Participation on the Northern Highlands of Bolivia." *Land Economics*, 44 (May 1968), 153–172.

———. "Problems and Conflicts over Land Ownership in Bolivia." *Inter-American Economic Affairs*, 22.4 (Spring 1969), 3–18.

———. "Reforma Agraria y integración campesino en la economía boliviana." *Estudios Andinos*, 1 (1970), 5–22.

Claure, Toribio. *Una escuela rural en Vacas.* La Paz: Universo, 1949.

Condarco Morales, Ramiro. *Zarate, El Temible "Willka.* La Paz: Talleres Gráficos Bolivianos, 1966.

Contreras, Manuel E. "A Comparative Perspective of Education Reforms in Bolivia: 1950–2000." In Merilee S. Grindle and Pilar Domingo, eds., *Proclaiming Revolution: Bolivia in Comparative Perspective.* London: Institute of Latin American Studies, University of London; Cambridge, UK: David Rockefeller Center for Latin American Studies, Harvard University, 2003, 259–283.

Cote, Stephen. "Bolivian Nationalism and the Chaco War." In Bridget María Chesterton, ed., *The Chaco War: Environment, Ethnicity, and Nationalism.* London, 2017.

Crabtree, John and Laurence Whitehead, eds. *Unresolved Tensions: Bolivia Past and Present.* Pittsburgh, PA: University of Pittsburgh Press, 2008.

Crandon-Malamud, Libbet. *From the Fat of Our Souls.* Berkeley, CA: University of California Press, 1993.

Cull, Nicholas John. *Selling War: The British Propaganda Campaign Against American Neutrality.* New York: Oxford University Press, 1996.

Dandler, Jorge. "'Low Classnes' or Wavering Populism? A Peasant Movement in Bolivia (1952–1953)." In June Nash, Juan Corradi, and Hobart Spedding Jr., eds., *Ideology and Social Change in Latin America.* New York: Gordon and Breach, 1977, 142–173.

———. "Peasant Sindicatos and the Process of Cooptation in Bolivian Politics." In June Nash, Jorge Dandler and Nicholas Hopkins, eds., *Popular Participation in Social Change.* The Hague: Mouton, 1976, 341–352.

———. "Politics of Leadership, Brokerage and Patronage in the Campesino Movement of Cochabamba, Bolivia, 1935–1954." Ph.D. dissertation, University of Wisconsin, 1971.

———. *El sindicalismo campesino en Bolivia: los cambios estructurales en Ucureña.* Mexico, D.F: Instituto Indigenista Interamericano, 1969.

Dandler, Jorge and Juan Torrico A. "From the National Indigenous Congress to the Ayopaya Rebellion: Bolivia, 1945–1947." In Steve J. Stern, ed., *Resistance, Rebellion, and Consciousness in the Andean Peasant World, 18th to 20th Centuries*. Madison, WI: University of Wisconsin Press, 1982, 334–378.

Dangl, Benjamin. *The Five Hundred Year Rebellion*. Chico, CA: AK Press, 2019.

———. *The Price of Fire*. Chico, CA: AK Press, 2007.

Davis, Angela, Noam Chomsky, et al. "Repressive Violence is Sweeping Bolivia. The Añez Regime Must be Held to Account." *The Guardian*, 24 November 2019, 1–3.

Daza Barrenechea, Capitan Óscar. *Sistematización Armada de la Revolución Nacional*. La Paz: n.p., n.d.

De Shazo, Peter. "The Colonato System on the Bolivian Altiplano from Colonial Times to 1952." *Land Tenure Center*, 83, n.d. Madison, WI.

Derysh, Igor. "'Cyber Rambo: How a US Army Vet Aided the Right-wing coup in Bolivia." *Salon*, 24 January 2020, 1–6.

Diez de Medina, Fernando. *Ainoka*. La Paz: Imprenta y Editorial Artística, 1950.

———. *Pachakuti y otras paginas polemicas*. La Paz: Imprenta y Editorial Artística, 1958.

———. *Siripaka*. La Paz: Imprenta y Editorial Artística, 1950.

———. *Thunupa*. 2nd ed. La Paz: Gisbert, 1956.

Dinges, John. *The Condor Years: How Pinochet and his Allies Brought Terrorism to Three Continents*. New York: The New Press, 2004.

Dorn, Glenn J. *The Truman Administration and Bolivia: Making the World Safe for Liberal Constitutional Oligarchy*. University Park, PA: Pennsylvania State University Press, 2011.

Dorner, Peter. *Latin American Land Reforms in Theory and Practice*. Madison, WI: University of Wisconsin Press, 1992.

Dorsey, Joseph F. "A Case Study of Ex-Hacienda Toralapa in the Tiraque Region of the Upper Cochabamba Valley." *Land Tenure Center*, 65 (June 1975), University of Wisconsin.

———. "A Case Study of the Lower Cochabamba Valley: Ex-Haciendas Parotani and Caramarca." *Land Tenure Center*, 64 (June 1975), University of Wisconsin.

Duncan, Kenneth and Ian Rutledge. "Introduction: patterns of agrarian capitalism in Latin America." In Kenneth Duncan and Ian Rutledge, eds., *Land and Labour in Latin America*. Cambridge: Cambridge University Press, 1977, 1–20.

Dunkerley, James. "The Origins of the Bolivian Revolution in the Twentieth Century: Some Reflections." In Merilee S. Grindle and Pilar Domingo, eds., *Proclaiming Revolution: Bolivia in Comparative Perspective*. London: Institute of Latin American Studies, University of London; Cambridge, MA: David Rockefeller Center for Latin American Studies, Harvard University, 2003, 135–163.

———. *Political Suicide in Latin America*. London: Verso, 1992.

———. *Rebellion in the Veins: Political Struggle in Bolivia, 1952–1982*. London: Verso Editions, 1984.

Eckstein, Susan. "The Impact of Revolution: A Comparative Analysis of Mexico and Bolivia." *Studies in Comparative International Development*, 10 (Fall 1975), 4–53.

———. "Transformation of a 'Revolution from Below:' Bolivia and International Capital." *Comparative Studies in Society and History*, 25 (1983), 105–135.

Eder, George Jackson. *Inflation and Development in Latin America: A Case History of Inflation and Stabilization in Bolivia*. Ann Arbor, MI: University of Michigan Press, 1968.

Erasmus, Charles. "Upper Limits of Peasantry and Agrarian Reform: Bolivia, Venezuela and Mexico Compared." *Ethnology*, 6.4 (October 1967), 349–380.

Ewing, Andrew and Susan Goldmark. "Privatization by Capitalization: A Popular Participation Recipe for Cash-Starved SOEs." *Viewpoint, The World Bank*, FDP Note No. 31, November 1994.

Ezell, Paul H. "Man and Land in Bolivia: The Hacienda Orurillo Case." *Ethnohistory*, 13 (1966), 123–144.

Fabricant, Nicole. "The Roots of the Right-Wing Coup in Bolivia." *Dissent*, 23 December 2019, 2–6.

Fanon, Frantz. *The Wretched of the Earth*. New York: Groves Press, 1968.

Farcau, Bruce. *The Chaco War: Bolivia and Paraguay, 1932–1935*. Westport, CT: Praeger, 1996.

Farthing, Linda. "Bolivia has been Promised Elections. But will they be Fair?" *The Guardian*, 2 December 2019, 1–3.

Feder, Ernst. *The Rape of the Peasantry: Latin America's Landholding System*. Garden City, New York: Doubleday, 1971.

———. "Societal Opposition to Peasant Movements and its Effects on Farm People in Latin America." In Henry Landsberger, ed., *Latin American Peasant Movements*. Ithaca, NY: Cornell University Press, 1969, 399–450.

Fellman Velarde, José. *Víctor Paz Estenssoro: El hombre y la revolución*. La Paz: E. Burillo, 1955.

Field, Thomas C. Jr. *From Development to Dictatorship: Bolivia and the Alliance for Progress in the Kennedy Era*. Ithaca, NY: Cornell University Press, 2014.

———. "Ideology as Strategy: Military-Led Modernization and the Origins of the Alliance for Progress in Bolivia." *Diplomatic History*, 36.1 (January 2012), 147–183.

———. "Transnationalism Meets Empire: The AFL-CIO, Development, and the Private Origins of Kennedy's Latin American Labor Program." *Diplomatic History*, 42.2 (April 2018), 305–334.

Fifer, J. Valerie. *Bolivia: Land, Location and Politics Since 1825*. Cambridge: Cambridge University Press, 1972.

Finot, Alfonso. *Defensa de mi Relato Así Cayó Villarroel*. La Paz: n.p., 1966.

Flack, Joseph. "Diary of a Revolution." *Foreign Service Journal* (September 1946), 22–25, 54–58.

Flores, Edmundo. "Taraco: Monografia de un latifundio del altiplano boliviano." *El Trimestre economico*, 22.2 (April–June 1955), 209–229.

Flores, Gonzalo. "Levantamientos campesinos durante el perodo Liberal." In Fernando Calderón and Jorge Dandler Hanhart, eds., *Bolivia: La Fuerza Historica del Campesinado*, Geneva: Instituto de Investigaciones de las Naciones Unidas, 1984, 122–132.

Flores Moncayo, José. *Legislación Boliviana del Indio*. La Paz: Instituto Indigenista Boliviano, 1953.

Forbes, David. "On the Aymara Indians of Bolivia and Peru." *Journal of the Ethnological Society of London*, 2 (1870), 193–305.

Foreign Areas Studies Division, Special Operations Research Office. *U.S. Army: Area Handbook for Bolivia*. Washington, DC: American University, 1963.

Friedman, Max Paul. *Nazis and Good Neighbors: The United States Campaign Against the Germans of Latin America In World War II*. New York: Cambridge University Press, 2003.

Frontaura Argandoña, Manuel. *La Revolución Nacional*. La Paz: Editorial Los Amigos del Libro, 1974.

Fuentes, Carlos. "Viva Zapata: Zapata and the Mexican Revolution." *The New York Review of Books*, 13 March 1969, 5.

Galarza, Ernesto. "The Case of Bolivia." *Inter-American Reports*, 6 (May 1949), 5–30.

García, Antonio. "Agrarian Reform and Social Development in Bolivia." In Rodolfo Stavenhagen, ed., *Agrarian Problems and Peasant Movements in Latin America*. New York: Doubleday, 1970, 301–346.

———. *Reforma agraria y dominación social en America Latina*. Buenos Aires: Ediciones Siap, 1973.

———. "Los Sindicatos en el Esquima de Revolución Nacional: El Sindicalismo en la Experiencia Boliviana de Nacionalización y Desarrollo." *El Trimestre Económico*, 33.4 (October–December 1966), 597–629.
Garcia Arganaras, Fernando. "Bolivia's Transformist Revolution." *Latin American Perspectives*, 19.2 (Spring 1992), 44–71.
Garner, Bryan, ed. *Black's Law Dictionary*. 7th ed. St. Paul, MN: West Group, 1999.
Geographic Society of Santa Cruz. "Integration of the Lowlands." In Sinclair Thomson et al., eds., *The Bolivia Reader*, translated by Alison Spedding. Durham, NC: Duke University Press, 2018, 189–192.
Gildner, Robert Matthew. "Indomestizo Modernism: National Development and Indigenous Integration in Postrevolutionary Bolivia, 1952–1964." Ph.D. dissertation, University of Texas at Austin, 2012.
Gill, Lesley. *Teetering on the Rim: Global Restructuring, Daily Life, and the Armed Retreat of the Bolivian State*. New York: Columbia University Press, 2000.
Godoy, Ricardo. *Mining and Agriculture in Highland Bolivia: Ecology, History, and Commerce Among the Jukumanis*. Tucson, AZ: University of Arizona Press, 1990.
Golinger, Eva. "USAID's Silent Invasion in Bolivia." *NACLA*, 20 May 2009, 1–3.
Gonzalez Torres, René and Luis Iriarte Ontiveros. *Villarroel, mártir de sus ideales, y el atisbo de la Revolución Nacional*. La Paz: Talleres-Escuela de Artes Graficas del Colegio Don Bosco, 1983.
Goodrich, Carter. "Bolivia in Time of Revolution." In James Malloy and Richard Thorn, eds., *Beyond the Revolution: Bolivia Since 1952*. Pittsburgh, PA: University of Pittsburgh Press, 1971, 3–24.
Gordillo, José. *Campesinos revolucionarios en Bolivia: Identidad, territorio y sexualidad en el Valle Alto de Cochabamba, 1952–1964*. La Paz: Plural Editores, 2000.
Goudsmit, Into A. "Exploiting the 1953 Agrarian Reform: Landlord Persistence in Northern Potosí, Bolivia." *The Journal of Latin American and Caribbean Anthropology*, 13.2 (November 2008), 361–386.
Graeff, Peter. "The Effects of Continued Landlord Presence in the Bolivian Countryside During the Post-Reform Era: Lessons to be Learned." *Land Tenure Center*, 103 (October 1974), Madison, WI.
Granado, Eduardo del. "Landlord Counteroffensive." In Sinclair Thomson, et al., eds., *The Bolivia Reader*, translated by Alison Spedding. Durham, NC: Duke University Press, 2018, 274–277.
Grandin, Greg. *Empire's Workshop: Latin America, the United States, and the Rise of the New Imperialism*. New York: Henry Holt, 2006.
———. "What the New York Times Got Wrong on Bolivia." *The Nation*, 18 December 2019.
Grieshaber, Erwin. "Hacienda-Indian Community Relations and Indian Acculturation: An Historiographical Essay." *Latin American Research Review*, 14 (1979), 107–128.
———. "Survival of Indian Communities in Nineteenth-Century Bolivia: A Regional Comparison." *Journal of Latin American Studies*, 12 (1980), 223–269.
Griffin, Keith. "The State, Human Development and the Economics of Cocaine: The Case of Bolivia." In *Studies in Globalization and Economic Transitions* (London: Palgrave Macmillan, 1996).
Grindle, Merilee S. and Pilar Domingo, eds. *Proclaiming Revolution: Bolivia in Comparative Perspective*. London: Institute of Latin American Studies, University of London; Cambridge: David Rockefeller Center for Latin American Studies, Harvard University, 2003.
Gueiler Tejada, Lydia. *La mujer y la revolución; autobiografía política*. La Paz: Los Amigos del Libro, 1959.

Guevara Arze, Walter. *Manifesto de Ayopaya*, in Walter Guevara Arze, ed., *Bases para replantear la Revolución Nacional*. La Paz: Librería y Editorial Juventud, 1988.
———. *Plan de política económica de la Revolución Nacional*. La Paz: Editorial Letras, 1955.
Guillén Pinto, Alfredo. *Utama* (La Paz: Gisbert y Cassanovas), 1945.
Guillermoprieto, Alma. "The Altiplano." *National Geographic* (July 2008), 74–87.
Harris, Olivia. "Labour and Produce in an Ethnic Economy, Northern Potosí, Bolivia." In David Lehmann, ed., *Ecology and exchange in the Andes*. Cambridge, UK: Cambridge University Press, 1982, 70–96.
———. "Sources and Meanings of Money: Beyond the Market Paradigm in an Ayllu in Northern Potosí." In Brooke Larson and Olivia Harris, with Tandeter, eds., *Ethnicity, Markets, and Migration in the Andes*. Durham, NC: Duke University Press, 1995, 351–390.
Harris, Olivia and Javier Albó. "Monteras y guardatojos. Campesinos y mineros en el norte de Potosí." La Paz: CIPCA, no. 7, 1976.
Havet, José. "Rational Domination: The Power Structure in a Bolivian Rural Zone." Ph.D. dissertation, University of Pittsburgh, 1979.
Healy, Kevin. Power, Class, and Rural Development in Southern Bolivia. Ph.D. dissertation, Cornell University, 1969.
Heath, Dwight. "The Aymara Indians and Bolivia's Revolutions." *Inter-American Economic Affairs*, 18 (Spring 1966), 31–40.
———. "Bolivia: Peasant Syndicates Among the Aymara of the Yungas—A View from the Grass Roots." In Henry Landsberger, ed., *Latin American Peasant Movements*. Ithaca, NY: Cornell University Press, 1969, 170–209.
———. "Bolivia's Law of Agrarian Reform." In Dwight B. Heath, Charles J. Erasmus, and Hans C. Buechler, eds., *Land Reform and Social Revolution in Bolivia*. New York: Praeger, 1969, 29–51.
———. "Hacendados with Bad Table Manners: Campesino Syndicates as Surrogate Landlords in Bolivia." *Inter-American Economic Affairs*, 24 (1970), 3–13.
———. "Land Reform in Bolivia." *Inter-American Economic Affairs*, 12 (1959), 3–27.
———. "New Patrons for Old: Changing Patron-Client Relationships in the Bolivian Yungas." *Ethnology*, 12.1 (January 1973), 75–98.
Heath, Dwight, Charles Erasmus and Hans Buechler, eds. *Land Reform and Social Revolution in Bolivia*. New York: Praeger, 1969.
Hennesy, C.A.M. "Shifting Forces in the Bolivian Revolution." *The World Today* (May 1964), 197–207.
Herman, Edward S. and Noam Chomsky. *Manufacturing Consent: The Political Economy of the Mass Media*. New York. Pantheon Books, 2002.
Hernanz, Óscar A. "Los Laimes y Jucumanis." *America Indígena*, 32 (1972), 817–829.
Heyduk, Daniel. "The Hacienda System and Agrarian Reform in Highland Bolivia: A Reevaluation." *Ethnology*, 13.1 (January 1974), 71–82.
———. "Huayrapampa: Bolivian Highland Peasants and the New Social Order." Ph.D. dissertation, Cornell University, 1971.
Huizer, Gerrit and Rodolfo Stavenhagen. "Peasant Movements and Land Reform in Latin America: Mexico and Bolivia." In Henry Landsberger, ed., *Rural Protest: Peasant Movements and Social Change in Latin America*. New York: Harper and Row, 1973, 378–409.
Humphreys, R.A. *Latin America and the Second World War*, Vol. 1. London, 1981.
Hyde, H. Montgomery. *Room 3603: The Story of the British Intelligence Center in New York During World War II*. New York: Farrar, Strauss, 1963.
Hylton, Forrest and Sinclair Thompson. *Revolutionary Horizons: Past and Present in Bolivian Politics*. London: Verso, 2007.

Jackson, George, ed. "The Decline of the Hacienda in Cochabamba, Bolivia: The Case of the Sacaba Valley, 1870–1929." *Hispanic American Historical Review*, 69.2 (1989), 259–281.
———. *Inflation and Development in Latin America: A Case History of Inflation and Stabilization in Bolivia*. Ann Arbor: University of Michigan Press, 1968.
———. *Regional Markets and Agrarian Transformation in Bolivia: Cochabamba, 1539–1960*. Albuquerque: University of New Mexico Press, 1994.
Janvry, Alain de. *The Agrarian Question and Reformism in Latin America*. Baltimore, MD: John Hopkins University Press, 1981.
Janvry, Alain de and Lynn Ground. "Types and Consequences of Land Reform in Latin America." *Latin American Perspectives*. 5.4 (Autumn 1978), 90–112.
John, S. Sandor. *Bolivia's Radical Tradition: Permanent Revolution in the Andes*. Tucson, AZ: University of Arizona Press, 2012
Johnson, Chalmers. *Revolution and the Social System*. Palo Alto, CA: Stanford University Press, 1968.
———. *Sorrows of Empire: Militarism, Secrecy, and the End of the Republic*. New York: Henry Holt and Company, 2004.
Judt, Tony with Timothy Snyder. *Thinking the Twentieth Century*. London: Penguin, 2012.
Katz, Friedrich. *The Secret War in Mexico: Europe, the United States and the Mexican Revolution*. Chicago: University of Chicago Press, 1981.
Keenleyside, Hugh Llewellyn. *Informe Keenleyside*. La Paz: Editorial U.M.S.A., 1952.
Keller, Frank. "Finca Ingavi: A Medieval Survival on the Bolivian Altiplano." *Economic Geography*, 26 (January 1950), 37–50.
Kelly, Jonathan and Herbert Klein. *Revolution and the Rebirth of Inequality: A Theory Applied to the National Revolution in Bolivia*. Berkeley, CA: University of California Press, 1981.
Kinzer, Stephen. *All the Shah's Men*. Hoboken, NJ: J. Wiley and Sons, 2003.
———. *The Brothers: John Foster Dulles, Allen Dulles, and Their Secret World War*. New York: Henry Holt and Company, 2013.
———. *Overthrow: America's Century of Regime Change from Hawaii to Iraq*. New York: Henry Holt, 2006.
Kirkland, Robert O. "Fox of the Andes: Colonel Edward Fox and the Bolivian Coup of 1964." *Journal of Intelligence and Counterintelligence*, 18.3 (October 2005), 473–482.
———. *Observing Our Hermanos en Armas: U.S. Military Attaches in Guatemala, Cuba and Bolivia, 1950–1964*. New York: Routledge, 2003.
Kirshner, Joshua David. "Ciudad de Anillos (City of Rings): Internal Migration and Uneven Integration in Santa Cruz, Bolivia." Ph.D. dissertation, Cornell University, 2009.
Klein, Herbert S. *Bolivia: The Evolution of a Multi-Ethnic Society*. Oxford: Oxford University Press, 1982.
———. *Parties and Political Change in Bolivia, 1880–1952*. Cambridge: Cambridge University Press, 1969.
———. "Prelude to the Revolution." In James Malloy and Richard Thorn, eds., *Beyond the Revolution: Bolivia Since 1952*. Pittsburgh, PA: Pittsburgh University Press, 1971, 25–51.
———. "Social Change in Bolivia Since 1952." In Merilee S. Grindle and Pilar Domingo, eds., *Proclaiming Revolution: Bolivia in Comparative Perspective*. London: Institute of Latin American Studies, University of London; Cambridge: David Rockefeller Center for Latin American Studies, Harvard University, 2003, 232–258.
Knight, Alan. "The Domestic Dynamics of the Mexican and Bolivian Revolutions Compared." In Merilee S. Grindle and Pilar Domingo, eds., *Proclaiming Revolution: Bolivia in Comparative Perspective*. London: Institute of Latin American Studies; Cambridge: David Rockefeller Center for Latin American Studies, 2003, 54–90.

Knudson, Jerry. *Bolivia: Press and Revolution, 1932–1964*. Lanham, MD: University Press of America, 1986.

———. *Bolivia's Popular Assembly of 1971 and the Overthrow of Juan José Torres*. Buffalo, NY: Council on International Studies, 1974.

Kohl, Benjamin and Linda Farthing. *Impasse in Bolivia*. London and New York: Zed Books, 2006.

Kohl, James. "Antonio Mamani Álvarez: A Call to Bolivian Indians." *The Journal of Peasant Studies*, 4 (July 1977), 394–397.

———. "Bolivia: Andean Power Shift." *The Progressive* (February 1977), 39–42.

———. "Bolivia Begins the 1970's." *New Politics* (Fall 1973), 48–58.

———. "Che's Revenge: Trouble for Bolivia's Junta." *Ramparts* (October 1973), 18–20.

———. "The Cliza and Ucureña War: Syndical Violence and National Revolution in Bolivia." *Hispanic American Historical Review*, 62 (November 1982), 607–628.

———. "Peasant and Revolution in Bolivia, April 9, 1952-August 2, 1953." *Hispanic American Historical Review*, 58 (May 1978), 238–259.

———. "National Revolution to Revolution of Restoration: Arms and Factional Politics in Bolivia." *Inter-American Economic Affairs*, 39 (Summer 1985), 3–30.

Kohl, James and John Litt, eds. *Urban Guerrilla Warfare in Latin America*. Boston: M.I.T. Press, 1974.

Kovalev, E.V. "The Class Essence and the Significance of the Agrarian Reform in Bolivia." In Robert Carlton, ed., *Soviet Image of Contemporary Latin America*, translated by J. Gregory Oswald. Austin, TX: University of Texas Press, 1970, 189–200.

Ladman, Jerry, ed. *Modern Day Bolivia: Legacy of the Revolution and Prospects for the Future*. Tempe, AZ: Arizona State University Press, 1982.

Lagos, Maria L. *Autonomy and Power: The Dynamics of Class and Culture in Rural Bolivia*. Philadelphia, PA: University of Pennsylvania Press, 1994.

Landívar Flores, Hernán. *Terebinto; drama nacional*. La Paz: n.p, 1966.

Landsberger, Henry, ed. *Latin American Peasant Movements*. Ithaca, NY: Cornell University Press, 1969.

Landsberger, Henry and Cynthia Hewitt. "Ten Sources of Weakness and Cleavage in Latin American Peasant Movements." In Rodolfo Stavenhagen, ed., *Agrarian Problems and Peasant Movements in Latin America*. Garden City, New York: Doubleday, 1970, 559–583.

Langer, Eric D. "Andean Rituals of Revolt: The Chayanta Rebellion of 1927." *Ethnohistory*, 37.3 (1990), 227–253.

———. *Economic Change and Rural Resistance in Southern Bolivia, 1880–1930*. Palo Alto: Stanford University Press, 1989.

———. "Labor Strikes and Reciprocity on Chuquisaca Haciendas." *Hispanic American Historical Review*, 65.2 (May 1985), 255–277.

Langguth, A.J. *Hidden Terrors: The Truth About U.S. Police Operations in Latin America*. New York: Pantheon, 1978.

Lara, Jésus. *Repete: diario de un hombre que fué en la guerra del Chaco*. Cochabamba: Editorial Canelas, 1938.

———. *Surumi: novela quechua*. 2nd ed. Cochabamba: Los Amigos del Libro, 1950.

———. *Yanakuna*. La Paz: Librería y Editorial Juventud, 1958.

Larson, Brooke. "Capturing Indian Bodies, Hearths and Minds: 'El hogar campesino' and Rural School Reform in Bolivia, 1920's-1940's." In Merilee Grindle and Pilar Domingo, eds., *Proclaiming Revolution: Bolivia in Comparative Perspective*. London: Institute of Latin American Studies, University of London; Cambridge, MA: David Rockefeller Center for Latin American Studies, Harvard University, 2003, 183–209.

———. *Colonialism and Agrarian Transformation in Bolivia: Cochabamba, 1550–1900*. Princeton, NJ: Princeton University Press, 1988.
———. "Democratic Progress or Peril? Indigenous and Popular Mobilization in Bolivia." In Gary Bland and Cynthia J. Arnson, eds., *Demoratic Deficits: Addressing Challenges to Sustainability and Consolidation Around the World*, Woodrow Wilson International Center for Scholars, Latin American Program (January 2009), 183–194.
Larson, Brooke and Olivia Harris, with Enrique Tandeter, eds. *Ethnicity, Markets, and Migration in the Andes: At the Crossroads of History and Anthropology*. Durham, NC: Duke University Press, 1995.
Larson, Brooke and Rosario León. "Markets, Power, and the Politics of Exchange in Tapacarí, c. 1780–1980." In Larson and Harris, with Tandeter, eds., *Ethnicity, Markets, and Migration*. Durham, NC: Duke University Press, 1995, 224–255.
Lehm A. Zulema and Silvia Rivera Cusicanqui. *Los artesanos libertarios y la ética del trabajo*. La Paz: Ediciones del THOA, 1988.
Lehmann, Kenneth D. *Bolivia and the United States: A Limited Partnership*. Athens, GA: University of Georgia Press, 1999.
———. "Braked but Not Broken: Mexico and Bolivia; Factoring the United States into the Revolutionary Equation." In Merilee S. Grindle and Pilar Domingo, eds., *Proclaiming Revolution: Bolivia in Comparative Perspective*. Cambridge, MA: David Rockefeller Center for Latin American Studies, Harvard University Press, 2004, 91–113.
Lema Pelaez, Rául. *Con las banderas del movimiento nacionalista revolucionario: el sexenio: 1946–1952*. La Paz: Los Amigos del Libro, 1979.
Leonard, Olen E. *Bolivia: Land, People and Institutions*. Washington, DC: Scarecrow Press, 1952.
Leons, Madeline. "Land Reform in the Bolivian Yungas." *America Indígena*, 27.4 (1967), 689–713.
Leons, Madeline Barbara and William Leons. "Land Reform and Economic Change in the Yungas." In James Malloy and Richard Thorn, eds., *Beyond the Revolution: Bolivia Since 1952*. Pittsburgh, PA: Pittsburgh University Press, 1971, 269–299.
Leons, Madeline Barbara and Harry Sanabria, eds. *Coca, Cocaine and the Bolivian Reality*. Albany, NY: State University of New York Press, 1997.
Levine, Michael with Laura Kavanau-Levine. *The Big White Lie: The CIA and the Cocaine/Crack Epidemic, an Undercover Odyssey*. New York: Thunder's Mouth Press, 1993.
Levy, Ayda. *El Rey de la Cocaína: Mi vida con Roberto Suárez Gómez*. New York: Vintage Español, 2012.
Lieuwen, Edwin. "The Military: A Revolutionary Force." *Annals of the American Academy of Political and Social Science*, 334 (March 1961), 30–40.
Linklatter, Magnus, Isabel Hilton and Neal Ascherson. *The Fourth Reich: Klaus Barbie and the Neo-Fascist Connection*. London: Hodder and Stoughton, 1984.
López Murillo, René. *Los restaurados*. La Paz: Editorial Novedades, 1966.
Lora, Guillermo. *Sindicatos y revolución*. La Paz: Ediciones Masas, 1960.
———. *Tesis de Pulacayo*. La Paz: Ediciones Masas, 1949.
Lord, Peter. "The Peasantry as an Emerging Political Factor in Mexico, Bolivia, and Venezuela." *Land Tenure Center*, 35 (May 1965), Madison, WI.
Loveman, Brian. *No Higher Law: American Foreign Policy and the Western Hemisphere Since 1776*. Chapel Hill: University of North Carolina Press, 2010
Macleod, Murdo. *Bolivia: The Uncompleted Revolution*. Pittsburgh, PA: Pittsburgh University Press, 1970.
———. "The Bolivian Novel, the Chaco War and the Revolution." In James Malloy and Richard Thorn, eds., *Beyond the Revolution: Bolivia Since 1952*. Pittsburgh, PA: University of Pittsburgh Press, 1977, 341–365.

———. "Revolutionary Politics." In James Malloy and Richard Thorn, eds., *Beyond the Revolution: Bolivia Since 1952*. Pittsburgh, PA: Pittsburgh University Press, 1971, 111–156.

Malloy, James and Richard Thorn, eds. *Beyond the Revolution: Bolivia Since 1952*. Pittsburgh, PA: Pittsburgh University Press, 1971.

Mamani Condori, Carlos B. *Taraqu, 1866–1935: masacre, guerra y 'renovación' en la biografía de Eduardo L. Nina Qhispi*. La Paz: Ediciones Aruwiyiri, 1991.

Manchester, William. *American Caesar: General Douglas MacArthur, 1880–1964*. New York: Little, Brown, and Company, 1983.

Marof, Tristán. *La tragedia del altiplano*. Buenos Aires: Claridad, 1935.

Marsh, Margaret. *The Bankers in Bolivia: A Study of American Foreign Investment*. New York: Vanguard Press, 1928,

Maurer, Noel. *The Empire Trap: The Rise and Fall of U.S. Intervention to Protect American Property Overseas, 1880–2013*. Princeton, NJ: Princeton University Press, 2013.

McBride, George McCutchen. "The Agrarian Indian Communities of Highland Bolivia." *American Geographical Society Research Series*, No. 5, 1921.

McEwen, William et al. *Changing Rural Society: A Study of Communities in Bolivia*. New York: Oxford University Press, 1974.

Mendelberg, Uri. "The Impact of Bolivian Agrarian Reform on Class Formation." *Latin American Perspectives*, 12.3 (Summer 1985), 45–58.

Mendoza López, Alberto. *Doctrina del movimiento nacionalista revolucionario*. La Paz: Editorial La Paz, 1952.

———. *La Soberanía de Bolivia*. La Paz: np, 1942.

Meyer, Michael and William Sherman. *The Course of Mexican History*. New York: Oxford, 1991.

Migdal, Joel. *Peasants, Politics and Revolution: Pressures Toward Political and Social Change in the Third World*. Princeton, NJ: Princeton University Press, 1974.

Mitchell, Christopher. *The Legacy of Populism in Bolivia: From the MNR to Military Rule*. New York: Praeger, 1977.

Moller, Edwin A. *El cooperativismo y la revolución*. La Paz: Imprenta "Renovación." 1963.

Montenegro, Carlos. *Culpables*. La Paz: Publicaciones S.P.I.C., 1955.

———. *Nacionalismo y coloniaje*. Buenos Aires: Editorial Pleamar, 1967.

Moseley, Michael E. *The Incas and Their Ancestors: The Archaeology of Peru*. London: Thames and Hudson, 2001.

Murillo, Mario. *La bala no mata sino el destino: una crónica de la insurreción popular de 1952 en Bolivia*. La Paz: Plural Editores, 2012.

Murillo Cardenas, Eliodoro and Gustavo Larrea Bedregal. *Razón de Patria: Villarroel y nacionalismo revolucionario*. La Paz: Editorial Metodista, 1988.

Murra, John. "Verticality and Complimentary." Excerpted in Sinclair Thomson, et al., eds., *The Bolivia Reader*, translated by Alison Spedding. Durham, NC: Duke University Press, 2018, 27–33.

Nash, June. *We Eat the Mines and the Mines Eat Us: Dependency and Exploitation in Bolivian Tin Mines*. New York: Columbia University Press, 1979.

Núñez de Arco B. Carlos. *Relato gráfico de la Revolución de julio de 1946: el pueblo en armas*. La Paz: Editorial Illimani, 1946.

Oikinomakis, Leonidas. *Political Strategies and Social Movements in Latin America: The Zapatistas and Bolivian Cocaleros*. New York, 2018.

Olivera, Oscar in collaboration with Tom Lewis, *¡Cochabamba! Water War in Bolivia*. Cambridge, MA: South End Press, 2004.

Osborne, Harold. *Bolivia: A Land Divided*. 3rd ed. London: Oxford University Press, 1964.

Ostria Gutierrez, Alberto. *Bolivia: Una revolución tras los Andes*. Santiago, Chile: Editorial Nascimiento, 1944.
———. *The Tragedy of Bolivia*. New York: Devin-Adair, 1958.
Paige, Jeffrey. *The Revolution That Never Was*. New York: Grossman, 1972.
Patch, Richard. "Bolivia: Decision or Debacle?" *American Universities Field Staff: West Coast South America Series*, 6 (18 April 1959).
———. "Bolivia: The Restrained Revolution." *Annals of the American Academy of Political and Social Science*, 334 (March 1961), 123–132.
———. "Bolivia: The Seventh Year." *American University Field Staff: West Coast South America Series*, 6.1 (3 February 1959).
———. "Bolivia: U.S. Assistance in a Revolutionary Setting." In Richard Adams et al., eds., *Social Change in Latin America Today*. New York: Vintage, 1960, 108–176.
———. "Bolivia Today: An Assessment Nine Years After the Revolution." *American Universities Field Staff: West Coast South America Series*, 8.4 (17 March 1961).
———. "The Bolivian Falange." *American Universities Field Staff: West Coast South America Series*, 6.4 (May 1959).
———. "The Last of Bolivia's MNR?" *American Universities Field Staff Report: West Coast South America Series*, 11.5 (June 1961).
———. "Social Implications of the Bolivian Agrarian Reform." Ph.D. dissertation, Cornell University, 1956.
Pearse, Andrew. *The Latin American Peasant*. London: Frank Cass, 1975.
Peñaloza, C. Luis. *Historia económica de Bolivia*. 2 Vols. La Paz: Tallares Gráficos Bolivianos, 1953.
———. *Historia del Movimiento Nacionalista Revolucionario, 1941–1952*. La Paz: Editorial Libreria "Juventud." 1963.
Peon, César E. *Historia y mito en la conciencia de un líder campesino boliviano*. Buenos Aires: Instituto de Estudios Histórico-Sociales, 1995.
Pérez, Elizardo. *Warisata: La Escuela Ayllu*. La Paz: Empresa Industrial Gráfica E. Burillo, 1963.
Perkins, John. *Confessions of an Economic Hitman*. New York: Plume, 2006.
———. *The Secret History of the American Empire*. New York: Plume, 2008.
Pettee, George Sawyer. *The Process of Revolution*. New York: Harper, 1938.
Pineo, Ronn. "The Decline of United States Influence and the Rise of Evo Morales." *Council on Hemispheric Affairs* (22 October 2014). www.coha.org/the-decline-of-us-influence-and-the-rise-of-evo-morales/
Platt, Tristan. "The Andean Experience of Bolivian Liberalism, 1825–1900: Roots of Rebellion in 19th Century Chayanta (Potosí)." In Steve J. Stern, ed., *Resistance, Rebellion and Consciousness in the Andean Peasant World: 18th to 20th Centuries*. Madison, WI: University of Wisconsin Press, 1987.
———. *Estado boliviano y ayllu andino: tierra y tributo en el norte de Potosí*. Lima: Instituto de Estudios Andinos, 1982.
———. *Espejos y maiz: temas de la estructura simbólica andina*. La Paz: Centro de Investigación y Promoción del Campesinado, 1976.
———. "Liberalism and Ethnocide in the Southern Andes." *History Workshop Journal*, 17 (Spring 1984), 3–18.
———. "Pensamiento político Aymara." In Xavier Albó, ed., *Raíces de América: El mundo Aymara*. Madrid: Alianza Editorial, 1988, 365–443.
———. "The Role of the Andean Ayllu in the Reproduction of the Petty Commodity Exchange in Northern Potosí." *Cambridge Studies in Social Anthropology*, 41 (1982), 27–69.

Plummer, John. "Another Look at Aymara Personality." *Behaviorial Science Notes*, 1.2 (1966), 55–78.
Prado Salmon, Gary. *Poder y fuerzas armadas: 1949–1982*. Cochabamba: Editorial Los Amigos del Libro, 1984.
Preston, David. *Farmers and Towns: Rural-urban Relations in Highland Bolivia*. Norwich, UK: Geo-Abstracts, 1978.
———. "Life Without Landlords on the Altiplano." *Geographical Magazine*, 41 (1969), 819–827.
———. "New Towns: A Major Change in the Rural Settlement Pattern in Highland Bolivia." *Journal of Latin American Studies*, 2 (1970), 1–27.
Priegue Romero, F. *La Cruz de Bolivia: crónic de la revolución de julio*. La Paz: Editorial Renacimiento, 1946.
Prucha, Francis P. *The Great Father: The United States Government and the American Indian*. Omaha, NE: University of Nebraska Press, 1986.
Querejazu Calvo, Roberto. *Masamaclay: Historia Política, Diplomatica y Militar de la Guerra del Chaco*. La Paz: Empresa Industrial Gráfica E. Burillo, 1965.
Rabe, Stephen G. *The Killing Zone: The United States Wages Cold War in Latin America*. New York: Oxford University Press, 2012.
Ranaboldo, Claudia. *El camino perdido: biografia del dirignte campesino kallawaya Antonio Álvarez Mamani*. La Paz: SEMTA, 1988.
Rand, Christopher. "Letter from La Paz." *The New Yorker* (31 December 1966), 35–48.
Reinaga, Fausto. *La revolución India*. La Paz: Empresa Industrial Gráfica E. Burillo, 1970.
———. *Tesis India*. La Paz: Editoral Fénix, 1971.
———. *Tierra y libertad*. La Paz: Ediciones Rumbo Sindical, 1953.
Rivas Antezana, Sinforoso. *Los hombres de la revolución: memoria de un lider campesino*. La Paz: Plural Editores, 2000.
Rivera Cusicanqui, Silvia. "La expansión del latifundio en el altiplano boliviano: elementos para la caracterización de una oligarquia rural." *Avances*, 2 (1978), 95–118.
———. "Liberal Democracy and Ayllu Democracy in Bolivia: The Case of Northern Potosí." *The Journal of Development Studies*, 26.4 (1990), 97–121.
———. "Luchas campesinas contemporáneas en Bolivia: el movimiento 'Katarista': 1970–1980." In René Zavaleta, ed., *Bolivia Hoy*. Mexico, D.F.: Mex-Sur Editorial, 1982, 129–168.
———. *Oppressed but not defeated; peasant struggles among the Aymara and Qhechwa in Bolivia, 1900–1980*. Geneva: United Nations Research Institute for Social Development, 1987.
———. *Oprimidos pero no vencidos: luchas del campesinado aymara y qhechwa de Bolivia, 1900–1980*. Geneva: United Nations Institute of Social Development, 1986.
Rivera Pizarro, Alberto. *Los terratenientes de Cochabamba*. Cochabamba: CERES/FACES, 1992.
Rodman, Kenneth A. *Sanctity Versus Sovereignty: The United States and the Nationalization of Natural Resource Investments*. New York: Columbia University Press, 1988.
Rolón Anaya, Mario. *Política y partidos en Bolivia*. La Paz: Empresa Editorial Novedades, 1966.
Ruíz, Ramón Eduardo. *The Great Rebellion: Mexico, 1905–1924*. New York: W.W. Norton, 1980.
Sanjinés G., Alfredo. *El hombre de piedra y la revolución*. La Paz: Editorial Artistica, 1946.
Scott, James C. *Domination and the Arts of Resistance*. New Haven: Yale University Press, 1990.

———. *The Moral Economy of the Peasant: Rebellion and Resistance in Southeast Asia*. New Haven: Yale University Press, 1976.
———. *Weapons of the Weak: Everyday Forms of Peasant Resistance*. New Haven: Yale University Press, 1985.
Scott, Rebecca. "Economic Aid and Imperialism in Bolivia." *Monthly Review*, 24.1 (1972), 48–60.
Seleme Vargas, Antonio. *Memorias del Gral. Antonio Seleme Vrgas: mi actuación el la junta Militar con el pronunciamento revolucionario del 9 de abril de 1952*. La Paz: n.p., 1969.
Serrate Reich, Carlos. *¿Qué es profoundizar la revolución?* La Paz: Dirreción Nacional de Informaciones, 1964.
Serulnikov, Sergio. *Subverting Colonial Authority: Challenges to Spanish Rule in Eighteenth-Century Southern Andes*. Durham, NC: Duke University Press, 2003.
Shesko, Elizabeth. "Conscript Nation: Negotiating Authority and Belonging in the Bolivian Barracks, 1900–1950." Ph.D. dissertation, Duke University, 2012.
———. "Constructing Roads, Washing Feet, and Cutting Cane for the *Patria*: Building Bolivia with Military Labor, 1900–1975." *International Labor and Working-Class History*, 80 (Fall 2011), 6–28.
———. "Hijos del inca. El congreso indigenal de 1945." *Fuentes, Revista de la Biblioteca y Archivo Histórico de la Asamblea Legislativa Plurinacional*, 4.6 (2010).
———. "Mobilizing Manpower for War: Toward a New History of Bolivia's Chaco Conflict." *Hispanic American Historical Review*, 95.2 (May 2015), 299–334.
———. "Same as Here, Same as Everywhere": Social Difference among Bolivian Prisoners in Paraguay." In Bridget Mária Chesterton, ed., *The Chaco War: Environment, Ethnicity, and Nationalism*. London, Bloomsbury Academic, 2017.
Shils, Edward. *Political Development in the New States*. Paris: Mouton, 1968.
Siekman, Philip. "When Executives Turned Revolutionaries." *Fortune*, September 1964, 147, 214–216.
Siekmeier, James F. *The Bolivian Revolution and the United States, 1952 to Present*. University Park, PA: Pennsylvania State University Press, 2011.
Simmons, Roger. *Palca and Pucara: A Study of the Effects of Revolution on Two Bolivian Haciendas*. Berkeley, CA: University of California Publications in Anthropology, 1974.
Soliz, Carmen. "Fields of Revolution: The Politics of Agrarian Reform in Bolivia, 1935–1971." Ph.D. dissertation, New York University, 2014.
———. "'Land to the Original Owners': Rethinking the Indigenous Politics of the Bolivian Agrarian Reform." *Hispanic American Historical Review*, 97.2 (2017), 259–296.
Soria Choque, Vitaliano. "Los caciques-apoderados y la lucha por la escuela (1900–1952)." In Roberto Choque Canqui et al., eds., *Educación Indígena: ¿ciudadania o colonización?* La Paz: Aruwiyiri, 1992.
Stavenhagen, Rodolfo. *Las clases sociales en las sociedades agrarias*. Mexico, D.F: Siglo Veintiuno, 1969.
Stern, Steve J., ed. *Resistance, Rebellion, and Consciousness in the Andean Peasant World, 18th to 20th Centuries*. Madison, WI: University of Wisconsin Press, 1987.
Summers, Anthony and Robbyn Swan. *A Matter of Honor, Betrayal, Blame, and a Family's Quest for Justice*. New York: HarperCollins, 2016.
Taboada Terán, Néstor. *Indios en rebelión*. La Paz: Editorial Los Amigos del Libro, 1968.
Taffet, Jeffrey F. *Foreign Aid as Foreign Policy: The Alliance for Progress in Latin America*. New York: Taylor and Francis, 2007.
Thiesenhausen, William C. *Broken Promises: Agrarian Reform and the Latin American Campesino*. Boulder, CO: Westview Press, 1995.

Thomson, Sinclair, Rossana Barragán, Xavier Albó, Seemin Qayum, and Mark Goodale, eds. *The Bolivia Reader: History, Culture, Politics*. Durham, NC: Duke University Press, 2018.
Ticona Alejo, Esteban. "Conceptualización de la educación y alfabetización en Eduardo Leandro Nina Qhispi." In Roberto Choque, et al., eds., *Educación indígena: ¿ciudadanía o colonización?* La Paz: Aruwiyiri, 99–108.
Ticona Alejo, Esteban and Xavier Albó. *La lucha por el poder communal (Jésus de Machaca: La marka rebelde 3)*. La Paz: CIPCA/CEDOIN, 1997.
Toranzo Roca, Carlos F. "Informal and Illicit Economies and the Role of Narcotrafficking." In Madeline Barbara Léons and Harry Sanabria, eds., *Coca, Cocaine, and the Bolivian Reality*. New York, 1997, 195–209.
Turovsky, Paul. "Bolivian Haciendas: Before and After the Revolution." Ph.D. dissertation, University of California, Los Angeles, 1980.
Vallejos, Fermín, Juan Félix, and Pablo Regalsky, eds. *Tata Fermín: llama viva de un Yachaq*. Cochabamba: CENDA, 1995.
Vargas Llosa, Mario. *A Fish in the Water: A Memoir*. New York: Farrar, Straus, Giroux, 1995.
Volk, Steven. "Class, Union, Party: The Development of a Revolutionary Union Movement in Bolivia, 1905–1952." *Science and Society*, 39.1 (Spring 1975), 26–43.
———. "Class, Union, Party: The Development of a Revolutionary Movement in Bolivia (1905–1952): Part II." *Science and Society*, 39.2 (Summer 1975), 180–198.
Webber, Jefrey R. *From Rebellion to Reform in Bolivia: Class Struggle, Indigenous Liberation and the Politics of Evo Morales*. Chicago: Haymarket Books, 2011.
Weeks, David. "Land Tenure in Bolivia." *Journal of Land and Public Utility Economics*, 23 (August 1947), 321–336.
Weiner, Tim. *Legacy of Ashes: A History of the CIA*. New York: Anchor Books, 2008.
Wennergren, E. Boyd and Morris Whitaker. *The Status of Bolivian Agriculture*. New York: Praeger, 1975.
Weston, Charles Jr. "An Ideology of Modernization: The Case of the Bolivian MNR." *Journal of Inter-American Studies*, 10 (January 1968), 85–101.
Whigham, Thomas and Barbara Potthast. "The Paraguayan Rosetta Stone: New Evidence on the Demographics of the Paraguayan War, 1864–1870." *Latin American Research Review*, 34.1 (1999), 174–186.
Whiteford, John H. "Urbanization of Rural Proletarians: Bolivian Migrant Workers in Northeast Argentina." Ph.D. dissertation, University of Texas at Austin, 1975.
Whitehead, Laurence. "Basic Data in Poor Countries: The Bolivian Case." *Bulletin of the Oxford University Institute of Economics and Statistics*, 31.3 (1969), 205–227.
———. "Boliva." In Leslie Bethell and Ian Roxborough, eds., *Latin America Between the Second World War and the Cold War: Crisis and Containment, 1944–1947*. Cambridge: Cambridge University Press, 1992, 120–146.
———. "Bolivia since 1930." In Leslie Bethell, ed., *The Cambridge History of Latin America: Spanish South America*, Vol. 8. Cambridge: Cambridge University Press, 1991, 509–584.
———. "The Bolivian National Revolution: A Twenty-First Century Perspective." In Merilee Grindle and Pilar Domingo, eds., *Proclaiming Revolution*. London: Institute for Latin American Studies, University of London; Cambridge, MA: David Rockefeller Center for Latin American Studies, Harvard University, 2003, 25–53.
———. *A History of the Bolivian Labour Movement, 1848–1971: Guillermo Lora*. Edited and abridged by Laurence Whitehead, translated by Christine Whitehead. Cambridge: Cambridge University Press, 1977.

———. "National Power and Local Power: The Case of Santa Cruz de la Sierra, Bolivia." In Francine Rabinowitz and Felicity Trueblood, eds., *Latin American Urban Research*, 3 (1973), 23–46.

———. "The State and Sectional Interests: The Bolivian Case." *European Journal of Political Research*, 3 (June 1975), 116–146.

———. *The United States and Bolivia: A Case of Neo-Colonialism*. London: Haslemere, 1969.

Wilkie, James. *The Bolivian Revolution and U.S. Aid Since 1952*. Los Angeles, CA: University of California Press, 1974.

———. *Measuring Land Reform*. Los Angeles, CA: University of California Press, 1969.

Wolf, Eric. "Aspects of Group Relations in a Complex Society, Mexico." *American Anthropologist*, 58.6 (December 1956), 1065–1078.

Wood, Bryce. *The Making of the Good Neighbor Policy*. New York: Columbia University Press, 1961.

Worman, Arturo. *We Come to Object: The Peasants of Morelos and the National State*. Baltimore, MD: Johns Hopkins University Press, 1980.

Young, Kevin A. *Blood of the Earth: Resource Nationalism, Revolution, and Empire in Bolivia*. Austin, TX: University of Texas Press, 2017.

Zavaleta Mercado, René. *Bolivia hoy*. Mexico, D.F.: Mex-Sur Editorial, 1982.

———. "Bolivia: Military Nationalism and the Popular Assembly." *New Left Review*, 73 (May–June 1972), 63–82.

Zondag, Cornelius H. *The Bolivian Economy, 1952–1965: The Revolution and Its Aftermath*. New York: Praeger, 1966.

Zulawski, Ann. *Unequal Cures: Public Health and Political Change in Bolivia, 1900–1950*. Durham, NC: Duke University Press, 2007.

Zunes, Stephen. "The United States and Bolivia: The Taming of a Revolution." *Latin American Perspectives*, 28.5 (September 2001), 33–49.

INDEX

Note: Page numbers in *italics* indicate figures and page numbers in **bold** indicate tables on the corresponding page.

1910 Revolution and Bolivian National Revolution 88–89; agrarian reform and 370; ejido program and 361, 306n79; Emiliano Zapata and José Rojas 419–420; U.S. opposition to resource nationalism and 89

Achacachi (La Paz) 2, 7–8, 28–30; attack of 17; Flores, occupation by 311–312; hacendados 35; haciendas 4, 204; peasant invasion of 253; strikes in 124; terratenientes 210; *see also* Altiplano; Omasuyos Province; Salas, Toribio
Achacachi–Warisata conflicts 307–309
Acheson, Dean (U.S. Secretary of State) 160, 168
Achtenberg, Emily 371–373
Agrarian Census of 1950 205, 241n14
agrarian reform 6, 203–240, 344–345, 370; *vs.* agrarian revolution 266–279; and *ayllu comunarios* 243n41; Chuquisaca and Tarija 228–232; Cochabamba Department 224–228, 268–269; colonato regime 204–205; colonization 235–236; cooperatives 233–235; factional conflicts and 278–279; La Paz and Oruro 214–218; and Nationalist Revolutionary Movement (MNR) 173–176; northern Potosí 270–278; Potosí 220–223; regional land tenure variations 213–232; San Pedro de Buena Vista 272–273; Yungas 218–220
Agrarian Reform Commission 176
Agrarian Reform Decree 205–213; and agricultural production 201n57; Article no.132 208, 254; and ayllu communities 176, 204, 250; Barrientos Mamani 301; capitalist change 220; *cocales* (coca plots) 219; as compromise 176; and cooperatives 233; ex-colonos 228; implementation 208–211; indigenous cooperativism and 193; inequality generated by 232; land redistribution 211; land restitution 211–212; land tenure system 203, 205; large estates, exemptions granted to 345; Lower Valley response to 228; and migrants 236; objectives 205; overview 6; paradox of 6; proclamation 176, 192, 251, 264; *Servicio Nacional de Reforma Agraria* (SNRA) 205, 207, 210, 219; and sindicatos 218, 254, 362; social stratification 238; syndical movement 208
Agrarian Reform Law of 1915 142
agrarian revolution 188–191; Cochabamba Department 268–269; and factional conflicts 278–279; northern Potosí 270–278; San Pedro de Buena Vista 272–273

agrarian sindicatos 208, 253–258; administration of land group 256; corruption 257–258; positions 255–256; Spanish-speaking bureaucracy 256; struggle for 176–178; union structure 257; *see also* Agrarian Reform Decree
agrarian syndicalism 264; *see also* Ucureña
Agricultural Bank 60, 234; *see also* Bolivian Agricultural Bank (BAB)
agricultural banks 196n43
agricultural enterprises (Oriente) 236, 345; *see also* Oriente
Aguas de Tunari 366
AIFLD *see* American Institute for Free Labor Development
Albó, Javier *see* Albó, Xavier
Albó, Xavier 277–278, 306, 375n3, 376n19
alcaldes mayores movement *see* Marka T'ula, Santos
Alcaldes Mayores Particulares (AMP) 72, 131–134; feud with alcades mayores 140; and Toribio Miranda and Gregorio Titiriku 25, 152, 352–353
Allende, Salvador 89, 336n86, 355
Alliance for Progress 7, 373; civic action projects 312, 318; and Inter-American Development Bank (IDB) 328; Jukumani–Laymi feud 314–317; and Latin American governments 327–328; and Lechín 302–303; and Ovando 348, 349; and Paz Estenssoro 290, 314–317, 318, 323, 326–327, 331; policy design 8, 290; Triangular Plan 314, 317
Altiplano 214–218, 306–313; Achacachi–Warisata conflicts 307–309; Atahuallpani assassination 309–310; Aymara factionalism 306–307; disease and famine 243n46; factional storm 311–313
Altmann, Klaus *see* Barbie, Klaus
Álvarez, Antonio Mamani *see* Mamani Álvarez, Antonio
Álvarez, Waldo 31–32
Álvarez Plata, Vicente 267, 309
Amaru, Tupac 137, 139, 272, 287n113; Grupo Tupac Amaru 24
American Institute for Free Labor Development (AIFLD) 290
AMP *see* Alcaldes Mayores Particulares
anarchism 122–123, 154n42
Andean highlands 3, 142; Agrarian Reform Decree 235, 362; agrarian rising in 152; apoderados network 24; drought 359; Indian soldiers,

deployment of 17; "Manifesto" (Mamani Álvarez), impact of 69, 191; and Oriente, shift towards 235, 263, 331, 344–345; peasants' exodus from 6, 16, 360; sit-down strikes 62
Anderson, Jon Lee 374
Andes 10, 213–214; ayllus 228, 233, 270, 288n132, 307; beliefs and culture 131, 353; collectivism 22; cooperativism 141, 205; communal labor 234–236; creole-mestizos 176; designs from 72; factionalism 290, 307; "First People" 4; poverty 346; San Pedro de Buena Vista 272; tinku ritual 288n132
Andia, Manuel 132
Andrade, Víctor 49, 51, 91–92
Áñez, Jeanine 374
Anglo-American powers 289
Antezana Ergueta, Luis 84n78, 86n134, 240n9, 244n77
Antonio Arze, José 53
Apaza Mamani, Julio 69, 156n116
apoderado movement 23–27, 38
Aramayo, Carlos Víctor 20, 109n24, 150
Aranha, Oswaldo 51
Arce, Armando 19, 50
Arce Gómez, Luis 357, 358
Argentina 11, 12, 21, 93, 369; Bolivians migrant workers in 230; Operation Condor and 357; Villarroel regime and 51, 93
Arguedas, Antonio 321
Ari Chachaki, Waskar 24, 131, 134
armaments 12, 14, 317–318, 327; military purchase of 56; USAID 317
Arze Loureiro, Eduardo 31, 33, 34, 44–45n106
Asociación de Ex-Prisioneros 48
Asociación de Industriales Mineros 113
Atacama Desert 12, 39n5
Atahuallpani Incident 309–311
August Revolution of 1949 146–148
Auténticos 292, 296, 320
ayllu 5–6, 14–17; and Agrarian Reform Decree 176, 204, 250, 271; Ayca 136; Aymara 2, 35, 131, 133, 221, 270, 278, 306; Cakaj Ana 136; census 221; Challapata 76; Checa 21; Chuquisaca 132; Cochabamba 132; Constitution of 1938 22–23; and creole-mestizos, resistance to 223; dualism 278; Hilata 179; Ialaque 136; Incumbris 136; Jukumani 281, 314–315; Kakachaka 136; lands, fight for return of 89; land,

usurpation of 6, 16, 214–215; Laymi 281, 314–315; Pari 136; Potosí and Northern Potosí Department 220, 223, 271, 273, 313; Quechua 228; Uru 143; Warisata 7, 40, 30, 308; *see also* Andes; Disentailment Law
ayllu comunarios 5–6, 8, 15–16, 25; and agrarian reform 243n41; Charazani 204; and *colonos*, conflicts with 123, 180, 215, 239; and *colonos*, transformation into 122; crops grown by 228–229; and disentailment laws 212, 223; dispossessed 23, 122; disputes and conflicts between 136, 313; Hilata 179; identity as 250; land claims made by 209, 211, 343; land privatization, rejection of 204; sindicatos organized by 199n96, 273; violence against 29
Ayma, Evo Morales 1, 343, 344, 367
Aymara factionalism *see* factionalism
Aymara Indians 2, 3, 14, 17, 24, 25; Black Legend of 306; factionalism 306–307; Katarista movement 351–353; observers of 306
Ayopaya rebellion of 1947 129–131, 155n76, 185, 265, 285n72

Ballivian, Hugo 151, 160
Banco Boliviano Americano 348
Bank of America 348
Banzer Suárez, Hugo: and Carter (Unites States President) 355; dictatorship/military regime 8, 347, 350–351, 353, 363; human rights issues 355; neoliberalism 362; "Popular Nationalist Front" 350; Siracusa on 351; state terrorism 8, 350–351, 354; U.S. aid to 351
Barbie, Klaus 321–322, 357–358
Barrientos Mamani, Zenón 146, 165, 170, 276, 301–302, 304
Barrientos Ortuño, René 8, 147, 289, 319–321; Augusto Cuadros and 162; Brill on 330; and Central Obrera Boliviana (COB) 347; Che's guerrilla *foco* 348, 376n10; Cochabamba political fray 312; and communists 326; death of 348; and Fox 316, 329–332, 341n180; Henderson on 325–326, 330–331; "Magic Bullet" episode 320–321; "Massacre of San Juan" 348; on mines as military zone 347; Pacto Militar-Campesino 327, 347; Paz government, coup against 324–326, 329–331;

political ambitions 322; press description of 319; public works projects 319; Quillacollo coup 313; "Revolution of Restoration" 343; successors 347; USAID-inspired tax on peasant land plots 376n22
Belmonte Letter 52, 88
Belmonte Pabón, Elías 47–48, 52
Bilbao La Vieja, Roberto 113
Black Lung disease *see* silicosis
Blackutt, Jorge 165
Bohan Plan 235, 236, 345
Boland Amendment 358
Bolivian Agrarian Cooperative Bank 142
Bolivian Agricultural Bank (BAB) 345
Bolivian National Revolution 1
Bolivian Power Company 113
Bonsal, Philip W. 91
Braden, Spruille 90–91
Branco, Castelo 329
Brazil 12, 17–18, 52, 61, 89, 203, 329, 332n6, 341n176, 350, 369, 376n12
Brill, William 322, 330
British propaganda campaign 88
Busch, Germán 37, 99; Andrade on 91–92; control of the *divisas* 60; "Day of the Indian" 21; dictatorship 34; and Francisco Chipana 64; Indian marriages 42n53; labor code 21–22, 35, 55, 58; military rule/socialism 20, 21–22, 34–35, 81n27; monastery land sale 34; Nazi consultation and assistance 45n122; reforms 21–22; suicide 34, 35, 39, 45n123
Butrón, Germán 168

caciques (chieftains) 65, 67, 137, 193, 268, 280, 281, 300, 324, 327, 336n83
cacique apoderados 23, 42n54, 42n63, 42n68, 43n71, 46n135, 64
Caciques Inkaicos (*Consejo de Amautas*) 69, 85n115
caciquismo in Northern Potosi 273–278
Calderón, Jaime 324
Calvimontes, Leonidas 46n129
Camacho, Luis Fernando 374
Camiri–TinTin petroleum pipeline 60
Capriles, José A. 33
Caracas Declaration 259–260
Carapata 122, 125
Cárdenas, Víctor Hugo 365
Carita, Pedro 275, 277, 287n124
Carrasco, Julio 65, 117, 128–129
Carrasco, Nicolas 65, 117, 128

Carter, Jimmy 355
Carter, William 182, 198n86, 255
Castro, Fidel 89, 236, 289, 289, 310, 373
Catavi Massacre 114, 115
Catavi-Siglo XX mines 115, 271; 1949 MNR insurrection and 143, 145, 147; layoffs at 115, 121, 261, 359; massacres at 114–115, 271; miners' militias at 304, 317; POR and 114; tin content of 258
Cawasiri, Rosendo 277
Central Intelligence Agency (CIA) (United States) 348; and the Alliance for Progress 290, 313–317, 323, 328; and Barrientos coup 325–327, 329–331; and Barrientos, shooting of ("Magic Bullet" episode) 321–322; and Control Político 323; and the Cuban Revolution 289–290; Mossadeq, coup against 89–90, 94, 96; and the narco-state, creation of 8; and Paz Estenssoro, intelligence assessment of 321–323; Plan TPAJAX 89–90
Central Obrera Boliviana (COB) 360, 362; agrarian sector 264–266; anti-government demonstration 358, 368; Barrientos abolishing 347; *Bloques Reestructuradores* 292; Che Guevara's guerrilla insurgency 349; and CNTCP 254–255; and Cocaine Coup 357; creation 5; and CSUTCB 353; demands 171, 193; Eder's free enterprise agenda 262–263; federations, regional and departmental 177; inaugural session 169–170; leaders of 170; and Lechín 5, 187, 252, 301; and the left-wing 170, 177; and Mamani Álvarez 192; Marxist revolutionaries and 5; mine worker sindicatos under 271; and Natusch Busch 356; Ovando 348; and Paz 171, 314; peasant representatives 254, 255; "Program of Principles" 170; proletarian militias 170; and the right-wing 170, 177; and Rivas 177, 185–186, 187; Siles' "divide and conquer" strategy against 7, 263, 264, 267, 292; strike 263; Triangular Plan 314; Trotskyist and Stalinist politicos influence 169; *Unión Democrática y Popular* (UDP) coalition 359
Céspedes, Augusto 146; Argentine gendarmes, capture by 145; fascist sympathies and anti-Semitism of 51–52, 54–55, 57; as Movimentista 108n43; *Sangre de Mestizos* 19

Chaco Boreal 10–11, 14
Chaco, Generation of the 17–20
Chaco War (1932–1935) 1–2, 10–39; casualties of 13–14; and communism 17; disease 13–14, 37; education in 23–35; Generation of the Chaco 17–20; literature 19–20; resurgence of the Old Order 35–37; rumors of rebellions 17; widows and orphans 59
Chávez, Hugo 89, 369, 373
Chávez, Julian 300
Chávez, Ñuflo 5; and Álvarez 192; and Apanza 191; Cochabamba dispute 147, 180, 188–189; comunarios' appeal to 215; Intransigentes 320; memoirs 197n52; as Minister of Peasant Affairs 172, 174, 177–178, 215, 233, 254; on Plata, demise of 310; Ucureños' loyalty to 267; as Vice President of MNR 5, 170, 261–263, 292; work stoppages, denunciation of 194
Chayanta Province (Potosí Department) 8; ayllus in 221; rebellions 24, 223, 245n82, 272; sindicatos in 313
chicha 226–227, 264–266, 272, 295; taxes on 129, 152, 226, 265, 266, 284nn70–71, 285n72, 297
chicherias 226
Chila, Macabeo 353
Chile 12; Operation Condor 357; overthrow of Salvador Allende 338, 362; war against Bolivia 12, 17, 18, 40n5
Chipana Ramos, Francisco 23; land seizures and 77–78, 136; Ministry of Indian and Peasant Affairs and 174; National Indigenous Committee and 62; National Indigenous Congress and 71–75
cholo/chola 17, 131, 192, 346; acculturated 227; as capitalists and entrepreneurs 215, 219, 226–227; and Cochabamba movement 264; discrimination against 117, 119; in La Paz 119, 121; migrants understood as 246; pejorative connotations of 375n3; and the Rosca counterrevolution 118; *see also* Rivas, Sinforoso; Salas, Toribio
Choque, Lorenza 128
Choroma Central 274, 275–277
Chumacero, Juan 194, 223
Chuquisaca Department 228–230; 1947 rebellion 130–131; AMP Movement in 4, 131–132; sindicatos 199n96, 208
CIA *see* Central Intelligence Agency

Civic Action projects 8, 290, 312–313, 318, 324, 328, 351
Civil War (1949) 4, 146–151, 166, 319
Claure Montaño, Toribio 32–33, 45n110
Cliza 264, 265–266, 297–300; Battle of 7, 185, 264–265, 267, 276, 305; conflict with Ucureña 7, 294–300, 303, 305, 312; sindicato at 31–32, 34, 36, 136, 185, 190
Cliza and Ucureña War 294, 299, 303, 312
CNRA *see* National Agrarian Reform Council
CNTCP *see* Confederación Nacional de Trabajadores Campesinos de Bolivia
COB *see* Central Obrera Boliviana
coca 219–220, 363–364
Cocaine Coup 356–358
cocalero unions 344, 365, 366, 368, 370, 378n57
Cochabamba Department 2, 4, 23, *127*; agrarian reform/revolution 224–228, 268–269; cooperatives 233–234; Great Rebellion 126–130; nuclear school 30–35; peasant movement 264; *see also Razón de Patria*: RADEPA Revolution
Cold War 114, 152, 259, 289, 315, 327, 329, 363
colonization 235–236
COMIBOL *see Corporación Minera de Bolivia*
comunarios: 1953 Agrarian Reform Decree and 212, 239, 243n41, 280, 281n2; boundary disputes and 6, 136, 212, 226, 308, 335n70; conflict with hacendados 15–17, 124–126, 273, 308; conflict with *vecinos* 8, 29, 250, 253; Disentailment and 23, 223, 243n48, 273; Indigenous Committee and 64; land claims and 179–180, 209; National Indigenous Congress and 64, 71–73, 77, 79, 85n117; sindicatos and 199n96, 273; urban migration and 23, 220
Concordancia 35–37, 113
Confederación Nacional de Trabajadores Campesinos de Bolivia (CNTCP) 254, 255
Confederación Sindical Unica de Trabajadores Campesinos de Bolivia (CSUTCB) 353
Constitution of 1938 22–23
Corporación Minera de Bolivia (COMIBOL) 169, 359; creation of 167; effect on 279; income 260; National Revolution, impact on 257–258; Petroleum Code of 1955; rehabilitation of 314
Correa, Rafael 374

corregidores 15–16, 29, 40n30, 72, 130, 152, 308
counter-insurgency 8; ELN and 354; *see also* Alliance for Progress and Mann Doctrine
counterrevolution of 1946 3–4, 53, 57–58, 89–90; collusion between US military attaches and indigenous military officers 96–98; economic sanctions 90–92; financial aid to 98; historiographical note 99–103; isolation of the regime 90; mass demonstrations 95–96; modus operandi 89–90; propaganda campaign 92–95
CSUTCB *see Confederación Sindical Unica de Trabajadores Campesinos de Bolivia*
Cuadros, Augusto 162
Cuadros Quiroga, José: *Movimiento Nacionalista Revolucionario* 78, 83n48, 303; and Nationalist Revolutionary Movement (MNR), fascist wing of 54–56
Cuba 289; Achacachi and 310; cocaine and 356; Evo Morales and 89; Kennedy administration and 313, 327; nationalist revolutions in 290; U.S. opposition to Cuban Revolution 289, 327

Danhart, Jorge 128
da Silva, Luiz Inácio Lula 369
Delgadillo Vasquez, Desiderio 31
Delgadillo Vasquez, Pedro 31
delle Chiaie, Stefano 358
Diez de Medina, Fernando 19–20
Disentailment Law 23, 42n60, 204, 212, 215, 223, 229
Drug Enforcement Agency (DEA) 363, 373, 377n31, 378n48
Dulles, Alan 259
Dulles, John Foster 259

Eder, George Jackson 261–264
education 2, 18, 22, 62–65, 176–177, 212; *Alcaldes Mayores Particulares* and 131, 176; Antonio Mamani Álvarez and 69–70; Eduardo Leandro Nina Qhispi and 38, 43n76; *escuelas particulares* 132, 134, 176; Indigenous Committee and 66, 68; Methodist Church and 82n36; military and 20, 36, 324; MNR and 54, 239, 249n162, 257, 351–352, 375n5; Movement Towards Socialism (MAS) and 371, 374; National Indigenous Congress and 74; New Economic Policy (NEP) and 360; RADEPA and 48;

Santos Marka T'ula and 23–25, 27, 37, 152; Vacas school 31–34; Warisata and 27–29, 30
Eisenhower, Dwight 169, 236, 258–259, 279; and covert warfare 106n5, 289
Escobar, Federico 315
Escobar, Pablo 358
escuelas particulares (clandestine schools) 132, 134, 176
Espinal, Luis 357

factionalism 6, 8, 291, 352; Achacachi-Warisata conflict and 306–307; *ayllu* and 279, 307, 335n71; Cliza-Ucureña conflict and 298–299; Kataristas and 352, 365; Laymi-Jukumani feud and 192, 278–281; MNR and 50, 78, 90, 115, 281, 292, 303, 308; sindicatos and 184, 279, 292
FAD *see Federación Agraria Departamental*
Falange Socialista Boliviana (FSB) 54; 1953 revolt by 252; 1956 election and 258; 1958 revolt and Terebinto Massacre of 323; Banzerato and 350; death of Jefe Oscar Unzaga de la Vega 143, 323; MNR conspiracy with 54, 116, 160
Falangist uprising 251–252
Fanon, Frantz 156
fascism 54; Anglo-American propaganda and 92–93, 105, 259; MNR and 83n42
Federación Agraria Departamental (FAD) 121–126, 135–136, 140
Federación del Trabajo de Oruro (FOT) 17
Federación de Obreros Sindicales (FOS) 65–67, 70, 72
Federación Obrera Local (FOL) 121–126, 135, 136, 154n42, 164
Federación Sindical de Trabajadores Campesinos de Cochabamba (FSTCC) 177, 185–188, 293, 296, 298
Federación Sindical de Trabajadores Mineros de Bolivia (FSTMB) 114, 115, 313
Federación Syndical Agraria de Bolivia (FSAB) 138
Fellman Velarde, José 54, 145, 166, 330n134
Ferrufino, Octavio 132
Field, Thomas, Jr. 315, 316
Finot, Alfonso 102, 116
First City National Bank 348
First Inter-American Indigenous Congress 29
Flores, Felipe 310–312, 324

Flores, Genaro 352–353, 357
Flores, Gonzalo 86n134
FOL *see Federación Obrera Local*
Fortún Sanjinés, Federico 319
FOT *see Federación del Trabajo de Oruro*
Fox, Edward 316, 320, 329–331
Frente Democrático Antifascista (FDA) 3, 95–97, 100–102; counterrevolution and 102, 108n37, 109n52, 110n64; Sexenio and 112–116, 118–119
Friedman, Max Paul 52, 106n9
Frontaura Argandoña, Manuel 53, 87n148
FSAB *see Federación Syndical Agraria de Bolivia*
FSB *see Falange Socialista Boliviana*
FSTCC *see Federación Sindical de Trabajadores Campesinos de Cochabamba*
FSTMB *see Federación Sindical de Trabajadores Mineros de Bolivia*

Galarza, Alejandro 264, 276, 298, 302
Galarza, Ernesto 9n1, 93–94, 96, 107n24
Galindo, Nestor 52
Gallardo, Melitón 72, 132–134, 156n102, 196n49
García, Antonio 72, 131–134, 234
García Linera, Álvaro 368–369
García Meza, Luis 196n31, 356–358, 363
Gas War 367–368
Generation of the Chaco *see* Chaco, Generation of the
Godoy, Ricardo 278
Goitia, Sanjinéz 324–325
Golinger, Eva 373
Good Neighbor Policy 88, 92, 104
Gordillo, José 177–178, 190, 266, 274
Gosalvez, Gabriel 150–151
Gosalvez Indaburu, Luis 113
Gotkowitz, Laura: chicha tax and rebellion 285n72; dual power 46n135; hacendado legal domain 129; Villarroel decrees 86n141; Villarroel overthrow 102–103
government corruption 257–258
Grájeda, Hilarión 130, 135, 185; and Ayopaya rebellion 129–130, 185; and the hacienda, organized resistance to 117, 128; imprisonment and death sentence of 129, 135; National Indigenous Committee, member of 64–66, 70–71, 73, 105
Gran Chaco 12, 39n8, 148
Great Depression 10, 39n2
Great Rebellion 118–134; Chuquisaca Department 130–131; Civil War

146–151; Cochabamba Department 126–130; *escuelas particulares* 132; La Paz Department 119–126; prelude to 133–134
Guaqui 16, 25, 59, *120*; and anarchism 122; and Marxist revolutionaries 177; union organization in 121; unrest in 123
Guatemala: CIA and 86n144, 89, 106nn5–6, 259, 289–290, 330; MNR and 29, 89, 104, 106n5, 203, 204, 259, 260, 289
Gueiler Tejada, Lydia 145
Guerra, Juan 34, 36, 37, 268
Guevara Arze, Wálter 320; agrarian reform 22, 301–302; Auténtico Nationalist Revolutionary Movement (PMNRA) 292, 296, 302, 320; Cochabamba campaign 292–294; Cochabamba prefect 187; colonization of the Oriente 174; Eder's plan 262, 263; and *Federación Sindical de Trabajadores Campesinos Cochabambinos* (FSTCC) 293; Gildner on 198n80; as interim president 356; José Rojas on 300; Junta and 52; land reform 78, 177, 296; on military zones 298–299; on Nationalist Revolutionary Movement (MNR), utilization of military by 299; nationalization of mines 22; and Paz Estenssoro and 292, 294, 296, 302, 321; presidential campaign 302; as right-wing theoretician 172, 297; and Rosca, overthrowing of 166; and Salvador Vásquez 297
Guillen, Néstor 113
Gulf Oil 260, 279, 331, 348, 349
Gutierrez, Eliseo 311, 324
Gutiérrez, Monje 113

Hacienda Santa Clara 30–32, 38, 45n108, 179, 180, 184, 185, 187, 226
Harris, Olivia 277
Heath, Dwight 86n146, 198n86; on *patrón* as peasant *dirigent* 288n134; Yungas, study of 234
Henderson, Douglas 320–321, 324–327, 329–330
Hertzog Garaizabal, Enrique: agricultural cooperatives, plans for 156n110; Ayopaya rebellion, response to 129; "colonies" 126; Concordancia 113; *Federación Obrera Local* (FOL), clash with 124; indigenous threat, maneuvers to counter 118–119, 122; *Partido Unión Socialista Republicana* (PURS) 144; presidency, end of 145; reforms introduced by 134–135; regime of 113–114, 125, 135; Rosca repression 134; rural inspectors 153n8; "Sexenio" 58
Hochschild, Mauricio 34, 91, 99–100; arrest of 53; kidnapping of 52; law firm of 113; mines held by 149, 167
Hughes, Matthew 12
Hugo Cárdenas, Víctor 360–361
Hull, Cordell 50–51, 83n60, 90, 92
Hull Doctrine 168, 259, 260
Hylton, Forrest 41n45, 368, 378n60

Inca Empire 139, 142, 192, 228, 233, 266, 306
Indigenous Committee 3, 63–70, 84n87, 152, 185–186
indigenous nationalism 19, 43n83, 62, 132, 152, 191
Ingavi Regiment 165, 318, 326
INRA *see* National Agrarian Reform Institute
insurrection (9–11 April 1952) 4–5, 161–162, 195n17, 296; 1949 Civil War and 146, 151; FDA and 93, 95; FSB and 252, 282n9; Gas War and 367–368, 378n60
Inter-American Development Bank (IDB) 314, 328
International Mining and Processing Corporation 348
International Monetary Fund (IMF) 261, 331, 359, 360, 369
Iran 3, 89–90, 92, 94–96, 98, 104–105, 259, 289

Johnson, Chalmers 20, 41n46, 110n73
Johnson, Lyndon 328, 330, 355
José Torres, Juan 348–349, 376n10

Kallawaya 85n112, 156n116; *see also* Mamani Álvarez, Antonio
Katari, Tupac 73, 272, 286n96
Katarista movement 351–353, 365, 376n19
Kennedy, John F. 290, 313, 315–317, 327–328, 341n175
Kirkland, Robert 329–330
Kissinger, Henry 336n85, 351, 355
Kollasuyu Educational Society 26
Kovalev, E. V. 209

La Calle 19
land: distribution of **207**, 207–208; redistribution 211; *see also* agrarian reform

land ownership 370; by type of unit **208**
land tenure variations 213–232; Chuquisaca and Tarija 228–232; Cochabamba 224–228; La Paz and Oruro 214–218; Potosí 220–223; Yungas 218–220
Langer, Eric 229
Lansdale, Edward 329
La Paz: agrarian reform 214–218; anarchism 122; dress codes 119; Great Rebellion 119–126; land disputes 125–126; population of 121; sit-down strikes 124; violence 124–126
Lara, Jesus 19
Larson, Brooke 365
latifundia 63; agrarian reform and 205, 208, 211, 219, 229, 233, 238; COB and 170; MAS and 371; Oriente and 345, 362
Law of Popular Participation (LPP) 361, 377n41
Laymi *see* Jukumani–Laymi blood feud
League of Nations 12
Lechín Oquendo, Juan: and Álvarez, denunciation of 192; and Banzer (General) 355; and Barrientos 319; and capture of 252; chica tax, views on 285n72; as COB leader 252, 263, 271, 292, 301; Cochabamba Department, revolutionary struggle led by 233; coup against 329; Executive Secretary of COB trade union 169; *Federación Sindical de Trabajadores Mineros de Bolivia* (FSTMB), leadership of 58, 130, 145, 169, 313, 347; golpe against 319; Guevara Arze, accusations against 300; hostage crisis 317; Izquierdista support 311–313, 316; as Labor Minister 177, 254; as mestizo 60; militia protection of 339n138; as Minister of Mines and Petroleum 168, 172; as Nationalist Revolutionary Movement (MNR) leftist-Marxist leader 5, 54, 261–262, 281, 302–303, 305; and Paz Estenssoro 322–323; presidential bid 309, 329, 331; Radio Illimani, occupation of 162; and Rivas 186–188, 201n140; Sala's support of 8, 310; as senator of Ororo 114; and Torres (General) 349; Triangular Plan, thwarting of 261, 316–317, 331; United States actions against 316–317
Legión Cívica 15
Legión de Ex-Combatientes 20, 31, 38, 69–70, 191
Lenin, Vladimir 130

Leons, Madeleine Barbara 219–220, 253–254
Linera, Álvaro García 368–369
Llarrea Bedregal, Gustavo 53
Local Workers Federation *see Federación Obrera Local* (FOL)
López España, Ángel 163–164
López Murillo, René 340n149
Lora, Guillermo 114, 153n12, 153n13

Madero, Francisco 57, 80, 166, 269
"Magic Bullet" episode 320–321, 322
Mamani, Marcelini 134
Mamani Álvarez, Antonio 14, 85n117, *118*, 191–193; "A Call to Bolivian Indians," distribution of 146, 166; as "Chaco Generation" 18–19, 23; and Chávez (Ñuflo) 177; and Chipana Ramos 74, 135; education and literacy, support of and advocacy for 152, 157n20, 175; FAD rebellions, criticism of 140; with Gabino Apaza *173*, 177; and Grájeda, support offered by 128; as Kallaway 68–69, 71–72, 137, 152, 157n123, 191–193; marginalization of 201n152; as member of Ministry of Indian and Peasant Affairs 174; and National Indigenous Committee 63–65; and National Indigenous Congress 72–73; and National Revolution, oppression by 105; "Pact of Alliance," 196n43; and the Second Indigenous Committee 68–71; and *Tesis of Caranguillas* 136–139, 166, 193
Mamani Condori, Carlos 9n1, 40n23, 41n30
Mann Doctrine 8, 328–329, 331, 355
Mann, Thomas 161, 328
Marcos Mamani, Samuel 324
Marka T'ula, Santos 18, 24–26, 38, 69, 72; dual power and 46n135; FOL and 121–122; land revindication and 24–37, 42n66, 70, 131, 152; sitdown strikes and 72
Massacre of Terebinto 323
Melgarejo, Mariano 204, 221, 240n9, 244n77, 319
Mendoza, Jaime 17, 41n38
Mesa, Carlos 368
Mexican Agrarian Law 142–143, 157n124
Mexican Revolution of 1910 and Bolivian National Revolution 88–89; agrarian reform and 370; ejido program and 361, 306n79; Emiliano Zapata and José Rojas

419–420; U.S. opposition to resource nationalism and 89
Mexico 21, 29, 46, 57–58; Disentailment Law of 1856 204; Madero (President) 80; Mexico City 269; United States' intervention in 105
military institution 2, 5, 7, 20, 207; caudillismo and 97; MNR and 171–172, 179, 197n70, 197n73; Paz Estenssoro and 260, 322, 323, 331, 356; race and class in 41n34; RADEPA and 48, 58; Revolution of Restoration and 327; U.S. military assistance and 338n119
military socialism 20–23
military socialists 2, 20–22, 31–35, 37–38, 79
Mine Workers Federation *see Federación Sindical de Trabajadores Mineros de Bolivia* (FSTMB)
minifundismo 6, 141, 174, 209, 345; and agrarian reform 239; predicament of 302; and urban migration 235, 244n64, 347
Miranda, Dionisio 64–66, 73, 185–187
Miranda, Toribio 192; and *Alcades Mayores Particulares* 25, 131–132, 152, 353
mitinaje 63, 66, 72, 76, 119, 174; *see also pongueaje*
MITKA *see Movimiento Indio Tupac Katari*
MNR *see* Nationalist Revolutionary Movement
Mobile Police Unit for Rural Areas (UMOPAR) 365, 378n44
Monetary Stabilization Plan 260–264, 279–280
Monroe Doctrine 259
Monroy Block, Germán 178
Montenegro, Carlos 19, 51, 54–56, 81n13, 108n42
Morales, Evo 1, 9, cocaleros and 351, 367–370; Gas War and 373; MAS and 371–373; "Pink Tide" and 374; Plurinational State and 371–375; U.S. opposition to 373, 379n70
Mossadegh, Mohammed 3, 89, 106n6
Mostajo, Moreira 267
Movement Toward Socialism (MAS) 367; *see also* Morales, Evo
Movimientistas 4, 301, 307; and "Agrarian Party," response to 117; and Auténticos, contest between 296; and Civil War 146–148, 150–151; divisions, conflicts, and factionalism among 280, 295; exposure of and threats to 112–113,

115; government accusations against 136; indigenous agrarian revolutionaries betrayed by 188, 192–193; legislators 55; massacre of 145; militants 100, 143, 146; nationalism envisioned by 175; National Union of Factory Workers (USTFN), relationship with 116; and Pinto (Colonel), distrust of 50; profiteering by 262; reform, efforts at 176; and Revolution 159–166; right-wing 5, 7, 177, 264, 292, 309; the Rosca, oppression by 118, 152; Salas' assassination of 8; Sexenio, opposition to and repression by 143, 151, 171; sindicatos, organization and control of 253, 298; *see also* Álvarez Plata, Vicente; Barrientos, René; Céspedes, Augusto 108; Chávez, Ñuflo; Fellman Velarde, José; Finot, Alfonso; Guevara Arze, Walter; Lechín, Juan; Nogales, Edmundo; Paz, Victor; Peñaloza, Luis; Pérez Patón, Roberto; Rojas, José
Movimiento Nacionalista Revolucionario (manifesto) 56, 78
Movimiento Indio Tupac Katari (MITKA) 353
MRTK *see Tupac Katari Revolutionary Movement*
Muñoz, Gabriel 128–129, 135
Muñoz Roldan, Carlos 113
Murillo Cardenas, Eliodoro 53
Murillo Plaza *see* Plaza Murillo
Mussolini, Benito 9n2, 93, 109n61

National Agrarian Reform Council (CNRA) 266–267
National Agrarian Reform Institute (INRA) 362, 370
National Council of Education 35
National Indigenous Committee 63–68
National Indigenous Congress 3, 71–78; indigenous history and 62; nationalisms and 62; Supreme Decrees of 1945 75–78
nationalism, indigenous 62–78
Nationalist Revolutionary Movement (MNR) 3, 54–57, 115–117; agrarian reform 173–176; agrarian revolution 188–191; agrarian sector 264–266; August Revolution of 1949 146–148; Civil War 146–151; clandestine cell structure 161; command and control 116, 161; economic sovereignty 167–169; election of 1949 144–145; election of 1951 151; electoral victory of 1956 263–264; failures 116; finances

of 116; founding manifesto 56; hunger strike 117; insurrection (9–11 April, 1952) 161–165; internal conflict 116; leftists 261; military institution 171–172; Monetary Stabilization Plan 260–264; national elections of 1947 113; Oruro 165–166; peasantry 166–167; peasants and proletarians 169–171; Petroleum Code 260; right-wing 261; special sectors 116; strategy 145; survival 112, 115–116; tin mines 167–169; universal suffrage 171; U.S. government and 258–264; women 145–146; working class membership 145
National Revolution 1; Alliance for Progress 313–317; Altiplano 305–315; as authoritarian police state 290; and factionalism 290–305; final years of 289; overthrow 88–103, 317–323; redux 167; survival of 323–331; United States government 323–331
National Union of Factory Workers (USTFN) 116
Natusch Busch, Alberto 356
Navarro, Gustavo 94
Nazis: Anglo-American propaganda and 89, 90–91, 93–95; FDA and 93; Klaus Barbie/Altmann and 358, 377n33; MNR and 55, 57; Paz Estenssoro and 321, 339n137; RADEPA and 48–52, 81–82, 102; U.S. historiography and 102–103
neocolonialism 56, 258–262, 279, 315, 352
neoliberalism, indigenous opposition to 359–368; decades of 359–362; Gas War 367–368; unions, confederations, parties, and protests 365–366; war on drugs 364–365; Water War 366–367
Nery, Wilge 314–317
New Economic Policy (NEP) 360–361
Nicaragua 104, 283n45, 358, 373
Nina Qhispi, Eduardo Leandro 18–19; Centro Educativo Kollasuyu 26–27, 46n135, 352; Republic of Kollasuyu and 25–27, 38
Nixon, Richard 336n85, 355
Nogales, Edmundo 66–68, 73, 85n117, 163, 266–267
North, Oliver 358
Northern Potosí: ayllus in 220–224, 273–274; agrarian reform and revolution 270–278; caciquismo in 273–278; comunario-vecino conflict in 271–279; map of 270

nuclear schools 2, 29; creation of 29–30; hacendado assault on 35; sindicato 30–32

Office for Transition Initiatives (OTI) 373
Olivera, Oscar 368, 378n55
Olmos, Facundo 311, 312–313, 319
Operation Condor 357, 377n29, 377n31
Organizaciones Territoriales de Base (OTB) 361
Organization of American States (OAS) 259
Oriente 9; and the Agrarian Reform Decree (1953) 362; agro-business of 236, 320; Bohan Plan 345; and Carangas Province, trade with 214; cartels and cocaine 357, 360; colonization of 58, 174, 193, 235, 344–347, 373; Comité Pro Santa Cruz and 373; economic development 345; flooding in 359; and Guevara Arze 174; indigenous peoples of 132, 156n110, 362, 367; migration to 239, 373; missions, Franciscan and Jesuit in 137; and Movement Toward Socialism (MAS), threat to 371; and the National Revolution 354; and Nazi war criminals 331; oil production 10; peasants, migration to 6, 239, 370; and Potosí Department, trade with 220; prison camps of 135; and *Razón de Patria* (RADEPA) 58, 174, 193; shift of national power to 8; United States policy makers, interference with 263, 331; USAID and 263–264; *see also* cocaine; Hertzog
Ormachea Zalles, Héctor 95–96, 99–100, 109n52
Oruro: agrarian reform 214–218, 271; FOS in 66, 70; FSB revolt in 250; Katarista movement in 351–353; miners and 1964 coup in 325–326; MNR revolution and 165, 196n35, 303; peasant-miner alliances in 267, 295; peasant uprisings in 243n49; Republic of Peñas and 43n83; Rosca coup in 53, 94, 100; sit-down strikes 63, 65; U.S. military and 318
Oruro Federation of Union Workers 65
Oruro Rural Society 62, 63
Oruro Workers Federation 121
Ostría Gutiérrez, Alberto 47
Otazo, Rafael 52, 69, 116–118, 143
OTB *see Organizaciones Territoriales de Base*
Ovando Candía, Alfredo 171, 294, 320, 350; attempted coup (1953) led by

170; as conspirator in military *golpe de estado* 313, 326, 330; coup d'état (1964) led by 289, 325, 330–331, 341n179; institutionalist faction represented by 322; Military Institutionalist 322; Nationalist Revolutionary Movement (MNR)'s strategy 166; pacification commission led by 299–300; Presidency of 348–350; "Revolution of Restoration" 331, 334n37, 347–349

Pachakamak movement 135, 138–140, 142–143, 152
pachakuti 41n45
Pachamama 132, 134, 176
Pacto Militar-Campesino Anticomunista 322–323, 347, 349, 353, 376n22
Paraguay 10, 11, 12; *see also* Chaco War
Pareda Asbún, Juan 355
Partido Obrero Revolucionario (POR) 17, 31–32, 37; Agrarian Reform Decree and 176; *entrismo* and 197n61, 201n140, 253; Hertzog and 134; Indigenous Committee and 64; MNR and 170; sindicatos and 176, 188, 189, 271; *Tesis de Pulacayo* and 114
Partido Unión Socialista Republicana (PURS) 113, 144, 149–150
"Partners of the Americas" 373
Patch, Richard 322–323
Patiño, Antenor 115
Paz Estenssoro, Víctor 374; and agrarian reform 172, 205–212, 215, 239, 266; on Allies-Axis confrontation 55; armed forces, reinstitution of 194; assassination attempt on 95; and August Revolution 146, 148; and authoritarianism 320–323; and Central Obrera Boliviana (COB) 171, 314; civic action 318; Control Politico 260; corruption 257–258; coup/military overthrow of 324–326, 329–331, 343; divide and conquer strategy 190; as elected president 4; election of 1960 302–305; election of 1985 362; elections of 1947 113; elections of 1951 151, 160; *Federación Sindical de Trabajadores Campesinos Cochabambinos* (FSTCC) rally 187; and Guevara Arze 292, 294, 296, 302, 321; indigenous miners and peasants resistance 8; Izquierdista caciques 311; Jukumani–Laymi feud 314–317; and Junta 52; land reform 78; "Magic Bullet" episode 322; Marxist faction of Nationalist Revolutionary Movement (MNR) 54; militant miners and 347; military buildup 318; MITKA and 353; modernization of nation 22; nationalistic position 192; neoliberalism/Decree 21060 359–360, 362; as orator 49; and Otazo 116; Petroleum Code 260; and Pinto 50, 96–97; retaining military institution against Nationalist Revolutionary Movement (MNR) leftists 5, 172, 331; and Rivas 186; second term of 290, 292, 318; social welfare programs 59; state ownership of subsoil rights 22; and tin magnates 60; Triangular Plan 314, 316–317; United States aid/support 258–260, 313; United States' propaganda against 93; and Veizaga 296–297, 301, 303–304, 305; and Villarroel 49–50, 53, 102, 103; "war on drugs," indigenous resistance to 365
Pearse, Andrew 250, 256–257
Peñaloza, Luis 109n45, 113, 116, 143, 145, 170, 301
Peñaranda, Enrique 35, 47, 52, 55, 63, 81n25
Pérez, Elizardo 27–29, 35, 43n87, 307–308
Pérez Patón, Roberto 267
Perón, Juan Domingo 93
Petroleum Code 260
Philips Brothers Petroleum 348
Pinochet, Augusto 355–357
PIR *see* Party of the Revolutionary Left
Plan TPAJAX 89–90
Platt, Tristan 204, 223
Plummer, John 306
Plurinational State of Bolivia 38, 370–373, 375
Poder Democrático y Social (PODEMOS) 371
pongo 70, 76, 135, 277
pongueaje 117; abolition of 122, 135, 174, 204–205; absence of 271; attempts to abolish 34–37, 66, 68–70, 72, 76; as colonato obligation 63, 225, 230, 272; and hacendados 119; FAD and 122–123; Hertzog and 134; Indigenous Committees and 65–67, 68–69; National Indigenous Congress and 76, 117, 119; Villarroel decrees and 174, 205
poverty 346
power shift 354–358
prebendalismo 257, 268, 276–277; and political opportunism 280
Preston, David 308
Primera Asamblea de Directores Indigenistas 33

Pro-Santa Cruz Committee 371
PURS *see Partido Unión Socialista Republicana*

Qhispe, Mariano 72, 134
Qhispi, Nina 38
Quilluma (Hacienda) 122
Quintanilla, Carlos 34, 35
Quispe, Felipe 368
Quispe, Luciano 308
Quispe Yucra, Esteban 121, 125
Quispe Yucra, Marcelino 121–122, 125–126, 135

RADEPA Revolution 2–3, 47–49; decolonization and 79; Gualberto Villarroel and 49–61; indigenous nationalism and 62–76; indigenous responses to Villarroel Supreme Decrees 76–79; national integration and 61, 78, 79–80; resource nationalism and 60–61; social rights and social welfare 59–60
Radio Illimani: FDA and 95, 97; MNR and 101, 162–163
Ramos, Antonio 128–129
Ramos Quevedo, Luis 65, 66, 70, 185; Antonio Mamani Álvarez and 69–70; Rural Society and 67; Villarroel regime and 68, 73, 105
Razón de Patria (RADEPA) Revolution 2–3, 47–80; agenda 48; indigenous nationalism 62–78; indigenous social rights 61–62; Junta, non-recognition of 50–54; membership 48; national integration 60–61; Nationalist Revolutionary Movement (MNR) 54–57; Nazi-fascists, branding as 92; objectives of 58–62; resource nationalism 60–61; social revolution 57–58; social rights and welfare 59–60; sovereignty 60–61; and Villarroel 48–50
Reinaga, Fausto 116
Republican Society of Kollasuyu 25–27
resource nationalism 60, 62, 104, 106n4, 167–169; MAS and 369; Ovando and 348; U.S. and 104, 258, 262, 279, 289
Revuelta, Antonio 34
Revuelta Padilla, Wálter 276–277, 294
Rivas, Sinforoso 296, 311; and Bustamente 185; as Cochabamba sindicato leader 6, 177, 233, 264; as dirigente of Valle Bajo cuartels 192, 251; *Federación Sindical de Trabajadores Campesinos Cochabambinos* (FSTCC), leadership of and attempts to unseat 188; First Departmental Congress of Cochabamba Campesinos 190; Galarza, replacement by 264; National Agrarian Reform Council (CNRA), appointment to and removal from 266–267; Quillacollo militia, use of 281; and Rojas, rivalry with 186, 189, 193, 281, 293–294
Rivas Ugalde, Eduardo 299, 313
Rivera Cusicanqui, Silvia 281, 296
Rojas Guevara, José: arrest of 136; and Guerra 268–269; and indigenous rights, struggle for 18, 184–190, 193, 264, 265–266; as Jefe of agrarian revolution (Cochabamba Department) 6–7, 268–269; and López (Gregorio), competition with 324; and Massacre of Terebinto 323; Minister of Peasant Affairs 292; and Ucureña Central 276–277, 281, 292–300, 322; and Veigaza, vendetta against 304, 312–313; and Zapata, comparisons to 268–269; *see also Federación Sindical de Trabajadores Campesinos Cochabambinos* (FSTCC); Movimientista; Veigaza, Miguel
Roosevelt, Franklin 12–13
Royal Dutch Shell 260
Rusk, Dean 316, 320, 323, 331

Salamanca, Daniel 10–12, 16, 20, 264
Salas, Toribio 192, 308–309
San Pedro de Buena Vista 272–273, 277–278
San Román, Claudio 311, 316, 321–323; *Control Político* and 311, 317, 323; covert activity and 316; Nazis and 321; racketeering and 323
Santa Cruz de la Sierra 236, 354, 375n4
Second Indigenous Committee 68–71
Seleme Vargas, Antonio 160, 161–162
Servicio Nacional de Reforma Agraria (SNRA) 209, 213, 227; bureaucracy 210, 231; hacendados' influence on 207; land, powers to grant 219; purpose of 205; shortcomings 241n22
Sexenio 4, 58, 99; Civil War 146–151, 166, 319; indigenous resistance to Hertzog government 130, 151; MNR and resistance to 112, 116, 151, 161, 166, 174; *see also* Great Rebellion
Shell Oil Company 260
Siles Zuazo, Hernán: agrarian reform 173, 177, 230; agrarian revolution 7; amnesty, exclusion from 355;

Atahuallpani Incident 309–311; and Banzer (General) 355; *Bloque de la Revolución* 320; and the Cochabamba region 304; "divide and conquer" strategy 264, 267, 280; Insurrection of 1952 160, 162–163, 166–167; as mestizo 60; as Movimentiesta 150, 292; and Nationalist Revolutionary Movement (MNR) 54, 78, 302, 323, 347, 353; National Socialism, admiration for 82n38; pacification commission 300; as presidential candidate 160; regime of 292–293, 299, 304; and Seleme Vargas (General) 162; Stablization Plan 261–264, 314, 318; and Terrazas (General) 160; *Unión Democrática y Popular* (UDP) coalition 356, 359; vice-presidency 151
Siñani Cosme, Avelino 28, 29, 35, 44n89
Siñani, Julian 44n89, 44n91
Siñani, Miguel 44n91
sindicato *see* agrarian sindicatos
Sindicato de Agricultores y Educatores de Cliza 36–37
Sindicato de Labradores (Farmworkers' Union) 122
Sindicato de Trabajadores Agrarios de Vacas 33
Siracusa, Ernest 350, 351, 376n23
Sisa, Bartolina 272
sit-down strikes 62, 63, 65–67, 70, 122–124, 130–132; anarcho-syndicalists, promoted by 4; *Federación de Obreros Sindicales'* (FOS) promotion of 72; and the hacienda 117, 122, 152, 179, 185; "Indigenous Committee," initiated by 3; Manuel Andia, organized by 132; National Indigenous Committee, support of 64, 70; Nationalist Revolutionary Movement (MNR)'s denunciation of 31; proliferation of 77; Ramos Quevado as architect of 65
SNRA *see Servicio Nacional de Reforma Agraria*
social revolution 1–2, 10, 18, 37, 82n37; MNR redux of 161–167, 193, 343–347; RADEPA as 58–62; U.S. cooptation of 260–266, 289
social rights: indigenous struggle for 18, 22, 61, 152; Plurinational State and 370, 371, 375; RADEPA/Villarroel regime and 3, 58–61, 78–80
Sociedad Centro Educativo Kollasuyu 26, 352; *see also* Nina Qhispi

Sociedad Rural: and Altiplano, unrest in 123, 131, 135; Cochabamba 33; and the Kallawaya 191; military recruitment lobbying by 15; mission of 67; propaganda campaign 33, 183; and Ramos Quevedo 65–68, 73; schools, opposition to 33–35, 63; sit-down strikes, opposition to 65–66; Supreme Decrees of 1945, concessions to 75, 104
Soliz, Carmen 210, 212, 281n2
Southern Air Transport 358
Soviet Union, Cold War 289
Spaeth, Carl B. 90–91
Stabilization Plan *see* Monetary Stabilization Plan
Standard Oil Company 2, 11–12, 21, 260
State-Owned Enterprises (SOE) 360
Stephansky, Ben 316
Stettinius, Edward, Jr. 91
Suárez Gómez, Roberto 357, 358, 377n36
Sumala 72, 131, 132, 133, 134
Supreme Decree 28701 369
Supreme Decrees of 1945 75–78; repercussions of 76–78
Suruma 72, 133, 134

Taboada Terán, Néstor 315
Taborga, Alberto 143
Tarija Agrarian Law 61–62
Tejada Sorzano, José Luis 20, 21, 29
Territorio Indígena y Parque Nacional Isiboro Secure (TIPNIS) 371
Tesis of Caranguillas 4, 136–139; conquest of political power 139; cooperativism 140–142; land revindication 140; possession of economic power 141
Thomson, Sinclair 41n45, 368, 378n60
tin barons 15, 22, 25; Concordancia and 113, 149–150; nationalization of mines and 160, 167–168, 259, 262; Villarroel regime and 80, 91, 101, 105, 106n15, 107n24, 108n37
Titiriku, Gregorio 25, 132, 175–176, 192, 353
Tiwanaku Manifesto 352–353
Toro, David 20–21, 31–32
Torres Ortiz, Humberto 97, 160, 163
Torrico, Juan 128, 296
Torrico, Narciso 268, 273–275, 277, 286n105, 286n107; death of 277
Torrico, Octavio 275, 317
Torrico, Ramon 300, 313
Triangular Plan 314, 316–317, 328, 331
Trotsky, L. 130

Trump, Donald J. 374
Tupac Katari Revolutionary Movement (MRTK) 353, 361

UCAPO *see Unión de Campesinos Pobres*
Ucureña 7, 31–32; central school at 46n129, 285n84; chicha tax 265–266; conflict with Cliza 7, 294–300, 303, 305, 312; and Guerra 36; militia 305, 312; Movimientistas and Auténticos, conflict between 295, 297–300; Pacto Militar-Campesino Anticomunista 322; and Paz 317; peasant sindicatos linked to 184, 205, 264, 274; and Rivas 188; and Vásquez (Salvador) 304
Ucureña Agrarian Federation 200
Ucureña and Rojas (José): and the Nationalist Revolutionary Movement (MNR) 7, 184–187, 268–269, 276–277, 281, 292–300, 304, 322
Ucureña Central 188–191, 264–268, 265; Cliza, blockade of 297–300; militiamen 276; and Rojas (José) 281, 292–293, 297; sindicato revolutionaries 274, 294
Ucureña War *see* Cliza and Ucureña War
UMOPAR *see* Mobile Police Unit for Rural Areas (UMOPAR)
Unión Cívica Femenina 126
Unión de Campesinos Pobres (UCAPO) 349
Unión Democrática y Popular (UDP) 359
Unión Juvenil Cruceñista 374
United States 323–331; Cold War 289; contingency plans 315–316; military attaches and indigenous military officers 96–98; and Nationalist Revolutionary Movement (MNR) 258–264; national security policy 290; "War on Drugs" 363–365; *see also* Central Intelligence Agency (CIA)
United States Agency for International Development (USAID) 6, 8; Mann Doctrine and 328–329; Office of Public Safety and 290, 315–316, 328; Oriente and 236, 263, 347, 373; subversion of governments 341n176, 373; Triangular Plan and 316–317
United States Army Special Operations Research Office 327
United States Green Berets 318
United States Information Service (USIS) 290
United States Military Assistance Program (MAP) 317–318

United States Panama Canal Zone 88, 320, 321, 324, 325, 328, 331
United States Special Forces 316
universal suffrage 1, 171, 302–303
Universidad Mayor de San Andrés 54, 95, 100, 150, 163, 360
Universidad de San Simón 36–37
Urriolagoitia, Mamerto 113, 116, 145, 147–151, 179
USAID *see* United States Agency for International Development
USIS *see* United States Information Service
USTFN *see* National Union of Factory Workers

Vacas Indigenous School 32–35
Vargas, Eugenio 277–278, 286n107
Vargas, Felix 131
Vargas, Rufino 275–276, 277, 286n104
Vargas, Virgilio 135–136
Veizaga, Miguel 300–305, 311–313; arrest of 313; Auténtico Nationalist Revolutionary Movement (PMNRA) campaign, joining of 293–294; campesinos, views on 265–266; Nationalist Revolutionary Movement (MNR), desire to return to 303; pacification conference 305; Paz Estenssoro, criticism of 297; Rojas, criticism of and vendetta with 297, 300, 303–304, 312; Secretary General of the FSTCC, election and expulsion 293, 296–298; Vila Vila Massacre 304
Vila Vila massacre 183, 190, 300, 304
Villarroel, Gualberto 23, 186, 193, 219; coup of 1943 48; death/killing of 4, 99, 112, 180, 321; as hapless figure 54, 321; indigenous nationalism 62–68; memorial 113; military institution 71, 172; National Indigenous Congress 71–79; National Revolution 48–50, 167; peasant awakening 178, 179–180; personal services 135, 174, 185, 204–205; Ramos Quevado and 70; *Razón de Patria* (RADEPA) 3, 48; regime/government 3–4, 88–105, 171, 259, 289; social revolution 57–62; United States, non-recognition policy 52–54
Villa Victoria massacre 116, 150, 163, 195n12

Walters, Vernon 329
Warachi Condorcanqi, Asto 136–138, 156n116
Warisata school 2, 27–30

"War on Drugs" 363–365; indigenous resistance to 364–365
Warren, Avra 52
Waskar Ari *see* Ari Chachaki, Waskar
Water Law 2029 366
Water War 362, 366, 370, 378n54
Webber, Jeffrey 370–371
Weiner, Tim 330
Whitehead, Laurence 261
White Massacre 115
Wimert, Paul 318
Wolf, Eric 267

Yacimientos Petrolíferos Fiscales Bolivianos (YPFB) 60, 169, 260
YPFB *see Yacimientos Petrolíferos Fiscales Bolivianos*
Yungas 67, 123, *213*, 218–220; Aymara of 86n146, 218; Nationalist Revolutionary Movement (MNR) agents in 198n86, 219; Nor 218; peasantry 219; Sud 156, 179, 218; tropical 214

Zapata, Emiliano 7, 268–269
Zarate "El Temible Willka" 272

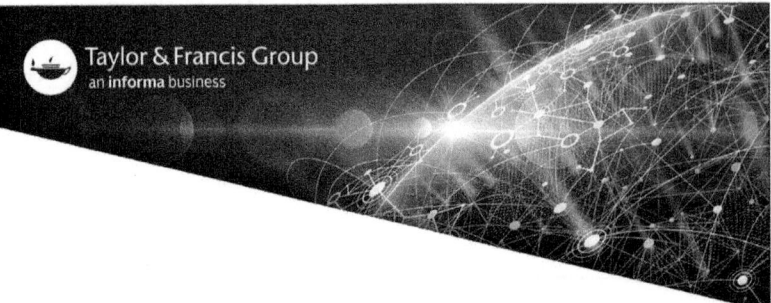